Studies in
Catholic History

John Tracy Ellis

Studies in Catholic History

In Honor
of
John Tracy Ellis

Edited by

Nelson H. Minnich
Robert B. Eno, S.S. &
Robert F. Trisco

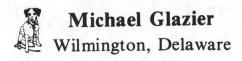 **Michael Glazier**
Wilmington, Delaware

The publisher wishes to thank and acknowledge the following copyright holders for material quoted in this book: America Press, Inc., 106 West 56th Street, New York, NY 10019, for permission to quote from "Have We Any Scholars?" *America* 33 (1925) 418-19 — pages 345-47. All rights reserved ©1925. Association of American Colleges, 1818 R Street, N.W., Washington, DC 20009, for permission to quote from "College Women and the War, *Bulletin* 28 (1942), 27-43 — page 357. Commonweal Foundation, 232 Madison Avenue, New York, NY 10016, for permission to quote from "The High Lights of Humanism," *Commonweal* 9 (1929), 674-75, and "Education and Wisdom," *Commonweal* 50 (1949), 36-45 — pages 354-55. American Academy of Arts and Sciences, Norton's Woods, 136 Irving Street, Cambridge, MA 02138, for permission to quote from "What is Education," *Daedalus* 88 (Winter, 1959), 25-39 — page 355. U.S. Catholic, 221 West Madison Street, Chicago, IL 60606, for permission to quote from "Catholic Culture in America," *Today* 8 (March, 1953), 12-13 — page 348, and "Recipe for Learning," *Today* 12 (November, 1956), 32-34 — page 348. United States Catholic Conference, 1312 Massachusetts Avenue, N.W., Washington, DC 20005, for permission to quote from "Opportunity of the Educated Layman," *Catholic Action* 14 (June, 1932), 5-6 — page 348. Harper and Row, Publishers, Inc., 10 East 53rd Street, New York, N.Y. 10022, for permission to quote from *Education and Moral Wisdom*, George N. Shuster, Copyright© 1960 — pages 354-355, 356, 359-360, 361, 365. And The University of Notre Dame Press, Notre Dame, IN 46554 — pages 352, 358-359, 360, 364-365.

First published in 1985 by Michael Glazier, Inc., 1723 Delaware Avenue, Wilmington, Delaware 19806. ©1985 by Nelson H. Minnich, Robert B. Eno, S.S. and Robert F. Trisco. All Rights Reserved. Library of Congress Card Catalog Number: 85-47754. International Standard Book Number: 0-89453-531-5. Typography by Susan Pickett. Cover design by Brother Placid, OSB. Printed in the United States of America.

Photograph page ii by Nick Crettier, The Catholic University of America, Office of Public Affairs.

Table of Contents

Acknowledgments

Many debts of gratitude have been incurred in the production of this volume honoring Monsignor John Tracy Ellis on the occasion of his eightieth birthday on July 30, 1985. Foremost is that owed to him for having inspired this collection by his dedicated labors and personal example as a church historian and teacher for over half a century.

This project was launched in December of 1982 with pledges of support from the Reverend William J. Byron, S.J., president of the Catholic University of America, and the Reverend Carl J. Peter, dean of its School of Religious Studies. From special funds he was able to raise, Father Peter provided for many of the expenses incurred prior to sending the manuscript to the printer. With assistance from Dr. David McGonagle regarding cost estimates on printing, from Mr. Philip T. Schavone of the university's Development Office, who supervised the preparation of a grant proposal, and from the Most Reverend James A. Hickey, Archbishop of Washington, who supported it, Father Byron was able to approach potential benefactors.

The Raskob Foundation for Catholic Activities, Inc., of Wilmington, Delaware, generously responded to Father Byron's request by providing the funds needed to help underwrite the publication costs of this *Festschrift*. A special word of thanks goes to Mrs. Patsy R. Bremer, Mr. Gerard S. Garey, and Mr. Anthony Robinson for their particular interest in and support for this project. Additional funding was generously contributed by Mr. Bernard O'Keefe, Mrs. Elizabeth Moore St. George, and the Reverend Timothy M. Dolan.

The editor is most grateful to his two associate editors, the Reverend Robert B. Eno, S.S., and the Reverend Robert F. Trisco, both colleagues in the Department of Church History at the Catholic University of America. Without their wise counsel, careful reading of manuscripts, correction of the galley proofs, and scholarly contributions to this volume, the *Festschrift* would have emerged a far poorer production.

In any project such as this the greatest thanks goes to those who contributed the articles. From the very beginning they have greeted the proposal for such a volume with overwhelming enthusiasm. Despite their busy schedules and prior commitments, they managed to produce a wide array of scholarly studies in the history of the Church. Two men in particular deserve special thanks for having graciously responded to specific requests: Archbishop Oscar H. Lipscomb for his insightful Foreword and the Reverend Mark A. Miller for his extensive and detailed bibliography.

Gratitude is also owed to a number of people who provided the essential technical and secretarial services. Sister Janice Farnham, R.J.M., translated into English on short notice the article in French by Canon Roger Aubert. Mr. Frank Hunt compiled the index to the volume. And the two secretaries of the Church History Department, Mrs. Helen Santini and Mrs. Evelyne Smith, typed the various draft proposals, extensive correspondence, and manuscript materials related to this project.

The publisher of this volume, Michael Glazier, Inc., has been one of the principal supporters of this project. Out of a personal respect for Monsignor Ellis it agreed to make an exception from its general policy not to publish *Fest-schriften* and instead undertook this project. When not all the contributions came in on time, it extended the deadlines while pledging to maintain the original publication date. For her understanding, patience, and repeated assistance on this project, the editor is particularly indebted to Eileen Daney Carzo.

May all of our combined labors have produced in some small way a fitting tribute of our affection and esteem for Monsignor Ellis on this occasion of his eightieth birthday.

Nelson H. Minnich
Editor

Foreword

Oscar H. Lipscomb

How does one memorialize a monument? How else, but by adding new stones. Hence, this *Festschrift* marking the eightieth birthday of the dean of American Catholic historians, John Tracy Ellis, is an altogether appropriate venture. This is more easily understood by a consideration given to the accomplishments apart from the man. For the half-century and more since Monsignor Ellis achieved doctoral status in church history at the Catholic University of America in 1930, his work as teacher, author, critic, and speaker has both shed light on the past and enriched the present. A bibliography of his published writings offered in the pages of this volume offers a corpus so marked by quantity and excellence as to merit easily the accolade: monumental.

In recognition of this fact now come former students, colleagues, and friends each with his or her own offering of scholarly effort: "stones" from which is fashioned this timely tribute. They come from across the nation and overseas inspired by motives of respect, friendship, affection, and gratitude. I count it a high privilege to be associated with their endeavor through these few words by way of a Foreword, readily admitting all of the above sentiments for one who directed my own graduate studies in American Catholic History some twenty years past. At the same time I must confess to a certain apprehension in their company. Though "honestly born" into the field of church history, I shortly thereafter "fell upon evil days" in administration and am now, I fear, set in my ways. In lieu, therefore, of the learned research and creative insights that will otherwise distinguish these pages, permit me to speak at another level from the perspective of twenty-seven years of friendship more to the monument that is the man.

Should the reader feel a need to consult a more scholarly approach to him whom we honor, might I make reference to such a critical evaluation by the late Archbishop Paul J. Hallinan of Atlanta which accompanied a collection published in 1963 of some of the articles, addresses, and sermons of Monsignor Ellis.[1] Additional personal details of the life of the priest-historian can be found in a series of detailed and entertaining responses, the result of an interview by Eugene C. Bianchi.[2] A conviction that it would be difficult for me to improve upon these two treatments of our distinguished subject reinforced my proposal to speak of him as I have know him personally: a major professor, a priest, and a friend. I hope the profiles that emerge from these recollections will add in their own way to flesh out the full measure of the man.

My first encounter with John Tracy Ellis took place in the autumn of 1957 after I had been given an assignment to do graduate work with a view toward writing diocesan history. Four of the next six years were spent in our nation's capital at Catholic University where already he was something of a legend. It is unfortunate that the part of the legend which dealt with his deft formation of future historians and teachers of history has never been seriously explored. This more than worthy successor to John Gilmary Shea and

---

[1] John Tracy Ellis, *Perspectives in American Catholicism*, Vol. 5 of *Benedictine Studies* (Baltimore, 1963), [i-v].

[2] Eugene C. Bianchi, "A Church Historian's Personal Story: An Interview with Monsignor John Tracy Ellis," *Records of the American Catholic Historical Society of Philadelphia*, 92 (1981), 1-42.

Peter Guilday taught as much by example as by precept. Certainly, however, there was none of the latter lacking, and I have yet to encounter anyone similarly situated who could convey so much so well with such interest in the space of a single hour. At his hands we learned that discipline of thought and effort was Clio's handmaiden. Who among his students can forget the casual shredding of meticulously handwritten notes as each lecture came to an end lest, as their author once explained, he might be tempted to use them at another time and so damage a future presentation by distancing it from richer sources? And we were expected to make such sources our own through the challenge of reading lists as wide as they were wise. Thus was the past not only recaptured in a way that somehow defies description, it was revived.

But it was in the seminars and through dissertation direction that Monsignor Ellis most influenced us. At such levels the numbers were fewer and the focus of study more concentrated, in time specified by the individual effort that is the heart of any graduate program. I remember a professor whose requirements of his students were constantly authenticated by his own careful performance. And yet high standards were enforced with a special charism of encouragement for the smoldering flax of talent and determination lest it be quenched. We were taught to walk before we were expected to run. This is not to say that honesty suffered for the sake of charity. He who was willing to disturb the complacency of the Catholic intellectual community on a national scale could be, for cause, equally disquieting at the individual level. It was not only in class that we encountered a favorite negative phrase that came to be a source of dread, even though it took its origin from the Scriptures: *In hoc non laudo!*[3]

[3]Cf. 1 Cor. 11:22.

At times the professor could be similarly open and direct with bishops and religious superiors. He not only solicited their support in the cause of the history of the Church in the United States by pointing out opportunities and identifying likely personnel, but also spoke up when he felt too much was demanded of a student, or that a candidate was being offered less than a reasonable chance for adequate development. In all such dealings, whether with students or others, Monsignor Ellis pursued a method of productive dialogue that was entirely in character. Later he said of composing differences, ". . . if they are put forth with reason and moderation, and with a courteous consideration for others' judgments, they can hardly prove anything but helpful to all concerned."[4]

It is no easy task to assess the effectiveness of a major professor through the success, or lack of it, of those who studied under him. There are too many variables. But by any reasonably applied standard John Tracy Ellis ranks among the finest in the field. His students have participated in the exciting task of revitalizing American Catholic history through research and skill in presentation. Their professional competence is recognized in colleges and universities both at home and abroad. The quality of a significant number of offerings from former students in this *Festschrift* speaks clearly to the point. Some have found themselves outside academic environments and discovered, like myself, that present responsibilities are better understood and more effectively faced because of so rich a frame of historical reference. And there are profound, if less tangible, benefits on a more personal level. One could not have completed successfully a course of graduate studies under Monsignor Ellis without a deep regard for truth and integrity, an equal aversion to dishonesty in all its forms, and a challenge to state the difference in words and deeds.

---

[4]John Tracy Ellis, "Sermon at the Diamond Jubilee Mass of Mt. Angel Abbey, St. Benedict, Oregon, May 13,1964," Boston *Pilot*, March 20, 1965, p. 8, col. 1.

Some people look askance at so-called hyphenated priests. There is sometimes a pejorative connotation given to such terms as: priest-social worker, priest-lawyer, or even priest-historian. While there are no doubt experiences that give cause for concern, so long as priesthood is given its proper place and priority the teaching and spirit of Vatican Council II clearly indicate that there is no basic opposition between ordination and a variety of entirely honorable professions. This is above all true of those that serve individual need and common good in our modern world. The life and work of John Tracy Ellis give clear evidence of an ability not only to harmonize two such callings but to excel at both. In his case well-deserved public distinction and professional acclaim have served to celebrate the historian; the historian himself with a continuing fidelity and commitment celebrates priesthood.

At the heart of that fidelity and commitment is the daily offering of Mass. By his own admission, the "practice of daily Mass and communion" was for Monsignor Ellis the proximate grace that moved the historian to accept God's call to priestly ministry.[5] He described the relationship of both vocations in this response to a query about religious and intellectual motives:

> It was, I think, a combination of the two. I have already mentioned that I told Bishop [Francis M.] Kelly frankly that I wished to teach rather than do parish work,...I was, of course, attracted to the religious aspects, and as time went on I grew to have more and more a love of the Mass as I assisted each morning in the seminary chapel. It was a slowly developing matter which, without trying to appear more pious than I am, I attribute to the grace of

[5]Bianchi, "A Church Historian's," 16.

the sacraments, the high morale of the seminary community, and a series of intangible factors that go to make us what we are.[6]

For all the years that I knew the priest-historian in Washington he was actively engaged in regular weekend priestly ministry at St. Matthew's Cathedral where a good friend, Monsignor John K. Cartwright, was pastor. An interesting indication of this continuing devotion to the Mass surfaced recently in some correspondence of mine to a mutual friend, now deceased. Writing to her on All Souls' Day, 1962, I described the following incident which took place in the chapel at Caldwell Hall: "Was more than a little embarrassed this morning when I started my Masses late, about eight, and Msgr. Ellis came over from his place and served all three of them. When I thanked him afterward he said it was a privilege."[7]

Two memories of pastoral response on the part of John Tracy Ellis come to mind vividly as the result of a visit he made to Mobile in May, 1960. Fresh from delivering the commencement address at Dominican College in New Orleans, he responded with grace and a happy result to a spur of the moment request in the sacristy to "say a few words" to some eighth-grade "graduates." And before his departure for home my friend turned his hand to a pastoral problem of more serious dimensions. At his request we made what I thought was a social call to a nearby community to visit relatives of a friend in Washington. Before this visit ended, thanks to Monsignor Ellis' initiative, a marriage difficulty that had estranged two Catholics from the active practice of their faith was at least on its way toward a solution. I was happy to be able to report to him by summer's end that the matter had reached a successful

[6]Ibid., 18

[7]Writer to Mrs. John A. Zieman, Washington, November 2, 1962.

conclusion. If only one among the friends of Monsignor Ellis can recall these several episodes of active priestly ministry, what, I wonder, would be the aggregate of such experiences? It is almost certainly true that the answer to that question will never be known. It is equally true that this dimension of the life's work of the priest-historian should not be overlooked at a time for remembering.

Finally, it is almost with hesitation that I speak of Monsignor Ellis as a friend. This is not due to a lack of closeness and affection implied in such a relationship; those elements have increased with the passing of years. But friendship implies a mutuality of giving and receiving, and I have been no match for his generosity. By way of illustration, let me cite three categories or signs of vitality in a friendship: presence, honesty, and self revelation. In each category John Tracy Ellis has never been found wanting to this friend.

Presence corresponds to need, or at least to convenience and comfort. I can think of no friend who has been more present in such circumstances than this mentor of many years. Regularly by correspondence, invariably when our paths crossed in Washington or San Francisco, extraordinarily twice in Mobile to add his own special contributions to a parish centennial and the sesquicentennial of the diocese, Monsignor Ellis has made himself available. Over the years there has hardly been a region in our nation to which he has not responded, giving unselfishly of time and talent as professor, scholar, speaker, and preacher.

One of the highest qualities of friendship is that it does not fear the truth. My experience of John Tracy Ellis as friend is that he would withhold neither blame nor praise provided either were honestly due. The value of such a reliable source of commentary and advice in today's world is self-evident. (I might add that the value of such a source in the life of a bishop is even more evident.) Within this context I feel one cannot ignore the profound, and at times painful, honesty that Monsignor Ellis has shown in his not infrequent comments on Church and nation. They are a sign of more than friendship; they are a manifestation of love. If in his critical judgments he has, at times, disturbed some of our co-religionists and our fellow-citizens it is because he cared too much to dissemble.

Closely akin to honesty among friends and, indeed, a form of its expression is self-revelation. Not that friendship requires the sharing of every secret and detail of another's life. It does imply a certain vulnerability that goes hand in hand with trust when one invites a friend into the otherwise hidden reserves of mind and heart and spirit. Monsignor Ellis is capable of this dimension of friendship with a grace and lightness of touch that establishes intimacy without imposition. It is a special gift and often accompanied by a masterful sense of humor that has served him well throughout these fourscore years.

It is with this sense of humor that I would like to bring these few personal remembrances to a close. If I have not mentioned it previously, it is because for those who know John Tracy Ellis well this special gift touches all others to improve them. Once he has set about the task of enlivening any conversation it cannot remain prosaic; more than once I have seen tension relaxed or possible embarrassment forestalled by the exercise of this happy faculty. Let me share one last episode for it evokes this good friend so completely that I feel it should be somewhere "written down." March, 1966, found Monsignor Ellis, Father James P. Gaffey, and myself in New Orleans where reservations had been made for a dinner at Antoine's. A cab deposited us at the main entrance where a sizeable crowd was waiting to be seated. When an obliging doorman admitted us at once it became apparent that more than one bystander was highly skeptical of reservations on behalf of the three Roman collars. As we were being shown to a table I can still hear, almost verbatim, the comments of the silver-haired historian: "Oscar, as I grow older I find it increasingly difficult to stand for long periods, so I thank you for this courtesy. However, in all honesty, I feel I should warn you that it was just such as this that caused the French Revolution!"

I know I speak for all who have contributed to this *Festschrift* in offering our prayers for continued blessings on one who has already received *multos annos* and used them well. May these pages do him honor whose gifts to students, colleagues, and friends have truly constituted part of the "hundredfold." And so might say the Church in our land.

Several Youth Sent from Here: Native-Born Priests and Religious of English America, 1634-1776

James Hennesey, S.J.

At a meeting of the Maryland Assembly on June 7, 1751, Colonel Hooper of the Grievances Committee warned of the Catholic menace:

> We see Popery too assiduously nurtured and propagated within this Province... subverting and withdrawing many of His Majesty's Protestant subjects, both from our holy Religion, and their Faith and Allegiance to his Royal Person, Crown and Family.

Hooper worried over "the Number of Jesuits and Popish Priests now in this Province and yearly coming in." But there was worse news: the "several Youth sent from here to St. Omer's and other foreign Popish Seminaries out of His Majesty's Obedience, to be trained up in Ways destructive to the Establishment of Church and State in His Majesty's Dominions." Some of them "return here as Popish Priests, or Jesuits, together with others of like Kind," to "live in Societies, where they have public Masshouses and with great Industry propagate their Doctrine."[1]

Maryland was an oddity among England's American colonies. Never in a political sense "Catholic," still it had a Catholic founder, Cecil Calvert, Second Lord Baltimore. For its first twenty years religious toleration obtained, and Catholics were prominent in government and society.[2] But by 1751 that was far in the past. Catholics were a tiny minority subject to penal laws in the colony their ancestors had helped found.[3] But they survived reasonably well, even prosperously. Their church was well organized. Some of the priests were their own sons; other sons and daughters followed a religious calling in Europe.

Maryland's first colonists landed on St. Clement's Island on March 25, 1634. In the 142 years between then and the Declaration of Independence, 113 Jesuit priests, a Jesuit scholastic, and thirty Jesuit brothers ministered to colonial Catholics in Maryland, Pennsylvania, and Virginia. Circuit riders traversed New Jersey and New York's Hudson Valley; a school functioned briefly in Manhattan. The mission was a self-supporting unit, living from gifts and farm income, directed by a superior dependent on the English Jesuit provincial in London. Most missionaries were English, joined by Germans after the work expanded in 1741 into "Pennsylvania Dutch" country.[4]

---

[1] William Hand Browne *et al.*, eds., *Archives of Maryland* (72 vols.; Baltimore, 1883-1972), XLVI, 593. Hereafter cited as *AM*.

[2] Robert Baird, *Religion in America*, ed. Henry Warner Bowden (New York, 1970), 50.

[3] Lawrence Henry Gipson, *The British Empire before the Revolution*, II: *The Southern Plantations* (Caldwell, Idaho, 1936), 64.

[4] Thomas Hughes, S.J., *History of the Society of Jesus in North America: Colonial and Federal*, 4 Vols. (New York, 1907-17), Text, II, 676-703, lists all Jesuits who served in colonial North America.

Relations between the Lord Proprietor and Jesuits were not always smooth, but efforts to attract other priests yielded sparse results. Two secular priests came out in 1642; their memory has vanished in the mists of history.[5] Scarcely more is known of the handful of English Franciscans who labored in Maryland between 1673 and 1718.[6] In an earlier report, Colonel Hooper had been on target when he singled out the émigré English Jesuit college at St. Omer in French Flanders as the chief "foreign Popish seminary" where Maryland Catholic boys were educated or, in the colonel's phrase, "imbib[ed] principles destructive to our Religious and Civil Rights."[7] American names occur on the St. Omers' register from the arrival there in 1681 of Robert Brooke and Thomas Gardiner. By mid-eighteenth century Marylanders crowded the rolls, and numbers stayed high after the college's move to Bruges in the Austrian Netherlands and then to the principality of Liège.[8]

St. Omers was not, however, the only school serving colonial American Catholics. Dom Henry Norbert Birt found five Americans at the English Benedictines' St. Gregory's College, Douai.[9] When, in the wake of Pope Clement XIV's suppression of their order, Austrian police expelled the ex-Jesuits from the Great and Little Colleges at Bruges, Dominicans took over. Most students followed their teachers to the Anglo-Bavarian Academy at Liège, but some

[5] John Tracy Ellis, *Catholics in Colonial America* (Baltimore, 1965), 330.

[6] Hughes, *History*, Documents, I/2, 134-35; Richard Trappes-Lomax, ed., *The English Franciscan Nuns, 1619-1821, and the Friars Minor of the Same Province, 1618-1761* (London, 1922), 294.

[7] *AM*, XLVI, 549. St. Omer is the town. Jesuits called the college St. Omers.

[8] Hughes, *History*, Documents, I/1, 137: Geoffrey Holt, S.J., ed., *St. Omers and Bruges Colleges: A Biographical Dictionary 1593-1773* (Thetford, 1979); Richard Trappes-Lomax, *Boys at Liège Academy, Their Parents, Guardians, etc.* (London, 1913).

[9] Henry Norbert Birt, O.S.B., *Obit Book of the English Benedictines 1600-1912* (Edinburgh, 1913), 73.

transferred to the Dominicans' college in Bornhem in a move which in time gave birth to a Dominican presence in the United States.[10] On the post-secondary level, some Americans qualified as Lawyers or physicians at Paris, Vienna, and London. Entrants into the Society of Jesus are first recorded at Watten, near St. Omer, or, after 1766 at Ghent. They studied philosophy and theology at Liège and made a final probationary year at Ghent. Aspirants to the secular priesthood studied at St. Alban's, Valladolid, and the Venerable English College, Rome.[11]

Principally from the ranks of these American students abroad came in colonial times forty-three Jesuit vocations, a single Benedictine monk, one doubtfully American Franciscan, and three secular priests. One secular seminarian died in his first year of divinity studies and another was dropped for academic reasons. Twenty-one Jesuits, including the future Archbishops John Carroll and Leonard Neale, worked in America. Thirteen served in Europe, chiefly in England. One died as a student; three scholastics and a brother left the order. One not yet ordained at the 1773 suppression died before ordination, another chose lay life. One priest a year ordained, at that time, became an Episcopal minister.

While their brothers and cousins headed for St. Omers and St. Gregory's, thirty-three women entered cloistered convents in France or Flanders. The first Maryland nun was Mary Digges, a canoness regular of the Holy Sepulchre at Liège in 1721. Seven Americans followed her to that monastery, which boasted the finest English Catholic girls' school, while nine became Carmelites, seven Benedictines, five Poor

---

[10]Holt, *St. Omers and Bruges*, 99.

[11]Edwin Henson, ed., *Registers of the English College at Valladolid* (London, 1930); *id., The English College at Madrid 1611-1767* (London, 1929); Henry Foley, S.J., *Records of the English Province of the Society of Jesus*, 8 Vols. (London, 1877-83), VII, 498.

Clares, and four Dominicans.[12] Pressure from Emperor Joseph II forced some of these convents to open schools, but they were in origin contemplative communities. No American entered an institute founded for the active apostolate. This contemplative bent was encouraged by their Jesuit advisers. When after Independence there was question of American nuns returning to introduce female religious life in the United States, it was done by cloistered Carmelites. John Carroll, wanting help in opening schools, commented tersely, "I wish rather for Ursulines," a teaching group.[13] But groundwork for that had not been laid in colonial days.

The first vocations came fifty years after the colony's founding, and were a direct result of the school opened on the Jesuits' Newtown Manor in 1677 by Brother Gregory Turberville. In 1680 the English Jesuit provincial reported to Rome: "I hear from the Maryland Mission that a school had been set up where humane letters are taught with great fruit. Everything is peaceable there."[14] The school was preparatory to St. Omer, and the provincial's report for 1681 announced the arrival at the latter school of the first Newtown alumni: "They yielded in ability to few Europeans for the honor of being first in their class."[15] The students were Robert Brooke and Thomas Gardiner. Brooke entered the Watten novitiate in 1684 and was the first Marylander ordained priest. Gardiner followed him "up the hill" to Watten the next year, but left the Jesuits before ordination.

Robert Brooke (1663-1714) had the usual course of studies at Liège and Ghent and was briefly a military chaplain

---

[12]Thomas W. Spalding, C.F.X., "Natives of Maryland in Religious Houses and Seminaries Abroad from 1684 to 1788," in Edwin W. Beitzell, *The Jesuit Missions of St. Mary's County, Maryland* (Abell, Maryland, 1976), 313-21; Peter Guilday, *The English Catholic Refugees on the Continent 1558-1795* (London, 1914), 121-421.

[13]Thomas O'Brien Hanley, S.J., *The John Carroll Papers*, 3 Vols. (Notre Dame, 1976), I, 312.

[14]Hughes, *History*, Text, II, 136.

[15]*Ibid.*, Documents, I/1, 136-37.

at Bruges before returning to Maryland in 1696. From 1708 to 1712 he was superior of the Maryland Mission. His grandfather, also Robert, was an Anglican parson sent over in 1650 by Lord Baltimore to help allay Protestant fears about Maryland's Catholicism. He settled on a 2,000 acre estate, "De la Brooke Manor," with a commanding view of the Patuxent River, twenty miles upstream from its mouth. His second son, Major Thomas, married a Protestant, Eleanor Hatton, but both husband and wife became Catholics. Their family included a son, Colonel Thomas, who converted to Protestantism, and three Jesuits.[16]

The Maryland rebellion of 1689 ended the Proprietor's government and signaled hard times for Catholics under Governor John Seymour (1704-09). An "Act to Prevent the Growth of Popery" forbade Catholic public and for a time private religious services. On September 11, 1704, the mission superior, William Hunter, and Father Brooke were brought before the council (on which Colonel Thomas Brooke sat, although he absented himself from this session) and charged with "dedicating a Popish chapel and for saying Mass." Brooke admitted the latter charge, pleading that "others had formerly done so." Since it was their first offense, the priests were let off with a warning, complete with tirade from the governor, who had the sheriff lock the chapel at St. Mary's City "and keep the key thereof." Maryland had its first native priest, but Mass was banned where the first chapel had opened seventy years before.[17]

By their father's will, Robert and Thomas Brooke divided De la Brooke and other lands. Robert had in 1689 made his share over to the Maryland Jesuits, with proviso for his mother's lifetime tenancy. Nine years after his death,

---

[16]"The Brooke Family," *Maryland Historical Magazine* 1 (1906), 66-73; 184-188. Beitzell, *Jesuit Missions*, 39, 50-53. The Brookes were a gentry family from Hampshire. Chief Justice of the United States Roger Brooke Taney descended from Major Thomas Brooke's half-brother Roger.

[17]*AM*, XXVI, 44, 161.

Colonel Thomas, already patentee of 11,000 acres, challenged the disposition on the ground that his late brother was a priest, "but never convicted of recusancy or any other crime." The case was tried in 1729, and the claim disallowed, the court holding that English laws against Catholics purchasing land and Jesuits inheriting it did not apply in Maryland.[18] Robert Brooke was the first of many Maryland Jesuits whose inherited estates financed the mission effort.

Thomas Gardiner (b. 1665), Brooke's companion at Newtown and St. Omer, was the second Marylander to become a Jesuit. He was Brooke's first cousin, son of Luke Gardiner and Elizabeth Hatton and godson of Major Thomas Brooke. Luke Gardiner had a reputation as an enthusiastic Catholic, at one time being charged with detaining his twelve-year old sister-in-law Eleanor (Major Brooke's future wife) to educate her as a Catholic. His will disinherited any of his four sons who might change his religion, "that he be no Catholic." Thomas Gardiner's career lasted nine years. He finished theological studies without being ordained, was released from his vows, and came home.[19]

While Brooke and Gardiner were at Watten, a brother-candidate, William Burley, began his noviceship in Maryland in 1685. He served the mission for forty years, the last reference to him being in 1725.[20] Mystery surrounds George Calvert (b. 1672), a Jesuit in 1690 who left the order in 1694. It is disputed whether he is the same George Calvert who

---

[18]Hughes, *History*, Documents, I/1, 224-28.

[19]Holt, *St. Omers and Bruges*, 110; Foley, *Records*, VI, 287; Hughes, *History*, Text, I, 137; McHenry Howard, "Some Early Colonial Marylanders," *Maryland Historical Magazine* 16 (1921), 319-24. Foley errs in saying he died a Jesuit in 1694. His name occurs on the list of those dismissed from the Jesuit order in the English Jesuit Archives, London. His descendants living in Maryland are mentioned in *Woodstock Letters* 61 (1932), 16.

[20]Hughes, *History*, Text, II, 682-83.

was the son of William Calvert and Elizabeth Stone and
grandson of Governors Leonard Calvert and William
Stone.[21]

The next two Marylanders took a more circuitous route.
They were Robert Brooke's brothers, Ignatius (1671-1751)
and Matthew (1672-1705). They probably followed him to
St. Omers, but from 1692 to 1699 were at St. Alban's, the
English college for secular seminarians at Valladolid.
Ordained there, they went to England in the spring of 1699
and entered Watten that summer. Ignatius was back at
Valladolid in 1701, escorting eight new students, among
them the future founder of the Pennsylvania missions,
Joseph Greaton. He stayed on until 1708 as minister, or
assistant rector, at the college and then was the first American assigned to the English Mission, where he served various chaplaincies in the Midlands until his death. He was
rector of the Derbyshire District and superior of St. Mary's
Residence, covering Oxford and Northampton, before he
died at eighty, retired at St. Omers.[22]

Matthew Brooke's career paralleled his brother's until their
noviceship ended. He then reviewed theology for a year
before beginning a three-year ministry in Maryland, dying
there in 1705, aged thirty-three. Both Brookes inherited
property, and Ignatius' transfer of his share to the order in
1732 is recorded.[23] During student days in Spain, Matthew
was involved in another financial dealing which sheds light
on the internal affairs of émigré English Catholics. St.
George's College, Madrid, was run by Spanish Jesuits, as was

[21]Hughes, *History*, Documents, I/1, 57-58. Foley, *Records*, VII, 112, claims he
died a Jesuit at Liège in 1696, but the English Jesuit Archives, London, list his
dismissal. A Calvert descendant, John B.C. Nicklin, "The Calvert Family," *Maryland Historical Magazine* 16 (1921), 192, denies that this Calvert belonged to the
family.

[22]Foley, *Records*, VII, 90; II, 1421; Henson, *Valladolid*, 170-79.

[23]Foley, *Records*, VII, 90: Hughes, *History*, Text, II, 684; Documents, I/2, 226,
255.

St. Alban's. Financial maladministration in Madrid had prompted removal of all English students, but St. George's remained responsible for supporting two of them at Valladolid. Brooke was one of these. His name appears on a bill for the mules on which he and his fellow pensioner travelled from San Sebastián on first arrival in Spain. The Madrid rector disputed the charge, and the matter had to be referred to the Jesuit general in Rome. When Brooke's fellow seminarian died in 1696, the rector of St. Alban's wrote drily to his counterpart in Madrid: "For the future, your reverence has only Mr. Matthew Brooke here, and consequently will not have to pay so much for maintenance." Matters were no better in 1701, when Thomas Powell succeeded Brooke as stipendiary. He needed breeches, doublet and hose and had to go about "in an evil-sleeved cloak, very short and torn, which he had brought with him and with which he covered his lack of breeches, etc."[24] The effect of all this on the apparently delicate Matthew Brooke can only be conjectured.

One casualty of Governor Seymour's antipopery crusade was the Newtown school. A ripple effect ensued, and for a decade and a half few American names graced the St. Omers roster. Joseph Dudley Digges (c. 1689-1771), who also used the name Hall, finished there in 1712 and continued studies for the priesthood at the Venerable English College, Rome, where he was ordained on April 20, 1715, the first Maryland secular priest. In 1719 he went to England, where he spent a half-century as chaplain to the Petre family at Ingatestone, Essex. Michael Herbert (1694-1720) of St. Mary's County and also from St. Omers followed Digges to the *Venerabile* in 1619, but was dead within the year.[25] It was Digges' sister

[24]Henson, *Madrid*, 160, 328, 331.

[25]*The Liber Ruber of the English College, Rome*, I: *Nomina Alumnorum* (London, 1943), 148, 163; Godfrey Anstruther, O.P., *The Seminary Priests: A Dictionary of the Secular Clergy of England and Wales 1558-1850*, 4 Vols. (Ware, Ushaw and Great Wakering, 1969-1977), III (1660-1715), 50.

Mary who in 1721 became the first Maryland nun when she joined the Sepulchrines at Liège, taking the name Sister Stanislaus.[26] Their first cousin, Dom Richard Paul Chandler (d. 1712), was colonial Maryland's lone male Benedictine, professed in 1705 and ordained in 1710 at St. Gregory's, Douai, where he died. His father, Colonel William Chandler, commanded the mixed Indian-English garrison at Charles County's Zachariah Fort; his mother, Mary Sewall, was a sister of the Diggeses' mother.[27]

Reliable local historians claim as a native Marylander Franciscan James Haddock (1671-1718, or 1720), but official Franciscan records call him a Lancashireman. He entered the Franciscans at Douai in 1689, was ordained in 1696 and commissioned for Maryland, where he died, in 1699.[28]

The generalate of Michelangelo Tamburini (1706-30) was a troubled time for the Jesuits. Quarrels over Jansenism raged in France, while difficulties over the Chinese Rites brought in 1723 formal censure of their missionaries in China, and of Tamburini, by the Sacred Congregation for the Propagation of the Faith. With Pope Innocent XIII's approval, the Society of Jesus was put on three years' probation and forbidden to accept novices. Although a new pope in 1724 lifted the censures, these factors, added to problems at home, may have produced a chilling effect on Jesuit vocations. Only in 1724, after a quarter-century gap, did Americans reappear at Watten.

[26]Spalding, "Natives of Maryland," 316.

[27]Bennet Weldon, O.S.B., *Pax: Chronological Notes on the English Congregation of the Order of St. Benedict* (Worcester, 1881), 10, 12; Ethelred L. Taunton, *The English Black Monks of St. Benedict: A Sketch of Their History from the Coming of St. Augustine to the Present Day*, 2 Vols. (London, 1897), II, 215-16; *AM*, VI, 309.

[28]Trappes-Lomax, *Franciscans*, 294. Spalding, "Natives of Maryland," 317, thinks him "probably" from Prince George's County, and Beitzell, *Jesuit Missions*, 340, agrees.

Henry Neale (1702-48) launched a multi-generational Jesuit tradition in his family, whose American founders, Captain James Neale and his wife, had settled Wollaston Manor in the future Charles County in 1642 after some years in the confidential service of King Charles I and Queen Henrietta Maria.[29] Henry Neale was at St. Omer's and later taught there as a scholastic. Nine of his students followed his example and became Jesuits. Allowed to cut short the tertianship, the final probationary year, after making the thirty-day retreat, he was by March, 1741 knee-deep in Philadelphia snow. The rest of his life he spent in Pennsylvania. In 1745 he helped open the school on St. Francis Xavier farm at the head of the Chesapeake. Noting that land prices were doubling, he urged property purchase as the "best and surest" way to establish missions. He acquired land at Conewago, Lancaster, and Goshenhoppen, all future mission centers, and secured from Sir John James, Bart., an annuity to support Pennsylvania country missions. In a begging letter he had explained to the English baronet that the "necessarys of Life" were "as dear, & several dearer, than at London itself." One expense was to keep a horse, so that he might minister to "poor people up and down ye country, some twenty miles, some sixty, some farther off."[30]

Neale's fellow novice in 1724, Arnold Livers (1705-67), was the son of a Dutch immigrant supporter of the lost Jacobite cause who came to Maryland indentured to John Carroll's Darnall grandfather, but died himself holding indentured servants. The son did not go to St. Omer's. He hurried through his Jesuit studies, since he was back at St. Thomas Manor in 1734. After thirteen years presiding over

[29] *Woodstock Letters* 7 (1878), 144.

[30] Hughes, *History*, Documents, I/1, 78, 285, 342-50. *American Catholic Historical Researches* 6 (1889), 182-83; 16 (1899), 96-97; Martin I.J. Griffin, "The Sir John James Fund," *Records of the American Catholic Historical Society* 9 (1898), 195-209.

Newtown Manor, he was accused before the Maryland legislature of having "perverted" Protestants and in 1754 he was, for his own safety, relegated to remote St. Inigoes, where he died. Livers was a genial entrepreneur under whom Newtown prospered. He raised horses and has left a record of their names. His plantation produced manufactured goods, medicines, and tanned hides. He cultivated flowers, raised birds, and wrote poetry. New England men brought their ships to his wharf to trade. In his exile at St. Inigoes he did forget. When in 1760 Governor Sharpe of Maryland took up a collection for the 220 families left homeless by the March 20th fire in Boston, Arnold Livers made three separate contributions.[31]

Bennet Neale (1709-87), Henry's younger brother, followed him to St. Omer and in 1728 to Watten. Ordained after two years' theological study, he took his final examination a year later and was home by 1742 after a tertianship commuted to the thirty-day retreat, all this accompanied by considerable handwringing on the part of Jesuit General Frantisek Retz, who, however, granted the necessary dispensations.[32]

Neale bought Deer Creek Plantation in present Harford County and worked there and at Newtown. John Carroll wrote in 1779 that he was one of those "in the lower part of the county" whom he seldom saw. In 1787 he reported that "good Mr. Bennet Neale finished a life of innocence with a holy death on March 27th."[33] He looks an unlikely candidate for his dramatic role in 1757, when he was arrested by the Baltimore County sheriff, accused in the aftermath of Braddock's defeat at Fort Duquesne of conspiracy with the

[31] Mary Louise Donnelly, *Arnold Livers Family in America* (n.p., 1977), 4-5, 24-30; Beitzell, *Jesuit Missions*, 61; *Woodstock Letters* 13 (1884), 292.

[32] Hughes, *History*, Documents, I/1, 80, 82-83.

[33] Hanley, *Carroll Papers*, I, 52, 254.

French and Indians and preaching treason. It was no light matter. Colonel George Washington was among those worried about "very unnatural and pernicious correspondence held with the French by some priests." Neale was bound over for trial at the Annapolis assizes, but won acquittal when his accuser, an English deserter, could not identify him.[34]

Bennet Neale was the senior American priest to live to the Revolution, but his longevity pales by contrast with that of Thomas Digges (1711-1805), nephew through his mother of the three Jesuit Brookes and member of a family whose American forebear was governor of Virginia.[35] He taught philosophy and was a missioner in Lancashire before coming home in 1742. He was mission superior, 1750-56, but spent most of his life as family chaplain at Mellwood, his widowed sister-in-law's estate on the Potomac, opposite Mount Vernon. The Duc de la Rochefoucauld met him there on a memorable Wednesday in Passion Week, 1797. The old man was a gracious host, but "the dinner was very sparing, quite Catholic and consequently not very restorative." Digges treated Louis XVI's onetime general to a lecture on France's iniquities: the country was peopled with "atheists and villains," the Revolution punishment for its sins, and the true cause of its calamity not the writings of Voltaire and Rousseau, but the destruction of the Jesuits.[36]

John Carroll's letters abound in news of Digges, "a most excellent, holy, & sensible man," impatient for news of the

[34]Hughes, *History*, Text, II, 546; John C. Fitzpatrick, ed., *The Writings of George Washington,* 39 Vols. (Washington, 1931-34), I, 498-99; *Pennsylvania Archives* (Philadelphia, 1853), II, 694.

[35]Foley, *Records*, VII, 203; Alice Norris Parran, ed., *Register of Maryland's Heraldic Families* (Baltimore, 1935), 145-47; Robert H. Elias and Eugene D. Finch, *Letters of Thomas Atwood Digges* (Columbia, South Carolina, 1982), xxiii-xxiv.

[36]François Alexandre Frédéric, duc de la Rochefoucauld-Liancourt, *Travels in North America*, II, 306-08, in *American Catholic Historical Researches* 8 (1891), 72-74.

English ex-Jesuits and anxious for the Society's restoration. As eyesight and memory failed, he was unable to say Mass, but still "loved to sit in company," where "his delight was to converse of the men of other times."[37]

Thomas Digges had gone to Watten in 1729. Next after him, in 1733, came Francis Digges (1712-81), possibly his brother. After years as a priest in northeastern England, he died at Berrington, near Durham.[38] Watten also welcomed in 1733 a cousin of the Potomac Diggeses, John Digges (1712-46), one of six children of John Digges who in 1735, twenty years before the Mason-Dixon survey, took up a 10,000 acre Maryland grant at the headwaters of the Monocacy in southern Pennsylvania's Conewago Valley. The invasion did not go unchallenged. A Digges son, Dudley, was shot and killed by "a Pennsylvania blacksmith," but the father held his ground, donated some of it for a Catholic church, and opened up the back country by building a wagon road to Baltimore. Young John, meanwhile, made quick work of his theological education. The Jesuit general objected in 1735 when superiors rushed him from the novitiate to philosophical studies, and a similar complaint was lodged in 1741, but he was soon back in America, where he shared in founding Deer Creek church on his father's Conewago-Baltimore road. He also attended the congregation in Baltimore, where he died in 1746.[39]

Robert Knatchbull (1716-82) represented a change of pace. From Queen Anne's County on Maryland's Eastern Shore, he was not related to the families from which levites had been coming. He was one of the nine students taught by Henry Neale who in 1735 entered Watten. In 1742 he was allowed a home leave, the general commenting that he was a

---

[37]Hanley, *Carroll Papers*, I, 166, 212; II, 384, 460.

[38]Spalding, "Natives of Maryland," 326.

[39]Hughes, *History*, Documents, I/1, 76; *Woodstock Letters* 34 (1915), 118; 63 (1934), 404-05.

scholastic in whom enormous hopes were placed, a person of "very great virtue and superior talent." Chaplain to the Lawsons at Brough Hall in Yorkshire, he was ousted in 1765 by the patron as too "busy." The Archbishop of York complained of his vigorous proselytizing and of the catechism program he had mounted. Rector and novice master at Ghent from 1765 to 1773, he died at Walton Hall, Yorkshire.[40]

A second American woman, Anna Maria Parnham (1716-84) entered religious life in 1742, this time at the Lierre Carmel where, as Sister Mary Teresa of Jesus, she held office as novice mistress and prioress.[41]

After a twelve-year hiatus, two Americans were at Watten in 1747, John Royall (1729-70), the only Jesuit from colonial Pennsylvania, and Joseph Cole (1727-63). Royall was later chaplain at English country houses like Plowden Hall and Swynnerton, seat of the Fitzherberts, and died at Husbands Bosworth in Leicester.[42] Cole, who had two brothers priests and a widowed sister a nun, taught humanities at St. Omers and died unexpectedly on a visit to Rome.[43] Eleanor Wharton (Teresa Joseph of the Incarnation, 1723-93) became Lierre's second American Carmelite in 1749, the year her brother Francis (1729-53) entered Watten. He died four years later at Liège.[44]

[40]Foley, *Records*, VII, 424; Hughes, *History*, Documents, I/1, 83, 259-60; Joseph Gillow, *A Literary and Biographical History, or Biographical Dictionary of the English Catholics, from the Break with Rome, in 1534, to the Present Time*, 5 Vols. (London, 1885-1902), IV, 66-67. For other members of his Kent family, *ibid*., 62-66. Hugh Aveling, *Northern Catholics* (London, 1966), 379.

[41]Spalding, "Natives of Maryland," 319; Guilday, *English Catholic Refugees*, 346-76.

[42]Foley, *Records*, IV, 562; VII, 674.

[43]*Ibid*., VII, 145-46; Russell L. Menard *et al.*, "A Small Planter's Profile: The Cole Estate and the Growth of the Early Chesapeake Economy," *William and Mary Quarterly* 40 (1983), 171-96.

[44]Foley, *Records*, VIII, 831.

A classmate of Wharton was Ralph Hoskins (1729-94), descended through his mother, Eleanor Neale, from the Calverts. As a fourth-year theologian at Liège he also taught sacred scripture, but his life was spent as chaplain to the Curzons in Oxfordshire and the Lawsons in Yorkshire. He wrote an account of the Jesuits' expulsion from St. Omers and a Latin life of a saintly relative, Brother William Couche, S.J. It was said he "wrote Latin better than English." Hoskins did not forget America. In 1790 John Carroll reported his promise to obtain a generous contribution for Georgetown College from Sir Thomas Lawson, but the money had not yet materialized.[45]

Also a Neale on the maternal side was Robert Cole (1732-1812), a Jesuit from 1752 who lived to rejoin the restored English Province and whose priesthood was spent ministering to the English gentry.[46] He was brother to Joseph Cole, S.J., and to the Reverend Henry Cole, both of whom died in 1763. Henry, a St. Omers and Valladolid alumnus, succumbed to smallpox while passing through England en route to the Jesuit novitiate.[47] Their sister Elizabeth (d. 1816), widow of of James Brooke, was professed as a Dominican nun (Ann Dominic) at the castlelike Spellekens convent in Brussels in 1757 and was twice elected prioress. Two Brooke sisters had preceded her in 1756, Mary (Mary Teresa, 1729-89) and Henrietta (Mary Rose, 1733-57), whose sister Jane (Mary Xavier of the Sacred Heart, d. 1771), joined the Lierre Carmel in 1749. A fourth Maryland Dominican, Mary Aloysia Spalding, made a deathbed profession at the Spellekens in 1757.[48]

[45]*Ibid.*, VII, 373; Guilday, *English Catholic Refugees*, 342-43; Gillow, *Biographical Dictionary*, III, 407-08; Hanley, *Carroll Papers*, I, 459.

[46]Foley, *Records*, VII, 146.

[47]Henson, *Valladolid*, 190-91; Anstruther, *Seminary Priests*, IV: *1716-1801*, 69.

[48]Spalding, "Natives of Maryland," 314-315, 321; Guilday, *English Catholic Refugees*, 420.

A nephew of the Coles, John Ceslas Fenwick (c. 1759-1816), was the first American Dominican priest. A student at the Great College, Bruges, when the Jesuits were suppressed, he transferred to Holy Cross College, Bornhem, and four years later took the Dominican habit. Back in Maryland, he worked with the Jesuits in the southern counties, who knew him as "good Father John." Bishop Edward Fenwick, O.P., of Cincinnati was his nephew.[49]

The 1750s saw a rise in female vocations. Besides the Brussels Dominicans, Mary Boone (Mary Rose, 1718-58) took the Carmelite habit at Lierre in 1750, while Mary Brent (Mary Margaret, 1734-84) and Margaret Pye (Mary Magdalen, 1724-77) did the same at Antwerp in 1751. Much of the surviving correspondence on these women deals with the dowries they had to bring with them. Pye was a special case. Her entrance had been long delayed because she had lost her parents and brother and had no financial resources. The English Lady Stourton finally made her a gift of the required amount.[50]

Ann Hill (Ann Louis, 1734-1813) and Anne Matthews (Bernardine Teresa, 1732-1800) were professed in the Hoogstraet Carmel in 1755. Ann Hill, John Carroll's cousin, was the prioress who led the community's flight to England in 1794; four years earlier Anne Matthews founded the first American Carmel. Another nun of the 1750s, Anne Neale (1736-84), who became Sister Mary, a Poor Clare at Aire, was grand-niece of two Jesuits and sister of four.[51]

The future Archbishop John Carroll (1736-1815) became a Jesuit in 1753. By 1762 his brother boasted: "My brother

[49]Holt, *St. Omers and Bruges*, 99; *Dominicana* (London, 1929), 135.

[50]Spalding, "Natives of Maryland," 314-19; Anne Hardman, S.N.D., *English Carmelites in Penal Times* (London, 1936), 106-110 — Mary Brent's voyage is described there. Thomas Hughes, S.J., "Educational Convoys to Europe in the Olden Time," *American Ecclesiastical Review* 29 (1903), 24-39.

[51]Charles Warren Currier, *Carmel in America* (Baltimore, 1890).

John...is now a Jesuit at Liège, teaching Philosophy and emminent [*sic*] in his profession." These Carrolls were sons of an immigrant Irish entrepreneur, related by marriage to *the* Carrolls and descended through their mother from the Darnalls and the Diggeses. In 1773 John Carroll was director of the sodality at Bruges. A year later he was home, and the rest of his life is the story of the organization of Catholicism in the United States.[52]

A first cousin of the Coles, Henry Neale (1733-54), after four years at St. Omer's became a novice brother at Watten in 1754, but died shortly thereafter.[53] Ralph Falkner (b. 1736) studied at Bohemia Manor and St. Omers before admission in 1755 to the English College, Rome. Ordained priest, he revisited Maryland and was at Newtown in 1761, proceeding from there to England, where he served at Brockhampton in Hampshire until at least 1772, when he was last heard from at a luncheon of the "Big M," the English secular priests' clergy fund.[54] A potential secular priest was Thomas Falkner, who went from St. Omer to Valladolid in 1756, but was dismissed in 1758, he and his professors agreeing that after two years of "logic and physiology" he "neither perceives nor understands anything nor does he have any chance of making progress in letters."[55]

The year 1756 saw arrival together at Watten of two blood brothers, Edward (1734-85) and John (1735-95) Boone, of the family after which Boone's Chapel, the original mission station in Prince George's County, was named. As priests

[52]Margaret Brent Downing, "The Earliest Proprietors of Capitol Hill," *Records of the Columbia Historical Society* 21 (1918), 16-18; James Hennesey, S.J., "An Eighteenth Century Bishop: John Carroll of Baltimore," *Archivum Historiae Pontificiae* 16 (1978), 171-204.

[53]Foley, *Records*, VII, 537.

[54]*Liber Ruber*, 215; Anstruther, *Seminary Priests*, IV, 100; *Woodstock Letters* 13 (1884), 290.

[55]Henson, *Valladolid*, 174, 190.

both went to England. Edward spent twenty years at Danby Hall, seat of Simon Scroope, Esq. in Yorkshire. His registers record an active sacramental ministry, but a dim view of the Established Church: "I administered the Viaticum to old Nelly Mud...the S[acraments], the H[oly] oils. She recovered — as many did." "Michael Errington foolishly married a Protestant." Another married a Protestant, "who afterwards broke his solemn word about changing his religion. Never again will I take a Protestant's word about religion." And, when a Catholic was rebaptized in the Anglican parish church: "O Tempora. O Person. O Shame."[56]

John Boone was in Maryland in 1765, but back in England by 1770. After the Revolution he met a chilly American reception. Carroll wrote to England: "As you could not prevent [him] from leaving you, so neither could we prevent his coming among us. If he will conduct himself well, we may perhaps find a station for him; if not he must provide a subsistance where he can." For the Maryland treasurer, Boone and Joseph Doyne were "burdensome members," owed support by the English ex-Jesuits. The unwelcome member had also been the unwitting occasion for setting in motion the appointment of Carroll as superior of the mission. He and another ex-Jesuit had applied for priestly faculties for America to the vicar apostolic at London, who declined to exercise that jurisdiction, and this led to Roman action to regularize the situation in the former English colonies. Boone found work at St. Inigoes and worked there until his death.[57]

Joseph Doyne (1734-1803) joined the noviceship the year after the Boones and was in Lancashire for eleven years, where "this eccentric character occasionally forgot the

[56]John Orelebar Payne, *Old English Missions* (London, 1889), 31-36.

[57]Hughes, *History,* Documents, I/2, 659; Hanley, *Carroll Papers*, I, 150-51; Archives of the Sacred Congregation for Propagation of the Faith, Rome, Scritture riferite nei Congressi, America Centrale, Section I, fols, 328r to 331v; *Woodstock Letters* 33 (1904), 381.

respect due to himself and others." He was eventually admitted among the Maryland clergy, worked in the "lower counties," and was active in plans for a Jesuit restoration.[58]

George Hunter, mission superior in the 1760s, actively promoted religious vocations. He organized the finances, once warning the nuns at Aire that their dowry demands were too high, and arranged group passages to the Low Countries, complete with instructions on how to act if captured by French privateers.[59] In 1760 Sarah Edelen (Mary Teresa, c. 1740-1826) and Susanna Spalding (Mary Clare, 1715-1813) became Poor Clares at Rouen. Anne Boone (Anne Joseph, 1733-1811) followed her sister, "the famous Mary Boone," to Lierre Carmel, Elizabeth Rozer (Scholastica, 1746-91), and Rachel Boone (Mary Xaveria, 1743-98) joined the Brussels Benedictines. Four Hagan sisters became nuns. Mary Anne (Mary Louisa, 1740-1811) became a Benedictine at Cambrai. In 1794 she was imprisoned with the sixteen Carmelite martyrs of Compiègne. When they went to the guillotine, their secular dress was distributed to the nuns left in the prison. Elizabeth (Elizabeth Clare) Hagan (d.1808) and her sister Monica (Monica Clare, d. 1807) were Poor Clares at Rouen, while Henrietta (Teresa) Hagan was subprioress of the Benedictines imprisoned in 1794-95 at the Château de Vincennes. Two Hagan cousins were Liège Sepulchrines: Elizabeth (Mary Longina, 1741-78) and Martha (Mary Jane Regis, 1733-91). A widow from Northampton County, Pennsylvania, Ann Kelsey Dougherty (1743-89) became Sister Bridget there in 1771.[60]

[58]George Oliver, *Collections towards Illustrating the Biography of the Scotch, English and Irish Members of the Society of Jesus*, 2nd ed. (London, 1845), 83; *Woodstock Letters* 13 (1884), 294.

[59]Hughes, *History*, Text, II, 521-23; *id.*, "Educational Convoys."

[60]Joseph T. Durkin, S.J., "Catholic Training for Maryland Catholics 1773-1786," *Historical Records and Studies* 32 (1941), 70-82; Robert Eaton, *The Benedictines of Colwich 1829-1929* (London, 1929), 43-60; Guilday, *English Catholic Refugees*, 398.

Three Semmes sisters were Benedictines and four Sepulchrines: Rachel (Mary Xaveria, 1736-89); Elizabeth (Mary Magdalen, d. 1780), and Catherine (Mary Frances, 1743-1824) at Paris; and, at Liège, Clare (Mary Ursula, 1745-1820), Martha (Mary Rose, 1746-68), Mary Anne (Constantia, 1739-67), and Teresa (Mary Frances, 1750-69). Their brother Joseph (1743-1809) taught philosophy at Liège until advancing French armies drove the Jesuits out. He died at Stonyhurst College, of which he was a founder.[61]

At least one American a year entered the Jesuits between 1760 and 1767. Six did so in 1766, the year after the novitiate was driven from Watten to Ghent. In 1760 arrived the first in a parade of sons of William and Anne Brooke Neale of Port Tobacco, William Chandler Neale (1743-99). Of their thirteen children, Anne was already a Poor Clare, two died students at St. Omer's, one of them, Joseph, making vows of devotion as a Jesuit on his deathbed, and four were Jesuits: William, Leonard (1747-1817) in 1767, Charles (1751-1823) in 1771, and Francis (1756-1837) in 1806.

William Neale worked in Lancashire until his mind gave way; he died in a Manchester asylum.[62] Leonard, ordained a month before the Jesuit suppression in 1773, was a missionary in England and Guyana and then at Philadelphia before becoming president of Georgetown College, coadjutor bishop (1800) and archbishop of Baltimore (1815-17).[63] Charles, a novice in 1773, was ordained at Liège. In 1790 he escorted the Carmelites to America and in 1805 made his

---

[61]Spalding, "Natives of Maryland," 320; anon., "The Migration of the Canonesses Regular from Liège to England in 1793," *Letters and Notices* 8 (1872), 136-57, 292-308; Foley, *Records*, V, 187; Hubert Chadwick, S.J., *From St. Omers to Stonyhurst: A History of Two Centuries* (London, 1962), 384-402.

[62]Hughes, *History*, Documents, I/2, 721; Oliver, *Collections*, 148.

[63]Foley, *Records*, V, 187; James Hennesey, S.J., "First American Foreign Missionary: Leonard Neale in Guyana," *Records of the American Catholic Historical Society of Philadelphia* 83 (1972), 82-86.

Jesuit vows. He was twice superior of the restored Maryland Mission.[64] Francis, denied entrance by the suppression, became a major Jesuit figure after the restoration.

Henry Pile (1743-1813), a Jesuit in 1761, spent the war years at Stubbs Walden in Yorkshire, but came home in 1784. John Carroll described him: "The worthy Mr. Pile has resided on his own estate since his return to Maryland but without indulging in idleness, having constantly performed the work of the ministry." Pile's ancestry traced to John Pile, a Maryland councilor in 1649. He lived alone and kept twenty-eight slaves at Salisbury Manor on Cobb Neck overlooking the Wicomico.[65]

Three Boarmans became Jesuits: John (1743-97), in 1762, and the brothers Sylvester (1746-1811) in 1765, and Charles (1751-1819) in 1770. The family plantation, "Boarman's Rest," was the site of an early chapel. Sending him to St. Omers, John's father insisted that he "stay his time out," and he forbade him dancing lessons. "Without much pretension to talents," he was nevertheless a successful missionary in Maryland.[66] Sylvester followed him to a like ministry,[67] but Charles, just starting philosophical studies when the blow struck in 1773, gave up the ecclesiastical career, married, and later taught at Georgetown.[68]

Ignatius Matthews (1730-90) was ordained at Valladolid in 1763 and was on his way with Henry Cole to the novitiate

---

[64]Holt, *St. Omers and Bruges*, 188-89; Foley, *Records*, VII, li; Geoffrey Holt, S.J., "The English Province, Ex-Jesuits and the Restoration," *Archivum Historicum Societatis Jesu* 42 (1973), 291-92.

[65]Hanley, *Carroll Papers*, II, 36; U.S. Bureau of the Census, Heads of Families at the First Census of the United States Taken in the Year 1790, Maryland (Baltimore,1965), 52.

[66]Oliver, *Collections*, 56; Foley, *Records*, V, 187; Hanley, *Carroll Papers*, I, 52.

[67]Foley, *Records*, V, 188; *Letters and Notices* 17 (1884), 215-16.

[68]John M. Daley, S.J., *Georgetown University: Origin and Early Years* (Washington, 1957), 117. But Daley is mistaken in saying he was "a student at St. Omers with Bishop Carroll." A quarter-century separated them — see Holt, *St. Omers and Bruges*, 41-42, 59.

when both came down with the smallpox which carried Cole off. Back in Maryland in 1766, Matthews was pastor at Newtown and Deer Creek, responsible in the latter post for the territory between the Patapsco and the Susquehanna. He died while his sister was on the high seas, coming to found Port Tobacco Carmel.[69]

A year after Matthews' arrival, a novice from the wealthy Sewall family of Mattapany arrived at Watten. His progenitor, Henry Sewall, was the Third Lord Baltimore's stepson, their Patuxent estate property once given by Indians to the Jesuits and confiscated by the Calverts. Charles Sewall (1744-1806) was a tertian at Ghent in 1773. Back in America he was priest at Deer Creek and then first resident pastor in Baltimore. A strong anti-Bonapartist, he wrote his brother of the presence there of Jerome Bonaparte, "a little, insignificant, dissipated youth of about 19 years of age." In 1805 Sewall was among the first three Americans to renew their Jesuit vows.[70]

France ousted the English Jesuits from St. Omer in 1762. Five Americans who shared that experience finished up at the Great College in Bruges and in 1766 reported to the newly named American novice master at Ghent, Robert Knatchbull. A sixth joined them, John Mattingly (1745-1807), a transfer from St. Omer to Valladolid in 1763. The others were Charles Sewall's brother Nicholas (1745-1834), Charles Thompson (1746-95), Austin Jenkins (1742-1800), John Digges (b. 1746), and Charles Wharton (1748-1833).

Sewall, a Bruges teacher in 1773, spent his life in Lancashire. In 1803 he entered the restored English Province, where he was twice rector of Stonyhurst and, from 1821 to 1826, provincial. A strong royalist of pronounced anti-

[69]Oliver, *Collections*, 139; Henson, *Valladolid*, 190.

[70]Foley, *Records*, V, 187; *Woodstock Letters* 7 (1878), 145-46; 34 (1904), 120; John Walter Thomas, *Chronicles of Colonial Maryland* (Baltimore, 1900), 290-92; English Jesuit Archives, London, Maryland File, Charles to Nicholas Sewall, November 12, 1803.

republican views, he advocated grassroots vigilante reaction to the "Sheffield Levellers" and the writings of "T. Paine & such fellows," although after the 1807 *Chesapeake-Leopard* battle he thought the British ministry wrong not to hear proposals made by U.S. Minister (and fellow Marylander) William Pinkney. This did not prevent the comment that "I think my Countrymen a set of violent, wrong-headed fellows, vindictive to the extreme." Until his death, Sewall received regular income from family property in Maryland.[71]

Thompson, descended from Leonard Calvert and a cousin of Ralph Hoskins, was a master at Bruges in 1773. Resisting John Carroll's entreaties to come home, he worked in Suffolk and died at Bristol.[72]

Mattingly had an adventurous career. He transferred to Valladolid in 1763, but was dismissed from St. Alban's in 1766 by the new secular administration for refusing the oath to serve as a secular priest in England. By 1773 he was dean and professor of controversial theology at the English College, Rome, an institution reduced by those days to eight students. After their suppression, the ex-Jesuits were allowed three days to acquire secular priests' garb and leave. Six of them moved into a nearby apartment, but Mattingly, "being yet young, about twenty-eight, and of a strong constitution," opted to take a proffered pension in a lump sum and began a career as travelling tutor to English gentry which ended only with his death in Ireland. For reasons unknown, the "Congregation for the Affairs of the Extinct Society of Jesus" forbade his return in 1774 to Maryland. An account by him of the work in Maryland is found in the Archives of the Congregation for the Propagation of the Faith.[73]

[71]Foley, *Records*, VIII, 701-02; English Jesuit Archives, London, Stone-Sewall-Connell File, Nicholas Sewall to Joseph Dunn, November 11, 1790; January 7, 1809.

[72]Foley, *Records*, VIII, 769-70; Hanley, *Carroll Papers*, I, 192.

[73]Henson, *Valladolid*, 190-91; *Woodstock Letters* 15 (1886), 241-48; Secret Vatican Archives, Fondo Gesuiti, Carte diverse della Congregazione per la sop-

John Carroll greatly admired Jenkins, "that man without guile...almost adored by his acquaintances." The little Welshman had "labours enough to kill a less zealous man," but a century later he was remembered as "sweet, affable and gentlemanly in all his ways....The charm of his manners was universally felt. He had a winning grace about him that won the affection of all who came in contact with him. His generous heart overflowed with kindly feeling." He was pastor at Newtown, near the estate, "White Plains," where he had been raised.[74]

Two in the class of 1766 took other vocational ways. John Digges left the Jesuits in 1769.[75] Charles Wharton, of whom Carroll wrote, "he is neither visionary nor fanatick, *un peu philosophe*, but I hope not too much so," was ordained in 1772, spent the war years in Worcester, and returned to America in 1783. In Carroll's mind, "he left behind him few of our antient brethren his equals, none, I believe, his Superiors." But he became an Episcopal clergyman, active in the inaugural conventions of the Protestant Episcopal Church. His apologia prompted Carroll's 1784 *Address to the Roman Catholics of the United States of America.* Wharton married twice, was briefly president of Columbia College, and died rector of St. Mary's parish, Burlington, New Jersey.[76]

Apart from novice brother John Deas, a Bruges student who entered in 1767 and departed two years later, and Dame Xaveria Boone's brother Joseph (c. 1750-1779), in 1772 the last Jesuit to enter the "Old Society" — he died a student at

pressione de la Compagnia di Gesù; Archives of the Sacred Congregation for Propagation of the Faith, Scritture riguardanti l'esecuzione del breve di soppressione, 1774, Missioni miscellan. V, fol. 22; Congressi, America Centrale, I, fols. 557r-v and 558r; Hughes, *History*, Text, II, 554-56; Anthony Laird, "The English College, Rome, under Italian Secular Administration, 1773-1798," *Recusant History* 14 (1977), 127-47.

[74]Foley, *Records*, VII, 402; Hanley, *Carroll Papers*, I, 56; *Woodstock Letters* 13 (1884), 291-92.

[75]Foley, *Records*, VII, 202.

[76]*Dictionary of American Biography* (New York, 1936), XX, 20; Hanley, *Carroll Papers*, I, 146-47.

Liège[77] — the tale ended where it had begun, with the Brooke family. Leonard (1750-1813) became a Jesuit novice at Bruges in 1769 and his brother Ignatius Baker (1751-1817) joined him a year a later. Their ancestor, Baker Brooke, had been immigrant Robert Brooke's eldest son. Their aunts were nuns at Brussels and Lierre.

Leonard worked most of his life in England, praised for his catechetical skill. He died chaplain to the Welds of Lulworth Castle.[78] Ignatius Baker Brooke returned to Maryland and married, but after his wife died was ordained at Baltimore. At Newtown from 1805-11, he then lived on his estate near Port Tobacco Carmel. He kept twenty slaves and ran a boarding house for young ladies, for whom Bishop Carroll once offered him a French nun as tutor. He apparently left the ministry for a time, but returned by 1815.[79]

After the catastrophe of 1773, the English ex-Jesuits continued their schools under the protection of the prince-bishop of Liège. Priests for the American mission were ordained there. France's revolutionary armies ended that sanctuary and disrupted the exiled English colony. Convents, American nuns included, fled from France and Flanders to England. The ex-Jesuits set up at Stonyhurst in Lancashire. For 110 years religious vocations had come from leading American families steeped in an austere continental Catholicism. The immediate future for an American clergy now lay with the academy at Georgetown and the Sulpician seminary established at Baltimore in 1791. After a contemplative start, female religious life in the United States would develop new, more activist, beginnings.

---

[77]Holt, *St. Omers and Bruges*, 84; Hughes, *History*, Documents, 1/2 661, 724.

[78]"The Brooke Family," 376; Foley, *Records*, V, 188; Hughes, *History*, Documents, I/2, 661; Oliver, *Collections*, 60-61.

[79]Foley, *Records*, V, 188.

John Carroll and Interfaith Marriages: The Case of the Belle Vue Carrolls

*Robert F. McNamara**

Cecilius Lord Baltimore established the colony of Maryland in 1634 on the sensible basis of civil religious liberty. Unfortunately, his innovative experiment was halted by Britain after only two generations. In 1692, under William and Mary, the Anglican church was officially established in Maryland, and a series of penal laws was initiated to press its Catholic minority, if possible, into Protestant conformity.

The faith of these beleaguered Catholics now faced two threats in particular. The first and more obvious was the attractive social and political advantage that religious conformity offered. The second threat, more subtle, was the religious gamble of Catholic-Protestant marriages. While

*The present writer wishes to express thanks to all who assisted him in preparing this essay, particularly Rev. Mark Miller, Rev. R. Emmett Curran, S.J., Bro. Thomas W. Spalding, C.F.X., and the late Edwin Warfield Beitzell, who kindly read and critiqued its preliminary draft.

such "mixed marriages" (the traditional Catholic term) did not necessarily result in the lapse of the Catholic partner, they could easily deprive his children of a firm and bequeathable Catholic identity. Futhermore, in not a few such matches in Maryland between 1760 and 1850, the contracting couple reached an agreement, surely without official church sanction, to raise the male offspring in the religion of the father and the female offspring in the religion of the mother. In these cases, denominational division became institutionalized at the outset.[1]

It must be said to the credit of the Catholics of Maryland that although a small percentage (including some prominent gentry) abandoned their Catholicism for social and economic reasons, the majority stood firm.[2] As for mixed marriages, Maryland's colonial Catholics were certainly not in the dark about their hazards. For instance, in 1762,

[1]Edwin W. Beitzell, *The Jesuit Missions of St. Mary's County, Maryland*, 2nd ed. (Abell, Md., 1976), 338. Mr. Beitzell informed the present writer that there were not a few cases of this compromise solution. One illustration was the apparent agreement between the Catholic chief justice, Roger Brooke Taney (1777-1864) and his Episcopalian wife, Anne Phoebe Charlton Key (1783-1855), married January 7, 1806 — see, e.g., Bernard C. Steiner, *Life of Roger Brooke Taney, Chief Justice of the United States Supreme Court* (Baltimore, 1922; Westport, Conn., 1970), 43-47; Carl Brent Swisher, *Roger B. Taney* (New York, 1937), 49-51 and passim; [Martin I.J. Griffin?] "'Star Spangled Banner' Key and Chief Justice Taney — Did Taney Make a Pre-nuptial Agreement with the Wife?" *American Catholic Historical Researches* (Philadelphia), New Series Vol. 8, No. 1 (January 1912), 87-90. Another case was a "Dr. Wilson"[Dr. Thomas Bennett *Willson*] of Queenstown, Queen Anne's Co., Maryland. Archbishop Ambrose Maréchal wrote of him that he was married to a Protestant lady "who brings up her girls in her persuasion" — see the "Diary of Archbishop Maréchal, 1815-1825," *Records of the American Catholic Historical Society of Philadelphia* 11 (1900), 417-54, here 432 (October 9, 1819).

[2]Peter Guilday, on the basis of John Carroll's 1785 report to Rome, seems to say that a large number of Maryland Catholics had left the Catholic faith under penal pressures — see his *Life and Times of John Carroll of Baltimore, 1735-1815* (New York, 1922), 770-71. Carroll wrote quite otherwise in his 1789 "Response to Patrick Smyth," in Thomas O'Brien Hanley, S. J., ed., *The John Carroll Papers* (Notre Dame, 1976) I, 337-46, here 341 — hereafter cited as *J.C.P.* A certain number of the gentry conformed, some ignobly. But more recent genealogical

Charles Carroll of Annapolis shrewdly advised his student son, the future Charles Carroll of Carrollton, "I earnestly Recommend it to you on no Consideration to Marry a Protestant for besides the Risque yr offspring will Run, it is certain that there Cannot be any solid Happyness without an Union of Sentiments on all Matters Especially Religion.... It will be an advantage if yr Lady should have been bred in a Monastery, early good impressions are very lasting." (Apart from the monastic reference, a devout Anglican father might have written the same Chesterfieldian counsel, *mutatis mutandis*, to his own son.)[3]

One course that the American Catholic missionaries began to follow even before the Revolution, in order to dissuade interfaith marriages, was to favor the marriage of Catholics (black and white alike), to kinsfolk (within, of course, the degrees of kinship permitted by general church law and special dispensation). While "family" weddings could perhaps have less desirable side-effects, they were already quite common, for various reasons, among British subjects, Catholic and Protestant alike.[4]

Intrafamilial marriages were bound to become a less practicable alternative after the United States won its inde-

---

studies indicate that the majority clung to their Catholicism, and that there was even a numerical increase of the Catholic minority. See Beitzell, *Jesuit Missions*, 48; and Thomas W. Spalding's "John Carroll: Corrigenda and Addenda," forthcoming in the *Catholic Historical Review*.

[3]Charles Carroll of Annapolis to Charles Carroll of Carrollton, September 1, 1762, in Maryland Historical Society, Baltimore, Md., Carroll Papers, MS. 206, Vol. 1, #84.

[4]John Carroll to Leonardo Antonelli, March 1, 1785, *J.C.P.* I, 179-85, here 181-82, 184-85. Guilday, *John Carroll*, 774, says "there is scarcely a letter [from Carroll] to Rome which does not ask for a stipulated number of dispensations for mixed marriages." Now, a spot check of Carroll's regular and special prelatial faculties from 1784 to 1810 has failed to turn up any authorization to dispense from the "impedient" impediment of *mixta religio* (the mixed marriage of a baptized couple of different denominations). What he did request were faculties to dispense from the closer degrees of consanguinity and affinity often involved in matches

pendence. Many seaboard natives, especially the less well-to-do, tended to move away from their kin and their old neighborhoods. Immigrants, naturally, had left most of their relatives in the Old World.

The pastoral career of Bishop John Carroll (1735-1815), who was the primary molder of the American Catholic Church, bridged the colonial and early federal periods of United States history. No longer a Jesuit after 1773, as a result of the papal suppression of that order, Carroll returned from Europe in 1774 and began missionary work as a secular priest in Maryland. In 1784, Pope Pius VI named him "Superior of the Mission of the Thirteen Provinces of Confederated North America." In 1789, the same pope appointed him the first bishop of Baltimore. Pope Pius VII raised him to the rank of archbishop in 1808; and he served as metropolitan of the province of Baltimore until his death on December 3, 1815.

between Maryland Catholics and Protestants, black as well as white. The faculties to dispense from the second degree of consanguinity (in pre-1983 computation, first cousins), and of affinity were first granted Carroll by Rome on July 17, 1785, for twenty cases apiece (Archives of the Archdiocese of Baltimore [here cited as AAB], Sp B A 9). On May 30, 1802, his faculties were renewed for 200 cases of each impediment; at the same time the faculty granted him on June 6, 1794 to dispense from the impediment of disparity of cult (baptized marrying non-baptized) was renewed for three years (Archives of the Sacred Congregation de Propaganda Fide, Vol. VII, *Udienze*, 1802, No. 48, fols. 355rv, 356r). Only in the wartime special faculties granted on January 10, 1810 to the Catholic bishops of England, Scotland, Ireland, and the United States, is the faculty granted to dispense from the *impedimento di matrimonio misto* in marriages already contracted, and in twelve cases of those to be contracted. The document says that this faculty had been given earlier to the vicar apostolic of the Midland District of England and to certain bishops in Ireland (Propaganda Fide Archives, Vol. VII, *Udienze*, 1810, No. 74, fols. 5r, 6v). Are we to conclude that up to then, mixed marriages, though reluctantly permitted, did not require a dispensation from *mixta religio*? Perhaps because the matrimonial legislation of the Council of Trent was not considered binding in British and Anglo-American territories? (I am indebted for the Propaganda documents to Dr. Wendy Schlereth, archivist, University of Notre Dame; and for the incoming Carroll correspondence, to the past and present archivists of the Archdiocese of Baltimore, Father John J. Tierney and Sister Felicitas Powers, RSM.)

An examination of Carroll's published writings throughout his American ministry shows that he took a consistent stand against interfaith matches. Not only did his Church frown on them; he had come to oppose them from his own pastoral experience. The aim of the present essay is, first, to gather from the bishop's utterances the evidences and rationale of his stance; and second, to outline, by way of illustrating his concern, the Catholic pedigree of one Maryland family of the colonial gentry that was much given, in the early federal period, to interfaith marriages.

John Carroll on Mixed Marriages

We have already noted that the Maryland Catholic clergy sought to discourage mixed marriages by favoring Catholics' marrying Catholic relatives. It was John Carroll who described this custom to the Holy See in his report of March 1, 1785. In the same report, Father Carroll, as Superior of the American Mission, requested papal faculties to dispense, for the benefit of betrothed kinsmen, from the impediments of consanguinity (blood relationship) in the second degree, as then computed (first cousins); and affinity (in-law relationship), also in the second degree. Evidently Carroll, at that point, still hoped that intrafamilial weddings might diminish interdenominational ones.

Pursuing his official review of the American church, he wrote frankly about the traits of American Catholics and of their milieu.

> As for their observance, in general they are rather faithful
> to the practices of their religion, and in frequenting the
> sacraments. All fervor, however, is lacking... since many
> congregations attend Mass and hear a sermon [only]

once a month or every two months. To this extent are we
overwhelmed by the scarcity of priests....The abuses
among the Catholic population are those above all which
spring from the necessity of familiar relations with the
non-Catholics and from the ideals derived from them.[5]

This absence of spiritual warmth obviously caused Carroll pastoral disquiet. What was now to become of his people, still old-line Catholics for the greater part? With the constraint of persecution lifted, would they be seduced into a mental attitude of indifference, as a result of the peer-pressure of the non-Catholics who daily surrounded them? The liability would surely be lessened if the clergy could give them full-time guidance. But in this crucial era of American Catholicism, priests were so tragically few!

In pointing out the spiritual risk of close interfaith association, Father Carroll doubtless had the increase of mixed marriages particularly in mind. He himself preached against these unions in and out of season. In one undated sermon, he begins with the statement that divine Providence instituted matrimony for the purpose of "consolation" and "hope of posterity." For that reason, he said, the Church has ruled "that its members should choose for their indissoluble companions throughout life only such as are united in the profession of the same faith." The Old Testament had made interfaith marriages a strict taboo; in New Testament times they were no more commendable:

In this dispensation of grace under Jesus Christ, to
deviate from this rule is to expose your own happiness, as
well as that of the children you may have, to the greatest
danger. The opposite religious opinions of the father and
mother serve to perplex, and finally to make their chil-

dren indifferent [,] about the tenets or practices of christianity; and being thus indifferent they fall an easy prey to
the artificial sophistry of deists, and finally discard from
their minds even the belief of God's moral government.

"I have spoken so often and so much," he continued,
"against marriages thus contracted, as to render it the less
necessary to add more at present, . . . except [to] express my
deep concern, that we are so often compelled for fear of
greater evils, to lend our ministry to their celebration." He
granted that some interfaith matches work out well enough;
but these exceptions should not cloud the painful rule: "If
some of them be attended with salutary consequences, many
leave us cause for the most poignant sorrow, and almost
induce us to repent that we concurred in forming them."[6]

In November, 1791, scarcely a year after his consecration
as bishop, Carroll communicated the same sentiments to his
clergy in the form of diocesan law. Gathering his priests in
the first diocesan synod of Baltimore, he laid down precise
regulations regarding mixed marriages.

Pastors, he declared, were to see to it, first of all, that
Catholics *avoid* marriage with non-Catholics. Since American Catholics were so few, however, and their social contacts with Protestants were so constant, it was impossible to
prevent a certain number of such matches. But priests
should agree to them only under rigorous conditions.

First, they were to admonish the Catholic party of the
great "inconveniences" of mixed marriages. If the Catholic
was not moved to reconsider by this exhortation, the pastor
was to study how much of a threat the marriage would
involve to the religion of the Catholic party in the case in
hand. The non-Catholic was to be asked to put no obstacle
in the way of raising *all* the children in the Catholic faith.
The pastor should also judge whether the couple, if refused a

[6]*J.C.P.*, III, 424-531, here 430.

Catholic marriage, would be liable to turn to a Protestant minister. Once the priest had satisfied himself on these points, he might proceed to schedule the wedding (provided, of course, that there were no other impediments to prevent it). The solemn nuptial blessing, reserved for fully Catholic marriages, was not to be given.[7]

There was no innovation here; the precautions were predictable. It goes without saying, however, that the laws of the synod did not put an end to interfaith marriages. American Catholics increased in number through natural growth and immigration, but the non-Catholic majority also increased, with the result that the number of requests for mixed marriages rose rather than declined. In 1803, Bishop Carroll unburdened himself on the whole topic to his English friend and confidant, Father Charles Plowden.

> Here our Catholics are so mixed with Protestants in all the intercourse of civil Society & business public and private, that the abuse of intermarriage is almost universal; and it surpasses my ability to devise any effectual bar against it — No general prohibition can be exacted, without reducing many of the faithful to live in a state of celibacy, as in sundry places there would be no choice for them of Catholic matches: and tho sometimes, good consequences follow these marriages, yet often, thro the discordancy of the religious sentiments of parents, their children grow up without attachment to any, & become an easy prey to infidelity or indifferentism, if you will allow the word.[8]

"In sundry places." With the constant expansion of the United States, Catholics both native-born and newly immi-

---

[7]*J.C.P.*, I, 526-45, here 530-31, 538.

[8]John Carroll to Charles Plowden, Baltimore, February 12, 1803, *J.C.P.*, II, 407-09, here 408.

grated would find on the frontiers fewer Catholics to marry. Carroll felt particular concern for Catholic young women who had been raised in a Catholic parish or mission but accepted the proposal to marry non-Catholic residents of districts far from a Catholic church. In 1809, a Baltimore grandniece of his, Maria Digges, gave her hand to a Protestant congressman, Robert Livingston, who lived in Holland-Dutch country at Hudson, New York. Most disturbed by this news, the bishop wrote of his deep anxiety to his sister Elizabeth,

> ...terrifying is the idea of a young woman being seated down in the hotbed of presbyterianism, at least one hundred miles from a Catholic church or clergyman, or perhaps the habitation of a Catholic. No worldly advantage or satisfaction, even if it were to be as real, as it is often only delusive[,] can make compensation for this evil.[9]

The interfaith wedding of Elizabeth and Robert Livingston was probably all the more upsetting to Carroll because it was one of several such matches among his own kindred. As the head of the Catholic Church in the United States, he had solemnly warned the American faithful to marry Catholics only; but he sometimes seemed a prophet without honor in his own tribe.

The bishop was all the more careful to maintain contact with this network of gentry kinsmen, so as to guide them in matters religious. For example, he kept in touch with his opulent cousin, Charles Carroll of Carrollton, and with Charles's high-society descendants, ever watchful of their spiritual welfare. But there are few evidences that this family

---

[9]John Carroll to Elizabeth Carroll, Baltimore, August 18, 1806, *J.C.P.*, III, 91-93, here 92.

apostolate was very effective. In 1806, the Signer's grand-daughter Mary Ann Caton had announced her engagement to a Baltimore Protestant, Robert Patterson (brother of Elizabeth Patterson, whom Carroll himself had married to Jerome Bonaparte, Napoleon's brother). Carroll commented gloomily on the engagement to his Washington friend, James Barry.

> The alliances of that branch of the Carrolls prognosticate the loss of their religion: Mary's mother, Uncle & Aunt have all formed connections, as you know, out of the Church; I endeavor, whilst I live[,] to save their children; but cannot hope much from my weak endeavors; and the most that can be said for the young people now coming forward, is the scarcity of suitable matches of their own profession, which is a ruinous evil.[10]

Three weeks later he expressed his continuing chagrin over the Caton-Patterson wedding to Father Ambrose Maréchal.

> Tomorrow Miss Mary Caton is to be married to a B[rother]. of Mad[am]. Jerome Bonaparte, as we call her here. Thus one after another, all this family drops into the hands of protestant partners for life, and must in the end lose all attachment to the religion of their forefathers.[11]

---

[10]John Carroll to James Barry, Baltimore, April 8, 1806, *J.C.P.*, II, 509-11, here 510. The Patterson-Bonaparte wedding took place on December 24, 1803. The Bishop's notification is quoted in *J.C.P.*, II, 427-28. His dim view of the match proved prophetic. As he wrote to James Barry from Baltimore two days later, "I wish well to the young Lady, but cannot help fearing, that she may not find all the comforts hereafter, which she promises herself." *J.C.P.*, II, 428. Napoleon "dissolved" the marriage!

[11]John Carroll to Ambrose Maréchal, Baltimore, April 30, 1806, *J.C.P.*, II, 513-15, here 514.

Had the archbishop lived past mid-century, he might have been pleasantly surprised by the relatively strong Catholicism of Maria Digges Livingston and of at least some of the Signer's breed. He would have been even more gratified by the steady increase of conversions through mixed marriages in the Catholic counties of southern Maryland. However, during his own last years, 1800-1815, he could see little in an expansionist and leveling America that would discourage his bleakest forebodings about Catholic-Protestant marriages.

A scientific "denominational genealogy" of a number of old Maryland Catholic families could make fascinating reading. Given the delicacy of such a project, however, it would probably be very difficult to research. Here we propose a simpler task: an outline of the religious associations of one family of the gentry between — roughly — 1767 and 1865. It is a branch of the Duddington Carrolls, the Carrolls of Belle Vue, with whom migration was almost a way of life and mixed marriages were the rule. How does their history relate to John Carroll's contemporary apprehension?

Maryland Catholics in Transition:
the Belle Vue Carrolls

The Charles Carroll who later assumed the style "of Belle Vue" and founded the Belle Vue Carrolls, was the youngest of the three sons of Mary Hill and Charles Carroll of Duddington II and Carrollsburg (1729-1773). Charles the younger was born on November 7, 1767, at his father's manor house near the Anacostia River in what is now the city of Washington's Southeast. Charles, Senior, was a first cousin of Charles Carroll of Carrollton; their paternal grandfather was Charles Carroll the Attorney General (1660-1720), who in 1688 had introduced into America this branch of the genteel Irish O'Carrolls. Like the Carrollton

Carrolls, the Carrolls of Duddington were also blood-relatives of Bishop John Carroll, at least on the side of the bishop's mother, Eleanor Darnall.[12]

During Maryland's years of colonial anti-Catholicism, the Duddington Carrolls appear to have remained actively Catholic. Attending Mass most likely in the chapel of the nearby Young family, they would have been ministered to, it seems, by Jesuits stationed at Whitemarsh, now a part of Bowie, Prince George's County. However, the Whitemarsh registers that would have recorded the baptisms of Charles and his brothers have disappeared. In 1783, the widowed Mary Carroll sent young Charles to Liège [Belgium] to attend the Catholic preparatory school conducted there by a group of former Jesuits. The Liège academy was, of course, the college originally established by English Jesuits at St. Omer, France, in 1593. It served a host of British and colonial Catholic youths, even after the suppression of the Jesuit order. Like his own pre-Revolutionary kinsmen who had gone to St. Omers, Charles was a boarding student, for whom his mother paid an annual *pension* of some 32 guineas. He spent two years at Liège (April 27, 1783 to September 10, 1785). The curriculum was strongly humanistic, but the background was just as strongly Catholic.

Charles probably devoted his next two years to touring Europe. He returned to America early in 1787. In 1788 he reached his majority and came into possession of the three large estates in Frederick County bequeathed to him by his father.

By 1788, various new borderlands were beginning to be opened to enthusiastic pioneers, and many of the less prosperous Marylanders started to move west. Young Charles also contracted the migratory fever and decided to seek his

---

[12]For a fuller, documented account of Charles Carroll of Belle Vue, see the present writer's "Charles Carroll of Belle Vue, Co-founder of Rochester," *Rochester History* (Rochester, N.Y., Public Library), 42 (October, 1980), 1-28.

fortune in western Maryland. He settled at Hagerstown, a busy frontier outpost in Washington County. In its environs he purchased a farm of over 1,000 acres, and here he erected a very large manor house which he named (perhaps as a memento of his Liègeois years) "Belle Vue." From that time on he signed himself "Charles Carroll of Belle Vue."

Catholics in and around Hagerstown in Charles's days constituted a small minority, few of them people of means. In 1790, John Carroll, by now bishop of Baltimore, sent Father Dennis Cahill, an Irish-born priest, to reside at Hagerstown and serve as a missionary to the Catholics of the district. Charles of Belle Vue was happy to cooperate with Father Cahill, who set about raising a log chapel. When the congregation bought land in 1794 for further church use, Charles was one of the trustees to whom the seller deeded the property.[13]

Carroll was on still closer terms with Father Charles Duhamel, the worthy French priest-educator who succeeded Father Cahill. Unfortunately, the Hagerstown congregation was too poor to support a pastor with any constancy. Charles therefore undertook to write his "kinsman," Bishop Carroll, on May 26, 1807, to inquire whether the diocese could contribute $80 a year toward the maintenance of Father Duhamel. If Duhamel had to leave, he said, it would be "truly deplorable"; but his continuance would offer "great comfort to the poor Catholics of this back country."[14]

Bishop Carroll was apparently unable to provide any regular subsidy, but Charles Duhamel did stay on at Hagerstown until 1810. When the priest was finally obliged

[13]Dennis Cahill to John Carroll, Hagerstown, November 9, 1795, AAB, 3R7. Rita Clark Hultzell, *Mother of Churches. A History of St. Mary's Church, Hagerstown, Maryland* (Hagerstown, 1976), 12, 47. See also J. Thomas Scharf, *History of Western Maryland* (Philadelphia, 1882; Baltimore, 1968), II, 1018.

[14]Charles Carroll of Belle Vue to John Carroll, Belle Vue, May 26, 1807, AAB, 11T9.

to leave Washington County, Carroll wrote to the bishop, "Mr. Duhamel's departure will be extremely regretted by this congregation. I have offered him a home in my home & wish some mode could be devised to keep him among us."[15]

Not long after electing Hagerstown as his seat, Charles of Belle Vue took a bride. The wedding records have not been preserved, but the marriage probably took place in 1790 or 1791. His wife was not a blood-relative, as Bishop Carroll would likely have preferred; she was a Washington County girl whose parents had migrated thence from Prince George's County at the outset of the Revolution. Ann Sprigg (1769-1837) was socially acceptable, a member of an old colonial family. Her father Joseph was a county judge; her half-brother Samuel would become governor of Maryland, 1819-1822.

Now, Ann was Protestant — of the Anglican faith, to judge from her ancestral church, St. Barnabas, in Queen Anne's Parish, Prince George's County. There is no positive evidence that she joined the Catholic Church at the time of her marriage or later. Even though the church record is missing, we can fairly assume the wedding to have been a Catholic ceremony, since Charles and Ann raised both their sons and daughters in the Catholic faith.

The Carroll couple had eight children, all born in Washington County: Henry (1792-1820); Jane Maria (1793?-1833); Charles Holker (1794-1865); Hannah Lee (1797?-1835); Dr. Daniel Joseph (1801?-1860); William Thomas (1802-1863); Ann Rebecca (1803?-1846); and Elizabeth Barbara (1806-1866). Their baptismal records are not extant.

Major Carroll (he acquired his commission in the Washington County militia) had lived at Hagerstown for scarcely a decade when he began to yearn for new (and more

---

[15]Same to same, Belle Vue, May 5, 1810, AAB, 11T10. See also Charles Duhamel to John Carroll, Hagerstown, February 16, 1807, AAB, 3F4; February 24, 1810, AAB, 3F6.

gainful) borderlands to conquer.[16] By the turn of the century he had developed an interest in the "Genesee Country" of western New York, lately made accessible to settlers. As a consequence, he persuaded his two Hagerstown colleagues and best friends to join him in inspecting and purchasing lands along the Genesee River. The friends were Col. Nathaniel Rochester (1752-1831) and Col. William Frisby Fitzhugh (1761-1839). Both men were devout Episcopalians. In 1800-1802, the trio viewed and bought thousands of fertile acres in the present Livingston County; and in 1803 they invested jointly in a tract of one hundred acres beside the falls of the Genesee River in what is now Monroe County. Nine years later, Col. Rochester, as agent of this partnership, founded on the falls-side tract the milling town of Rochesterville, out of which developed the city of Rochester, New York.

All three gentlemen had intended to move from Hagerstown to their New York State properties soon after the purchase was made, but only Col. Rochester trekked north before the outbreak of the War of 1812. The others waited for peace — Carroll until 1815, Fitzhugh until 1817. During the war years Charles and his family went to Georgetown to live. Here he bought a handsome residence to which he also gave the name "Belle Vue." (Today it is known as Dumbarton House.) The Georgetown Belle Vue was within the neighborhood of Holy Trinity Catholic parish, but the Trinity records for 1811-1815 have no reference to Charles's family; nor should they, necessarily.[17]

Neither Charles Carroll nor William Fitzhugh had intended to settle in Rochesterville. Their dream was rather to set up as Maryland-style planters on their superb new

[16]"Field Officers of Regiments. Militia Appointments," date of record 1794, I, 6, 8th Regiment of Washington Co., Hall of Records Commission, Dept. of General Services, State of Maryland, Annapolis, Md.

[17]Margaret H. McAleer, Special Collections Division, Georgetown University Library, to present writer, May 3, 1983.

acreage forty miles upstream from the Genesee Falls, at Williamsburg, a "ghost village" in the Town of Groveland. On arrival, Carroll and Fitzhugh began to turn their largely primeval acres into productive farms.

Now, if Hagerstown had been a frontier settlement, the Town of Groveland, New York, was even more truly "back country." Its inhabitants were sparse, and its Catholic inhabitants were fewer still; hence, when the Catholic Carrolls arrived in 1815 they were utterly without spiritual provision. However, in 1818, John Connolly, the bishop of New York, sent the vigorous young pastor of St. Mary's, Albany — New York State's only upstate church — on a trip to western New York to search out newly-arrived Catholics. The *Ontario Messenger* of Canandaigua, New York, carried in its issue of June 30 the following notice:

> The Rev. Dr. O'Gorman, a Roman Catholic Priest and Rector of St. Mary's Church, Albany, will preach at the Court House in this village THIS DAY at six o'clock in the afternoon — and in the village of Williamsburg in the Town of Groveland, on Sunday, the 5th day of July next, at 11 o'clock in the forenoon.

A parallel notice in Canandaigua's *Ontario Republican* said that the service in Groveland would be "at Williamsburg near Major Carroll's."

Father Michael O'Gorman's plans must have worked out well, for on January 16, 1819, the "First Catholic Church of the Western District of the State of New York" was officially incorporated, with "Charles Carroll of the Genesee Valley" as one of the trustees. Actually, the new church was to be erected no farther west than Utica. St. John's Roman Catholic church, opened in that city in 1821, was some 150 miles east of Williamsburg and thus not very serviceable to Groveland Catholics. The "Third Roman Catholic Church of the Western District" was organized in 1820 in Rochester, only two-score miles distant from Williamsburg. Out of that would come, three years later, St. Patrick's, Rochester's first Catholic church. But it was not until the 1850s that Catholic parishes were founded within a Sunday-morning ride from the Carroll plantation.

However, by the time St. John's was dedicated in 1821, Major Carroll had already moved off to a third frontier. In 1818, his friend President James Monroe named him register of lands for Howard County in north-central Missouri. He accepted for several reasons, one of which was financial.[18] The newly-appointed register, it seems, opened his office in Franklin, Missouri, that same year. Then he left his oldest son, Henry, as "acting register," and returned east to arrange for transporting to the West his wife and three younger daughters, Hannah Lee, Ann Rebecca, and Elizabeth Barbara.

Franklin was indeed the remotest borderland that Charles had yet entered. A crossroads for adoptive Missourians and for those bound farther afield, this riverside village possessed as yet no church of any denomination. A Catholic missionary who made a preliminary visit to Franklin in 1819 found only fifteen Catholics.[19] It would be a good while before priests missioned out of St. Louis were able to include the Franklin neighborhood among their regular stations.

[18]Neil Adams McNall, "The Landed Gentry of the Genesee," *New York History* 26 (1945), 162-76.

[19]Fr. Charles De la Croix (1792-1869), a zealous Belgian secular priest, made a mission tour up the Missouri River in late 1818 or early 1819, and reported to Bishop Joseph Rosati of St. Louis from Florissant, Mo., March 2, 1819, "I have a mission at Côte Sans Dessein, almost 100 miles from here, and at Franklin, commonly called Boone's Lick, about 90 miles further, both situated on the banks of the Missouri...As to Franklin, there are only fifteen Catholics there. I stayed in the place four days...." He was the first priest to visit the settlement, and no record indicates that he himself ever returned. Gilbert J. Garraghan, S.J., *St. Ferdinand, Florissant. The Story of an Ancient Parish* (Chicago, 1923), 157-61. See also "De la Croix, Charles," *New Catholic Encyclopedia* (New York, 1967), IV, 725.

Carroll did not remain in Missouri as long as he had anticipated. During his extended initial absence from Franklin, his son Henry, though popular among some Franklinites, had become the object of mounting antagonism on the part of many others. His enemies eventually denounced Henry to the federal government, and asked that he be ousted from the register's headquarters. On February 29, 1820, this movement against Henry reached a bloody climax. The leader of the opposition, Major Richard Gentry, shot and killed him outside the village. Major Carroll saw to it that Henry's killer was brought to trial; but since there had been no witnesses to the slaying, the court dismissed the case on March 30, 1821.

Charles Carroll chose to resign his registership late in 1821, and by the end of 1822 he and his "Missouri family" had returned to the Groveland home of his son Charles Holker Carroll. There the Major died on October 28, 1823. In his brief will, he invoked the name of God, but made no other reference to religion.[20] The inventory of his property, which might have included religious allusions, has been lost. Charles was interred in the little Williamsburg/Groveland burial ground. The admittedly skimpy records of his death and funeral say nothing of Catholicism. This is not surprising, however. There was still no Catholic missionary priest resident in western New York in October, 1823.[21] Therefore, Charles's last Catholic act of record was his standing as godfather to his granddaughter Mary Tabbs, when she was

---

[20]Livingston County Clerk, Will Book 1, 30.

[21]However, there was a local Catholic tradition that Father John Dubois, Henry Carroll's mentor at Emmitsburg and later bishop of New York (1826-1842), blessed the grave (or plot) of Major Carroll during a pastoral visitation — see James T. Dougherty to Frederick J. Zwierlein, Canandaigua, N.Y., September 1, 1917, relating a statement of Rev. John J. Donnelly, pastor of St. Patrick's church, Mt. Morris, N.Y., 1875-1880, Archives of the Diocese of Rochester, Zwierlein papers. Dubois is known to have visited the Genesee Country in 1827, 1828, 1829, and 1837. Post-burial blessings of Catholic graves were a regular practice in missionary days.

baptized at the church of St. Francis Xavier, Vincennes, Indiana on June 20, 1819. (On that occasion the baptizing pastor was Anthony Blanc, a French missionary who later became the first archbishop of New Orleans.)[22]

Charles Carroll of Belle Vue, a man highly esteemed by those who knew him, was to prove a bridge-figure in his family's Catholic history. Born a Catholic in pre-Revolutionary Maryland, he was educated in the Catholic faith in Europe, and exerted positive Catholic leadership on two of the three American frontiers into which he moved. Despite his marriage to a Protestant, he raised his children as Catholics. Specific Catholic data are fewer during his last years, 1818-1823; but we shall later see further indications that, even though he had lived from 1815 to 1823 in priestless hinterlands, he died in the faith in which he had been baptized.

The Belle Vue Carrolls and Catholic Identity

Charles Carroll of Belle Vue's two brothers had not shared his migratory disposition. Daniel Carroll of Duddington II remained in the District of Columbia; Henry Hill Carroll, in Baltimore County. There seem to have been interfaith weddings in both of their families; but perhaps because they stayed in close contact with the Maryland Catholic community, they had less difficulty in passing the faith on to their descendants. What, then, do the documents say about the Catholic convictions of Charles's widely scattered progeny?

Henry, the Major's firstborn, was the object of his father's deepest affection and hope. In 1809, Charles sent him to Mt.

[22]Basilica of St. Francis Xavier, Vincennes, Ind., Baptismal records, Vol. B (1814-1837), 32. Godfather (signing the record) was Charles Carroll, Belle Vue; godmother was Ann Rebecca Carroll (Moses Tabbs signed as proxy).

St. Mary's, a Catholic boys' school just opened at Emmitsburg, Maryland, by a French émigré priest, Father John
Dubois. Henry had not been there long when he felt a strong
attraction to the diocesan priesthood. Naturally, Dubois, an
educator of priests, encouraged him.

However, when Major Charles heard this news, he was
upset. He penned a rather excited letter to Archbishop
Carroll, not, he told him, to seek his advice, but to open his
own mind on the matter. An eighteen-year-old like Henry,
he said, is still too untested by "the temptations and allure-
ments of the world" to make so grave a decision. "I abhor an
apostate clergyman," Charles wrote; and he opined that
some such "apostates" owed their lapse to a lack of timely
counsel from their parents. He had decided, therefore, to
take Henry out of Mt. St. Mary's, and to send him to
Carlisle, Pennsylvania, for a period of secular experience.
Should the youth still feel called to the priesthood after that
period of trial, he would not stand in his way, even though
he had had other plans for his son.[23]

If Henry actually did go to Carlisle, it was not for long.
We find him next at the Catholic college of St. Mary's,
Baltimore, where he won his A.B. in 1813. After that year
there is no further mention of a priestly calling in his brief
annals. In 1814, Henry Carroll seemed on the threshold of a
diplomatic career. When Henry Clay asked him to serve as
his private secretary in the current negotiations at Ghent to
terminate the War of 1812, Archbishop Carroll gave his
young relative letters of recommendation to European
friends which spoke of Henry in terms of talent, piety, and
high promise.[24] Young Carroll had the thrill of bringing

[23]Charles Carroll of Belle Vue to John Carroll, Belle Vue, May 5, 1810. AAB,
11T10. The student business records of Mt. St. Mary's list a number of devotional
books purchased in 1809-1810 by Henry Carroll.

[24]John Carroll to Thaddaeus Brzozowski, S.J., n.p., January 28, 1815, *J.C.P.*,
III, 252-54 ("my relative and a youth of great promise"). Same to Charles Plowden,
Baltimore, February 3, 1814, *J.C.P.*, III, 256-58 ("a young gentleman of amiable
manners, considerable acquirements in litterature [*sic*] & above all, commendable
piety and regularity of life...").

back to President James Madison the official text of the peace treaty of Ghent; but that was apparently the end of his diplomatic employment.

Henry Carroll's activities during the years 1814-1818 are obscure save in one respect. According to family tradition, around 1816 he fell in love with his Catholic cousin Louisa Caton, granddaughter of Charles Carroll of Carrollton. Unfortunately for Henry, Louisa jilted him, and went on to become, eventually, Duchess of Leeds.[25] The few documents about his turbulent career in Missouri say nothing about Henry's status as a Catholic in 1820, or about any Catholic aspects of his tragic frontier death and burial. Still, there is no real reason to doubt that he died a Catholic.

Jane Maria was the second of the Belle Vue children. What sort of education she and her sisters were given is not clear, but it was most likely at the hands of private tutors.[26] Jane first came into public notice in 1811 when, at the age of about eighteen, she married Moses Tabbs.[27] Tabbs, an attorney, was then a state senator from his home county, St. Mary's; but he had earlier practiced law in Washington County, where he served as its representative in the Mary-

[25][Ellen McWilliams], "The Tabbs Family, " written c. 1865 by Moses Tabbs's niece, and presented for publication by Mrs. Philip Ford Combs, *Chronicles of St. Mary's* (St. Mary's Co. [Md.] Historical Society) 13, No. 6 (June 1965). Ellen's chatty family memoir is valuable but incorrect in several details. Thus, for example, she identifies Henry's cousin as "the beautiful Emily Caxtan, afterwards the Marchioness of Carmarthen." The *Caton* (not Caxtan) girl who married the Marquess of Carmarthen and future seventh Duke of Leeds was not *Emily* Caton (Mrs. John MacTavish), but Louisa.

[26]Had Charles sent his daughters to convent schools, the handiest would have been St. Joseph's, conducted at Emmitsburg, Md., by St. Elizabeth Seton's Sisters of Charity; or Georgetown Convent of the Visitation. The archivists of neither school could find positive references to the Belle Vue girls in their (admittedly incomplete) records.

[27]*Maryland Herald and Hagerstown Weekly Advertiser*, October 9, 1811; Washington Co. Marriage Records, same date. For the religious objections, see McWilliams, "The Tabbs Family."

land House of Delegates, and also, of course, made the acquaintance of his future wife.

The Tabbs family was strongly Episcopalian. When Moses proposed to Jane Maria, both the Tabbs and the Carroll families objected to the match on religious grounds. The marriage did come off, however, on October 8, 1811, with Father Charles Duhamel, the old family friend, presiding. However, when Moses took his bride back to St. Mary's County to introduce her to his father, stern Dr. Barton Tabbs gave her the iciest of receptions. Jane broke into tears, and Moses' brothers and sisters shared her pain.

Around 1817, Moses and Jane decided to start afresh on a new frontier, Indiana. Vincennes welcomed them as Maryland aristocrats, and they quickly became popular. This old French settlement was supportive of Jane's Catholic faith. She affiliated with the ancient French parish of St. Francis Xavier. Here the couple had their daughter Mary Carroll Tabbs baptized, on June 20, 1819; and their daughter Ann Elizabeth Tabbs, on April 30, 1820. When Charles Tabbs, their Maryland-born son, died on September 10, 1820, they laid the boy to rest in the old French cemetery behind the parish church.[28]

For a variety of reasons, some quite dramatic, the Moses Tabbses moved back east a few years later, and by 1828 were living in Washington, D.C. Both Moses and Jane were in poor health. Jane lost infants in rapid succession. She died in childbirth on March 4, 1833 and was buried in the Congressional Cemetery. Moses, carried off by tuberculosis on May 21, 1836, was interred in the same burial ground.[29]

[28]See note 22 for Mary Tabbs' baptism. Ann Elizabeth's baptism (by Andrew Ferrari, pastor) is recorded in the register of St. Francis Xavier Basilica, Vol. B (1814-1837), 50. Godparents (no proxies indicated) were Daniel Carroll and Elizabeth [Barbara?] Carroll. Ferrari (1792?-1820) was an ordained priest who was a Vincentian novice (James Graham, C.M., to the present writer, St. Louis, Mo., May 18, 1983). For Charles Tabbs' burial, see the St. Francis Savier burial records, Vol. 5 (1704-1838), 554.

[29]For Jane's death, see *National Intelligencer*, Washington, D.C., March 5, 1833; for Moses' death, same newspaper, May 26, 1836. Their burials are listed in

It seems that on April 4, 1831, Jane Maria had become a member of Christ Episcopal church, on Capitol Hill.[30] Three daughters survived the couple. Ann Elizabeth, who never married, died on September 9, 1884 in a sanitarium at Danville, New York, not far from the Town of Groveland where her grandfather Carroll had settled and some of the family of her uncle, Charles Holker Carroll, still lived. She was buried in the Carroll lot of the Williamsburg/Groveland Cemetery. There are no indications of Ann's religious affiliation at the time of her decease.[31] After the death of the Tabbses, Judge Carroll apparently took in the orphaned teenaged Mary Carroll Tabbs. It was at Judge Carroll's home, "The Hermitage," that she was wedded, on May 29, 1845, to Thomas Tasker Gantt, a St. Louis lawyer and future judge. Gantt had no denominational commitment, and "inclined toward Unitarianism." Their marriage, however, was an Episcopal rite, with the Reverend Henry B. Bartow of St. Michael's Episcopal church, Geneseo, New York, as officiant.[32] By that time, a Catholic priest would have been available; but Mary had evidently affiliated with the Episcopal Church. The third surviving Tabbs daughter, Alida, was born on April 30, 1825. Her baptism is not

the Congressional Cemetery's "Interments and Removals," Book No. 1, pp. 56 and 81. The present writer is indebted to the late Francis A. Raven, Arlington genealogist, for data on the Moses Tabbs family during their Washington sojourn; and on the W. T. Carrolls.

[30]Christ Protestant Episcopal church records, 1793-1921, compiled by Livingston Manor Chapter, D.A.R., District of Columbia, vol. 69, P. 136 (April 4, 1831); also, perhaps, under "Mary Gabbs [sic]," p. 97. As noted later, Jane's Washington brother William had probably already become an Episcopalian by that time, as her brother Charles certainly had.

[31]*Dansville Express* (Dansville, N.Y.), September 18, 1884; Williamsburg/Groveland cemetery record, Livingston Co. History Research office, Geneseo, N.Y. The death records, Town of North Dansville, say she died in the Dansville, N.Y. sanitarium (record thanks to Town Historian Wilford J. Rauber). The cemetery record says Ann Elizabeth was 60 at death — which, if correct, would mean that she was born in 1824 rather than 1820. It is possible, of course, that the Tabbses lost the Ann Elizabeth of 1820 and gave the same name to a later child.

[32]*Rochester Democrat* (Rochester, N.Y.) records the wedding, issue of June 5, 1845. For T. T. Gantt, see J. Thomas Scharf, *History of St. Louis City and County*

recorded in the Catholic parish register at Vincennes, perhaps because the Tabbes had already returned east before her birth or baptism. When her parents died, Alida went to live in Oswego, New York, with her aunt Elizabeth Barbara Carroll Fitzhugh. In 1847, she married DeWitt Clinton Littlejohn, an Oswego business associate of her uncle Henry Fitzhugh. DeWitt and Alida came to be prominent members of Christ Episcopal church, Oswego.[33]

Charles Holker Carroll, the second son of the Major, who on his father's death became pretty much head of the family, was to have a decisive influence on the religious directions of most of the Carrolls of Belle Vue. When his father moved to Missouri in 1819, Charles, Jr., just come of age, was concerned about his ability to supervise the Major's New York and Maryland estates. However, he grew gracefully into his new role. Like Henry Carroll, Charles Holker had received an A.B. from St. Mary's College, Baltimore — with honors, according to his obituarists.[34] After Major Carroll's departure for the West, Holker, in the spring of 1820, married Alida Van Rensselaer of Utica, a member of the old New Amsterdam patroon family. Jeremiah Van Rensselaer, Jr., Alida's father, was a Presbyterian. However, the Carroll-Van Rensselaer nuptials were celebrated in Utica in a Catholic ceremony presided over by the Reverend John Farnan. Father Farnan was pastor of St. John's, the Utica Catholic

(Philadelphia, 1883), II, 1486-87; obit, *St. Louis Daily Globe-Democrat*, June 18, 1889. The Gantts were buried in Bellefontaine, a general cemetery, 1920-3175, Block 26. She died in 1884, he in 1889. They were childless.

[33]See obit and funeral notices of Alida Littlejohn in *Oswego Daily Palladium*, April 30, May 2, 1872; and of D. C. Littlejohn, *Palladium*, October 27, 28, 29, 1892. Their two children, Hugh and Lucy A., died single. (I am indebted to Mrs. Beulah S. Schroeder, Oswego genealogist, for much information on the Littlejohns and the Henry Fitzhughs of Oswego.)

[34]Charles Holker Carroll and Henry Carroll are recorded as graduates of St. Mary's College, Baltimore, the former (1811-1813) at p. 30, the latter (1809-1812; 1813) at pp. 86, 91, of *Memorial Volume of the Centenary of St. Mary's Seminary of St. Sulpice* (Baltimore, 1891). Judge Carroll's career is treated in obits (Rochester, N.Y. *Union and Advertiser*, July 24, 1865; *Livingston Republican* [Geneseo, N.Y.], July 27, 1865); likewise (inadequately) in Lockwood L. Doty, *A History of*

parish of which Major Charles Carroll had been one of the founding trustees.[35]

Holker read law and was admitted to the bar. He practiced private law very little, but he was named judge of Livingston County in 1826. In the same year he built a handsome house, "The Hermitage," at Groveland. Appointment to the court launched him on a political career that led him to the New York Assembly, the New York State Senate, and finally the U.S. House of Representatives.

In 1826 or early 1827, Judge Carroll joined the Protestant Episcopal Church, affiliating with St. Michael's Episcopal church, Geneseo, New York. When St. John's Episcopal church was founded in 1833 at Mt. Morris, closer to "The Hermitage," Charles transferred to the junior parish. In both churches he was an active member. He served as a delegate to the 1852 General Convention of the Episcopal Church, and at his death in 1865 he was a warden of St. John's.[36]

Ten years later there was a tradition among Catholics at Mt. Morris that Charles Holker Carroll had remained Catholic "till he was elected judge and Episcopalianism was most fashionable."[37] It does seem significant that he did not take this step until after the death of his father; and denominational change for secular advantage is not an unusual

Livingston County, New York (Geneseo, 1876, 1979), 567-71, and Lockwood R. Doty, *History of Livingston County* (Jackson, Mich., 1905), 940. See also Ann Patchett, "Valley Folk," *Livingston County Leader* (Geneseo, N.Y.), October 24, 1957.

[35]The Carroll-Van Rensselaer wedding is noted, without precise date, in the *Ontario Repository* (Canandaigua, N.Y.), May 23, 1820.

[36]Judge Carroll's name appears in a list of families of St. Michael's Episcopal church, Geneseo, N.Y., compiled by the rector, Rev. L. P. Bayard, in autumn, 1827. For his later affiliation with St. John's Episcopal church, Mt. Morris, N.Y., see Levi Parsons and Samuel L. Rockefellow, *Centennial Celebration, Mt. Morris, N.Y.* (Mt. Morris, 1894), 137-38. The Rochester *Daily Union* mentions the judge's service as a delegate to the Episcopal convention, August 23, 1852.

[37]James T. Dougherty to Frederick J. Zwierlein, Canandaigua, N.Y., September 1, 1917. See note 21 above.

phenomenon. Other factors, however, may have played a role in this case. The continuing lack of Catholic missionary service could have been one. The religious attitude of the Major's widow, Ann, could have been another. Her denominational connection after their marriage is obscure, as we have said; but there is a good chance that she always remained Protestant. Judge Carroll's change did not deter him from giving aid to local Catholics. When the Genesee Valley Canal was under construction in Livingston County between 1838 and 1842, he provided land for a temporary chapel at Brushville (now Tuscarora) for the convenience of the many Irish Catholics engaged in digging the waterway.[38] On the other hand, the judge was not unwilling to serve in 1856 as a presidential elector of the American (Know-Nothing) party, which was explicitly anti-Catholic.[39]

A natural consequence of Holker's church shift was that his children, all daughters, followed him. Cornelia, the oldest, born in 1826, had apparently been baptized as a Catholic. Now she was enrolled at St. Michael's church, where she was later confirmed. Anne Elizabeth (born 1828), Adeline (born 1830), and Alida (born and died 1831) were baptized at St. Michael's. Cornelia (Mrs. Edward Philo Fuller) and Anne Elizabeth (Mrs. William Dana Fitzhugh) were subsequently married in Episcopal rites. Their mother Alida, who died young in 1832, had likewise been buried from St. Michael's church.[40]

Charles's choice also prompted his two sisters, who were

[38]John Timon, *Missions in Western New York and Church History of the Diocese of Buffalo* (Buffalo, 1862), 220.

[39]*Biographical Directory of the American Congress, 1774-1971* (Washington, 1971). This incomplete sketch follows Lockwood L. Doty in calling the judge Charles *Hobart* Carroll, an error repeated in *Who Was Who? Historical Volume, 1667-1896.*

[40]Records of St. Michael's church, Geneseo, where all these rites took place. In the parishioners' list of 1864, Cornelia's entry reads "Fuller, Cornelia, bap. C.C.," which seems to mean "in the Catholic Church." Born in Groveland on April 9, 1826, Cornelia died in Grand Rapids, Michigan on June 6, 1909 — see the *Evening Press* [Grand Rapids], June 7, 1909.

living with him, to follow suit. The Major's fourth child, Hannah Lee, who remained single, received confirmation at St. Michael's church on February 2, 1827.⁴¹ Elizabeth Barbara, the baby of the Belle Vue family, took the same path. Her last recorded action as a Catholic was to participate (personally?) as the godmother of her niece Ann Elizabeth Tabbs in the baptism administered at Vincennes on April 30, 1820. When she was married at Groveland on December 19, 1827 to Episcopalian Henry Fitzhugh, it was in an Episcopal ceremony presided over by the Reverend L. P. Bayard, rector of St. Michael's church. Henry became a leading citizen of Oswego, New York. All five of the children of Henry and Elizabeth Barbara seem to have been raised in the Anglican tradition.⁴²

The Major's sons Daniel and William lived in less close contact with their brother the judge. What was their religious affiliation in later years?

Daniel, who never married, may have attended Mt. St. Mary's College, Emmitsburg, as a youth. Later he became a physician, and moved from upstate New York to New York City, where he practiced medicine until his death in 1860.⁴³

---

⁴¹St. Michael's registers.

⁴²*Ontario Repository* (Canandaigua, N.Y.) December 19, 1827; St Michael's parish records. At least two of their children are definitely known to have been given Episcopalian burial.

⁴³The student records of Mt. St. Mary's list two Carroll boys from Washington, D.C., Daniel and William, whose father was named Charles and who also had a brother Charles. Their period of attendance fits in well with the known history of the Belle Vue family: Daniel, January 6, 1811 to June 30, 1814; William from September 6, 1811 to June 30, 1814, and again from March 23, 1816 to January 24, 1817. The main objection is that Daniel, who was born 1800/01, is listed as aged 14, and William, who was born March 2, 1802, is listed as aged 16. Since these two Washington (Georgetown?) Carrolls were the only pupils of their name at Emmitsburg during this period, one is inclined to conclude that the ages are given incorrectly. The fact that Archbishop Carroll sent special greetings to a pair of Carrolls studying there on December 22, 1811, encourages our conclusion, because of his continual interest in his Belle Vue relatives. He wrote on that date to Father John Dubois, president of Mt. St. Mary's, "My love likewise to my nephews, to Chs Harper, Wmson, *the two Carrolls* and all my young friends with you — let them all to pray for; [sic] Dr. Sir, Your friend and Svt in Xt, J. Abp of Bre"(*J.C.P.*, III, 165. Emphasis added).

The only evidence of his adult Catholic connection is his serving (in person?) as godfather at the baptism of his niece Ann Elizabeth Tabbs at Vincennes, April 30, 1820.[44] Despite his living many miles away from the "head of the family," Charles, Dr. Daniel nevertheless held him in high esteem; and in his will, drawn up after Holker had left the Catholic Church, he bequeathed all his property to this "beloved brother."[45]

William Thomas Carroll was the only child of the Major's to remain permanently in the South. He, too, may have attended Mt. St. Mary's in his youth. When the family decamped for New York State in 1815, William stayed behind, studied law, and was admitted to the bar. In 1827, through the influence of Moses Tabbs, his brother-in-law, with Henry Clay, he was appointed to the prestigious post of clerk of the United States Supreme Court. He discharged this office ably until 1862, the year before his death.[46]

On October 7, 1828, William Thomas Carroll married Sarah ("Sally") Sprigg, the daughter of Samuel Sprigg, former governor of Maryland, and his own half-first-cousin. It was an Episcopalian wedding, in a part of the

---

Dr. Daniel Carroll's name appears in the New York city directories of the 1850s, with residence at 97 Chambers Street. Oddly, he is not listed in the medical directories.

[44]See note 28.

[45]Daniel Carroll's will, signed on January 25, 1830, was admitted to probate on October 21, 1865, after the death of Charles H. Carroll, his beneficiary (New York County Surrogate Court, Liber 157, p. 284).

[46]Regarding W. T. Carroll's possible attendance at Mt. St. Mary's, see note 43. For Henry Clay's role in his appointment to the clerkship of the Supreme Court, see McWilliams, "The Tabbs Family."

Despite his relative prominence, William Thomas Carroll seems to have eluded biographers. The notice of his death and funeral plans is a bare announcement (*Daily National Intelligencer*, Washington, D.C., July 14, 1863). He usually receives passing notice in biographical sketches of his son, Maj. Gen. Samuel Sprigg Carroll (see especially *Appleton's Cyclopedia of American Biography*, I [New York, 1888], 539). Somewhat fuller details of his life appear in a MS. article, "Willie Lincoln," by Mathilde Williams (Peabody Collection, D.C. Public Library, Georgetown Branch). In 1857, Carroll purchased lot 292 in Oak Hill Cemetery, a general cemetery in Georgetown. Here are interred not only his family but Gov. and Mrs. Samuel Sprigg.

country where there was certainly no shortage of Catholic clergy. When their son William Thomas, Jr., was baptized on February 16, 1834, the christening took place at Christ Episcopal church in Washington. It is likely that their seven other children were christened into the same faith. In the 1840s we find Clerk Carroll an active parishioner of the Episcopal church of St. John, Washington.[47] Therefore, William, like his brother Charles Holker of Groveland, had become an Episcopalian. We have no way of knowing, at present, which of them first took the step, or which influenced the other. However, some of the clerk's descendants have been Catholic, whether through an undetermined thread of continuity or through a later conversion.[48]

Ann Rebecca is the only Belle Vue Carroll whom we have not yet discussed. On April 19, 1819, while still living in Groveland, she had stood as godmother, by proxy, in the Catholic baptism of her niece Mary Tabbs at Vincennes.[49] She was about sixteen that autumn, when her parents took

[47]William T. Carroll and Sally Sprigg were married on October 14, 1828, at the Sprigg residence, "Northampton," Prince George's Co., Maryland. It was a Protestant ceremony (*Baltimore American*, October 20, 1828). The baptism of William Thomas Carroll, Jr., born July 10, 1833, was administered by the Rev. Frederick W. Hatch, according to the parish register of Christ Episcopal church, Capitol Hill, Volume 1795-1838. For Clerk Carroll's later association with St. John's Episcopal church, see Alexander P. Hagner, "History and Reminiscences of St. John's Church, Washington, D.C.," *Records of the Columbia Historical Society*, Washington, D.C., 12 (1909), 89-114, here 96.

[48]The children of William and Sally Carroll were: Gen. Samuel Sprigg Carroll (1832-1893) (m. Helen Bennett); William Thomas Carroll, Jr. (d.s. 1857); Violetta Lansdale Carroll (m. Dr. Thomas Swann Mercer); Sarah Carroll (m. [1] Maj. Gen. Charles Griffin [1826-1867]; [2] "Count Esterhazy of Austria"); Caroline Carroll (m. "Lieutenant Boles"); Alida Carroll (m. Gen. John M. Brown). Major Carroll Mercer, the older son of the Dr. Mercer, was a close social friend of Franklin D. Roosevelt. If he was not himself Catholic, his daughter Lucy was. Lucy Mercer (Mrs. Winthrop Rutherfurd, 1891-1948) had a private Catholic chapel in her residence at Tranquility, N.J., and was buried in a Catholic rite in the local cemetery, where her family plot had been blessed as a Catholic graveyard. (See Joseph P. Lash, *Eleanor and Franklin* [New York, 1971], 220-21; Elliott Roosevelt and James Brough, *A Rendezvous with Destiny. The Roosevelts of the White House* [New York, 1975]; also, Rev. Richard Steiger, Andover, N.J., to the present writer, November 28, 1981 and December 4, 1981.)

[49]See note 22.

her, her older sister, Hannah Lee, and her younger sister, Elizabeth Barbara, out to Missouri.

In 1822, when the disheartened Major Carroll brought his wife and two of his daughters back to New York State, Ann Rebecca stayed behind. She had married Dr. Hardage Lane, a Franklin physician, on November 7, 1821. Lane was highly respected as a medical man. He was also a leading figure in Freemasonry, both at Franklin and at St. Louis, whither he and Ann removed in 1826. The newspaper notice of the wedding stated that a "Rev. Mr. Williams" had received the couple's vows. There is no Catholic priest by that name in contemporary records. Quite likely he was the Rev. Justinian Williams, a Methodist missionary then preaching along the Missouri River.[50]

It would seem at first glance, then, that Ann Rebecca, in marrying a Mason before a non-Catholic minister, was implicitly severing her connections with the Catholic Church. Later events proved otherwise. Ann Lane raised her daughter, at least, as a Catholic. When that daughter was married on February 2, 1843, it was a Catholic wedding, performed at St. Francis Xavier, the college church of St. Louis University. The record says that the bride, Elizabeth Carroll Lane "of the Catholic Church," was united in marriage with Samuel S. Peake "of the Protestant Episcopal Church."[51] Furthermore, on October 11, 1855, Hardage Lane, Jr. (who, like their other son, Harvey Lane, died single) purchased a plot in the new Calvary Catholic cemetery at St. Louis. Admittedly, neither son was buried there (perhaps the boys had not been brought up in their mother's faith); but one of the two children interred in the plot was a Leoni Isabella Peake (August 13, 1863). This burial serves

[50]*Missouri Intelligencer* (Franklin, Mo.), November 13, 1821. The identity of Rev. Mr. Williams has been suggested by Alma Vaughan, formerly reference specialist, State Historical Society of Missouri, Columbia, Mo.

[51]Marriage Records, St. Francis Xavier (College) Church, St. Louis. Presiding was the then pastor, Rev. George A. Carrell, S.J. (1807-1868), future first bishop of Covington, Ky.

to confirm that Hardage Lane, Jr. and Elizabeth Lane Peake were brother and sister.[52] Ray Denslow, Dr. Lane's Masonic biographer, states that the doctor and Ann were themselves laid to rest in Calvary cemetery.[53] There is some confusion here. Denslow gives a picture of the vault in which they are buried, but the inscription indicates that it belongs to a Harty family. Furthermore, Calvary cemetery was opened in 1854, several years after the deaths of the Lane couple. The grain of truth here seems to be that Hardage and Ann were interred in *some* Catholic grave-yard. What appears sure is that Ann Rebecca Carroll's Catholic commitment withstood both the tensions of an interfaith marriage and the latitudinarianism of the frontier.

* * * * *

The "denominational genealogy" of these earlier Carrolls of Belle Vue tells its own story. Of course, John Carroll did not live to see the denouement; but the Belle Vue case provides a dramatic illustration of just what he most feared from mixed nuptials, particularly in the frontier conditions of a young America.

Beneath the bishop's official pastoral concern about such marriages, there ran a deeper current of personal perplexity and pain. Here was a priest who had experienced the malice of Maryland's anti-Catholic penal laws. He was stirred by the firmness his fellow-Catholics had shown during that epoch of religious and cultural war. As he later wrote, these "Catholics, oppressed and persecuted, were reduced to poverty and contempt. . . . It is surprising that, notwithstanding

[52]Ann Goessling, Catholic Cemeteries of the Archdiocese of St. Louis, to the present writer, St. Louis, October 27, 1981.

[53]Ray V. Denslow, *A Missouri Lodge. The Story of Franklin Union Lodge No. 7, at Old Franklin, Missouri, 1822-1832* (n.p., 1929), 65-70. Dr. Lane was given a "dimit" from his St. Louis Lodge on September 16, 1837. Whether he died a Mason, says Denslow, is unknown. Denslow would probably not have written thus if he had learned that Lane had entered the Catholic Church. It is quite possible, then, that when the Lanes were married, the Rev. Mr. Williams performed the role of a civil rather than a religious official.

all these difficulties, there were still so many Catholics in
Maryland who were regular in their habits, and at peace
with all their neighbors. The propriety of their conduct was
a subject of edification to all.... "[54]

His generation, therefore, had preserved "the religion of
their forefathers," and passed it on, as a treasure, to their
heirs. What the old archbishop could not comprehend, in
the federal times that had brought back religious liberty,
was the apparently blithe willingness of Catholic "young
people now coming forward" to enter marriages that could
easily jeopardize that religious patrimony. The grandpar-
ents had refused to conform to Anglicanism under severe
legal pressure. Why were the grandchildren so incautious
about conformity through default?

John Carroll was a sophisticated man, and, in the best
sense, a man of the world. He rejoiced in the civil religious
liberty that the American constitution had established. He
was remarkably ecumenical in his dealings with Americans
of other faiths, including his own non-Catholic relatives.

For all that, the first bishop of Baltimore was personally a
man of tested and unswerving Catholic conviction. Had he
foreseen, then, the gradual alienation from Catholicism,
through interfaith marriages, of his dear and rather prominent kinsmen of Belle Vue, he would surely have found here,
too, a cause for "the most poignant sorrow."

---

[54]"The Establishment of the Catholic Religion in the United States," essay
attributed to John Carroll, in *J.C.P.*, I, 403-08, here 405.

THE CARROLLS OF BELLE VUE*

Charles Carroll the Attorney General (1660-1720)
m. Mary Darnall I (1678-1742) (grandaunt of Abp. John Carroll)

Charles of Annapolis (1702-82)
Charles of Carrollton (1737-1832)

Daniel of Duddington (1707-34)
Charles of Duddington II & Carrollsburg (1729-73)
m. Mary Hill (1744-1822)

Daniel of Duddington II (1764-1849) — Henry Hill (d. 1804) — Charles of Belle Vue (1767-1823) m. Ann Sprigg (1769?-1837)

Children of Charles of Belle Vue:

- Henry (d.s.) (1792-1820)
- Jane Maria (1793?-1833) m. Moses Tabbs (1780?-1836)
- Charles Holker (1794-1865) m. Alida van Rensselaer (1801?-32)
- Hannah Lee (1797?-1836)
- Daniel, M.D. (d.s.) (1801?-60)
- William Thomas (1802-63) m. Sally Sprigg (1812-93)
- Ann Rebecca (1803?-46) m. Hardage Lane, M.D. (d. 1849)
- Elizabeth Barbara (1806-66) m. Henry Fitzhugh (1801-66)

Children of Charles Holker & Alida van Rensselaer:

- Mary Carroll (1819-84) m. Thomas T. Gantt (1814-89)
- Alida (1825-72) m. DeWitt C. Littlejohn (1818-92)
- Cornelia Granger (1826-1909) m. Edward P. Fuller (1820-86)
- Ann Elizabeth (1826-1905) m. Wm. Dana Fitzhugh (1824-89)

Children of William Thomas & Sally Sprigg:

- Gen. Samuel S. (1831-95) m. Helen Bennett (dates?)
- Violetta Lansdale (dates?) m. Thomas Swann Mercer, M.D. (dates?)
- Sarah (dates?) m. (1) Gen. Charles Griffin (1826-67) (2) "Count Esterhazy of Austria" (dates?)
- Caroline (dates?) m. "Lieut." Bates, U.S.N. [Matthew Bolles, d. 1875?] (dates?)
- Alida (dates?) m. Gen. John M. Brown (dates?)
- Elizabeth (dates?) m. Samuel S. Peake (dates?)
- Gerrit Smith (1834-83) m. Harriett M. Crandall (dates?)
- Gen. Charles (1838-1923) m. Emma Shoenberger (1842-1923)

*This chart lists only those Belle Vue grandchildren known to have married.

Some Aspects of Bishop DuBourg's Return to France

Annabelle M. Melville

It is a truism to state that the Catholic Church in the United States was a beneficiary of the arrivals of French clergy who, like Louis William Valentine DuBourg, found refuge in the New World during the French revolutionary upheavals of the 1790s. It is likewise generally known that some of these exiles returned to France after the Concordat of 1801 which, in asserting the two fundamental principles of freedom of religion and the right of public worship, seemed to predict less stringent proscription of the Church's authority under Napoleon. These returns to France, sometimes occasioned by the dictates of French superiors,[1] the urgings of fond relatives, or a simple personal preference for the homeland, continued for several decades after 1802. Without intending to derogate from the value of any general study of the return to France of *émigrés* priests, this essay is

---

[1] Jacques Emery, the Sulpician Superior in Paris, for example, recalled Ambrose Maréchal, Michel Levadoux, and Antoine Garnier from the United States in 1803.

confined to the return of one Franco-American bishop whose action, rather than illustrating a more extensive exodus, presents a singular and still interesting question of motivation.

Of DuBourg's French contemporaries reaching American shores between 1791 and 1801, six became bishops in the United States.[2] Of these six, four remained in their sees until removed by death. One, John Cheverus of Boston, somewhat against his will, returned to France in 1823, summoned by King Louis XVIII.[3] William DuBourg was the only one of the six to return to France of his own volition. His decision, which came on the heels of his determination to resign his American see, was reached a quarter of a century after the Concordat of 1801, and a dozen years after the restoration of the Bourbons to the French throne.

When DuBourg landed at Le Havre on July 3, 1826, "after a most happy voyage," he wrote at once to Rome announcing that he had come to Europe to secure permission to resign;[4] on July 8 Propaganda, responding to his previous pleas, notified him that his resignation was

[2] Arranged according to the dates of their consecrations, they were: John Chéverus of Boston, 1810; Benedict Joseph Flaget of Bardstown, 1810; Louis William DuBourg, of Louisiana and the Floridas, 1815; Ambrose Maréchal of Baltimore, 1817; John Baptist David of Mauricastro, coadjutor of Bardstown, 1819; and John Dubois of New York, 1826.

[3] For a detailed study of Cheverus' return, see Annabelle M. Melville, "Some Aspects of the Return of Bishop Cheverus to France," *Historical Records and Studies* (United States Catholic Historical Society) 45 (1957), 2-32.

[4] Archives of Propaganda Fide, DuBourg to Caprano. Since these archives have been calendared and microfilmed for documents relating to the Church in the United States, to simplify references to the microfilms housed at the University of Notre Dame, items hereafter will be identified by the volume and document numbers as they appear in Finbar Kenneally, O.F.M., ed., *United States Documents in the Propaganda Fide Archives; a Calendar* (Washington, D. C., 1966ff.). The present reference, for example, would read: **Kenneally,** *Calendar,* **1, 983.**

accepted.[5] The question which has interested historians since then has been : *why* did Bishop DuBourg resign from the diocese of Louisiana and the Floridas, the most extensive diocese in the United States and one over which he had been shepherd, either as administrator apostolic or bishop, for over a dozen years.[6]

Oddly enough, DuBourg's episcopal confrères in the United States knew nothing of DuBourg's intentions. The Archbishop of Baltimore, Ambrose Maréchal, in reporting DuBourg's "precipitously" undertaken departure from New Orleans, complained to Saint-Sulpice in Paris: "What are his motives? I know of none. Some say he goes to solicit the dignity of archbishop. Others think that through his schemes he is on the verge of making a heap of ruins in New Orleans as he did in St. Louis." The most charitable guess Baltimore could venture was that the Bishop of Louisiana was perhaps going on a general search for funds.[7]

Benedict Flaget, the Bishop of Bardstown, Kentucky, uneasily reported to DuBourg's coadjutor in St. Louis that DuBourg had vouchsafed only that he undertook the trip "at the instance of his clergy; but did not state the purpose of that trip." Flaget feared that DuBourg was going to try once more to get a postponement of the division of his vast Mississippi Valley jurisdiction.[8]

[5]DuBourg Family Papers, D-78, Somaglia to DuBourg, Rome, July 8, 1826 — the DuBourg Family Papers are in the possession of Georges de Sainte Marie and are presently located at 64 Rue Aristide Briand, 92300 Levallois Perret, France; for the date of July 2, 1826 for the acceptance of DuBourg's resignation, see Kenneally, *Calendar*, III, 1938. The pope accepted his resignation on July 2-3. Pietro Caprano, Secretary of Propaganda, writing for Giulio M. Somalia on July 8 from Rome, notified DuBourg.

[6]DuBourg was named Administrator Apostolic of Louisiana on August 18, 1812, was consecrated bishop of the see on September 24, 1815, and departed for France from New York on June 1, 1826.

[7]Sulpician Archives in Paris (hereafter cited as SAP), Maréchal to Garnier, Baltimore, June 20, 1826.

[8]Archives of the Archdiocese of St. Louis (hereafter cited a AASL), Flaget to Rosati, Bardstown, May 26, 1826.

Bishop Joseph Rosati in St. Louis was closer to DuBourg's larger intentions when he told his Vincentian superior in Rome that DuBourg's purpose was to assure the continuation of the good already done in Louisiana;[9] and said more explicitly to the superior of the Vincentian college at Piacenza: "The purpose of his journey is to consolidate our establishment in his vast diocese. We need subjects."[10] Yet even Rosati, who had seen DuBourg off from St. Louis in May, was unaware of DuBourg's determination to resign his post, and as late as October 1826 refused to believe the news from Europe that DuBourg had gone to France to stay.

However mystified DuBourg's contemporaries may have been by his behavior in 1826, in the century and a half since DuBourg's death as Archbishop of Besançon in 1833, American Catholic historiography has not hesitated to assign to DuBourg a variety of motives, both personal and administrative, for going. Among those peculiar to the man himself are found: ambition, poor health, pusillanimity, and persistent financial distresses brought on by his own extravagance and imprudence. Administrative problems cited as reasons for his resignation include: trusteeism, the opposition of his clergy, estrangement from his episcopal confrères, and Rome's determination to divide the diocese of Louisiana prematurely. The most provocative motive of those deduced is that curious mischance, the "Inglesi affair," in which an ingratiating young Italian impostor victimized the Bishop of Louisiana.

Cited in whatever combinations, these suggested motives do not present a man of exceptional attractiveness or worth;

---

[9]Anon., ed., "Documents from Our Archives: Diary of Bishop Rosati, 1822, 1825,1826," *St. Louis Catholic Historical Review* (hereafter cited as *SLCHR*) 3 (1921), 311-69; 4 (1922), 76-108, 165-84, 245-71; 5 (1923), 60-88, here 4 (1922), 248 n. 89 (an extract from Rosati's summary of his correspondence kept in Notebooks — see *ibid.*, 168 n. 16)

[10]*Ibid.*, 248 n. 92.

and in the absence of a full-length biography of the bishop, either in the United States or in France, DuBourg's reputation has suffered to some degree. Since he was in fact a man of brilliant talents, enormous zeal, and the conceiver of many institutions to which he contributed, and which survive him today, in the sesquicentennial year of his death DuBourg's return to France merits reconsideration.[11]

The amorphous charge of ambition arises from the word of two men who, as far as any personal contact was concerned, knew DuBourg chiefly as a schoolman in Baltimore vigorously trying to make Saint Mary's College during the years 1800 to 1812 the most distinguished secondary school of the Atlantic seaboard. Benjamin Henry Latrobe, who sent his son to DuBourg's college and assisted DuBourg in the decoration of Saint Mary's Chapel, some ten years later jotted down in his journal that DuBourg's ambition was "equal to his talents" and that both were "of the first magnitude."[12] Ambrose Maréchal, who disliked DuBourg and did all he could in later years to minimize DuBourg's episcopal influence in Rome, [13] constantly suspected him of ambition, warning Cardinal Fesch in Rome, "He has the miserable weakness of wanting to be Archbishop."[14] Pervading ambition as a motive in human affairs, however, remains difficult to confirm or refute, as Shakespeare's *Julius Caesar* perennially argues. In 1826 one thing was clear: that in DuBourg's return to France he was opting to relinquish whatever power and prestige he may have had as bishop of an Ameri-

[11]This essay was undertaken in 1983.

[12]Benjamin H. Latrobe, *Journals,* Vol. III of the *Papers of Benjamin Henry Latrobe* (Baltimore, 1980), 214.

[13]Ronin John Murtha, "The Life of the Most Reverend Ambrose Maréchal, Third Archbishop of Baltimore, 1768-1828," unpublished Ph.D. dissertation at the Catholic University of America (Washington, D. C., 1965), 153-54. Murtha cites letters to Rome to show that by 1826 "Archbishop Maréchal had become completely opposed to any influence DuBourg might have in the American Church."

[14]*Ibid.*, 143.

can frontier diocese for a totally uncertain future in retirement. "Ambition should be made of sterner stuff."

The charge that DuBourg retreated to France to escape the financial chaos resulting from his extravagance and poor business judgment is equally tenuous. Accusations of liberal spending and accumulating debts were certainly leveled against him by his contemporaries. From Issy, his first educational enterprise, to the college in New Orleans, his last in the United States, he did indeed leave a trail of debts behind him. His twentieth-century defenders in both Maryland and the Mississippi Valley, on the other hand, after carefully examining accounts and assessing the economic conditions of the times, have exonerated DuBourg from any taint of heedlessness or folly in his financial transactions.[15]

More relevant to the question of motivation is DuBourg's own attitude toward money. On one occasion when European recruits were arriving in St. Louis with no means available for their support, DuBourg defended himself to his brother, saying:

> I wished prudently to have funds before looking for men. But here the men are, come before the funds. It's God's way of disconcerting the plans of our poor human prudence; may His holy will be done!...Could I refuse this saintly band of apostles under the unworthy pretext that I do not know where to get the means to nourish them? It is God who has called them, it is He who has sent them. He will not let them die of hunger.[16]

[15]Joseph W. Ruane, *The Beginnings of the Society of St. Sulpice in the United States, 1791-1829* (Washington, D.C., 1935), 128-30; Paul C. Schulte, *The Catholic Heritage of Saint Louis: a History of the Old Cathedral Parish of St. Louis, Mo.* (St. Louis, 1934), 113-17; Charles L. Souvay, "Around the St. Louis Cathedral with Bishop DuBourg, 1818-1820," *SLCHR* 5 (1923), 158-59.

[16]*Annales de l'Association de la Propagation de la Foi* 1 (1825), 462, L.W.V. DuBourg to Louis DuBourg, Baltimore, March 13, 1823.

Financial insecurity never mattered to DuBourg at any time when decisions for the good of religion were involved. There is no evidence to support the theory that it directly motivated his actions in 1825-1826.

The motive of health is not so easily discounted. Not long after DuBourg's death on December 12, 1833, the physician who had attended him was moved by both medical interest and personal affection to write and have published an account of DuBourg's last days, which included a retrospect of DuBourg's health throughout adult life. According to Dr. Joseph Auguste Gaspard Pécot, at the age of fourteen DuBourg had been strong but of short stature. All at once, during a bout with quartan fever he shot up to the unusual height for which he was distinguished as a man, and this rapid growth enfeebled his nervous system.

As an adult DuBourg was never able to enjoy uninterrupted vigor. In his thirties he was attacked by an inflammation of the lungs of a most virulent kind, from which he recovered only by a sort of miracle. In his mid-forties he suffered acute attacks of rheumatism and could scarcely use his arms. Praecardial anxieties and agonizing pangs brought on complete exhaustion and fainting.

> These prostrations more or less complete returned unexpectedly, sometimes at several days' intervals, sometimes several times a day. They surprised him in the midst of liturgical ceremonies or in the course of crossing forests and streams in visiting his wilderness missions. Those who witnessed these terrifying crises often believed him dead. Some spiritous drink and a morsel of coarse bread, which he instinctively requested, seemed to restore him.[17]

[17]Dr. [Joseph Auguste Gaspard] Pécot, "Notice sur la maladie et les derniers moments de Mgr. Dubourg, Archevêque de Besançon, 1766-1833," *Académie de Sciences...de Besançon,* Séance publique du 28 janvier, 1834 (Besançon, 1834), 60-72.

In March 1983, Dr. Gordon McHardy of New Orleans, an internationally known gastroenterologist, offered some tentative interpretations of Pécot's account of DuBourg's health. McHardy began by commenting that the period of startling growth in adolescence was not particularly unusual, but that the fever — which could have been quartan malaria or yellow fever — may have left an endocrine abnormality, perhaps an occult thyroid disturbance. McHardy viewed DuBourg's lung condition as inflammatory pulmonary disease. (One recalls that it was an era when tuberculosis was prevalent, and that in midlife DuBourg was associated with the Setons, so many of whom died of that disease.) McHardy continues:

> His adult life illness brings one to the possibility that his rheumatoid manifestation in the forties may have been acute rheumatic fever, despite the age factor, and that in his adult life hc was developing manifestations compatible with mitral valve disease....The possibility of its being rheumatic heart disease is supported by his exhaustion, fainting, and his intolerance to both physical and emotional exertion.[18]

After DuBourg entered his sixties and returned to France, there was a rapid deterioration of his health. He tried various spas, hoping to restore his energies, but to no avail. As McHardy points out, "At many of the spas, the water had a high iodine content, which would have favored control of a thyroid disturbance. At the same time, if he had tuberculosis, which is suggested by the glandular involvement at this time, it may have worsened with iodides." This would explain DuBourg's loss of voice after taking a river steamer to Bordeaux, when he caught cold, contracted an

[18]The evaluation by Dr. McHardy was secured through the courtesy of Dr. Robert Judice of the Medical Center of New Orleans.

inflammation of the bronchi and larynx, and ran a fever. Dr. Pécot recalled that "his voice, three-quarters gone, never reappeared completely."

The autopsy performed after DuBourg's death in 1833 showed inflammation of the stomach, intestines, liver, pancreas, and additionally lymph node and respiratory tract inflammation, all of which suggested a diffused tuberculosis. "But the heart," Pécot recorded, "was found to be the organ the most anteriorly and gravely attacked. It showed all the alterations characteristic of chronic periocarditis. ..." The noticeable change in his features during DuBourg's last months confirmed, for McHardy, the possibility of endocrine disturbance, particularly hyperthyroidism "or any other bizarre endocrinopathy."

This analysis of DuBourg's health obviously leaves much to be desired. In the first place, Pécot's summary of the American years was based upon DuBourg's account of them given in the year of his death. It should be stated, nevertheless, that accounts of DuBourg's contemporaries on the American scene during his ministry bear out Pécot's later descriptions. Another difficulty lies in the variety of symptoms presented. As McHardy notes, "It would be almost impossible to consider the entire life span and illnesses as one entity." In the end, whether the man's health was largely the result of youthful fever (rheumatic, malarial, or yellow), a subsequent endocrine disturbance, or persistent tuberculous involvement, is not essential to the question of his motivation in returning to France. Suffice it to say that poor health *could* have been a reason to resign in 1826.

Yet it was not. Shortly after DuBourg's arrival in Paris that year *L'Ami de la religion et du Roi* commented on his resignation, "One believes that the state of the health of the prelate has been one of the motives for this measure."[19] DuBourg hotly and hastily denied this, asserting:

[19]*L'Ami* 48 (1826), 295. After the July Revolution, this journal dropped the words "et du Roi" from its title.

The motives of my resignation are of a higher order; and they were presented to the Holy See, to which they appeared so just that His Holiness the Pope did not hesitate a moment...to dissolve the sacred ties that bound me to that important but laborious mission. But in ceasing to be head of it, I have not ceased to feel the most tender solicitude for it....It is that solicitude which forced me to leave it, since on the one hand it was evident my presence there would be more prejudicial than useful, and on the other hand, I flatter myself that I would be able from Europe to render that mission more important services.[20]

It appears that although his medical history attests poor health, the bishop clearly rejected it as a motive at the time of his return to France.

John Gilmary Shea in the later nineteenth century claimed that "discouraged at the difficulties which arose to thwart him," DuBourg at last "lost all heart and energy," and thus abandoned his assignment.[21] Shea's imputation of a lack of fortitude found favor with later writers, especially those of the distaff side. Sister Mary Teresa Carroll in her *Catholic History of Alabama and the Floridas* published in 1908 claimed that DuBourg was always in terror for his life;[22] and fifty years later the biographer of Philippine Duchesne found it helpful to history to discover in his portraits that DuBourg had a "weak chin."[23] Content to reproach Louise Callan with the poet's dictum, "There's no

[20]*Ibid.*, 336.

[21]John Gilmary Shea, *The History of the Catholic Church in the United States,* 4 vols. (New York, 1886-1892), III, 390.

[22]Mary Teresa Austin Carroll, *A Catholic History of Alabama and the Floridas* (New York, 1908), 253.

[23]Louise Callan, R.S.C.J., *Philippine Duchesne: Frontier Missionary of the Sacred Heart, 1769-1852* (Westminster, Maryland, 1957), 313.

art to find the mind's construction in the face," one may properly raise the question: was DuBourg at any time in danger in Louisiana? The evidence seems to support an affirmative reply.

On July 2, 1814, having been in New Orleans as administrator apostolic less than two years, DuBourg reported to Archbishop Carroll that he had fled the city, owing to an eruption of violence encouraged by Father Antonio de Sedella. The mayor, who upheld the rebellious faction, had threatened to throw DuBourg bodily from the pulpit of the cathedral if he dared ascend it to preach; and many other rioters had gone to the church armed with stones to pelt DuBourg.[24]

Nevertheless, DuBourg soon returned to the city to rally support for Andrew Jackson as the British approached; and, after the Battle of New Orleans in January 1815, welcomed the hero of that victory to the cathedral. Saint Louis church, in which DuBourg's life had been threatened a few months earlier, was now the scene of splendid liturgies of thanksgiving for the defeat of the British with all parties for the moment united in the outpouring of national pride and joy.

The trustees of the cathedral, however, under Sedella's leadership, were only momentarily subdued. While DuBourg was in Europe recruiting workers for the diocese in 1816, his brother Louis from New Orleans confided in Bishop Flaget that violent opposition was again on the rise. No bishop except Père Antoine was acceptable to the *marguilliers*. For some time Sedella's supporters had been sending money to the French Minister of Cults, Jean-Étienne Portalis, to obtain the episcopate for Sedella. Should DuBourg, who had been consecrated the previous year in

[24]Archives of the Archdiocese of Baltimore (hereafter cited as AAB),3-E-10, DuBourg to Carroll, County of Acadia [La.], July 2, 1814.

Rome, return to New Orleans as Bishop of Louisiana and the Floridas, his family would be exposed to the hatred of the intriguers, and the bishop himself might be sacrificed. Louis ended his report to Flaget, "I do not fear the danger myself since I have decided to join my sister in France; but I leave here my brother [Pierre-François], a father of five children, and a nephew who has already been obliged to impose silence on one of these men hired to spread calumny."[25] That a bishop's nephew should engage in duels to defend his uncle's honor suggested how far things had gone.

The bishop, recruiting missionaries in Italy, Belgium, and France, was quite aware of all this; and he did notify Rome of his plans to make his residence, for the time being, at St. Louis on his return to the Mississippi Valley. Yet he categorically declined the proposal of Louis XVIII that he accept a see in France; and, in reporting the invitation to Propaganda, assured Lorenzo Cardinal Litta that he had no intention of accepting, and had only mentioned the matter in case the French government should appeal to the pope.[26]

The king's offer was well known in Paris, for Antoine Garnier relayed it to Maréchal, saying that DuBourg was making a brilliant impression in Paris, and that people were talking of his settling there.[27] Philippine Duchesne, who followed DuBourg to Louisiana in 1818, remembered it well, writing from the American frontier in later days, "The example of our holy bishop, who might have had a brilliant career and chose poverty, toil, and suffering instead, is an inspiration to us."[28] A fearful man seeking to avoid a dan-

[25]*Ibid.*, 16-A-2, Louis DuBourg to Flaget, New Orleans, August 1, 1816. The recipient of this letter was earlier identified as Maréchal, but internal evidence shows it to have been Benedict Flaget.

[26]Kenneally, *Calendar*, V, 1538, DuBourg to Propaganda, Paris, September 30, 1816.

[27]Sulpician Archives in Baltimore (hereafter cited as SAB), Antoine Garnier to Maréchal, Paris, May 11, 1817.

[28]Callan, *Duchesne*, 258.

gerous assignment in the United States would have found the suggestion of an easy berth in France enticing. DuBourg did not. He returned to his diocese, and in 1823 returned to New Orleans as his permanent seat of operations, where the aged Père Antoine at last collaborated with the bishop and his European recruits.

Trusteeism, unhappily, was not vanquished in Lower Louisiana, and renewed threats of violence two years later were, indirectly, in fact one of the causes for DuBourg's decision to resign. He told Rome in a succession of letters[29] prior to his departure, "A longer stay in this country is incompatible with both the good of Religion and the safety of my family." His brother Pierre-François' numerous daughters were by then married, and the number of grand-children was increasing. Since his nephew Arnould had become a justice of the peace and Pierre-François served as consul for Sardinia in New Orleans, the name DuBourg was more prominent than ever. When their episcopal relative was calumniated, tempers rose; and DuBourg wrote uneas-ily to Propaganda, "How long I shall be able to restrain my natural defenders, I know not; but the mere thought that on my account blood — the blood of my relatives — may be shed does not leave me a moment's rest."

Two developments in particular augmented high feeling against the bishop in New Orleans in the year preceding his departure. The first was the gift by the Ursulines of their old convent to serve as an episcopal residence for the bishop and his successors. The thought that DuBourg had an *évêché* roused the *marguilliers* to a fury not displayed since they had threatened to stone him in 1814. As one Louisiana historian comments:

[29]Letters of DuBourg to Peter Caprano, New Orleans, December 20, 1825; January 6, 10, 1826; and February 17, 1826, in Kenneally, *Calendar*, V, 1900-02; the Latin text and an English translation of the letter of February 17, 1826 are printed in anon, ed., "Documents from Our Archives: Bishop DuBourg's Corre-spondence with Propaganda," *SLCHR* 1 (1918-19), 73-80, 127-45, 184-96, 300-11:2 (1920), 43-52, 130-50, 210-24 ; 3 (1921), 106-50, 191-222, here at 3 (1921), 201-04, nr.XLIII.

It is not surprising to find them explosively condemning
Bishop DuBourg in the newspapers and pamphlets like
Nos Libertés Vengées and charging that he had either
deliberately robbed the Sisters of their property or insi-
diously prevailed upon them to forfeit it to him, interlop-
ing foreigner that he was, seeking to enrich himself, lining
his purse and that of the clergy, and ready to make his
escape, well-fixed, as soon as there was a chance.[30]

The second violent outburst attacking the bishop was
provoked by his refusal to give a place to a newcomer to
Louisiana. DuBourg explained to Propaganda in February
1826:

I have had a great deal of trouble lately stopping my
nephews nay even my dearest brother from taking
revenge on those who attack me; and now scarcely a week
passes that I am not grossly insulted in the newspapers
because of that miserable priest (Sigura), who was foisted
upon the church of one of the suburbs by the trustees;
even though this man is utterly despised by his abettors,
still these, out of hatred toward me, make themselves
openly his supporters.[31]

The crisis over Segura, as the name is more often spelled,
developed during the summer of 1825. In June the Spanish
priest arrived in New Orleans and asked for permission to
officiate in the diocese. He had come from the French
diocese of Aire, admitting that because of an intrigue
against him he was without an *exeat*, but claiming that his

---

[30]Roger Baudier, *The Catholic Church in Louisiana* (New Orleans, 1939), 302.
Baudier here combines the charges made by a wide variety of newspapers and
pamphlets.

[31]Anon., ed., "DuBourg's Correspondence," *SLCHR* 3 (1921), 204, DuBourg to
Caprano, New Orleans, February 17, 1826.

bishop had not censured him. DuBourg assured Segura that he would write to Aire regarding an *exeat*, and in the meantime Segura could offer Mass but perform no other function.

While DuBourg was away on an episcopal visitation he received two letters from Destrehan on the "German Coast" of the Mississippi River, one from Segura and one from the trustees of the church of Saint Charles Borromeo, announcing that the Spaniard was pastor of the church and demanding the bishop's approval. On returning to New Orleans DuBourg laid the matter before his council consisting of Père Antoine (the pastor of the cathedral parish), Louis Sibourd (the vicar general of the diocese), and Benedict Richard (chaplain of the Ursuline convent). The council unanimously concurred with the bishop that without an *exeat* Segura could not be installed as pastor.

Ignoring the bishop and his council, the trustees of Saint Charles installed Segura and let loose a barrage of letters and articles in the papers of New Orleans stating that:

In the United States of America the voice of the people was sovereign, that the use of the term "hierarchy" was contrary to the principles of American democracy, that the people had a voice under American institutions to choose their pastor, that Father Segura was a regularly ordained priest, hence did not need the approval of foreign interlopers, nor did such foreigners have any right to interfere with the practice of religion.[32]

Just why the bishop, who had been in the United States since 1794 and was of French origin, as were many Louisiana citizens, should have been dubbed a "foreign interloper," while Segura, a newly arrived Spaniard, became the

---

[32]Baudier, *Church in Louisiana*, 301-02.

symbol of American democracy at bay remains enigmatic. But fanatics are no respecters of reason, and their scurrilous attacks on DuBourg in this instance made it very difficult for the bishop to dissuade his hotheaded nephews from challenging the editors who printed the calumnies.[33] In this sense, fear — fear of violence and danger to his family — combined with trusteeism, was a contributing factor to DuBourg's resignation.

Peter Guilday in 1927 held that Rome accepted DuBourg's resignation because Propaganda "had learned through letters from Bardstown and New Orleans that DuBourg had reached such a state of suspicion and sensitiveness that cooperation with other bishops and priests was almost at an end."[34] While Rome's motives are not at issue here, the matter of DuBourg's relations with his co-workers in the vineyard is pertinent. For a man of his nature, thriving on appreciation and admiring smiles, accustomed to exerting great charm over those he sought to influence, easily wounded by criticism and opposition, his last years in Louisiana were certainly not unfailingly rewarding. He did face opposition from his priests; and, as the only American prelate not a suffragan of the Archbishop of Baltimore, his views were not always supported by the hierarchy of that province. Yet the extent to which this lack of rapport became a motive for DuBourg's departure remains moot.

It can be argued that the opposition of DuBourg's clergy arose chiefly from the notorious Inglesi affair. Angelo Inglesi had arrived in St. Louis in the autumn of 1819, toward the end of DuBourg's second year in Upper Louisiana. He immediately impressed the bishop, who wrote jubilantly to Simon Bruté in Maryland:

[33]Kenneally, *Calendar*, V, 1900, DuBourg to Caprano, New Orleans, January 10, 1826.

[34]Peter Guilday, *The Life and Times of John England: First Bishop of Charleston, 1786-1842*, 2 vols. (New York, 1927), I, 584.

A very distinguished [subject] aged 26 has just come to me. A Roman count, sharing richly the gifts of fortune and an admirable physique, to wide knowledge, above all, that of the world and the three languages Latin, French, and English, he unites a rare devotion and modesty. He will be, I believe, an acquisition of the first rank. He has already made his studies for the ecclesiastical state, even part of his theology. Family circumstances compelled him to suspend them; and for 6 years he has traveled all over Europe and North America as an observer and man of quality. Having arrived in New Orleans he was inclined to return to Rome, when the needs of this diocese...decided him to settle in Louisiana. He is here to finish his studies.[35]

Count Inglesi had been well received in New Orleans, and Louis Moni, DuBourg's first assistant at the cathedral there, had enthusiastically recommended him to the bishop in St. Louis. In no time Inglesi, "because of his education and conversational ability, which had always been highly regarded by the French, was able to gain access to the fashionable society of this growing town on the Mississippi."[36]

On March 20, 1820, DuBourg "with unseemly and uncanonical haste"[37] ordained the fascinating newcomer at St. Louis, and immediately gave him permission to return to Italy to settle some family affairs. While in Europe Inglesi was also authorized to collect money and recruits as DuBourg's vicar general.

[35]Archives of the University of Notre Dame, DuBourg to Simon Bruté, St. Louis, October 4, 1819.

[36]F. G. Holweck, "Ein dunkles Blatt aus DuBourgs Episkopat," *Pastoral-Blatt* 52 (1918), 17-20, here 17.

[37]William Barnaby Faherty, S.J., "The Personality and Influence of Louis William Valentine Dubourg," *Frenchmen and French Ways in the Mississippi Valley,* ed. John Francis McDermott (Chicago, 1969), 43-57, here 51.

The unsavory story of this handsome young charmer need not be dwelt upon here,[38] but two details are pertinent. The first is that Inglesi's reputation was destroyed in Rome shortly after his arrival by a husband's accusation that Inglesi had seduced his wife,[39] and ambassadors to Rome in September 1821 speedily dispatched the brow-raising news to their own capitals. The second relevant fact is that DuBourg that very spring had proposed to Rome that Inglesi be made his coadjutor bishop,[40] and this proposal was simultaneously being discussed on both sides of the Atlantic.

Among his clergy in Louisiana DuBourg had made no secret of his proposal, and had persuaded himself that they favored it. The truth was that in New Orleans some did not, and these priests avidly listened to the rumors about Inglesi arriving with almost every ship from Europe. The leader of those decrying Inglesi's nomination was Bertrand Martial, who had come from Bordeaux in 1818 to conduct a school for boys and who had DuBourg's respect and affection. Long before the bishop was finally convinced of Inglesi's deceit,[41] Martial was lengthily writing to Rome and Québec, seeking information about Inglesi, relaying rumors, protesting the bishop's blunder, and reporting the disaffection among the clergy.[42] Records do not indicate how much

[38]A lengthy essay on the Inglesi affair is presented in Chapter 25 of the manuscript biography, "DuBourg of Louisiana," by the present writer.

[39]Kenneally, *Calendar*, III, 1611, Propaganda Fide to Cardinal Consalvi, Particular Congregation of Propaganda, Rome, September 22, 1821, to deal with reports of the misconduct of Angelo Inglesi.

[40]*Ibid.*, I, 701, DuBourg to Cardinal Fontana, New Orleans, May 3. 1821.

[41]*Ibid.*, I, 822, Bishop DuBourg to brother Louis DuBourg, Washington [Baltimore], February 6, 1823, is the first document revealing DuBourg's realization that Inglesi had duped him.

[42]Martial letters to B. Billaud from New Orleans are dated July 12-14, October 20, and November 30, 1822 — cf. Kenneally, *Calendar,* I, 550, 795, 804. The Archives of the Archdiocese of Québec preserve letters dated November 13 and 24, 1822.

DuBourg eventually learned of Martial's role in aggravating the situation in Lower Louisiana; but once DuBourg fixed his permanent residence in New Orleans in 1823, Martial accompanied by part of his school's pupils and faculty withdrew to the diocese of Bardstown, apparently without an *exeat* from DuBourg.[43] Something of DuBourg's sentiments at this juncture may be surmised from his remark to Joseph Rosati, "May he not plague the Bishops there as he has plagued me!"[44]

The notion that DuBourg suffered a wholesale desertion of his clergy rests largely upon three remaining documents: Martial's claim in 1822 that he could not prevent some priests from deserting over the Inglesi business,[45] Maréchal's gratuitous comment to Cardinal Fesch on July 11, 1823, that DuBourg had lost the confidence of both the clergy and laity of New Orleans,[46] and DuBourg's own assertion in a letter to the pope that he felt he had deserved to forfeit his clergy's respect and loyalty because of his errors in regard to Inglesi.[47] Other evidence, however, suggests that of the more than fifty men who came from Europe under DuBourg's auspices, and formed the active clergy of his eight-year episcopate in the Mississippi Valley, more were lost to death or poor health than to disaffection and desertion.

DuBourg himself nevertheless suffered keenly in the aftermath of the Inglesi affair. Peter J. Rahill, who contributed the essay on DuBourg to the *New Catholic Encyclope-*

---

[43]SAB, Flaget to D'Aviau, Bardstown, October 10, 1825, indicates that Flaget at Martial's urging requested an *exeat* for him from Bordeaux. Two priests who left with Martial for Bardstown were Simon Fouché and Evremond Harrissart.

[44]AASL, DuBourg to Rosati, New Orleans, December 23, 1823.

[45]Kenneally, *Calendar,* I, 795, Martial to Billaud, New Orleans, July 13-14 and into the month of August, 1822.

[46]*Ibid.,* VII, 2273, Maréchal to Fesch, Baltimore, July 11, 1823.

[47]F.G. Holweck, "Contribution to the 'Inglesi Affair'," *SLCHR* 5 (1923), 14-39, here 17, DuBourg to Leo XII, New Orleans, February 1, 1825.

dia and wrote a monograph on DuBourg's St. Louis episcopacy, held that the "one depressant never lifted was the remorse of the bishop at his having been deluded by the duplicity of Angelo Inglesi."[48] Rahill saw the mistake of ordaining Inglesi in 1820 as the "enduring impulsion for the resignation by DuBourg of the Diocese of Louisiana." Rahill's view has certain merit, particularly if DuBourg's Roman correspondence alone forms the basis for theorizing.

Almost as soon as DuBourg received incontrovertible evidence of Inglesi's true character early in February 1823, he sent to Rome his first suggestion of resigning over Inglesi. To Philip Borgna, C.M., who was intending to go to Italy, DuBourg wrote a long instruction on matters he wished presented to Propaganda, among them his revulsion at having ordained Inglesi. He directed Borgna:

> Say that I acknowledge my mistake and deplore it, and that such is the confusion and sorrow into which this sad disclosure has plunged me, that I have several times been tempted to beseech His Holiness' permission to retire...; that only the fear of seeing my Diocese lost by that request prevented me; but if His Eminence deems it fitting to relieve me of a place of which I made myself unworthy by such great imprudence, I am ready to resign, and will be most thankful to him.[49]

A year later DuBourg sent a letter directly to Propaganda stating that he wished to resign.[50] On May 29, 1824, Propaganda reassured DuBourg with the words, "His Holiness

---

[48] Peter J. Rahill, "The St. Louis Episcopacy of L. William DuBourg," *Records* (American Catholic Historical Society of Philadelphia) 77 (1966), 67-98, here 91.

[49] Kenneally, *Calendar*, I, 827, DuBourg to Borgna, Washington [Baltimore], February 27, 1823.

[50] *Ibid.*, 568, DuBourg to Propaganda Fide, New Orleans, March 8, 1824.

says to remain tranquil in spirit and do not let the Inglesi blunder be a reason for resigning the episcopacy."[51] On July 9, 1825, Rome forwarded the pope's reiteration that DuBourg be comforted in that regard.[52]

During the year and more that Inglesi lived in Philadelphia, DuBourg kept Rome informed of whatever news he had of his former protégé, a process which reopened old wounds. On February 1, 1825, DuBourg revealed most clearly the depth of his sorrow as he addressed Leo XII:

> Your Holiness,
> Much consolation have I derived from your kind letter, by which Your Holiness commands me to be of good cheer and to persevere in ruling the flock entrusted to me. But I confess that the arrow is fixed too deep in my heart ever to be withdrawn entirely. Since that day when I put aside the wise sanctions of Canon Law and hastily ordained an unworthy man who later scandalized the Catholic world (by which action I became an accomplice of the sins and shame of that man) not only the office of bishop but life itself has become hateful to me.[53]

Rahill was correct in presenting remorse over Inglesi as a recurring and depressing influence on DuBourg's state of mind; but was this remorse the chief reason for DuBourg's eventual return to France? It was not. It would be misreading the man's whole life to picture him, when he finally chose to leave Louisiana, as a man with head hanging in defeat, driven by the spectre of an impostor who had deceived him in the past. In attributing ultimate motives one should consider not only the annual letter to Rome decrying his offense and offering his resignation, but also DuBourg's

[51]*Ibid.*, III, 1795, Propaganda Fide to DuBourg. Rome, May 29, 1824.
[52]*Ibid.*, 1870, Propaganda Fide to DuBourg, Rome, July 9, 1825.
[53]Holweck, "Inglesi Affair," *SLCHR* 5 (1923), 17.

episcopal career in the Midwest from February 1823 to May 1826. Those years of DuBourg's New Orleans residency were a period of steady progress in the cause of religion, particularly in Lower Louisiana, where opposition could always flare anew. After DuBourg's departure, one of his priests writing to a friend in France listed the twenty parishes of the new diocese of New Orleans, all served by young and virtuous priests, and continued:

> All the parishes that I have just named, except two...are served by priests who were placed there by Mgr. Dubourg. You can judge by that the good he achieved in New Orleans during the few years he lived there. Some of these parishes did not exist before his arrival...and others, where there was a miserable wooden church, maintain very pretty brick ones which he himself consecrated.[54]

In addition, religious houses flourished. The Ursulines built a new, larger convent; the Religious of the Sacred Heart established their second house in Lower Louisiana— their third in the whole diocese; and the Lorettines, already established in St. Louis, began a second house in Assumption Parish at La Fourche, Louisiana. The energy with which DuBourg pursued the development of new institutions, made physically harrowing visitations of the remote regions of his extensive diocese, supervised the renovation of the old convent which was to serve as both his residence and a college, and proposed judicious plans for improving the effectiveness of the American hierarchy, belies the image of a man mournfully marking time until Rome accepted his pleas to resign.

---

[54]*Annales de l'Association de la Propagation de la Foi* 3 (1829), cahier 18, Bouillier to [?], New Orleans, March 1, 1828.

It was only when DuBourg tried to found a second Vincentian house and seminary that he came up against a strong wall of opposition, and began to question seriously his further usefulness. The opposition in this case came from his good friend and coadjutor, Bishop Rosati, who was also the superior of the Congregation of the Mission in the United States. The two men clashed, not over the need for a seminary in Louisiana, but rather over the practical possibility of establishing one before the diocese of Louisiana was to be divided in 1826, as Rome had decreed. To DuBourg, who would remain in Lower Louisiana as Bishop of New Orleans, it seemed only just that, after all the efforts he had made to found the Vincentian seminary in Missouri and to encourage his recruits to join their congregation, the Vincentians should sacrifice in his interest to provide his future diocese with a nursery for priests. He saw two alternatives: either syphon from the northern institution some men to man a new school, or transfer the Missouri seminary to Louisiana until new professors could be acquired. To Rosati it seemed that to weaken, perhaps destroy, the existing seminary in Missouri by attempting to run two schools without enough Vincentians, especially one capable of heading the new seminary, in the end would prove fatal to religion in the diocese of St. Louis, which he expected to head after 1826.[55]

By 1825 relations between DuBourg and Rosati had become rather strained on the questions of a second seminary and the timing of the division of the diocese. Rosati turned more and more toward Flaget when he needed to open his heart on these painful matters. In spite of his devotion to DuBourg, Flaget's sympathies were with the coadjutor's views, and on February 7, 1826, the Bishop of

---

[55]For a balanced treatment of this complex subject, see Frederick J. Easterly, C.M., *The Life of the Rt. Rev. Joseph Rosati, First Bishop of St. Louis, 1789-1843* (Washington, D. C., 1942), 83-87.

Bardstown decided to take a hand in settling matters. Speaking for himself and his own coadjutor, John B. David, Flaget gave Rosati's Vincentian superior in Rome their opinion of what ought to be done. "It is our firm conviction," he began, "that the projects explained by Bishop DuBourg to Bishop Rosati are prejudicial in every respect." Kentucky opposed the transfer of the major seminary and any postponement of the division of the diocese. "This is our conclusion, founded principally on the perfect knowledge we have of Bishop DuBourg." Bertrand Martial, who was going to Rome, would clarify things so that Rosati might be extricated from "his painful position."[56] Ten days later Flaget told Rosati what he had done, explaining, "Since I do not wish you. . .to move your Seminary to New Orleans, I have already written to your superior in Rome to tell him to insist that the division of the two bishoprics be made as soon as possible."[57]

In his discussion of DuBourg's return to France, Charles L. Souvay, C.M., in 1917 suggested that the shock produced by this defection of Flaget exacerbated the "smarting pain caused by the manifold difficulties besetting" DuBourg and led him on February 27, 1826, to ask for permission to resign. "His resolution to go to Europe," Souvay held, "was the logical consequence of this first step."[58]

Several things combine to negate this theory. In the first place, there is no evidence that DuBourg knew of Flaget's intervention at the time he wrote to Rome on February 27. Even if the mails were more speedy than usual, it is unlikely that Rosati would have informed DuBourg in New Orleans of Flaget's action. Certainly DuBourg made no reference to it in his last letter to Flaget before his departure for France.

---

[56]Kenneally, *Calendar,* V, 1903, Flaget to Baccari, Bardstown, February 7, 1826.

[57]AASL, Flaget to Rosati, Bardstown, February 17, 1826.

[58]Charles L. Souvay, "Rosati's Elevation to the See of St. Louis," *Catholic Historical Review* 3 (1917), 165-86, here 180.

The most that can be attested is that on his way to New York DuBourg did not leave his steamboat at Louisville to visit Flaget at Bardstown; and, once settled permanently in France, DuBourg did not write to Flaget directly for five years.[59] More detrimental to the Souvay theory is the fact that DuBourg prior to February 27 had already on at least fourteen other occasions mentioned resigning to either Propaganda or to the pope.

Finally, a more recent examination of all the documents presently available supports the month of December 1825 as the time of DuBourg's firm decision to withdraw from his jurisdiction. The catalyst was not Flaget's meddling but Rosati's announcement that he and his seminary council had decided that they could not consent to DuBourg's proposals regarding a seminary in Louisiana at that time. On receipt of this news DuBourg on December 9 replied amicably to his coadjutor, "I have said *Fiat* to the deliberation of your Council. Having few years to live I will probably not see the extinction of the Diocese. And if I see it, I will have nothing for which to reproach myself."[60] Beginning on December 20, 1825, DuBourg wrote in swift succession nine letters to Rome urging his resignation. On January 30, 1826, he informed Propaganda of his impending departure for Europe, which would take place "immediately after Easter."[61] From Europe he would still urge the necessity of a seminary for Louisiana.[62]

One further thing needs to be said about DuBourg's relations with his episcopal confrères as a possible motive

[59]SAP, Flaget to DuBourg, Bardstown, March 1, 1832. In this letter Flaget expresses his pleasure at hearing from DuBourg at last. In letters to mutual friends DuBourg had previously sent Flaget his regards.

[60]AASL, DuBourg to Rosati, New Orleans, December 9, 1825.

[61]Kenneally, *Calendar,* V, 1899, DuBourg to Pietro Caprano, New Orleans, January 30, 1826.

[62]DuBourg's correspondence with Rosati after 1826, preserved in AASL, attests to DuBourg's continued interest in this seminary.

for his going, and that is the relevance of Maréchal's intervention in matters affecting DuBourg's diocese, particularly his two attempts to have DuBourg's European recruits removed from the diocese of Louisiana to be made heads of dioceses created totally or in part from Maréchal's jurisdiction. In the first instance, the attempt to make Rosati a bishop of Mississippi and Alabama in 1822, Maréchal failed, owing to the immediate and outraged protests of DuBourg and Rosati within the diocese of Louisiana, and those of Flaget and David in Kentucky. Rosati became, instead, DuBourg's coadjutor bishop and after 1823 relieved DuBourg of much of the administration of Upper Louisiana.[63]

In the second case, Maréchal's attempt to make Michael Portier vicar apostolic of Alabama and the Floridas in 1825 eventually succeeded. The chronology of the Portier nomination, however, makes clear that DuBourg had reached his determination to resign before learning of Rome's action in Portier's regard. Although DuBourg for two months refrained from alluding to the matter at all, when he did write, his protests showed a mounting anger.[64] Clearly he was "sensitive"; he did indeed have "suspicions" — and rightly so — that Maréchal had misled Rome about Portier.

To imply, however, as Guilday did, that by 1826 DuBourg was isolated from the other American bishops is inaccurate. In the Portier affair Kentucky again sided with DuBourg, with Flaget telling Maréchal forcefully that it would need a miracle for Portier to accomplish anything in the new diocese.[65] As late as January 18, 1826, the western bishops were

[63]For a detailed account of this matter, see Charles L. Souvay, "Rosati's Election to the Coadjutorship of New Orleans," *Catholic Historical Review* 3 (1917), 3-21.

[64]For a detailed account of the Portier appointment, see Oscar H. Lipscomb, "The Administration of Michael Portier, Vicar Apostolic of Alabama and the Floridas," an unpublished Ph.D. dissertation at the Catholic University of America (1969), 36-42.

[65]AAB, 16-U-20, Flaget to Maréchal, Bardstown, June 22, 1827.

replying favorably to DuBourg's suggestions for facilitating the selection of American bishops.[66] To be sure, from time to time there were differences between DuBourg and his priests, as well as with his fellow bishops. That these differences were a motive for his departure in 1826 is simply not demonstrable.

The one underlying principle to which DuBourg adhered throughout his career as prelate, and which finally led him to his decision in December 1825, was that episcopacy must be established with authority and dignity in a country where bishops were scarcely known and not infrequently humiliated. During his years in Maryland DuBourg had perceived the first Catholic bishop of the United States suffering indignities more than once. DuBourg had filled in at the German church in Baltimore when Father Cesarius Reuter rebelled against his bishop. In New York schismatic Catholics interrupted Carroll's Mass, compelling him to complete it in the chapel of the Spanish embassy. In Philadelphia quarreling trustees even brought a civil suit against the bishop in a dispute over the control of church properties.[67]

Before he entered his own diocese as bishop, DuBourg had learned of the deep-rooted opposition in New Orleans to a bishop appointed by and consecrated in Rome. He told the Prefect of Propaganda on June 24, 1816:

> The ringleaders have so aroused all classes of people against the admission of a Bishop, that my friends believe it would be unsafe for me to go there. . . . Access to the Cathedral would be denied me and the Episcopal dignity would be ignominiously outraged. When my Vicar General brought to Father Antonio the Testimonial of my

[66]Kenneally, *Calendar*, I, 949, Flaget to DuBourg, Nazareth, Ky. [Bardstown], January 18, 1826.

[67]For details of Carroll's difficulties with trustees, see Annabelle M. Melville, *John Carroll of Baltimore* (New York, 1955), 203-13.

Consecration and the Brief of His Holiness raising me to the Episcopate...one of the trustees afterward took these documents to a Café and made jokes about them insulting to His Holiness and the Bishop. Father Antonio boasts that he has nothing to do with the Pope or Bishops of his making.[68]

In the face of such insubordination DuBourg's arrival could only have jeopardized the respect due episcopal dignity and the vital interests of religion, "a danger," he insisted, "which ought to be avoided at all costs because once the mischief was done it would be impossible to remedy."[69] He had made his temporary headquarters at St. Louis to prevent that danger.

It had proved a wise decision. When DuBourg made a visitation of Lower Louisiana three years later he was everywhere given a warm reception, especially by Père Antoine in New Orleans. DuBourg told Propaganda:

This example has given the tone to the whole city, so that I was not afraid to celebrate publicly a synod in that same city where a year ago, merely to show myself would have meant extreme danger. This Synod was made up of some twenty priests from Lower Louisiana. All manifested in unison both their obedience to me and their zeal for the maintenance of Ecclesiastical discipline.[70]

To Philippine Duchesne he reported, "Episcopal authority is today respected and recognized by even those who were its most ardent detractors. I have reason to hope for the happiest results for religion."[71]

Realistically, he retained some reservations about the

[68]Kenneally, *Calendar,* I, 221, DuBourg to Dugnani, Bordeaux, June 24, 1816.

[69]*Ibid.*

[70]Anon., ed., "DuBourg's Correspondence," *SLCHR* 2 (1920), 132-36, here 135, DuBourg to Cardinal Fontana, Upper Louisiana, February 24, 1821.

[71]Roman Archives of the Religious of the Sacred Heart, DuBourg Letters 21, DuBourg to Duchesne, New Orleans, February 21, 1821.

permanence of the good-will displayed in the winter of 1820-1821, telling the Bishop of Québec more soberly, "Yet how many things are everywhere to be done!...How many evils to repair. You are quite right, my lord, that I am only preparing the way for my successors. Pray that I shall acquit myself so as not to increase the difficulties for them."[72] Unless future shepherds could work in peace, the flocks would be scattered; he judged his successes and failures by that criterion.

In moments of melancholy over his own deficiencies he could cry out to the pope, "I see that the hatred which, right or wrong, from the very beginning of my administration, inspired the various classes of our population against me, will never die out and that, whatever I do, the progress of religion will be thwarted." If he were the obstacle to that progress then he ought to be replaced. "Any other Bishop may take my place," he argued, "especially that angelic man, the Right Rev. Mr. Rosati...a man, who on account of his inborn meekness and for his great knowledge and virtue, is most welcome to all the clergy and is not hated by any of the laymen; by him the Church will certainly be well provided."[73]

After the personal opposition to DuBourg was resurrected in 1825, as he later explained to the head of the French Ministry of Ecclesiastical Affairs, the conviction grew that:

> All that I could have done of benefit to that poor country, and which perhaps could never have been done by another, is already done or on the way to completion....My presence could only hinder or harm. My

[72] Lionel St. G. Lindsay, ed., "Some Correspondence Relating to the Dioceses of New Orleans and St. Louis (1818-1843): From the Archiepiscopal Archives at Québec," *Records* 19 (1908), 185-213, here 189, DuBourg to Plessis, Lower Louisiana, February 25, 1821.

[73] Holweck, "Inglesi Affair," *SLCHR* 5 (1923), 17, DuBourg to Leo XII, New Orleans, February 1, 1825.

successor, on the contrary, has in his hands all the elements needed to accomplish great good without having to struggle against personal opposition.[74]

DuBourg was correct in concluding that his presence in New Orleans was once more a hindrance to peace and progress. Philip Borgna expressed the same conviction when he told Propaganda after DuBourg's departure:

In this city, this sewer of all vice and refuse of all that is worst on earth, the prejudice against him is so strong that in spite of all his sacrifices and all his exalted ability, he could not have effected any good here. The very name of DuBourg has an irritating sound in the ears of ...this new Babylon. You can not imagine all the abominations which fill the newspapers.[75]

When in December 1825 DuBourg perceived that the last thing he had hoped to accomplish for his successor, a seminary for the diocese of New Orleans, could not be achieved, he believed it was time to step down.

There has never been any question of DuBourg's zeal for souls nor of his devotion to the Church; there has never been any doubt that he spent his energies lavishly in serving his flock. Even his most extravagant projects and dreams were single-heartedly undertaken for the good of religion. It is only reasonable to suppose that in making the most important decision of his mature years he was impelled by the guiding principle of his life. His was not a desertion for the sake of self. Writing to Pietro Caprano, the Secretary of Propaganda, on March 10, 1826, he said, "Even though the bonds uniting me to this church are to be severed, yet I shall never cease to wish it well, and promote its increase by all

[74]SAP, DuBourg to Frayssinous, La Trappe near Laval [France], July 20, 1826.

[75]Kenneally, *Calendar,* I, 997, Borgna to Propaganda, New Orleans, October 17, 1826.

the means in my power."[76]

After his return to France he continued his care for Louisiana, sending men and money to Bishop Rosati and to the Jesuits, furnishing recruits for Portier in Alabama, welcoming Osage Indians to Montauban and securing aid for their return to Missouri, and in his last *mandement* — written for his installation as Archbishop of Besançon — he revealed his steadfast love for all those entrusted to his care, whether in the New World or the Old:

> O, Churches of *Louisiana* and *Montauban!* Dissolved is the holy alliance which in succession identified my existence with yours. But the ties of paternity will never by severed; it will always be true that I was your spouse and your children still mine. Always your welfare and theirs will be the object of my most ardent wishes, and for my heart a never-failing joy. Louisiana, Montauban — cherished names — I can not separate you in this effusion because you were never separated in my tenderness. In passing from one to the other I felt nothing changed in my first affections—only the sphere had been enlarged and I understood how a father can retrieve all the same intensity of love for the children of his later life as that he held for his first-born.[77]

Louis-Guillaume-Valentin DuBourg was only a few months away from death when he wrote those words. It requires a particular hardihood to doubt his sincerity. This essay holds that the welfare of his flocks was ever the object of his "most ardent desires," and that his return to France in 1826 should be seen in the light of that unquenchable flame.

[76] Anon., ed., "DuBourg's Correspondence," *SLCHR* 3 (1921), 207-12, here 211-12, nr. XLV for DuBourg to Peter Caprano, New Orleans, March 10, 1826.

[77] A complete text of this *mandement* is preserved in the Archives of the University of Notre Dame. The most extensive quotations from it appeared on October 19 in *L'Ami* 77 (1833), 545-49. It was read in the cathedral at the installation of DuBourg on October 10, 1833.

American Catholic Approaches to the Sacred Scripture

Gerald P. Fogarty, S.J.

Sacred Tradition and Sacred Scripture make up a single sacred deposit of the Word of God, which is entrusted to the Church. By adhering to it the entire holy people, united to its pastors, remains always faithful to the teaching of the apostles, to the brotherhood, to the breaking of the bread and the prayers.[1]

The Second Vatican Council's constitution on divine revelation, *Dei Verbum*, represented a victory for the progressives at the Council. The first draft of the schema had been entitled "on the Sources of Revelation" and reflected the conservative orientation of Cardinal Alfredo Ottaviani and the council's theological commission. It spoke of scripture and tradition as separate sources of revelation. From the American hierarchy, it evoked divergent responses reflecting different theological understandings of the question. Cardinal James McIntyre praised it for representing

[1] Austin Flannery, O.P., ed., *Vatican Council II: The Conciliar and Post Conciliar Documents* (Collegeville, Minn., 1975), 755.

91

the teaching of the Church. Cardinal Joseph Ritter and Cardinal Albert Meyer called for the schema's rejection.[2] Probably without realizing it, the American bishops at Vatican II were debating issues which bore striking similarities to the disputes at the end of the nineteenth and beginning of the twentieth centuries. In both periods, the conservatives displayed their total ignorance of an older American Catholic theological tradition, which was lost by the end of the last century.

The bishops of the nineteenth century envisioned a strong bond between scripture and tradition. As they noted in the Second Provincial Council in 1833: "We know not that it is the word of God, except by the testimony of that cloud of holy witnesses which the Saviour vouchsafed to establish as our guide through this desert over which we journey towards our permanent abode."[3] While not using the term "tradition," the bishops saw the need not only for testimony as to what was the word of God, but also for its proper interpretation. On this point, they reflected their own strong sense of episcopal collegiality. As they put it:

> Thus the recorded testimony of those ancient and venerable witnesses, who in every nation and every age, proclaimed in the name of the Catholic Church, and with its approbation, the interpretation of the Holy Bible, whether they were assembled in their councils or dispersed over the surface of the Christian world, is an harmonious collection of pure light, which sheds upon the inspired page the mild lustre which renders it pleasing to the eye, grateful to the understanding, and consoling to the heart.[4]

---

[2]Vincent A. Yzermans, *American Participation in the Second Vatican Council* (New York, 1967), 97-101.

[3]Hugh J. Nolan, ed., *Pastoral Letters of the American Hierarchy, 1792-1970* (Huntington, Ind., 1971), 51.

[4]*Ibid.*, 52.

The bishops, then, envisioned tradition as the process of preserving the truth of scripture rather than being a separate source of revelation.

The bishops' pastoral letter was probably written by Bishop John England of Charleston, but it reflected the theology of Bishop Francis Kenrick of Philadelphia. In treating scripture in his *Theologia Dogmatica,* Kenrick relied heavily on the Fathers of the Church and ignored the scholastics. In dealing with tradition, he referred his readers to Johann Adam Möhler's *Symbolik.* In Kenrick's exposition,

> We have demonstrated that the written word cannot be the basis for a perfect and unique rule of faith; for it needs both a witness and an interpreter. What then is that certain basis which Christ established, in order that men could attain revealed truths? It is, as we have proven, the harmonious preaching of the Apostolic ministry, public and solemn doctrine. Morever, since inspiration and revelation lay claim not to individuals, nor even to the gathering of the Pastors, but is only a type of assistance, by which they can once for all preserve the faith handed down to the saints, therefore the rule which they follow in the very act of teaching is *tradition,* that is the very doctrine of their predecessors, the very faith of the whole Church, derived all the way from the Apostolic age.[5]

Kenrick and his contemporary American bishops, then, considered tradition to be the process of preserving and interpreting scripture. The primary norm for the proper interpretation of scripture was the consensus of the Fathers.[6]

[5]Francis Patrick Kenrick, *Theologia Dogmatica,* 2nd ed. (Mechelen, 1858), I, 288.

[6]*Ibid.* 365-70.

Kenrick was widely regarded as the leading theologian among the American bishops. His theology, so strongly dependent on the Fathers, provided a basis for the strong sense of collegiality which he and his American confreres were then developing. In addition to his strictly theological work, he also undertook to bring out an American version of the Douay-Rheims-Challoner edition of the Bible. The work raised new questions for him. In 1843, he told his brother, Archbishop Peter R. Kenrick of St. Louis, that he was impressed with the theory of J. G. Eichhorn, who suggested that Moses had composed the Pentateuch from pre-existing sources.[7] When he published his version of the Pentateuch in 1860, however, he was more cautious. He acknowledged that the theories of the new "rationalistic school" could be reconciled with "the authority, or even the inspiration of the work," but adhered to the Jewish and early Christian testimony of the Mosaic authorship of the books. In his mind, "Eichhorn and others who regard it as a compilation, are forced to admit many things which it requires great ingenuity to reconcile with their theory."[8]

In dealing with the literal interpretation of the scripture, however, Kenrick acknowledged the difficulties presented by modern science. According to the chronology of Genesis, the world was created about 4000 years before Christ, but science, particularly geology, challenged that position. Kenrick had two observations to make about the problem. First, he said,

> We feel bound to respect the judgment of the learned, when they agree so decidedly in declaring the results of their investigations. Their discordance, however, in theory, and the conflict of their views, detract from the

[7] *The Kenrick-Frenaye Correspondence,* ed. F.E. Tourscher (Philadelphia, 1920), 174.

[8] Francis Patrick Kenrick, *The Pentateuch* (Baltimore, 1860), vii-viii.

weight which they might otherwise have, and our venera-
tion for the sacred text does not allow us hastily to
abandon its letter, or absolutely to embrace what does
not appear to harmonize with it.[9]

In short, Kenrick was opposed to jumping on the band
wagon of novelty or to adhering slavishly to the literal
interpretation of the scripture. Just as the consensus of the
Fathers was the norm for the interpretation of the scripture,
the norm for accepting science over the literal interpretation
was the consensus of learned men.

Kenrick's second observation more directly pertained to
the nature of tradition. Though the ancients had not known
the science of geology, he said, "the Mosaic narrative was
not understood by all the Fathers of the Church as implying
the creation of the universe in six days." Citing several
Fathers, he concluded,

> The diversity of views entertained in regard to the length
> of the days, which some held to be merely imaginary,
> whilst others understood them of indefinite spaces of
> time, shows that on this point the tradition of the Church
> was not absolute and dogmatical, so that if, with the
> progress of science, it become manifest, that a vast suc-
> cession of ages can alone account for the structure of the
> earth, and the phenomena discovered on its surface and
> in its depths, as far as they can fall under observation,
> such indefinite periods may be admitted, without depart-
> ing in any respect from the authoritative teaching of
> antiquity.[10]

By the standards of later nineteenth-century historical
criticism, Kenrick was conservative, but he did manifest a

[9]*Ibid.,* 17-18.
[10]*Ibid.,* 18.

theological mind open to new developments. He died in 1863 and his version of the Bible was virtually forgotten. At both the Second and Third Plenary Councils in 1866 and 1884 respectively, the bishops recommended its adoption, but Peter Kenrick, for unknown reasons, vehemently opposed it.[11] By then, the shape of the American hierarchy was beginning to change. After the First Vatican Council, the American tradition of collegiality gradually all but disappeared.[12] More importantly, the Thomistic revival introduced a theology different from that of Francis Kenrick — a theology which could not grapple with the issues raised by historical criticism of the scripture and related questions. As Gerald McCool has noted, the Thomism which was revived under Leo XIII was not so much a return to Thomas Aquinas himself as to the school of Cajetan, who emphasized the act of conceptualization rather than judgment.[13]

At the turn of the century, that form of Thomism led to the battle for the Bible in the American Church. It was essentially a conflict between a static, a-prioristic theology, reflecting a Church on the defensive against the forces of European liberalism, and a theology which was open to new developments and to the potentiality of human nature. In the United States, the controversy was between the Jesuits and the liberal party in the hierarchy — a party which not only espoused Americanism but was also open to new discoveries in scripture studies and science. The Jesuits' principal theological center was Woodstock College, founded in 1869 by Italian refugees from the *Risorgimento.* Its first dean, Camillo Mazzella, had been a leader in the Thomistic

[11]*Acta et Decreta Sacrorum Conciliorum Recentiorum: Collectio Lacensis* (Freiburg im Br., 1875), III, 357; *Acta et Decreta Concilii Plenarii Baltimorensis Tertii* (Baltimore, 1884), lxvi-lxvii.

[12]See my *Vatican and the American Hierarchy from 1870 to 1965* (Stuttgart, 1982), 1-26.

[13]Gerald A. McCool, *Catholic Theology in the Nineteenth Century* (New York, 1977), 13, 234.

revival and was summoned back to Rome to implement Thomism in the Gregorian University in 1879. In 1886, Leo XIII named him a cardinal and he subsequently became prefect of the Congregation of the Index.[14] In 1893, he drafted at least part of Leo's encyclical on the biblical question, *Providentissimus Deus,* and incorporated into it the theory of inspiration developed by Cardinal Johann Franzelin, S.J.[15] Simply put, Franzelin started with the principle that God is the author of scripture and from this he derived his theory of "content inspiration." Inspiration was the charism which enlightened and stimulated the mind of the human author to write down only those truths which God wished to communicate to the Church. This constituted the "formal word" or element of the scripture. Inspiration was distinguished from "assistance" which extended to the "material words," by which the human instrument conveyed the inspired truths.[16] In the hands of lesser theologians, Franzelin's theory minimized the role of the human author and ran into conflict with historical criticism.

Much of Mazzella's and other Jesuits' theological orientation was shaped by their own political experience of having been expelled from their own countries and of seeing papal temporal power wrested away by the liberal Kingdom of Italy. Even without Mazzella and the original Italian founders, Woodstock remained a bastion of reaction. Anthony J. Maas, S.J., Westphalia-born professor of scripture, was a prime example. In 1893, he published the first of a two-volume study, *Christ in Type and Prophecy.* His approach to the topic came through clearly in an article the

[14]Anon., "Two of Woodstock's Founders," *Woodstock Letters* 29 (1900), 296-308.

[15]Francesco Turvasi, *Giovanni Genocchi e la Controversia Modernista* (Rome, 1974), 93.

[16]James Tunstead Burtchaell, C.S.C., *Catholic Theories of Biblical Inspiration since 1810: A Review and Critique* (Cambridge, 1969), 98-99.

same year, "Adam's Rib — Allegory or History." For him, the story of the origin of man and woman in Plato's *Symposium* represented "the distorted record of a tradition," which Genesis narrated with the "sober earnestness of the inspired writer."[17] Though commentators such as Origen and Cajetan had considered the story an allegory, he believed it essential to take it as historical or else the relationship between type and anti-type would be jeopardized. Paul, Augustine, Jerome, Bernard, and Thomas had all agreed in seeing that Eve being fashioned from the rib of Adam was the type of the Church being fashioned from the side of Christ.[18]

As if Maas' treatment of the Old Testament were not bad enough, he had also published in 1891 the first edition of *The Life of Jesus Christ According to the Gospel History*. With no attempt to recognize the particular theological nuances of each of the evangelists, he wove together one continuous narrative from the various accounts. He illustrated the theological premise of his work in his treatment of the synoptic problem in *The American Ecclesiastical Review* in 1895. From the patristic testimony, he believed it obvious that the synoptic gospels were "the records of the catechetical instructions of the Apostles." These instructions, in turn, "were based on that of St. Peter, but were developed according to the needs of the catechumens." He reached his conclusion from "the two facts of St. Peter's residence in the three principal primitive churches in Jerusalem, Antioch, and Rome, and of St. Peter's primacy in the apostolic college." Even Paul showed his dependence on Peter, if one compared "his discourses in Pisidia, at Athens,

[17]Anthony J. Maas, S.J., "Adam's Rib — Allegory or History,"*The American Ecclesiastical Review* 9 (Aug., 1893), 88-102, here at 88; for an excellent survey of the treatment of scripture in American periodicals, see Bernard Noone, F.S.C., "American Catholic Periodicals and the Biblical Question, 1893-1908," *Records of the American Catholic Historical Society of Philadelphia* 89 (1978), 85-108.

[18]*Ibid.*, 91-93.

and before Festus and Agrippa, with those of St. Peter before Jewish audiences and the Gentile Cornelius."[19] It is difficult to determine whether Maas was seriously trying to understand the scripture or whether he was intent on defending Petrine primacy as a bulwark of papal primacy. The Roman question — the status of the pope within the Eternal City — and the *Kulturkampf* — Bismarck's attempt to subjugate the Church to the Prussian State — seem to have influenced his approach to scripture more than knowledge of the historical method then being brought to bear on the synoptic problem.

Maas would ultimately dominate *The American Ecclesiastical Review's* reports on biblical scholarship, but only after 1900 when the editor, Hermann Heuser, assigned him a regular column. In the 1890s, the journal was more open to developing trends in biblical studies. Alfred Loisy, former professor at the Institut catholique in Paris and the very symbol of Modernism, contributed three articles between 1896 and 1898: "The Scriptural Account of the Disciples of Emmaus,"[20] "The Transfiguration of Our Lord,"[21] and "Gethesmane."[22] Closer to home, the French-born Joseph Bruneau, S.S., professor of scripture at St. Joseph's Seminary, Dunwoodie, New York, introduced the *Review's* readers to the theory of "verbal inspiration" then being proposed by the progressive European scholars.

In an article in 1896, Bruneau noted that Maas had considered "verbal inspiration" an "abandoned theory," but he went on to analyze the work of various scholars who developed a new form of the theory as a means of making the human writer a true author and of avoiding any sugges-

[19]Anthony J. Maas, S.J., "The Synoptic Problem," *The American Ecclesiastical Review* 13 (1895), 171-81, here 171-73.

[20]*Ibid.*, 14 (1896), 446-57.

[21]*Ibid.* 17 (1898), 169-78.

[22]*Ibid.* 18 (1898), 225-33.

tion of divine dictation. Some of Bruneau's favorite authors would not win him friends in Rome. He noted that Giovanni Semeria, an Italian Barnabite, approached the subject in terms of saying that "God, the primary author of Scripture, *allowed* the writer to choose the words; but He *did not make him choose them;* otherwise we would find no imperfection at all."[23]

Even more to Bruneau's liking was Hermann Schell's approach to inspiration in his *Dogmatik*, where he said that inspiration "materially ... extends as far as the human authorship, including the *will,* the plan of *thought,* and the execution or *words*; for these three activities are not only synchronous, but conditional, and influence each other mutually, so that no one or no two of them would suffice as the sole vehicle of Inspiration."[24] The Sulpician was still more sympathetic with "the prominent biblical scholar Alfred Loisy," who had attempted to answer Semeria "in his unfortunately discontinued magazine *L'Enseignement biblique*." As Bruneau quoted Loisy, "both God and man have (but in a widely different manner) a right to be called authors of the Bible in its entirety — of its ideas and words — substance and form, religious truths and historical or cosmological data. Neither ancient tradition, properly interpreted, nor reason sanction the divisions which modern writers under the influence of polemical bias have tried to effect in the Bible."[25] Bruneau was treading on dangerous ground, for Loisy had been criticizing Franzelin's theory of inspiration.

Bruneau cited other lesser authors in his analysis of the problem, but he was concerned with explaining to his readers that, if inspiration was essentially the communication of

[23] Joseph Bruneau, "A Page of Contemporary History," *ibid.,* 14 (1896), 240-54, here 244-45.

[24] *Ibid.,* 245.

[25] *Ibid.,* 247-48.

revelation, then the words were an essential part of inspiration. To illustrate his point, he introduced his readers to the brilliant Dominican exegete, M.-J. Lagrange, founder of the École biblique in Jerusalem. Writing in the *Revue biblique* in 1895, Lagrange had challenged the theories of non-verbal inspiration as "an administrative compromise ...created by men who, wrongly imagining inspiration to be a mechanical pressure, attempted to resolve some difficulties in referring to the writer *at least* the choice of words." For Lagrange, this would "deny the inspiration of thoughts, when not necessarily revealed" and did not conform with the exegetical method of the Fathers. Bruneau favorably quoted Lagrange's conclusion that the new historical method would re-establish "some ancient systems on a more scientific basis" and that "apologetics would not suffer, but will feel more comfortable in the large edifices of traditional theology, than in the modern halls, hastily built up, as a provisional refuge by Cardinal Franzelin."[26]

In thus translating for his American audience Lagrange's criticism of Franzelin, Bruneau may have contributed to the Jesuit opposition to the progressives. He was not himself an original scholar, but he symbolized the Sulpicians' sympathy for the new criticism and for Lagrange, who had spent a year at their seminary at Issy before entering the Dominicans. Bruneau's most original contribution to the field was his *Harmony of the Gospels,* published in 1898. He arranged the synoptics in parallel columns and amply sprinkled his notes with quotations from Richard Simon, Lagrange, and Loisy. As he stated in his preface, he did not intend to settle the synoptic problem, but to let students know how the problem has arisen. "All that may be good in this little publication," he said, was due "to the lessons and

[26]*Ibid.,* 252.

works of my former professors: MM. Fillion, Vigouroux, Martin, Loisy."[27]

Maas and Bruneau, both seminary professors, represented two opposing views of the biblical question in the American Church. But their differences reflected the division within the Church on other issues. The Sulpicians supported the liberal bishops, led by John Ireland, Archbishop of St. Paul, Cardinal James Gibbons, Archbishop of Baltimore, Bishop John J. Keane, rector of the Catholic University of America, and Monsignor Denis J. O'Connell, rector of the American College in Rome. As early as 1890, O'Connell, who maintained a correspondence with Loisy, recommended him for Ireland's new seminary as "the leading Biblical scholar in the church."[28] Opposed to the American liberals were Archbishop Michael A. Corrigan of New York, Bishop Bernard McQuaid of Rochester, and the German-American clergy. The conservatives had the complete support of the Jesuits. Though the historiography of the liberal-conservative dispute is extensive, the relationship with the biblical question is seldom pointed out. Both the liberals and the exegetes would run afoul of the same conservative theologians.

As the biblical question unfolded, the reports of Bruneau and the writings of other Sulpicians were not the only examples of the relationship of the liberal party to the new criticism. The Catholic University of America, opened in 1889, was intended to be the expression of the American bishops' commitment to the intellectual life; it rapidly became the intellectual center for the liberals. *The Catholic University Bulletin,* founded in 1895, became a vehicle for presenting the new ideas on scripture scholarship. In 1895, Charles Grannan, graduate of the Urban College of Propa-

---

[27]Joseph Bruneau, *Harmony of the Gospels* (New York, 1898).

[28]O'Connell to Ireland, Rome, Sept. 21, 1890, Archives of the Archdiocese of St. Paul.

ganda and professor of dogma at the university, openly espoused "the critical history of the origin of the sacred books."[29] He also took his sympathies into the classroom.

Archbishop Francesco Satolli, the first apostolic delegate to the United States, who had begun his tenure as a friend of the liberals, had shifted to the conservatives. He expressed his concern about the university's approach to scripture studies to Monsignor Joseph Schroeder, a conservative member of the university faculty. Schroeder reported his findings to Satolli on June 18, 1895. He was concerned about a thesis chosen for defense by Father William Russell of Baltimore, later the Bishop of Charleston. The thesis read: "While the Council of Trent does not admit any difference in point of canonicity, it does not expressly condemn the opinion held by Jerome and the Greek fathers that there is a distinction of authority between the Protocanonical and the Deuterocanonical books of the Old Testament." Schroeder remonstrated with Russell that the thesis was taken from a work of Loisy. He then protested to the faculty, but found his only ally to be Joseph Pohle, professor of Thomistic philosophy and a fellow conservative.[30] Schroeder's letter to Satolli was one of several documents which occasioned the forced resignation of Keane as rector in the fall of 1896.[31]

Keane's resignation, however, did not change the university's attitude on the biblical question. In 1897, Grannan published his further reflections on inspiration in the *Bulletin*. More courageously than before, he embraced higher criticism. Though God could have written the Bible Him-

[29]Charles A. Grannan, "A Program of Scripture Studies,"*Catholic University Bulletin* 1 (1895), 35-52, here 39.

[30]Schroeder to Satolli, Washington, June 18, 1895, Archivio Segreto Vaticano, Rub. 43 (1903), fasc. 2, 78-80.

[31]Patrick H. Ahern, *The Life of John J. Keane, Educator and Archbishop, 1839-1918* (Milwaukee, 1955), 178-79.

self, he said, "he preferred to write it with the cooperation of a human intellect, and with the consent of a human will, and with the resources of a human memory."[32] To illustrate his point, he drew the "analogy between the divine and human in the Bible and the divine and human in Jesus Christ." He pointed out, however, that the union of the two natures in Christ was "hypostatical or personal," while the union of the two elements in the Bible was "merely verbal."[33]

In a subsequent article, Grannan acknowledged that the sacred writers used existing secular works which they "copied out into Scripture under the influence of Inspiration."[34] "Historical criticism," he wrote, "has placed the books of the Bible on a level with the most reliable human documents."[35] Grannan, nevertheless, made no effort to explain what he meant by inspiration nor to grapple with the problem of its compatibility with error. His knowledge of exegesis remained primarily second-hand.

As a biblical theologian, Grannan would have been unimportant, had he not been one of several links between biblical criticism and the liberal movement, which had then emerged as Americanism. In August, 1897, he and Edward A. Pace, a confrere at the university, attended the Fourth International Catholic Scientific Congress held at Fribourg, Switzerland. The congress gathered together virtually everyone with progressive ideas in the Church. Denis O'Connell, who had been dismissed as rector of the American College, read a paper entitled "A New Idea in the Life of Father Hecker." It argued for the value to the Church of the American separation of Church and State, which flowed

---

[32]Charles A. Grannan, "The Two-fold Authorship of Scripture," *Catholic University Bulletin* 3 (1897), 131-60, here 138-39.

[33]*Ibid.*, 154.

[34]Charles A. Grannan, "The Human Element in Scripture," *ibid.*, 4 (1898), 167-82, here 174.

[35]*Ibid.*, 181.

from the Common Law. John A. Zahm, C.S.C., American procurator in Rome for the Holy Cross Fathers, spoke on evolution and dogma. Maurice Blondel discussed subjectivity in philosophy. On biblical studies, Lagrange delivered a discourse on historical criticism of the Pentateuch and Baron Friedrich von Hügel sent a paper, read for him by Semeria, on the sources of the Hexateuch.[36] Grannan arranged for the *University Bulletin* to publish excerpts of Lagrange's paper and the full text of von Hügel's.[37]

At first glance, the ideas presented at the Fribourg congress seem disparate; yet there was an interlocking consistency — at least in the minds of the conservatives. To speak, as O'Connell had, of the separation of Church and State and religious liberty seemed to surrender the very rights the Church in Europe was seeking to defend from the usurpations of the European liberal State; it appeared to be an American form of the rationalism which the European Church was trying to combat. To show the compatibility of evolution with the Church's doctrine, as Zahm had asserted, seemed to endanger the notion of God as creator. Von Hügel and Lagrange's acknowledgment that the Old Testament, as it exists, was the product of several sources raised the question of who was the inspired author. Blondel's notion of philosophical subjectivity appeared nothing more than subjectivism and individualism. For the Fribourg progressives, the heart of the issue was the potentiality of human reason under grace or inspiration. For their opponents, the emphasis on human reason was the very basis of all the problems the European Church confronted.

[36]Lawrence F. Barmann, *Baron Friedrich von Hügel and the Modernist Crisis in England* (Cambridge, 1972), 68-69; Fogarty, *Vatican and American Hierarchy*, 153-56.

[37]Friedrich von Hügel, "The Historical Method and the Documents of the Hexateuch," *Catholic Univeristy Bulletin* 4 (1898), 198-226. The summary of Lagrange's paper appeared in "Miscellaneous: On the Pentateuch," *ibid.*, 115-22.

The first of the new ideas emanating from Fribourg to be condemned was Americanism. The European critics of the movement included the Jesuits, led by Cardinal Mazzella, and a variety of other opponents. Charles Maignen wrote *Père Hecker: est-il un saint?* to challenge the spirituality of the Paulists and to condemn the American notions of religious liberty.[38] A.-J. Delattre, S.J., professor of Hebrew at the Jesuit scholasticate at Louvain, contributed his *Catholicisme américain* accusing the Americanists of individualism.[39] Both would also write against the biblical critics.

For the time being, none of the progressives sensed the relationship in the minds of conservative theologians between Americanism and the biblical question. In the United States, John B. Hogan, S.S., former professor at Issy and then rector of St. John's Seminary in Brighton, Massachusetts, published in book-form a series of articles originally written for *The American Ecclesiastical Review* on "Clerical Studies." His proposals for seminary education were decidedly historical and he lamented that since the Middle Ages the Bible had "ceased to be at the centre of clerical studies, and this was the direct result of the new movement which gave birth to scholastic theology."[40] He traced the development of biblical scholarship from the Renaissance, through the discoveries of archeology, to the application of the historical method to the sacred books themselves. "The devout reader of the Bible," he wrote, would find no difficulties with the new criticism, because, for such a reader, "the human element of the Scriptures vanishes, as it were, laying bare the divine, and setting the reader, like Moses on the mountain, in the dread presence of

[38]Thomas T. McAvoy, *The Great Crisis in American Catholic History: 1895-1900* (Chicago, 1957), 189-99, 211-17.

[39]Alphonse J. Delattre, S.J., *Un Catholicisme américain* (Namur, 1898); see McAvoy, *Great Crisis*, 224-26.

[40]John B. Hogan, *Clerical Studies* (Boston, 1898), 427-28.

God himself."[41] Scientific study of the scripture was essential, he continued, for "edification must ultimately rest on truth."[42]

In Hogan's mind, those who found a threat to the faith in the findings of astronomy and geology and in the theories of evolution had forgotten "that God in the Bible accommodates Himself to the minds of men, and follows the laws of their language; that other meanings besides the literal had, at all times, been admitted in certain cases."[43] The whole contemporary debate over inspiration, he believed, resulted from two different methodologies, that of the theologians and that of the biblical scholars. He admitted that either side could go to extremes, but he thought the controversy had arisen from the fact that, while inspiration was "an article of faith,... what is implied thereby has never been defined, nor, perhaps, can it be defined, except by approximation." His sympathies clearly lay with the biblical scholars, for, "because of all the work that has been done on the Bible in recent times, with results which are no longer seriously questioned, theologians have to acknowledge, however reluctantly, that henceforth much less can be built on the Bible than has been done in the past." For Protestants, this might cause "dismay," he concluded, but Catholics could "contemplate it with perfect equanimity. Their faith is based, not on the Bible, but on the Church."[44]

Hogan may have intentionally skirted the issues raised by the debate over inspiration by emphasizing the role of the Church. Early in 1900, however, he received word that he might be under investigation. As he wrote Denis O'Connell,

[41]*Ibid.*, 457.
[42]*Ibid.*, 458-59.
[43]*Ibid.*, 471-72.
[44]*Ibid.*, 480-81.

Somebody in Rome — your successor [William H. O'Connell, then rector of the American College] I believe — has sent word here that people connected with the Index are looking after my "Clerical Studies" — in connection with poor Mivart's quotation from them. In one sense I should be very glad that some of these people would read the book — if they know English enough to do so — it would perhaps broaden them a bit.[45]

Nothing more was heard of any investigation and Hogan died the following year. But a French translation of his book, with certain important omissions, won a favorable review from Loisy, who later remarked, Rome "condemns in me what it approves in M. Hogan."[46]

Hogan's American confrere, Francis E. Gigot, S.S., was more venturesome still on the biblical question. Professor of scripture at Dunwoodie, he published his *General Introduction to the Study of the Holy Scriptures* in 1900. It had the *imprimatur* of Corrigan and the *nihil obstat* of Hogan. Like Hogan, he emphasized that Catholics had less to fear from modern criticism than Protestants, for "Catholics built their faith primarily on the teaching of a living Church, whereas Protestants rest their whole belief on the written word of God."[47]

Gigot was impressed with the more modern theories of men like Cardinal John Henry Newman, Canon Salvatore di Bartolo, whose book, *I Criteri Teologici,* had been placed on the Index, and Maurice d'Hulst, rector of the Institut catholique in Paris. All had held some form of

---

[45] Hogan to O'Connell, Brighton, April 29, 1900, Archives of the Diocese of Richmond. On Mivart, see John D. Root, "The Final Apostasy of St. George Jackson Mivart," *Catholic Historical Review* 71 (1985), 1-25.

[46] Alfred Loisy, *Mémoires pour servir à l'histoire religieuse de notre temps,* 3 vols. (Paris, 1931), II, 73.

[47] Francis E. Gigot, S.S., *General Introduction to the Study of the Holy Scriptures* (New York, 1900), 517.

inspiration limited to faith and morals, but not applicable to science or history. Opposed to this view were Franzelin, Mazzella, and others, who treated the question "from the safe harbor of dogmatic theology," as the Tübingen theologian, Peter Dausch, had noted. It was because of such disagreement over inspiration, said Gigot, that Leo XIII had issued *Providentissimus Deus,* which effectively supported the conservative views. The papal pronouncement had made Catholic scholars more cautious, he said, but there was still no unanimity about precisely what inspiration meant.[48]

Gigot's *General Introduction* was a relatively safe work, in which he took no definitive position on the question of inspiration. But he intended the book as the first in a three-volume study of Scripture. In 1901, he published his *Special Introduction to the Study of the Old Testament: Part I. The Historical Books.* Here he made it obvious that his sympathies lay with those scholars who held that the Pentateuch was not written directly by Moses, but was a compilation from at least four sources.[49]

Gigot's work was widely used in Sulpician and other diocesan seminaries and was indicative of the openness of the American Church at the time toward the new scholarship. This openness could be further seen in the reaction of *The American Ecclesiastical Review* toward the condemnation of five of Alfred Loisy's books by the Congregation of the Index in 1903. The author of the comments, probably Hermann Heuser, the editor, praised Loisy as an apologist, for "to oppose mere tradition against scientific investigation is like combatting a man who confronts you with a pistol by means of a stout stick." The author feared that, because Cardinal Andreas Steinhuber, S.J., was prefect of the

---

[48]*Ibid.,* 511-14.

[49]Francis E. Gigot, S.S., *Special Introduction to the Study of the Old Testament: Part I. The Historical Books* (New York, 1901), 85-141.

Index, those unsympathetic with the Church would say, "Rome has allowed itself once more to come under the spell of the Jesuits as in so many other cases." He wished to avoid the extremes of both those who decried any use of criticism and those who challenged the validity of the Church's actions. In his mind, the Church condemned Loisy, "because his statements not only lack sufficiently convincing proofs, though he himself may have an instinctive certainty regarding them, but because they are an injury to the children of her household."[50]

While Heuser may have appeared relatively open to the critical method, he directly contributed to the shift in the American Catholic theological mentality. In 1900 he asked Anthony Maas to be the exclusive writer for the *Review*'s "Recent Bible Study" column and suggested, as he later recalled, that Maas write anonymously, because "otherwise there was likelihood that controversies would be stirred up, owing to differences of opinion regarding the extent of Biblical inspiration and kindred topics of Exegesis, among representatives of scholastic groups who claimed for them superior merit of patristic tradition."[51] Maas' bias against historical criticism, however, was well known, for he had already written against it in the *Messenger of the Sacred Heart*. [52] Maas and several Jesuit successors at Woodstock would assure that the clergy of the United States were ignorant of the contemporary issues in biblical criticism.

Maas' conservative reports on biblical scholarship reflected the Roman build-up against exegetes, the initial

---

[50][H.J. Heuser?] "The Books of the Abbé Loisy on the Index," *The American Ecclesiastical Review* 30 (Feb., 1904), 174-76.

[51]H.J. Heuser, "Father A.J. Maas, S.J. — An Appreciation," *Woodstock Letters* 58 (1929), 417-23, here 417.

[52]See for example, Anthony J. Maas, S.J., "Recent Phases in Bible Study," *American Catholic Quarterly Review* 22 (1897), 832-50; "Higher Biblical Criticism," *Messenger of the Sacred Heart* 33 (1900), 51-59; "Divisive Criticism," *ibid.*, 116-26; "Biblical Criticism," *ibid,* 239-46, 512-22, 627-33.

phase of which was the condemnation of Loisy. In 1904, Alphonse J. Delattre, S.J., one of the first to enter the lists against Americanism, published his *Autour de la question biblique*. His primary target was Lagrange's *Méthode historique*. But the secondary object of his sally was a man of greater significance to the American Church, the young Dutch scholar, Henry Poels, who had published a brochure entitled *Critiek en Traditie, of de Bijbel voor de Roomschen*. He took Poels to task for arguing that, while there could be material errors in the Scriptures, they were not formal ones as long as the sacred writer incorporated them "without making them the object of critical judgments."[53] Where Poels argued from Jerome's recognition that there were "insoluble difficulties" in Scripture and even contradictions, Delattre countered that this would make of the scriptural writer a true author and not a copyist. For Poels, "the defenders of so-called tradition" ran counter to Jerome's "great freedom" in speaking of "the history contained in the biblical books." For Delattre, "the real defenders of tradition" had Jerome as their "most glorious ancestor," who had set forth as a creed that the Scripture was to be interpreted literally.[54] Lagrange subsequently answered Delattre, who, in the meantime, was appointed to the Gregorian University in Rome.

Back in the United States, Maas enthusiastically reviewed Delattre's book and took the opportunity to warn his readers against Lagrange and the "new exegesis." The school, he admitted, had a strong defender in Eudoxe-Irénée Mignot, Archbishop of Albi, but he commended the answer given Mignot by Charles Maignen — a name familiar to Americans as the author of *Père Hecker: est'il un saint?*[55] Maas

---

[53] A.-J. Delattre, S.J., *Autour de la question biblique* (Liège, 1904), 176.

[54] *Ibid.*, 176-82. See also below note 55.

[55] Anthony J. Maas, S.J., "Ecclesiastical Library Table: Recent Bible Study," *The American Ecclesiastical Review* 31 (1904), 395-402, here 395-97.

would continue to reflect the attacks of his European confrere. At this point, however, he focused almost exclusively on Lagrange. He soon had a target closer to home.

In 1904, the Catholic University appointed Henry Poels professor of Old Testament. In *The Catholic University Bulletin* for January, 1905, he wrote the first of three articles on "History and Inspiration." Just as the Church faced Hellenistic philosophy at the beginning of the third century, Poels wrote, it confronted literary and historical criticism at the beginning of the twentieth. He praised the work of the Fathers and acknowledged that "the wall built by the giants of the Middle Ages, will weather the storms of time . . ., but they did not and could not make a bridge between Christianity and modern science."[56] The theological crisis of his day, Poels felt, was due to the study of history "according to new and truly scientific methods." Though, indeed, the "enemies of Christianity" may well have acclaimed the new methods, "truly scientific criticism *can be nothing else* than an apology for truth; and every apology for truth is, of course, an apology for Christianity itself."[57]

Poels' treatment of inspiration reflected his affinity with Lagrange. "The whole Bible is inspired, in all its parts, in all its sentences, and even in its *obiter dicta,"* he wrote, but biblical statements "must needs be true only in that sense in which God and the inspired author wished it to be understood. Error existed only where there was "a *judgment* or affirmation." It was the role of the critic to determine the sense affirmed by the author.[58] It was on this point that Poels set himself at odds with his theological opponents. To determine the true sense "intended and expressed by the sacred writer," it was "not sufficient. . . merely to examine

[56]Henry Poels, "History and Inspiration," *The Catholic University Bulletin* 11 (Jan., 1905), 19-67, here 22.

[57]*Ibid.,* 22-23.

[58]*Ibid.,* 27.

the words and grammatical construction of single sentences. We must also consider the *context;* not only the immediate context, but at the same time — what theologians frequently seem to forget — the more *remote* context, that is to say, *the literary character* of the whole book."⁵⁹

Poels drew the distinction between the "author" and "the man...as he is the representative of his generation." As an example outside the biblical field, he chose St. Thomas Aquinas who reflected the common opinion of his age in citing the works of Dionysius as though they were written by a contemporary of Christ's. Thomas also accepted the scientific opinions of his age and relied on the Vulgate, which "all scholars agree...is not a correct rendering of the original text."⁶⁰ Poels then applied to the Bible the distinction between "author" and the "man" as representative of his age. He stated that he had derived this distinction from Jerome. Where the Scripture called St. Joseph "the *father* of Christ and the Virgin Mary the *wife* of St. Joseph," Jerome had commented that, aside from Joseph, Mary, and Elizabeth and perhaps a few others, "*all considered Jesus to be the Son of Joseph. And so far was this the case that even the Evangelists, expressing the opinion of the people, which is the true law of history...,* called him the father of the Saviour...."⁶¹ On the basis of Jerome's "law of history," Poels concluded that "we do not see any reason, why we should admit that generally they [the inspired authors] knew more than their contemporaries about profane things, which God did not reveal to them."⁶²

Poels went on to develop his position in his subsequent article on "The Fathers of the Church." Like Hogan, Bruneau, and Grannan, he argued that Christ "did not found

⁵⁹*Ibid.*, 28.
⁶⁰*Ibid.*, 33-40.
⁶¹*Ibid.*, 50-51.
⁶²*Ibid.*, 56.

His Church upon dead writings but upon living teaching, the transmission of which was entrusted to "official teachers."[63] While revelation had been entrusted only to the authors of Scripture, it was clear that there had been "an *'evolution'* of Christian doctrine" from the first to the twentieth century. Here, too, Poels foresaw conflict with theologians. While there could be no valid evolution or development of doctrine which was not "a branch of the tree of Christ. . ., for the theologians, who study the principles, branch and bud are one; while historians compare the tree in its maturity to the mere sapling."[64] The development of doctrine was another sticking point with the type of theology which Poels and his contemporaries were confronting.

Just as he distinguished between the author of Scripture and the man of his age, Poels now drew the distinction between the Fathers as "witnesses of the Church" and "as scholars of their day."[65] Inasmuch as the Fathers sought to acquire "knowledge of the biblical teaching on 'faith and morals'," they were "scientific," but they had no knowledge of the twentieth-century science of literary and historical studies. Instead, they simply accepted the views of history common in their age.[66] When confronted with difficulties about a particular passage of Scripture, they therefore resorted to a spiritual interpretation. This approach led a certain "class of 'prudent' Catholics" in Poels' own age to adhere to the historical character of every passage of Scripture. "If there should be a clash between true historical science and a theological school," he said, "the responsibility for the dishonor and for the far-reaching consequences of such a condition of affairs, would fall upon this theologi-

---

[63]Henry Poels, "History and Inspiration. II. The Fathers of the Church," *The Catholic University Bulletin* 11 (Apr., 1905), 152-94, here 153.

[64]*Ibid.*, 156-58.

[65]*Ibid.*, 161.

[66]*Ibid.*, 165-67.

cal school."[67] He was worried that this type of theology made Catholic students in universities incapable of reconciling their faith with the findings of the natural sciences and history. "Catholic scholars," he asserted, "ought to be more 'prudent' than, in our opinion, Father Delattre was in writing his *Autour de la question biblique.*"[68] Poels was simply trying to defend the validity of the new historical method and to explain that it was not against the Church's tradition of the living word of God, but he had drawn to himself the antagonism of conservative Jesuits.

In the June issue of *The American Ecclesiastical Review,* Maas took the offensive against both Lagrange and Poels. Unfortunately, the Jesuit archival sources are no longer extant, but it is highly probable that Maas was in correspondence with Delattre or other Jesuits in Europe. Maas subjected Lagrange to the very type of syllogistic logic which the French Dominican said could not be applied to the study of the Scriptures. He first took Lagrange's statement: "God teaches whatever is taught in the Bible, but he does not teach anything more than what is taught by the sacred writer, and the latter teaches only what he intends to teach." Maas challenged the use of the term "teach" and Lagrange's statement that everything in the Bible was inspired but not everything was revealed. In Maas' mind, Lagrange's method could not determine when God was teaching and could not solve the historical and scientific problems.[69] The Jesuit argued that there was no justification in claiming

> that the writer did not intend to say what is actually said
> in the passage, and this merely in order to get rid of
> extrinsic difficulties. Recent apologists appear to sin in

[67]*Ibid.,* 173.

[68]*Ibid.,* 175.

[69]Anthony J. Maas, "Ecclesiastical Library Table: Recent Bible Study," *The American Ecclesiastical Review* 32 (June, 1905), 647-49.

this respect when they solve scientific and historical difficulties by maintaining that God did not intend to teach
science or history in the scriptures, or that the sacred
writers did not intend to write science or history in the
modern critical acceptance of the word.[70]

Maas had presented virtually a caricature of the way in
which theologians regarded history. The question of historical appearances and "implicit citations," he said, had been
definitively settled by the decision of the Biblical Commission in February, 1905. The decision required that his fellow
Jesuit, Franz von Hummelauer, abandon his liberal tendencies, he noted, but he saved his real invective for "the poison
that certain readers might gather out of Dr. H.A. Poels' two
articles." Though Poels might not agree with the commission's decision, Maas patronizingly concluded: "if Dr. Poels
does not quarrel with the Biblical Commission, we will not
quarrel with him."[71] For the next year, Maas carried on a
long and tedious debate with Thomas a Kempis Reilly,
O.P., an American then studying at the École biblique in
Jerusalem, who attempted to show how Maas misinter-
preted and mistranslated Lagrange. The exchange was a
prime example of the inability of the prevailing theological
school, represented by Maas, to hear what the historical
critics were saying.[72]

In the meantime, on June 27, 1906, the Biblical Commission issued its decree stating that Moses was substantially
the author of the Pentateuch.[73] This seemed to sound the
death knell for the new critics. Sometime either that year or
early the next, Lagrange expressed his concern to Father

[70]*Ibid.,* 650.

[71]*Ibid.,* 654.

[72]See Thomas à K. Reilly, O.P., "What Father Lagrange Says and Thinks," *The American Ecclesiastical Review* 33 (Oct., 1905), 422-30.

[73]DS 3394-3397.

Henry Hyvernat, a former classmate at Issy and then professor of Semitic languages at the Catholic University of America. The problem, Lagrange believed, was that Rome was so fearful that the development of dogma meant its alteration that it believed "the remedy to the situation is the bloc of Fr. Delattre." He urged Hyvernat, if he had any "zeal for the good of the Church," that he make it known that the "bloc" stood for little and that far from extinguishing any "conflagration," it was actually setting "part of the fire. The question here is to sustain the entire dogmatic structure with little freedom in the criticism of history." Lagrange was worried that "we who wish to work for the good are counterbalanced by the imprimaturs of those who do not care for it."[74]

Lagrange was not alone in his assessment of the influence of Delattre. Baron Friedrich von Hügel in England linked the Jesuit with the biblical commission's decision on the Mosaic authorship of the Pentateuch. Writing to his friend Charles Augustus Briggs of Union Theological Seminary in New York, he said he had been informed

> that this decision and the appointment at the Roman Gregorian University of that thoroughly reactionary and obscurantist Père Méchineau, S.J. in succession to that already, one would have thought, sufficiently Philistine Père Delattre, S.J. who was given that Professorship of Scripture held by that fine, candid, critically competent scholar, Padre Enrico Gismondi, S.J. (whom I have the honour to call my friend) are intended as attempts to impose this kind of toothless blind apologetic upon us as *scholarly* and by the authority of *scholars*."[75]

[74]Lagrange to Hyvernat, Roybon, August 16 [1906 or 1907], Archives of the Catholic University of America.

[75]Von Hügel to Briggs, Hindhead, Surrey, August 28, 1906, Briggs Papers, Union Theological Seminary, New York.

Von Hügel also suggested that he and Briggs collaborate on a critique of the commission's decision. This took the form of an exchange of open letters between himself and Briggs in September, 1906, and was published as *The Papal Commission and the Pentateuch.*[76]

Maas had already accused Briggs of denying inspiration in 1891; now he ignored von Hügel altogether and concentrated his attacks only on Briggs.[77] The following year, an anonymous reviewer in *The Catholic University Bulletin,* usually friendly to the new exegetes, took issue with both Briggs and von Hügel. The Baron, said the review, "takes for granted" that, if "the so-called historical method" were "applied to the Pentateuch," it "will surely disprove its Mosaic origin."[78] The Catholic University was clearly beginning to go through a new reactionary phase in regard to the biblical question. In this, it mirrored the reaction of the American Church to Modernism.

The university had drawn Roman attention to its approach to biblical studies through the writings of Poels. In 1907 Delattre published *Le Critérium à l'usage de la mouvelle exégèse biblique.* It was a response to Lagrange's answer to his earlier *Autour de la question biblique,* but he reserved some of his venom for Poels, whose reproach for "lack of prudence" he found "very gratifying," coming as it did from a scholar who denied that the scripture writers and the classical historians, like Thucydides and Herodotus, were writing true history.[79] Poels had thus drawn the attention of conservative theologians not only in the United

[76]The Rev. Charles A. Briggs and Baron Friedrich von Hügel, *The Papal Commission and the Pentateuch* (London/New York/Bombay, 1906)

[77]Anthony J. Maas, "Ecclesiastical Library Table: Recent Bible Study," *The American Ecclesiastical Review* 36 (Mar., 1907), 55-71, For his earlier attack on Briggs during the latter's charge with heresy by the Presbyterian Church, see "Professor Briggs on the Theological Crisis," *ibid.* 5 (1891), 198-211.

[78]*The Catholic University Bulletin* 13 (1907), 495.

[79]A.-J. Delattre, S.J., *Le Critérium à l'usage de la nouvelle exégèse biblique: réponse au R.P.M.-J. Lagrange, O.P.* (Liège, 1907), 70.

States but also in Rome. The complicated case of his dismissal from the Catholic University was one of two scholarly crises in the American Church over Modernism; the other was the demise of the short-lived *New York Review,* published at Dunwoodie.

The New York Review was perhaps the foremost example of how derivative from Europe American scholarship was in the beginning of this century. Founded and edited by James T. Driscoll, S.S., the rector of the New York archdiocesan seminary, with the approval of Archbishop John Farley, the *Review* published articles from almost every leading liberal European scholar. The seminary, then under the direction of the Sulpicians, included on its faculty Francis Gigot. In addition to book reviews, Gigot published multi-part articles on "Studies in the Synoptic Gospels," "The Authorship of Isaias," "The Higher Criticism of the Bible," and "Divorce in the New Testament: an Exegetical Study;" he also wrote articles on the books of Jonas and Job and on Abraham. Bruneau, too, was on the faculty until 1906 when he went to St. John's Seminary, Brighton, Massachusetts. His principal contribution to the *Review* was a series of book reviews. The founding of the journal caused a painful episode for the Sulpicians.

In 1906, Gigot published the third volume of his study of Scripture: *Special Introduction to the Study of the Old Testament,* Part II. *Didactic and Prophetical Writings.* It was a relatively cautious work. While, for example, he treated Isaiah 1-39 separately from 40-66 and mentioned the arguments of the higher critics in favor of separate authorship, he came down in favor of there being one author.[80] The book had not, however, received the official sanction required of Sulpicians in the United States, but, instead, had been approved by Gigot's superior, Driscoll. In the mean-

---

[80]Francis E. Gigot, *Special Introduction to the Study of the Old Testament, Part II. Didactic Books and Prophetical Writings* (New York, 1906), 249-65.

time, the first volume of Gigot's study of the Old Testament had been sent to Jules Lebas, S.S., the superior general in Paris, and failed to receive his approbation. For some time, Gigot had been bristling at the increasing conservatism of the Sulpicians' French superiors and requirements of censorship different from what the Church at large required. He had therefore already informed Edward R. Dyer, S.S., the American vicar general in Baltimore, that he was considering withdrawing from the society. The publication of his second volume and the founding of the *Review* brought the issue to a head. Dyer had praised the intentions of Driscoll in establishing a scholarly review, but challenged its being published at the seminary. Early in 1906, Driscoll, Gigot, and three other Sulpicians at Dunwoodie withdrew from the society to be incardinated in the archdiocese of New York. Bruneau then left Dunwoodie.[81]

The New York Review, however, continued for another two years. Its demise occurred in the aftermath of Pius X's encyclical *Pascendi Dominici Gregis,* issued on September 8, 1907. The official reason given for ceasing publication was the lack of financial support, but Modernism was also involved. The journal had published a three-part article by Edward J. Hanna, professor of dogma at St. Bernard's Seminary in Rochester, on the human knowledge of Jesus. Hanna, then under consideration for coadjutor Archbishop of San Francisco, had been delated to Rome and, in a fourth article, had virtually retracted what he had earlier written. The more immediate occasion for the journal's demise, however, was its advertisement for George Tyrrell's *Lex Credendi,* which had recently been placed on the Index of Forbidden Books. The publication of the advertisement had been due to an oversight, but it drew yet further Roman

[81]E. R. Dyer, S.S., *Letters on the New York Seminary Secession* (Baltimore, 1906). Originally published in English and French, this was circulated among Sulpicians in the United States and France, the former Sulpicians at Dunwoodie, and the apostolic delegate.

attention to the *Review*.[82] As the *Review* ceased publication and as the *The Catholic University Bulletin* became more of an in-house organ, the American Church was left without a scholarly publication until the 1940s.[83]

At the Catholic University, the dismissal of Henry Poels was yet another indication of the intellectual retreat of the American Church. Poels was a consultor of the Biblical Commission and, in the summer of 1907, had an audience with Pius X at which he said he had difficulty abiding by the commission's decision regarding the Mosaic authorship of the Pentateuch. The pope first asked him if he would consider teaching another branch of theology. When the interpreter, Giovanni Genocchi, also a consultor of the commission, pointed out that these were all specialized fields, the pope said that Poels could remain teaching as long as he did not formally deny the commission's decision. Poels' understanding of the pope's wishes was confirmed in a letter from Lawrence Janssens, O.S.B., secretary of the commission in May, 1908. In the meantime, Denis O'Connell, then the rector of the university, was having a personality conflict with Charles Grannan, his former supporter during the Americanist crisis. In the summer of 1908, O'Connell had an audience with the pope. Having Grannan in mind, he said that a professor was raising questions about scripture with his students, but providing few answers. Presuming O'Connell meant Poels, the pope said he ordered the exegete not to teach. The situation remained in suspense until the fall of 1909 when Poels was abruptly told not to offer his courses. Eventually, the board of trustees and the chancellor, Cardinal James Gibbons, arrived at a compro-

---

[82]Michael J. DeVito, *Principles of Ecclesial Reform According to the 'New York Review'* (New York, 1978).

[83]Michael V. Gannon, "Before and after Modernism: The Intellectual Isolation of the American Priest," in: John Tracy Ellis (ed.), *The Catholic Priest in the United States: Historical Investigations* (Collegeville, Minn., 1971), 292-383, here 343, 362.

mise and allowed Poels to remain teaching until his contract expired in June, 1910. Poels published all his correspondence on the issue under the title "A Vindication of my Honor." He circulated it among the bishops on the university board of trustees and a few colleagues.[84] Poels was a victim of a reactionary purge, in which almost all the principals were guilty of less than honesty. For his own part, he returned to his native Holland, where he became a leader in Catholic social action and the labor movement. Despite being forced to resign from the Catholic University for heterodoxy, he remained a consultor of the Biblical Commission until his death in the 1940s.

The intellectual life of the American Church virtually ceased to exist. Biblical studies tended to reflect what was taught in Rome at the Pontifical Biblical Institute, opened in 1909. As originally envisioned by Leo XIII, the Biblical Institute was not to be under a single religious order. Leo himself spoke to Lagrange about teaching there. Giovanni Genocchi later told Briggs that Leo intended also to appoint Poels and Umberto Fracassini to the faculty, but that Pius X, under the influence of Cardinal Raffaele Merry del Val, placed the institution under the direction of the Jesuits. The first rector, Leopold Fonck, S.J., followed in the tradition of Delattre and made Lagrange the particular object of his assault in the name of orthodoxy. The École biblique he characterized as having a "deadly spirit" which ought to be "expunged from the land."[85] In the United States, the open-

---

[84]The complex story is given in Colman J. Barry, O.S.B., *The Catholic University of America: 1903-1909: the Rectorship of Denis J. O'Connell* (Washington, 1950), 177-81. See also John Tracy Ellis, *The Life of James Cardinal Gibbons; Archbishop of Baltimore, 1834-1921,* 2 vols. (Milwaukee, 1952), II, 172-81. Poels' pamphlet was republished in 1982 by Frans Neirynck, professor of scripture at Louvain, in *Annua Nuntia Lovaniensia* 25 (1982).

[85]L. Hughes Vincent, O.P., "Le Père Lagrange," *Revue biblique* 47 (1938), 321-54. here 347. Curiously the English version of this obituary omits specific reference to Fonck's statement — see *Blackfriars* 19 (1938), 475-86, here 477; on Genocchi's remark, see Genocchi to Briggs, Rome, June 11, 1909, Briggs Correspondence, 2.50, Union Theological Seminary, New York.

ness of the theological method which had characterized American Catholic theology from Kenrick to Poels was replaced by the aprioristic and a-historical approach of theologians like Maas. The Sulpician tradition, however, was not totally destroyed. It was kept alive by men like Edward Arbez, who began teaching at St. Patrick's Seminary, Menlo Park, California, in 1904. His lectures to the seminarians presented all the arguments of the higher critics and it was clear where his own sympathies lay. But he would not publish any of his ideas until well into the 1940s.[86]

Unfortunately, what most priests and lay people learned about Scripture was gleaned from the pages of *The American Ecclesiastical Review,* where Maas continued to write from time to time until 1912, when, after serving as rector of Woodstock College, he became provincial superior of the Maryland-New York Province. His place in the *Review* was taken by the equally obscurantist Walter Drum, S.J. Unlike Arbez, who was at least alerting his students to the problems of historical criticism, Maas and Drum preferred to assassinate the character of those with whom they disagreed. In notes possibly taken when he was a student under Maas, Drum recorded the reaction to Lagrange and Gigot's statement that criticism had begun in Catholic circles with Jean Astruc and J. Geddes. Drum (or Maas) challenged how either could be considered Catholic when Astruc had left his wife and children and Geddes was suspended from the priesthood and refused a Christian burial.[87]

The conservative approach to Scripture also marred the otherwise scholarly *Catholic Encyclopedia,* for which Maas wrote the articles on "Deluge," "Deuteronomy," "Exegesis," "Logia Jesu," "Knowledge of Jesus Christ," "Pentateuch," and "Scripture." There was no separate article on "Genesis"

[86]Arbez lecture notes, Sulpician Archives, Baltimore, RG 12.

[87]Walter Drum, notes on the Pentateuch, Jan. 20, 1904, Woodstock College Archives, Washington, D.C., II A 10.1d(4).

— Maas treated it under "Pentateuch." With the characteristics of this theological approach, which was in fact an innovation in the American Church, it would come as no surprise that the American Catholics were ill-prepared for the espousal of higher criticism contained in Pius XII's encyclical, *Divino Afflante Spiritu* in 1943 and for other developments which took place at Vatican II.

The interrelationship between religious liberty — the basic premise of Americanism — and the biblical question has been seldom seen. They have been treated as separate issues. Yet, at the beginning of the century both fell victim to a theological method, which denied the development of doctrine, wished to make the Church a museum piece, and, in view of problems confronting the Church in Europe, down-played the role of human reason. Religious liberty was thus seen as religious subjectivism and the denial of the need for external authority. The possibility that Moses was not the author of the Pentateuch in its present form raised the question that human reason had somehow reflected upon, developed, and therefore modified the writings of the original recipient of divine revelation — it was important that one man be the inspired author and that his name be known or otherwise the whole notion of inspiration and revelation was jeopardized, at least within that theological system. What was needed was a whole new theological system, but when it emerged on the American scene, its practitioners faced problems similar to those of their predecessors at the beginning of the century.

In the years immediately preceding Vatican II and during its first session, the issues of religious liberty and biblical studies again caused controversy in the American Church. The situation was almost a repeat performance of the early part of the century — only the names of the protagonists were different, but the theological premises were similar and this time the Jesuits were on the side of the liberals. In 1943, John Courtney Murray, S.J., professor of dogmatic theology at Woodstock, began writing on the American separation of Church and State and the religious liberty which resulted from it. In 1955, he ceased writing at the request of his Roman superiors. In the United States, he had run into opposition from Monsignor Joseph Fenton, editor of *The American Ecclesiastical Review.* Fenton reflected the mentality of Cardinal Ottaviani, who argued that Catholics, when in the majority, had the obligation to work for the official union of Church and State.[88]

In the late 1950s, Fenton launched an attack on biblical scholars, which was reminiscent of Maas. He reflected in the United States the conservative reaction which had taken place in Rome after the death of Pius XII. In 1958, moreover, Archbishop Egidio Vagnozzi, a supporter of Ottaviani, became apostolic delegate. Two years later the Pontifical Biblical Institute in Rome and its faculty came under attack from Monsignor Antonio Romeo, professor of scripture at the Lateran University and consultor to the Sacred Congregation of Seminaries and Universities. He accused the Jesuit institution of promoting criticism "inconsistent with the traditional doctrine." In the United States, Vagnozzi and Fenton created a mirror-image of the Roman controversy with assaults on biblical scholarship in general and the Catholic Biblical Association in particular. At their annual meeting in 1961, the American biblical scholars passed a resolution condemning the attacks in *The American Ecclesiastical Review.*[89]

The replayed story this time had a happier ending for scholars of both religious liberty and the Bible. When the first session of the council opened, Fenton was present as a

[88]On Murray, see Donald E. Pelotte, S.S.S., *John Courtney Murray: Theologian in Conflict* (New York, 1976), 3-73.

[89]"Pontificium Institutum Biblicum et Recens Libellus R.mi D.ni A. Romeo," *Verbum Domini* 39 (1961), 3-17. See Joseph A. Fitzmyer, S.J., "A Recent Roman Scriptural Controversy," *Theological Studies* 22 (1961), 426-44; *The Catholic Biblical Quarterly* 23 (1961), 470.

theologian for Ottaviani. Murray remained at Woodstock, "disinvited," as he put it, by Ottaviani and Vagnozzi.[90] The first session of the council was a turning point. Not only was Murray invited to be a *peritus* through the influence of Cardinal Francis Spellman of New York, long an opponent of Vagnozzi's, but the first schema "on the Sources of Revelation" was withdrawn.

The council's acceptance of both religious liberty and the critical method in biblical studies depended on a change in theological method — a method open to the development of doctrine, to the potentialities of human reason, to the recognition that scripture and tradition must be closely connected. It required a Church which did not see itself beleaguered by the forces of rationalism and the attacks of the nineteenth-century liberal State — issues which had so shaped "orthodox" theology.

For American Catholics, the council's words may well have been surprising that "indeed the words of God, expressed in the words of men, are in every way like human language, just as the Word of the eternal Father, when he took on himself the flesh of human weakness, became like men."[91] Yet, these words were quite similar to what Grannan, Gigot, and Poels had been trying to say to the American Church at the turn of the century. The twentieth-century rediscovery of the Fathers provided a theological basis for some of the developments at Vatican II. The Fathers also provided many of the arguments of the progressive Catholic exegetes in the early part of the century and were the primary theological locus for Kenrick. For the American Church, the battle for the Bible at the beginning of this century and on the eve of the council did not so much represent the introduction of a new theological method, as a return to an older one.

[90]Pelotte, *Murray,* 77.
[91]Flannery, *Vatican II,* 758.

Protestant Church Historians Interpret American Roman Catholic History, 1844-1950

Robert T. Handy

What has been called "the great tradition of American church history" began with Robert Baird, whose work marks the real beginning of the effort to tell the overall story of religion in America in one volume.[1] For a hundred years, all such endeavors were done by Protestant church historians.[2] The way such scholars perceived and interpreted the history of Catholicism [3] in America not only revealed much about Protestant attitudes toward the Catholic Church, but also helped to shape public opinion concerning it, and was used by general historians as they interpreted American religious life. Much American Catholic church historiography was shaped in reaction to the patterns set by the

[1] Martin E. Marty, in Jerald C. Brauer, ed., *Reinterpretation in American Church History* (Chicago, 1968), 205.

[2] In 1946 a brief, interpretive book by a Catholic historian appeared: Francis X. Curran, *Major Trends in American Church History* (New York, 1946).

[3] There are various types of Catholicism in the United States; in this essay hereafter the word is used to refer to Roman Catholicism.

Protestant church historians as they undertook to survey the whole story of religion in America, focusing primarily on the history of Christianity. Soon after the middle of the twentieth century, however, the long-dominant tradition of American church history as epitomized in widely-read one-volume surveys began to change. In this essay, the focus will be on the way prominent Protestant church historians from 1844 to 1950 presented and interpreted Catholicism in their one-volume surveys.

I. Robert Baird (1798-1863)

The Rev. Robert Baird was a Presbyterian who became a missionary agent for the American and Foreign Christian Union in Europe, where for sixteen years he promoted Protestant evangelicalism, the organization of Sunday schools, and the distribution of Bibles. Finding considerable European interest in the American religious scene, he lectured on the topic, and in 1844 published in Scotland a work of over 700 pages, *Religion in the United States of America*.[4] The work was republished in the United States in 1844 and was soon translated into French, German, Swedish, Danish, Dutch, and Italian. Baird utilized the work of denominational historians in this first attempt to tell the comprehensive story of Christianity in America. For more than a century, those who followed him in that effort drew on his comprehensive effort with varying degrees of critical insight.

Baird's strongly evangelical Protestant perspective was made explicit in his preface, for in acknowledging with

[4]Robert Baird, *Religion in the United States of America: Or an Account of the Origin, Progress, Relations to the State, and Present Condition of the Evangelical Churches in the United States, with Notices of the Unevangelical Denominations* (Glasgow, 1844); reprinted as *Religion in the United States of America* (New York, 1969).

particular pleasure the many helpful suggestions given to him by Robert Walsh, he observed that the latter was "a Roman Catholic, and yet with a kindness and liberality in every way remarkable, he tendered his assistance with the full knowledge that the Author is a decided Protestant, and that his work, however liberal the spirit in which it is written, was to be of a thoroughly Protestant character."[5] That bias soon manifested itself in the text in such observation as that at the time of the Spanish discovery of America "all Christendom at that day bowed its neck to the spiritual dominion of the vicar of Christ, as the bishop of Rome claimed to be." That the Cabots rather than a Spanish explorer claimed a large slice of North America for England was provided as an illustration of his broadly providential interpretation of history as he spoke "of that superintending providence which rules all things."[6] His attention was focused thereafter on the colonies under English control, and hence he paid no attention to the work of Catholic missions in Spanish and French territories. He did praise the tolerant spirit of the Calverts in settling Maryland, and criticized what happened when Protestants took over in that colony, as they "with shame be it said, enacted laws depriving the Roman Catholics of all political influence in the colony and tending to prevent their increase."[7] Though Catholicism was not wholly neglected, the bulk of his work was devoted to the story of evangelical Protestantism.

Only with that task done did he turn in Book VII to a discussion of "Unevangelical Denominations in America." He was apparently a little uneasy at putting Catholics with Unitarians and others in the same category, saying "the former, doubtless, as a church, hold those doctrines on which true believers in all ages have placed their hopes for

[5] *Ibid.*, xi.
[6] *Ibid.*, 16-17.
[7] *Ibid.*, 22.

eternal life, yet these have been so buried amid the rubbish of multiplied human traditions and inventions, as to remain hid from the great mass of the people." But as they have not denied "the Lord that bought them," in a curious double negative he concluded that "we would not say that an enlightened mind may not find in their church the way of life, obstructed though it be by innumerable obstacles."[8] His brief chapter on Catholicism then noted that in the colonial period Catholics did not receive their fair share of political rights "unless in Pennsylvania and Rhode Island," but stated with apparent sincerity that he believed that by his time "they are everywhere upon the same footing with others, and enjoy all the political privileges that our constitution affords." A long footnote discussed the burning of the convent at Charlestown, Massachusetts, in 1834, and asserted that it "was destroyed under the conviction that it was an immoral institution, and not because it was a Roman Catholic one." Assuming that the political fears of "controversial opponents" of Catholics were based on the presumed hatred of the priests to republican institutions, he observed that "not a few valuable citizens and stern patriots" in the country "have professed, at least, to belong to the Romish church, and it remains to be seen how far it is possible for the Romish priests to obtain or exercise the same influence over their followers" that they possess in some European countries. He concluded his brief chapter by noting that Catholic growth was primarily by immigration and not by proselytism, that the Church had gained a firm and extensive footing, and that the absence of religious processions and services in the streets, so familiar in Catholic Europe, was not because "the religion of Rome changes its nature on crossing the Atlantic, but only that it has comparatively few adherents in the States."[9] For him, Catholicism posed no serious threat to Protestant America.

[8]*Ibid.*, 612-13.
[9]*Ibid.*, 614-18.

In 1856 a second edition of the book appeared, with a slightly altered title, updated statistical material, and "a large amount of new matter."[10] Baird found that immense changes had taken place in the nation and the churches in twelve years, and he had become somewhat alarmed at the rapid increase of Catholicism. A new tone marked some of his editorial changes and additions. An added footnote to his brief account of colonial Maryland pointed out that though Lord Baltimore was undoubtedly a man of liberal and tolerant views, it was, after all, Protestant England that had granted the charter.[11] The brief chapter on Catholicism had several new pages; the changed situation of growing Catholic strength no longer permitted his earlier conclusion about "comparatively few adherents." Instead there was a statement "that there is no well-informed American who does not rejoice in the perfect religious liberty which exists for all; nor is there wanting a good degree of kindness and social intercourse among men of all religious opinions." This was followed directly by a paragraph that began: "Of all forms of error in the United States, Romanism is by far the most formidable, because of the number of its adherents, the organization, wealth, influence, and worldly and unscrupulous policy of its hierarchy." He suggested that Catholic claims about numbers were often inflated and did not take proper account of the "falling away," which happened in part, as he saw it, because of "the manifest superiority of the Protestant population in intelligence, enterprise, wealth, and general influence." He concluded the chapter by calling attention to three things that have

[10]Robert Baird, *Religion in America; or, an Account of the Origin, Relation to the State, and Present Condition of the Evangelical Churches in the United States, with Notices of the Unevangelical Denominations* (New York, 1856), vii. Henry Warner Bowden has prepared a critical abridgment of this edition with an introduction: Robert Baird, *Religion in America* (New York, 1970).

[11]Baird, *Religion in America* (1856), 127.

aroused the American people "in relation to Rome and her movements": the efforts to secure public funds for sectarian schools, the attempt to bring all church property into the possession of the bishops, and the willingness of the hierarchy to play the political "balance of power" game.[12] The revised edition of this Protestant endeavor to tell the overall story of Christianity in America thus presented what had become America's largest church in an even more limited and negative light than had the earlier version; clearly religious commitments were shaping historical judgments at this point. The positive contribution of his pioneer work lay in other areas of his extensive volume.

II. Philip Schaff (1819-1893)

Born in Switzerland and educated at Tübingen, Halle, and Berlin, Schaff had studied with many of the German theological giants of his time, and in extensive European travels had conversed with many of the leading religious figures of his time, including Pope Gregory XVI. Possessed of a developmental view of church history which looked toward an "evangelical Catholicism," he emigrated to America to teach in the theological seminary of the German Reformed Church at Mercersburg in 1844.

Schaff was a scholar of great breadth who was to produce many volumes in his long career as church historian, including a multi-volume *History of the Christian Church.*[13] Late

[12]*Ibid.,* 545-47.

[13]See David S. Schaff, *The Life of Philip Schaff, in Part Autobiographical* (New York, 1897); James H. Nichols, *Romanticism in American Theology: Nevin and Schaff and Mercersburg* (Chicago, 1961), esp. chaps. 3, 5.

in his life (1888) he founded the American Society of Church History and served as the first of a long line of Protestant presidents of that organization; it was not until after the period treated in this paper that the first Catholic to become president of the society was elected — John Tracy Ellis, who served in 1969. Yet that development was not out of harmony with Schaff's ecumenical interests, for in his last public appearance at the World's Parliament of Religions in Chicago in 1893 he spoke eloquently on "The Reunion of Christendom."

Schaff's book on American church history, however, was written early in his career, before his ecumenical interests had matured. Like Baird's volume, his was addressed primarily to European audiences, having been originally given in lecture form in Germany in 1854. But *America: A Sketch of Its Political, Social, and Religious Character* was quite different from Baird's work in that it was much shorter and more interpretive; it was written when the author was far from his library, and was minimally documented. Yet there are good grounds for the conclusion of Perry Miller, who edited a modern version of Schaff's classic, that he "very likely had in mind, when trying to reach the comprehensions of the Germans, a book he is said to have admired, Robert Baird's *Religion in America.*"[14] Though originally published in Europe, in German, Schaff's book was quickly translated and published in the United States in 1855.

The book was interpretive and analytical and did not contain much historical narrative or detail. When he touched on Catholicism in the first part, he was emphasizing the Protestant character of the United States, as can be seen from these words:

[14]Philip Schaff, *America: A Sketch of Its Political, Social, and Religious Character,* ed. Perry Miller (Cambridge, Mass., 1961), xxxi.

> While in Europe ecclesiastical institutions appear in historical connections with Catholicism, and even in evangelical countries, most of the city and village churches, the universities, and religious foundations, point to a mediaeval origin; in North America, on the contrary, every thing had a Protestant beginning, and the Catholic Church has come in afterwards as one sect among the others, and has always remained subordinate. In Europe, Protestantism has, so to speak, fallen heir to Catholicism; in America, Catholicism under the wing of Protestant toleration and freedom of conscience, has found an adopted home, and is everywhere surrounded by purely Protestant institutions.[15]

He went on to admit that Maryland was one of the earliest settlements, but reported that it was founded on the thoroughly anti-Roman and essentially Protestant principles of religious toleration, and that it never had any specific influence on the life of the country. He insisted rather on the Protestant spirit and character of the land, observing that "The Roman Church has attained social and political importance in the eastern and western States only within the last twenty years, chiefly in consequence of the vast Irish emigration; but it will never be able to control the doctrines of the New World, though it should increase a hundred fold."[16]

In the second part of the book, Schaff contrasted the two systems: Protestantism as Christianity in the form of free subjectivity, Catholicism as taking Christianity in an entirely objective sense; "in the first, the centrifugal force predominates, in the second, the centripetal — there freedom, here authority." To harmonize perfectly these two opposite but correlative principles, he declared, "is the high-

[15]*Ibid.*, 72.
[16]*Ibid.*, 73.

est, but also the most difficult, problem of history."[17] But he saw the forces of history moving, under divine providence, not back to Roman Catholicism, but ahead to an enriched "evangelical Catholicism": "Out of the most confused chaos God will bring the most beautiful order; out of the deepest discords, the noblest harmony; out of the most thoroughly developed Protestantism, the most harmonious and at the same time the freest Catholicism."[18]

In the Baird pattern, toward the end of the book he discussed the major denominations *seriatim*. Looking now at American Catholicism more on its own terms, he observed that it was older on the continent than Protestantism itself; he spoke with appreciation of the deep piety of Columbus, of Isabella and Ferdinand, and rejoiced in what he called "this beautiful prelude of American history."[19] He regretted the brutalities of the Spanish conquest, citing Hefele as to its terrible cost. In a quite characteristic Protestant opinion of his time, he interpreted the loss of North America to Spain by saying, "God in his providence had destined the northern half of the New World as a hospitable asylum for all nations and churches of Europe, and more especially for the Anglo-Saxon race and for Protestantism, which so soon followed the discovery of America, as if this had prepared a new home for it."[20]

In this setting he felt the Catholic Church was almost an anomaly, but allowed it a somewhat negative role — as a necessary and useful check and corrective for the extremes of Protestantism and religious radicalism. Though it remained in some contradiction with earlier remarks, in this context he praised the founders of Maryland, who, more fully than Roger Williams, proclaimed the principle of the

[17] *Ibid.*, 101.
[18] *Ibid.*, 103.
[19] *Ibid.*, 179.
[20] *Ibid.*, 180.

fullest religious liberty, and acted upon it until the Protestants overthrew it. Some Protestant and ethnic biases conjoined in his judgment of the Irish, who "do not seem to be morally improved by any number of masses and confessions, which they scrupulously attend." He interpreted American Catholicism as progressive, in part because of "the jealous watching of thousands of Protestant eyes," and spoke appreciatively of the higher clergy.[21] He commented on the the Church's industry in building imposing cathedrals, establishing schools, and multiplying publications, noted also its growing political influence, but wondered if that might not prove dangerous, if not fatal. The great hopes Catholics have for their future in western nations Schaff saw as strengthened by the Romanizing movements within Protestantism, especially in Lutheran and Episcopal churches, one by-product of which was a number of converts to Catholicism, notably Brownson.

In a dramatic passage, the eminent historian declared it was very probable that the ultimate fate of the Reformation would be decided in America, and that the last decisive engagement between Romanism and Protestantism will occur not in Europe, "but on the banks of the Hudson, the Susquehannah, the Mississippi, and the Sacramento; and that it will result in favor not, as the sanguine Papists think, of the Roman, but of an evangelical Catholicism."[22] In that consummation, he predicted, what is true, great, good, and beautiful "in the hoary but still vigorous Catholic church" will be preserved, but its temporary form (the papacy) and some of its practices and attitudes must go. The Americanization of the Church will give it a more liberal character than in Europe, he predicted, even as the jejune and contracted theology of popular American Protestantism will

[21]*Ibid.,* 183, 185.
[22]*Ibid.,* 191.

undergo a considerable revolution. All this, he concluded, "would no doubt also affect the religious sentiment, and greatly contribute towards removing the bigoted prejudices of the two confessions, until the present relation of bitter enmity be exchanged for one of mutual respect and love."[23] Though lacking the precision of his interpretations of the past, his glimpses into the future have not proved wholly wrong.

III. Daniel Dorchester (1827-1907)

To look at works of Baird and Schaff as they discussed Roman Catholic history is to see them at a weak point as they dealt in minimal fashion with matters about which their biases were especially evident; their creative contributions to the emerging study of American church history show better at many other points. But the writings of some who came after them copied some of their weaknesses without improving greatly on their strengths. Jerald C. Brauer was referring primarily to Dorchester when he wrote, "What Baird and Schaff developed as a stimulating perspective in the hands of creative and skilled historians provided only a handy framework for men who could not rise beyond chronicle to history."[24] Some of Dorchester's work did, however, enrich the field.

Daniel Dorchester, who had studied at Connecticut Wesleyan and later received several honorary degrees from that institution, was a Methodist pastor who also served several terms in political office and was superintendent of Indian Schools during the administration of President Harrison. As church historian, he was self-consciously in the Baird tradition of American religious history. In the preface to his

[23]*Ibid.,* 198.
[24]Brauer, in Brauer, ed., *Reinterpretation in American Church History,* 4.

Christianity in the United States he referred to correspondence with Baird before the latter's death, and cited him a
number of times in his volume of nearly 800 pages, but made
only a passing reference to Schaff. His threefold typology of
religions followed the Baird lead and reflected the competi-
tiveness between "Protestantism, Romanism, and a variety
of Divergent Elements."[25] But he was an industrious reader,
and his treatment of Catholicism was informed by Catholic
scholarship. At the outset, drawing on the writings of John
Gilmary Shea, he emphasized that the first discoveries and
settlements of the territories that became the United States
were under Roman Catholic auspices. Informed also by the
works of such historians as Bancroft and Parkman, he
discussed both Spanish and French colonial efforts in some
detail. He continued the providential interpretation of history as his predecessors had done, but it was being slanted in
a progressive direction, evident in such a statement as this:
"Columbus and his successors in discovery accomplished
great Providential purposes, opening up pathways for
nations and imparting new impulses of progress to the
world."[26] He called attention to the brutalities, the thirst for
gold and love of power that went with those conquests, but
he also greatly admired the heroism and faithfulness unto
death of many Catholic missionaries. In discussing New
France, he provided vivid documentation for his generalization that "It would be difficult to do justice to some great
examples of self-forgetfulness and devotion in this truly
heroic period of Jesuit missions."[27] He had little sympathy
with what those missionaries actually accomplished among
the Indians, observing that "The intrepidity and enterprise
of the Jesuits have drawn forth our encomiums, but the
moral results were meager and full of blemishes," and that

[25]Daniel Dorchester, *Christianity in the United States: From the First Settlement down to the Present Time* (New York, 1888), 4.
[26]*Ibid.*, 23.
[27]*Ibid.*, 48.

among the tribes won they "fostered their hatred of the English."[28]

Dorchester gave much more attention to Catholic history than Baird had — five chapters were devoted wholly to it, and references occurred in other places. He paid tribute to Catholic participation in the Revolution, and briefly told the story of the establishment of the hierarchy in the United States, citing Catholic sources. He called attention to the work of the missionaries in the West in the nineteenth century, pointing out that "a zealous and self-sacrificing spirit, not excelled by any Protestant pioneers, was exhibited by its emissaries on the wild and broken frontiers."[29] There were passages on prominent church figures, such as Archbishops Carroll and Hughes, and Bishop England, whom he especially admired.

As the story drew near to his own time, however, the tone changed, and a note of alarm was sounded as he described the influx of immigrants and the increase of the type of Catholicism long prevalent in Europe with its festivals, public processions, and display of symbols. The orders were now pictured in an unfavorable light: "The activity of the Jesuits, and other orders, in bringing forth their peculiarities has at times awakened serious apprehensions in many minds lest European Romanism should be fully and permanently established among us." Hence he could interpret nativist legislation and such movements as the Know-Nothing party as "the jealousy naturally engendered by the bold, defiant, and revolutionary conduct of Roman Catholics."[30] He pressed hard a rather narrow range of evidence, centered chiefly in New York, to make the case that the Catholic Church was well on the way to establishment, that

[28]*Ibid.*, 77.
[29]*Ibid.*, 544.
[30]*Ibid.*, 586.

is, to becoming a state religion, by securing a lion's share of public donations, by interfering in the political process (quoting Fr. Edward McGlynn on that point), by controlling chaplaincies, and by organizing "Roman Catholic regiments."[31] In the concluding chapter of his long book his fear of the European immigrants, three-fifths of whom he reported as coming from Catholic stock, was reiterated: "How grievously have morals been debauched, pauperism, insanity, and crime augmented, and moral progress retarded by these exotic masses!" But his faith in divine providence gave him hope "that Romanism has already lost much of her hideous character; that it is not a question of choice on her part, but an inevitable necessity, that she must be still more radically modified and improved, and that all such changes will bring her nearer to the likeness of apostolic Christianity."[32]

IV. *Leonard Wolsey Bacon (1830-1907)*

Before his death, Philip Schaff came to the conclusion that an important step toward the reunion of Christendom would be the publication of a series of volumes on the histories of the denominations in America. Under his general editorship the project was taken on by the American Society of Church History and the writers chosen, including Leonard Wolsey Bacon as the author of a final, summary overview. The thirteen volumes were originally published in New York between 1893 and 1897; not surprisingly they were cast largely in the Baird-Schaff frame of reference. Bacon, a Yale graduate who went on to study theology at Andover Seminary and Yale Divinity School, also earned the M.D. degree at his *alma mater*. He was ordained as a

[31]*Ibid.*, 591-95.
[32]*Ibid.*, 764, 780.

Congregational minister, served a number of pastorates, and wrote many books. He did a competent job of summarization in *A History of American Christianity,* but, as William A. Clebsch has observed, his volume "introduced a scissors-and-paste method of writing 'general' as opposed to denominational histories of American religion, by clipping episodes from many denominational chronicles and gathering them into one chronological sequence."[33] Hence there were few surprises in his work of just over 400 pages; the generalizations in what became the standard one-volume survey of American church history for three decades were based largely on what had gone before.

The familiar providential-progressive perspective was in evidence from the start; that the "secret of the ages" had long been kept from premature disclosure was interpreted as "high strategy in the warfare for the advancement of the kingdom of God in the earth."[34] Only two chapters, on Spanish and French Christianity in America, were focused wholly on Catholicism; colonial Maryland shared a chapter with the Carolinas; otherwise the relevant passages were inserted in various chapters. As would be expected, there were a number of references to Thomas O'Gorman's *A History of the Roman Catholic Church in the United States,* the ninth volume of the American Church history series. The seamy side of the Spanish conquest was duly noted. Bacon was much more partial to the French effort: "a more magnificent project of empire, secular and spiritual, has never entered into the heart of man."[35] But it was all for the good, as Bacon saw it, for the loss of the French Catholic power made possible the later large and free development of

[33]William A. Clebsch, *From Sacred to Profane America: The Role of Religion in American History* (New York, 1968), 6.

[34]Leonard Wolsey Bacon, *A History of American Christianity* (New York, [1897], 1900), 2.

[35]*Ibid.,* 18.

the Catholic Church in the United States. In his words, "If there are those who, reading the earlier pages of this volume, have mourned over the disappointment and annihilation of two magnificent schemes of Catholic domination on the North American continent as being among the painful mysteries of divine providence, they may find compensation for these catastrophes in later advances of Catholicism, which without these antecedents would seem to have been hardly possible."[36] He believed that the trend in the Church in the newly independent nation was toward an absolute government administered on republican principles; hence "American ideals and methods were destined profoundly and beneficially to affect the Roman Church in the United States, but not by the revolutionary process of establishing 'trusteeism,' or the lay control of parishes."[37]

Bacon was a consistent enemy of intolerance, race prejudice, and religious antipathy. For example, he interpreted the burning of the convent in 1834 as the work of fanatics and demagogues; he saw the infamous woman named Maria Monk as "the Titus Oates of the American no-popery panic, in 1836" through her monstrous stories; he explained that the serious hindrance to the "noble advances" the Church made in serving hordes of immigrants through a network of institutions was "bigoted Native-Americanism."[38] He looked for a closer relationship between Catholic and Protestant. As he put it, without any sacrifice of principle "the Roman Catholic, recognizing the spirit of Christ in his Protestant fellow-Christian, is able to hold him in spiritual if not formal communion, so that the Catholic Church may prove itself not dissevered from the Church Catholic."[39]

[36]*Ibid.,* 185.
[37]*Ibid.,* 216.
[38]*Ibid.,* 312-13, 320-21.
[39]*Ibid.,* 324.

V. William Warren Sweet (1881-1959)

The next major effort to interpret the overall story of religion in America was by William Warren Sweet. Between Bacon and Sweet an historiographical revolution occurred —the rise of critical, scientific history promoted by a guild of professional historians, most of them graduates of Ph.D. programs. That story has been told many times; its impact on the study of church history has been analyzed in considerable detail by Henry Warner Bowden. That church history should be done by the same exacting methods used in general history was articulated sharply by Ephraim Emerton, a graduate of Harvard who then studied at Berlin and Leipzig (Ph.D., 1876). In 1882 this Unitarian layman was called back to Harvard to teach church history at the Divinity School. Here for thirty-six years he utilized the seminar method, insisted that "concrete evidence substantiate the truth of every generalization," and "denied that supernatural elements played any part in historical events or that they could figure in a historian's judgment."[40] His approach was followed in somewhat modified form by Williston Walker and Arthur C. McGiffert, both Congregationalists, one a layman, the other ordained. None of them undertook to write a general history of religion in America, but the new viewpoint was applied in a somewhat preliminary way by another layman, Henry Kalloch Rowe, a graduate of Brown who earned his doctorate at Boston University and taught church history and social sciences for more than three decades at Newton Theological Institute, later Andover Newton Theological School. In 1924 he wrote a brief history of religion in America, without documentation or bibliography, which he called "merely an essay in interpretation." The tone of his sparse remarks on the Catholic Church can

[40]Henry Warner Bowden, *Church History in the Age of Science: Historiographical Patterns in the United States, 1876-1918* (Chapel Hill, 1971), 95, 101.

be seen in his observation that it "suffers continually from its lack of kinship with the spirit of freedom and democracy. Its genius is European, not American."[41]

That same year Sweet, a graduate of Ohio Wesleyan, Drew Theological Seminary, Crozer Theological Seminary, and the University of Pennsylvania (Ph.D., 1912), then teaching at DePauw University, published an even shorter book, *Our American Churches,* which outlined the approach he was to develop in the remainder of his long career. In 1927 he began his work at the University of Chicago, holding the first professorship in the history of American Christianity, serving there until his retirement in 1946, undertaking many research projects, directing a number of doctoral dissertations, and producing a series of works that dominated the growing discipline of American church history for several decades. Best known among his many books was his one-volume survey, *The Story of Religions in America,* published in 1930. Nine years later a revised and enlarged edition was published with a slightly modified title, and in 1950 a third edition, further enlarged, appeared. As the author explained, the writing of dissertations and books in the field had greatly increased, producing materials helpful to those who undertook the preparation of such general works.

Sweet had been schooled in the tenets of "scientific history" at Pennsylvania, where John Bach McMaster, with whom he took a course, was especially famous. He was also influenced by Frederick Jackson Turner who stressed the importance of interpretative hypotheses in historical investigation, and who is remembered for his famous and much-debated thesis on the importance of the frontier in American history.[42] At Chicago, Sweet took his place

[41] Henry Kalloch Rowe, *The History of Religion in the United States* (New York, 1924), viii, 119.

[42] Sidney E. Mead, "Prof. Sweet's Religion and Culture in America," *Church History* 22 (1953), 33-49.

among a group of church historians who accepted the importance scientific history placed on inductive reasoning based on empirical data, but who also recognized the significance of generalization and interpretation. An ordained Methodist minister, in his interpretation of American religion Sweet located its main constitutive elements in evangelical Protestantism, and was aware of the work of his predecessors in this tradition. His one-volume text was a success from the beginning; the 1950 edition was especially popular, selling annually nearly three thousand copies a year for a decade.[43]

The focus of his attention at the outset was on the English colonies; he gave only passing attention later in the book to missions under the Spanish and French, observing that "the French Jesuits were intrepid explorers as well as devoted missionaries."[44] He noted but did not identify with the providential interpretation his Protestant predecessors gave to the fact that Luther posted his ninety-five theses just twenty-five years after Columbus' discovery of America, adding "but whether providential or not, it is a significant fact that these two great historic events, taken together, contain the key which explains to a large degree the establishment of the English colonies in America."[45] The story of Maryland's founding is told in a chapter on the first experiments in religious liberty, in which it is explained that Lord Baltimore, "a practical and hardheaded investor," founded the colony "upon the principle of religious toleration in spite of his religion rather than because of it," while Williams in Rhode Island "based his position on great fundamental truths." He also affirmed that though toleration in Maryland was primarily for business reasons, yet "it was also the

[43]James L. Ash, Jr., *Protestantism and the American University; An Intellectual Biography of William Warren Sweet* (Dallas, 1982), esp. xvi, 67, 82, 96.

[44]William Warren Sweet, *The Story of Religion in America* (New York, 1950), 165, cf. 310, 338.

[45]*Ibid.*, 8.

outcome of his convictions and kindly nature."[46] He utilized Catholic sources in discussing the role of Catholics in the Revolution, appreciating their practically unanimous support for it, observing that the American people then learned that "people could be good citizens and good Catholics at the same time; and they could be good neighbors and good friends in spite of their Catholicism," and criticizing as inflated some claims about the Catholic share in winning the war. He briefly recounted the career of John Carroll, finding him "a leader admirably fitted for the peculiar task which America presented."[47]

The Chicago professor told the story of the period of Irish and German immigration dispassionately, describing John England and John Hughes "as men of decided character and great ability, bold, fearless and independent"; he discussed the controversies over trusteeism and public schools without comment, but criticized the Know-Nothing movement as "unjust and ill-timed."[48] Sweet cited Catholic sources in dealing briefly with "Negro Catholicism," and with the vast and complex patterns of immigration in the later nineteenth century. He interpreted the upsurge of anti-Catholicism in the late nineteenth century as a rural protest against the Catholic influx into the cities, declaring that "the dominance of the Irish Catholic politician in such cities as Boston, New York and Chicago, and the corrupt municipal governments which so often resulted from this control aroused real fear on the part of many that American institutions were in danger."[49] Obviously impressed by the numerical and institutional growth of the Church, he praised Cardinal Gibbons, saying that "it was particularly fortunate that the American Catholics should have had such wise and

[46]*Ibid.,* 77, 80.
[47]*Ibid.,* 185, 203.
[48]*Ibid.,* 270-73.
[49]*Ibid.,* 331, 379.

patriotic leadership at the time that Catholic immigration was pouring into the country in such unprecedented streams."[50]

In a concise discussion of the presidential candidacy of Governor Alfred E. Smith in 1928, he summarized both sides of the debate as to whether Catholics had really accepted toleration and the complete separation of church and state. His views were more clearly put in a little book that grew out of lectures given in England in 1946, in which he said "it is becoming quite apparent that the Roman Catholic hierarchy are aiming at a kind of world domination, inimical to the basic freedom of all our freedoms, religious liberty."[51]

His final comments on Catholicism in the third edition of *The Story of Religion in America* reflected that position: after observing that Catholics "now feel perfectly at home in America," and referring back to the days of fraternization in the nineteenth century, he concluded that "when the Catholic crosses the threshold of his church he puts an almost impassable barrier between himself and his Protestant neighbors....Thus there has been created a broad and impassable cleavage in American society which inevitably creates suspicion, if no open enmity." The rising tide of resentment against Catholic power he saw not as another crude outbreak of anti-Catholic hysteria nor as an attack on Catholicism as a religion, but as an aggressive opposition to Catholicism in politics. Reviewing the various controversies of 1949, he concluded by anticipating "a period of bitter controversy, the end of which no one can foresee."[52] Like his predecessors, he allowed his own religious understandings and commitments to influence his interpretation of Catholic history.

[50]*Ibid.*, 380, 382.

[51]William Warren Sweet, *The American Churches: An Interpretation* (New York, 1948), 108.

[52]Sweet, *Story of Religion in America,* 442, 448.

After Sweet, the situation rapidly changed for a number of reasons, among them the ecumenical impact of Pope John XXIII and the Second Vatican Council, new attention to ecumenical and theological history, fresh interpretations of American Catholic history by such scholars as Thomas T. McAvoy and John Tracy Ellis, increased attention to historiographical problems in the writing of church history, and the growing role of the academic study of religion in university life. General interpretations of religion in America took on a different tone in dealing with Catholicism and with certain other topics, as can be seen in the works by such authors as Sydney E. Ahlstrom, Catherine L. Albanese, Edwin S. Gaustad, Winthrop S. Hudson, Clifton E. Olmstead, and H. Shelton Smith and his colleagues. Yet their work too is indebted to the authors who have been discussed here, even as they have corrected past mistakes and limitations, especially in their treatment of Catholicism.

Chicago and Milwaukee: Contrasting Experiences in Seminary Planting

Philip Gleason

The study of seminary education is one of the most neglected subfields in the whole underdeveloped area of American Catholic historiography. The pioneering essays of John Tracy Ellis are the only works presently available that deal with the topic in a comprehensive or synthesizing manner, and there are not many competent treatments of individual institutions. Two major research projects are presently under way; when completed they will perhaps stimulate further interest in this important area which Msgr. Ellis has done so much to open up.[1] The present sketch of early

---

[1]Msgr. Ellis' principal contributions to the field are his *Essays in Seminary Education* (Notre Dame, Ind., 1967), which brings together a number of studies previously published in various places, and his "The Formation of the American Priest: An Historical Perspective," in John Tracy Ellis, ed., *The Catholic Priest in the United States: Historical Investigations* (Collegeville, Minn., 1971), 3-110. The two projects presently under way are: Joseph White's project to write a general history of Catholic seminary education in the United States, which is being carried

efforts at seminary education in Chicago and Milwaukee, both of which were established as dioceses in 1843, illustrates some of the hazards that beset the enterprise. It is a study in contrasts, since Chicago was unable to sustain a seminary, while St. Francis de Sales in Milwaukee became one of the nation's leading Catholic seminaries in the late nineteenth century.

Although it was to suffer practically every misfortune imaginable, the Catholic Church in Chicago got off to an excellent start under its first bishop. William Quarter was an Irish-born priest educated at Mount St. Mary's College and Seminary in Emmitsburg, Maryland; he labored productively in New York for fifteen years before being named Bishop of Chicago.[2] Finding only two priests on hand when he arrived in his see city in May of 1844, Quarter concluded that providing a reliable supply of clerical manpower should be his number-one priority. Within a month of his arrival he therefore established a college designed to be the first stage of a seminary system. Although it was chartered by the state of Illinois as "The University of St. Mary of the Lake," this institution was in reality a conventional college/seminary of the "mixed type" that bishops had been establishing since the days of John Carroll.[3]

out under the auspices of the Cushwa Center for the Study of American Catholicism at the University of Notre Dame, and Christopher J. Kauffman's project to write the history of Sulpician work in seminary education in the United States, which was commissioned by the Society of St. Sulpice.

[2]The most extensive treatment of Quarter's administration, which reproduces his diary, is found in James J. McGovern, "The Catholic Church in Chicago," in *Souvenir of the Silver Jubilee in the Episcopacy of His Grace the Most Rev. Patrick Augustine Feehan, Archbishop of Chicago* (Chicago, 1891), 16-87. See also Gilbert J. Garraghan, S.J., *The Catholic Church in Chicago, 1673-1871* (Chicago, 1921), 108-36. Charles Shanabruch, *Chicago's Catholics: The Evolution of an American Identity* (Notre Dame, 1981), 1-30, provides background on the period discussed here.

[3]D. J. Riordan, "University of St. Mary of the Lake," *Illinois Catholic Historical Review* 2 (Oct., 1919), 135-60, includes the text of the charter, dated Dec. 23, 1844. The most recent and informative treatment of this institution is Harry C. Koenig's

St. Mary of the Lake progressed rapidly under Quarter, who devoted his personal funds to diocesan needs, raised money among his friends in New York, and received help from French and Austrian mission-aid societies. The city was growing with amazing speed, assuring a steady flow of students, and the whole community took an interest in a "university" which added to its civic attractiveness. Hence Quarter was able to dedicate an impressive three-story frame structure on July 4, 1846, just two years after initiating his college in the wooden chapel that was the first Catholic church built in Chicago. The grounds of the University comprised an entire city block, half of which had been donated by Chicago's booster mayor, William B. Ogden, and Catholics living in that part of the city worshiped in its chapel. Eventually a separate church was built on the grounds and staffed by priests from the University.[4]

Under Bishop Quarter, the college/seminary was the most important undertaking of the diocese, and it was making impressive progress. But as the fourth anniversary of his arrival in Chicago drew near, Quarter suffered a stroke and died in a matter of hours. His death has justifiably been called "a calamitous tragedy."[5] He was only forty-two years old at the time of his entirely unexpected death; had he lived to guide the diocese over the next twenty years or so, the Catholic Church in Chicago might have been spared some of the worst ills that plagued it for a generation

unpublished "History of Saint Mary of the Lake Seminary, Mundelein, Illinois," 1-41. I am grateful to Msgr. Koenig for providing me with a copy of this manuscript. Ellis, *Essays*, 160-62, also discusses St. Mary of the Lake, but I believe he over-emphasizes the degree to which it departed from the standard college/seminary model. On the types of seminaries characteristic of this era, see William S. Morris, *The Seminary Movement in the United States: Projects, Foundations, and Early Development, 1833-1866* (Washington, 1932), 83-91.

[4]Garraghan, *Chicago,* 112-16; Koenig, "History," 1-10.

[5]Koenig, "History," 9.

and left it without its own seminary from 1868 to the opening decades of the twentieth century.

The University of St. Mary of the Lake was intimately connected with the difficulties of the diocese because the priests associated with it were unable to work cordially with Quarter's successors. The first of these was James O. Van de Velde, S.J., one of the original group of Belgian novices recruited in 1817 who became the nucleus of the Missouri Province of the Society of Jesus.[6] Van de Velde had held positions of responsibility among the Jesuits, including those of professor and president at St. Louis University. One might therefore have assumed that he would be well qualified to nurture the growth of the college/seminary. But there had been almost a year's hiatus between Quarter's death and Van de Velde's installation, during which time the diocese was administered by Father Walter Quarter, the deceased bishop's brother, who was the local favorite to succeed him.[7] Walter Quarter was closely associated with the priests of St. Mary of the Lake, and there was doubtless some disappointment that he had been passed over for an outsider who was also a member of a religious community often regarded by the secular clergy as excessively devoted to its own corporate interests. But it was the disposition of diocesan property provided for in Bishop Quarter's will that made tension inevitable between the new bishop and the priests of the college/seminary.

According to Quarter's will, "all real estate and personal property" held by the first Bishop of Chicago was

[6]On Van de Velde, see Garraghan, *Chicago,* 137-66; and McGovern, "Catholic Church in Chicago," 98-184, which reproduces Van de Velde's diary.

[7]See Jeremiah A. Kinsella to Paul Cullen, June 3, 1848, Archives of the Irish College in Rome, in which Kinsella asks Cullen to use his influence to get Walter Quarter named Bishop of Chicago and says that a petition to that effect had already been sent by Chicago priests to the Archbishop of Baltimore. (A microfilm of the letters to the Irish College in Rome is among the Manuscript Collections, University of Notre Dame. Hereafter cited MCUND.)

bequeathed to the University of St. Mary of the Lake "to be used by that institution for the purposes of the Catholic Religion and worship." Walter Quarter and Jeremiah A. Kinsella, president of the University, were named by Bishop Quarter to be executors of his will.[8] When Van de Velde arrived on the scene, he thus found that the priests who constituted the corporate body of the University were in legal possession of much of the ecclesiastical property of the diocese, including the house occupied by the Bishop himself. This situation was naturally unacceptable to Van de Velde, who drew up a constitution and by-laws for the University according to which he, and his successors as Bishop of Chicago, were designated ex-officio president of the board of trustees of St. Mary of the Lake. At the same time, he requested from the priests of the University deeds conveying to him and his successors the ecclesiastical property to which Quarter's will had given them title.[9]

Although Kinsella and his confreres at St. Mary of the Lake showed a cooperative spirit by acquiescing in the reorganization and turning over the deeds to the property as requested by Van de Velde, the situation bred continuing suspicion and tension. From the Bishop's point of view, a cohesive body of priests had ensconced themselves in a key institution from which they could mount an opposition to his authority. He would have been happy to replace them; indeed, he tried unsuccessfully to get both the Jesuits and the Congregation of Holy Cross to take over the operation of the college/seminary. These efforts confirmed the suspicion of the priests at St. Mary of the Lake that their bishop was prejudiced against them and stiffened their resistance to

[8] Koenig, "History," 13 n., gives the text of Quarter's will.

[9] *Ibid.*, 13-16. This account is based on Van de Velde's statement of the situation in an undated document entitled "The Bishop of Chicago to the Congregation *de gravaminibus*," MCUND, Natchez Papers, which Koenig believes was sent to the Bishops of the Province of St. Louis. See also Van de Velde's diary for July 18 and 19, 1849, in McGovern, "Catholic Church in Chicago," 109.

what they regarded as his misguided policies. Kinsella was in a particularly strong position since he could make a legal case for salary owed him as president of the University, and he threatened to resort to the civil courts if Van de Velde attempted to dismiss him. An open conflict of that sort could precipitate a schism, for the Kinsella group had both clerical and lay sympathizers.[10]

Van de Velde had been most reluctant to leave the Jesuits and assume episcopal responsibilities, and he had no stomach for the kind of battle that would be required to establish his authority over the priests of St. Mary of the Lake. In 1852 he travelled to Rome to request a transfer from Chicago. While he was there, a letter from Kinsella and three other priests of the University complaining of his administration reached Propaganda. Van de Velde was assured that Roman officials did not take seriously the complaints made against him, and he was promised release from the burdens of Chicago. The following year he was transferred to Natchez, one of the most inconsiderable dioceses in the country. Before leaving, the unhappy bishop let fly a Parthian shot in the form of a farewell sermon informing the faithful of the difficulties that had prompted him to seek a transfer and saying that he was leaving to his successor the task of enforcing episcopal authority upon the refractory members of the clergy.[11]

[10]Koenig, "History," 16-19. In an undated statement addressed "To the Congregation of the Most Rev. Archbishops," MCUND, Natchez Papers, Van de Velde said that he was forced to keep Kinsella in office "for fear of having a suit instituted against him [i.e., the Bishop of Chicago], and of perhaps seeing the Catholics that favor the party opposed to the Bishop involved in a schism or acting in open opposition to his authority."

[11]See Kinsella *et al.* to Propaganda, May 28, 1852, MCUND, microfilm, which is calendared in Finbar Kenneally, O.F.M., *United States Documents in the Propaganda Fide Archives: A Calendar,* First Series, 7 vols. (Washington, 1966-77), II, item 572. This letter details the case of the priests of St. Mary of the Lake. In a later letter, dated May 18, 1855 (Kenneally, *Documents,* II, item 906), Kinsella and his friends complained that Van de Velde had published in the diocesan paper,

Van de Velde left Chicago in November, 1853; his successor, Anthony O'Regan, was not installed until September, 1854. The diocese was thus without authoritative leadership for almost a year. Part of the delay resulted from the fact that O'Regan, an Irish-born priest who had been rector of the seminary in the archdiocese of St. Louis, at first refused the position on the grounds that he was a bookish and retiring person and had no pastoral experience. He finally accepted the mitre when commanded to do so by Rome, but his instincts had been sound. His administration was no improvement over Van de Velde's and was equally brief; he too resigned after only fours years in office.[12]

As Bishop, O'Regan wasted little time in grasping the nettle so far as St. Mary of the Lake was concerned. After a five-month interlude during which he made new appointments to its board of trustees, he summarily dismissed Kinsella and the other three priests who constituted the faculty of the college/seminary and the staff of the church annexed to it. His specific complaint was that they had deceived him about the debt contracted in the building of a new church of the Holy Name, which had been undertaken during Van de Velde's administration and apparently with his approval. The church debt was probably less the cause of O'Regan's action than the pretext for it, however, since he spoke generally of the "misdeeds" of Kinsella and the others and said it would have been a blessing if they had been gotten rid of earlier.[13] The priests' version of events was

The Western Tablet, "a severe article on us, in which he stated that we had written 'falsehoods against him to the Holy See,' and that 'we were virtually schismatic,' " MCUND, microfilm. Garraghan, *Chicago*, 164, alludes cryptically to Van de Velde's blast. A copy of the farewell sermon in Van de Velde's hand is in MCUND, Natchez Papers.

[12]Garraghan, *Chicago*, 167-79; Koenig, "History," 20-26.

[13]O'Regan to John B. Purcell, Jan. 20, 1855, MCUND, Cincinnati Papers. For other complaints against the "College Priests," see O'Regan to Francis P. Kenrick, May 19, 1855 and April 11, 1857, Archives of the Archdiocese of Baltimore. Martin J. Spalding to Purcell, Sept. 12, 1855, MCUND, Cincinnati Papers, refers

quite different; they protested to Rome that the financial situation was manageable, that O'Regan had been prejudiced against them from the outset, and that he did them an injustice in ejecting them from the diocese.[14] While the rights and wrongs remain murky, it is clear that Kinsella and the others were not simply clerical trouble-makers for they left Chicago without stirring up factions among the laity to resist the Bishop's action, and they served honorably in the eastern dioceses to which they moved.

The mass dismissal of the faculty of course precipitated a crisis at St. Mary of the Lake. O'Regan replaced them on a temporary basis with other diocesan priests, while simultaneously appealing to Bishop John Henni in Milwaukee to send his seminarians down to Chicago to help revive the establishment. Henni, who was on the point of opening St. Francis Seminary in his own diocese, was uninterested in this proposition, and for several years Chicago's ecclesiastical prospects either received instruction in the Bishop's newly enlarged residence or were sent out of the diocese for their training. The more numerous lay students, in the meantime, were confided to the care of the Congregation of Holy Cross, with whom O'Regan concluded an agreement in August of 1856. The Bishop's action thus effectively ended seminary education in Chicago and led to the transfer of the University of St. Mary of the Lake to the control of a religious community. This was the situation when O'Regan

---

to a deficit of $30,000 "wholly unaccounted for by Kinsella & Co.!!" Writing from Chicago just as Bishop Van de Velde left, Archbishop Purcell of Cincinnati voiced the opinion that the troubles in Chicago were much exaggerated, and could be solved without great difficulty if handled with charity and prudence. Purcell to Anthony Blanc, Nov. 7, 1853, MCUND, Louisiana Papers.

[14]Kinsella *et al.* to Propaganda, April 17 and May 18, 1855, MCUND, microfilm (Kenneally, *Documents,* II, items 900 and 906).

went to Rome in 1857, at which time the Pope permitted him to resign as Bishop of Chicago.[15]

If things had gone rather badly under Van de Velde and O'Regan, they ultimately took an even worse turn under James Duggan, the fourth occupant of the see, although his administration promised well in the first few years.[16] Another Irishman, Duggan had completed his theological preparation in Missouri and filled a variety of responsible posts in the archdiocese of St. Louis. He was familiar with the situation in Chicago, since he was a friend of O'Regan and had twice served temporarily as administrator of the diocese after the resignations of his two immediate predecessors. While still acting as administrator, Duggan conceived the idea of recovering control of St. Mary of the Lake in order to make it into a diocesan seminary. Within three months of his installation as Bishop in January, 1859, he put the Holy Cross fathers on notice that they would be required to vacate the University and all other places in the city where members of the community were working. There followed a series of interviews and letters which Father Edward F. Sorin, the superior of the Congregation of Holy Cross and founder of the University of Notre Dame, regarded as unjust and mortifying. As the deadline for Holy Cross evacuation approached, however, the quarrel was resolved through the good offices of Archbishop Francis P. Kenrick of Baltimore, who was passing through the region.[17]

[15]Koenig, "History," 24-26. For the appeal to Henni for seminarians, see Peter Leo Johnson, *Halcyon Days: Story of St. Francis Seminary, Milwaukee, 1856-1956* (Milwaukee, 1956), 48.

[16]Garraghan, *Chicago,* 180-218, for a general treatment of Duggan's administration; for Duggan's handling of St. Mary of the Lake, *ibid.,* 210-16.

[17]Edward F. Sorin, "Chronicles of Notre Dame du Lac, Ind., from the year 1841," Archives, UND, 361-94, reviews the involvement of the Holy Cross community with St. Mary of the Lake from 1852, when Van de Velde first approached Sorin on the subject, up through year 1859. See also Koenig, "History," 28-31, which is mostly based on Sorin's "Chronicles."

Duggan was far from being reconciled to leaving the Holy Cross community permanently in control of St. Mary of the Lake. After what Sorin interpreted as harassing tactics in 1860, the Bishop returned to the charge the following year and this time enforced the expulsion of all Holy Cross personnel from his diocese. Sorin was in default in payment of the annual fee specified in the lease of the University of St. Mary of the Lake (some $2,100), but he was no doubt correct in believing that this was not the real reason for Duggan's fixed resolve to drive the Holy Cross fathers away. More important was Duggan's determination to convert the University into a diocesan seminary, and his conviction, probably correct, that so long as Sorin's priests were in control of it, St. Mary of the Lake would remain more a feeder for Notre Dame than a significant institution in its own right.[18] The Bishop's action was high-handed, and Sorin considered it quite unfair, but it was by no means irrational. The sequel was to demonstrate, however, that Duggan could not continue on satisfactory terms with those in charge of St. Mary of the Lake, even when they were his own appointees and priests of his own diocese.

The person placed in charge was John McMullen, a Chicago priest and one of the first A.B.'s to graduate from St. Mary of the Lake. Sent by Bishop Van de Velde to Rome, McMullen received a doctoral degree in divinity from the Urban College of Propaganda in 1858. On his return to Chicago he did routine pastoral work until his appointment as president of the University in 1861. He found the place in need of improvement. According to his biographer, who was a close associate of McMullen, St. Mary of the Lake had become little more than "a select day-school for a few Catholic young men of the Holy Name Parish."[19] This state-

[18]Sorin, "Chronicles," 415-34.

[19]James J. McGovern, *The Life and Writings of the Right Reverend John McMullen, D.D., First Bishop of Davenport, Iowa,* (Chicago, 1888), 144.

ment, and the fact that much refurbishing was needed to fit the place for boarders, suggest that the Holy Cross community had done little to develop its potentialities.

Within six months of assuming the reins, McMullen had assembled a faculty that included four lay professors, and the student body had risen to a respectable 160, of whom thirty-three were boarders. The next year growing enrollments required the building of a new wing; this expansion made it possible, McMullen announced, to add law, medicine, and divinity to the offerings of St. Mary of the Lake. Only the latter was to be taught at the University, however, since the law lectures were to be delivered at the court house and medical work was provided through cooperation with Rush Medical College.[20]

The theological faculty consisted of McMullen himself; James J. McGovern, Chicago's first native vocation and a fellow student with McMullen in Rome; Thaddeus J. Butler, another Roman student; and a priest named John P. Roles, who also served as rector of the Cathedral. Later Patrick W. Riordan, the future Archbishop of San Francisco, who had studied in Rome and at the American College at Louvain, was added to the seminary faculty. To round out the offerings of the University, and to help recruit German-speaking prospects for the seminary, a special German "High School" was opened up. A final indication of McMullen's ambitions for the University was the launching in January, 1865, of *The Monthly,* a high-level magazine intended to fill the gap left in the field of serious Catholic literature by the demise of *Brownson's Quarterly Review,* which had just taken place.[21]

[20]*Ibid.,* 145-47. See also, Koenig, "History," 31-36.

[21]Koenig, "History," 36-37. The remarks of Richard Burtsell, the New York clerical diarist, give a picture of McMullen and suggest some of the problems faced by *The Monthly:* "Dr. McMullen of Chicago called to see me. He is a stern, self asserting man, very patronising, [who] thinks that by the Monthly which he has lately commenced to edit, he is going to fill up the gap of Catholic literature in this

It is not too surprising that this venture failed after twelve issues, since the life-expectancy of such a journal was bound to be uncertain. Quite inexplicable, however, was the closing down of the University itself, which followed hard on the heels of *The Monthly*'s termination. The older accounts are no help here, for they would have us believe that St. Mary of the Lake was brought down by its inability to pay "a floating debt of six thousand dollars."[22] This was not a heavy burden, nor was it new, as Msgr. Harry C. Koenig points out in his unpublished history of seminary education in Chicago. Hence we must infer that the closing of the University was the opening episode in the bitter controversy that arose between Bishop Duggan and a group of prominent priests, of whom McMullen was the leading figure. No details concerning the University's closing have been uncovered; but the Bishop's action was so drastic and apparently uncalled-for that it does not seem unreasonable to interpret it as an early symptom of the mental imbalance that would lead to Duggan's confinement for insanity three years later.[23]

Although the University was suppressed, the seminary associated with it continued for two more years. Its closing is part of the tragic story of Duggan's mental breakdown, certain aspects of which resemble a nightmarish repetition of Van de Velde's and O'Regan's battles with the priests of St. Mary of the Lake.[24] The crisis came in 1867-68, after

country. Dr. Keogh told him that the Monthly was a failure: that Chicago was not the place where it should originate; that not a single good article had yet appeared in it. Dr. McMullen gives out as a new idea, whatever appears new to himself." Entry for August 15, 1865, in *The Diary of Richard L. Burtsell, Priest of New York: The Early Years, 1865-1868*, edited by Nelson J. Callahan (New York, 1978), 126-27.

[22]McGovern, *Life of McMullen*, 159-60; Riordan, "St. Mary of the Lake," 153.

[23]Koenig, "History," 38-41, adopts this view, and it is accepted by Ellis, *Essays*, 162.

[24]The two paragraphs that follow are based primarily on James P. Gaffey's detailed study, "Patterns of Ecclesiastical Authority: The Problem of the Chicago Succession," *Church History* 42 (June, 1973), 257-70. Gaffey's *Citizen of No Mean City: Archbishop Patrick Riordan of San Francisco, 1841-1914* (Wilmington,

Duggan had gone to Europe on his doctor's advice. He had been suffering from a variety of physical and nervous afflictions, and was reported as saying that if his health did not improve he would resign the see. Hearing that no improvement had occurred, and concerned over his erratic decisions and the state of things in the diocese, McMullen, McGovern, and two other priests on the board of trustees of the seminary wrote to Rome urging that Duggan's resignation be accepted, and detailing the aberrations of his conduct in Chicago, expecially his neglect of the seminary.

Duggan's denial of these allegations and the fact that he was defended by his patron, Archbishop Peter R. Kenrick of St. Louis, placed Rome in perplexity, and the Bishop was permitted to return to his diocese in August, 1868. After an investigation by Kenrick which vindicated Duggan, the latter struck back at his critics by closing the seminary, suspending the four priests, and then expelling them from the diocese. This in turn prompted McMullen to undertake a journey to Rome to present the priests' case and to petition for Duggan's removal. The mission succeeded to the extent that Duggan was prevailed upon to receive back into the diocese the three surviving critics (one had died in December, 1868), and the Bishop's removal was soon effected by other means. Early in 1869, Duggan's mind gave way completely; he was placed under the care of the Sisters of Charity in St. Louis, "hopelessly gone mentally."

The public battle between the Bishop of Chicago and four of his leading priests was regarded by responsible churchmen as a national scandal, and its consequences lingered for years in the form of factional suspicions and clouded reputations.[25] From our viewpoint, however, the most signifi-

N.C., 1976), 22-34, covers the episode more succinctly. Thomas W. Spalding, *Martin John Spalding: American Churchman* (Washington, 1973), 265-69, 274-79, also provides much detail and a perspective different from Gaffey's.

[25]In January, 1869, Martin J. Spalding reported to Rome that the dissident Chicago priests were responsible for the greatest scandal in the public prints since the notorious Hogan schism in Philadelphia in the 1820s. Spalding, *Spalding,* 269.

cant result was that seminary education ceased to exist in Chicago for half a century.[26] One could hardly ask for a clearer illustration of the disastrous effects of weak and inconsistent episcopal leadership. Conversely, vigorous leadership in Milwaukee enabled that diocese to profit from Chicago's loss, for when St. Mary of the Lake Seminary was suppressed, its twenty-eight theological students were sent to St. Francis Seminary.[27] The story of this institution affords an instructive contrast to the case we have just reviewed, especially in the crucial area of leadership.

John M. Henni, first Bishop of Milwaukee, took possession of his see the same year Bishop Quarter did and, for the first decade of its history, his diocese gave no indication that it would be more effective in seminary education than its ecclesiastical neighbor. Bishop Henni started out with a few seminarians living in his residence, and this arrangement persisted with minor variations over a decade. A total of thirty-nine seminarians are recorded for the years 1845-55, virtually all of whom were European recruits almost ready for ordination, whose training consisted primarily in study of the English language and an orientation to the pastoral conditions they would encounter in Wisconsin.[28] Only with the erection in 1854-55 of a magnificent seminary named in honor of St. Francis de Sales and popularly known as the Salesianum did developments in Milwaukee diverge markedly from what was happening in Chicago.

Three factors combine in the success story of seminary education in Milwaukee. Continuity of leadership at the top was the first and indispensable condition. Henni was a

[26]A minor seminary was opened under Archbishop James E. Quigley in 1905; the major seminary of St. Mary of the Lake was re-established by Archbishop (later Cardinal) George Mundelein in 1921. Koenig, "History," 46, 87 ff.

[27]*Ibid.,* 40.

[28]Johnson, *Halcyon Days,* 46. This is a valuable history of St. Francis Seminary, but the material is confusingly presented.

Swiss-born priest seasoned by fifteen years of pastoral experience in Cincinnati before being elevated to the hierarchy. He was the same age as Quarter; but where Quarter's administration was cut short after only four years, Henni guided the destinies of the Catholic Church in Milwaukee for thirty-seven years. Before his death in 1881, he had seen Milwaukee made an archdiocese and been honored as its first metropolitan.[29] Simple episcopal longevity thus spared Milwaukee the woes that followed from frequent changes at the top and the ineffectiveness of Quarter's successors. Since leadership is crucial in the early stages of any undertaking, this factor alone goes far to explain why Milwaukee did so much better than Chicago in seminary education.

But continuity of episcopal leadership in itself was not enough to guarantee success in this area. Peter Richard Kenrick ruled St. Louis longer than Henni did Milwaukee, and was equally committed to seminaries, but he had to abandon the struggle to maintain his own diocesan system.[30] Two additional factors — ethnic feeling and vigorous second-level leadership — enter the Milwaukee story at this point. A quick sketch of the background and founding of the Salesianum will bring out the role played by these two factors.

There had been much talk in the 1840s, both in this country and in Europe, about the need to train priests to work among German-speaking immigrants. Short-lived attempts were made to establish mission seminaries at Muenster in Westphalia and Altoetting in Bavaria. The Redemptorists, a heavily German order active in the United States, were involved in the work at Altoetting, and a

[29]Peter Leo Johnson, *Crosier on the Frontier; A Life of John Martin Henni* (Madison, 1959), is a scholarly biography.

[30]Seminary development in St. Louis under Kenrick is difficult to unravel; for the most recent contributions, see John E. Rybolt, C.M., "Kenrick's First Seminary," *Missouri Historical Review* 71 (Jan., 1977), 139-55: and Rybolt, "The Carondelet Seminary," *ibid.* 74 (July, 1980), 391-413.

Redemptorist seminary also operated for a time in Baltimore.[31] Boniface Wimmer, O.S.B., was familiar with the work in Bavaria, and his aim in bringing Benedictine monks to Pennsylvania in 1846 was to establish a base to carry on missionary work among German Catholic immigrants. He aspired to set up a seminary for Germans in the United States, and in publicizing his plans he did not fail to appeal to the national sentiments of his German constituency.[32]

Bishop Henni himself had labored to set up a seminary for Germans before he left Cincinnati, and he very likely prompted Bishop John B. Purcell of that city to propose such a project to the prelates assembled at the Fourth Provincial Council of Baltimore in 1840. Nothing came of this idea, but Henni pursued the matter himself, and had bought property to house a seminary for Germans shortly before his removal from Cincinnati by episcopal appointment. Indeed, an ultranationalistic German charged that Henni was being banished to the wastes of Wisconsin by the Irish bishops because they wanted to frustrate his efforts to open a special seminary for Germans.[33] This groundless allegation was refuted by the *Wahrheits-Freund*— the German Catholic newspaper which Henni had founded — but when he took over his duties in Milwaukee so many other needs clamored for his attention that he had to put aside for the moment his plans for a German seminary.[34] As bishop, Henni recruited missionaries in Ireland as well as on the

[31]Johnson, *Halcyon Days,* 6-10, 15-24; Morris, *Seminary Movement,* 89-91.

[32]On Wimmer's career, see Jerome Oetgen, *An American Abbot: Boniface Wimmer, O.S.B., 1809-1887* (Latrobe, Pa., 1976). The promotional appeal he published in a German newspaper shortly before setting out for America is reproduced in John Tracy Ellis, *Documents of American Catholic History* (Milwaukee, 1956), 286-95.

[33]Johnson, *Halcyon Days,* 9, 13-15, 20-21; Johnson, *Crosier,* chaps. 4-5, for Henni's work in Ohio.

[34]*Wahrheits-Freund,* May 30, June 6, 1844.

Continent; of the twenty-nine priests he ordained in the first ten years of his episcopacy, sixteen were German-born and eleven Irish-born.[35] But in the early 1850s, the special needs of the Germans came in for renewed attention.

Prominent among the factors that made a German seminary seem needful then was the anti-Catholic agitation carried on by radical refugees from the German revolution of 1848. Milwaukee attracted a concentration of these Forty-Eighters, many of whom were bitterly anticlerical. A German-language Catholic paper, *Der Seebote,* was established in 1851 to counteract their polemics, and the hostility of the radicals made other defensive institutions, such as a seminary, seem vital.[36]

While the German Catholics felt they had to defend themselves against fellow Germans who were not Catholic, they were not prepared to identify themselves unreservedly with fellow Catholics who were not German. For that reason they were unenthusiastic about a school called St. Peter's Institute, a short-lived college-seminary affiliated with the cathedral parish and staffed by predominantly English-speaking faculty. This place remained open only a single year because, among other reasons, it did not offer a "sufficiently strong appeal to German-speaking folks."[37] As it passed off the scene, a new campaign was launched to build a special seminary for training German priests.

The leading promoter of this project, Joseph Salzmann, was the outstanding exemplar of the kind of energetic second-level leadership needed for success in seminary-planting. A young Austrian priest who came to Wisconsin in 1847, Salzmann held a doctoral degree in theology from Vienna. He had brought with him to Milwaukee two semi-

[35]Johnson, *Halcyon Days,* 46.

[36]See M. Hedwigis Overmoehle, F.S.P.A., "The Anti-Clerical Activities of the Forty-Eighters in Wisconsin, 1848-1860" (Ph.D. diss., St. Louis University, 1941).

[37]Johnson, *Halcyon Days,* 39-42.

narians whose preparation he completed informally while on his first parochial assignment. In addition to this work, Salzmann distinguished himself in the polemical battle with the anticlerical Forty-Eighters. It was he who founded the *Seebote,* and while on a money-raising tour on behalf of the paper he was struck by the shortage of priests to work among the German Catholic settlers in the country districts of Wisconsin and Iowa. On his return to Milwaukee, he won Bishop Henni's approval for a campaign to establish a seminary adequate to the pressing needs of the diocese.[38]

It is clear from the way he went about the task that Salzmann was thinking of a special German seminary. He launched the campaign by an appeal directed to all the German priests of the diocese who were assembled for a retreat just before the dedication of the new cathedral in July 1853. The English-speaking priests of the diocese were also in Milwaukee for the occasion, but their retreat was held separately and Salzmann made no effort to enlist their support. To the German priests, however, he painted an affecting picture of the pathetic situation of their immigrant countrymen, lacking the solace of the sacraments and exposed to the mockery of unbelievers who filled the columns of the radical German-language press with ridicule of their faith and calumny of their leaders. In these circumstances, the "quasi seminary" associated with St. Peter's Institute could hardly be deemed adequate, and Salzmann called upon his fellow German priests to support the campaign to build the sort of place that was really needed. They responded enthusiastically, pledging some $3,100 on the spot to inaugurate the fund-raising campaign.[39]

---

[38]*Ibid.,* 31, 51, 55-56; Joseph Rainer, *A Noble Priest; Joseph Salzmann, D.D., Founder of the Salesianum* (Milwaukee, 1903), 56 ff., 83-85. Salzmann was twenty-eight years of age when he came to Milwaukee.

[39]Johnson, *Halcyon Days,* 53-55; Rainer, *Salzmann,* 88-98. The expression "quasi-seminary" was applied to the arrangement at St. Peter's Institute by Father Michael Heiss, first rector of the Salesianum and Henni's successor as Archbishop of Milwaukee. See "Letters of the Late Archbishop Michael Heiss," *The Salesia-*

Two other German priests were associated with Salzmann's project; between the launching of the campaign and the formal opening of St. Francis Seminary two-and-a-half years later they followed a clear-cut division of labor. Salzmann's role was most crucial since, besides having initiated the whole enterprise, he was also the fund-raiser. His exertions in this field were impressive in scope and results. In addition to setting up the Salesian Society as a seminary-support association whose members pledged regular contributions, Salzmann canvassed throughout the state of Wisconsin and made a number of swings to more distant cities. In an 1854 tour of more than four months, for example, he travelled to Chicago, Cincinnati, Louisville, Memphis, and New Orleans. More than half the total collected on this trip (some $4,000) came from Cincinnati, the oldest western center of German Catholicism and a place where Bishop Henni was fondly remembered from his days as a devoted pastor. Before his death in December, 1873, Salzmann collected more than $100,000 for the Salesianum.[40]

Since Salzmann's "begging," as he called it, kept him on the go most of the time, preparatory work in Milwaukee fell on his two collaborators, Michael Heiss and Francis X. Paulhuber, both of whom were university-trained priests from Bavaira. They were matched opposites: Heiss, scholarly and cautious; Paulhuber, bold, dynamic, and abrasive. There was eventually a falling out that led to Paulhuber's withdrawal from the project, but in the autumn of 1853 he threw himself into the work and made the dirt fly. An attractive site for the seminary had been selected on the shore of Lake Michigan; here Paulhuber supervised the clearing and leveling of the land, the setting up of a brickyard, and other preliminaries of construction. Heiss's role,

num 10 (Jan., 1915), 24-25. See also M. Mileta Ludwig, F.S.P.A., *Right Hand Glove Uplifted: A Biography of Archbishop Michael Heiss* (New York, 1968), 202-03.

[40]Johnson, *Halcyon Days*, 57-58; Rainer, *Salzmann*, 103, 106 ff.

at this stage of operations, was confined to record-keeping and other clerical details.[41]

In the spring of 1854 the picture was complicated by the opening in Milwaukee (about four miles distant from the seminary site) of another "school for scientific studies," which Bishop Henni apparently intended to make use of as a temporary seminary until the Salesianum was completed. The new, in-town school was of the "mixed" college/seminary type; it was prepared to accept students as young as twelve years of age, but promised that instruction would be carried on with "true German thoroughness and solidity."[42]

The notice of this school's existence was issued in the names of Heiss and Paulhuber, but the former did not know that it was to appear and he was unenthusiastic about the project. He cooperated to please the Bishop, but complained in midsummer that the situation was "very burdensome." Although there were only twelve students, their preparation was so uneven that, while teaching theology to one, "with others I read Caesar and Xenophon, and with still others I decline *musa*."[43] When cholera struck a few weeks later, carrying off three of the students, the school was shut down. Heiss refused to acquiesce in its being reopened; he did, however, offer to take the three seminary prospects who were furthest along in their studies and continue their preparation for ordination at the seminary-site, where he was living with a group of Franciscan brothers. This was done, but for some reason it precipitated a split with Paulhuber. The latter drops out of the seminary story at this point, although it seems that he continued to teach the

[41]Johnson, *Halcyon Days,* 44, 56-57, 59-61; Rainer, *Salzmann,* 85; Ludwig, *Heiss,* 203-06; and *Seebote,* February 1, 1854.

[42]*Seebote,* May 10, 17, 1854; Johnson, *Halcyon Days,* 42-44; Rainer, *Salzmann,* 101-03.

[43]Rainer says that the appearance of the notice was a "great surprise" to Heiss — *Salzmann,* 102. For his comments on the students, see Ludwig, *Heiss,* 205-06.

younger students and at the same time embarked on the construction of an orphanage near the new seminary.[44]

After a comparatively quiet fall and winter, work on the new seminary got under way in earnest in the spring of 1855. Heiss reported in June that some eighty workmen were going at it "with full steam."[45] Although the four-and-a-half story structure was not completely ready for occupancy for another six months, the cornerstone-laying on July 15, 1855, was the most impressive public celebration connected with the establishment of St. Francis Seminary. The speeches given on this occasion included remarks touching on the sensitive matter of ethnicity. Father Heiss, who served as rector of the Salesianum until named Bishop of LaCrosse in 1868, was the principal orator. Addressing the crowd of four or five thousand in German, he alluded to the importance in religion of scholarship as well as faith. According to the report of the *Seebote,* which seemed to be paraphrasing his words, Heiss went on to say:[46]

> German faith and German scholarship are the two pillars upon which Christianity will continue the building of her world-structure. And if the young man who studies here is equipped with these, then the objection voiced from time to time that the seminary will become *Irish* collapses of its own weight. The reverend speaker was guided by this train of thought as he sought to refute the objections mentioned above, and as he likewise showed that our seminary, which is indeed the work of German Catholics exclusively, will become a nursery in which German thoroughness and German scholarship will be scrupulously fostered and sacredly preserved.

[44]Johnson, *Halcyon Days,* 45-46; Rainer, *Salzmann,* 102-03.

[45]Johnson, *Halcyon Days,* 64; "Letters of Heiss," *Salesianum* 10 (April, 1915), 21.

[46]*Seebote,* July 20, 1855, as reprinted in *Wahrheits-Freund,* Aug. 2, 1855.

Clearly, Heiss was concerned to reassure the German Catholics of Milwaukee that the Salesianum would not be permitted to slip under the domination of the Irish. But neither did he conceive it as a strictly German institution, for in a letter written less than a week after his dedicatory address he made the point that the seminary was to serve the entire diocese and not just the Germans. Here is how he explained the situation to officers of the Ludwig Mission Society in Bavaria:[47]

> Incidentally, we removed a misunderstanding which might have become a drawback for us. Until the present, as German priests, we appealed principally to the charitableness of the Germans, and figured that we might expect aid from the Irish and other nationalities after we had shown that the enterprise was not impossible. And so some thought that the seminary would become an institution solely for the Germans. When, however, we also accepted Irish youths, certain priests spread the suspicion that it was planned to displace the Germans gradually and make the seminary Irish. Both these suspicions were unfounded. We desire to establish a diocesan seminary, that is to say, one which is adequate for the needs of the diocese the faithful of which are chiefly German and Irish. The preacher, Father Riordan, explained this clearly, and I am informed that everybody was satisfied with the pronouncement that in the future seminary the German element would be always amply considered, but indeed without neglecting other nationalities.

Without impugning Heiss's sincerity, we may doubt that all misgivings were laid to rest by these assurances. Yet the

---

[47]Quoted in Johnson, *Halcyon Days*, 68; Ludwig, *Heiss*, 203-09, gives a slightly different version.

conclusion that it was impracticable to establish and maintain an exclusively German seminary had also been reached by another staunch representative of German Catholicism, Abbot Boniface Wimmer in Pennsylvania. He too had begun with the idea of ministering strictly to German Catholic immigrants; but experience had taught him that the Germans and Irish were so intermingled in the United States that churchmen had to be prepared to deal with both. Hence Wimmer informed the same benefactors in Munich, that training bi-lingual priests would constitute a boon to the American Church by bringing about an amalgamation of two nationalities whose quarrels had too often retarded the progress of faith.[48]

In the case of the Salesianum, things worked themselves out pretty much along the lines suggested by Heiss's letter. The place retained its markedly German character for many years. The Irish, who were not accustomed to being the minority, sometimes found the German flavor a little *too* strong, but it was a diocesan seminary from the start, serving the needs of all Catholics and accepting candidates of diverse ethnic backgrounds.[49] With the coming of seminarians from St. Louis, Chicago, and elsewhere, it soon became the leading establishment of its kind in the Middle West. It lost something of this regional pre-eminence in the twentieth century because strong diocesan seminaries had developed by that time in neighboring dioceses, including Chicago. Its ethnic distinctiveness likewise gradually faded over the years, but the names of Aloisius Muench and Albert Meyer — both former rectors who went on to become outstanding American churchmen in the immediate

[48]Henry A. Szarnicki, "The Episcopate of Michael O'Connor, First Bishop of Pittsburgh, 1843-1860" (Ph.D. diss., The Catholic University of America, 1971), 179-80.

[49]For allusion to tensions between Irish and Germans over St. Francis, see Johnson, *Crosier,* 133-34; M. Justille McDonald, F.S.P.A., *History of the Irish in Wisconsin in the Nineteenth Century* (Washington, 1954), 206-07.

pre-Vatican II era — attest to the continuing tradition of German Catholic leadership associated with St. Francis Seminary.

* * * * * *

This comparative review of seminary-planting in Chicago and Milwaukee only hints at what we might call the external history of both institutions, and leaves untouched internal aspects of their development such as curriculum, recruitment patterns of students, and so on. But sketchy as it is, the comparison suggests some general reflections about the beginnings of seminary education on the American frontier. These points may be worth listing for their possible heuristic usefulness to future students of the activity.

First, the comparison dramatizes the importance of energetic episcopal leadership exercised consistently over a number of years. Surely the single most important difference between the two places was that Bishop Henni lived long enough to permit the seminary situation to stabilize itself, whereas Bishop Quarter's untimely death removed a man who had made a fine beginning and ushered in an era of inconsistency and conflict between Quarter's successors and the seminary staff. Given the tendency in recent years to deprecate overemphasis on episcopal biography by writers of American Catholic history, this finding is of some importance. Bishops may have gotten more attention than they deserved in the past, but in correcting that distortion we must not lose sight of the vital leadership role they played — or failed to play — especially in the early days of Catholic development in a region, when everything had to be established from the ground up.

Secondly, there is the point about the key role of second-level leadership. Precisely because the early bishops had to do so much, they could not devote themselves entirely to any single task — even one as important as establishing a seminary, which virtually all of them regarded as crucial to assuring an adequate supply of priests. Hence they had to rely on subordinates, and finding, or retaining, the right kind was an uncertain affair. Quarter apparently got off to a good start in this matter; his successors, however, regarded the seminary priests as unsatisfactory, although it is not possible, at this distance in time, to say whether their view of the situation was justified. Bishop Henni was extraordinarily fortunate — and, to repeat, chance seems a major factor here — in finding a trio of priests whose combined talents were almost made to order for the task of establishing a seminary. The difficulties of establishing, or even staffing, a seminary prompted many bishops to try to persuade religious communities to take over the task of preparing their candidates for the priesthood. Sometimes this worked very well, but what were perceived as conflicts of interest often developed, of which the Holy Cross experience in Chicago can serve as an illustration, although an imperfect one, since the religious community in this case was not engaged in seminary education as such.

Finally, the Milwaukee story draws attention to the complexities of ethnicity as it interacts with religion in the history of American Catholicism. Ethnic feeling certainly figured prominently in the mix of factors that entered into the establishment of the Salesianum. Henni had a long record of concern for the establishment of a seminary to serve the needs of the German Catholics, and ethnic feeling was one of the animating forces in Salzmann's involvement in the project. The same combination of religious and ethnic sensibility may be assumed on the part of the German Catholic faithful who contributed to its realization, and on the part of Heiss and Paulhuber as well. Echoes of resentment at Irish predominance in the American Church are unmistakable in the accounts that have come down to us, and it is reasonable to infer that a species of German Catholic minority-consciousness helped to fuel the seminary campaign. The Germans were the predominant element in

Wisconsin, however, and that was one place where the seminary could be *theirs*. Yet precisely for this reason — because Wisconsin was theirs, and this pre-eminence had been confirmed by the appointment of a German-speaking bishop — the seminary could not be *exclusively* German. Having reached the position of pre-eminence, the Germans were responsible for the welfare and development of the *whole* Church in Wisconsin, and they could not therefore disregard the needs of coreligionists of other ethnic derivations.

In a way it was easier to be in the minority in a multi-ethnic Church. For a group in that situation, there was no strain between ethnic and religious feeling; the two meshed together and reinforced each other — or were not even thought of as being distinguishable. But when a group attained a position of predominance, the particularistic claims of nationality-feeling might move in a direction contrary to that required by religious responsibilities that transcended the boundaries of the ethnic group. If they were conscious of such a conflict's arising, there is no question that for Henni and Heiss and the other German Catholic leaders associated with the Salesianum, religious responsibilities took precedence over purely ethnic considerations. But the story of St. Francis Seminary affords us a new insight into the subtleties of ethnicity and religion. Deeper study of other such institutions throughout the whole span of American Catholic history would, I am convinced, enrich our understanding of many other aspects of the past besides seminary education as such.

The Holy See and the First "Independent Catholic Church" in the United States

Robert Trisco

The first attempt to form an "Independent Catholic Church" in the United States was made in 1819, when an Irish Franciscan, Richard Hayes, known more for his ardent nationalism than for humble deference to the Holy See, was invited to have himself consecrated bishop of South Carolina by the Jansenist bishop of Utrecht. This recourse to an extreme measure was the climax of the troubles instigated by two insubordinate Irish priests and by refractory Irish trustees in Charleston. The threatened schism did not come to pass, however, because the designated candidate of the dissidents, who was completely uninvolved and even surprised by their choice, promptly denounced the scheme to the Holy See. The Sacred Congregation de Propaganda Fide, which supervised the Church in the United States until 1908, was so alarmed by the imminent danger, nevertheless, that it recommended to the Pope

175

the erection of a new episcopal see at Charleston and the appointment of an Irish priest, John England, as the first bishop in 1820.[1]

When the first "Independent Catholic Church" in the United States actually came into existence toward the end of the nineteenth century, the candidate of the separatists was willing — indeed, he had abetted their movement — and the creation of a new diocese was not a possible solution of the problem. In certain other respects, however, parallels can be drawn, for in both cases the laity rebelled against their respective archbishops, who differed from them in national origins, wished to get rid of their lawful pastors and to choose their ecclesiastical leaders, and sought to control the church finances on their own authority. Again in the 1890s too, the Holy See endeavored first to prevent the secession and then to contain the harmful effects.

The first actual establishment of an "Independent Catholic Church" in the United States occurred in St. Hedwig's Parish of Chicago. There had been earlier instances of independent congregations in several American cities, but in none of those cases had the illegitimate pastor had himself consecrated a bishop. The main events in the drama that unfolded on the North Side of Chicago have been narrated and analyzed by several historians, but the source-materials preserved in Roman archives have not been utilized until now. The purpose of this essay, therefore, is to study the role played in this tragedy by the Holy See through its officials at different levels — the Apostolic Delegate in Washington, the Propaganda in Rome, the Papal Secretary of State in the Vatican, and Leo XIII himself.

St. Hedwig's Parish was founded in 1887 by Vincent Barzynski, C.R., the most prominent religious leader of the

---

[1]Peter Guilday, *The Life and Times of John England, First Bishop of Charleston (1786-1842)*, 2 vols. (New York, 1927), I, 262-90.

Poles in Chicago and the pastor of the original Polish parish of the city, St. Stanislaus Kostka. A division of his immense parish was necessitated by the rapid influx of immigrants who were fleeing the harsh economic conditions in their partitioned homeland. To accommodate those living farther than a mile from St. Stanislaus' church, Father Barzynski purchased a square block of land in the northwestern part of his territory for the new parochial buildings and lent additional money for the construction of a church combined with a school. At his request the Archbishop of Chicago, Patrick A. Feehan,[2] then appointed his younger brother, Joseph Barzynski, C.R., pastor of St. Hedwig's Parish and dedicated the building on December 4, 1888. In the following month the Sisters of the Holy Family of Nazareth opened the parochial school, and a rectory was built around 1890. From the original 230 families the parish grew to 1,300 families by 1894.[3]

St. Hedwig's was the ninth Polish parish to be established in the city and its suburbs, and they were all served either by Resurrectionists or by secular priests approved and recommended by the Resurrectionists. In 1871 the Superior General of the Congregation of the Resurrection, Jerome Kajsiewicz, had entered into an agreement with the administrator of the diocese of Chicago, Bishop Thomas Foley, by which the Resurrectionists were given the right to staff the Polish parishes in the diocese for the next ninety-nine years.[4] Since the young religious order, however, was unable

---

[2]On Feehan's relations with the Poles, see Charles Shanabruch, *Chicago's Catholics: The Evolution of an American Identity* (Notre Dame, Ind., 1981), 94-98.

[3]Harry C. Koenig (ed.), *A History of the Parishes of the Archdiocese of Chicago* (Chicago, 1980), I, 333-35; Joseph John Parot, *Polish Catholics in Chicago, 1850-1920: A Religious History* (De Kalb, Ill., 1981), 102-03; John Iwicki, C.R., *The First One Hundred Years. A Study of the Apostolate of the Congregation of the Resurrection in the United States, 1866-1966* (Rome, 1966), 79.

[4]Iwicki, *First One Hundred Years*, 57-58.

to provide enough men out of its own ranks to satisfy the ever increasing needs of the Polish immigrants, it had to seek the collaboration of secular or other regular priests. Since 1874 the Resurrectionists in Chicago had been guided by Vincent Barzynski, who espoused a policy of assimilation of the immigrants united with the retention of their language and customs. In the developing tension over the relative importance of Catholicism and nationalism as factors in the identity of the Polish-Americans, the Resurrectionists became the pillars of the religious or clerical party. The nationalists, who did not consider Catholicism essential to Polishness, were not the only ones, however, who resented the Resurrectionists' predominance. Many immigrants who had deposited money in the parish bank founded for their benefit by Barzynski in 1875 could not withdraw it by the late 1880s and early 1890s, when the bank was in debt to the extent of more than $400,000. It was $15,000 of the bank's funds that Barzynski had used to buy the lots for St. Hedwig's Parish. Loans of this kind almost equalled the bank's total assets. The distress of those who stood to lose their savings through the failure of the badly managed bank was aggravated by the panic of 1893 with its concomitant unemployment. The Resurrectionists in general and the Barzynski brothers in particular thus became the objects of widespread discontent in Chicago Polonia for several reasons. They did not lack means of self-defense, nevertheless, for in addition to their pastoral ministrations they could avail themselves of their publications. Father Barzynski founded the Polish Publishing Company in 1887; it immediately began to issue a weekly newspaper, *Wiara i Ojczyzna* (Faith and Fatherland), and continued it until 1899. In 1890 the company launched a daily, *Dziennik Chicagoski*, in the columns of which the Resurrectionists engaged in bitter combat with the anticlerical and liberal nationalists.[5]

[5]*Ibid.*, 203-08.

The one who exploited this sentiment and gathered support among the opponents of the Resurrectionists was a Polish priest, Anthony Kozlowski, who arrived in Chicago in 1894, when Father Joseph needed a new assistant to replace one who had been transferred to another parish. Father Vincent prevailed on his brother to accept the newcomer, and the pastor of St. Hedwig's reluctantly consented. His initial aversion to the energetic, handsome, charming, thirty-seven-year-old priest was soon confirmed as Kozlowski won the affection of many parishioners, especially of women, and by the same token alienated them from their overburdened, business-like, gruff, and sometimes moody pastor. The mounting antipathy between the two priests naturally became known to the parishioners, and some of the latter who were already hostile to the Barzynski brothers began to criticize the two Resurrectionists in personal and vicious ways. Finally, supporters of Kozlowski circulated among the parishioners a petition to the archbishop, which has not been found; it probably contained the same requests as their next petition, namely, that Father Joseph Barzynski be removed from the parish and that a priest who was not a member of a religious congregation be appointed in his place. It is not clear whether this petition was ever actually presented to the archbishop, but it is a fact that Feehan, having consulted the Barzynski brothers, dismissed Kozlowski, whom he presumably regarded as the instigator of the dissension in the parish, on December 18, 1894. On Sunday, December 30, Kozlowski's supporters held a "mass meeting" (as they later called it) in the school house after the High Mass; they sent a delegation to the pastor, inviting him to the meeting for the purpose of explaining, "if he knew, why Father Kozlowski had been removed."[6] According to

---

[6]Petition to Feehan, undated, typewritten, carbon copy, Archivio Segreto Vaticano (hereafter cited as ASV), Delegazione Apostolica, Stati Uniti, Diocesi, Chicago, folder 32a (hereafter reduced to "Chicago" with the folder number).

these critics, Barzynski "not only refused to attend the meeting but assailed the committee who waited on him with the most vile language and epithets, and refused to have any conference" with them. Thereupon a committee claiming to represent "the whole congregation" of St. Hedwig's church drew up a new petition and presented it to the archbishop, begging him to investigate "the charges and allegations" set forth therein to the end that he substitute "some secular priest" in place of their present pastor. They asserted that their intention was "not to cause trouble or foment strife, . . . but rather to avoid public scandal and disgrace" and to give the archbishop "the opportunity to hear in private or in an Ecclesiastical Court" their complaints and reasons. Then they set down their grievances against their pastor. (1) They said that he was not "in accord with his congregation, in sympathy or in work," and that he was "given to using very rude and improper language in his public sermons and when acting as a pastor before his people." (2) They asserted that in the confessional he used "the most terrible language," abused the penitents, called them "all manner of names," and spoke "in so loud a voice that everyone in the room" could hear him; consequently, people feared to go to confession to him lest he upbraid them. (3) They accused him of refusing to listen to any of their complaints, petitions, or suggestions. At this point inserted by hand in the typewritten petition was the sentence: "And he has never rendered or published any account of the debts or financial condition of the parish, although often requested so to do." (4) The petitioners characterized him as a man "of violent temper" which he exhibited in public, "in the Pulpit and out of it," and in consequence, they wrote, the people went to another priest. They added: "The people were all very much pleased with Father Anton Kozlowski, as they had been with two former priests, but that our present Pastor. . . as soon as he sees the people evince any inclination or love for another Priest. . . does everything he can to have that Priest

removed...." They affirmed that the members of the congregation all liked Father Kozlowski and gladly went to
their "duties" to him. They did not explicitly ask that the
younger priest be appointed their pastor, but they expressed
their "opinion" that relations between the pastor and the
people were so strained that the cause of the Church and of
religion was being harmed and that it was to the best interest
of the Church and of the spiritual welfare of the parish that
Barzynski be removed. They continued:

> And should your Grace deem such action necessary, we
> pray you, if possible, to send us a Priest who is not a
> member of any Religious Society, and suggest to your
> Grace that among the Polish people there is a great deal
> of politics in these Religious Societies; that it is the out-
> growth of old country politics, and that members of
> Religious Societies will always find factional and politi-
> cal differences with various members of their congrega-
> tion, and we pray to have our religion kept out of Politics
> as much as it possibly can be.

Perhaps the petitioners were alluding to Vincent Barzynski's dominant role in the organization of the Polish League,
the first national convention of which had been held in
Chicago the preceding May; although the League was to
promote the cause of Polish nationalism, it also upheld the
authority of the Church and provided a special place for
pastors of Polish parishes or their assistants. These guarantees of clerical influence caused disaffection among the
"progressive" nationalists, many of whom became less
inclined to follow their traditional religious leaders. In any
case, the committee concluded their address to Feehan with
the sentence: "Your petitioners in all humility submit this
petition, and hereby now promise faithfully to abide by the
decision of your Grace in this matter." In the light of their

future conduct, the sincerity of this engagement may be doubted.

On January 3, 1895, they presented a new argument to the archbishop. They alleged a discrepancy of $500 in the parish account ledger and urged that their pastor be removed for fiscal mismanagement. After investigating the charge, the chancery office cleared Joseph Barzynski of any wrongdoing.

Perceiving that they could not induce Feehan either to remove their pastor or to reinstate Kozlowski, the dissidents decided to appeal to a higher ecclesiastical authority. Since January, 1893, there had been an Apostolic Delegate in the United States, and the first holder of this office, Archbishop Francesco Satolli, had already settled one dispute among the Polish Catholics of Chicago, videlicet, the one concerning Holy Trinity church, which was the first parish to be broken off from St. Stanislaus Kostka's in 1874 and to be organized by nationalists opposed to the Resurrectionists' hegemony. The faction resisting Barzynski had nominated as their pastor a secular Polish priest who had come from New York, and when Bishop Foley refused to appoint him they appealed to the prefect of the Propaganda; after their third petition was submitted they received an affirmative reply. Accordingly, the nominee of the "Trinitarians" was installed in 1877, but when he later attempted to reciprocate the favor shown him by his supporters by having the name of the parish and his own name included in the deeds of the church property in addition to that of the Catholic Bishop of Chicago (the corporation sole), Foley's successor, Archbishop Feehan, suspended him in 1881, and when the censured pastor refused either to leave the parish or to change the deeds, the archbishop closed the church; this action provoked riots in the streets in front of both Holy Trinity and St. Stanislaus' churches. The refractory priest soon died of a stroke of apoplexy, and Father Barzynski persuaded the archbishop to restore control of Holy Trinity church to the pastor of St. Stanislaus. Unwilling to acquiesce in this decision, the Trinitarians staged another scene of disorder when the archbishop sent his vicar-general to them, and Feehan then closed Holy Trinity church again; this time it remained closed for eight years. In 1889 the Trinitarians obtained the reopening of the church by turning the deed over to the archbishop and by promising to accept a Resurrectionist as pastor. Upon learning, however, that their church was not recognized as that of an independent parish but rather only as a succursal church of St. Stanislaus Kostka, they rioted again in the streets. After they protested with wild demonstrations against the archbishop's further regulations, he ordered the church to be closed once more. At this juncture they appealed to the prefect of the Propaganda, asking that Holy Trinity be constituted a separate parish and that the pastor be independent of the Resurrectionist Congregation. Two representatives of Holy Trinity church even journeyed to Rome to present their grievances and petitions to the Propaganda in person. Since by this time the Pope had decided to establish the Apostolic Delegation in the United States, the Delegate was directed to investigate the matter. Hence, when he went to Chicago in June, 1893, to take part in ceremonies at the World's Columbian Exposition, he listened to all the parties concerned. With Archbishop Feehan's consent he received a delegation representing the church and granted their petition for the reopening of the church on condition that the title to the property be changed in conformity with archdiocesan requirements, that obedience to Archbishop Feehan be unqualified, and that the pastor appointed by him be accepted. Then Satolli offered Mass himself in Holy Trinity church and afterwards went to South Bend, Indiana, where he persuaded the Fathers of the Congregation of Holy Cross to take charge of the church. After a Polish priest of that congregation was named, the parish was at last canonically erected. Thus the Apostolic Delegate ended the controversy by compelling the Resurrectionists to relinquish authority over Holy Trinity church, the Foley-Kajsiewicz pact notwithstanding, and by having the parish made independent of St. Stanislaus Kostka's.[7] Although in this war the nationalists had defeated the clericals, some of them were dissatisfied with the cession of the parish property to the archbishop and became more attracted to "Independentism" as the only feasible ultimate redress of their grievances.

The sympathetic hearing that Archbishop Satolli had given to the spokesmen of the congregation of Holy Trinity church must have encouraged the dissidents of St. Hedwig's Parish to lay their case before him. Also proving that he was favorably disposed toward the Polish laity was his resolution of a protracted conflict between the Bishop of Detroit, John S. Foley, and the pastor of the independently organized congregation of the Sweetest Heart of Mary, Dominik Kolasiński, in February, 1894, on terms acceptable to the errant Poles and disagreeable to the ordinary.[8] Whether these precedents emboldened them or not, the dissidents of St. Hedwig's Parish, as has been seen, appealed to Satolli in January, 1895. A committee went to Washington that month and obtained an appointment. Apparently the Apostolic Delegate consulted Archbishop Feehan before giving them any answer, for the latter wrote to him on the 28th, saying (in his rudimentary Latin), "These are the facts," and proceeding to set forth the relations between the pastor,

[7]Parot, *Polish Catholics*, 51-52, 55-57, 63-65, 69-74, 80-83, 85-87, 91, 105; Koenig, *History of the Parishes*, I, 403-07; Iwicki, *First One Hundred Years*, 68-71; Victor Greene, *For God and Country: The Rise of Polish and Lithuanian Ethnic Consciousness in America, 1860-1910* (Madison, Wis., 1975), 74-83.

[8]See Lawrence D. Orton, *Polish Detroit and the Kolasiński Affair* (Detroit, 1981), 120-44; and Leslie Woodcock Tentler, "Who Is the Church? Conflict in a Polish Immigrant Parish in Late Nineteenth-Century Detroit," *Comparative Studies in Society and History* 25 (1983), 241-76, here 270-71. See also Eduard Adam Skendzel, "The Kolasiński Story. Priest-Protector of Detroit's Pioneer Polish Immigrants or Father of Polish American Church Independentism" (pamphlet; Grand Rapids, Mich., 1979).

Joseph Barzynski, and the *sacerdos vagus*, Anthony Kozlowski, to whom the pastor had given hospitality for a few months. "Now it seems," he continued, "that that priest spent his time mainly in stirring up some of the congregation against Father Barzynski with the intention of obtaining his place after the pastor would be removed." Feehan assured Satolli, however, that "by far the larger and better part" favored Barzynski. The archbishop testified that he had never heard anything against the Resurrectionist in the many years of his service in Chicago and that the priest was zealous and hard-working. Although the pastor would "absolutely not be removed," the superior of the Congregation of the Resurrection had sent to that church "another good priest" who would have a large share of the pastor's charge. Feehan predicted that the trouble-makers (*turbulenti*) would keep quiet.[9] As the sequel was to show, the archbishop was not gifted with prescience.

As soon as the Apostolic Delegate received Feehan's letter, he wrote to the parishioners of St. Hedwig's church as follows:

> I have carefully considered the matter you presented to me, and I find that the Most Rev. Archbishop seems already to have taken such steps as should satisfy all reasonable demands. As to his having removed another priest who had labored among you for some little time, that was done with sufficient reason, and a Bishop cannot be interfered with in the assigning of his priests to their fields of work in his diocese as his prudence advises. From all I learn Father Barzynski is a pious and zealous priest. Moreover, you have been sent another assistant who will have most of the work to do and you will undoubtedly find that the difficulties of which you com-

[9]Feehan to Satolli, Chicago, January 28, 1895, ASV, Chicago, folder 32a.

plained will be overcome. I pray you to submit in patience and charity as good Catholics should do to the guidance and government of your Archbishop.[10]

Upon receipt of this exhortation a committee of the parish called on the archbishop on February 1. By their own admission he received them "very kindly" and expressed his regret at the recent occurrences. According to their report of the interview, he promised to do everything in his power to satisfy the congregation but refused to reinstate Kozlowski. They said that he had advised them to apply to the Apostolic Delegate for the satisfaction of their desires. If Feehan actually gave them such advice, he was apparently confident that the Apostolic Delegate would again sustain his decision. In any case, "the committee and the whole Congregation" immediately petitioned the Apostolic Delegate anew for the substitution of Kozlowski in place of Joseph Barzynski. The only reason that they gave (in ungrammatical English betraying their haste) was that the whole congregation "liked Father Kozlowski ever-so-much and gladly went to their duties to him," because he instructed them properly and led them on the way to God; they especially needed his assistance at that time because the Easter season was approaching and they all wanted to go to confession, but they could not go to their pastor or any of his assistants because, they alleged:

> they all bear the most patent hatred against us and do not listen to the penetents at all; but instead they use the most terrible language towards the penetents and sends them away without any hope; why! they even refuse to babtise our children and when they do babtise a child they use a terrible language caling the child all manner of names. . . .

[10]Satolli to Parishioners of St. Hedwig's church, Washington, D.C., January 30, 1895, carbon copy, *ibid.*

They went on to plead piteously for the recall of their beloved Kozlowski:

> Father Kozlowski was and is a good priest yes indeed he was our leader in him we have found a good shepherd in him we have found a true Minister of God and in him we have laid confidence but nevertheless he has been taken away from us and through such a deed our hope and our joy has faided away; and will not return until Rev. Antoni Kozlowski is returned to us. There fore we aply to your grace to send to us our sheapard that we may again rejoice and be happy; why! even the school children fall on their knees and are beging of your grace that Rev. Father Kozlowski may return.

They besought the papal representative to let them know within one week whether he would send Kozlowski to their parish in order that they might be able to keep peace among the parishioners. They foresaw that unless their favorite priest returned in a short time or Satolli answered, there would be renewed disorder and their church would be closed.[11]

The committee was obviously aware of the rising anger of the congregation. The very next morning, in fact, at the Sunday Mass, some of the people interrupted Father Barzynski while he was preaching, and when the police tried to prevent a disturbance of the peace, bedlam ensued. That evening a number of Kozlowski's supporters gathered outside St. Hedwig's rectory, shouting taunts and threats of death to Father Barzynski. A contingent of police was sent from the local station to guard the pastor, but he preferred to withdraw to his brother's rectory at St. Stanislaus Kostka's, leaving his two assistants in charge. In desperation the committee wired Satolli:

[11]Peter P. Bloch, Secretary, to Satolli, Chicago, February 2, 1895, *ibid.* The spelling errors are in the original.

> We are in danger. We need your assistance at once. The priests Barzynskis and their helpers teach us politics & storys in church. The parishioners have stopped such nonsense in church. The city police threatened to shoot in church. We beg of your Grace to assist us.[12]

On the next day, Monday, the committee expanded their urgent petition to the Apostolic Delegate through their secretary. They tried to explain the disorder of the previous morning by blaming their clergy:

> The Resurrection priests talk to us in Church as though it was a political meeting. Rev. Joseph Barzynski and his assistant priests teach us politics and storys in church, and they tryed to do so last sunday they have criticised the Russian polish people calling them all manner of names. They were also telling us lot of storys about the old-country. But the parish did not want to listen to such noncence, so they told the priest to stop such talk, because they think that the Catholic church is a house of God. And not a place to speak politics but there were several City police officers which Barzynski always keeps on hand. And they with their revolvers and clubs and by shouting made more disturbance, and the priest was not allowed to finish his political speech in church.

They then entreated Satolli again to send Kozlowski to them and gave him the priest's current address in Mt. Pleasant, Pennsylvania. They also declared that they did not want any of the Resurrectionists in their parish, and promised that if Kozlowski would be sent to them without delay, everything would be quiet again. They concluded the letter with an invocation that foreshadowed the name of their

---

[12]Committee and Parishioners of St. Hedwig's church to Satolli, Chicago, February 3, 1895, telegram, *ibid.*

future schismatic church: "We beg of your Grace in the name of God and All-Saints please help us this week."[13]

Meanwhile Satolli had learned from the newspapers about the disturbance of the religious service and wrote to Feehan in Latin, deploring the scandals and excesses which had taken place in St. Hedwig's church the preceding day. "Certainly those Poles who so violently disturbed the sacred temple and the sacred functions are to be severely rebuked," he said and recounted his previous dealings with them. He also asked Feehan, however, to let him know what plans he had made to prevent a recurrence of such violent outbreaks. "And if Your Excellency should also desire my co-operation to restore peace and tranquility, I would gladly comply with your wish."[14]

In reply Archbishop Feehan informed Satolli that Joseph Barzynski had resigned the pastorate of St. Hedwig's Parish of his own accord and had completely left the church. Two priests, both Resurrectionists, who had previously had nothing to do with that congregation, had taken over his responsibilities. Remarking that some of the malcontents wanted to have Kozlowski as their pastor, Feehan wrote that that priest had no connection with the Archdiocese of Chicago, and he forwarded to Satolli two documents pertaining to him.[15]

---

[13]Bloch to Satolli, Chicago, February 4, 1895, *ibid.*

[14]Satolli to Feehan, n.d. (February 4, 1895), draft, *ibid.*

[15]Feehan to Satolli, Chicago, February 7, 1895, Latin. *ibid.* One of the two documents (which were actually enclosed with Feehan's letter of February 8) was a letter from John Machnikowski, pastor of St. Stanislaus Kostka's church in Shamokin, Pennsylvania, dated February 2, 1894 (should be 1895) and translated into English from the original Polish; the addressee is an unnamed priest. The writer said that he was sorry to hear of Kozlowski's conduct toward Joseph Barzynski, especially because Machnikowski had procured "good testimonial letters" for him from his bishop. He continued: "But what was I to do? This worthless man, whom I received into my house out of christian charity, immediately began to tell falsehoods about myself. He flattered the women exceedingly .... When he was residing with me, Rev. A. Koslowski [*sic*] walked from house to house, and devoted his time to telling different stories about me. During his stay at my house, he pretended to be sick. I believed it, for some time, to be true that he

Whether or not Satolli waited for this reply, he decided on February 8 to reprimand and admonish the unruly parishoners of St. Hedwig's himself. Addressing his letter to the secretary of the committee, he wrote:

> I am grieved more than I can tell you at the scandalous performance which took place in the church of St. Hedwig last Sunday. It is too bad that your people cannot control themselves sufficiently at least to respect the sanctity of the House of God, and the celebration of the Divine Mysteries. You must understand that the government of the diocese and the removing or changing of pastors and other priests belongs to the Bishop. If the parishioners have any valid reason for objecting to the priests assigned to them they should present those reasons to the Bishop and he is bound to give them his careful consideration. When he has done so, the people are bound if they wish to remain good Catholics, to abide by his decision. I beg you and the others who are discontented with the priests you now have to be patient, and assure you that proper consideration will be given to the matter and such provision made as will secure peace and harmony. It is to be hoped that there will never be a repetition of the scandal of last Sunday.[16]

was really sick, but I found that the sickness came from whiskey taken before breakfast. He was accustomed to take several glasses. Many times he did not return home until 12 oclock, and even after 12 oclock and 1 oclock at night. He never studied anything. When I politely advised him to study the tract 'De Poenitentia,' he replied that he had studied theology seven years." Machnikowski forwarded "the original letter written by the Archbishop of Taranto," Pietro Jorio, who had ordained Kozlowski, in order to show what studies the young priest had pursued. This Latin letter, presumably addressed to Machnikowski and undated, was Feehan's other enclosure. Archbishop Jorio asserted that Kozlowski ought to continue his studies in order to be fit for his ministry, and he asked the recipient to instruct him; otherwise neither the Italian archbishop's nor the Pennsylvanian pastor's conscience would be safe. "Tardo ingenio praeditus, latino sermone vix vix instructus non potuit scientias sacras, ut oportet, apprendere [*sic*]. . . ." *Ibid.*

[16]Satolli to Bloch, [Washington, D.C.], February 8, 1895, carbon copy, *ibid.*

Satolli sent this letter to Feehan and asked him to convey it to the committee.

The Apostolic Delegate did not issue his rebuke early enough to prevent another grave incident at St. Hedwig's church. On the same morning as he wrote to the secretary of the committee, February 8, at seven o'clock, several hundred people, led by women and armed with household implements, stormed the rectory, broke down the doors, and threatened the lives of those inside, shouting, "Turn the priest over! Lynch him!" Two police officers arrived and tried to protect the priests and others, but they were themselves assaulted by the irate mob; a woman threw a handful of ground red pepper into the eyes of one officer, temporarily blinding him, and the other was severely injured by being struck on the head with a hammer. The first officer, having recovered his sight, had to defend himself at gunpoint when the crowd attacked him with bricks and stones. As soon as news of the riot reached the local police station, the captain rushed to the scene with as many men as he could muster, but even these were not sufficient to restore order. A third policeman fell to the ground blinded with pepper, although he succeeded in arresting two of the women who were leading the charge. After two more patrol wagons came from other stations, the police dispersed the mob, and several patrolmen remained behind to guard the church and rectory.[17]

That same day the archbishop reported to Satolli that Kozlowski had recently returned to Chicago and was busy among the people of St. Hedwig's, stirring them up and inciting them to riot. He added, "I think that in order to prevent disturbance (*tumultum*) and perhaps violence, it is prudent and necessary to close that church for a short

---

[17]*Chicago Tribune*, February 9, 1895, quoted by Iwicki, *First One Hundred Years*, 85-86. On the significance of the role played by women in such riots, see Tentler, "Who Is the Church?" 254-55, 274-76.

time."[18] In fact, he immediately notified the local superior of the Resurrectionists of his decision prohibiting religious services of any kind in the church "for the present time."

While these shocking events were being publicized in the newspapers not only in Chicago but also elsewhere in the country, the Apostolic Delegate sought ampler information about Kozlowski. He asked the Bishop of Harrisburg, Thomas McGovern, in whose diocese the Polish priest had previously labored (at St. Stanislaus Kostka's church in Shamokin), whether he was ordained for that diocese or belonged to another and how he had conducted himself while living in that diocese.[19] McGovern replied that Kozlowski had been in his diocese at the beginning of the preceding year, saying that he had been ordained in Italy and had worked for the Church in Taranto; he had served the parish in Shamokin for several months as an assistant. Without the pastor's advice he established the Third Order of St. Francis among the women of the parish and laid down rules for them, one of which was that the women should practice continence toward their husbands a few days each week; the husbands refused to become parties to these conditions in silence and made an outcry. In other ways too he had behaved strangely. From then on, the bishop denied him hospitality, and Kozlowski went on to Pittsburgh.[20] He never returned to the diocese of Harrisburg.

In spite of the bloody riot that had occurred on February 8, Archbishop Feehan soon had reason to expect a pacification. When he thanked Satolli for the letter of February 8 which he had personally handed to the secretary of the

[18]Feehan to Satolli, Chicago, February 8, 1895, Latin, ASV, Chicago, folder 32a; Iwicki, *First One Hundred Years*, 86-87.

[19]Satolli to McGovern, [Washington, D.C.], February 12, 1895, Latin, draft, ASV, Chicago, folder 32a.

[20]McGovern to Satolli, Harrisburg, February 13, 1895; same to same, Harrisburg, February 14, 1895, Latin, *ibid.*

committee, Peter Bloch, he expressed hope that it would have a very good effect. He reported that on the preceding Sunday (February 10) the dissident faction at St. Hedwig's intended to install Kozlowski in the church by force and in a solemn manner, but they failed because the church was closed and guarded by the police. In the following week they petitioned the City Council to empower them to manage and administer all the property of the church and congregation independently of any other authority, but their petition was immediately rejected. Feehan deemed it prudent to keep the church closed for a short time until they would think better of their position.[21] The archbishop was clearly looking forward to an amicable termination of the dispute.

On the very next day he announced to the Apostolic Delegate with pleasure that "that Polish difficulty of St. Hedwig" appeared to be ended. Some of the faction had just called on him, professing repentance and promising obedience for the future. In return, Feehan promised to reopen the church at once and to give them new and, insofar as he could, good priests; then the past would be entirely forgotten.[22]

It was really more to Satolli's credit than to Feehan's that a reconciliation became possible. Peter Bloch, "the leader of the recalcitrant party" (as a newspaper identified him), and some other members of the committee went to Washington for the second time to seek the intervention of the Apostolic Delegate. When they returned to Chicago, they called a mass meeting, but only a few persons were present. Bloch reported that they had had a brief interview with Satolli on Saturday morning (February 16). In Bloch's words, the Apostolic Delegate said "that he had left the task of settling our troubles to Archbishop Feehan and that he would not interfere for the present." He promised to go to Chicago and

[21] Feehan to Satolli, Chicago, February 13, 1895, Latin, *ibid.*
[22] Feehan to Satolli, Chicago, February 14, 1895, Latin, *ibid.*

look into them, however, if they were not settled by May. Afterwards the committee discussed the matter at greater length with Satolli's secretary (presumably Frederick Z. Rooker), who told them that they could do nothing better than become reconciled to whatever priest the archbishop might choose to send them. Bloch replied that if arrangements were not made to suit them, they would bring the matter into the courts. At the meeting held in Chicago on February 18, Bloch said that a letter was being prepared containing charges against the pastor of St. Hedwig's church and after being signed by the committee would be forwarded to Archbishop Satolli on the following evening; according to the reporter, Bloch "intimated that the document would be sensational."[23] No such letter has been found; perhaps none was ever sent because the dissidents were confident that a diocesan priest, maybe even their own nominee, would be appointed pastor.

On Sunday, February 24, at Archbishop Feehan's behest, the chancellor of the archdiocese, Peter J. Muldoon, went to St. Hedwig's church to announce the archbishop's decision. It was not yet publicly known that Feehan, upon the recommendation of Vincent Barzynski, had appointed a new pastor and a new assistant who were both Resurrectionists. Muldoon narrated the episode to Satolli's secretary, Dr. Rooker, the next day in this way:

> As soon as we reached the parish house, the committee of
> the disaffected met us and made their demand that no
> Polish priest of the C.R. should be placed over them. I
> refused to deal with them. I then went to the church &
> asked the people as good Catholics to disperse & as good
> citizens to disperse, and all passed out quietly. I might
> have named the pastor but I feared what might take place

[23]*Chicago Herald*, February 19, 1895.

if some of the evil minded objected — as the church was packed with men, women & children. Prudence dictated to send them home & close the church. The great bulk of the congregation are fervent & peacable [*sic*].

Muldoon admitted:

...We are all much disappointed at the action of the disaffected because we were certain that the affair was peacably [*sic*] settled — and that without the sacrifice of any principle.

Why the committee changed we do not know! They solemnly promised the Archbishop last week that they would gladly accept any priest except Rev. Joseph Barzynski, C.R. Two young and able Polish priests were selected; one who has been here only two years, and another called from a college in Canada. We hoped that these would give satisfaction, but in vain.

The chancellor wanted the Apostolic Delegation to be informed in case the dissidents should send another embassy to Satolli. He acknowledged the disagreeableness of the situation, for the newspapers were publishing "many garbled accounts" and the daily expense for the salaries and meals of the constables guarding the property was large.[24]

When ten days passed without further incidents, Satolli seems to have concluded that the crisis had been surmounted. At least he reported to the prefect of the Propaganda, Cardinal Mieczyslaw Ledóchowski (the former Archbishop of Gniezno and Poznań), who might have been presumed to be particularly interested in the welfare of his fellow Poles in the United States, that through the efforts of Archbishop Feehan, whom he had assisted by his counsel,

---

[24]Muldoon to Rooker, Chicago, February 25, 1895, ASV. Chicago, folder 32a. Parot, *Polish Catholics*, 116, has given yet another garbled version of his own.

the difficulties in St. Hedwig's church had been resolved. To eliminate the partisan feelings, the priests who had been attached to that church had been removed and others substituted, he wrote, and he hoped that peace had been effectively re-established through that action of the archbishop, who had thanked him for his help in this affair.[25] Within a week the Apostolic Delegate was to rue this premature reassurance of his Roman superiors.

Just as Muldoon had expressed the views of Archbishop Feehan in his letter, so in his reply Rooker spoke for the Apostolic Delegate. He did not write, however, until new developments caused greater anxiety. On March 14 the parishioners of St. Hedwig's church wired Archbishop Satolli that on February 24 Father Muldoon had "said to the Congregation before the altar that if the Congregation was not satisfied with Father Barzynski from Noble Street the church would be closed until Archbishop Feehan opened it himself." They asserted that "last Monday" (March 11) a delegation of the parishioners took a letter to the archbishop, but he refused it and "would have nothing to say until Satolli came himself and opened the church." They informed the Apostolic Delegate that that morning approximately fifteen constables and some officers "with a priest from Barzynski" came and opened the church without the key. They insisted that Satolli tell them whether he would "come and settle this affair," and they warned that "any other but a secular priest" would be in danger of his life. Not having received an answer by the end of the day, they wired Satolli again: "Please advise regarding telegram this morning what would you have us do. Answer quick."[26]

[25]Satolli to Ledóchowski, Washington, D.C., March 8, 1895, Italian, Archives of the Sacred Congregation de Propaganda Fide (hereafter cited as APF), N.S., Vol. 57 (1895), fol. 45v, Rub. 13 (Prot. 12156).

[26]Parishioners of St. Hedwig to Satolli, Chicago, March 14, 1895, telegram. Delegates of St. Hedwig's Parish to same, Chicago, March 14, 1895, telegram, ASV, Chicago, folder 32a.

This time the Apostolic Delegate did reply at once, but his advice was not what his petitioners wished to hear: "Act like good Christians and Catholics and submit to the Archbishop who is your lawful superior, and who knows the needs of your parish."[27]

The Apostolic Delegate's stern admonition arrived too late to deter the dissidents from attempting anew to regain possession of St. Hedwig's church by force. On March 15 shortly after dawn approximately 200 of them marched four abreast on the sacred edifice and occupied it, subduing the policemen on duty. When more police arrived, however, the attackers surrendered; although some threw rocks outside the church, no one was injured. Several of the trespassers were arrested, and again the newspapers carried the scandalous reports far and wide. The church was closed again.

Aroused by these latest events, Rooker wrote to Muldoon, but the communication was really going from Satolli to Feehan:

> Mgr. Satolli is surprised and pained to know that the arrangement attempted by the Most Rev. Archbishop was so unsuccessful in terminating the affair. He thought from the Archbishop's letter that a complete settlement had been made, and a perfect and amicable understanding had been reached. Now he learns that the remedy offered by the Archbishop was altogether ineffectual. That some at least of the complaints of the people against the Rev. Barzynski were reasonable can hardly be doubted. It seems certain that he was unreasonably harsh in his treatment of the people, and that his manner of addressing them was to say the least unecclesiastical. It appears too that he had obstinately refused to give any

---

[27]Satolli to Committee St. Hedwig Parish, Washington, D.C., March 15, 1895, telegram, copy, *ibid.*

account of his administration of the temporalities of the Church, and since the money comes from the people, it is perfectly just that they should know what is done with it. There was consequently some ground for their desire that he should be removed and another pastor appointed in his place. For some reason they seem to have taken a serious dislike to the Resurrectionists in general. It is of little avail to enquire too strictly whether this dislike is a reasonable one or not. Considering the character of the Poles, it is plain that it is an insuperable one. It has always been the custom of the Church to take into account the likes and dislikes of the people in giving them pastors, when it was possible to do so. If it were absolutely impossible to find them any other priest than one belonging to an order or a congregation, then of course they would have to be patient and accept the best that the Ordinary could do for them. But when their request to have a secular priest assigned to them can just as well be granted as not, it seems unwise to insist on their taking one they do not want at the cost of exciting such scandalous proceedings as have now been going on in Chicago for so long a time. When Mgr. Satolli heard that other priests had been sent them he thought that these were seculars and blamed severely the people for not submitting to the arrangement made by the Archbishop. It seems that it would have been much better to have yielded a point and given them seculars, rather than to have had this continuance of the trouble. It is now a question whether the present violent state of things is to go on at the risk of great injury to religion and of the loss of so many souls, or whether an effort shall be made by giving them a secular priest to remove the grave scandal which exists. Mgr. Satolli has in everything given his unqualified support to the Archbishop, and yesterday wired them to act like good Catholics and submit to their lawful superior. He is very anxious, however, that the matter should be adjusted.[28]

No doubt, he was also chagrined by this reverse which made his complacent report of the preceding week to the Propaganda now sound hollow.

This forthright criticism of the archdiocesan authorities' policy naturally called forth a prompt and frank response. Muldoon wrote back to Rooker on the very day on which he received his letter:

> ...We also are pained and surprised that the Polish affair has not been settled. We have used every kind considerate and just means within our power to induce the people to submit but in vain thus far. The Archbishop wrote the Most Rev. Apostolic Delegate after he had a long and plain talk with the committee, and relying upon their word of submission he sent the note concerning the scttlement. He was too sanguine for they broke all their pledges, before Sunday came. You will say, "well why not give them a secular priest and thus settle the contention?" There is the real point *at present*. At first they only required the removal of Father Joseph Barzynski, but when this was granted they advanced a step and took as their motto "No Resurrectionist." Why then has the Archbishop held out against this request? For the sole reason that for the government of this most complex and cosmopolitan Diocese, the request involved a principle that he could not cede without doing almost irreparable damage to local church discipline. When they advanced that proposition they brought into the matter a principle that affected all the foreign congregations of the city, but especially those governed by religious orders. As proof of this the Polish pastors have come individually and beseeched us not to yield this point, for if yielded, they

[28]Rooker to Muldoon, [Washington, D.C.], March 16, 1895, carbon copy, *ibid.*

might as well give up endeavoring to rule a difficult people, for it meant that the congregation could virtually choose its own pastors, or could object to any religious order that might become distasteful to them. This same principle might if granted be applied by Germans and Bohemians when dissatisfied with some temporary pastor — and the Rt. Rev. P. N. Yeager, O.S.B., of St. Procopius Parish could tell you of the difficulty in guiding his parish unless the strictest (although kind) government were employed. We feel assured that if this point be ceded them at present it will not be years before the same request be made at the mother church of St. Stanislaus, for if the pastor offend or displease (and even the best may) any portion of the congregation, they would follow the example of St. Hedwig and ask for the removal of the entire order from the parish. This of course would be a sad calamity for the Diocese and for the Poles. No body of men has done such hard and constant labor for their countrymen as this order from the very beginning of the Polish colonization of the city, and we feel that no body of men could work more successfully than they have done. Until late days they have been entirely free from any contentions.

Dear Dr. Rooker, I ask you to consider Chicago and its peculiarities. No city in the world like it. Its foreign (non-English speaking) population (Catholic) amounts to 250,000. They are here in America leading in great part the same life as in Europe. In free America, and enjoying its benefits without at times fully understanding the full meaning of the term. Of this mass, the Poles are, at least 100,000. Not from the same parts and bringing with them consequently not only Polish customs but superadded the customs of the portion of the old country from which they hailed. A German Pole has an influence with his set too; hence often not fully understanding and often through ignorance, they follow blindly the leadership of a few deciding ones. As the Archbishop often says, "if any one told me before coming to Chicago the many sides to the Polish character, and the many perplexities in dealing with them I would not credit it," but this is absolutely true. They come to you kissing your hand but if you refuse their requests they go from you muttering maledictions.

We have quite a number of American Polish priests and several Poles who have been educated in America, and they all will tell you without qualification that the Poles must be governed with a strong, firm hand, gloved in velvet. Every just concession should most surely be granted them, but these priests repeat that in questions of discipline, no concessions should be made, for if they gain what they term a victory they are looking forward for another point. If this present point of contention should be ceded, we are confident that they will demand strict church committees in the future. Such committees as render the priest no longer a pastor but a servant, in fact they have already intimated their intentions, and you are aware of the great scandal and abuse that once arose from such intermeddling in New York and Penn., a half a century ago. Granted that Father Barzynski did not give them annual statements, and this in fact is the worst that could be proved against him, it is a mistake that may be easily corrected. But although he gave them no report, he sent his annual statement to the Chancery which evidences a large amount of work and a just use of the funds.

With all due humility I must most earnestly say that we are deeply pained and humiliated at the actions of the people of St. Hedwig but still I feel that every due concession has been made the disaffected, and that if the affair be settled on the lines given them by the Archbishop it will be the cause of easy future government, and will give ease and confidence to every Polish pastor, but if on the contrary their present contention be granted, I do fear for the future.

I know the Archbishop is deeply grateful to Most Rev. Francis Satolli, the Apostolic Delegate, for his salutary advice, and now I am pleased to state in conclusion that in all probability the affair will be settled within the next few days. After receiving the last dispatch from Archbishop Satolli, they felt they must obey, and they waited upon Father Sedlacek [*sic*] C.R. and told him that if he assured them that he would not be ruled by the pastor of St. Stanislaus, but would act only on the advice of Archbishop Feehan that they would receive him. Father Sedlacek C.R. told them it would be so, and we hope that the Church will be peacably [*sic*] opened next Sunday.

Muldoon trusted that he would be able to announce a satisfactory conclusion of these troubles "within a short time."[29] This unbounded and unfounded confidence shows how badly he and his superior underestimated the tenacity of their adversaries.

On the same day as the chancellor sent this *plaidoyer* to Washington, the parishioners of St. Hedwig's again wired Satolli, begging him "in the name of God" to send them Father Kozlowski as soon as possible. Undoubtedly they understood that the Apostolic Delegate was the only one capable of satisfying their demands who might be moved by their entreaties. They pleaded, "We have suffered almost too much and cant stand it much longer." Complying with their request for a prompt answer, Satolli wired back the same day: "Kozlowski in person has declared to me that he will not accept your parish even if it were offered him. It is your duty as Catholics to obey your Archbishop."[30] Regardless of his personal opinion of Feehan's intransigence, the Apos-

[29]Muldoon to Rooker, Chicago, March 19, 1895, *ibid.*

[30]Parishioners of St. Hedwig's to Satolli, Chicago, March 19, 1895, telegram; Satolli to Committee St. Hedwig's church, Washington, D.C., March 19, 1895, telegram, copy, *ibid.*

tolic Delegate did not deviate from his rule of not interposing between the shepherd of a diocese and his wayward sheep.

The protesting parishioners, not surprisingly, were unwilling to heed his exhortation. Their rejoinder was yet another telegram, sent the next day. Once again they "most earnestly" begged his Grace to send Kozlowski to them. They expressed their conviction that he would accept their parish if the Apostolic Delegate and Archbishop Feehan would permit him to come to them. They reiterated their supplication: "Please appoint him our pastor as soon as possible; we will be obedient to Archbishop Feehan and to you."[31] This time apparently Satolli thought it useless to reply.

As Satolli hinted to the parishioners of St. Hedwig's, he had had direct contact with the subject of all this contention. Anthony Kozlowski had called on him on March 15 and had presented to him a long memorial, written in sometimes imperfect but always intelligible Italian and in a respectful tone. The Polish priest set forth "the facts" which had brought about his departure from Chicago and all the disturbances that had occurred in St. Hedwig's Parish as well as the disagreements between himself and Joseph Barzynski. He wrote that after coming to Chicago toward the end of April, 1894, he had found a place as assistant to that pastor. He claimed that he had discharged his duties scrupulously and that the most perfect harmony had reigned between him and his pastor until early December. Then one evening after being called to a sick person at nine o'clock, he stopped on his way back in a pharmacy to buy some medicine for himself and engaged in conversation there for a while. He returned home toward eleven o'clock. Father

[31] Parishioners of St. Hedwig's to Satolli, Chicago, March 20, 1895, telegram, *ibid.*

Barzynski then began to scold him for coming home so late and called him a night tramp (*vagabondo notturno*). The next morning Kozlowski begged his pardon, but Barzynski replied by forbidding him to say Mass and then dismissed him. Kozlowski then went to Holy Trinity church, where he celebrated Mass and heard confessions almost the whole day long because the Forty Hours' Devotion was being observed there. When he later returned to St. Hedwig's rectory to inquire whether Barzynski had gotten his papers back from the archbishop, the pastor told him that he wished him to remain in his place as before, and he remained. But when the parishioners heard of the quarrel, they began to collect signatures for a petition that he should remain in their parish. He averred that they signed this petition without his knowledge and that if he had known that such things were happening, he would never have said a word to anyone. At the end of December, when Barzynski found out what was going on, he really did dismiss Kozlowski and told him that it would be better for both of them if Kozlowski were to leave Chicago. He then spent a few days with Father Nawrocki (presumably Stanislaus Nawrocki, pastor of St. Mary of Perpetual Help church) and afterwards stayed with another priest-friend in Manitowoc, Wisconsin, for approximately ten days. Subsequently he went to several other cities, including La Crosse, St. Paul, and Milwaukee, to find a place, but wherever he went he was told that he could not be accepted because his interlocutors had learned from the newspapers that he had been suspended *a divinis* and excommunicated, that he was an agitator and wished to chase Barzynski away in order to remain in his place — all this, he said, was put in the papers by Vincent Barzynski — and also that he was living in Chicago and saying Mass in private homes and hearing confessions without permission. The result was that he could not find any position and he had to seek refuge and hospitality from a friend, the Reverend Francis Pikulski, pastor in Mt. Pleasant, Pennsylvania. He lamented:

I cannot in any way find a position because I am continually persecuted by the Resurrectionists and slandered in all the newspapers of America. In the past days I went to Chicago to see Archbishop Feehan, begging him to oblige the Resurrectionists to retract all the lies written in their newspapers, but he replied to me that he could not and did not wish to. Then I asked him to hold a trial according to the rules of canon law, but he replied that he himself was the supreme judge. I begged for any position in his diocese, since in the Diocese of Chicago there was need of priests, and a certain Reverend Zalenski wished to accept me as an assistant, but the Archbishop replied that he absolutely did not want me to remain in his diocese, and he issued to me a certificate stating that I may celebrate Mass and that I have never been suspended by him.

Kozlowski, therefore, turned to Satolli and called on him as the judge in his case. He asked him to oblige Vincent Barzynski to retract in his newspapers all that he had written against the plaintiff, and added: "and if Your Excellency will not have pity on me, I am a lost man, because I have lost the esteem of my fellow countrymen. I ask of Your Excellency not a favor but justice, and if I am the guilty one, I accept any punishment whatever." Not having the means to support himself in America or to return to Europe, where he had "also been slandered by the same newspapers," he asked Satolli to provide him with some position or to rehabilitate his reputation in order that he might find one for himself and thus be able to work again and serve the glory of God.[32]

Even though Kozlowski's account of his tribulations was unquestionably one-sided and self-serving, it seemed to be so simple, disingenuous, and piteous that it could easily

---

[32]Memorial of Kozlowski to Satolli, n.p., March 15, 1895, Italian, *ibid.*

have moved the Apostolic Delegate to compassion. In a subsequent communication the unfortunate priest wrote that he was still awaiting a reply from Texas, and he promised to inform Satolli before he would leave Mt. Pleasant. Not long thereafter he actually went to Thurber, Texas, but apparently *en route* he passed through Washington and solicited an audience with the Apostolic Delegate. Satolli refused to receive him, and Satolli's secretary called him a liar in front of others. (Perhaps Satolli had concluded that Kozlowski was duplicitous in saying that he would not accept the pastorate of St. Hedwig's Parish even if it were offered to him or that he had misrepresented the Apostolic Delegate after their last conversation.) Kozlowski claimed that his motive was that the people had suffered so much, but having said that, he had done what his conscience told him to do, and he added, "and I am not afraid, not only not of the world but not even of hell or of God, no! because he is just, and this seems to me to be enough for my defense." In conclusion he said that his last prayer to Satolli was that the Delegate for love of God look kindly upon the people of the Polish church of St. Hedwig.[33]

When he arrived in Texas, he spoke with the Bishop of Dallas (Edward Joseph Dunne, who had served in the Archdiocese of Chicago until he was promoted to the episcopate in 1893). According to Kozlowski, the bishop permitted him to exercise his priestly powers, but on March 27 told him that he could remain only until April 23, because another priest was expected to come within a few days to join the Carmelites already working in Thurber. Kozlowski professed not to know where he would go after his month's sojourn in that town,[34] but in his desperate plight he would inevitably have thought of returning to St. Hedwig's, where he would be warmly welcomed by many of the parishioners.

[33]Kozlowski to Satolli, Mt. Pleasant, Pa., March 16, 1895, Italian, *ibid.*
[34]Kozlowski to Satolli, Thurber, Tex., April 18, 1895, Italian, *ibid.*

In fact, the people loyal to Kozlowski in that parish still refused to recognize the pastor recently appointed by Archbishop Feehan. When they heard that a delegation of their opponents, probably including Father Sedlaczek, would go to Washington and wait on the Apostolic Delegate, they wired him that they would not accept this Resurrectionist "under any condition," and they begged Satolli again "to come to Chicago and investigate the matter so that it could be settled."[35] At the same time the "Committee of St. Hedwig's Parish" wrote him another letter, appealing to him once more to redress their wrongs. They claimed to represent the parish, for they numbered thirteen hundred families as compared with "thirty or forty people." They stated boldly:

> The whole parish is one upon the question of whether a Resurrectionist shall be in charge of the parish or not. And upon that question all say, no. The fact that such an overwhelming majority are against the Resurrectionist order, and that they have held out so long should show that the determination cannot be broken and that there are some good reasons for it.
>
> In spite of the misrepresentations and false stories circulated and made to the archbishop which he seems to believe, the cause for this trouble was the fact that the collections were made for the church debt and money contributed but that the debt instead of decreasing, kept on increasing.
>
> The ones who are sympathizers of the Resurrectionists have been those who helped to bring about such state of affairs or those who have obtained political positions under the influence of the Rev. Barzynski.
>
> We desire a priest, and surely there are plenty, any

---

[35]Parishioners and Committee, St. Hedwig's church, to Satolli, Chicago, April 16, 1895, telegram, *ibid.*

body, we are satisfied with anyone your Excellency will send us with the exception of one belonging to the Resurrectionist order.

We do not desire to rebel against the Church but only expect our wishes to be consulted in this matter.

Under no conditions will the parishioners accept a priest of that order.

We are authorized to state that if this parish will not be given a priest soon that the parish will be compelled to use measures to recover its property and to do the best it can without the bishop.[36]

This final threat of schism could hardly be ignored by the ecclesiastical authorities.

The Apostolic Delegate even in this critical situation maintained his policy of non-intervention. He answered the Committee of St. Hedwig's church sternly:

In reply to your last petition and to your telegram of yesterday, I desire once more to insist that you shall put aside all spirit of opposition and submit to the decisions of your Archbishop, whatever it may be. I assure you again that it is useless for you to have any further recourse to me, since I have determined to leave the matter entirely to the Archbishop and not to interfere in any way at all. When you get ready to act as all good Catholics should act, the Archbishop will open your church and see to it that your spiritual wants are provided for. While, however, you continue to place yourselves in an attitude of rebellion to lawful authority you can expect no recognition.[37]

---

[36]Committee of St. Hedwig's Parish to Satolli, n.d. (received April 16, 1895), *ibid.*

[37]Satolli to Committee of St. Hedwig's church, [Washington, D.C.], April 17, 1895, carbon copy, *ibid.*

While the Apostolic Delegate was careful not to countenance the parishioners' insubordination, he also understood the necessity of taking some positive steps to placate them. Hence, on the same day he wrote to Feehan that they were continuing to send him petitions, and he complained, "It is unfortunate that this trouble should drag along so tiresomely, and if your Grace could find some means of settling it, I should be exceedingly pleased."[38]

The archbishop, on the contrary, did not admit the need for any change of course. He recalled in his reply to Satolli:

> This Polish faction has endeavored from the beginning to gain their point by violence and threats.
>
> The Police suppressed their riots. Among other things they threatened to destroy — to "dynamite" they said, the Archbishop's residence.
>
> Everything possible was conceded to them. To yield to them absolutely, would, it seemed to me, be a surrender to anarchy. Besides a very dangerous precedent would be given to various peoples. There are said to be in Chicago one hundred thousand Poles. There are probably seventy five thousand various other Slav peoples: such as Bohemians, Hungarians [!], Lithuanians, Ruthenians, Slavonians, Croatians, etc.
>
> All have their own priests and churches, and most of them schools and sisterhoods.
>
> They resemble each other in many points, but the Poles seem to be the most turbulent.
>
> At present a large number, I am told, of St. Hedwig's people attend Mass and the various duties of religion, in a large chapel given to their use.
>
> The malcontents go to other Polish churches in that region. Their baptisms, sick calls, funerals, etc. are attended to.

[38]Satolli to Feehan, [Washington, D.C.], April 17, 1895, carbon copy, *ibid.*

I believe it is better to have that church closed, if necessary, for a time, than to admit a principle which might render it most difficult to preserve order and church discipline among those numerous and various peoples, who form so large an element of the Catholic population of Chicago.

The malcontents are in reality but a few hundred, and I think it can be said there is little, if any scandal.[39]

Feehan promised to continue to strive "to bring them to a better sense."

Seeing that the Archbishop of Chicago was inflexible in his dealing with the recalcitrant parishioners, the Apostolic Delegate acquiesced in his decision. He commented that although it was highly desirable that such difficulties be removed, in the actual circumstances the more opportune and prudent way to forestall a renewal of the scandals was the one indicated by Feehan, namely, that St. Hedwig's church should remain closed, especially since the spiritual needs of the people seemed to be sufficiently provided for.[40]

Actually, a delegation of the loyal party, composed of two laymen and the new pastor, did go to Washington in April with Feehan's permission. Apparently their purpose was to prevent the Apostolic Delegate from siding with the dissidents. He received them and, according to a newspaper story, said that "he was entirely misrepresented by Father Kozlowski" and by the previous delegations of dissidents in their reports of their conversations with him; he declared that he had no intention of interfering in the matter as long as the majority continued to disregard the command of Archbishop Feehan. By contrast, when a delegation of the dissidents also tried to call on Satolli, he "declined to grant

---

[39]Feehan to Satolli, Chicago, April 25, 1895, *ibid.*

[40]Satolli to Feehan, [Washington, D.C.], April 30, 1895, Latin, draft, *ibid.*

any further interviews" and expressed the hope that the recalcitrant party would soon come to a sense of the duty they owed their archbishop.[41] That was the last attempt of the rebels to win the support of the Apostolic Delegate.

Around the beginning of May Kozlowski returned to Chicago. As he later explained to Satolli, after departing from Thurber he went to Galveston, but because of the spite of Vincent Barzynski, the Bishop of Galveston was unwilling to let him serve there although there were two vacant positions. He then went to other places, but he searched in vain because of "the diabolical envy of the Resurrectionists." He thought that he could earn enough money in Chicago to pay for his passage back to Europe, "rather than die of hunger." But the people, he wrote, came begging him not to abandon them, and he, seeing "the injustice" that they and he had experienced, was inclined to remain with them. He attributed the fault to Archbishop Feehan, who had had five months to give them another priest, since the people wanted any secular priest. He disclaimed responsibility, for he wished to be subject to the Holy Roman Catholic Church, and the people did also. "If I exercise my priestly ministry without permission," he asked rhetorically, "am I at fault? No!" He said that he had gone so many times to the archbishop but the latter had refused to see him. He added that he would have to administer the seven sacraments publicly from June 1 on, because the provisional chapel (which the seceders had been preparing) would be finished and ready. He concluded the letter by saying that the people did not want him to abandon them and he could not do so because he knew that the voice of the people was the voice of God; he saw this clearly because there was no justice on the part of the Resurrectionists and of the archbishop. Suggesting his reluctance to break his ties with the Catholic Church,

----

[41]*Chicago Times-Herald*, April 25, 1895, p. 12.

he emphasized that there was still time (apparently meaning that a final rupture was not ineluctable), but only one week.[42] Although Kozlowski was hoping, he affirmed, in the mercy of God and of Most Holy Mary that the Apostolic Delegate would take care "of us wretched sinners," Satolli did not respond, no doubt regarding the case as hopeless. Indeed, the "Independents" dedicated their new place of worship, temporarily located in a rented store and named in honor of All Saints, on June 16. Kozlowski was assisted by two Polish priests, Francis Kolaszewski of Cleveland and Stephen Kaminski of Omaha, who had established independent churches in their respective cities amid violent disturbances.[43]

Meanwhile Archbishop Feehan had decided that St. Hedwig's church should be solemnly reopened on the same day, presumably to deter the people from going to All Saints. On June 15, however, the "Independents" filed a civil suit for an injunction that would stay the opening of the church on the grounds that they held legal title to it, and the judge issued a temporary restraining order. Five days later, however, the judge ruled in favor of the Catholic Bishop of Chicago (the corporation sole), considering only the question of property rights and refusing to interfere in such internal matters as the appointment of pastors and assistant pastors. The judge also warned the complainants that if they caused any riot or bloodshed when St. Hedwig's church would be reopened, they would simply be disloyal citizens and entitled to no sympathy from the court. They heeded his admonition and created no uproar on the following Sunday. Meanwhile the archbishop had accepted Sedlaczek's resig-

---

[42]Kozlowski to Satolli, n.p., n.d. (written in pencil: June [should be May] 25, 1895), Italian, ASV, Chicago, folder 32a.

[43]On Kaminski, see Henry W. Casper, S.J., *History of the Catholic Church in Nebraska*, Vol. III: *Catholic Chapters in Nebraska Immigration, 1870-1900* (Milwaukee, 1966), 186-87. On Kolaszewski, see John J. Grabowski *et al.*, *Polish Americans and Their Communities of Cleveland* (Cleveland, 1976), 176-81.

nation and upon nomination of the Resurrectionists had appointed another member of that order, John Piechowski, pastor of St. Hedwig's Parish. He was installed and the church was reopened by the chancellor of the archdiocese with impressive ceremonies on June 23. A more capable and conciliatory priest than his predecessor, Piechowski then began the arduous task of rebuilding the shattered parish, and he labored at it with patience, kindness, and diligence for fourteen years.[44]

After Kozlowski had blessed the seceders' temporary church on June 16, Archbishop Feehan consulted the Apostolic Delegate. Besides recounting the contumacious priest's latest acts, he said that Kozlowski had previously written him a letter of defiance. He asked Satolli whether under these circumstances Kozlowski should not be "publicly excommunicated — and also the leaders and abettors of this movement?" Feehan denounced the priest as "the original fomentor of this trouble" which he had continually excited during the past months. Feehan desired "the advice and sanction" of the Apostolic Delegate in order that any necessary action might have his approval.[45] Evidently he was not sure that Satolli would agree with him on the appropriateness of this severe censure.

The archbishop's question gave Satolli an opportunity to open his mind at length. He replied that he was sad to learn that the condition of the Poles at St. Hedwig's church had gone from bad to worse. Using Latin, with which he was more familiar than English, he wrote:

> Your Excellency is not unaware that I always insisted that these Poles submit to your authority, but such efforts have not produced the desired effect. At the outset of the

---

[44]Iwicki, *First One Hundred Years*, 88-93.

[45]Feehan to Satolli, Chicago, June 20, 1895, ASV, Chicago, folder 32a.

turmoil I indicated that the more suitable way of resolving the difficulties seemed to me to be that there be assigned another pastor who would not belong to the Resurrectionist order against which, although perhaps unjustly, not a small part of the congregation was aroused. What was not done then could perhaps be tried at present, scilicet, that the rector be neither that Kozlowski nor a Resurrectionist but some priest chosen by Your Excellency before recourse is had to inflicting the most grave penalty of excommunication on the leaders of the rebels and their abettors. And if Your Excellency judges it opportune for an easier settlement of these affairs, after duly forewarning Kozlowski to desist from his perverse way of acting against ecclesiastical authority, and if these admonitions prove fruitless, you may punish him with the penalty of excommunication. Furthermore, Your Excellency will see whether for the spiritual good of these people it would be better to use the greatest kindness and to employ all the means apt to avert the necessity of separating very many from the unity of the Church. Hence, a division of the quasi-parish of St. Hedwig could also be considered and proposed, so that those who wish may remain and the rest may form a new congregation. I have thought that these things should be suggested to Your Excellency because it does not seem good to take the extreme measure of excommunicating very many except after all other means of reconciliation have been tried. For the rest, may Your Excellency do what he deems to be advantageous in the Lord.[46]

The archbishop, however, adamantly refused to adopt any expedient that might appear to be a concession or compromise, and thus, as has been seen, simply appointed

---

[46]Satolli to Feehan, n.d., Latin, draft, *ibid.*

another Resurrectionist pastor of St. Hedwig's Parish, although only about 300 families remained attached to it, while nearly 1,000 followed Kozlowski into schism.

The Apostolic Delegate may have learned much about these developments from the newspapers, but he also had a more personal source of information. The Reverend Bernard M. Skulik of Shamokin, Pennsylvania, who was spending several months in Chicago, had already reported to Satolli at the end of May on the progress of the independent movement. He wrote that at a meeting held a few days previously and attended by almost all the men, it was resolved to found an independent church, and all present swore fidelity to Kozlowski and named him their pastor. They then bought a lot for the church, rented a house , and acquired the sacred furnishings. Skulik went on to pose this question:

> Who is the principal cause of this new schism? Who has pushed these people to this point?...Who has made them lose the faith? It is not for me to ask or answer certain questions, to mix myself up in certain things, to scrutinize and judge these facts. But since I am their fellow countryman (almost all are from my province, upper Silesia in Prussia, from my area, from my native city and its environs) I know them better than all the other priests do...and having studied the facts from all angles, and now being at hand to organize two new Slavic parishes with the permission of the local Archbishop, I see everything that is being done; moreover, seeing that you, Monsignor, have been misinformed on many points, and also this Archbishop of Chicago, who, however, does not wish to be convinced, and even seeing the injustice and great wrong that he has done to these people, does not yield, and seeing how the injustice has been done especially by some priests and how nobody wishes to

explain the things to you as they are, I believe it to be my duty to inform you. . . .

All the parishioners of St. Hedwig's are very good people, almost without exception (perhaps there are among them a dozen perverse people, and that is all), very kind and religious, as perhaps no other people in the world (I have never seen a people so good, faithful, especially to the Church and to a good priest), pious and devout, patient and generous, especially to the Church, . . .attached to their habits and the customs of their own country. . . .The principal cause of the schism, that the Silesians of St. Hedwig wish to found an independent church, that the 1,000 families — about 7,000 souls — are embracing the schism, renouncing obedience to ecclesiastical authority, to the Pope, and that hundreds are losing the faith and going to hell. . .is the Reverend Barzynski and the order of the Resurrectionists; the Archbishop indirectly inasmuch as he is misinformed and places too much faith in them. These people want nothing more than any secular priest whatever; he can be from any part of Poland [as long as he is] not a Resurrectionist priest, and they will be good and faithful as before. And they are right inasmuch as the Resurrectionist Fathers have been here in Chicago the ruin of many parishes; they have often given bad example, grave scandals; they are unjust with the people; they have never given accounts of the receipts; they have made debts upon debts,. . .etc., etc.; they cannot forgive especially the closing of the Church of the Holy Trinity for very many years, which was the height of injustice and the beginning of the complaints among the people. . . .The principal reason why they do not want them is that all the money which they must pay for the church does not go for the church but for the order of the Resurrectionists. If Your Excellency will command the Archbishop of Chicago to give them a secular priest, there will be a peace such as there never was before; otherwise all these 7,000 souls will be lost.[47]

Even if allowance be made for the writer's excusable partiality toward his fellow countrymen and his unaccountable prejudice against the Resurrectionists, his interpretation of the dissension and his proposal of a remedy were bound to make an impression on Satolli. In reply the Apostolic Delegate urged Skulik to "be ready to do something to prevent such a grave scandal." In particular he directed him to put himself in agreement with the archbishop and to act according to the latter's intentions.[48]

When Skulik wrote to Satolli again, he said that he alone could do nothing; he had gone to Feehan several times — especially after receiving Satolli's directive — but he had not been able to obtain anything; Feehan did not wish to listen, and all the other priests were afraid to tell him anything lest they be chased out of the diocese. "The authorities in Chicago are the archbishop and Father Barzynski," he stated, putting the burden back on Satolli's shoulders. "Only you, Monsignor, can do something and put an end to this schism."

In this same letter Skulik provided the Apostolic Delegate with more information about the new independent church of All Saints. He described the blessing of the cornerstone by Kozlowski on August 11, of which he had been an eyewitness. All of *Jadwigowo* (the village or colony of St. Hedwig) — more than 5, 000 persons — took part in the celebration; they paraded through the streets, protested publicly and demonstrated against the archbishop and Father Barzynski. Skulik claimed to have been in the parish several times and to have talked with the Resurrectionists and with secular priests of the city, and they had told him

[47]Skulik to Satolli, Chicago, May 30, 1895, Italian, *ibid.*

[48]Satolli to Skulik, [Washington, D.C.], June 3, 1895, Italian, *ibid.*

that the people were good and very religious and wanted nothing but to free themselves from the yoke, from the tyranny and despotism of the Resurrectionists. Skulik then proceeded to repeat the alleged failings of these religious priests, especially in financial matters. In addition to the old charges, he stated that instead of building a church (divine worship was conducted in the school), the Resurrectionists had built a palace for about $27,000 which served as the parish house for two priests, and that when the people complained to the archbishop, the latter consulted Vincent Barzynski, who deceived him. The disorder had started when the archbishop closed the church and told the people that if they did not want the Resurrectionists, he would never give them any priest. The infuriated people reasoned that if the archbishop was unwilling to give them a secular priest, if he closed the church for which they had contributed more than $100,000, they would build a new church which would be independent of him and would have Kozlowski as their pastor. The new church, Skulik wrote, would cost about $60,000; he called the parishioners "rich enough"; very many were property owners and very generous to the church; he thought that they could easily support three churches and at least four priests. He also admitted that the people had been duped by Kozlowski, who claimed to be in communication with the Pope and the Propaganda and to be a missionary apostolic independent of the archbishop and of the Apostolic Delegate; they were also misled by the liberal newspapers. Skulik recommended that the Resurrectionists be permitted to keep St. Hedwig's church, school, and rectory with the 300 families adhering to them — the other people would also be content with this arrangement — and that a secular priest be authorized to found a new parish and to build a new church; Skulik was confident that in that case Kozlowski would be abandoned by the people and would resign and that the schismatics would offer the deed to the archbishop, and all would be well. Otherwise, he predicted somberly, the schism would never end. He promised that if Satolli would make Feehan carry out this plan, Satolli would be blessed by all of Chicago Polonia, which numbered 150,000 souls, as he was for having opened the Polish church of the Holy Trinity, which had since then become one of the best parishes in the whole city. Hence, he urged Satolli to take the initiative in this instance.[49] Even if this letter does not present a balanced exposition of the facts, it affords a clear insight into the mentality of the rebels.

It is strange that Skulik failed to tell the Apostolic Delegate that when Kozlowski preached at the ceremonies of dedication on August 11, he disclosed for the first time that the new congregation would sever its connection with the archdiocese of Chicago and affiliate itself with the Old Catholic Church under Joseph René Vilatte, the *soi-disant* Archbishop of the Old Catholic Church in America, who had previously visited Chicago to fish in troubled waters and to induce the disaffected Poles to establish an "independent Polish National Church."[50]

As soon as Satolli received Skulik's letter, he wrote in alarm to Archbishop Feehan:

> I desire officially to inform Your Grace that reports have come to me regarding the trouble in the Polish parish of St. Hedwig, in Chicago, according to which the disorders instead of decreasing are growing more serious. I have learned that nearly the entire population of that parish, amounting to more than five thousand souls, have united themselves to the priest Koslowski [*sic*], and have formed an independent and schismatic church. These

[49]Skulik to Satolli, Chicago, August 12, 1895, Italian, *ibid.*

[50]Parot, *Polish Catholics*, 119. See Henry R. T. Brandreth. *Episcopi Vagantes and the Anglican Church* (London, 1947), 31-35. See also Claude B. Moss, *The Old Catholic Movement, Its Origins and History*, 2nd ed., (London, 1964), 291-92; this author asserts that Vilatte was a Jacobite, not an Old Catholic, after his consecration in Colombo, Ceylon, in 1892.

people have recently, I am told, made a public demon-
stration of some magnitude. I beg Your Grace to give me
information concerning this matter, telling me what you
may have done or intend doing to remove if possible this
scandal.[51]

The archbishop's reply to this peremptory question, if ever
any was sent, has not been preserved in the papers of the
Apostolic Delegation.

Father Skulik had also written about "the new scandal in
the Polish colony" directly to Cardinal Ledóchowski. He
said that Kozlowski had incited the people of St. Hedwig's
Parish against their pastor, and he described in vivid detail
the fracas in which "about 500 men and women, armed with
sticks, pitchforks, knives, and revolvers in church, made a
great uproar" and wanted to kill the pastor. In the battle
with the police that ensued, he asserted, many were
wounded and four were killed. He went on to recount
Kozlowski's activities in May. As in his letter to Satolli of
the preceding day, Skulik contended that the ecclesiastical
authority itself had pushed the people into schism. The
people hated the Resurrectionists "like the devil himself," he
reported, because, as they all said, "The Resurrectionist
Fathers do not care at all about the parish, about the people;
they do not think of their children, about paying the debts;
they think only of themselves, of their monastery." Skulik
went on to assert that both the archbishop and the Apostolic
Delegate were misinformed and had rejected the independents' pleas. After repeating many of the observations he had
made to Satolli, he begged the Propaganda to investigate
the affair "and to save these people." The only way, he
insisted, was to order the archbishop of Chicago to appoint
a secular priest, especially a fellow countryman of theirs,

---

[51]Satolli to Feehan, [Washington, D.C.], August 15, 1895, carbon copy, ASV,
Chicago, folder 32a.

pastor. (One wonders whether he coveted the position for himself.) He predicted that if the archbishop would permit a mission to be held among the people, Kozlowski would soon go away and the people would be converted.[52]

Disturbed by this report, Cardinal Ledóchowski promptly sought verification and further information from Archbishop Feehan. Without revealing his source, he wrote that he was surprised to read that the Resurrectionists had provided the remote occasion for the dissension by their neglect of the people, for he had known in other ways that they were well deserving of religion through their zeal. Summarizing Skulik's account as well as his allegations and predictions, the prefect asked Feehan to enlighten him about the truth of this report and to do whatever might seem good to him to avert this danger to souls and to restore tranquility to the people.[53]

Feehan, naturally, presented his side of the dispute in reply. He asserted, "The true and, as I believe, only cause of those [difficulties] was the Reverend Anthony Kozlowski." After reviewing the history of the discord, he wrote, "I have made every possible concession to them, but they would not listen." The archbishop emphasized the fact that St. Hedwig's church had been reopened and that religious services were being peacefully conducted there under the legitimate pastor, and he stated that those services werc being attended by the larger and better part of the people; furthermore, he wrote, the school was in operation with a large number of children. Attributing the continuation of the rebellion and schism to the fact that Kozlowski pretended "to have full powers and independence," Feehan requested the cardinal's advice as to whether the priest should not be punished, and indeed publicly, with some ecclesiastical censure of excom-

[52]Skulik to Ledóchowski, Shamokin, Pennsylvania (or Chicago?), May 31, 1895, Italian, APF, Acta, Vol. 269 (1898), fols. 358r-59r.

[53]Ledóchowski to Feehan, Rome, June 30, 1895, Latin, *ibid.*, fol. 359r.

munication or other. He defended the Resurrectionists as good and zealous priests who had done very much for the spiritual benefit of the Polish people; he could not discover the reason for the dissenting faction's opposition to them except the instigation of Kozlowski and perhaps of others.[54] It is noteworthy that Feehan still held, against the evidence, that the schismatics constituted only a minority of the original parish.

The archbishop was also wrong in his superficial analysis of the cause of the schism. Overlooking the more basic ideological differences, he singled out a person as the chief force behind the movement. This investigation, on the contrary, confirms the conclusion reached by Victor Greene:

> Although it is difficult to determine precisely the origin of the parish's discontent, the preponderance of evidence suggests that Kozlowski was an important catalyst in the independent movement, but not its initiator. Independentism in Chicago was a general lay reaction to a religious issue, not a conspiracy of clerical malcontents. Kozlowski was a beneficiary of the movement, not its founder. . . . Kozlowski's activities and counsel were simply not those of a determined revolutionary.[55]

After Feehan's letter was received in Rome, the secretary of the Propaganda, Archbishop Agostino Ciasca, replied on behalf of the prefect toward the end of August. Without doubting the archbishop's roseate description of the situation of St. Hedwig's Parish, he answered the question regarding the proper way to punish Kozlowski: "Your Excellency, after having issued the warnings prescribed by

---

[54]Feehan to Ledóchowski, [Chicago], August 1, 1895, Latin, *ibid.*, fols. 359v-60r.

[55]Greene, *For God and Country*, 108.

law, may use your right of proceeding against him with ecclesiastical censures."[56]

Confident of being supported by both the Apostolic Delegate and the Propaganda, the archbishop prepared to excommunicate the schismatic priest. Lest the procedure be flawed in any respect, however, he first wished to resolve a doubt by asking Satolli's advice: "whether before publication of the censure, after the three canonical warnings have been issued, he should still be given an investigation before the episcopal court of the diocese?" He thought that this was not necessary because Kozlowski's offense was so grave and so public and notorious for many months; furthermore, delay ought to be avoided in his case. Feehan wished to be sure, nevertheless, of proceeding properly.[57] Satolli replied with almost curt brevity: "I would say that it seems that a juridical process is necessary," and he referred the archbishop to Sebastian B. Smith's *Compendium Juris Canonici* as an authority, citing the exact page and paragraph numbers.[58]

It can be assumed that Kozlowski failed to answer the summons and to appear at his trial. The archbishop formally excommunicated him on September 27, 1895, and ordered that the decree be read from the pulpit in every Polish and Bohemian church of the archdiocese two days later at the Sunday Masses.[59] After this censure was promulgated, some of the renegade's followers who had believed that he was in communion with the Catholic Church aban-

[56]Ciasca to Feehan, Rome, August 26, 1895, Latin, APF, Acta, Vol. 269 (1898), fol. 360r.

[57]Feehan to Satolli, Chicago, September 13, 1895, Latin, ASV, Chicago, folder 32a.

[58]Satolli to Feehan, [Washington, D.C.], September 16, 1895, carbon copy, *ibid.* The fourth edition of Smith's *Compendium* had been published at New York in 1890; the reference was to p. 413, No. 1262.

[59]The text is given in Parot, *Polish Catholics*, 119-20.

doned him and returned to their traditional faith, but the majority remained loyal to him.

Archbishop Satolli's terse reply to Feehan was, as far as has been discovered, his last word on the subject. He was elevated to the cardinalate on November 29, 1895, and he left the United States in October, 1896. Although he was not as well acquainted with the internal divisions of the Poles in America as he should have been, he offered the archbishop of Chicago sound advice. If it had been followed, the schism might never have occurred.

His successor in the office of Apostolic Delegate, Archbishop Sebastiano Martinelli, O.S.A., who arrived in the United States in October, 1896, seems to have paid no attention to the Kozlowski affair during his first fifteen months in Washington. Shortly after he assumed office, the excommunicated priest sent him a telegram requesting an audience to discuss his situation; perhaps he thought that he would receive a more sympathetic hearing from the new Delegate. No reply was given to Kozlowski; on the back of the sheet the words "address unknown" were written with the date, October 26, 1896. That was the end of Kozlowski's contacts with the Catholic Church. He then proceeded to have his supporters elect him their bishop, and next he applied to the Old Catholic Council in Bern, Switzerland, for episcopal consecration. After Vilatte recommended his petition, it was formally approved. Thereupon Kozlowski journeyed to the Swiss capital and was consecrated bishop there in the Cathedral of SS. Peter and Paul on November 21, 1897, by the Old Catholic bishops of Bern (Eduard Herzog) and Bonn (Theodor Weber) and the Jansenist archbishop of Utrecht (Gerard Gul); the American ambassador to Switzerland attended the ceremony. It seems that Kozlowski went to Rome after his consecration, for he sent a telegram from that city to Chicago on November 26, but the purpose or results of his visit are not known.[60]

After Kozlowski returned to Chicago, where he was enthusiastically welcomed by his adherents, he issued a pastoral letter. "The Right Reverend Anthony Kozlowski, Bishop of the Independent Catholic Diocese of Chicago," here reviewed the causes which had induced his followers to elect a bishop, emphasizing the "intolerable religious despotism, which oppressed with the heavy chains of slavery" their consciences and, if possible, their bodies. "Abuses," he wrote, "offending your religious sentiments, as well as your material interests brought you at last to the resolution to abandon the communion of a church, in which you were deprived of your double liberty as free citizens, and as men whom Christ has set free, and you gathered to form new congregations." He assured them that they had not "intended to form a new religion or new creeds, nor to reject the faith which was transmitted" to them by their fathers. Accordingly, they retained their belief in the episcopacy with apostolic succession, and they considered "the episcopal form of church government and church organization as the only possible form" consistent with their doctrinal standpoint. He promised to be a true shepherd to them until death, unlike those strangers to whom they had for so long been subject, men calling themselves shepherds even though they did not share their flock's joys or sufferings. To strengthen their constancy he exhorted them:

> Do not be dismayed nor afraid, if uncharitable men should persecute you, and even abusing the name and the authority of Christ pretend to excommunicate you. You are resting on a sure foundation which is Christ Jesus Himself. . . .

[60]Il Direttore, Direzione delle Poste e dei Telegrafi di Roma, to Secretariat of State of the Vatican, Rome, March 10, 1898, ASV, Segreteria di Stato, anno 1898, Rubrica 280, fasc. 1, fol. 100r.

My dearly beloved brethren! It was assuredly the death of our Spiritual liberty, which preceeded [*sic*] the death of our national independence in the old country.

May the Spiritual independence, which you now regained here in the land of the free, expiate in you and in your children the old fault and may this noble independence remain with you as a perpetual blessing, so that you indeed rejoice in the liberty of the children of God and be filled with the abundant richess [*sic*] of the Holy Spirit. Amen.[61]

When a copy of Kozlowski's pastoral letter was sent to the Apostolic Delegation, Martinelli promptly reported the matter to the prefect of the Propaganda, Cardinal Ledóchowski. He thought that the information which he was providing might be useful, especially in view of the development that could occur in the future. Obviously drawing upon the archives of the Apostolic Delegation, Martinelli reviewed the case at considerable length and with remarkable objectivity (commensurate with his documentary sources); he passed no judgment on Feehan or the Resurrectionists. He observed that from the beginning the Apostolic Delegation had upheld the archbishop's authority without failing at the same time to inculcate tact and prudence in order to avoid exciting the people; on the one hand Martinelli's predecessor insisted on the people's duty to obey, and on the other he urged the archbishop to find a way of ending the strife as quickly as possible. The new Delegate admitted that he did not know whether or in what way Satolli's instructions to Feehan had been put into execution. At the end of his narrative he added that according

---

[61]"Pastoral Letter of...Kozlowski," Chicago, December 19, 1897, two printed pages joined, ASV, Chicago, folder 32a; Italian translation, handwritten, ASV, Segreteria di Stato, anno 1898, Rubrica 280, fasc. 1, fols. 88r-90v; printed in APF, Acta, Vol. 269 (1898), fols. 362r-63r.

to information given him by Feehan, it appeared that Kozlowski's adherents were decreasing because they were disgusted by the fact that he had been consecrated by ministers whom they regarded as Bismarckians.[62]

Cardinal Ledóchowski in turn deemed it his duty to draw the attention of the Secretary of State, Cardinal Mariano Rampolla del Tindaro, to the "sad happening" in Chicago because of the "rather grave consequences" that it could entail. He enclosed an Italian translation of Kozlowski's pastoral letter which he said had been published in Polish. Ledóchowski asked Rampolla to apprise the Pope of this serious matter in order that he might take whatever measures he would judge opportune to prevent as much as possible the lamentable effects that could be feared, especially considering the large number of Polish Catholics who had let themselves for several years already be dragged into schism.[63]

After the Secretary of State had acquainted Pope Leo with the contents of the prefect's letter, he replied to Ledóchowski that His Holiness had felt the most acute pain and enjoined the Sacred Congregation to give the Apostolic Delegate in the United States and the archbishop of Chicago the instructions that it would think necessary to prevent the sad effects that could be feared from so serious a state of affairs.[64]

Before executing the papal directive, the prefect of the Propaganda, it seems, waited for a response to the request for further information which, as he had mentioned in his letter to Rampolla, he had sent to the archbishop of Chi-

[62] Martinelli to Ledóchowski, Washington, D.C., January 14, 1898, Italian, original in ASV, Segreteria di Stato, anno 1898, Rubrica 280, fasc. 1 (Prot. 42139); printed in APF, Acta, Vol. 269 (1898), fols. 360v-61v.

[63] Ledóchowski to Rampolla, Rome, January 29, 1898, Italian, ASV, Segreteria di Stato, anno 1898, Rubrica 280, fasc. 1, fols. 86r-87v.

[64] Rampolla to Ledóchowski, Vatican, January 31, 1898, Italian, *ibid.*, fol. 96r-v.

cago. In his reply Feehan succinctly reviewed Kozlowski's past, commenting that he had come to the United States "to create disturbances among the Poles." Consistent with his habit of making as light as possible of the affair, Feehan asserted that until then Kozlowski had made no impression on the Polish people outside his original followers. "The Poles believe that he is not a real Catholic bishop and does not have communion with the Holy Apostolic See." Feehan said that according to some estimates there were 100,000 Poles in Chicago, according to others, 120,000; out of these Kozlowski had about 800 families or about 4,000 persons of all ages. Aside from the Poles no one, whether Catholic or non-Catholic, gave any thought to him; not even the newspapers mentioned him. The archbishop stated his opinion that at that time there was no danger for the mass of Poles; they had many churches, which they attended, he argued, and alongside each one a school in which a multitude of children was being educated in the Catholic faith. He admitted, nevertheless, that Kozlowski and his followers were liars and were constantly trying to deceive the people; therefore, "good priests" thought, and he himself felt, that to protect the faithful people it would be good if "some authoritative voice coming from Rome were to condemn Kozlowski and his followers." He believed that the mass of the Polish people would listen to the voice of the Holy See and would obey, but he said that he deferred to the prefect's wisdom.[65]

Upon receipt of this letter, Ledóchowski transmitted a copy of it to Rampolla. Since Feehan had suggested that it would be opportune for Rome to condemn Kozlowski and his followers, the prefect of the Propaganda asked the Secretary of State to let him know what orders the Pope

[65]Feehan to Ledóchowski, Chicago, February 19, 1898, Latin, copy in ASV, Segreteria di Stato, anno 1898, Rubrica 280, fasc. 1, fols. 106r-07r (Prot. 42964); printed in APF, Acta, Vol. 269 (1898), fols. 363v-64r.

might give on the matter.[66] Rampolla hastened to lay the question before Leo XIII and then to reply to Ledóchowski that in view of the gravity of the matter the Pope had ordered that it be examined in a general (plenary) meeting of the cardinals composing the Congregation de Propaganda Fide.[67] Thus the stage was set for the last act in the drama.

Among the documents collected and circulated in print for the cardinals to study in preparation for their meeting was a petition submitted to the Holy Father by the Polish priest of the Diocese of Scranton, Francis Hodur, "in the name of three churches built in the State of Pennsylvania against the will of the ordinaries." Hodur wrote that the Polish people scattered throughout the United States had built more than 200 churches, but that in some towns these churches had become dens in which the people were scandalized; quarrels between the faithful and their pastors and ordinaries were not uncommon. Hodur assigned the following causes for this sad state of affairs: (1) the bishops and their consultors did not know the language or character of the Poles living in America and therefore often could not be mediators between the faithful and the pastors; (2) many pastors, even the most unworthy, real tyrants, enjoyed the greatest possible favor of the bishops, and if the people murmured against those impious servants of God, they were compelled to obey even by civil force; and (3) very many priests were occupied more with the collection of money than with labor in the Lord's vineyard, and hence on Sunday instead of preaching the Gospel they scolded the people, invited them to games, lotteries, and other worldly amusements directed by the priest in the name of the Church. Consequently, he averred, the Polish people were day by day losing the reverence due to bishops and priests, and

[66] Ledóchowski to Rampolla, Rome, March 14, 1898, Italian, ASV, Segreteria di Stato, anno 1898, Rubrica 280, fasc. 1, fol. 103r-v (Prot. 42964).

[67] Rampolla to Ledóchowski, Vatican, March 16, 1898, Italian, *ibid.*, fol. 108r.

their faith in the Catholic Church could be shaken unless the Pope would turn his eyes toward these wretched people. Specifically Hodur made three requests: (1) that the Pope give the Polish people in the United States a bishop or representative to the Apostolic Delegation in Washington who could use the Polish language; (2) that the material goods of the churches, namely, the schools, houses, and sacred edifices, be entirely the property of the faithful; and (3) that the people have some influence on the election of their pastors.[68] These were principles which were to be put into practice in the Polish National Catholic Church, of which Hodur became the first bishop in 1907 after the death of his archrival, Kozlowski.

Hodur also brought to Rome a memorial composed by some dissident Poles, and this was also included in the printed *Sommario* distributed to the cardinals of the Sacred Congregation. It contained a broad survey of the conditions in which the Poles, said to number between one and a half and two millions, lived in the United States, and it deplored the "false foundations" on which the Polish parishes rested from the beginning, that is, that the church property was held by the bishops who for the most part were of Irish origin. It also criticized the priests who in many cases were

[68] Hodur to Leo XIII, Rome, February 16, 1898, APF, Acta, Vol. 269 (1898), fol. 364r-v. Hodur, who had been suspended by his bishop in the previous year for abandoning his parish in Nanticoke, Pennsylvania, and accepting the pastorate of a new, independent church in South Scranton, St. Stanislaus, which had been founded by a group of dissidents, went to Rome in 1898 to win the Pope's favor. He did not succeed in obtaining an audience from the Pope, but he told reporters that he had presented a petition to Cardinal Vannutelli (whether Serafino or Vincenzo is not specified), who assured him that it would be given due consideration. Hodur was excommunicated in September, 1898. See John P. Gallagher, *A Century of History: The Diocese of Scranton, 1868-1968* (Scranton, 1968), 215-23. See also William Galush, "The Polish National Catholic Church: A Survey of Its Origins, Development and Missions," *Records* of the American Catholic Historical Society of Philadelphia 83 (1972) 131-49, here 134-36; and Warren C. Platt, "The Polish National Catholic Church: An Inquiry into Its Origins," *Church History* 46 (1977), 474-89, here 477-78.

more interested in currying favor with the bishop than in taking care of the people. The bishops, it was alleged, refused to listen to complaints against the priests, many of whom deserved to be called tax exactors and bloodsuckers. Hence, the people, pushed to the extreme limit, staged public demonstrations, but then they were constrained by the police to submit to the hated priest and bishop as the owners of the church property. To put an end to these disorders and scandals, the more enlightened among the Polish Catholics, according to this exposition, proposed to ask the Holy See to reform the administration of the Church in regard to Polish congregations. Then followed the same three demands as Hodur had laid down plus a fourth, namely, that the financial administration of the parish should be entrusted to men elected by the parishioners and approved by the priest. It was stated that these requests did not touch the dogmas of the faith or the constitution of the Catholic Church, but aimed only at restoring tranquility among the people and confidence between them and the clergy. The petitioners closed the memorial by submitting to the direction of Holy Mother Church and promising "to live and die as faithful confessors of the only true congregation of Jesus on earth."[69]

The Pope transmitted these two documents to the Propaganda in order that opportune provisions might be adopted. Supposing that Hodur belonged to the archdiocese of Chicago, Cardinal Ledóchowski wrote to Feehan, asking him to inform the Polish priest that the petitions presented by him and the other signers were in opposition to the laws and canons in force in the Church and therefore were not

[69]"Traduzione del Memorandum mandato da alcuni polacchi dissidenti alla S. Sede: Memorandum nell'affare della Chiesa Polacco-Cattolica negli Stati Uniti indirizzato alla Sede Apostolica dalla Chiesa Nazionale," unsigned and undated, APF, Acta, Vol. 269 (1898), fols. 364r-65v. On the difficult situation of the priests, see William Galush, "Both Polish and Catholic: Immigrant Clergy in the American Church," *Catholic Historical Review* 70 (1984), 407-27.

accepted by the Holy See. Feehan was also to say that the Holy See exhorted them for the spiritual good of their souls to be submissive to the legitimate ecclesiastical authorities and to their decisions with the necessary tranquility and docility.[70]

Cardinal Lucido Maria Parocchi was designated as the *relator* or *ponens* for the session of the Sacred Congregation in which these questions would be discussed. In his *relazione* he adverted to "the ease with which the Bishops of the United States welcomed into their dioceses Polish clerics and priests without being well informed beforehand about their condition and tenor of life." To remedy this failing, he proposed that a printed circular be sent to all the ordinaries of the United States commanding that in the future they not accept Polish clerics or priests who were not furnished with testimonial letters from the Propaganda certifying their legitimate departure from their dioceses, their freedom from censure, and the regularity of their conduct. Secondly, in regard to the disorders that had occurred, Parocchi noted that either the individual ordinaries had taken measures or opportune instructions had been given by the Propaganda and remedies were supplied, but these did not prevent some Polish priests from remaining rebellious toward ecclesiastical authority and dragging many of their fellow countrymen with them. Coming then to the case of Anthony Kozlowski, the cardinal reviewed the documentation already furnished to his fellow members in print. Finally, he asked them to answer three questions, as follows: (1) whether and what provisions it was proper to adopt "against the pseudobishop Kozlowski"; (2) whether and what provisions were to be taken regarding the Polish churches in the United States that were in rebellion against their ordinaries; and (3)

---

[70] Ledóchowski's letter to Feehan on this subject has not been found. The facts are taken from the *relazione* cited in the following note.

whether and what other provisions it was advisable to adopt.[71]

Besides Parocchi, nine cardinals, including Ledóchowski and Satolli, took part in the general congregation held on April 18, 1898. To the *relator*'s first question they replied affirmatively and decided that through a decree of the Propaganda it should be declared in the name of the Pope that the pseudobishop Kozlowski had incurred major excommunication reserved to the Supreme Pontiff, and that it should be promulgated and explained by the ordinary of Chicago. The second question was also answered in the affirmative, and it was ordered that the sentence of excommunication be published in all the dioceses of North America along with an appropriate instruction. Finally, in response to the third point, it was resolved that the bishops of Italy should be warned not to admit to sacred orders foreign young men, especially Poles, without testimonial letters of their own ordinary, much less to recommend them to the bishops of America without the previous permission of the Propaganda. Likewise, the ordinaries of places in which congregations of Poles existed were to be instructed to deal more mildly with those faithful, to assign them suitable rectors endowed with zeal and charity and well regarded by the people, and, where necessary, to transfer to another mission at an opportune time the rectors whom the people disliked. In addition, the Apostolic Delegate in the United States was to be informed about all these provisions. All these resolutions were ratified and approved in every respect by the Pope in an audience granted to the secretary of the congregation, Archbishop Ciasca, on April 26.[72]

[71]"Ponente Lucido Maria Parocchi. Relazione con sommario. Sullo scisma causato negli Stati Uniti dal sedicente 'Vescovo della Diocesi Cattolica indipendente di Chicago' Antonio Kozlowski," April, 1898, APF, Acta, Vol. 269 (1898), fols. 354r-55v.

[72]*Ibid.*, fols. 356r-57r.

It is to be remarked that only Kozlowski was excommunicated by the Holy See and not his followers, as Feehan had suggested. Furthermore, it is understandable that the cardinals refused to adopt the measures demanded by Hodur and other dissidents which were contrary to ecclesiastical law, such as that the property of the parish be legally held in the name of trustees elected by the parishioners, or that a right of patronage, based on the contributions by which the people built and maintained the church, be recognized so as to give them a voice in the appointment of their pastors, or that laymen control the financial management of the parish exclusively. But no law forbade the choice of a Polish bishop in the United States; as the anonymous memorial pointed out, such a Polish representative in the midst of the American hierarchy could be a mediator between the Polish people, the Apostolic See, and the American bishops, as well as an advocate for his fellow countrymen's rights. Yet ten more years were to pass before the first Polish-American priest was elevated to the episcopate. After Paul P. Rhode was consecrated a bishop in 1908 to serve as an auxiliary to Feehan's successor, many of the schismatic Poles returned to the Catholic Church. The same result could undoubtedly have been obtained a decade earlier.

The decisions of the Propaganda were executed by means of three documents signed by the prefect and secretary and dated May 2, 1898. One was a decree declaring in the name of Pope Leo XIII that Kozlowski had incurred major excommunication reserved to the Roman Pontiff. It said also that His Holiness had ordered that this sentence of excommunication along with an appropriate instruction be promulgated not only by the ordinary of Chicago in his diocese but also by all the ordinaries of the United States in their respective dioceses. The instruction of the Sacred Congregation, which was the second document, was addressed to all the ordinaries of places in which congregations of Poles existed. It recalled with sadness the not infrequent dissensions between the rectors and the people of Polish parishes from which tumults, rebellions, and other grave evils of that kind resulted. To preclude repetitions of such disturbances, the Propaganda implored the local ordinaries, "for the outstanding charity and zeal for souls with which they were inflamed," to assign to those faithful suitable rectors who would seek the things of Christ, not their own, and would know how to benefit the people entrusted to them. It also advised the bishops not to hesitate at the proper time to remove rectors who did not live up to their expectations. Finally, the Propaganda urged them to enter into such arrangements as in their judgment might advance the cause of religion among the Polish-speaking people, without infringing in any way on the rights of episcopal authority. The third in this series of official pronouncements was a letter to be sent to the ordinaries of Italy. Deploring the woes caused in the United States by the bad conduct of certain priests who, though foreigners and frequently natives of Poland, were ordained in Italy, the Sacred Congregation stated that the Pope had ordered that the ordinaries of Italy be admonished not to admit to sacred orders foreign young men, especially Poles, without authentic testimonial letters of their own ordinary, much less to recommend them to bishops in America without the previous permission of the Propaganda.[73] The cardinal prefect sent copies of all three documents to Martinelli and asked him to watch over the execution of the first two, which were addressed to the ordinaries of the United States.[74]

It may seem that the Holy See was locking the stable door after several horses had already been stolen, but at least it was taking some action at last. How effective these precautions were it is not easy to determine. Kozlowski continued to expand his empire. More than a year later a "Catholic

---

[73]Copies of the decree, instruction, and letter in ASV, Chicago, folder 46. The letter to the ordinaries of Italy was published in *Acta Sanctae Sedis* 31 (1898-99), 320, and in the *American Ecclesiastical Review* 19 (1898), 632.

[74]Ledóchowski to Martinelli, Rome, May 23, 1898, ASV, Chicago, folder 46.

priest of the Archdiocese of Chicago" who did not dare to sign his name wrote to the Apostolic Delegate about the progress of the independent movement:

> Fake-Bishop Kozlowski is continuing his devilish work. To-day's papers announce the blessing of a church for the Italians who joined his movement, and Mr. D'Andrea, a former student of St. Mary's Seminary, Baltimore, ordained by Kozlowski, is made their pastor. If the Church will not do more than she has hitherto done, Kozlowski will find more and more followers and do still more harm to the Catholic religion.
>
> He is going to start several new churches in different places of Chicago, in Joliet, East Chicago, in the diocese of Fort Wayne, etc. He intends to buy a Protestant church not far from Holy Trinity Polish church, Chicago, which the Catholic Poles of the vicinity would like to buy, because Holy Trinity Church is too small, but our Most Reverend Archbishop refused to give his consent. The Poles are thus compelled to go to German churches where they cannot understand the sermons. No wonder that they get crazy and join the Independent church where they get preachers of their own tongue.
>
> Poles, as a rule, are good Catholics but with regard to certain things they have queer notions. They are fond of ceremonies and external splendor and when they see Kozlowski dressed as a bishop, speaking to them in their own tongue, acting according to their customs, etc., they follow him in spite of the instructions they receive in the Catholic churches.
>
> Now, if the Catholic Church cares for immortal souls, she ought to check Kozlowski's work. But the only way of doing this, is to elect a Polish bishop or some higher authority in Chicago, who would understand the wants of his people, work among them, speak to them as in authority and in this way, the just complaints that the Poles are treated by the American bishops somewhat like

orphans by their stepmothers, would be set aside. Something ought to be done by all means if we want to arrest the influence of Kozlowski and save many unmindful people from spiritual ruin. By the way, the same Polish prelate could serve other nationalities as a Pole always speaks different European languages.[75]

Such advice fell on deaf ears in Washington, and no further remedies were attempted by the Holy See as long as Martinelli was Apostolic Delegate. Meanwhile Kozlowski incorporated into his diocese twenty-three parishes located as far east as New Jersey and as far west as Manitoba, comprising between 75,000 and 100,000 communicants. After his demise most of his adherents became members of the Polish National Catholic Church organized by Hodur, and his cathedral in Chicago, All Saints, eventually became the cathedral of the Polish National Catholic bishop in that city.

This narrative suggests some differences between the local ecclesiastical authorities and the officials of the Holy See with respect to the values that were perceived to be at stake. Neither understood all the divisive factors motivating the parishioners, and both, of course, regarded peace as the immediate goal to be attained. They both sought a swift termination of the public disorders not only because in the eyes of the non-Catholics of the city and the country the Church was being embarrassed and disgraced by the uncivilized conduct of a certain body of its members and by the suits brought by them before civil courts, but also because spiritual harm was being wrought on the dissidents themselves by the hatred, violence, malevolence, jealousy, and calumny to which they had succumbed. To restore the desired tranquility, amity, and charity, the archbishop of

[75] Anonymous "Catholic priest of the Archdiocese of Chicago" to Martinelli, Chicago, June 25, 1899, *ibid.*

Chicago and his chancellor had recourse mainly to punitive or coercive measures such as closing St. Hedwig's church, calling the police to prevent or quell riots, having the leaders of the disturbances arrested, and excommunicating Kozlowski (and, if they had prevailed, even his chief abettors). The only concession they were willing to make was to replace one Resurrectionist with another in the pastorate; they refused to bow to the recalcitrant group's insistence on having a secular priest in that office. The Apostolic Delegate, on the contrary, would have compromised on that crucial point by granting them a secular priest, though not Kozlowski. The fundamental divergence, however, lay in the ultimate goods that the churchmen on the two levels were pursuing. For the archdiocesan authorities what mattered most was the maintenance of proper discipline; they feared that to yield to any demand would undermine the whole organizational structure; they were determined to uphold it at all costs, even if they had to pay the price of losing, at least temporarily, several hundreds or even thousands of those whom they considered obstinate malcontents. For the papal officials, on the other hand, what outweighed all other considerations was the preservation of the unity of the Church, which appeared to them to be worth more than the affirmation or enforcement of unquestionable episcopal authority over the laity. Even when the Holy See complied with the archbishop's request for a solemn pronouncement of censure, it excommunicated only Kozlowski, who had already flagrantly broken his bond with the Church by his illicit consecration, and not his followers, whom it hoped to draw back to their original allegiance. It might be concluded that those locally responsible were more concerned with the short-term advantage of ensuring smooth governance of their heterogeneous flock, and that those viewing the discord from a higher vantage point were more apprehensive about the long-term effects of alienating those inclined to independentism, knowing that it is easier to intensify than to overcome an estrangement and that a schism quickly tends to become permanent.

From Saints to Secessionists: Thomas Hughes and *The History of the Society of Jesus in North America*

Robert Emmett Curran, S.J.

"I miss the story," an historian commented in 1913 about the latest volume of Thomas Hughes' *History of the Society of Jesus in North America*.[1] Many readers have had the same frustrating experience in trying to use, much less read through the four volumes of text and documents that Hughes published on the North American Jesuits of the Colonial and Federal periods. Hughes himself confessed to his editor that there was "no story," but "odds & ends scraped up everywhere; I had no narratives to give, except in the Canadian section," where Hughes contended that he had no intention of "repeating ten-times-told tales."[2]

In an age in which even "Popes admit everyone into the private archives of the Holy See," Hughes prided himself on

---

[1] Georgetown University Archives, Washington, D. C. (hereafter cited as GUA), William Poland, S.J. to Edward Devitt, S.J., St. Louis, May 19, 1913.

[2] GUA, Thomas Hughes, S.J. to Devitt, Rome, July 21, 1918.

being a modern scientific historian who mined the field for original sources and respected their integrity too much to force them into patterns simply for the sake of a narrative.[3] Nor did he hesitate to include the unpleasant. "I should like it to be seen," he once wrote, "that I never omit anything because I may not happen to like it...."[4] "To allow of tampering...with these Documents," he protested when some Jesuits were expressing concern about his publishing the records of the acrimonious dispute between the Society and the Archbishop of Baltimore, Ambrose Maréchal, "would be like permitting each story of a house as it rises to have its bearings knocked out, columns dispensed with, arches kicked away — & there would be no reason for going to other stories at all. ..."[5] What those documents in their totality would reveal to the discerning reader, Hughes was confident, was "the circumstances, ...[the] environment, and habits of thought" that had prevailed in the world the American Jesuits worked in from the seventeenth to the nineteenth centuries.[6]

Discerning readers might protest that any such patterns were hopelessly buried in the sheer weight of Hughes' poorly

---

[3]Thomas Hughes, S.J. *The History of the Society of Jesus in North America: Colonial and Federal, Text* (hereafter cited at *History*), Vol. I (London, 1907), 25.

[4]GUA, Hughes to Devitt, Rome, April 19, 1913.

[5]GUA, Hughes to Devitt, Rome, June 26, 1906. Hughes felt that John Gilmary Shea, "to please his patrons." had sanitized his histories. "I have pleased no one," Hughes wrote after publishing the fourth volume, "neither Cath. nor Prot., neither South nor North, neither inside nor outside, but only the truth, and *ruat coelum*" (GUA, Hughes to Devitt, Rome, July 21, 1918). The critical reception of Hughes' first two volumes was much more positive than he implies here. The initial volume won Columbia University's Loubat prize in 1907 and was widely and favorably reviewed. When the companion volume of documents was largely ignored, Hughes became convinced that there was a boycott of his work, especially in Maryland, because of his treatment of the Maréchal affair (GUA, Hughes to Devitt, Rome, April 6, 1908.)

[6]*History, Text,* I, 79.

organized material and convoluted prose. An irrepressible bent for polemics and digressions only further obscured his subject. But from the beginning there were larger themes present. Hughes himself confessed that he realized the full implications of those themes only after he had completed the fourth volume. He subsequently incorporated them more explicitly into a fifth volume of *The History* that was never published. That volume in its two redactions, like its predecessors, told more about Roman perceptions of the Society and Church in Rome and America in the early twentieth century than it did about Society and Church a hundred years earlier.

Born and raised in Liverpool, Thomas Hughes (1849-1939) upon his graduation from Stonyhurst College entered the English Province of the Society of Jesus in 1866. During his novitiate he volunteered to transfer to the Missouri Province in order to work with Indians in the American West. The pages of his histories were the closest he came to realizing this ambition as his intellectual promise quickly caught the eye of his superiors. Once he completed his studies he was assigned to teach, first at the Jesuit novitiate at Florissant, Missouri, and then at St. Louis University. At St. Louis he was particularly remembered for having begun a prestigious graduate lecture series in the 1880s which helped to lay the groundwork for graduate studies in that institution.[7]

In 1894 he was called to Rome to work with a team of Jesuit historians preparing to write the history of the Society. The following year he was charged with doing the history of the Jesuits in North America in the nineteenth century. Hughes accordingly concentrated his research on that more recent history with particular attention upon the long controversy the Jesuits in the Maryland Mission had

[7]William B. Flaherty, S.J. *Better the Dream: St. Louis University and Community, 1818-1968* (St. Louis, 1968), 175-79.

had with Archbishop Maréchal over their property. The general of the order, Father Luis Martín, wanted that delicate matter to be "altogether exhausted."[8] Apparently sometime in the latter nineties, Hughes was told that he was now to do the early history of the Maryland Mission as well, beginning in the seventeenth century. According to Hughes, Martin indicated that "the old history should be treated as a mere preliminary to the nineteenth century."[9]

With one assistant in Rome and two in America, Hughes accelerated his research on two continents. By 1906 he had two volumes ready for the publisher, Longmans, Green and Co. of London, one a collection of documents and the other a text. In his preface to the text, Hughes presented the two volumes as companion pieces, but acknowledged that the documents went beyond the matter treated in the text. In fact fewer than 200 of the 600 pages of the volume of documents dealt with the history of the Jesuit mission in the seventeenth century. Most of the volume concerned Jesuit property and the Maréchal controversy.

Father General Martín's interest in the old property fight was in large portion a practical one. The Jesuit generals had long wanted the Maryland Jesuits to free themselves from the farms and country parishes in Southern Maryland and on the Eastern Shore. Martín particularly wanted Hughes to ascertain whether the lands were held in fee simple or in trust. If the latter, he intended to press the Archbishop of Baltimore to take over the parishes and at least some of the land. Ironically, that had been the basic issue of the controversy, whether the lands belonged to the Society or were merely held for "the Church."[10]

---

[8]Thomas Hughes, S.J. "Reminiscences." *Woodstock Letters* 51 (1922), 181.

[9]The colonial history of the Maryland Mission was originally to have formed part of the history of the English Province, but the Jesuit doing that history found Maryland "a very jejune subject." Hughes confessed that he himself might have been "the origin of that impression" (Hughes, "Reminiscences." 182).

[10]*Ibid.*, 180-81.

Hughes saw more in the question than a matter of title or settlement of property. Having lived in Maryland (he was in the first class at Woodstock College), he knew the stories that still circulated among clergy and laity about Jesuits retaining property that belonged to the diocese. As he got deeper into the research of the early nineteenth century, he became more convinced that the Jesuit reputation had been unjustly damaged by the affair. When some Jesuits in Maryland began to pressure the provincial to use his influence to stop Hughes from stirring embers of a fire that had long since died, Hughes had little patience with those who counseled that "it was much ado about a little paltry property." Was it inconsequential, he protested, to bring

> charges against religious men, that they were 'guilty of a breach of a religious trust,' that they 'purloined,' that they were 'perjurers,' that they should be 'unfrocked' — or made bishops — and this spread through Italy, France & England, of a whole Regulars' Mission, so that American Jesuits travelling through Europe had to go slinking through, and apologizing, & averring that they had never been cut off from the body of the Society! I am of the same mind— so much ado about a little paltry property. The English Parliament was of the same mind in another case: So much ado about a paltry Stamp Act! But, if the offset to such a paltry thing was an American Republic, it is not strange that the offset, after a hundred years, to the wholesale arraignment of a Mission of religious men should be a little rectification.[11]

Hughes wasted no opportunity in editing the documents to provide just that. As John Carroll had incorporated the property to preserve it for the Society against all interlopers,

[11]GUA, Hughes to Devitt, Rome, January 25, 1908.

including papal congregations, so, Hughes argued, the Maryland Jesuits, foreigners and natives alike, justly resisted Ambrose Maréchal's claims, even when their own general and the pope himself told them to yield. As Hughes reconstructed the long affair, Father General Aloysius Fortis was "buying peace at any price"; the pope was getting one-sided information from the bishop and his agent; Maréchal was arbitrarily using his juridical power to force the Jesuits to meet his demands. Only the Maryland Jesuits appreciated that the very life of the Mission was at stake.[12]

For Hughes the meaning of the controversy transcended Maryland and the early nineteenth century, as he intimated to Edward Devitt, S.J. The extraordinary threat that Maréchal had represented in Maryland in 1820 was a daily fear that the Society lived under in Italy by 1908. "The demand on the Jesuits for the episcopal mensa in Maryland corresponded to what a progressive Government like that of Italy to-day exacts of the episcopal mensa itself for the lay treasury...," he noted.[13] Both were species of arbitrary government and tyranny.

The first volume of text covered only the first eleven years of the Maryland Mission and most of the pages (320 of 564) dealt with another controversy, that of the Jesuits with the Second Lord Baltimore, Cecil Calvert. By the late nine-

---

[12]Hughes, *History, Documents,* Vol. I (London, 1908), 571-75.

[13]*Ibid.,* 543 n. 25; GUA, Hughes to Devitt, Rome, January 25, 1908. Occasionally the note of being under siege crept into his correspondence with Devitt. "How politics stand & will turn." he reported in 1909, "is all in the hands of the Lord. There is no Catholic party to save anything. And the Socialists & anticlericals are bent on carrying out the French antecedents here. The ministries always go from bad to worse...." (GUA, Rome, November 24, 1909). When there were rumors in 1912 that the government was about to pass a law confiscating the property of religious orders, Hughes was convinced that the reasons for it were the war debts and a desire to eliminate private education. "All will be State and atheistic," he commented. "New vested interests will be created in the army of hungry brevetted teachers waiting for a place. And then the whole story of France can be rehearsed...." (GUA, Hughes to Devitt, Rome, November 30, 1912).

teenth century, Baltimore was already well noted for having introduced the concept of religious toleration into British America. In his introduction Hughes pointed out that the Maryland experiment of "practical toleration" was the precursor for "every clime in our day" and a microcosm for judging how religious orders could expect to fare with "a dozen European monarchies, empires, or republics, in the matter of general religious politics...."[14]

What Hughes found in Cecil Calvert was a Gallican Catholic whose treatment of the Jesuits showed his intentions of subduing religion to the state. Religious toleration, Hughes was convinced, was the legacy of the Catholic gentry, not the Baltimores. Hughes cited with approval the Jesuit general's appraisal of Calvert that

> he has drunk of the muddy waters in the way of Egypt, and is imbued with principles not at all sound; and it is to be feared that not a few others are infected with the same. But I do not see what remedy can be applied, especially in these dubious times, and in a place where every body thinks with impunity what he likes.[15]

That Cecil had not had the advantage of studying at St. Omers, as his younger brothers did, told Hughes much. Baltimore remained a Catholic out of self-interest, but his real convictions were Protestant and his political principles were Erastian. To Hughes it was no accident that Lord Baltimore's chief associate, John Lewger, was a converted rector of the Church of England.[16]

[14]Hughes, *History, Text,* I, 137.

[15]Vincent Carafa, S.J. to Henry Silesdon, S.J., Rome, November 7, 1648, cited in Hughes, *History, Documents,* I, 37.

[16]Hughes, *History, Text,* I, 350-53. "I take him to have been an ill-formed Catholic, entirely in the hands of the anti-Jesuit party of Engl.," he commented to Devitt in 1899 (GUA, Hughes to Devitt, Rome, December 16, 1899). Hughes had suspected Cecil Calvert's orthodoxy long before he began his study of Maryland. "It appears." he wrote in 1878, "that Lord Baltimore was a liberal Catholic, and

Calvert's dispute with Thomas Copley over the land the Jesuits had acquired from the Piscataway not only revealed to Hughes Lord Baltimore's contemptuous attitude toward the natives, but more importantly his Erastian ambitions of a Church establishment controlled by the proprietor. Nor was it only the property of Jesuits and Indians that Calvert was bent on confiscating according to Hughes. Baltimore's feudal designs, which imposed taxes upon property and military service upon the population, clergy included, were to Hughes a seventeenth-century brand of socialism in its absolute claims upon land and persons.[17] Copley, on the other hand, was making but one absolute claim, the principle (as Hughes reminded) "which cannot be denied by a Catholic, that the Church is not under the State."[18]

In this struggle for state control, Hughes noted that "the venal proletariate [*sic*], which had the numbers and votes" were in the pockets of Calvert and Lewger. The quality people in the province were all with the Jesuits.[19] When in 1645 Virginians challenged the proprietor's authority, his "new majority" showed the extent of its loyalty by quickly going over to the invaders.

The change of government was hardly a liberation for the Jesuits. At the end of Hughes' first volume, Andrew White and Copley were being shipped back to England in chains; the other Jesuits had fled into Virginia. Of the first twelve Jesuits to serve in Maryland, eight had died on the mission within the first decade. Five were under forty, a testament to

temporized much and was ready to temporize more, in order to save his property in troublesome times....[T]he history of St. Mary's city is rather that of a city blighted for liberal Catholicism and apostasy." (Hughes to Daniel Considine, Woodstock, Md., August 29, 1878, in Anon., ed., "Maryland: Letter from Father Thomas Hughes to Mr. Considine." *Letters and Notices,* 12 (1878-79) 171-75, here 172).

[17] Hughes, *History, Text,* I, 399-404.

[18] *Ibid.,* 405.

[19] *Ibid.,* 439.

the Society's commitment to send some of its most promising young men to the New World, despite the hardships and dangers.

In the second volume of text, Hughes followed the precarious fortunes of the Maryland Jesuits and Catholic gentry through the overthrow of the Calverts to the suppression of the Society in 1773. Although the Catholic planters soon lost power and became a tiny minority of the colony, they continued to be a moral and cultural force with the superior education that the English recusant schools at St. Omer and Bruges gave them. From this saving remnant ("the solid and sterling Catholicity of Maryland") came a large number of vocations to the Society, persons of "first-class understanding and judgment" like Robert Brooke, the first native vocation.[20] He and his fellow Jesuits quietly went about the business of their ministry in Maryland in the face of penal laws, attempts to wrest away their property, and the general anti-popery that Hughes saw plaguing the colony through the late colonial period. To the faithful Maryland Jesuits and Catholic gentry he applied the words of the Assyrians about the Israelites: "Who can despise this people? Is it not right that we should fight against them, and leave not a man alive; or they will circumvent the whole world with their chains!" (Judith 10:19)[21]

The second volume of documents, issued in 1910, covered events from the suppression of the Society to the settlement of Archbishop Maréchal's claims in 1838. Again a major focus was the controversy over the property, but the scope was larger and the tone decidedly different. Hughes now suggested that the Maryland Jesuits might have been wiser had they reached an early accommodation with Maréchal. "Whatever they gained in maintaining their rights," he con-

[20] Hughes, *History*, Text, II (London, 1916), 137-38.

[21] *Ibid.*, 607. Hughes had foreshortened the first sentence of the quote. It reads in full: "Who can despise this people that has such women among them?"

cluded, "they lost in reputation. . . ."[22] Actually Hughes was now more sympathetic with the archbishop's arguments. The property *was* indeed ecclesiastical in nature, he pointed out, no matter what the American Jesuits and United States' law said about it. It *should* have been under canonical jurisdiction, as Maréchal was contending and the Maryland Jesuits denying.

Regardless of the canonical rights, Hughes noted that the Jesuits were crippling themselves by so concentrating on the farms and undermining the attempts of enlightened foreign Jesuits like Anthony Kohlmann who wanted to shift the center of operations from Maryland to New York. Hughes obviously shared Kohlmann's judgment that of the states, Maryland was "the worst and poorest in the Union, from which even seculars retire into the wilderness of Kentucky. . . ."[23] The Maryland Jesuits were beginning to pay the price of provincialism, poor management, and the distrust of foreigners who by 1820 were a strong majority of the Mission. Locked into the past, they maintained the autonomy of the corporation they had set up to protect the property after the suppression, even though that legal body should have come under the authority of the religious superior after 1805 when the Society was revived in Maryland. Nevertheless, Hughes had to admit that "the blessed Corporation" (one exasperated superior's term for it) was a *felix culpa* insofar as it saved the estates.

As Hughes was completing the fourth volume in 1913, he learned that Father General Franz Wernz wanted all the histories to terminate with the suppression. "I was immensely relieved," Hughes later claimed.[24] Five years later he was told to resume the story. Hughes confessed to Devitt that he had little idea what particular focus it would take or how it

[22]Hughes, *History, Documents,* I, Part II, 1030.
[23]*Ibid.,* 945 n. 14.
[24]Hughes, "Reminiscences." 183.

would differ from the provincial history that Devitt was publishing *seriatim* in *Woodstock Letters* at the time.[25]

The theme he took up was one that he had planted over a decade before in the first volume. There he had observed the importance of studying the period that had led to the American Republic. It was vital to study the impact of this milieu upon "the life and destiny of one religious institute," he had argued, seeing how large that order had become in the United States by the early twentieth century and what influence it had across the country. But, he continued, "if this religious Order is fated to decay, its decline and fall do not seem likely to occur through agencies from without. . . . No; the possibility of decline must be limited to the alteration of internal life or the process of decay from within."[26]

Toward the end of the second part of the documents, Hughes had observed that the Maréchal controversy had saddled upon the Jesuits the reputation of "not being Jesuits at all, but a kind of broken limb barely hanging on to the Society."[27] Hughes himself now seemed determined to substantiate that reputation. If the image of the Maryland Jesuits in the first volumes had been triumphal, one of men who were "superior in learning and ability," zealous, obedient, and heroic, that of their successors in the nineteenth century was one of children dissipating the legacy of their fathers.

Relying on more extensive material than had appeared in the volumes of documents, Hughes portrayed a post-Restoration Society in Maryland that was materialistic and ignorant of its traditions. The Neale brothers, Charles and Francis, who held the vital posts of mission superior and novice master respectively, were basically strangers to the

[25]GUA, Hughes to Devitt, Rome, November 17, 1918.

[26]Hughes, *History, Text,* I, 137-38.

[27]*History, Documents,* I, Part II, 1030.

Society's laws and tradition. Charles, Hughes pointed out, had been a mere novice at the time of the Suppression. His younger brother had joined the Society only after the Maryland ex-Jesuits were allowed to affiliate themselves with the Society in Russia in 1805. Despite being superior three times, Charles knew so little about the laws of the Society that he had possessed private property until his death and willed it to his family.

The Neales, the Fenwicks, and their Maryland confreres were depicted as clerical planters, so preoccupied with their property that they were willing to jeopardize everything else to preserve it, whether it be their standing in the Church during their dispute with Archbishop Maréchal or their very future as a body by following a policy of closing the novitiate as an economy measure. They opposed the farsighted foreigners among them, especially Anthony Kohlmann, in Hughes' judgment the unmatched "light in his generation" intellectually and spiritually.[28] Men like Kohlmann, Pierre Epinette, and John Henry had been trained in Russia and knew the Society from the inside, but they were pushed aside by the native faction. On the other hand, the native Jesuits were all too ready to minimize their differences with Protestants, a tendency, Hughes observed, "which is violently alien to the purposes of the Society of Jesus."[29]

Given these tendencies it was no surprise to Hughes that the foreigners found the younger Jesuits lacking in any spirituality. They were receiving no formation, "had to make bricks without straw, teach without capital and live by their wits."[30] The novices were largely unsupervised when they were not being pulled away to teach at Georgetown or New York. They were admitted virtually without scrutiny and they left as freely. Some very promising young Ameri-

---

[28] Hughes, "History, Text III" (Redaction of 1926), 925, ms. copy in GUA.

[29] *Ibid.,* 533 bis.

[30] *Ibid.,* 393.

cans were being drawn to the Society, Hughes found, but tiring of their exploitation and "finding nothing of what they expected," most of them soon left.[31]

The foreigners found that laissez-faire formation promoting contempt for the traditions of the Society. One of them reported that "One would be ashamed to speak of the rule. Rodríguez [Alfonso Rodríguez, S.J., who wrote *The Practice of Perfection and Christian Virtues*] would have raised a laugh."[32] The quality of Jesuits produced by such a system that rarely dismissed anyone was predictable. A John McElroy somehow managed to survive it. More typical in Hughes' eyes was a Joseph Carberry, "an ignoramus" who could barely read and had no formal novitiate or training in the Society. What attracted the Marylanders to Carberry was that he was a first-class farmer who would give them another vote on the corporation.[33] Even worse was Adam Marshall who became for Hughes the *reductio ad absurdum* of this new generation denied "an honest and genuine formation." An avowed Jacobin who rarely said Mass, went to confession, or exhibited any signs of a religious spirit, Marshall nonetheless became the most powerful figure in the Mission as procurator of the corporation. It was appropriate, Hughes wrote, that he had died teaching "as a secular professor" on a United States' naval ship. "He was fit for a frigate," he concluded, but "had nothing in common with the Order."[34]

An excessive love of liberty and nation were two results of the lack of formation. The Maryland Jesuits' machinations to retain control of their property, despite the commands of general and pope, revealed their true identity as "ecclesiasti-

[31] *Ibid.*, 748.

[32] Stephen Dubuisson, S.J. to Aloysius Fortis, S.J., cited in Hughes, "History, Text III," 664.

[33] *Ibid.*, 581-83.

[34] *Ibid.*, 662-63, 673.

cal democrats" whose ultimate goal was autonomy.[35] Without the proper training to counteract American pressures, Hughes suggested, such behavior was inevitable.

As he had done with the previous volumes, Hughes submitted his manuscript to be reviewed by two censors within the Society. One of those appointed was Gilbert Garraghan, who was himself in the process of researching the history of the Society of Jesus in the United States. Garraghan reported anonymously that once again Hughes' work was a model of "thoroughgoing research and scholarly detail." That made it all the more painful, he went on, to return an unfavorable verdict. Not only was Hughes unfair to Carroll, but he was distorting the record in portraying the opposition to Maréchal and Rome over the property as a strategy peculiar to the Americans. Most of the foreigners, including Kohlmann, had agreed with their stance, he commented.

Garraghan detected a striking shift in tone between Volume III of the *History* and the documents upon which it purported to be based. "One gets an entirely different view of men or things," Garraghan remarked, "as he uses one or the other source." In this latest volume the "incompetency, the mismanagement, the erroneous views, the sharp practice, the moral delinquencies" so burdened the story that the reader must conclude that "scarcely any one thinks, says or does anything through a spiritual or supernatural motive." Surely, Garraghan observed, even in Maryland things could not have been this bad. The censor noted that Hughes was now applying to the Society itself the polemics that critics of his earlier works had accused him of engaging in against adversaries of the Jesuits. "[I]f any chapter in the history of the Society calls for broad and sympathetic treatment, he suggested, "it is that which records the efforts of a little group of well-intentioned, but, if you will, misguided men to

[35] *Ibid.*, 604.

revive the Society of Jesus in the United States; and broad and sympathetic treatment is precisely what they have not received."[36]

The other censor shared Garraghan's judgment that the manuscript should not be published. Father General Wlodimir Ledóchowski told Hughes that he could not publish it in its present form. Hughes agreed that "there are indeed limits" to what should be made public, but he reminded the new general that Father Martín's intention in starting the historical project was the instruction of "our rising generations."[37] Hughes, however, was aiming higher than novices or scholastics in his efforts to instruct. "[O]nly in discovering the historical roots of illnesses can one begin to cure them," he suggested to the general.[38] The Society of Jesus in the United States was not only sick, Hughes contended, but very likely in a state of secession from the Society in Rome.

In an 82-page memorial to the general, Hughes attempted to show that his history of the Maryland mission had been no exaggeration, but a revelation of the roots of a crisis among Jesuits in America that Father General Martín himself had recognized by the end of the century. In part it was autobiographical, Hughes' personal discovery of "the Maryland tradition." He recounted the cultural shock of coming from the novitiate in England with its mature candidates, a third of them converts, to its counterpart in Florissant where all seven novices were adolescents from Xavier College and the atmosphere stiflingly provincial. Recreation periods were interminable; religious instruction was minimal. The master of novices, Hughes recalled, "communicated no idea either about religion, the Society of

[36]GUA, [Garraghan], Censor's report, n.d.

[37]GUA, "De Abusibus." an 82-page typewritten Latin copy of a memorial to Wlodimir Ledóchowski, S.J., dated July 4, 1930; GUA, Hughes to Devitt, Rome, April 19, 1913.

[38]Hughes, "De abusibus." 5.

Jesus, or any other thing...."[39] When the young Hughes complained about the lack of order, the novice master peevishly responded: "They will have to experience everything afterwards; therefore better begin now."[40]

The casual manner in which Americans approached the liturgy and other spiritual exercises scandalized him: provincials saying Mass in less than twenty minutes, priests racing to finish the divine office to win a bet, superiors sending mail during retreat. Hughes claimed that his real awakening to the spiritual deterioration took place at Woodstock where he began theology in 1869. A classmate was enthusiastically urging him to read a novel by George Eliot. Finally succumbing to his appeal, Hughes indicated that he would seek permission to read it. "Oh! No!" the other Jesuit exclaimed; and disappeared with the book. "This brought on my first suspicion," Hughes remembered, "of the turbulent waters swirling beneath the surface of the Society of Jesus."[41]

Subsequent trips to America at the turn of the century only provided additional evidence of the extent of Jesuit declension. The inroads of secularization were even more palpable. Going to the theatre was now common; the reading of newspapers took the place of meditation and community recreation; confession was becoming a rare exercise; priests were saying Mass once a week. The splendid cuisine and the enormous trunks that carried Jesuit belongings revealed the level of poverty they observed. They were obsessed with money.

In the colleges Hughes alleged an attempt to "modernize" in order to compete with the Harvards and Yales. At Georgetown Hughes found that modernization largely meant

[39]*Ibid.*, 28.
[40]*Ibid.*,
[41]*Ibid.*, 22.

baseball. The daily order he encountered there in 1899 included nearly as many hours for baseball as for class. The team spent weeks on the road pursuing the Holy Grail of baseball supremacy in the moral wildernesses that Hughes considered New Haven and Cambridge to be. The high point of the day, he reported, was the rector's reading of the telegram relating the latest victory to the thunderous applause of the students. The image he best remembered was that of the rector sitting "alone, full of the majesty of Religious Order," watching 100 boys playing baseball.[42] "Now is baseball queen of studies," he concluded.[43]

The intellectual vacuity of the colleges was for Hughes only a symptom of a larger blindness to the culture that held them captive. He recalled from his diary Father General Martín's words: "They see no dangers in America; more than that, they see nothing. They say we don't understand them in America."[44] Indeed, Hughes found very much alive the contempt for Rome that had perplexed former generals like Roothaan and Martín. It had been no accident, Hughes pointed out, that nine of the thirteen superiors of the Maryland Mission/Province from 1823 to 1901 had been outsiders.

If truth be told, Hughes contended, many Americans had succumbed to Americanism and Modernism. The passive virtues associated with prayer, contemplation, and obedience were obsolete in America; the active virtues, "those which best agree with the national genius: to act, make noise, make money, build, be bound hand and feet to the people, whoever they may at length be," were regnant, not only among the populace but, he suggested, even within the Society.[45] That retreat directors were omitting the exercises

[42]*Ibid.*, 44.

[43]*Ibid.*, 77.

[44]Hughes' Diary, February 15, 1896, cited in Hughes, "De abusibus," 74.

[45]Hughes, "De abusibus," 74.

on hell told much about the decline of faith ("pure and simple modernism").[46] The understanding of the Mass as a mere symbol also had lessons for the discerning. American Jesuits, he concluded, were unconscious Modernists. Even the German-American Jesuits, renowned for their fidelity to the Society's rules and spirit, were more and more conforming "to the common life of America, not to the common life of the Society of Jesus."[47]

A large part of the trouble was the leadership in the Society in America. The penchant for choosing superiors who had business acumen was the best assurance of perpetuating spiritual and intellectual mediocrity, Hughes contended. Worse still was the appointment of converts like Edward Purbrick and John Whitney, who had been Maryland provincial and rector of Georgetown respectively in the 1890s, and abetted the corrosive influence of Protestantism upon the Society there. The worst consequence of this influence, Hughes implied, was the individualism that had marred the Jesuit character in America since the restoration.[48] A "home-rule" spirit was prevailing that could be traced back at least as far as John Carroll, "the most American" of the American Jesuits.[49]

As early as the second volume of documents (1910), Hughes had noted "some shadows" upon Carroll's character. Carroll, Hughes admitted, was scrupulously correct in trying to restore the property to the Society, but he also manipulated the corporation to advance his own interests. Buried in Hughes' notes was his concern about the archbishop's Gallican tendencies. Carroll's conviction that papal congregations had no just claim upon the temporal possessions of the American Church or indeed any share in the

[46]*Ibid.,* 25.

[47]*Ibid.,* 52.

[48]*Ibid.,* 54.

[49]*Ibid.,* 5.

pope's spiritual authority was to Hughes the equivalent of the assertion of episcopal autonomy from papal control.[50] By the 1926 redaction, Carroll had become an episcopal boss, fighting the reconstitution of the Society, waging a campaign to keep young men from joining it, starving Georgetown, while he more and more attempted to accommodate the Church to the Protestant milieu.

In a final redaction which he completed in 1933 Hughes put the nineteenth-century history of the American Jesuits within the context of the Age of Revolution which he offered as the key to the shape the Society had come to take in the New World. Carroll himself was a child of that age, imbibing the individualism and zest for religious innovation that had marked the first revolution that came to be known as the Enlightenment. By the time he returned to America in 1774, Carroll's secular tendencies were clearly set to embrace the American Revolution with its illusive promises of religious liberty and separation of Church and State.[51] Finally in the year that Carroll was elected bishop by his fellow priests, the third revolution occurred in France, "a world-wide convulsion, a mass of symptoms & eruptions, social, civic and religious, under the effects of which we are laboring a century and a half later."[52]

Only in America had the Society "saved" its property. Property, however, was no substitute for the character of the Society, and here was the real loss the Jesuits in America had suffered, Hughes concluded. Kohlmann and Francis Dyzierozynski had waged a futile struggle to transplant the ideals of the Society and a knowledge of its fundamental body of laws, the *Constitutions,* to the Americans. Personal and economic interests had instead triumphed and the com-

---

[50]Hughes, *History, Documents,* I, Part II, 619 n. 2.

[51]Hughes, "History, Text III" (Redaction of 1933), ms. copy in GUA, 81, 442.

[52]*Ibid.,* 315.

munal character of the Society, the epitome of which was its "devotion to the Church, [and] to its visible head the Papacy," effectively died with the foreigners.[53]

Or rather escaped with them to the West in 1823 when Charles Van Quickenborne led his party of seven novices into Missouri after the corporation closed the Maryland novitiate. But Hughes left the reader doubtful whether these western Jesuits would long be able to resist the poisons from the east. How pessimistic Hughes had become about the state of the Society in the United States he made clear in his memorial to Ledóchowski. There he held out two hopes for the American Society: recruits from the sons of first and second generation immigrants and training for them in Rome.[54]

It may seem ironic that Hughes wrote his history in the service of an ultramontane tradition that little valued it.[55] His own vision, however, was on the permanent principles which gave life to the Church and the Society. The "secret" of the Jesuits was "the organization of daily life and work, whether common, exceptional or heroic, on the solid basis of spiritual motives and supernatural aids."[56]

Uniformity was the key, and its source for the Society, as for the Church, was Rome. Had Hughes known better the history of the Society, he would have perhaps better appreciated Carroll's conviction that the Society needed to adapt itself to place and time. Even one of Hughes' heroes, Francis Dzierozynski came to realize in action the Ignatian principle of adaptation according to circumstances. What worked in Europe, Dzierozynski tried in 1841 to convince another Eurocentric general, John Roothaan, would not necessarily

[53]*Ibid.*, 106, 421.

[54]Hughes, "De abusibus," 78-81.

[55]See Stephen J. Tonsor, "Lord Acton on Döllinger's Historical Theology," *Journal of the History of Ideas* 20 (1959), 329-52.

[56]Hughes, "History, Text III" (Redaction of 1933), 6.

work in the United States.[57] A later European superior in Maryland who had shared Dzierozynski's insight predicted that "in time the Americans will be equal to the Europeans but give them time."[58]

Such a separate but equal status made no sense to Hughes either in terms of his understanding of the Society's tradition nor his experience of America. He had never been at home there; and it was impossible for him to believe that there could be an authentic American Jesuit tradition, faithful to the spirit and *Constitutions* of the Society, but reflecting its unique environment. What he could see all too clearly was a growing American influence, both in the world and in the Society. By 1920 America was a world power and the American Jesuits accounted for a sixth of the members of the Society of Jesus. The five members in 1805 had grown to nearly 3,000, almost double those in the English Assistancy. Hughes was all too aware that their time had come. The combination of his vestigial colonialism and radical ultramontanism made this American advent about as welcome as a new suppression. The ultimate irony was that by the time Thomas Hughes died in 1939 no part of the Society was more oriented toward Rome than the American Assistancy.

[57]Archivum Romanum Societatis Jesu, Rome, (hereafter ARSI) *Provincia Marylandia* (hereafter MD) 5 III 6, Dzierozynski to Roothan, Frederick, Md., June 29, 1841.

[58]ARSI, MD 8 IV 9, Burchard Villiger to Peter Beckx, Baltimore, September 7, 1860.

Peter Guilday:
The Catholic Intellectual in the
Post-Modernist Church

David O'Brien

At its 1984 annual meeting, the Association of Catholic Colleges and Universities presented its Theodore M. Hesburgh award for outstanding contribution to Catholic higher education to Monsignor John Tracy Ellis. On that occasion, James Hennesey, S.J., delivered an address, "Our Zeal for Excellence: Have We Made a Hospitable Home?" The first phrase of that title was taken from a speech of Bishop John Lancaster Spalding a century earlier. Hennesey described the nineteenth-century bishop, one of the founders of the Catholic University of America, and Ellis, as men "convinced of the importance for the Catholic Church in the United States of intellectual excellence and of Catholic education as its proper home." Hennesey did well to associate the two men; Ellis has long admired the Peoria bishop and frequently pointed to his "zeal for excellence" as an inspiration for his own career. Furthermore, Ellis' introduction to the scholarly pursuit of church history came at the university Spalding helped to found. There the man with whom Ellis studied provided a living bridge between the drive for scholarship and intelligent leadership in the Church, which characterized Spalding's dream for Catholic America, and the concern with intellectual freedom, scholarly research, and simple honesty which have characterized Ellis' distinguished career. That teacher was Peter Guilday, founder of the *Catholic Historical Review* and the American Catholic Historical Association, the leadership of which he passed on to John Tracy Ellis, a man he called his "providential successor." What many would today say of Ellis was said of Guilday in 1945 by another distinguished historian, Thomas T. McAvoy: "for a generation you have been American Catholic Church history personified."[1]

Born and raised in Chester, Pennsylvania, Guilday attended the nation's first free diocesan high school, in Philadelphia; among his teachers was Charles McCarthy, who later served with him on the history faculty at the Catholic University. In 1902, at the age of 18, he entered the diocesan seminary at Overbrook. Five years later, he was awarded one of two places maintained by the diocese at the American College at Louvain. After ordination, Guilday spent a year studying in Germany, then returned to Louvain to pursue his doctorate in history, under some of the university's most notable scholars, including Alfred Cauchie, who remained a lifelong friend.[2] In March of 1910, concerned about the shortage of priests, Archbishop Patrick Ryan summoned Guilday back to Philadelphia, where he was

[1] James Hennesey, S.J., "Our Zeal for Excellence: Have We Made a Hospitable Home?" *Current Issues in Catholic Higher Education.* IV (Winter, 1984), 39-42; Peter Guilday to Msgr. Edward Hickey, February 21, 1945, Guilday Papers, Catholic University of America (hereafter cited as GP); Thomas T. McAvoy to Peter Guilday, February 28, 1945, GP.

[2] "Autobiographical Statement, 1927" in GP; biographical information can be found in John Tracy Ellis, "Peter Guilday: March 25, 1884 — July 31, 1947," *Catholic Historical Review* 33 (1947), 257-68; Hugh J. Nolan, "Peter Guilday," *Records of the American Catholic Historical Society of Philadelphia* 55 (1944), 385-87 and 56 (1945), 233-35.

appointed assistant rector of St. Thomas Aquinas church. In July, he was transferred to the Cathedral parish. Meanwhile, Bishop Thomas Shahan, rector of the Catholic University of America, was negotiating with Ryan for Guilday's services. In January, 1911, he wrote congratulating Guilday on his appointment to the faculty of the University and announcing that he was to return to Louvain, where the rector hoped he could complete his doctorate in two years. Guilday responded enthusiastically. As it turned out, doctoral work took longer than Shahan had hoped. In 1912 and 1913 Guilday was granted permission to remain an additional year. Finally, in 1914, he completed a dissertation on English Catholics on the continent from Elizabeth to the French Revolution, and returned to Washington to take up his new duties.[3]

In his early years at the University Guilday taught modern church history and completed a biography, never published, of Martin Luther. At the same time he settled on American Catholic history as his field of study. Trained at Louvain in the critical examination of historical texts, he wished to organize a seminar to train historians in critical methods, and to build archives to preserve important documents of American church history. This meant, in turn, the need to organize historical work in much the same way that such organization had taken place in the previous generation among American historians, finding a home for scholarly work in the university, building support for archives and documentary publication, training professionals skilled in the techniques of critical or scientific history, and launching journals to provide outlets for this research. Guilday, who was to be the guiding spirit of this organizational work, was therefore an institutional intellectual, dedicated to

---

[3]Archbishop Ryan to Guilday, March 1, 1910; April 3, 1910; and July 22, 1910; and Bishop Shahan to Guilday, January 7, 1911; January 15, 1911; April 2, 1911; April 11, 1911; and May 5, 1913, GP.

scholarship, intellectual excellence, and cultural progress solidly within a linked set of institutions, most importantly the church and the university.[4]

Guilday was a priest, a professor in an ecclesiastical university, and professional historian deeply committed to his work. It was a new and somewhat unusual combination, at least in the United States, where priesthood had long been associated primarily with pastoral work, social service, and teaching. As a priest he was responsible to his archbishop and had been trained in a seminary to uphold orthodox Catholic doctrine, obey his religious superiors, and pursue a life of holiness, self-discipline, and dedication to the well-being of the Church. As a professor he was accountable to university authorities who, in the case of the Catholic University, were in turn responsible to the American hierarchy and the Holy See. As a scholar, he was the product of an intellectual environment which emphasized ideals of objectivity and respect for evidence, an ethic emerging as a moral ideal for historical work in the United States as well. Reconciling these obligations to truth with those to the Church, to its leaders, and to the faith, however possible in theory, is always difficult in practice. Guilday's fellow historians elsewhere in America, with their colleagues in other fields, would have to fight some serious battles for recognition of the value of scholarly independence and academic freedom, to say nothing of mobilizing support for the expensive work of research and graduate study. Guilday would have similar problems, made even more difficult and complex by the fact that his experience of academic professionalism and university work would take place in a setting so intimately linked

[4]On the development of research and graduate study in the modern university, see Laurence R. Veysey, *The Emergence of the American University*, Phoenix Books edition (Chicago, 1965), especially chapter 3.

to the Catholic Church and to the peculiar needs of the Catholic subculture in the United States.[5]

Outwardly, Guilday was well prepared to pioneer, for he was highly motivated, extremely well trained, deeply loyal to the Church, and thoroughly committed to scholarship. Personally, however, he found it difficult, in part because he was a lonely man often plagued by self-doubt. When he first arrived at the Catholic University in September, 1914, he noted in his diary he felt "no enthusiasm, no joy," although the new post represented the fulfillment of his dreams. He worried that he would not be at the University very long; he began many projects but completed few. Convinced that he would never do "anything great," he noted that he was melancholy and "sick with the sickness of no confidence in myself." Yet he threw himself into his work with tremendous energy, exhausting himself in teaching, developing plans for a church history program, and launching an historical journal. In December his tiredness led to renewed expressions of loneliness. He longed for friends but could not suffer company; he thought perhaps he was better suited for parish work, but he would be unable to stand the "turmoil and unrest of diocesan intrigue." He lacked the intelligence required by the university position and was tired for the "constant work." "This must be something like Hell on the miniature scale," he noted in mid-December.

Intrigue, it turned out, was not confined to parish rectories. In the spring of 1915 he found himself trying to be like other members of the faculty, "trusting no one and being on guard to avoid suspicion and misinterpretation." He knew that if he wished to be successful, he would have to discipline himself to writing and publishing, but work seemed only to accentuate his loneliness. This in turn led to further self-

[5]See Michael V. Gannon, "Before and After Modernism: The Intellectual Isolation of the American Priest," in John Tracy Ellis, editor, *The Catholic Priest in the United States: Historical Investigations* (Collegeville, Minn., 1971), 293-383.

doubt; he thought himself unpopular, seen by others as "full of superiority," while his students saw through his "flimsy scholarship." He knew no one who loved him for himself and worried that his relationship even with God was dominated not by love but by fear of Hell. At the heart of his inner loneliness and uncertainty, he came to believe, was the ambition which fueled his enormous energy and hard work. He worried that God would punish him for this fault; yet he took no pleasure in his own achievements. In 1919, at the height of his activity, he noted in his diary:

> I never can, nor could take the least pleasure without having the feeling that sin somewhere lurked in it and I have never succeeded in any single thing without feeling sure I should be knocked in the head by the One who sees everything.

Delighted with the anticipated success of the new American Catholic Historical Association, he was sure something would happen to rob him of his pleasure. Fear of the Lord, he concluded, was the beginning of many things, but not of wisdom.[6]

Students in Guilday's classes, subject to his rigorous demand for precision and accuracy, his refusal to embellish or even to lecture in his graduate classes, did not find him a cold or distant man. On the contrary, they found him kind, generous, and personally concerned for their welfare. His heart and soul were in his work; his books, for all their "life and letters" style, evoked a sympathetic identification of reader and subject because the author so obviously placed himself in his subject's shoes. In September, 1925, finishing

[6] Diary entries for September 17, 1914; November 7, 1914; December 12, 1914; April 15, 1915; June 10, 1916; November 12, 1916; May 1, 1917; and November 19, 1919, GP.

his biography of John England, Guilday reflected how England's life mirrored his own. What a failure England's had been, Guilday mused, his many projects constantly thwarted by more worldly ecclesiastics. "Happiness goes the moment you put your head above the crowd," he concluded. "I watched him die again all day today and I questioned everything — the church, her organization, her polity, the very Christ who inspires her."[7]

There is far too little of this kind of evidence to draw any serious conclusions about Peter Guilday's spiritual or psychological condition. Nevertheless, his occasional diary entries, along with emotional outbursts in letters to close friends, suggest the profound personal costs which arose from a lifelong struggle to combine the values of priesthood, scholarship, and faithful service in a university setting closely related to the hierarchy at a time when the Church was hardly noted for its sympathy to scholarship. In any cultural situation, priesthood itself exerts an enormous pressure upon an individual, who must constantly measure himself against his own high ideals, those of the Church which ordains him, and those of the larger public, which judges him by often unrealistic standards. When that same person is also a scholar, with fundamental commitments to intellectual honesty and scholarly objectivity, that pressure is increased. Add to that the problems associated with the felt need to break new ground promoting what would later be called the intellectual apostolate, and the setting for an individual human life becomes even more complex and demanding. It is hardly any wonder that Peter Guilday's judicious scholarship and gentlemanly appearance masked considerable inner turmoil and agony of spirit.

Guilday was the organizer of modern American Catholic historical scholarship. Shortly after arriving at the Univer-

[7] Diary entry for September 1, 1925.

sity he launched the *Catholic Historical Review,* whose first number appeared in the spring of 1915. Bishop Shahan announced the purposes of the new journal, to provide an outlet for the growing body of scholarly work and raise the standards of historical understanding in the American church. Guilday was managing editor, persuading a variety of writers to submit materials, printing notes of historical interest and crucial documents he was gathering for his own work. A board of editors, composed of other Catholic University faculty, provided little help, a sign of problems to come. Nevertheless, the new journal was immediately successful, winning respectful attention throughout the historical community.

For Guilday the *Review* was the first step towards organizing historical work among American Catholics. He told Bishop Austin Dowling of Des Moines that it would "combine scientific work with a popular presentation." He would have preferred a more strictly professional journal, with emphasis on bibliographic information and publication of critical texts, but he knew in the beginning that he would have to combine this "scientific work" with articles of broader appeal. Shortly after the first issue appeared, he reported proudly to Dowling that non-Catholic historians were "glad to see that we have come out into the open in the latest scientific dress." Admitting that the early articles were "somewhat shoddy" he felt there was promise of better work in the future from the students studying at the University.[8]

There Guilday was organizing his historical seminar, very like the early seminars at Johns Hopkins which had molded modern American historical research. Each year a report of the seminar appeared in pamphlet form, with reports on student research, course outlines, and notes on the "scientific progress of historical research." The first report, in

[8]Guilday to Bishop Dowling, January 19, April 19, May 31, 1915, and June 15, 1916, GP.

1915, featured a guest lecture by Monsignor H.T. Henry of Philadelphia, one of Guilday's early seminary teachers. The paper reflected Guilday's own view of the need to organize and unify scholarly work in order to strengthen the Church's position in American society. "Too long have American Catholic apologists been content to wage guerrilla warfare against their enemies," Henry wrote. "We have failed to organize our activities of self-defense. It was everybody's business to defend us, and the result was, of course, that it really was nobody's business, or worse still, perhaps, it seemed to become the business of incompetent and self-appointed marksmen." Around the years of World War I, such considerations were giving rise to an array of new organizations in the Church and for the next decade Guilday would be at the center of more than one.[9]

By this time World War I was underway in Europe and Guilday, considered pro-German and in fact deeply sympathetic to the Irish, had further reason to feel isolated among the University faculty. Still, he was a very patriotic American and when the war came he found service as secretary to the committee on historical records of the National Catholic War Council, later serving in Philadelphia as assistant educational director of the Student Army Training Corps. Guilday combined a powerful concern for Irish freedom with an equally passionate chauvinism about his own nation. Writing Shane Leslie in England in January, 1918, Guilday argued that the war would never be won by the "Anglo-Saxon" alone; England must learn that victory would come only when she "repaired her mistake by giving Ireland her freedom." It was "Ireland at home and Ireland abroad" that would "carry the armies of the Allies over the breastworks of the Huns." As for the United States, Washington now was the "Rome of the political world," an agent not just of

[9] Msgr. Hugh T. Henry, " History and the Catholic Apologist," American Church History Seminar *Report,* I (1915), 67, GP.

victory but of renewed idealism requiring total commitment. What was needed for the new Rome, he wrote emotionally, "was dogma, excommunication, interdict, suspension — all the weapons Rome uses to keep the faith pure."[10] The comment undoubtedly reflected the exaggerated patriotism of the day rather than any pronounced tendency toward authoritarianism, but it did indicate how Guilday, like so many Catholics of this period, was coming to identify Catholic progress with national idealism, providing a symbolic structure for the combination of Catholic triumphalism and American nationalism which characterized the Catholic subculture between the wars.[11]

In April, 1917, Cardinal John Farley of New York asked Guilday to help him prepare a biography of the first American cardinal, John McCloskey. At Farley's request, Guilday was released from teaching duties and lived for a time at the Cardinal's New York home, in effect ghost writing the book. For all his complaints about "intrigue," Guilday seemed to enjoy ecclesiastical gossip. As he told Shane Leslie a few years later, he was more interested in what Farley "knew or thought he knew" about church affairs than he was in McCloskey's "inane and colourless doings." The work that emerged under Farley's name was a competent sketch of McCloskey's life, but hardly a work of scholarship. Despite his commitment to "scientific" history, Guilday felt little anxiety about pulling punches when dealing with bishops, especially living bishops. Ironically, a year later Guilday was asked to write a piece on Farley for the new *Catholic Encyclopedia* being prepared under the direction of his friend, John Wynne. When he submitted the article, Wynne complained about Guilday's flowery praise of the New York archbishop. Guilday responded candidly: "My idea of the

[10]Guilday to Shane Leslie, January 25, 1918, GP.
[11]William Halsey, *The Survival of American Innocence* (Notre Dame, Ind., 1980).

whole matter was that the Cardinal was to be praised and praised highly and that as far as possible anything detrimental to his good fame was to be quietly overlooked."[12]

Guilday began attending meetings of the American Historical Association in 1914 and regularly complained to friends that there were so few priests in attendance. On several occasions he indicated a desire to begin a similar national organization to promote historical work among Catholics. In the winter of 1917-1918, he presented the idea in papers to the New York and Philadelphia Catholic historical societies. The idea was well received by the former group, whose representatives were satisfied that the new organization, national in membership, would cover all of church history, not just that of the United States. In March he spoke to a small turnout in Philadelphia and was not at all pleased with the response. Friends, puzzled by his reaction, told him there was no significant opposition, though some felt his "good plan" had little hope of success. Guilday explained that he valued local historical societies which stimulated interest in history and encouraged historians to become less antiquarian and more scholarly or, as Guilday put it, "induce us here to become theoretical." Scientific work, however, still appealed only to a few people. The *Review* had been designed to cover the whole spectrum of church history because Guilday believed that the number of topics which could be treated scientifically in American church history would soon be exhausted. There was a need, therefore, to "gather in all who are interested in church history of whatever period or nation." They might start with those attending the annual meeting of the American Historical Association, a group that would likely number no more than twenty. Beyond providing a base of support for serious

[12]Cardinal Farley to Guilday, April 15, 1917; Farley to Shahan, April 28, 1917; Guilday to John J. Wynne, November 4, 1918; Guilday to Shane Leslie, February 1, 1921, GP.

work, such an association would offer an antidote to the occasional anti-Catholicism voiced at the larger meeting. "If you have ever attended any of the American Historical Association meetings, you know that they can get away with murder," he told Arthur Preuss. "If a body similar in design but with a parallel scope should meet contemporaneously, it would do much good both ways."[13]

In October, 1919, Guilday wrote a number of historians proposing a "Catholic society similar in design and outlook to the American Historical Association," meeting side by side with it, and assured of a welcome by the larger group. By the end of November he had forty-one promises to attend the first meeting and was working hard to drum up support, find someone from outside the Catholic University to serve as President, and arrange a program. Lawrence Flick, a Philadelphia physician and leader of the Philadelphia society, was asked to serve as President, because Guilday wished to honor the Philadelphia group whose people "started the historical work" in the United States. Flick accepted the offer. Another early supporter was the convert and historian, Carlton J. H. Hayes of Columbia, who responded warmly to Guilday's invitation: "Any organization that can increase the interest of Catholics in historical study seems to me very much worthwhile."[14]

Guilday's presentation at the first meeting, December 30, 1919, made no mention of apologetics, but set the new association directly in the context of the larger American

[13]Guilday to William Basch, January 1, 1917; Guilday to Lawrence Flick, March 19, 1918; Flick to Guilday, May 7, 1918; James Wilcox to Guilday, May 1, 1918; Guilday to Arthur Preuss, September 6, 1919. The Flick and Wilcox correspondence is in the papers of the American Catholic Historical Association at the Catholic University; other items in GP.

[14]Guilday to Father O'Daniel and others, October 30, 1919; Guilday to Mr. Galbally, December 3, 1919; Carleton J. H. Hayes to Guilday, December 16, 1919; Memorandum "The Origins of the American Catholic Historical Association." All items in ACHA Papers.

Historical Association. When the latter was organized in 1884, it introduced a new era of objective scholarship which had its counterpart in Leo XIII's decree opening the Vatican archives the previous year. The same year the AHA was organized, the first meetings were held of the local Catholic historical societies in New York and Philadelphia. More professional historians had nowhere to go to support the organization required by scientific work. Religion was ruled out of the *Reports* of the American Historical Association, while the American Society of Church History was made up almost entirely of Protestants. In addition to local societies, then, the time had come for a national organization which would promote interest in Catholic history, so that the Church would "be recognized in her true position as the sacred and perpetual mother of all that is best and holiest in civilization."[15]

Guilday was in many ways the Catholic counterpart of J. Franklin Jameson, the guiding spirit of the American Historical Association as it gradually came to be dominated by university-trained scientific historians. For Guilday, the really pioneering work was the gathering, preservation, and publication of documents, and the production of scholarly monographs on limited subjects. This was Jameson's love as well. The similarity was not fortuitous, for Jameson, in his welcoming remarks at this first meeting of the Catholics, informed them he had been greatly influenced by the Bollandists, the scholarly historians whose work in critical evaluation of sources pioneered serious historical investigation among Catholics; their love for documents and rigorous canons of evidence dominated Guilday's own historical studies at Louvain.[16]

[15]Peter Guilday, "The American Catholic Historical Association," *Catholic Historical Review* 6 (1920), 3-14.

[16]Jameson's remarks are in the transcript of the first meeting in the ACHA papers; on Jameson's career see John Higham, *History: The Development of Historical Studies in the United States* (Englewood Cliffs, N.J., 1965), 1-145.

Many of those attending the first meeting were not historians of this sort, but men like Doctor Flick, amateurs devoted to historical study, or priests who linked historical research to apologetics and to an aura of Catholic romanticism. Anxious as he was to promote professionalization of historical studies, Guilday was nevertheless forced to depend upon these and other non-professional supporters, and at times bend the organization and his own work to their perception of what was needed. When doing so, he had to proceed cautiously to retain the support of more scholarly Catholics and preserve for the new Association a cordial relationship with the larger body, the AHA. Hayes, for example, was elected secretary but soon felt frustrated by the fact that several priests had not answered his letters. He was convinced, he told Guilday, "that a layman teaching in a non-Catholic University is not a suitable person to act as secretary of an organization, the great majority of whose officers are clergymen and not vitally interested in historical scholarship." Guilday carefully soothed Hayes' feelings, pointing out that his election had raised the tone of the organization and promising to help lighten the load of his work.

Guilday himself had not yet sorted out the purposes of the organization. In a letter to his friend Thomas Meehan on February 4, 1920, he said he had been sick since the Cleveland meeting, but was elated at its success. "I see such wondrous possibilities in the movement for the honor of the Church that no effort of my part will be spared to make our first annual meeting here a success," he wrote. "Naturally, such success will always be local and provincial; the American Historical Association hardly expects more. But in twenty-five years time, 25 meetings in 25 different cities, with a year of preparation for each one, are bound to leave their impress on those for whom the ACHA was founded: the non-Catholic historical student and teacher." Yet, in a memorandum written about the same time, he listed among the "Practical Aims" for the new organization increasing historical knowledge through research, and diffusing the results through popular books, articles and educational materials. The Association was not just to answer non-Catholic objections, as his letter to Meehan suggested, but to promote positive historical knowledge: "We must try to create an atmosphere of historical interest, a kind of 'historical mindedness' in our Catholic community."[17]

Privately, Guilday remained far from satisfied through the early years of the Association. Reviewing the New Haven meeting of 1922 with Dr. Flick, he admitted the apparent success of the meeting in impressing the AHA. Non-Catholic scholars had sensed "a power in scholarship which, if once poured out generously, would be liable to crowd their Association off toward the wings." Moreover, Catholic "non-scholars" had learned the value of "centralization" and "rejoiced in the display." Unfortunately, Guilday thought, both reactions were "dangerous to our success." What was vitally necessary, Guilday argued, was to stay "strictly within our own field," taking an equal place "but never forcing ourselves upon the larger group" and most important, trying to "hold fast against any tendency to make the meeting a 'Catholic Christmas social treat.'" The Association could not afford to have the work of James Walsh, an amateur historian whose book on the thirteenth century was enormously popular, "put forward as typical of the scholarship we are seeking." He went on to evaluate the papers given at the meeting, finding few beyond criticism. One was "too legal" for real history, another, by an Irishman, "the last echo of an old time paddy," a third "a bit snappish." One seemed to reduce "all sociology to an act of contrition" while the address of a well-known Boston priest-

---

[17]Hayes to Guilday, February 18, 1920; Guilday to Hayes, February 19, 1920, Guilday to Thomas Meehan, February 4, 1920, GP; Manuscript "Some Practical Aims of the American Catholic Historical Association," ACHA Papers.

historian "was a bit too much like a chance opportunity to make a profession of faith."[18]

Like the earlier organizers of the American Historical Association, Guilday remained trapped in a dilemma. On the one hand he wished to promote "scientific history" of the kind best done in a university setting, but his organization and *Review* needed the financial backing of non-professional historians and a broad reading public, in his case, for the most part priests. Behind the articles, speeches, and papers in which both groups praised each other, there were real differences, both in the approach they took to history and in the priorities they set for the Association and *Review*. In 1920, Guilday surrendered control of the *Review* to a new managing editor, in order to make time for the work of the Association, his teaching, and his own research and writing. Unfortunately, he soon found the journal leaning toward a more popular format, a drift supported by its readers. In 1926, he appealed to Shahan with a plan for reorganization intended to preserve the *Review*'s scholarly objectives. That summer he travelled to Europe recruiting scholars to serve as contributing editors; the Catholic University group was eased out and Guilday resumed control. But the problem persisted. In 1931, reviewing three decades of work on American church history, he appealed to the priest readers of the *American Ecclesiastical Review* to support development of a "scientific center" of Catholic historical studies in Washington to promote serious scholarship, provide a basis for a national library and archives, train younger men in the work, and build "a corporate Catholic consciousness" of the need to preserve historical sources. Such a center, he contended, would help "gradually eliminate the amateurs who in so many cases have misused their opportunities and have so pitiably confused the terrain

---

[18]Guilday to Flick, January 12, 1923, GP.

of a subject which should be sacred to every Catholic heart."[19]

While all this organizing work was going on, Guilday was a professor at the Catholic University of America. The University he found when he arrived in 1914 was still less than three decades old, and throughout its history it had been a storm center of controversy. Established in 1886 with the support of the liberal leaders of the American hierarchy, most notably John Lancaster Spalding, Cardinal James Gibbons, and John J. Keane, the first rector, the University won papal backing and the endorsement of the body of bishops. The University was intended, in Spalding's words, to be "at once a scientific institution, a school of culture, and a training ground for the business of life." Without an undergraduate college, it would be a "true university," dedicated to research and graduate study. However, the Catholic University fell victim to the controversies that stirred the American church in the 1890s, climaxing in Pope Leo XIII's condemnation of "Americanism" in 1899. Lacking the support of a united hierarchy, plagued by financial problems and internal divisions, the University soon added undergraduate studies, began regular programs of seminary education, and added professional schools of education and social work to provide trained leadership for new church agencies.[20]

[19]Guilday to Arthur Preuss, Feburary 1, 1921; Guilday to Father Betten, November 29, 1925; Guilday to Bishop Shahan, November 11, 1926, GP; "Recent Studies in American Catholic History," *Ecclesiastical Review* 84 (1931), 545-46.

[20]The Spalding quote is from a speech at the laying of the cornerstone, on May 24, 1888, printed in John Tracy Ellis, editor, *Documents of American Catholic History,* II (Chicago, 1967), 465; the history of the University in its early years may be found in: John Tracy Ellis, *The Formative Years of the Catholic University of America* (Washington, 1946); Patrick H. Ahern, *The Catholic University of America, 1887-1896: The Rectorship of John J. Keane* (Washington, 1949); Peter E. Hogan, *The Catholic University of America, 1896-1903: The Rectorship of Thomas J. Conaty* (Washington, 1949); and Colman J. Barry, *The Catholic University of America, 1903-1909: The Rectorship of Denis J. O'Connell* (Washington, 1950). See also my paper "The Catholic University of America and the 'Organizational Revolution' in American Catholicism" delivered to the annual meeting of the Organization of American Historians, 1980.

Shahan's efforts to recruit Guilday, and his support for the *Review* and the Association, indicated that the original dream of a "true university" had not altogether disappeared. Moreover, the University had many advantages over other Catholic institutions; when Guilday arrived it was still one of only two Catholic institutions offering a significant number of advanced degrees. As a pontifically chartered and episcopally sponsored university, it enjoyed the patronage of the Holy See and the hierarchy. On the other hand, the condemnation of modernism a decade earlier had thrown a pall of suspicion over all universities, an atmosphere made worse by an incident which had forced one professor to leave the Catholic University under a cloud of accusation arising from mistaken identity.[21] Episcopal support meant an annual financial drive to raise money, but it also meant caution lest the suspicions of an increasingly unimaginative and unadventurous group of bishops be aroused. Finally, the long series of controversies left many faculty and administrators exhausted, some cynical, as Guilday's early diary entries indicated. Finally, the financial problems of the University were forcing increased attention to undergraduate education, which seemed to offer the surest route to stability in the period after World War I.

It is hardly surprising that in this atmosphere the young historian fresh from Louvain, filled with plans for the modernization of historical studies, should feel almost immediately a sense of loneliness and estrangement. Just as in the secular historical community, the rise of scientific history was linked directly to the emergence of the modern university, centered in the graduate school and the research seminar, so in the Catholic community the struggle for a new scholarship was bound up with the fate of the nation's single Catholic institution with a pretension toward

---

[21]On the impact of the modernist controversy, see Gannon, "Intellectual Isolation of the American Priest."

advanced studies and research. For Guilday, from the very beginning, the work of the *Review* and the Association were means to promote the new history, which meant to build up a constituency for his university-based program of gathering documents, training researchers, and producing scholarly monographs. Unfortunately, the battle to overcome the amateurs in the Association was a trifle compared to the struggle to vindicate scholarly ideals amid the practical and human problems confronting the University.

From the beginning Guilday chafed under what he considered the sluggish progress of the University. He felt that some of his colleagues believed he was launching into too many projects at too young an age but, as he told his friend Arthur Preuss, if he waited until he was "seasoned the spirit of inertia which seems to have settled down over the University would have me by the throat." In his diary in October, 1917, he noted that he had visited at the home of William Kerby, a distinguished moral theologian, where he had spoken "in disgust" of the "spiritual, moral, intellectual and administrative bankruptcy of the University." He urged Kerby to organize the younger faculty and force reforms on the University, but unfortunately "it had no more effect on him than water on the proverbial duck's back." Kerby, Guilday wrote cruelly, seemed "as rooted in medievalism as the others."[22]

In 1919 Guilday was again experiencing unpopularity in the University; he even believed there was an "anti-Guilday faction." "My chief sins have been discontent voiced in criticism of things at Catholic University and in the Church of God at large," he wrote. Perhaps one reason was his passionate concern for history as a field of study. In September, he wrote in his diary that a University was primarily a place for research and any particular university should

---

[22]Guilday to Arthur Preuss, February 25, 1916; Diary entry October 13, 1917, GP.

concentrate on those fields in which it was best suited to make a contribution. The Catholic University was not suited for science, because it was not wealthy, and it could not compete with European universities like Louvain in philosophy and theology; the Catholic University should instead be a center for historical studies. "An arsenal, a fortress, could be built here with the historical sciences," he wrote. "We could do good by brushing away ignorance, prejudice and bigotry and by stimulating a love for the story of the Church."[23] "The philosophy of the situation to me is this," he wrote Monsignor J. L. Kirlin of Philadelphia. "Here in the United States, the practical, pragmatic turn education in non-Catholic institutions assumed around the eighties has created a new and distinct kind of Protestant mind." In Europe, "the doctrinal, liturgical and disciplinary sides of the church are the subjects of controversy," but in the United States "it is the history of the Church which is mainly attacked. Now, those who are attacking us from the historical standpoint are scholars," he added. "Our purpose then is to create [a] group of scholars able and competent to answer these historical objections."[24] Scientific history, then, was one element in the larger task of defending the Church and bringing it to an effective encounter with modern culture. Like his secular historical counterparts, Guilday believed that after gathering documents, sifting them for the facts, and subjecting them to canons of evidence, a single, true story would emerge and it would vindicate the Church and win attention for her claims. But where could one find support for that work? As a priest he could hardly turn to a non-Catholic university; among the Catholic schools only the Catholic University had even a verbal commitment to higher studies, research, and graduate edu-

[23] Diary entry for September 8, 1919, GP.
[24] Guilday to J. L. F. Kirlin, September 21, 1922, GP.

cation. Thus Guilday fought to save the original commitment of the University to advanced studies and to win that fight he needed support among the bishops. Thus he cultivated the support of powerful bishops and those less powerful who shared his interest in historical studies, shaping his argument to meet their concerns.

Several bishops provided financial contributions for Guilday's own work. One, John T. McNicholas, then the bishop of Duluth, was cultivated in terms echoed in Guilday's correspondence with others. In 1920 Guilday told McNicholas the University should, as its founders intended, be "a school of research, of graduate work, of contribution not alone to the general educational progress of the Church, but of influence and effort upon the nation at large." Praising McNicholas for a recent sermon at the University in which he had emphasized the "directive influence of Catholic doctrine, of Catholic law and discipline, and of Catholic history," Guilday noted that it was precisely its Catholicity which provided the University with the foundation for this contribution:

> To me it is of little value to the Church or to the nation, if for example, our Engineering School should turn out a genius. But it is of prime importance that in the intellectual world today, we should be recognized as *orthodox,* that is as showing to the nation the *right way* and the *straight way* amid all the mental unrest around us.

Toward that end, Guilday hoped "to lay the foundation of a strong school of historical study at the University." From the beginning his plan moved in two directions: "a national association of everyone interested in the past history of the Church, with a constructive, *apologétique* platform, and a national magazine." The Association was now well underway, while the *Review,* six years old, was meeting the standards of the best European journals.

But these accomplishments were only the external, visible aspects of his program. "The intrinsic part of the plan is to create a school of trained historians here," he added. "These will always be in the highest majority priests, and their work will be a blending of theology, canon law, and history. To proceed on constructive, edifying, stimulating, *apologétique* lines is the *mot d'ordre*," he concluded.[25] In the twenties Guilday multiplied projects for the history program. A privately printed circular "On the Creation of an Institute for American Church History" contained proposals for archives, research, graduate study, and publication which he hoped would catch the attention of the trustees. Later, he wrote another pamphlet on graduate studies, again hoping it would show those responsible for the University that the "old ideal" was not dead. Most faculty were unsympathetic, he wrote a friend, some because they were afraid, some because they wished to become rector, and others because they had grown defensive and angry that anyone should raise the question. Yet, if it was not faced, he feared that Walter George Smith's description of the University as "an advanced high school" would come true.[26]

In 1921, as the University searched for a new rector, Guilday told the Chancellor, Archbishop Michael J. Curley of Baltimore, that the University was in danger of becoming an "intellectual failure." He traced its problems to two sources: initiating an undergraduate program, thus breaking faith with the nation's Catholic colleges, and tolerating an unproductive graduate school faculty. A few weeks later he wrote his colleague, John A. Ryan, soliciting his support for another term as rector for Bishop Shahan. Financial problems, a project to build a national basilica on the grounds, discipline, and concern over "the academic value of work done" had persuaded many to go along with Shahan's desire

[25]Guilday to Bishop McNicholas, November 1 and 15, 1920, and November 28, 1928, GP.

[26]Circular is in GP; Guilday to Msgr. Richard J. Haberlin, May 21, 1924, GP.

to pass the burdens of the leadership to a younger man, but Guilday was concerned that the favored candidates had less appreciation of the value of serious scholarship.[27]

In 1925, the internal battle grew heated and some faculty were convinced that the administration wished to abandon graduate study altogether. Shahan, Guilday's original mentor, was by then aligned on the other side. In March, 1925, the senior faculty rejected a new constitution, which sharply reduced the power of the faculty and institutionalized the commitment to undergraduate and seminary education. Instead, they voted to establish the centralized graduate program Guilday favored. Guilday was ecstatic until, in April, the trustees rejected the faculty proposal without discussion. Guilday noted angrily in his diary that Shahan's policy of supporting the status quo was victorious, overriding the united voice of the staff asking for a "higher and better centralization of our Graduate work."

> The failure is complete. . . . The day will come when all those who are involved in this tragic break with higher Catholic scholarship will be held up to scorn and ridicule.

Later he told a friend that he had held back from criticizing Shahan openly because he was close to him and appreciated the circumstances and problems which faced him. The University was a "shadow" of what it might be, but it was not Shahan but Edward Pace, the University's vice-rector, who "has been the evil genius of the past twenty years."[28]

[27]Guilday to Archbishop Curley, September 27, 1921, and to John A. Ryan, October 27, 1921, GP.

[28]The fight can be traced through the diary in the spring and summer of 1925. The following entries are particularly important: February 16, April 26, and June 24, 1925, and March 7, March 20, April 14, 1926. He spoke of holding back in attacks on Shahan in a letter to Arthur Preuss on December 7, 1927. For Guilday the problem centered on the undergraduate curriculum; he told J. Hugh O'Donnell, C.S.C., on October 16, 1925, that the university faced the choice of "abolishing completely the undergraduate department or of sinking into second rate educational work," GP.

By 1925 it was clear Guilday was fighting a losing battle. His comments on university affairs became increasingly bitter. He still wished that the original plans had been fulfilled, "a selected group of scholars, with the apparatus necessary, freed from all academic duties, living in a community as a phalanx for information on all Catholic subjects and as an arsenal for the defense of the church." Instead, the process of "intellectual suicide was well underway." Worse, it seemed that the stand he had taken had isolated him within the University and even jeopardized support for his work. In 1925 a proposal for assisting apologetical work through the Paulists was turned down by the rector, "the last of a series which in my regard bears an invidious interpretation," opposition that stemmed from his stand on "university studies."[29]

In the spring of 1927, Guilday told Wilfrid Parsons, S.J., that publication of his biography of John England had been delayed by the financial problems of the University and its inauguration of a six-year seminary program, another step towards ending "higher work" at the University. One reason the bishops and faculty had failed to support his plea for graduate studies was his association with the Jesuits, perceived by many to be enemies of the Catholic University. Charges were made that John Carroll was pro-Jesuit, that Guilday covered this up in his book on Carroll, and that the *America* press had taken *England* in order to censor anything against the Society. Guilday admitted he regarded the Jesuits as among the sole supporters of serious scholarship and admitted his "heresy," his belief that the only means to foster real scholarship at the Catholic University was establishment of a house of studies for Jesuit scholastics and the presence of Jesuits on the faculties of theology and philosophy. Guilday enthusiastically endorsed the Jesuits'

[29]Guilday to Dominican Provincial, August 5, 1929; Guilday to Joseph McSorley, August 24, 1925, GP.

new quarterly *Thought* and contributed an article to its first number. At the same time he warned Shahan that the new publication would include an historical section and could well become a rival to the *Review* unless Guilday's plans to improve the *Review*'s quality were adopted.[30] He told J. Franklin Jameson his stand against augmenting undergraduate work and for centralizing the administration of research and graduate study had cost him any chance to become university rector. Placing his career in a context Jameson could appreciate, Guilday noted that "it has been a hard fight to save historical study here from becoming a species of Catholic chauvinism." On the brighter side there were many young priests dedicated to the work; he was trying to choose the best and channel their energy into history, "not primarily as duty to the Catholic Church but to the American Republic."[31]

Yet if Guilday was indeed a victim of university politics, he was also an agent of that subordination of scholarship to church purposes which was at the heart of the whole problem. He cultivated the bishops, even though he knew that few really understood or shared his commitments. Dowling, an early supporter, wrote a harshly critical review of Guilday's biography of John Carroll, a step which the author believed greatly pleased his enemies both in the American Historical Association and at the University. Dowling and Archbishop John J. Glennon of St. Louis had urged him to establish a center to study the problem of leakage, the loss of immigrants to the Catholic faith, but when Gerald Shaughnessy wrote a dissertation on that subject under the direction of another professor, Guilday was angry and determined to suppress the results. He solicited financial assistance from Boston's Cardinal William H. O'Connell

---

[30]Guilday to Wilfrid Parsons, May 24, 1927; Guilday to Francis LeBuffe, October 29, 1925; and Guilday to Bishop Shahan, January 11, 1929, GP.

[31]Guilday to J. Franklin Jameson, December 10, 1927, GP.

and wrote fulsome letters of praise to priests close to the Boston Archbishop. In 1921, he told one Boston priest O'Connell was "the best hated man in America and yet he has such wondrous powers." Yet O'Connell was no friend of the University and an active opponent of the National Catholic Welfare Conference. Nor was he a true friend of historical scholarship. Delighted with a gift of Guilday's biography of John England, the monarchical O'Connell surprisingly identified with the democratic England, apparently because he saw himself and England as victims of the conspiracies of lesser men. His predecessor, Archbishop John Williams, had destroyed "every vestige of documents that had any relation to his life except the purely official," O'Connell told Guilday. After reading *England*, O'Connell was convinced Williams was right to do so.[32]

Guilday must have flinched at this remark; yet he was himself concerned with the image of respectability and unity O'Connell thought necessary for the well being of the Church. He had told McNicholas he was concerned with the "orthodox" and "right way" and he seemed to agree that the bishops knew this best. In 1927, he told his friend Justin McGrath of the NCWC News Service that he always had a member of the hierarchy read over his work before publication: "I think it may be quite possible that there are some who would accept things from my pen as authoritative and I think one has to hesitate on what can be said and how it should be said."[33]

This attitude was evident again and again in Guilday's correspondence and published work. Sympathetic though he was with the dreams of Spalding and the ideals of the Americanists of the previous generation, he carefully

---

[32]Guilday to Msgr. Edwin Burton, February 28, 1921; Guilday to O'Connell, November 9, 1922; diary entry February 25, 1922; and O'Connell to Guilday October 28, 1927, GP.

[33]Guilday to Justin McGrath, April 4, 1927, GP.

avoided discussion of the events of those years. Admitting to Shane Leslie that he had suppressed references to Edward McGlynn and Archbishop John Ireland from an article he had written, Guilday indicated his sympathy with Ireland but regret that the liberal leader was incompetent in church politics: "there was not enough of John Carroll in him." To a non-Catholic historian who had asked about McGlynn, Guilday stressed the fact that the New York priest had been punished not for his social and economic ideas but for "insubordination" which, in a priest, was an "unforgiveable offense." When Eduardo Soderini, who was writing a biography of Leo XIII, wrote asking for information on the Americanist episode, Guilday was frank about the need for caution. The period had not yet been treated by historians, he told Soderini, because some of the principals were still alive. Furthermore, the association of Americanism and Modernism and the personal conflicts which these condemnations had caused made scholars "feel that the questions involved in our progress from 1878 to the death of Pius X should not be made the matter of public discussion for some years yet." He went on to comment, however, that Archbishop Francesco Satolli, who arrived as Apostolic Delegate in 1893, played a crucial role. He was a man whose "personal habits and ethical viewpoints were somewhat at variance with American customs." Such personal considerations were so interwoven with events, he concluded, that it would be years before things could be sorted out. Indeed, even writing about these things in a friendly letter "should be condemned by some of our leaders." His own essay on the period, which appeared in the *Review* in 1921 and avoided serious discussion of church divisions, "was gone over carefully by Cardinal Gibbons before his death."[34]

[34]Guilday to Dr. Henry Jones Ford, August 18, 1925; and Guilday to Eduardo Soderini, January 13, 1922. He spoke further of his "contempt" for Satolli in Guilday to Thomas F. Meehan, March 2, 1926, GP. Guilday to Shane Leslie, February 2, 1921, GP.

Guilday was equally reluctant to share his full views of nativism and anti-Catholicism. When Edward F. McSweeney of the Knights of Columbus asked Guilday to write a book on the subject, Guilday responded: "I must warn you...that my studies in the subject...do not lead me to the traditional attitude of American Catholics. The extenuating circumstances are too great." He could only write of the Know Nothings, for example, with a strong condemnation of Roman officials "who sent Bedini here to spy out the country." He would find it "equally hard to read the traditional bigotry into the citizenship plank of the Native American party without showing clearly the total disregard of conscience and honor on the part of Irish immigrants coming into the country." Most surprising, Guilday told McSweeney he could not "treat the whole question of anti-Catholicism without placing clearly where it belongs the blame for keeping Catholics *exiled* in their own country: this means Rome and the hierarchy here."[35] When historian Peter Johnson commented to Guilday that American bishops had been silent before Protestant attacks in the early nineteenth century not because of their faith in Protestant fairness but their fear of persecution, a lack of fearlessness seen again during the 1928 campaign "when everything dear to Catholics was trampled upon," Guilday ignored the historical point, but simply noted that "much could be written on episcopal silence in certain periods, my dear friend, but there would be little silence afterwards for the man who dared to tell the story."[36] Guilday himself regularly complained about episcopal silence and caution, but he also went to some pains to justify their behavior when writing about the Church's history, presumably because he shared their concern for the unity of the Church and its need for

[35]Guilday to Edward F. McSweeney, December 18, 1922; see also Guilday to Carleton J. H. Hayes, March 6, 1933, GP.

[36]Guilday to Peter Leo Johnson, December 14, 1933, GP.

careful accommodation to the demands of the American environment. Nowhere was this more evident than in his praise for the bishops for their refusal to confront the greatest public issue in nineteenth century America, slavery. Writing of the Plenary Council of 1852, he concluded:

> Perhaps the outstanding proof of the wisdom of our prelates lies in their silence on the slavery question, then dividing political parties and the Churches of other denominations into antagonistic groups which have never been wholly reconciled. Many expected at the time that this largest and greatest of all Christian official assemblies... would take cognizance of the political debates on the slavery question, and would issue a definite statement on the Church's position; but the hierarchy rejected the apparent demand for such a decision and refused to break with the traditional policy of the Church which excluded rigourously all discussions or political debate. The prelates were face to face with problems of far greater moment in their effort to keep abreast of the tide of immigration to our shores. No other Church in the land, then as now, has realized the supreme need of keeping itself free from political questions; and no other church has sympathized more profoundly with the basic American distrust of ecclesiastical interference in public life.[37]

Occasionally Guilday's caution could get him into trouble. When a writer in the Brooklyn *Tablet* criticized an article Guilday had written which ignored the large number of Irish in America at the time of the Revolution, Guilday wrote to Monsignor McGolrick of the Brooklyn diocese to complain that his critic had "opened up one aspect of the

[37] Peter Guilday, *A History of the Councils of Baltimore, 1791-1884* (New York, 1932), 182.

question of American Catholicism which I have done my
best to silence." While the sources were uncertain, he
accepted the possibility that such large numbers of Irish
were present, "but my attitude is not to stress this fact too
much lest the obvious conclusion be made by our people,
namely why did so many Irish Catholics lose their faith so
quickly. It is not a pleasant aspect of Catholic devotion to
the faith." McGolrick responded, apologizing for the
"blunder" of printing the letter, but editor Patrick Scanlan
was furious. He protested to Guilday for going over his head
and wrote McGolrick presenting his author's credentials
and complaining that Guilday seemed to be the first contributor to the paper whose work could not even be discussed.[38]

The episode must have been particularly distressing for
Guilday, as ordinarily he looked to lay Catholics like Scanlan to bring into the open the hidden problems of the
American Church. Invited to join the initial discussions
which led to the formation of *Commonweal*, he hoped the
new journal would be an instrument for arousing the laity.
He wrote Yale chaplain T. Lawrason Riggs: "My thesis is
this: if it catches up the voices of Catholic unrest in the land
and articulates them in an irenic, constructive way, I believe
you have a glorious mission to fulfill." He explained to
Doctor James Walsh that he believed that American
Catholics needed a lofty, inspiring sense of their mission and
they were not getting it from their leaders:

> Rome is misunderstanding us, and our clerical leadership
> is unfortunately misunderstanding us. Please do not put
> me down as one of the young upstarts who want to
> revamp everything but as I see the Catholic situation in
> the United States....we are not being strengthened in
> our Americanism. Even that word has a bad meaning

[38]Guilday to Msgr. McGolrick, April 11, 1928; McGolrick to Guilday, April 12,
1928; and Scanlan to Guilday, April 13, 1928, GP.

.... If the review manages to give the little fellows like me just that peculiar drop of ambrosial confidence.... it will be a blessing. I don't want it to take me up off my knees but I do want it to put some gumption into my prayers.

In late November, 1924, depressed by events at the University and upset by the Democratic convention at which Al Smith had been rejected after 103 ballots and the delegates split badly over the Klu Klux Klan, Guilday was "eagerly awaiting the Commonweal," hoping it would meet "all the hopes spoken about it." "There is talent aplenty in the land," he told John Wynne, "but I doubt if there is as much courage in dealing with American Church matters." Once again, there was the problem of leadership: "Our traditions are being formed without guidance or foresight and the mould the Church is taking is not a progressive one."[39]

Submission to episcopal review, cautious presentation of controversial issues, political intrigues within the University, and careful balancing of professional and amateur interests in the Association were only a few of the compromises and accommodations forced upon Guilday by the circumstances in which he worked. Even his own research interests had to give way to the conditions of the Church in the interwar years. His best works were his biographies of *Carroll* and *England,* initially understood as building blocks toward a full history of the American Church, to be completed with studies of John Hughes and Cardinal Gibbons. Yet this was not the work he wanted to do or thought himself qualified to do.

In 1924 he complained to his old friend Hermann Heuser of the *American Ecclesiastical Review* that he had begged bishops to back him in doing the work "Louvain prepared me to do — not to *write* history but to publish a critical text

[39]Guilday to T. Lawrason Riggs, February 15, 1923; Guilday to James J. Walsh, January 12, 1923; and Guilday to John J. Wynne, November 6, 1924, GP.

of the *Analecta Ecclesiastica* of the United States." He noted that Archbishop Glennon of St. Louis had told him that the way was not yet prepared for such work, so he should blend it with episcopal biography. In *Carroll* he had "published *in extenso* all the documents of that period" and if his interpretation "ran astray at times, later writers may correct that." Similarly, if anything went wrong with his interpretation of John England, he would nevertheless have achieved his "only purpose — the collection and presentation of all the manuscript sources of the period." When Arthur Preuss complained of the excessive use of documents in the texts of *Carroll* and *England*, Guilday characteristically replied that he had placed the problem of the construction of the volumes before "four of our best archbishops" and all agreed that the separation of the documents into an appendix would be a mistake. Guilday had reluctantly accepted this advice: "What I have hoped for, prayed for, talked for is that I will not be obliged to continue doing something for which I have not the slightest gift — biography — and be supported in the work of publishing documents with notes etc.," he wrote. If he were free tomorrow, he told Preuss wistfully, "I should do nothing else but publish volume after volume of documents and leave the writing to the others." Louvain had sent him home "as a skilled worker in the auxiliary sciences, not as a writer. I might as well have been trained in Sanskrit."[40]

Yet the biographies allowed him to present not only many of the documents, but also to shape an historical interpretation of the American church which reinforced his convictions about its mission, and he was by no means unconscious of this purposefulness in interpretation. In late 1922, Peter Guilday wrote an article describing Bishop John England's experiment in constitutional government a cen-

---

[40]Guilday to Msgr. Arthur Connolly, November 9, 1922; Guilday to Hermann Heuser, March 18, 1924; and Guilday to Arthur Preuss, November 17, 1927, GP.

tury before, for his friend Heuser's *American Ecclesiastical Review*. Guilday had originally entitled the article "America's First Welfare Council," a reference to the recently established National Catholic Welfare Council, whose short existence was then threatened with Roman suppression. Heuser was afraid the title would inject the article into the controversy surrounding the NCWC and Guilday agreed. He suggested instead a title drawn from an England letter cited in the article: "Fighting in Detached Squads."[41] The phrase aptly described Guilday's own attitude toward the Church of his day and provides a good description of a central thrust of his own work. Like many progressive Catholics of his day, Guilday believed that the Church in the United States needed to develop a more organized approach to its mission to defend itself against non-Catholic attacks, which had arisen once again in the period after World War I, and to bring the full resources of its tradition to bear on American cultural and political life. To attain such an active stance the Church desperately needed to overcome its own internal divisions, its psychology of defeat, and its continual bickering and mobilize its best talents. These views of the contemporary Church shaped, and were shaped, by Guilday's historical interpretations.

It would be possible to characterize these views as Americanist, in the sense that he read American Catholic history in terms of adaptation of a more or less unchanging Church to the demands of an ever changing American environment, adding to that adaptationist framework a normative sense of the greatness and potential of America, and therefore of the American church. As he put it in his biography of John Carroll, the historic problem of the Church was "to adjust

---

[41] Heuser to Guilday, November 13, 1922; and Guilday to Heuser, November 16, 1922, GP. "Detached squads" quote from a letter of England to Archbishop Ambrose Maréchal in 1823, in Guilday, *The Life and Times of John England, First Bishop of Charleston (1786-1842)* (New York, 1927), I, 408.

its traditional and quite perfect form of government to the situation of the new nation." It was not primarily a problem of Church and State, but a problem of administration. To draw the proper "demarkation of the spiritual and the temporal," Carroll understood the need to Americanize the population and adjust the structures of the Church to the unique demands of the new society:

> America, to be America, to admit what was even then apparent to all, could not be made up of juxtaposed little nations. America, to follow the providential guidance which has been bestowed upon its great leaders, should become one nation made up of a people speaking the same tongue, enjoying the same privileges and living for the same purpose: the glory and prestige of the new Republic. The Church in America, to fulfill to the utmost its destiny as the most compact religious body in the nation, should be American in its appeal, American in its sentiments and its spirit.[42]

He found in John England a model for this blend of loyal Americanism and fervent Catholicism. During his lifetime, England was "unquestionably the foremost ecclesiastic in the Catholic Church in the United States," Guilday believed. Zealous for the ideals of the American republic, he had the same "mystical love of America" which marked Carroll. The problem of the latter had been that while "no further experiment in the art of ruling the Catholic faithful was needed," American government was in an experimental stage. Dissensions he had been able to keep silent broke out into the open after his death; what the Church thus needed was a strong central government, "profound in its loyalty to the Holy See, wholeheartedly in unison with the

---

[42]Peter Guilday, *The Life and Times of John Carroll, Archbishop of Baltimore 1735-1815)* (Westminster, 1954), 773.

dominant anti-foreign and national policies of the day, with all parts properly subordinated by the laws of ecclesiastical authority." It was England who pointed in this direction and, despite his setbacks, offered the surest road to securing the place of Catholicism in American life. What enabled him to do so was that, unlike his French opponents, he was thoroughly American:

> It is on account of his untrammeled Americanism, on account of his thorough grasp of American idealism, and above all because of the unique place he made for himself in American history by interpreting justly and accurately to his own epoch the harmony between Catholic principles and the constitutional bases of American government.[43]

Even non-Catholics of the day understood that the bitter attacks launched against Catholics disturbed social conditions to the detriment of all parties. They feared "foreign spiritual interference in American temporal affairs, or foreign temporal interference in American spiritual affairs," and these fears reflected a "grave problem," the "Americanization of alien Catholics who came in such numbers after the war of 1812." No bishop understood as clearly as England the need for such Americanization. As Guilday saw it, England found in America a foreign church and he devoted his life to making it American. He understood that the greatest dangers came not from external attack but internal resistance. Carroll's successors organized the Church "partly in the European system"; they emphasized "parochial and institutional life and neglected to seek a substitute for public opinion." Reducing the foreign loyalties of the clergy, forming a more cooperative laity by granting them a share of administration, and constant efforts to reduce Protestant

---

[43]Guilday, *England,* I, vii-viii.

prejudice and fears would enable the Church to better assimilate its members and grow in the respect and confidence of other Americans.[44]

Work on England thus confirmed some of Guilday's most basic assumptions about the situation of the American Catholic Church. In the period 1820 to 1840, the American Church "practically stagnated," he believed, because French bishops and clergy succeeded in keeping England in Charleston, and left him almost alone to defend the Church against revived anti-Catholicism. As he brought the book to a close in 1925, he wrote a friend:

> I do not know how far I shall go in speaking my mind frankly, but my belief is that the Roman Catholic Church lost America between 1820 and 1840 and that highly instrumental in that loss was the determination on the part of the French Prelates who were here to keep John England out of national affairs. No more open attempt to found a dynasty could be seen than in these years in the see of Baltimore.[45]

The combination of defensiveness and latent triumphalism was even more evident in a "sesquicentennial essay" Guilday prepared for the first issue of the new Jesuit quarterly, *Thought*, in June, 1926. The fact that the Church's "center of government was in a foreign land" often led to mistrust, Guilday argued. Nowhere had the "Catholic Question" of dual allegiance occasioned "more dangerous mistakes" among non-Catholics and "even to a certain extent among many ill-instructed Catholics" than in English-speaking lands. As a result, "the history of the Catholic Church in the United States from colonial times to our own

---

[44]*Ibid.*, 68-72.
[45]Guilday to W. H. Grattan Flood, August 18, 1925, GP.

lies in the explanation of the delicate and supremely necessary adjustment of its spiritual obedience to the temporal claims upon Catholic civil allegiance." Long-standing Protestant prejudice accounted for the fact that many Americans had "never accepted whole-heartedly the historic fact of American Catholic love for America." Nor had they understood "how naturally and integrally the spiritual allegiance of [the Church's] members knits into their national allegiance so as to round each other out."

Guilday then went on to divide American Catholic history into three periods. The first, from 1778 to 1826, was one of "comparative calm"; the second, extending to 1876, was marked by "much violence, the purpose of which was to halt the spread of the Church." The final period, since 1876, was "justly estimated in the balance of disintegrating Protestant doctrines and in the realization that morality and religion are closely interwoven with the survival of the Republic." Citing John Lancaster Spalding's appeal to Catholics "to enter more fully into the public life of the country," Guilday noted the increasing national organization of the Church and the "cautious and orthodox" direction given by church leaders to insure that the new nationalism did not injure "the delicate fabric of its inner organization which must always depart from and return to the parochial and diocesan limitations to which all national movements in Catholicism are rightly subject." Nowhere in the nation, he claimed, was there "any institution which has so steadfastly and so eminently advanced the best interest of the country." Its unifying and stable organization contributed to national unity and stability through the civil war, industrial conflict, immigration, and made it America's "most sacred national asset."

America can never forget God with one-fifth of its citizens holding a supernatural aim as their chief purpose in life. America can never be effectually divided so long as these millions who adore God in the same spirit, partake of the same sacramental life, and are all the children of the one true God and brethren of the one Christ, remain faithful to the teaching of the great Church of the ages; obedience in spiritual matters to Jesus Christ, the King of the Universe, and steadfast loyalty to the Republic in national and civic concerns.[46]

In a letter to a Philadelphia lawyer, Thomas H. Meagher, a year earlier, Guilday similarly divided American history into three phases: one to 1815, when America established its independence from Europe, a second to 1895, when the United States stood aloof from European affairs, and a third since, when the nation was merging back into western civilization. In this new era of entry into world affairs, Guilday argued, the nation had two duties, in each of which the invaluable role of the Church was clear, "to keep sacred national ideals by the Americanization of every element in the land and carrying to the world the humanitarian lessons of American democracy."[47] Thus Guilday, like so many others, found the integration of religious and national loyalty in an Americanized and Americanizing church whose unity and discipline contributed stability to the nation and preserved a set of moral values and cultural standards which offset the disintegrating moral and religious influence of Protestantism. Later, in the 1930s, he would begin to take greater note of the dangers of secularism, apparent for him most notably in the work of some of the nation's leading historians. Throughout, he represented that "survival of American innocence" which William Halsey has characterized as the stance of Catholic intellectuals in the interwar years.[48]

[46]Guilday, "The Catholic Church in the United States," *Thought,* I (June, 1926), 3-20.

[47]Guilday to Thomas Meagher, March 10, 1925, GP.

[48]Halsey, *Survival of American Innocence,* 47-48.

Like the Americanists of the previous generation, then, Guilday saw the American Catholic experience as unique, but without their tendency to generalize upon it for the benefit of the universal Church. On Church and State, for example, he simply found the tradition of the Church irrelevant to the American experience. He did not deny the fact that the Church taught the necessity of union; he simply argued that in the United States the problem was not theory, but practice. On that level, it was Protestants who advocated union, Catholics whose life demanded freedom and independence from state control and a continuing effort to Americanize its own members. This issue, of course, became of major public significance during the twenties and, once again, there was a considerable difference between Guilday's writings, which attacked Protestant intolerance, and his private views, which emphasized Catholic responsibility. When William Franklin Sands wrote a conventional article in *Current History,* answering Protestant Charles C. Marshall's famous challenge to Alfred E. Smith, Guilday wrote to complain that he had not gone far enough, especially considering the fact that he was a layman and might have done so. What the whole dispute came down to, Guilday believed, was whether or not the Church "held to a doctrinal theory, as expanded by her theologians, that the perfect social and political condition of mankind, living under organized government, is a union of Church and State," and, secondly, "does not such a union implicitly and for all practical purposes place the political government of a state at the mercy of those who represent the Church, namely Churchmen?" Guilday was direct: "There is only one honest answer to these two questions and that answer corroborates all that Mr. Marshall said — and did not say, either out of charity or forethought." The Church could "not put its head in the sand" and think others would ignore its past, Guilday wrote.

If it can be shown that the Church ever avoided the consummation of such a union, and if it can be shown that even in a single case where such a union, while it existed, did not interfere with the normal processes of free government, then I believe Catholics have the right to argue the problem.

As a professor of church history, he "could not in conscience" answer either question "in favor of Churchmen."

The only answer to the attack was one "implied in Mr. Marshall's letter"; the Church had clung to "an utopian ideal that has never once worked well in practice." In her "blind insistence" on that ideal, she had "deliberately sacrificed" persons of conscience. In controversy, there was "only one answer, and it is a vulgar one," that all other Christian denominations had "strived...to bring about the very union of State and Church they condemn when the Catholic Church is considered." Tracing the history of the issue from early times through the Reformation to the nineteenth century, Guilday argued that "the Protestant sects" required state support, lost it in the United States Constitution, and "have been squirming ever since to find a way out," hiding "their own dependency...by flinging the Middle Ages at us American Catholics."[49]

The best defense was a good offense, it seemed; this was clear in a series of articles on "the Catholic Question" Guilday prepared for the National Catholic News Service for use during 1928. Although Justin McGrath, who arranged publication, claimed they would "carry well through the campaign," Guilday denied, "without any mental reservations whatsoever," that the series had any connection with the election. Rather they were intended to stimulate interest in American Catholic history while exposing "the persistency

[49]Guilday to William Franklin Sands, May 26, 1927, GP.

of Puritan intolerance toward Catholicism." On that topic, he had few reservations. Guilday wanted to encourage Catholics. "What I am debating over is the tenor of the *language* to be used toward our enemies," Guilday wrote McGrath. After discussing the question with his graduate students, "all agreed it was time for 'gloves off'." The series was strong, with little of the self-criticism which marked the historian's private correspondence. Perhaps Guilday pushed this approach too far, for in December McGrath advised him to soften his argument that Protestants consistently challenged Catholics on the basis of "dual allegiance." McGrath pointed to a number of ministers who spoke fairly and even favorably of the Church and the numerous Protestant politicians backing Smith. Moreover, he argued, Catholics in Germany and Holland had persuaded many Protestants of their patriotism and loyalty, and such an outcome was surely possible in the United States. He urged Guilday to modify his language a bit in order not to "alienate" Protestants of goodwill who were openly willing to support "Catholics seeking political favor."[50]

Despite Guilday's disdain for Catholicism's traditional theory of Church and State, he was deeply troubled by Smith's answer to Marshall's attack, written by Fr. Francis Duffy. By claiming a Catholic basis for religious liberty and Church-State separation, it flew in the face of historical evidence and contemporary theological orthodoxy. Guilday was alarmed, fearing, as he told Arthur Preuss, that it would become "the direct cause of a theological house-cleaning in this country." He even suggested "Smithism" might well take the place of another word "seldom heard nowadays," presumably Americanism. Later, he called the letter a "tissue of heresies." "No one of us would dare (in print) to

[50]McGrath to Guilday, November 5, 1928; Guilday to Arthur Preuss, November 17, 1927; Guilday to McGrath, May 24, 1927; and McGrath to Guilday, December 6, 1927, GP.

vindicate the theology of that Answer," he told Ellen Flick, who was considering a biography of Father Duffy. "It is the letter of an opportunist and if you were to make it a focus, too many theological eyes would find flaws."[51]

Guilday, then, believed that the union of Church and State was indeed theologically orthodox, a view held also by liberal Monsignor John A. Ryan. Both men based their "theological argument" on authority; union remained the ideal position outlined in the teachings of the Popes, including Leo XIII. Like Ryan, however, Guilday argued against this position in practical terms; he knew of no situation in which union had worked out successfully and he believed the United States would "escape" such union even if its people became "completely Catholic." In a letter to historian Joseph Schaeffer in early 1928, he claimed fear that if Catholics gained control of the American government they would abolish religious liberty was "the basis of all non-Catholic fears of the Roman Catholic Church in this country," but it could not be proven. In fact, he stated dramatically that, if Schaeffer could prove that Catholicism was "inimical to our republican institutions of liberty and equality," he would "become a charter member of any association you found for the purpose of resisting the growth of Catholicism in the United States."[52]

Ryan, Guilday, and other Catholic intellectuals, though troubled by their Church's position on Church and State, felt that Protestants had treated the Church unfairly during the campaign. Guilday worried that the unfair charges leveled against the Church had set back work for a more open Catholicism. In a speech to a Holy Name convention in Cincinnati shortly after election day, Guilday was asked if the failure of priests to cooperate with ministers on a local

[51]Guilday to Preuss, March 27, 1928; Guilday to Christopher Perotta, March 27, 1928; and Guilday to Ella Flick, April 5, 1922, GP.

[52]Guilday to Joseph Schaeffer, February 23, 1928, GP.

level was not one cause of the animosity that had arisen. Guilday answered that there had in fact been a great deal of cooperation on matters of civic concern. "Look what we have got in return," he continued. "They have allowed their ministers and bishops to vilify our Church." As a result, he predicted, "there is going to be a change. We are going to hesitate after this to give them the slightest bit of encouragement. We can't do any more than we have done." In contrast to his long work to overcome Catholic isolation, he now concluded, "We have to be separatists. We cannot cooperate with those who are unwilling to disavow an UnAmerican thing."[53]

He was even more disillusioned by developments within the historical profession, especially by the positivism he detected in the work of James Harvey Robinson and Charles Beard. He was "genuinely shocked by the general tone" of papers given at the 1929 American Historical Association meeting in Durham, North Carolina. "One fact became clear," he told P. J. O'Keefe:

> Christian principles and philosophy have little, if any, hold upon these outstanding historical leaders. To believe all that was said meant one conclusion — Christianity is out worn and the only successful philosophy of life is that which begins and ends with the animal in man.

Nevertheless he was more convinced than ever that the Catholic historians had "a great work to accomplish"; after "going softly the past ten years" they should now "prepare to carry the Christian message of life both in the past and the present into the ranks of our best historical scholars."[54]

[53]Transcript of the speech to the Holy Name Convention, Cincinnati, November 20, 1928, GP.

[54]Guilday to P. J. O'Keefe, January 7, 1930; see also Guilday to Francis Steck, January 16, 1930; and Guilday to Wilfrid Parsons, January 21, 1930, GP.

Yet Guilday's enthusiasm dimmed as the Church entered the years of the great depression, another national crisis which failed to stir the Church to life. In London the "apologetical movement" of street preaching was successful because of the remarkable "spirit of freedom granted to this rising group of priests and laymen on the part of higher ecclesiastical authorities." Living in "a different atmosphere" in the United States he could not honestly say that "the American ecclesiastical ethos is such that a priest and laymen feel unfettered to go out and meet the growing disorder. I take it for want of a better name — Sacramentalism, or pragmatism under a Catholic doctrinal cloak."

In this same letter to Lucien Johnson, Guilday summed up his frustration after twenty years of active work. Under the rectorship of James H. Ryan, with Roy Deferrari, "a real scholar," as Dean, the University was making "great progress," but it was "all intramural and within the walls. We are working in detached squads. There is no great central idea dominating our ranks." He went on to illustrate the connection between the University's problems and those of the larger Church:

> Two men came to the University for the doctorate. One majors in Church History — a priest; the other, a layman, majors in the social sciences. Both maybe even attend the same professors, sit in the same classroom or around the same Seminar table; but later on the priest can be in the pulpit, and the layman in the front pew, and yet, even up to that moment, they have not met or talked or shared any mutual desire to give of their best for Christ's sake.

Sadly, Guilday lamented that "we have everything here for a successful adventure...toward a more vocal leadership, but we have not yet reached any one dominantly central purpose. Each one works *pour soi-même*."

He pointed out that those on the outside of the University looked for intellectual leadership to their fellow priests on whose training "the Church has spared nothing." Such scholars were placed "in enviable circumstances" of "academic calm," with resources of books and materials and well-trained, zealous colleagues. Then those responsible for administration "crowd the days and nights with a hundred and one duties which shatter gradually all physical ability to produce the scholarly work" the Church had a right to expect. In the Jesuit houses of England, noted for their scholarship, one found the "highest conception of *leisure*" yet not one was, like Guilday, running an historical journal and association and a graduate group "twice as large as would be permitted in any German University." Sadly, he closed on a personal note:

> Intellectual scholarship rests upon specialization, leisure for investigation, freedom for contribution and productivity. Take my word for it, after twenty years here, whatever contribution has been made to any field, has been made at the expense of nervous energy, health and comfort.[55]

If occasionally Guilday gave way to self-pity, he had reason to be sad about the state of the Church and even about his own work. Substantial as it was, it seemed little in comparison with his youthful dreams, a judgment made more poignant by his own inner melancholy. He saw himself as a victim, as did so many liberal priests of that era. Like all victims, however, he had become an agent of his own oppression, for he had internalized many of the values and attitudes which motivated those whose leadership caused him so many problems. He had shaped his arguments for historical research around themes of apologetics and orthodoxy, and had proven his dedication to those values by submitting some work to episcopal review and all of it to his

---

[55]Guilday to Lucien Johnson, August 3, 1933, GP.

own review in terms of avoiding controversy, criticism, and division. Like other liberal Catholics, he had narrowed the dreams of Spalding and Ireland within ecclesiastical fences, producing a defensiveness against church authorities inside and outside the University and real or imagined enemies in society at large. The irony of Peter Guilday's career, perhaps, lay in the fact that, almost in spite of himself, he helped sustain and legitimate the solidarity of the Church under episcopal domination which all but insured that good people like himself would fight in "detached squads."

Sidetracked from the type of scholarship he most loved, he devoted his life to organizing the Catholic historical profession under auspices which demanded orthodoxy and apologetics. A scholar and an honest man, he saw many of the flaws in the Catholic subculture, but he was Irish and Catholic enough to speak of non-Catholics as "our enemies," to submit his writing to episcopal review, and to tailor his appeals for support to the group-centered prejudices of his ecclesiastical superiors. To avoid scandal, and to limit the criticism to which he was regularly subjected, he suppressed some parts of the Catholic story and avoided others which might prove embarrassing. Privately he decried episcopal silence and clerical caution, and he hoped that lay scholars like Sands and the backers of *Commonweal* would gather up the secret discontents of Catholics like himself. A priest and a professor at the Catholic University, he was forced to approach such things indirectly, by printing in his books documents which told their own story, without need for his comment, by gathering and supporting Catholic historians and affirming *Commonweal, Thought,* the Catholic Association for International Peace, and other works he thought would move the Church toward courage and honesty and, perhaps, toward that "great central idea" which would stir the scattered goodness and talent to action. Perhaps his teaching did the same. John Tracy Ellis has testified to the open, candid, honest tone of his teacher's classes and conversations, and the passion for truth, fairness, and honesty which he sought to instill in his students. Peter Guilday suffered, compromised, and persisted. John Tracy Ellis would undoubtedly agree that he reached great eminence on the shoulders of Peter Guilday. The rest of us, who have been the beneficiaries of Ellis' talent, dedication, and charity, may also acknowledge our debt to Guilday, who in a real sense made our work in American Catholic history possible.

Cardinal Mercier's Visit
to America in the
Autumn of 1919

Roger Aubert

Both "triumphal and tiring" (A. Simon), the journey of Cardinal Mercier[1] to the United States constitutes an unforgettable page in the life of the Archbishop of Mechlin and in the history of the United States Catholic Church.[2] The prestige of the patriot-cardinal, a symbol to Americans of courageous resistance to brute force in the name of law and liberty, would inevitably reflect on the whole Catholic community. It was an enviable status, given the tendency within

[1]Désiré-Joseph Mercier (1851-1926), founder of the *Institut supérieur de philosophie* at Louvain, where for twenty-five years he was one of the leaders of its neo-Thomist revival, became Archbishop of Mechlin in February, 1906. For an abundant bibliography, see Alois J. Simon, *Le cardinal Mercier,* in *Collection "Notre Passé"* (Brussels, 1960).

[2]There are various sources for information about this journey. The principal ones include the following: a) The *Fonds Mercier* of the Archives de l'Archevêché de Malines (hereafter cited as A.A.M.): Box 12 (a few pieces of correspondence, texts of some speeches, and an account of the reception in Chicago); Box 23 (printed material about receptions, the doctorate *honoris causa* at Yale, and three folders on the visits to Québec, Ottawa, and Toronto); Box 119 (clippings from newspapers and journals given by the Dessain family).

the American climate of opinion to suspect Catholic citizens, many of whom were of Irish or German origin, of indifference to the Allied cause.[3]

The initiative for the cardinal's visit, moreover, had come from the American side. In the early years of the war, members of the Commission for the Relief of Belgium had gone to that country to organize the distribution of supplies during the occupation. They had been duly impressed by the

b) The dossiers entitled *Correspondance politique: Étas-Unis* (hereafter cited as *Correspondance*) folder "Septembre-décembre, 1918," and B. 347 (file marked *Belgique-États-Unis/Propagande,* folder "Voyage du Cardinal Mercier," in the Ministère des Affaires Étràngères de Bruxelles (hereafter cited as A.M.A.É. Br.).
c) Two accounts written by traveling companions of the cardinal, Antoine De Wachter, vicar general and auxiliary bishop since 1909 ("En Amérique," manuscript kept in A.A.M., Box 98, folder "De Wachter II"), and Professor Maurice De Wulf ("Le voyage de S.É. le cardinal Mercier aux États-Unis et au Canada," in the commemorative album, *Le cardinal Mercier, 1851-1926* [Brussels-Paris, 1927], clxv-clxxxiv, with numerous illustrations).
d) Three volumes of press clippings: one sent in November, 1919, by P.R. Blount, entitled "To the Ethical Hero of the Great War" (in A.A.M., Box 12); two others, with more complete information, entitled "To His Eminence D.S. [*sic*] Cardinal Mercier, Archbishop of Malines — Presented by the Department of State in commemoration of the visit of his Eminence to the United States of America, 1919" (A.A.M., Boxes 19 and 20). These were sent to Mercier by Ambassador Brand Whitlock on July 28, 1920, with the accompanying note:
 I have just received from my government two volumes of newspaper clippings that chronicle the visit of Your Eminence to the United States last year. The Secretary of State has asked me to send them to Your Eminence with his compliments, and with the wish that they will provide you with as happy and lasting a memento as that treasured by all in America who had the honor of meeting you (A.A.M., Box 12).
e) A few documents in Vol. VI of *Oeuvres pastorales,* by Cardinal D.J. Mercier (Louvain, 1926), 164-72 and 185-88.

[3]It is well known that there was some Catholic opposition to the entrance of the United States into the war. Shortly after the Armistice, one of the highly-placed officials in the Belgian Ministry of Foreign Affairs, recalling some warnings that had issued from the Belgian Legation in Washington, called Mercier's attention to the fact that "American Catholic circles are often under the influence of the Irish, who themselves have close acquaintance with German nationals or naturalized German-Americans" (Letter dated February 12, 1919, in A.A.M., Box 12).

eminent moral character of the archbishop of Mechlin.[4] As soon as the war ended, numerous Belgian nationals residing in the United States, along with Americans sympathetic to Belgium, were calling for Cardinal Mercier to come on a publicity tour as soon as possible. Bishop Carton de Wiart, a Belgian who had become auxiliary bishop of Westminster, visited the United States on behalf of the Belgian government to congratulate Cardinal Gibbons on the occasion of the fiftieth jubilee of his consecration.[5] From there, he wrote on November 28, 1918, to the Belgian Minister of Foreign Affairs: "I am asked everywhere that His Eminence Cardinal Mercier visit the United States. In my opinion, nothing would be more helpful, not only for our religion, but for the Belgian cause. The American people would welcome him warmly."[6] Two days earlier, Baron Ernest de Cartier de

[4] In the brief account of the cardinal's tour published shortly after his return, one of his traveling companions reported:

> When His Eminence thanked them for their services, all without exception told him of the enthusiasm his name inspired in the United States, and of the unanimous sentiments of friendship of which he was the object. They were of one accord in expressing the desire to welcome him someday and to hear him thank their fellow-citizens for their charitable efforts. Several had insisted as well on the important moral value such a visit could have. Mrs. Kellogg, wife of one of the leaders of the Commission for Relief, had made hundreds of speeches in the United States on behalf of occupied Belgium. She feared that the young people of America were becoming absorbed by concerns for the economic prosperity of this wealthy nation. She hoped they would become more idealistic, with a more intense spiritual life (*Oeuvres pastorales*, VI, 164).

[5] James Gibbons (1834-1921) was Vicar Apostolic of North Carolina in 1868 and in this capacity attended the First Vatican Council. He became Bishop of Richmond in 1872, coadjutor and finally, Archbishop of Baltimore in 1877. He was named a cardinal in 1886. His influence on the Catholic Church in the United States was remarkable, to the point that some bishops even resisted what they called "the Baltimore Vatican." He enjoyed considerable prestige at the White House and in various spheres of American society, where he was respected for his breadth of vision and his concern for the "Americanization" of Catholics. See John Tracy Ellis, *James Cardinal Gibbons*, 2 vols. (Milwaukee, 1952).

[6] Bishop Carton de Wiart to Paul Hymans, November 28, 1918 (A.M.A.É.Br., B. 347, folder "Jubilé du Cardinal Gibbons").

Marchienne, Belgian Plenipotentiary Minister to the United States,[7] had telegraphed as well:

> American newspapers are publicizing many projected trips here by various highly-placed officials and notable persons for war relief. Their purpose would be to interest the American public in the economic restoration of their respective countries of origin. Our friends here are concerned that we will be upstaged in this appeal for American assistance. All have advised me that the presence of popular Cardinal Mercier would be most useful to help with our economic restoration in the broadest sense. Our friends insist that the cardinal be the first of the important visitors, if possible, and that he come without further delay.[8]

In a letter of December 2, the Belgian diplomat, preoccupied with the tendency of American opinion to lose interest in European problems after the war,[9] summarized his views:

[7]Ernest de Cartier de Marchienne (1871-1946), had become legate in Washington in 1917, and attained the rank of ambassador in 1919. From 1927 through 1945, he served as ambassador to London. A masterful defender of Belgian interests in the United States, Cartier de Marchienne was deemed "an eminent diplomat" (J. Willequet, in *Biographie Nationale*, XXXII, 68-69).

[8]Telegram No. 530, dated November 26, 1918 (A.M.A.É.Br., B. 347, folder "Voyage du Cardinal Mercier"). A month later, he would repeat: "All here hoping arrival soon of our cardinal" (Telegram dated December 28, 1918, A.M.A.É.Br., *Correspondance*, folder "Septembre-décembre, 1918").

[9]A few examples indicate this. "Now that the waves of patriotic enthusiasm have receded, it is necessary that we take every opportunity to keep alive the new American national impulse" (Telegram dated November 25, 1918, A.M.A.É.Br., *Correspondance,* folder "Septembre-décembre, 1918"); "With the halt in hostilities, public opinion has returned to a practical realism that could provoke a reaction to the humanitarian and idealistic goals of the war, which President Wilson has extolled with the eloquence and noble detachment with which you are familiar" (Letter of November 30, 1918, *ibid.*).

I have hoped for a long time that the primate of Belgium might assist the nation at the end of the war by arousing American sympathies. He could also channel their support, which is certainly generous and well-intentioned but latent and uninformed, towards the most important goals of our national restoration....You know by my reports that Cardinal Mercier is very popular in America. He still personifies heroic Belgian resistance to the occupying forces, and to Americans was a spokesman for the Allied cause. If he were able to come here shortly, with the official mission of thanking Americans for their assistance, it seems to me that it would help if the journey were made with a certain éclat. I think the cardinal could be the guest of Cardinal Gibbons and take part in civic and religious demonstrations in large cities. I would not see these projects as limited to particular areas, e.g., predominantly Catholic sectors. We cannot forget that in this country the cardinal is regarded above all as a great patriot, one of the most heroic figures of the war.[10]

He added, referring to a piece published prematurely in the *New York Herald*,[11] that it would be preferable for the

[10]Cartier de Marchienne to P. Hymans, December 2, 1918 (A.M.A.É.Br., *Correspondance*, folder "Septembre-décembre, 1918").

[11]On December 1, 1918, the *New York Herald* announced: "Cardinal Mercier is coming to the United States to thank the American people for the succor given to Belgium. His stay here will be brief, as he has made it emphatic that he feels he is urgently needed in helping to restore Belgium....Just when the Cardinal will get here is not known. It is expected this will be late in the winter or early next spring. The famous prelate will come here under the auspices of the Belgian Relief Bureau and the National Belgian Church of St. Albert, 431 West Forty-Seventh Street. The two are under the same roof and have the same persons in charge. The Reverend Joseph Francis Stillemans, pastor of the church and president of the Belgian Relief Bureau, has gone to Belgium to arrange the details of the journey of the Cardinal." Father Joseph Stillemans (d. 1933), a priest of the diocese of Ghent, was involved for a long time before the war in the mission of welcoming Belgian emigrants to New York. During his stay in Europe, he was raised to the rank of prelate.

cardinal to come as an invited guest of the United States, rather than as an official under Belgian sponsorship. He also mentioned two eminent Americans who would be able to facilitate the cardinal's visit. Thomas F. Ryan,[12] a wealthy Catholic layman, was willing to place at the cardinal's disposal his own residences in New York and Washington, as well as his special railroad coach. Cardinal Gibbons of Baltimore, Mercier's long-standing admirer,[13] and an enthusiastic supporter of the Belgian cause from the outset of the war,[14] had already personally invited his colleague from Mechlin to come to the United States to plead his country's cause.[15]

[12]Thomas Fortune Ryan (1851-1928), a self-made man, had made his fortune in the transportation business, and later headed the American Tobacco Company. He had interests in the Belgian Congo, especially in the Forminière. He was very generous to the Church: his benefactions were estimated at $20 million, from net assets worth over $200 million. He served on the Board of Trustees at the Catholic University of America. See *Dictionary of American Biography,* XVI, 265-68. On Ryan's offer, see telegram of Cartier de Marchienne, dated December 10, 1918 (A.M.A.É.Br., *Correspondance,* folder "Septembre-décembre, 1918").

[13]Gibbons had met Mercier during the Eucharistic Congress at London in 1908, and again at the election of Benedict XV in 1914. At an earlier date, when he was passing through Belgium prior to the war, Gibbons made a detour to Mechlin to talk with Mercier, a fact he would recall when he introduced his guest to the gathering at the Lyric Theater in Baltimore, on September 16, 1919. (See *The Baltimore American,* September 17, 1919.)

[14]Gibbons had a special interest in the rebuilding of the University of Louvain. (See Ellis, *Gibbons,* II, 263-64). The sentiments of Gibbons towards Belgium were well known at the Belgian Ministry of Foreign Affairs. When considering the usefulness of sending a representative to congratulate Cardinal Gibbons on his episcopal jubilee, the General Director of Policy, Bassompierre, spoke of "the American cardinal, who has done so much to show his sympathies toward Belgium. . . ." (Draft of September 26, 1918, in A.M.A.É.Br., B. 347, folder "Jubilé du Cardinal Gibbons"). In a note dated October 15 (*ibid.*), he added, "It must be remembered that Gibbons had frequently manifested Belgian sympathies."

[15]This letter seems not to have been preserved, but Mercier alludes to it in his response on March 9, 1919, cited by Ellis, in *Gibbons,* II, 264 n. 15. Pierre Orts, Secretary General *ad interim* at the Belgian Ministry of Foreign Affairs, reminded Mercier a few weeks later: "Cardinal Gibbons ardently hopes that Your Eminence will visit the United States. Along with all our friends, he wants to take advantage of the occasion to arouse the enthusiasm and support of Americans everywhere in

In the ensuing weeks, Baron de Cartier frequently returned to the question. He telegraphed on December 10: "Yesterday I met many notable persons in New York who urged me to appeal to you for a visit from Cardinal Mercier as soon as possible."[16] And again, ten days later, "I want to point out that for the past two weeks, all the newspapers refer to an approaching visit by the cardinal and that this is ardently desired by our American friends, regardless of their religion or political party."[17]

There was pressure on Mercier from Belgium as well. Soon after the signing of the Armistice, his Dominican friend Georges Ceslas Rutten encouraged him to go without delay:

> M. Van de Vyvere[18] came to the United States while I was there. He is convinced, as is Father Stillemans,[19] that a visit on the part of Your Eminence would do much good. M. Van de Vyvere, who has always been interested in our workers' projects, shares my anxiety over their future financial security. The war wiped out all the resources of our labor unions. It will take at least a year to replenish

favor of Belgium" (Letter of February 12, 1919, A.A.M., Box 12). There is no denying Gibbons' desire to assist the Belgian cause. The question is raised, however, whether the former champion of American nationalism against the machinations of German-American Catholics was not equally sensitive to the fact that the prestige of the defender of Law against German aggression could reflect on the Catholic Church in the States as a whole.

[16]Telegram No. 572, dated December 10, 1918 (A.M.A.É.Br., *Correspondance,* folder "Septembre-décembre, 1918").

[17]Telegram No. 608, dated December 20, 1918 (A.M.A.É.Br., B. 347, folder "Voyage Mercier").

[18]Aloys van de Vyvere (1871-1961), Administrator of Societies, Catholic parliamentary deputy for Roulers-Thielt since 1911, and Minister of Fianance throughout the war, was closely allied with Christian democratic organizations. See P. Van Molle, *Le Parlement belge, 1894-1969* (Brussels, 1969), 347-48.

[19]Father Stillemans, president of the Belgian Relief Bureau in New York, had gone to Europe to convince Mercier that he should journey to the States (see n. 11, above).

even a part of their funds. For now, the unions are not in
a position to pay their publicizers, even though these are
more indispensable than ever. M. Van de Vyvere, who is
knowledgeable, assures me that M. Vandervelde[20]
brought back a lot of money. For this reason above all we
earnestly hope for a visit from Your Eminence to the
United States.[21]

Those who were interested in the re-establishment of the
University of Louvain insisted in much the same vein. The
cardinal was especially sensitive to that aspect of the issue;[22]
nevertheless, he hesitated. On one hand, he saw the reorganization of his widespread diocese in the wake of the war as
an all-engrossing task. He knew that "his detractors in
Mechlin considered this journey an exaggerated manifestation of egotism."[23] On the other hand, the cardinal must
have been aware of the unfavorable response given by the
Belgian Minister of Foreign Affairs to the suggestion of
Baron de Cartier de Marchienne. On a telegram from the
Belgian diplomat dated November 26, there is the following
marginal note: "The Minister does not consider it advisable
to follow up on this suggestion."[24] A few days later, the

[20]Emile Vandervelde (1866-1938), a socialist leader, had served as parliamentary
deputy since 1894, and was Minister since January, 1916. He became president of
the International Socialist Bureau. See P. Van Molle, *Le Parlement belge,* 344-47.

[21]Rutten to Mercier, December 6, 1918 (A.A.M., Box 29, folder "Correspondance Rutten").

[22]On January 5, 1919, he wrote to the Bishop of Bruges: "The newspapers
announce that I shall go to the United States. I am not thinking of it at this time. It
is *possible* [underlining is Mercier's] that I go later on, in the interest of the
University and of general works" (A.A.M., Box 78, folder "Correspondence
Évêques"). On his return, he would write to Msgr. Hebbelynck: "All through my
journey, the first of my concerns was the rebuilding of our Alma Mater" (Letter of
November 14, 1919, draft in A.A.M., Box 85, folder "Restauration de la
Bibliothèque").

[23]Simon, *Le cardinal Mercier,* 162.

[24]A.M.A.É.Br., B. 347, folder "Voyage Mercier." The marginal note is dated
December 2, 1918, followed by these words: "Obert, telegraph this decision to
Cartier."

minister specified his reasons in a telegram to Baron de Cartier: "I do not consider it useful to sound out the cardinal regarding a journey to the United States. The cardinal is needed here and cannot embark on such a journey. It is preferable not to insist on such an unrealistic undertaking."[25]

Was this a pretext offered by the liberal minister, who was little inclined to see the leader of the Belgian Church collect more honors in America, along with funds for Catholic works? Or was he convinced that the cardinal could best promote the Belgian cause by remaining at home and receiving at Mechlin the acclaim of many eminent foreign visitors who were passing through Belgium during those weeks? Or again, was it the simple fact that the minister knew what a high priority the cardinal gave to his immediate pastoral goals? Whatever the reason, the minister's stance shifted in the weeks that followed. On December 23, Baron de Bassompierre, Director General of Policy, sent a telegram to Cartier de Marchienne: "I hear unofficially that the cardinal would not be opposed to visit United States in a month or two. Minister absent. At his return I shall suggest he sound out the cardinal. Matter suspended, awaiting further instructions."[26] On his return to Brussels, Foreign Minister Paul Hymans consulted King Albert. Having received a favorable nod,[27] he wrote a letter to the cardinal:

[25]Telegram dated December 13, 1918 (A.M.A.É.Br., B. 347, folder "Voyage Mercier").

[26]Telegram dated December 23, 1918 (*ibid*). Hymans divided his time between Brussels and Paris, where the Peace Conference was in preparation.

[27]On December 28, 1918, the King's Chief of Staff, Count Guillaume d'Arschot, wrote to Hymans: "After I left you, I reported to the king what you told me concerning a journey of the cardinal to the United States. His Majesty prefers that you send a letter to Cardinal Mercier, written along the lines that you suggested to me" (A.M.A.É.Br., B. 347, folder "Voyage Mercier"). A. Simon, who utilized sources that are normally inaccessible, adds this detail: "The king suggested the journey to the cardinal, with the understanding that the Archbishop would not be fulfilling an official mission" (Simon, *Le cardinal Mercier,* 162).

Your Eminence:

The King's minister in Washington has informed me of the keen desire on the part of the people in the United States to have Your Eminence visit America so that they may directly express their sentiments.

I have learned indirectly that Your Eminence would yield to insistent requests for a voyage to America. I want to state that the Royal Government believes such a visit would greatly enhance the Belgian cause, by the fulfillment of the project at hand and by the manifestations of friendship and admiration with which Your Eminence would be met across the Atlantic.

I would be pleased to be able to inform M. Cartier de Marchienne whether Your Eminence would consider going to the United States, and, if possible, the date upon which the journey would be taken."[28]

The cardinal answered several days later that he had "a desire and a hope to respond to the kindly and urgent invitations from the U. S.," but that it was impossible for him to specify an exact date for the trip, which in any case could not take place "before springtime."[29]

Two days later, he wrote in much the same vein to Étienne Lamy, the French academician who was president of the committee to rebuild the library of Louvain. The prelate mentioned that the former rector, Msgr. Adolphe Hebbelynck, and Professor Alfred Nerincx, of the Law School at Louvain, were leaving for the United States with a mission to initiate widespread support for the University: "I am not

[28]The original has been lost. Draft copy is in A.M.A.É.Br., B. 347, folder "Voyage Mercier." The text had been written the day before by de Bassompierre, who immediately advised Cartier de Marchienne of his action (Telegram dated December 31, 1918, *ibid.*).

[29]Autographed letter, dated January 8, 1919 (*ibid.*).

giving up the hope and desire of going later, once the preoccupations and turmoil of this time have passed."[30]

In the ensuing months, the still-hesitant Mercier was regularly approached by those who were concerned for the future of Louvain[31] and by friends of Belgium in the United States, led by Gibbons. There were others who wanted the visit for less idealistic reasons. A contributing journalist of the liberal daily, *L'Indépendance belge,* recalled a visit made to Mechlin in April, 1919, by one of the "bosses" of American journalism, the founder of *McClure's Magazine.* He wrote:

> MacClure [sic], former editor of Robert Louis Stevenson, Mark Twain, and Kipling, proposed a series of conferences that the archbishop could make in key cities of the United States. It was quite unusual to see a literary agent employing all his eloquence and skills to convince the placid prelate, more accustomed to speaking in dark churches than in lighted halls before audiences of three or four thousand. MacClure had brought huge colored posters, and thought to impress the cardinal with the display. Without taking offense, Cardinal Mercier was nonetheless disconcerted, and changed the conversation. . . . The uncertain MacClure left without knowing whether he had obtained the archiepiscopal promise of a conference tour.[32]

---

[30]Letter dated January 10, 1919, Draft copy (A.A.M., Box 85, folder "Restauration de la Bibliothèque").

[31]At the beginning of April, an alumnus of Louvain and member of the Belgian delegation at Versailles telegraphed to Mercier that Cartier de Marchienne "is very worried that, if Your Eminence does not go himself to America, there will be little chance to get important contributions for Louvain" (Telegram from Paul Van den Ven, dated April 9, 1919; A.A.M., Box 12). He would have wanted Mercier to leave at the end of April, but the cardinal replied: "Sincere regrets, need to confirm impossibility departing presently. Serious obligations retain me here" (*ibid.*).

[32]*L'Indépendance belge,* January 26, 1926. The editor was with McClure at Mechlin, and witnessed the scene personally.

Sometime during May, the cardinal finally decided to take the journey,[33] prompted by complex motives that have been well summarized by Simon: "The explicit aim was to express thanks from a Belgian citizen to American citizens for military and financial aid during the war; but the implicit hope was to create a movement of fervent and lucrative support for Belgium, its social works, and the University of Louvain."[34]

At first, it seems that the cardinal hoped to make the journey sometime in August, a holiday period during which he had less work.[35] Word came immediately, however, that Washington would be out of the question at that time: "Unanimous opinion here that visit [of] Cardinal Mercier not take place before end [of] September. Extreme heat makes trip impossible before autumn. Notables to be met by Cardinal Mercier are out of cities during this time."[36] Professor Nerincx added a further reason, that the universities did not reopen until the end of September.[37] Now from the

[33]He wrote to Cardinal Gibbons on May 23: "Dear and revered Eminence, Belgium owes a great debt of gratitude to the Great Republic of the United States. I consider it a duty to go myself and express our appreciation for the armies and the generous support of its citizens. God willing, I shall board ship at the end of August and arrive in New York around September 8" (A.A.M., Box 12).

[34]Simon, *Le cardinal Mercier,* 162.

[35]An official of the Belgian Ministry of Foreign Affairs wrote to Foreign Minister Hymans on June 14, 1919: "Upon receipt of information from M. De Wulf, professor at the University of Louvain, I had written on May 29 to the chargé d'affaires in Washington, announcing that the visit of Cardinal Mercier to the United States would take place next August" (A.M.A.É.Br., B. 347, folder "Voyage Mercier").

[36]Telegram from chargé d'affaires, dated June 11, 1919 (*ibid.*).

[37]Nerincx to Mercier, May 13, 1919 (A.A.M., Box 23). Had the Minister of Foreign Affairs, Paul Hymans, intervened again at some point or other to sway the decision of the cardinal? There is strong evidence for this in the following lines from Cartier de Marchienne, who was spending the summer in Belgium where he heard the rumors: "I can only congratulate and thank you for having convinced His Eminence to have personal contact with his admirers in the United States, who were so taken with his strength of spirit and his outstanding character during the war." (Letter of September 24, 1919, A.M.A.É.Br., B. 347, folder "Voyage Mercier").

outset, Cartier de Marchienne had pointed out the importance "of the cardinal's being assured here of a broad and profitable support from the university community."[38] Consequently, there was agreement on a two-month delay, when a new telegram arrived from Cardinal Gibbons, announcing that on September 24 an extraordinary meeting of the American hierarchy was to take place, and it was hoped Cardinal Mercier could attend.[39] Without further ado, Mercier sent his consent,[40] and preparations for the visit got under way.

Professor Nerincx had warned the cardinal against the danger of his journey's appearing as a publicity venture.[41] Planning, he wrote, should be left to the Belgian embassy and to the American ecclesiastical authorities. In fact, Mercier wrote to Cardinal Gibbons asking him "to have one of his secretaries draw up a helpful itinerary that I could follow for September and for the first half of October," adding

[38]Telegram of December 3, 1918 (A.M.A.É.Br., *Correspondance*, folder "Septembre-décembre, 1918"). Not only in the interests of Louvain was the ambassador concerned to promote this aspect of the visit. A few months later, referring to the success of Mercier's visit, he wrote to the minister: "We should be proud that the university communities have welcomed Cardinal Mercier so warmly. The congenial atmosphere he is sure to find and the impression he makes on his audiences will have a profound influence in these centers that are often closed to us. The thinking of intellectuals at Harvard, Yale, Princeton, Columbia and other places today becomes public opinion tomorrow" (Letter of September 24, 1919, A.M.A.É.Br., B. 347).

[39]Telegram sent on June 17, 1919, by the Belgian chargé d'affaires at Washington and re-routed to Mechlin by Baron de Borchgrave (A.M.A.É.Br., B. 347, folder "Voyage Mercier").

[40]Telegram from Mercier, dated June 28, sent through the Ministry of Foreign Affairs: "Hope to arrive several days before September 24th. My delegate will come and see Your Eminence in July to arrange my stay in America" (*ibid.*).

[41]"I feel I should insist that Your Eminence not agree to appear 'under the auspices' of Mr. McClure or of the Lee Keedick Agency. If M. de Cartier accepts the arrangement, this woman — as she has offered — will handle only the practical organization of the journey and of a few of the public addresses (four or five at the most). For these sessions, the agency will rent the hall and sell tickets for seats (necessary to avoid a crush). The profits will be used exclusively for the works of Your Eminence" (Letter of May 13, 1919, A.A.M., Box 12).

that he hoped "to visit as well our Canadian benefactors in Québec, Montréal, Toronto."[42] Cardinal Gibbons, for his part, preferred to allow great freedom for his own colleagues.[43] Local committees were set in motion in various cities, and it soon became apparent that the receptions would take place on a grand scale. Thus, in Baltimore, where Cardinal Gibbons had asked the former governor, Phillips Lee Goldsborough, to be president of a 100-member committee, the governor announced to the press "that it is his intention to give the distinguished visitor a reception that will far exceed anything of its kind that was ever held in Baltimore."[44]

Some had hoped at the outset that the cardinal might travel throughout the United States, noting that he might want to visit those places in the far West where one of his uncles had come to work as a missioner.[45] The archbishop of New Orleans wrote a personal letter to Mercier, inviting him to come South.[46] But these were unrealistic hopes, and the

[42] Mercier to Gibbons, May 23, 1919 (A.A.M., Box 12). In fact, as soon as there was question of an impending trip as reported in the American press in December, 1918, the Belgian consul at Ottawa had telegraphed: "Lively hopes expressed here on all sides that he visit Canada as well. Considering profound gratitude we owe Canadian people, desirable that Cardinal Mercier spend at least 48 hours in Canada if he visits United States" (A.M.A.É.Br., B. 347, folder "Voyage Mercier").

[43] Nerincx to Mercier, May 15, 1919 (A.A.M., Box 12): "His Eminence does not seem to want to dictate to the other dignitaries or local committees about what they should or could do in their own localities when Your Eminence visits them."

[44] Reported in the Baltimore *News*, August 7, 1919.

[45] Mrs. Kellogg confirms such a wish in the few pages she wrote for the commemorative album, *Le cardinal Mercier, 1851-1926* (Brussels, 1927), 204. The cardinal's maternal uncle, Adrien Croquett (1818-1902), was a missionary in the Rocky Mountain region from 1858 to 1898. Mercier held him in great admiration and had often visited him in his last years at Braine-l'Alleud, where he had retired. See J. Bosse, *Mgr. Adrien Croquet, le "saint de l'Orégon"* (Braine-l'Alleud, 1977), mimeographed.

[46] Letter of March 2, 1919 (A.A.M., Box 12). Throughout the cardinal's tour, invitations multiplied to visit other parts of the country. De Wulf notes that

visit was to be limited to the Northeast, Midwest, and southern Canada.

In July, the vice-rector of the American College at Louvain, Father Pierre de Strijcker, came as the personal representative of Cardinal Mercier to help those who were charged with organizing the trip. An exact departure date could not be arranged until the last minute, because transatlantic traffic still suffered from postwar irregularities, and priority of space was given for the repatriation of troops. On August 25, the Belgian ambassador in Paris sent a letter to the military attaché of the United States, announcing that the cardinal and his entourage could board the *Agamemnon,* "which leaves Brest around September 2."[47] Actually, the cardinal was to make the crossing on the *Northern Pacific*, a comfortable and speedy vessel.[48]

Mercier left Mechlin the morning of September 1 and spent the night in Paris, where he was assailed by "a cloud of reporters and photographers" before taking the thirteen-hour rail journey to Brest. He boarded ship in the late morning of September 3, accompanied by Bishop De Wachter, one of his auxiliaries,[49] the lawyer Francis Dessain who

"California was especially insistent, promising anything to get the cardinal to the Pacific Coast" (*Le cardinal Mercier, 1851-1926,* cxxiv).

[47] From Gaiffier to Hymans, August 25, 1919 (A.M.A.É.Br., *Correspondance politique : France,* folder "1919").

[48] De Wulf wrote that "it is the fastest of the transport ships. An oil-burning vessel, it speeds over the ocean at 21 knots per hour" (*Le cardinal Mercier, 1851-1926,* clxvi). Bishop De Wachter made the following entry in his diary: "They are trying to catch up to the *Leviathan,* which left two days earlier than we did, with General Pershing on board."

[49] Antoine Alphonse De Wachter (1855-1932), former dean of Vilvorde, was vicar-general and had served as auxiliary to Cardinal Mercier since 1909. He spent the war years in England, where he was the cardinal's representative on behalf of Belgian refugees. He spoke English fluently, and had been in frequent contact with American groups that were supportive of Belgium.

was to serve as secretary,[50] Professor Maurice De Wulf,[51] two priests,[52] and a servant. Baron de Cartier de Marchienne was also on board, returning to his post in Washington where he was to welcome King Albert.

The sentiments of Mercier as he set out on this voyage are reflected in one of the first speeches he gave when he arrived in the United States:

> When we started from Brest and our boat had entered upon the immense ocean, I felt sad at the thought of being away from my flock and from all those with whom I lived.
>
> But as we received by wireless news from different parts of the world and word from passing steamers, I began to realize that, though apparently isolated from humanity, I was in real connection with the whole world. All my invisible brothers and I were resting on the same terrestrial globe and breathing the same atmosphere. Finally, a wider horizon of thought opened out before me — the conception of the unity and catholicity of our divine Church.[53]

[50]Francis Dessain (1875-1951), attorney and promoter of the Football Club at Mechlin, had worked closely with Mercier during the war, and decided in 1919 to enter the priesthood. In June, 1920, he became Mercier's personal secretary. It was generally thought that the cardinal cared for him like a son (A.A.M., Box 9, folder "Mort. condoléances"). Having completed his secondary studies in Birmingham, England, Dessain was perfectly fluent in English and was able to assume most of the secretarial tasks during the American tour.

[51]Maurice De Wulf (1867-1947), professor at the University of Louvain, had been one of the early collaborators of Mercier at the *Institut supérieur de philosophie*. Member of the Belgian Royal Academy since 1913, and author of a history of medieval philosophy that was recognized worldwide, De Wulf had taught many courses in North America during the war years, particularly at Harvard and Toronto. (See Fernand Van Steenberghen in *Biographie Nationale*, XXXIII, 755-62).

[52]The two priests were Father Nys, who had replaced Mercier as rector of the Séminaire Léon XIII at Louvain, and Father Roosen.

[53]Allocution to the seminarians at Baltimore, September 12, 1919 (manuscript text in A.A.M., Box 12). On his return, in a conference to the seminarians at

Weather was unfavorable for the first part of the crossing. The cardinal felt sick the first evening, and the sea was so rough the next two days that three-fourths of the crew succumbed to seasickness. Calm returned by Saturday, September 6, and Sunday was a magnificent day. The cardinal celebrated Mass at 10 A.M. in a hall filled to capacity; after lunch, he spoke to the soldiers and officers. As this was his first attempt to speak English in public, there were a few problems, later recalled by Professor De Wulf:

> An officer on board was assigned to the cardinal, and he began immediately to speak English, which he had forgotten from lack of practice. The beginnings were painful. His Eminence had not had the time to prepare himself for the exacting tasks of public speaking that awaited him. He reacquainted himself with the language while on board. The first day, he was mixed-up and hesitant. Eight days later, the same man would be addressing thousands. Within two weeks, he would speak up to five times in a single day, improvising, moved by the faith of the throngs. All who heard him would be struck by the clarity of his diction and the correctness of his grammar.[54]

Mechlin, the cardinal would recall that impression: "There in the middle of the sea, a sensation of isolation, of being lost — the majesty of God, *mirabiles elationes maris*...and the immensity of the horizon. Yet each day the captain posted items of world news: strikes, railway accidents...I began reflecting on the electric currents that reach everywhere, their harmony untroubled by winds or storms. In nature, all is in everything! What a marvel of unity! Yet sometimes we have trouble imagining the universal presence and action of the Prime Mover, or the communion of saints....(scribbled notes, dated December 2, 1919, in A.A.M., Box 86, folder "Allocutions aux séminaristes, 1914-24").

[54]See *Le cardinal Mercier, 1851-1926,* clxvii-clxviii. His indisposition over, the cardinal, who enjoyed people, used every opportunity to chat in English with soldiers going home on the *Northern Pacific.* "He had been among them daily on the voyage, talking with them and walking the decks with them" (*The Sun,* September 10, 1919).

According to De Wulf, the short allocution in which the cardinal expressed his feelings of gratitude and admiration for the Americans[55] became the inaugural of his speaking tour:

> His voice was hardly louder than a whisper, and seemed not to carry to the last row of the audience. Yet it truly echoed throughout a continent. We knew that the wireless was sending his words to New York, where they appeared in the next day's papers along with details of life on board. It wasn't long before we realized that all the attention of the American public was focussed on this little warship. That same day, at noon, a cable was sent from Cape Cod by a group of 300 journalists: 'Please send us by wireless expression of goodwill and greetings to America.' Seventy-two dollars was enclosed for the response.[56]

The arrival in New York was planned for the morning of Wednesday, September 10. Cardinal Gibbons had insisted from the outset that prior to any official meetings in New York, "the first visit of (Mercier) should be with the primate of the United States in Baltimore, with plans for a return visit to New York later."[57] All had been organized with this in mind, but circumstances intervened. The *Northern*

[55]The text of his speech to the officers has been preserved (A.A.M., Box 12). Among other things, he said: "In fact all of them [the soldiers] gave their lives or were ready to give their lives for the triumph of our common cause, for justice and civilization. On that point I want to say to you my gratitude. But especially I want to say my gratitude to your American people. I knew better than anyone that if Belgium were saved from starvation, if the lives of the women and children were spared, that we would be indebted to you and that magnificent institution, the Commission for the Relief of Belgium, presided over by Mr. Hoover. It is one of the most wonderful institutions for humanity that ever existed in the world."

[56]In *Le cardinal Mercier, 1851-1926,* clxviii.

[57]Nerincx to Mercier, May 13, 1919 (A.A.M., Box 12).

Pacific gained speed, arriving a half-day early and reaching New York late Tuesday afternoon.[58] It was necessary to modify the plan at the last minute. The cardinal would spend his first night in New York and would leave for Baltimore on the following day. A delegation gathered on the New York police boat that came to meet the steamer as it entered the harbor. There were two welcoming groups from New York and Baltimore, some Belgian priests — Father de Strijcker, the former rector Msgr. Hebbelynck, and Father Stillemans — who had been involved in organizing the journey, John Francis Hylan, the mayor of New York City, and Archbishop Hayes[59]. Hayes, "speaking into a giant megaphone the length of a chimney stack, shouted words that seemed to issue from a giant's throat: 'You are very welcome in America'."[60] Mercier had scarcely disembarked onto the crowded pier before reporters surrounded him. One of them had the singular lack of understanding to ask about his impressions of the New World![61] Others were more interested in knowing whether the visit had an official character. "Did you come here on a special mission for the Belgian government?" asked a reporter from *The New York Times.* The cardinal answered, "No. I come as a Belgian in

[58] *The New York Herald* reported on the morning of September 9: "Wireless messages received last night from the steamship *Northern Pacific* said the liner was making new records on her trip from France to this port." That same day, *The Evening Globe* added this: "As the liner was not expected to arrive before tomorrow, this necessitated a hurried change in the plans of the reception committee."

[59] Patrick Hayes (1867-1938), of Irish origin, spent his entire career in New York. From November, 1917, he headed the military chaplaincy there. Auxiliary bishop to Cardinal Farley since 1914, he succeeded him as Archbishop on March 10, 1919. Hayes was one of the four co-signers of the Program of Social Reconstruction in 1919, and a staunch supporter of the temperance movement. See J.B. Kelly, *Cardinal Hayes* (New York, 1940).

[60] M. De Wulf, in *Le cardinal Mercier, 1851-1926*, clxviii.

[61] See the letter of June 1, 1920, from Mercier to the Director of the Belgian Touring Club, in *Oeuvres pastorales*, VI, 185. The cardinal adds: "So I answered, 'Please! give me time to breathe and look around'."

the name of the whole of the people, both Catholic and Protestant, to convey to the people of America their gratitude and admiration and love because of what you have done for us all." He hastened to add that Belgium was still counting on American aid to get the country on its economic feet.[62] Another journalist, referring to a recent dispatch from the Associated Press,[63] commented, "It is reported that you are here on a mission from his Holiness the Pope?" Mercier's answer was even more precise. "No, no. I am here only as a Belgian, in the name of all the Belgians to express to America the gratitude of Belgium."[64]

Mercier's first communications with the press are preserved in the news accounts. He shared his anxiety that the attitude of Germany had not changed and that it was already preparing a revenge. Furthermore, he was concerned over the serious danger posed by "radical socialism," meaning communism. Asked how America could continue to help Belgium, he answered that his country was not seeking alms, but assistance for getting itself back to work. "Send us machinery. In our schools, we need something new. We need industrial schools where our children can learn to do skillful work."[65] He spoke equally of the needs of the universities.

The first formalities over, the cardinal was taken to the archbishop's residence. The understanding was that

[62] *The New York Times,* September 10, 1919.

[63] According to a Paris correspondent for the Brooklyn *Eagle* on September 2, 1919, the cardinal had been "entrusted with a delicate mission in that country by the Holy See," related to the League of Nations.

[64] *The Boston Post,* September 10, 1919. The Belgian representative to the Vatican, Count d'Ursel, confirmed the statement telegraphically to the minister on September 13: "Cardinal Mercier has received no mission from the Holy See" (A.M.A.É.Br., *Correspondance politique: St-Siège,* folder "1919-1922"). D'Ursel added in another letter on the same day that he knew this "from information given me at the Secretariat of State" (A.M.A.É.Br., B. 347, folder "Voyage Mercier").

[65] *The Baltimore Sun,* September 12, 1919.

throughout the journey, though civil authorities might be closely linked with the festivities, Mercier would always stay with the local Catholic bishop. Professor De Wulf describes a typical arrival:

> The procession of automobiles would begin, and an extraordinary spectacle would occur, one to be repeated daily in various ways and places. Advance police dispatchers organized motorcades through cities crowded with traffic. Police on motorcycles preceded the cars along the route. With sirens wailing, they would stop or re-route traffic. The roadways cleared as if by magic; for a few moments noisy streets became still as the cars glided quietly by.[66]

Because of the change in plans and the subsequent delay of his arrival in Baltimore, it was thought that the cardinal could attend the "Pershing Parade," celebrating the return from Europe of the First Army Division, led by General Pershing. The general rode by the cathedral plaza where the cardinal stood, flanked by Mr. Brand Whitlock, United States Ambassador to Belgium, and Archbishop Hayes. He stopped, got down from his chestnut horse and shook hands with the prelate amid thunderous applause.[67]

After that ceremony, Mercier left by train for Baltimore, accompanied by the mayor and a few members of the welcoming committee. Mr. Ryan, the wealthy businessman mentioned earlier, had provided Mercier with his own comfortable railway coach for the duration of his American stay.

[66]See *Le cardinal Mercier, 1851-1926,* clxviii.

[67]In addition to newspapers, see also M. De Wulf, *ibid.,* clxx; and F. Dessain, *ibid.,* 136.

This elegant car served as a special train or became an addition to a speedier train that we would sometimes leave behind to rejoin later. It provided an excellent hotel-restaurant, with four commodious sleeping berths, a reception room to the rear, a balcony on which the bolder reporters would board the train en route, a dining room, and a kitchen with three negro servants. This was enhanced by all the comforts of American life: a bathroom, hot and cold water, electric lights and fans, icebox, telegraph, and telephone.[68]

The reception at Baltimore was grandiose. Cardinal Gibbons presided from a throne-like chair set up in the train station. Outside, tens of thousands waited on the grassy slope, led by children waving Belgian and American flags, singing and applauding. The first three days provided some respite. Mercier had long private conversations with Gibbons,[69] interspersed with tours in the vicinity of the city. There was also a visit to the major seminary where the cardinal spoke briefly to priests on retreat. Finally, there were receptions in the homes of wealthy Catholic families who could offer financial assistance to the Church in Belgium.

The official visit began on Sunday, September 14. Mercier made his first public address during the solemn high Mass, before a crowd larger than any seen at the cathedral since the Third Plenary Council in 1884. He began by acknowledging Cardinal Gibbons, "that wonderful man who is the most glorious witness of Catholic faith in the New

---

[68]M. De Wulf, *ibid.*, clxxii-clxxiii, clxxxiii.

[69]On September 13, Mercier sent his friend Canon Van Ballaer a postcard with this message: "Pleasant crossing, very good health, delightful welcome. I am spending a few days with my dear colleague Cardinal Gibbons, who is 85. The hours of conversation with him have beeen among the loveliest of my life" (Archives of the Monastery of Chevetogne, Van Ballaer Papers).

World,"[70] and went on to thank the American people and to develop the theme of unshakable confidence in God in the midst of the worst trials.[71] The following evening, an "absolutely informal" reception took place in the cavernous Fifth Regiment Armory, during which 30,000 to 40,000 persons, Catholics and non-Catholics alike, filed by the platform flanked by sailors and soldiers. Some held rosaries, others lifted books or flags to be presented for a blessing. Although there was no speech planned, the cardinal was moved to say a few words expressing his emotion at this outpouring of friendship. In the late afternoon of September 16, the elite of Baltimore gathered in the Lyric Theater with Cardinal Gibbons and former governor Goldsborough to hear Mercier's first lengthy public discourse, entitled "Why I Have Come Over Here."[72] He answered the question in three points. First, "to express my admiration for America," which, though it had no direct financial or political interests in the war, had taken up arms to defend the right. Then, he wished "to express my thankfulness," because not only had American intervention in 1917 been a providential agent of victory, but the food supplies sent from the United States in the first months of the war had also staved off famine for the Belgians. Finally, he hoped "to express the need of American help for the social reconstruction of Belgium." The cardinal recounted the ravages of war in his country, stressing the destruction of numerous homes and schools, of 800 churches, and in particular, of the University of Louvain. "The University of Louvain asks for its library, its laboratories, its instruments of scientific research, the necessary

[70] *The New York Tribune,* September 15, 1919. M. De Wulf notes: "As Americanism never gives up its rights, the pulpit was rolled into the middle of the Church." (*Le cardinal Mercier, 1851-1926,* clxxix).

[71] Diary of Bishop De Wachter.

[72] Text in A.A.M., Box 12.

[73] Diary of Bishop De Wachter.

funds to ensure its economic life." He did not hesitate to challenge the audience that sought only to applaud him: "Allow me to be frank: after all that you have done, your work is not complete." Following the ritual which was to become routine in the next six weeks, namely, to "shake hands with thousands of people," the cardinal boarded the train at 10 P.M. and arrived in New York the morning of September 17. There he attended a solemn anniversary service for Cardinal Farley[74] and went to City Hall where he was made an honorary citizen of New York. That evening, the mayor hosted a banquet in his honor for 1,500 guests. Draped in a cloak of watered silk, the cardinal addressed his "fellow citizens" for almost an hour, speaking of the Belgian resistance movement, of workers' deportations, of the sacred pledge of all political parties to uphold the king, and of the patriotic spirit of the Belgian clergy.

On the 18th, the cardinal visited Albany and received his first doctorate *honoris causa* during a reception at the Educational Hall, where he heard speeches by the governor, the Catholic bishop, a delegate of the Episcopalian bishop, and a rabbi. He was back in New York by 10 P.M. the same evening. On the following day, as the luncheon guest of the Wall Street Bankers Club, he took the opportunity to arouse the generosity of the business community towards Belgium. That evening was spent at a dinner given by the Belgian Consul General at the Hotel Astor, attended by "a hundred or so of the most important names in the legal professions, the clergy, business and financial affairs, letters and journalism."[75] Later there was a reception for the Belgian community, whom he addressed in French, Flemish, and English.

[74]Archbishop of New York from September 15, 1902, to September 17, 1918.

[75]Cartier de Marchienne to Hymans, September 24, 1919, in A.M.A.É.Br., B. 347, folder "Voyage Mercier." The cardinal, who for many years had fought against alcoholism, noted with satisfaction on his return "that at all the public banquets, only water was served: spring water, bottled water, seltzer water, in sparkling crystal glasses that decorated the festive tables" (*Oeuvres pastorales*, VI, 188).

On September 20, the cardinal returned to the south. After a short stopover in Baltimore, where he celebrated the pontifical Mass on Sunday morning, he left for Annapolis to be welcomed by the governor of Maryland. He visited the Naval Academy, where he told the young midshipmen of his admiration for the American Navy. By evening of September 22, he arrived in Washington, but a previously-planned official reception by President Wilson had been cancelled because of the President's ill health. The reception at the Belgian Embassy, however, gave the cardinal a chance to meet all kinds of political figures, who were deeply impressed with him.[76]

The next day, Mercier assisted at the first plenary assembly of the American hierarchy,[77] an occasion he used to address the ninety-two bishops meeting at the Sulpician Seminary located at the Catholic University of America. Great was the cardinal's surprise to note that the talk was being filmed,[78] a departure from the closed European episcopal meetings, to which he was accustomed. His speech was

[76]Ambassador de Cartier de Marchienne wrote enthusiastically to Minister Hymans on September 24, describing the "warm welcome" everywhere for the cardinal: "I observed this again yesterday, at a reception I gave for Cardinal Mercier at the Embassy, to which I had invited Members of Congress, Senators and Deputies with whom I have personal contact, ambassadors and heads of missions, Cabinet members and high government officials, our own compatriots and persons from every level of society" (A.M.A.É.Br., B. 347, folder "Voyage Mercier").

[77]Prior to this, only the archbishops met annually. After the war, Cardinal Gibbons deemed it important to engender unified action among the hierarchy. At this meeting, the National Catholic Welfare Council was inaugurated (See Ellis, *Gibbons,* II, 303-04).

[78]Letter to the Director of the Belgian Touring Club, quoted in *Oeuvres pastorales,* VI, 188: "How surprised I was when, as soon as the door opened and before I stood up to speak, workmen arrived to install photographic equipment for 'moving pictures' there in the meeting room. One of my confrères explained it like this: 'Yes, we want our people to see us at work. We Americans live a very social existence. Tomorrow in all the major American cities, our faithful and fellow-citizens will be able to witness the Catholic hierarchy at work. They follow us with interest because they know how interested we are in them'."

divided into two parts.[79] In the first, he developed the three points summarized above, which became a kind of thematic constant throughout his tour of the United States, with adaptations for various audiences. Thus, he began by expressing his admiration at the vitality of the American Church, which he was now experiencing first-hand rather than through reading. In the third point, he restated "in the name of the Belgian Catholic hierarchy" the great needs of the Catholic University of Louvain. The second part of his address, however, took a completely different direction. He recommended that his colleagues examine a topic to which he had been attached for many years; namely, the eventual definition of Mary as universal Mediatrix,[80] a point he proposed for their study.[81]

The cardinal left for a day's rest at Mr. Ryan's estate at Oakridge. On the 26th, he arrived in Philadelphia, where he was met at the train station by a hundred festooned automobiles.[82] All the factories had closed for two hours, to allow their workers to greet the cardinal along his route, a length of ten kilometers. There was a "monster banquet," Friday abstinence notwithstanding, during which toasts were offered by the mayor, the governor, the archbishop, the Episcopalian bishop, and the rabbi, who, according to Bishop De Wachter, gave "a wonderful speech."[83] The cardi-

[79]The first draft, dated September 20, was changed considerably. The definitive text and the original draft are preserved in A.A.M., Box 12.

[80]On Mercier's particular interest before the war in the doctrine of Marian mediation, see R. Laurentin, *La question mariale* (Paris, 1963), 54-55. In October, 1924, the cardinal would appeal to the hierarchy all over the world for petitions to Rome favoring the definition of Mary as universal mediatrix.

[81]Bishop De Wachter noted in his diary, with an element of shrewdness: "I doubt that the assembly has interest in this issue so dear to the heart of His Eminence."

[82]One of the most striking phenomena for Mercier and his traveling companions was the nearly total absence of horse-drawn carriages in the larger cities.

[83]At one point, he exclaimed: "Thanks to you, distinguished son of a distinguished faith, for the blessings that your heroic example gave to all humanity."

nal then went to the office of Belgian Relief, and in the evening he spoke at the Opera House.

The next day was very full indeed. There were visits to the city hall, the seminary, the hospital, and the university, where the cardinal attended a football game, during which the 100,000 spectators frequently cheered him enthusiastically. Finally, he attended a reception given by a Ladies' Committee, a type of group that was flourishing in the States, and whose dynamic quality often impressed the cardinal. The day ended with a visit to two convents.

Another honorary doctorate was bestowed upon the cardinal on September 28 at Princeton University, where the *Veni Creator* was sung at his entrance and university president John Grier Hibben gave a remarkable speech.[84]

Passing briefly once again through New York, Mercier visited the oil magnate, John Rockefeller,[85] and then went on to Providence, Hartford, Yale University at New Haven — where he received another honorary doctorate,[86] — and Springfield, Massachusetts. On October 4, he came to Boston as the guest of Cardinal William H. O'Connell.[87]

---

[84]Among other things, Hibben told Mercier: "You not only belong to the Roman Catholic Church, but to all Churches everywhere that pronounce the name of Christ."

[85]Rockefeller made statements on the altruistic use of his wealth which impressed Mercier to the point that he noted them down during the return crossing, among his impressions of America. See, at the end of my text, item No. 3 of "General Impressions."

[86]President Hadley remarked that "to find in the history of Yale University a ceremony that approaches today's celebration, we must retrace a century, to the visit of Talleyrand, or even two centuries, to that of Berkeley. For in you we discover the merit of both these men: the qualities of the statesman and the intuition of the philosopher" (Cited by De Wulf in *Le cardinal Mercier, 1851-1926,* clxxvi).

[87]William H. O'Connell (1859-1944), former rector of the North American College in Rome from 1895-1901, became Archbishop of Boston in 1907 and cardinal in 1911. Theodore Roosevelt, who criticized him for his pro-Spanish leanings, considered him "very narrow" and "a medieval reactionary" — see *The Letters of Theodore Roosevelt,* ed. by E. E. Morison, VII (Cambridge, 1954), 437.

As the cardinal's visit gained impetus, the number of spontaneous receptions at railway stations increased. Two extracts from diaries kept by his traveling companions describe the general atmosphere on these occasions:

[October] 3. Departure for Springfield — all along the route schoolchildren are lined up. Workers and the whole population are crowded into the station and all around it to hail the cardinal. Arrival at Springfield, 12:15 P.M.. . . .

[October] 4. We leave Springfield at 9:10. Dense crowds in all stations along the route. Ovation for His Eminence at the Worcester station by the students of Holy Cross College, run by the Jesuit Fathers. Arrived Boston at about 11:30.[88]

The great speed of the tour gave us firsthand knowledge of the impressive organizational genius of this great people. Crowds, previously informed by the newspapers, waited at the stations to greet the train. In Hamilton, a five-minute stop sufficed to have a brief reception. At times, the train slowed up and passed through smaller towns on the way so that the cardinal could step out onto the platform at the back of his car. On the way to Albany, at Peckhill, clusters of people crowded on the banks near the tracks, and crowds climbed up on the ramps to get a better view. At Blackstone, the railway employees had been given a half-day off to greet the cardinal. At Albany, the reception committee tried to extend the visit by a half-hour, holding up a special locomotive that was to take our car 350 kilometers beyond our scheduled journey![89]

[88]Diary of Bishop De Wachter.
[89]M. De Wulf in *Le cardinal Mercier, 1851-1926,* clxxiv.

Mercier's stay in Boston, from October 4 to 6, was marked by two important events. On the morning of Sunday the 5th, in the diocesan cathedral, the cardinal met members of the Belgian royal family who were on a six-week tour of the United States.[90] During the solemn high Mass celebrated by Cardinal O'Connell, King Albert and Mercier sat facing each other in the sanctuary.[91] After Mass, Mercier mounted the pulpit to express his gratitude to the people of Boston, and then the king and his retinue filed into the sacristy to meet some public functionaries. The next day, Mercier was awarded *honoris causa* a doctoral degree by Harvard University, truly an exceptional honor.[92] Cardinal O'Connell, hardly renowned for his breadth of vision, and eager to keep young Catholics out of this "Protestant" university, had let Mercier know that he did not approve of the reception at Harvard.[93] Mercier had discussed the issue with Gibbons at one of their first meetings, but he had been quickly reassured: "If you refuse the invitations of American universities, that will be regarded not only as an insult to the universities but to the entire nation."[94] One can easily

[90]King Albert, with Queen Elizabeth and the Crown Prince Leopold, had boarded at Ostende on September 17. On the 31st of October, he started for home from a journey that had taken him all the way to California. See P. Goemaere, *À travers l'Amérique avec le roi des Belges* (Brussels, 1923). It was claimed that the king "felt some resentment" over the warm welcome accorded to Mercier by the Americans. See Joseph Dessain, "Les progrès de l'Oecuménisme: l'incidént Mercier 1919-1922," *Revue théologique de Louvain* 5 (1974), 469-76, here 469.

[91]There is a photo of the ceremony in *Le cardinal Mercier, 1851-1926,* clxxvi.

[92]"Only four times in its previous history had Harvard called an extraordinary convocation similar to the one organized in honor of the cardinal. In 1776 and in 1833, it had received two Presidents of the Republic, George Washington and Andrew Jackson. In 1902, it welcomed Prince Henry of Prussia, and in 1917, Marshal Joffre" (M. De Wulf, in *Le cardinal Mercier, 1851-1926,* clxxvi-clxxviii).

[93]During the war, O'Connell complained to Mercier that De Wulf had agreed to give courses at Harvard. Because he thought De Wulf was a priest, O'Connell had notices posted in all the sacristies of his diocese forbidding De Wulf to say Mass!

[94]Mercier told this to Pius XI at his first audience on February 7, 1922 (A.A.M., Box 24, folder "Conclave, 1922," No. 4 in the report on his audience). In a draft of

imagine that under these circumstances, the conversations between the two cardinals during the Boston visit were somewhat strained, especially since O'Connell had never hidden his antipathy towards the Allied cause during the war.[95]

From October 7 to 11 there were full days, once again in New York. On his arrival, after lunch sponsored by the Merchants' Association, at the Hotel Astor, the cardinal went to Columbia University to receive another honorary doctorate. The Belgian ambassador noted that "this ceremony held a special importance for us because Mr. Murray Butler, President of Columbia, is also president of the American committee for the rebuilding of the University of Louvain. During the ceremony, the reconstruction of the library was mentioned."[96] The next day, there was a pontifical Mass at St. Patrick's Cathedral, a reception at the Colony Club, and dinner at the home of Mr. and Mrs. Nicholas Brady, followed by a reception at the Catholic Club. On the 9th, Mercier was the guest of the Chamber of Commerce[97] and went to a banquet for 1228 guests, sponsored by the

---

the letter to Benedict XV on March 4, 1920, Mercier wrote: "With only one exception, all the bishops in the United States were unanimous in their gratitude to me for having broken down some of the Protestant prejudice towards the Catholic Church" (cited by Dessain, "Les progrès," 471).

[95]For example, see Cartier de Marchienne to Hymans, November 27, 1918, in A.M.A.É.Br., *Correspondance,* folder "September-décembre, 1918": "The cardinal archbishop of Boston, undoubtedly because of his links with Sinn-Fein, was never anything but lukewarm towards us. His more or less cold treatment of Father Rutten led one to believe that Bishop Carton would be received in much the same way. This was such a painful contrast to the friendliness and warmth we found in Cardinal Gibbons."

[96]Cartier de Marchienne to Hymans, November 19, 1919, in A.M.A.É.Br., B. 347, folder "Voyage Mercier." The following appeared in the *Evening World* of October 6, 1919: "Cardinal Mercier will visit Columbia tomorrow, open the national project to raise $500,000 for a new library at the University of Louvain, and receive the degree of LL.D. from the hands of President Butler."

[97]This typical American ceremony is described by M. De Wulf, in *Le cardinal Mercier, 1851-1926,* clxxii.

Knights of Columbus whose members had gathered from everywhere in the United States. After a breakfast on the 10th, co-hosted by the Church Peace Union and the New York Federation of Churches, Mercier attended a reception in Central Park given by the children of New York; he crowned a statue of Joan of Arc, and assisted at an evening reception given by the New York Bar Association. At this ceremony, the president of the association recalled that during the war, "one word from [Mercier's] mouth weighed more than tons of enemy propaganda,"[98] and read a message from the noted jurist and statesman, Elihu Root.[99] Finally, at noon on the 11th, there was a banquet given by the Pennsylvania Society, attended by the most influential business people in the United States, including Thomas Edison, "who disturbs himself for no one."[100]

Later that afternoon, the cardinal left for a tour of the Great Lakes region, with a brief detour into Canada. He passed through Scranton ("20,000 people stood in the rain to greet the cardinal," noted Bishop De Wachter); Syracuse ("tremendous crowd"); Rochester ("day too full but magnificent"). There was one day in Toronto, followed by visits to Niagara Falls, Buffalo, Cleveland (where he stayed for a couple of days), Toledo ("whistling of all the locomotives"), Monroe, and Detroit.

The Detroit stop, on Monday, October 20, was an important one. The General Convention of the Episcopalian

[98] He added, recalling the invitation addressed by the American hierarchy to the young Mercier to teach at The Catholic University in Washington: "If 30 years ago he had yielded to the pressing requests to come to Catholic University, what a treasure that would have been for the spiritual and intellectual life of our country! But Providence disposed otherwise, and thanks be to God, in the war to end all wars, he was found at his important post, serving his own country, accomplishing tasks with strength and devotion of the highest supernatural order" (*ibid.*).

[99] *Ibid.*

[100] M. De Wulf adds, "A Belgian flag hung from the hotel facade. My table companion noted, with undisguised satisfaction, that it was the biggest Belgian flag in the world" (*ibid.*).

Church in the United States was meeting at the time.[101] Through the intermediary of the Catholic Bishop Michael J. Gallagher, the cardinal had been invited to receive the esteem of the assembly members, many of whom had served on committees for Belgian relief during the war. Mercier addressed the lower chamber of priests and laypeople, gathered in a public hall rather than a church. Having recalled some of his wartime memories and thanked his audience for their generosity to the Belgians, Mercier sketched the harmful characteristics of Kantian philosophy, stressing the important role it had in the misdirection of the German mind and in the development of subjectivist modernism.[102] The remarkable thing about this allocution, intended to be apologetic in tone, was the terminology employed by the cardinal in greeting his audience: "I have greeted you as brethren in the worship of common ideals, as brethren in the love of liberty and, let me add, brethren in the Christian faith."[103] That a cardinal of the Church of Rome should address members of a Protestant Church in such fashion was without precedent since the Reformation. It was, however, most appropriate within the interconfessional atmosphere that had prevailed since Mercier's arrival from Europe, a phenomenon which presented a total novelty for him. At the beginning of his visit, he had heard himself described by the President of Princeton: "You belong not to the Roman church alone, but to all those churches in all nations that pronounce the name of Christ

[101]The Protestant Episcopal Church, USA — PECUSA — is the American branch of the Anglican communion.

[102]"Le voyage de S.É. le cardinal Mercier aux États-Unis," in *Oeuvres pastorales*, VI (Louvain, 1926), 166.

[103]The statement was cited by several papers in nearly identical phrasing. In using this expression, Mercier was echoing the welcome of the president: "The Church Cardinal Mercier represents and other Christian faiths are one in the fatherhood of God. We are brethren in the Christian faith. We are at this moment, I think, to unite our efforts to show the world that our brotherly feeling is only a corollary of the fatherhood of God."

and believe in his power to save the soul of the world."[104] Everywhere, even in Boston, the non-Catholic ecclesiastical leaders had taken part in the civic and religious ceremonial greetings for Mercier. The Episcopalians appeared particularly sensitive to this. A few days earlier, the Catholic bishop of Scranton had, during a public reception, turned to his Anglican colleague while he spoke of "the Church that is located at the next door."[105] Again, at a dinner in Baltimore, the Episcopalian Bishop Murray had declared: "Here are quotations of the pastoral letters of Cardinal Mercier which I have been reading to my diocesans. So that, Cardinal, my flock became your flock." All of these considerations aside, there were those described by *The Christian Century* as "the rather conservative clergy in America," who were shocked by Mercier's attendance at the Episcopalian Convention and even more so by the audacity he had shown in addressing his hosts as "brothers in the faith." Cardinal O'Connell was quick to delate Mercier to the Holy Office.[106]

The cardinal then spent two days in Chicago, where Archbishop George Mundelein accorded him a princely welcome. The journey continued through Moline, Davenport, Rock Island, Peoria,[107] St. Louis, Cincinnati, Dayton, Columbus, and Pittsburgh, where he received another honorary degree between a meeting at the Masonic Hall and

---

[104]Cited by M. De Wulf, in *Le cardinal Mercier, 1851-1926,* clxxviii.

[105]*Ibid.,* clxxix.

[106]The story and its sequel have been recounted, based on documents in the *Fonds Mercier* at Mechelen, by J. Dessain, "Les progrès," 469-76. Bishop Gallagher, who had accompained Mercier, was likewise disturbed. Among the nine motives for justifying the appearance, he mentioned that "a refusal on your part to attend ¿the Convention¡ would have aroused a storm of indignation against a Church whose members accept charity, but refuse to express thanks to their benefactors because they are Protestants."

[107]"Bishop Dunne of Peoria, —a true Yankee—stayed with our car for two days to be sure that His Eminence would stop in the cathedral city of his diocese. He managed to gain the four hours needed to give the reception he had planned and a special night train then linked up to our coach at St. Louis, where we resumed the scheduled journey" (M. De Wulf, in *Le cardinal Mercier 1851-1926,* clxxv).

an "imposing ceremony at the Cathedral." On Wednesday, October 29, Mercier was once again in New York.

According to the original plan, the cardinal was to have spent the day in Washington and be formally received by President Woodrow Wilson during a special session of Congress. But the aggravation of the President's illness occasioned another cancellation of that ceremony. Instead, a delegation of senators and members of Congress came to New York and presented the cardinal with the address that would have been read to him.[108] It was also impossible for him to visit The Catholic University of America in Washington, which had not yet reopened when he had passed through that city in September. A delegation from the University, led by the rector Bishop Thomas Shahan, came to New York to present him with a doctorate in theology, *honoris causa*. A total of sixteen universities had honored the prelate in this fashion.[109] Others, Cornell among them, would have wanted to do the same had the arrangements for the visit permitted it.

The last days of the visit had been reserved for Canada, with departure from New York on November 5. This time a dock strike upset the plans. Because the cardinal insisted on being back in Belgium for the elections on November 15, it happened that his visit to the United States ended on October 29, a glorious autumn day. Early in the evening, the special train took him to Ottawa. The next day, in sub-zero weather, he was the guest of the governor-general, the Duke of Devonshire. He spent the 31st in Montréal[110] and the next two days in Québec, as the guest of Cardinal Louis Nazaire Bégin. From Québec he sailed for England on the *Megantic*, a steamer of the White Star Line.

[108]Francis Dessain, in *Le cardinal Mercier, 1851-1926,* 136-37.

[109]See the letter of Bishop Shahan dated October 13, 1919 (A.A.M., Box 23). Among those universities conferring on him an honorary doctorate were: Harvard, Yale, Princeton, Columbia, Michigan, Chicago, Wesleyan, Brown, New York, the Catholic University of America, and Toronto.

[110]"At Montreal, the same testimonies awaited us, more reserved and sober than

If the journey had indeed been a tiring one,[111] it had also surpassed all expectations. True, there had been some reservations. We have already alluded to the disappointment of certain conservative Catholics over what they judged to be Mercier's exaggerated openness to Protestants. There were some who believed he had exceeded the religious boundaries to which he should have limited himself, and that his addresses were too political, too anti-socialist, and above all, too anti-German. This point of view is reflected in a press dispatch which, while biased, is nonetheless significant:

> The well-known Belgian socialist intellectual, Henri de Man, is now in America. He is sending back some very interesting letters on the economic and social situation in the United States. His latest letter refers to the American visit of Cardinal Mercier. He writes that the cardinal talks too much. To the great astonishment of the Americans, he speaks of matters that have nothing to do with theology. There is some amazement that he has discussed Belgian industrial needs. In America, where people like their Church to limit itself to religious matters, some are asking whether the seat of the Belgian government is in Brussels or Mechlin. People are also astonished to hear the Belgian primate discuss the struggle against socialism and the future of the League of Nations.
>
> Cardinal Mercier has apparently stated that another war will break out in Europe within fifteen years, that Germany is already preparing for it, and that Belgium would once again side with the French. He is said to have

those in the United States, but not less cordial or spontaneous" (M. De Wulf, in *Le cardinal Mercier, 1851-1926*, clxxxiv).

[111] Witnesses reiterated the fatiguing nature of this tour that lasted almost two months, but they also told of the ease with which Mercier sustained the stress of the journey. Journalists were impressed from the first: "The vitality and alertness of Mercier, his firm step and keen mind are not those of an old man" (*The Baltimore Star*, September 12, 1919).

warned the United States to be cautious in future dealings with Germany. Such prophecies have elicited smiles from those who are more knowledgeable.[112]

The historian should take reservations of this kind into account, but the general impression of a "triumphal march" remains. Professor De Wulf himself used that expression,[113] adding a further important note:

There was yet something more noteworthy than the processions and receptions, the speeches and the celebrations. It was the welcome accorded this man of God by the people, and the spontaneous quality of that welcome.... One does not orchestrate the soul of a crowd. Yet the soul of these crowds was conquered by the cardinal.[114]

The throngs had been struck especially by the combination in Mercier's personality of greatness, both physical and moral, and of a modest, smiling kindliness.[115]

[112]Translation of a dispatch from the *Deutsche Allgemeine Zeitung,* October 27, 1919, in A.M.A.É.Br., B. 347, folder "Voyage Mercier." Henri de Man (1885-1953), who would later write a celebrated book, *Au delà du marxisme* (1927), kept close contact with the German Left. He published his impressions of America in a work entitled *Au pays du taylorisme* (1919).

[113]De Wulf was not the only one to do so. Francis Dessain, at the onset of the voyage, wrote to a Belgian cloistered nun: "We go from triumph to triumph. It's incredible." (Postcard copied in the "Dossier rouge" of the Benedictine Monastery of Maredret).

[114]Article dated October 30, 1919, in *La Libre Belgique,* 1919, No. 327. See also the later reflections of Mrs. Kellogg in *Le cardinal Mercier, 1851-1926,* 202-03.

[115]Two further notes on this modesty: Francis Dessain wrote on October 17, 1919, to the Abbess of Maredret ("Dossier rouge" cited above), "Our great and dear cardinal goes through all this like a child, never doubting the extent or the power of his influence, yet aware of it in a most humble way, with astonishment, attributing it all to God." And to Dom Lambert Beauduin, linked to the origins of the famous pastoral letter, *Patriotisme et endurance,* Mercier sent a postcard on which he wrote, "You are the one who should be here." See S.A. Quitslund, *Beauduin, a Prophet Vindicated* (New York, 1973), 43. On the role of Beauduin in the redaction and diffusion of this famous pastoral letter, see L. Bouyer, *Dom Lambert Beauduin, un homme d'Eglise* (Tournai, 1964), 85-89.

And what of Mercier's own impressions during the eight weeks in which he had "discovered" America? Some of these formed part of a public discourse the day after his return.[116] Better still are those he noted in a few phrases on his homeward journey from Québec to Liverpool, when he wrote spontaneously of things that had struck him most, both positively and negatively. What more appropriate way to end this account, than to reproduce the jottings exactly as he set them down?[117]

GENERAL IMPRESSIONS

1. Agreeable surprise. This business nation with its marvelous initiative, where everything is in constant motion — with millionaires and billionaires — is also a nation more concerned and taken up with moral and religious ideals than any European society.
   Convictions more practical than speculative, but spontaneous and sincere.
   Evangelical simplicity; i.e., absence of pretense or dissimulation.
   St. Gregory: Treatise on morality —
   Morality, the source of religious inspirations and sincerity, seems to me the unique virtue of this American people.

2. Respect for law and authority — springing more from individual conscience than from constraint. Same for

---

[116]See especially "Réponse à l'adresse du bourguemestre de Malines," November 24, 1919, in *Oeuvres pastorales,* VI, 168-69, and "Une impression d'Amérique. Lettre au Touring Club de Belgique," January 1, 1920, *ibid.,* 185-88.

[117]The original, kept in the *Fonds Mercier* at Mechelen, disappeared a few years ago. Happily, Canon Joseph Dessain had made a copy and he was kind enough to let me use it. The rough sketch of two conferences the cardinal gave at the seminary early in December, 1919, are preserved in his own hand (A.A.M., Box 86, folder "Allocutions aux séminaristes, 1914-24"). The first contains a few recollections of his journey, and the second is on "Characteristics of the American people." The fuller text here reproduced can be found summarized therein.

importance of public opinion arising from personal responsibility (the self-made man).

3. From this, an altruistic concept of the function of wealth. Rockefeller: a) My principle has always been: If you've saved a dollar, use it to earn another. b) As for me, I have always considered myself as a servant of humanity.
    R: "I serve, I am a servant, you and I are servants."
    M: *"Qui major est inter vos fiat sicut minister."* (Let the greater among you be as the servant.)

4. Respect for the religious beliefs of others. Protestant bishops: at Baltimore, Bishop Murray who had dinner with us at the cardinal's, spoke to some of the guests after the meal: "Here are some extracts from the pastoral letters of Cardinal Mercier which I have read to my flock. So that, Cardinal, my flock became your flock."

5. Competition: to be first in this and in that.

6. Cult of the most, the biggest: a bishop has built X number of buildings, covered so many miles in a year, has so many different races in his diocese.

7. Weaknesses:
    The cult of morality is for many Americans more sentiment than conviction. Their spiritual brotherhood is an easy one because it is based on minimal ideals: justice, honesty, charity. We Catholic Christians should affirm our faith with conviction basing it on certainties. We should raise our souls to the supernatural plane. To lower our beliefs to the level of a naturalistic ideal would be a form of "Americanism," the "modernism" of Tyrrell.
    A fear: Are not these natural virtues too easily judged to be sufficient by Catholics? Spiritual liberalism has advantages for common life. It is deficient from the supernatural and Christian standpoint. It is merely a relative good, a step up from materialism.

Trans. by Janice Farnham, R.J.M.

George N. Shuster and American Catholic Intellectual Life

Thomas E. Blantz, C.S.C.

In a controversial article published in 1925, a young George N. Shuster, having taught English for only five years at the University of Notre Dame, leveled a devastating criticism at American Catholic scholarship:

> It appears to me...that if we try to view Catholic academic life as a whole, we shall find that during the past seventy-five years it has produced not a single great literary man or writer on literary subjects; not a scientist, excepting possibly two or three chemists and seismologists, who has made an original contribution to the vast catalogue of recent discoveries; not an historian whose study of a definite field has resulted in a new orientation of our minds towards the past; and, with one exception, no economist whose leadership has divined new and better social directions. If we are honest, we must admit that during seventy-five years of almost feverish intellectual activity we have had no influence on the general culture of America other than what has come from a

passably active endeavor to spread to the four winds knowledge accumulated either by our ancestors or by sectarian scholars.[1]

Shuster singled out his own academic field for special criticism. "I can only say," he noted, "that a relatively careful examination of some twenty-five doctorate theses prepared in Catholic colleges on subjects relating to English literature forced me to conclude that not a single one would have been accepted, simply as research, at a university of the first rank."[2] "Almost every one," he continued, "revealed a meager knowledge of historical background or linguistics; scarcely any were even comparatively original studies; and only three disclosed on the part of the authors a trained aptitude for investigating a problem."[3] The final tragedy, according to Shuster, was that doctoral work was rarely scholarship but only training for scholarship, and yet the Catholic graduate seldom continued serious research after receiving the advanced degree. "After that is carefully framed," Shuster continued, "he is assumed to be a master; he rides his oars merrily, teaches twice as many classes as any human being ought to teach, and by force of circumstances over which he has no control is borne into a mental desuetude which is sometimes pathetic and sometimes ridiculous."[4]

Shuster cited several reasons for this deplorable state — the recent origin of Catholic education in America, a lack of

---

[1] George N. Shuster, "Have We Any Scholars?," *America* 33 (1925), 418-19, here 418. This article was judged so controversial that the journal editors prefaced it with the following disclaimer: "[*America*, while not in agreement with all of Mr. Shuster's statements, publishes this article in the assurance that it will rouse keen discussion. — Ed., *America*.]" Hereafter Shuster's name will be omitted from footnote references to his publications.

[2] *Ibid.*, 418.

[3] *Ibid.*

[4] *Ibid.*, 418-19.

national prestige, and a shortage of money for scholarly research — but the major cause he suggested was the proliferation of Catholic colleges. "Scarcely has a Catholic college been established anywhere," he stated, "than it begins to dream of building up branch universities...on the plains, on the desert, on the mountaintops."[5] There were simply not that many qualified teachers available and, as a result, both lay and religious instructors were forced to teach far too many classes (for far too meager salaries) to leave time or enthusiasm for scholarly growth. Shuster had little use for the argument that such expansion was demanded by the large number of students seeking admission. "Many of our colleges," he concluded, "are barely able to collect enough matriculation fees to start a respectable savings account; and if they were sufficiently audacious to risk imposing the usual entrance standards, the enrollment would approach zero with amazing rapidity."[6]

This dearth of American Catholic scholarship was a topic to which Shuster returned frequently throughout his life. In *The Catholic Spirit in America,* written in 1927, he admitted that American Catholics generally lagged behind their fellow citizens in culture. They were an immigrant church and, as immigrants, they often arrived from poor educational backgrounds, were absorbed with making a livelihood, and, in a frequently hostile environment, felt greater need to justify and defend their religion than advance it creatively and culturally.[7] In an article in *Catholic Action* in 1932, he urged Catholics to grow in their religion and in their professional careers. "The opportunities to do this growing are at hand," he insisted. "What this country needs is people who do not stop a fifth of an inch below the surface. And I

---

[5] *Ibid.,* 419.
[6] *Ibid.*
[7] *The Catholic Spirit in America* (New York, 1927), 85-120. See also 163-204.

sincerely hope that one effect of this depression will be to diminish the number of Catholic go-getters and increase the total of doctors, lawyers, public servants..., writers, scholars, and journalists." He lamented especially the all-too-frequent low estimation of things of the intellect. "When I was professing at Notre Dame," he recalled, "nothing annoyed me more than the constant stream of old grads who were surprised to find me 'still teaching' when I might have been following in their footsteps as a bond salesman." "Part of this annoyance was due to the blow at my self-esteem," he admitted, "but part of it was also caused by the manifest dumbness of the human race."[8] In 1952, he noted with disappointment that "in some fields, a Catholic scholar is as hard to find as a Hittite hymnal"; but he praised the American Church's achievements also: "Our people has drunk in the smell of the stockyards without losing hope; it has worked in the coal-mines and kept its faith; it has stood all day and night in the heat of the steel mills without abandoning charity. It is a great people."[9]

Shuster returned to this discussion of Catholic scholarship in a symposium on "The Catholic Contribution to American Intellectual Life" in 1958.[10] Emphasizing the need for Catholic scholars, he suggested that they could come from only three sources. A few would come from religious orders, but the majority enter the religious life with other goals. The priesthood could supply a few, but scholarship is often continued in a family tradition and the celibate priesthood is an obstacle here. Thus, the primary source of Catholic scholars must be the laity, and these lay scholars need the assistance and stimulation of close contact with a vibrant

[8]"Opportunities of the Educated Layman," *Catholic Action* 14 (June, 1932), 5-6, here 6.

[9]"Catholic Culture in America," *Today* 8 (March, 1953), 12-13, here 13.

[10]"On Catholic Education," delivered at a symposium sponsored by the Thomas More Association and the Department of Library Science, Rosary College, River Forest, Illinois, and published in *Education and Moral Wisdom* (New York, 1960), 65-83, here 77-80. The quotations are from 79 and 80.

university. The problem once again was that "far too many so-called universities have reared their heads" and that in them the lay faculty was not often accepted as full partners and colleagues. Shuster still refused to justify this prolifera- tion of Catholic colleges on the grounds of a need for pastoral care. "In the long run," he insisted, "the only valid reason for going to a university is to obtain what a univer- sity, with its traditions, professors, laboratories, and library has to offer." Even in the popular *Ave Maria* he lamented in 1963 that "until recently something was obviously wrong because the number of Catholics who emerged as scholars or serious shapers of public opinion was far smaller than it should have been."[11]

But for all his criticisms and pleading, Shuster was proba- bly not primarily a research scholar himself, at least not in the strict sense of that term. For one reason, he held numer- ous responsible and demanding administrative positions throughout his life and these left him little of the leisure which research and scholarship demand.

Born in 1894, Shuster graduated from the University of Notre Dame in 1915, worked for a time as a newspaper reporter in Chicago, served with U.S. Army Intelligence in World War I, and returned to the faculty of English at Notre Dame from 1919 to 1924, chairing the department for four years.[12] He moved to New York in 1924, taught at Brooklyn

---

[11]"The School: Not Little and Red Any Longer," *Ave Maria* 97 (February 9, 1963), 9-12, here 10.

[12]An excellent source is Shuster's autobiographical *The Ground I Walked on*, 2nd enlarged edition (Notre Dame, 1969). See also his "An Autobiography," in *Leaders in American Education*, Seventieth Yearbook of the National Society for the Study of Education, Part II (Chicago, 1971), 277-305; Vincent P. Lannie, "George N. Shuster: A Reflective Evaluation," *ibid.*, 306-20; "George N. Shu- ster," *Current Biography Yearbook, 1960* (New York, 1960), 378-80; "George Nauman Shuster," *The National Cyclopaedia of American Biography*, Vol. H. (New York, 1952), 89-90; Barry D. Riccio, "American Catholic Thought in the Nineteen Twenties: Frederick Joseph Kinsman and George Shuster," *An Ameri- can Church*, ed. David J. Alvarez (Moraga, California, 1979), 113-23; and Wil- liam M. Halsey, *The Survival of American Innocence* (Notre Dame, 1980), 84-98.

Polytechnic Institute and St. Joseph's College for Women, and served first as associate editor and then managing editor of the recently founded *Commonweal* magazine from 1925 to 1937. He spent the next two years in Europe, received his Ph.D. in literature from Columbia University in 1940, and that same year was appointed president of Hunter College, then the world's largest public institution of higher education for women.[13] Shuster held this position until 1960 and somehow found time for numerous government assignments also. He served with Enemy Alien Board #2 in New York in 1942, chaired the War Department's Historical Commission to Germany in 1945, served on the United States National Commission for UNESCO and on UNESCO's Executive Committee after the war, was a member of the General Advisory Committee of the State Department's Division of Cultural Relations, and was appointed Land Commissioner for Bavaria in 1950-1951, the chief American administrator under Commissioner John McCloy during the Allied occupation. In 1960, he resigned the presidency of Hunter College and returned to the University of Notre Dame as Assistant to the President (Rev. Theodore Hesburgh, C.S.C.) and Director of the newly-established Center for the Study of Man in Contemporary Society. He died in 1977 at the age of 82.

Through all these administrative positions, Shuster continued to give encouragement and support to Catholic scholarship, and he managed to be more than prolific in his own writings. By the time he left the Notre Dame faculty in 1924, he had already edited a handbook for freshman writing courses, written articles on "The Tragedy of Mark Twain," "The Retreat of the American Novel," "Catholic Literature as a World Force," "Joris Karl Huysmans: Egoist and Mystic," and "The Surrender of Robert Louis Steven-

[13]Shuster was actually appointed acting president in 1939 and president in 1940.

son," and also published his first full-length book, *The Catholic Spirit in Modern English Literature.*[14]

Shuster's next twelve years, the *Commonweal* period, 1925-1937, were some of the most productive years of his life, and as the journal's associate and managing editor he offered a forum for Catholic scholars at home and in Europe. *Commonweal* published works of G. K. Chesterton, Jacques Maritain, C. C. Martindale, Luigi Sturzo, John La Farge, Agnes Repplier, Carlton J. H. Hayes, and John A. Ryan; and it encouraged younger writers to publish also: Paul Hanly Furfey, Joseph Fichter, Leo R. Ward, John Tracy Ellis, Max Jordan, Fulton J. Sheen, and John A. O'Brien. Continuing his interests in literature and humanism, Shuster himself published articles on "Newer Catholic Poets," "Thomas Hardy," "The High Lights of Humanism," "Jacques Maritain, Revivalist," "François Mauriac," "Paul Bourget and Reality," "A Novelist in Retrospect," "St. Thomas More," "G. K. Chesterton," "Patmore: A Revaluation," and "Thoughts on Francis Thompson."[15] Concerned with the responsibility of being both American and Catholic, especially during the controversy over Al Smith's possible presidential candidacy, he published *The Catholic Spirit in America* in 1927. Long interested in German history and culture, he made extensive trips to Europe in the 1930s and published three important works: *The Germans,* a detailed

---

[14] *The Chief Things about Writing* (Notre Dame, 1917). For these articles see *The Catholic World* 104 (1917), 731-37; *ibid.*, 106 (1917), 166-78; *ibid.*, 111 (1920), 454-62; *ibid.*, 113 (1921), 452-64; and *ibid.*, 120 (1924), 89-95. *The Catholic Spirit in Modern English Literature* was published in 1922.

[15] "Newer Catholic Poets," *The Catholic World* 122 (1925), 314-19; "Thomas Hardy," *ibid.*, 126 (1928), 721-29; "The High Lights of Humanism," *Commonweal* 9 (1929), 674-75; "Jacques Maritain, Revivalist," *Bookman* 70 (1929), 1-10; "François Mauriac," *ibid.*, 72 (1931), 466-75; "Paul Bourget and Reality," *ibid.*, 73 (1931), 273-83; "A Novelist in Retrospect," *Commonweal* 14 (1931), 418-19; "Saint Thomas More," *ibid.*, 22 (1935), 233-34; "G. K. Chesterton," *ibid.*, 24 (1936), 319-20; "Patmore: A Revaluation," *ibid.*, 24 (1936), 604-06; and "Thoughts on Francis Thompson," *ibid.*, 25 (1937), 431-33.

description of the political, economic, and cultural background of post-World War I Germany; *Strong Man Rules,* an interpretive account of the events leading up to the emergence of Adolf Hitler; and *Like a Mighty Army,* an examination of the impact of Hitlerism on established religion in Germany.[16]

Scholarship and the advancement of learning were clearly a major concern during his years at Hunter. Under his presidency, the college's graduate program was expanded, the Ph.D. continued to be required of all incoming faculty members, respected scholars like Hoxie Fairchild of Columbia University were hired from other institutions, and the custom was inaugurated of honoring at a special luncheon each Hunter faculty member on the publication of a book.[17] Shuster was now one of the country's most respected voices in the field of education and he spoke and wrote on the subject frequently: "Education and Religion: The Making of a Rounded Individual" (1944), "Education's New Responsibility" (1947), "Education and Wisdom" (1949), "Academic Freedom" (1953), "Recipe for Learning" (1956), "On Catholic Education" (1958), and "What Is Education" (1959).[18] During this same period, among other full-length books, Shuster published his doctoral dissertation, *The*

---

[16]*The Catholic Spirit in America* (New York, 1927); *The Germans* (New York, 1932); *Strong Man Rules* (New York, 1934); and *Like a Mighty Army* (New York, 1935).

[17]*The Ground I Walked on,* 24-25, 104-06, and 109; Samuel White Patterson, *Hunter College: Eighty-Five Years of Service* (New York, 1955), 182-91; entries in *Current Biography Yearbook, 1960,* 379-80, and *The National Cyclopaedia of American Biography* Vol. H, 90; and author's interview with Doris (Mrs. George) Shuster, South Bend, Indiana, September 2, 1983.

[18]"Education and Religion: The Making of a Rounded Individual," *The Saturday Review of Literature* 27 (September 16, 1944), 26-30; "Education's New Responsibility," *Survey Graphic* 36 (1947), 569-72; "Education and Wisdom," *Commonweal* 50 (1949), 36-45; "Academic Freedom," *Commonweal* 58 (1953), 11-13; "Recipe for Learning," *Today* 12 (November, 1956), 32-34; "On Catholic Education," 65-83; and "What is Education," *Daedalus* 88 (Winter, 1959), 25-39.

English Ode from Milton to Keats, a work still cited in scholarly treatises forty years later.[19]

As director of Notre Dame's newly-established Center for the Study of Man in Contemporary Society from 1961–1968, Shuster supported research and creative scholarship in a variety of areas, especially in the social sciences.[20] The Center administered grants from government departments and from the Carnegie, Ford, Rockefeller, and other foundations; it sponsored research in areas of world population, drug addiction, artificial intelligence, the non-violent resolution of human conflict, health care delivery, juvenile delinqquency, and government regulatory policies; and it published significant studies on evolution and on the American Catholic school system.[21] Shuster continued his own writing in the areas of American education, recent changes in Germany, and modern Catholicism, edited *Freedom and Authority in the West,* wrote a popular biographical sketch of Cardinal Albert Meyer of Chicago, and published *UNESCO: Assessment and Promise* and the autobiographical *The Ground I Walked On.*[22]

[19] *The English Ode from Milton to Keats* (New York, 1940). See John D. Jump, *The Ode* (London, 1974), 3, 22, and 64; and Paul H. Fry, *The Poet's Calling in the English Ode* (New Haven, 1980), 49.

[20] Shuster also served as Assistant to the President during this period and it is difficult at times to determine which activities he undertook as Director of the Center and which as Assistant to the President.

[21] Material in the Office of Information Services, University of Notre Dame; *South Bend Tribune,* November 21, 1969, p. 22, col. 4; and *New York Times,* January 26, 1977, p. B6, col. 4; *Evolution in Perspective: Commentaries in Honor of Pierre Lecomte du Nouy,* ed. George N. Shuster and Ralph E. Thorson (Notre Dame, 1970); and *Catholic Schools in Action: A Report: The Notre Dame Study of Catholic Elementary and Secondary Schools in the United States,* ed. Reginald A. Neuwien (Notre Dame, 1966).

[22] *Catholic Education in a Changing World* (New York, 1967); "German Catholic Voice," *Commonweal* 74 (1961), 149-51; *Freedom and Authority in the West* (Notre Dame, 1967); *Albert Gregory Cardinal Meyer* (Notre Dame, 1964); *UNESCO: Assessment and Promise* (New York, 1963); and *The Ground I Walked on.*

In all, George Shuster published more than thirty books and two hundred articles, in addition to countless book reviews and unsigned editorials in *Commonweal*. His works ranged from an examination of the philosophy of Plato to a novel set in Civil War America, from essays on Shakespeare to notes for an English edition of *Mein Kampf,* and from a scholarly introduction to *The Confessions of St. Augustine* to the light and imaginative *The Hill of Happiness* and *Brother Flo.*[23]

The number and range of these writings might indicate Shuster's own ideal of learning and the intellectual life. He realized that research and creative scholarship were essential for the advancement of both the Church and human society, but they were clearly not for everyone, and probably not for himself. Shuster at times criticized research scholarship as too narrow, too specialized, too incomplete — and Shuster was anything but narrow and specialized. In an article as early as 1929 he admitted that some "describe the American professor as a busy collector of foot-notes to nothing in particular," and he hoped any over-specialization in education would be tempered by the new movement toward "humanism."[24] "Perhaps the time has come," he declared fifteen years later, "to assume that although dissertations are valuable and pure scholarship a noble ideal, the central humanistic purpose is not implicit in these things."[25] "I think that at this point," he noted later, "we might well go back to Cicero and say that the pursuit of wisdom is not to be carried on through scholarship alone," because research scholarship might be weak in criticizing, in evaluating, in

[23]"The Legacy of Plato," *Commonweal* 15 (1932), 289-91; *Look Away* (New York, 1939); "The Silence of Shakespeare," *Sign* 15 (1935), 54-55; Adolf Hitler, *Mein Kampf,* (New York: Reynal and Hitchcock, 1939); *The Confessions of St. Augustine* (New York: Heritage Press, 1963); *The Hill of Happiness* (New York, 1926); and *Brother Flo: An Imaginative Biography* (New York, 1938).

[24]"The High Lights of Humanism," 674.

[25]"Man on the Campus," *Education and Moral Wisdom*, 31-40, here 32.

creating.[26] He returned to this question of creativity in a centennial address in 1950:

> Or suppose we turn to the realm of literature, and note for example that scholarship can collect every available shred of material about the life, language, and intellectual background of Geoffrey Chaucer. It can pretty well determine how the *Canterbury Tales* sounded when the poet himself spoke the lines, and it can almost tell you, if you are interested, what books he read before he sat down to write. These are matters of great interest and importance. But not all Chaucerian scholars round the wide world could produce *The Knight's Tale* or anything comparably good.[27]

"For the great Greek [Aristotle], even as for Confucius," he wrote later, "wisdom could never be synonymous with knowledge. The knower might be all else than wise in his knowing."[28]

For Shuster, therefore, the intellectual ideal seemed to be something broader, deeper, even more fully human than research scholarship — the quality or virtue he often called wisdom. This wisdom was the combination of a broadly liberal and humanistic education, of prudence and good judgment arising from practical experience, of theology and a grasp of divine revelation, and of a good life, progress in prayer, and participation in liturgy which led one closer to holiness and kept all life in proper perspective. For Shuster, this wisdom seemed to be the perfection of Christian culture and education.

Shuster's educational theory and view of the intellectual life were greatly influenced by the writings of Cardinal

---

[26]"Education and Wisdom," 44.

[27]Address at the centennial convocation at the University of Dayton, 1950, printed in *Education and Moral Wisdom*, 85-94, here 89.

[28]"What is Education," 37.

Newman, especially *The Idea of a University.* As early as 1925, Shuster had edited a collection of Newman's prose and poetry, he wrote an introduction for a new edition of *The Idea of a University* in 1959, he contributed a paper, "Reflections on Newman's *Idea,*"for a major symposium on Catholic higher education in the late 1960s, and he referred to Newman frequently in other writings.[29] Like Newman, Shuster founded his educational structure firmly on the liberal arts. These he defined in an address to Hunter College freshmen in 1956:

> They are studies, of language and literature, of mathematics and the sciences, of history and of the notable forms of social behavior — psychological, political, economic, sociological, anthropological, which if carefully pursued provide basic information, instruct in accuracy of thought and expression, and form judgment. With them the noble arts of music, painting, and sculpture are associated as forms of literature having their own lofty and distinctive being. We say not only that these constitute our legacy of human culture, but also that they are means through the use of which any one of us may attain unto a measure of personal cultivation.[30]

Shuster believed that such an education should actually begin before college:

> Prior to leaving high school the boys and girls I have in mind should certainly have been helped to gain knowl-

---

[29] *Newman: Prose and Poetry* (Boston: Allyn and Bacon, 1925); John Henry Cardinal Newman, *The Idea of a University*, Introduction by George N. Shuster, (New York: Image Books, 1959); "Reflections on Newman's *Idea*," *The Catholic University: A Modern Appraisal*, ed. Neil G. McCluskey, S.J. (Notre Dame, 1970), 104-17; "Of What Use Are Poets," *Ave Maria* 92 (September 10, 1960), 9-11 and 28.

[30] "To the Freshmen of Hunter College: I," *Education and Moral Wisdom*, 41-46, here 42.

edge of and insight into Homer, Virgil, Dante, Shakespeare and one major English or American novelist. They ought likewise to have studied in class one good short introduction to philosophy, have read the Nicomachean Ethics and selected Dialogues of Plato. If I had my way, they would also have concerned themselves in detail with at least one great artist — Giotto, perhaps, or Michaelangelo [*sic*], or if you prefer the Northern culture cycle, Dürer or Rembrandt. Naturally a feeling for genesis and progression in all forms of historic time will be stimulated by the teacher through imaginative sketching in of the background against which personages and themes loom up.[31]

"What counts in the secondary school," he added, "is reading a relatively few illustrious texts carefully, sensitively, and creatively, as the French for example do, and then relying on a young person's eagerness to read more books of his own choosing from a well-chosen and intelligently organized school collection."[32]

Even the exigencies of World War II did not lower the priority he gave to a liberal education. "The core of the liberal arts college is sound," he wrote in 1942. "Arts, literature, philosophies and sciences must survive in the minds and hearts of women, though they may need restatement now. No doubt we should develop in particular a sense of the interrelation of cultures, by fostering comparative literature and history."[33]

A grasp of this "interrelation of cultures" was an important part of Shuster's program, but not in any superficial sense:

[31]"Recipe for Learning," 34.

[32]*Ibid.*, 34.

[33]"College Women and the War," *Association of American Colleges Bulletin* 28 (1942), 27-34, here 29.

In the Western world, we have been rather arrogantly Western. Looking abroad, we Americans are likely to think only of Europe and the Near East, with a casual gesture in the direction of our Latin neighbors. Therefore, it is often urged that we must immediately include the Orient in our study books, and stress India, for example, as we do France. At the risk of inviting trouble, I shall dissent on the ground that the suggestion is quite impractical. We do not understand the French, despite our many teachers of their literature and history and our innumerable tourists. How then will a few random samplings of Indian lore help us to fathom the world of the Upanishads.

It seems to me imperative that education make a real effort to understand the French — or the British or the Russians or the Spanish. Once we succeed in this we shall have learned how to step outside ourselves, how to see an alien people clearly, with no illusions as to our own superiority or significance.[34]

Shuster included literature, history, the social sciences, mathematics, philosophy, and the natural sciences in this liberal education,[35] but he differed with Newman in insisting on music and the arts also:

I will conclude with a reference to what has long seemed to me a special weakness in Newman's book. This is a relegation to the university limbo of the aesthetic experience. He assumed (doubtless again because of the time in which he lived and of his special intellectual preoccupations), that the whole world of the arts was somewhere beyond the pale. The arts were properly servants to some

[34]"Education's New Responsibility," 571.

[35]See also "Of What Use Are Poets," 9-11 and 28, and "History: A Barrier or a Blessing," *The Catholic Historical Review* 22 (1936), 185-90.

other endeavor, for example, the Church. But they seemed to him obstreperous servants always putting on airs. He did not much care for Pugin's obsession with the restoration of Gothic art; in this he was, of course, right. But that seems an insufficient excuse.

Still — and I think that the younger generation would often agree with me here — one cannot well expect religion to humanize rigorous intellectualism (and in his own inimitable way he explained how difficult that is), unless one concedes to the arts a comparable role, though at a lower level, of course, in the order of being. I am not, may the Lord forbid, recommending art for art's sake or eulogizing the painter as a priest. But the fact remains that the music of Bach is the first coda in which Catholic and Lutheran experience came together in harmonious union. It was the first great page in the ecumenical movement. And I submit that it is not any easier to read that page aright than it is to wrestle with Whately's logic.[36]

"It almost seems as if the Cardinal, who loved to play the violin," Shuster wrote elsewhere, "thought that listening to what was produced on it was hardly compatible with the serious business of training the mind."[37] Shuster could not agree: "We also quite generally think that a man with no music in the soul is to be pitied."[38]

This education in the humanities did not single out only the religious, but it ennobled the secular; and this once brought Shuster to an interesting comparison between Newman and Christopher Dawson:

American Catholic educators have paid lip service to Newman's thesis that the proper business of education,

[36]"Reflections on Newman's *Idea*," 114.
[37]"Of What Use Are Poets," 9.
[38]*Ibid*.

insofar as 'secular' subjects are concerned, is to teach literature and science (both of which the social sciences straddle) in such a way that the student will have a comprehensive, critical awareness of the human and cosmic reality with which he must live. Yet in practice they have veered toward acceptance of Christopher Dawson's contention that what is desired is the teaching of Christian culture. To isolate from literature what is specifically Christian or Catholic and to teach 'Catholic social science' means, of course, cutting the core out of Newman's philosophy of education.[39]

If, as Shuster once suggested, "education is always human nature trying to become more human,"[40] it somehow had to be practical and experimental also. The truly wise person was a prudent person. "And, of course, action has its part in life," Shuster wrote in 1932. "This is Goethe year, and Goethe was a great and good man. His famous line, 'In the beginning was the act,' continues to be profoundly true. Of course the kind of inward growth outlined above implies constant activity of a sort, but there are other ways a-plenty in which the Goethean maxim can be applied."[41] "That is why, incidentally, the American system of vacations is excellent," he wrote in 1944, "provided it is properly utilized. Young men who work during the summers come to know the speech of common men, in which there is little learning but often much of shrewd, hard common sense. They drop the habit of exclusive association with abstractions, which is the inevitable characteristic of formal academic study, for a useful time, returning to it with mingled humility and realism."[42] Six years later he defended his emphasis on voca-

[39]"The School: Not Little and Red Any Longer," 11.

[40]*The Ground I Walked on*, 100.

[41]"Opportunities of the Educated Layman," 6.

[42]"Man on the Campus," 38-39.

tional courses or "vocational inlays" at Hunter College: "I have unshamefacedly urged all language and literature majors to take courses in typewriting and stenography, and I have just as persistently cajoled feminine students into finding out what a baby looks like, what has to be done to help it grow up, and what a strange sort of creature its father is likely to be."[43] "It seems to me inconceivable," he concluded, "that a college exists in order to help young people fail in everything else than their classes."[44]

Theology, the study of God through divine revelation, was central to Shuster's schema, as it was to Newman's. "The place of theology in education is at once simple and august," Shuster wrote. "It is to enable the pupil and teacher to dwell in the kind of light which will make manifest to them the glory of the supernatural life, the ability to see which in a glass darkly is God's greatest gift to man."[45] "There are vast realms of being which reason cannot explore," he stated. "The human spirit is able to reach down and touch the floor of the universe, but it must take the cellar for granted. It can likewise place its hand on the ceiling of human destiny and therewith know that God exists, but it is unable to fathom the hidden things which rest in the Divine Counsel. To fancy that reason is all of man's strength is just as limiting as is the denial of reason's existence."[46] "But someday it will dawn on people," said Shuster in 1963, "that the Catholic school has a dimension which many other schools have lost. This is compounded of reverence and freedom, of a desire for the whole as well as an intelligent understanding of the parts in which the whole is reflected. In short, the Catholic school will be one of the

---

[43]"The Administration of a Municipal College," *Education and Moral Wisdom*, 1-13, here 7. "Vocational inlays" are discussed on 9.

[44]*Ibid.*, 8.

[45]"The School: Not Little and Red Any Longer," 11.

[46]"Centennial Address," 92.

ways in which, as Père de Chardin has suggested, the human mind moves toward Christ taking the world to Him."[47]

Religion and theology also opened up new depths of insight in literature and art:

> If one surveys the differences between classic poetry, sculpture and painting and what has been done in the same arts since Christianity modified the outlook of mankind, one finds that the chief change has been a heightening, an intensification, of emotion. Greece made more beautiful statues than the *beau Christ* of Amiens or Rodin's *Thinker*, but it fashioned none in which so intense an expression of feeling is manifest. The frescos of Egypt are sublime, but passion surges nowhere in them as it does in even the transfigured affection of Raffael. There is brooding in antique portraiture, but it seems only a passing mood compared with the tremendous concentration of Leonardo da Vinci or Peter Brueghel. Calamity and desire, finally, crowd the lines of Aeschylus; but how much of poise they keep when compared with the doom and the wrath of *Macbeth*! In the *Salve Regina* there is unprecedented ecstasy; in the *Dies Irae*, unparalleled woe.[48]

But knowledge of God did more than broaden one's insights; it could also lead to holiness, to the perfection of what it meant to be human. For Shuster, there was no conflict between learning and holiness. "The educated man is to some extent at a disadvantage in the Catholic scheme," he admitted. "He finds it harder to become even as a little child; critical faculties awaken in him, often subjecting to harsh scrutiny beliefs which his humbler brethren find beautiful and consoling. The man in whom college training does

---

[47]"The School: Not Little and Red Any Longer," 12.
[48]*The Catholic Spirit in America*, 269-70.

not awaken a measure of skepticism is rare, indeed. Yet this more or less painful experience with the question mark is a necessary stage in that higher development without which, I think, the so-called 'faith of the Breton peasant' would soon evaporate."[49] "Religion speaks not of the dignity but of the holiness of man," Shuster declared elsewhere. "And by this it means not an assumption to which, perchance, the victim in a concentration camp might appeal against his tormentors, but a startling, inexorably costly discovery, implicit in the act of finding God." "The young man or woman wrestling with the choice to be made is influenced by personalities rather than by courses," he continued. "This means only that holiness, though discerned by the intellect, needs exemplification. It is the saint, the person of sanctity, who will always be the supreme teacher of the religious life, because he alone has insight into the whole experience — I might quite as well say the experiment — upon which verification rests."[50] He concluded elsewhere: "But that a scholar should, by reason of delving sacrificially into the secrets of nature, come to live by a purifying and ennobling law — that the great scientist is, in short, a kind of saint — happens to be a wonderful truth."[51]

For Shuster, the scholarly, the cultural, and the personally sanctifying could all come together in the Church's public worship, the liturgy. He lamented the fact that, at least in the first half of the twentieth century, the liturgy did not hold its proper place in American Catholic life:

> The leisurely, wise Old World Church had created a better system of popular education — the liturgy. In this marvelous, symmetrical blending of dogma and mystical

[49]"Opportunities of the Educated Layman," 5.

[50]"Education and Religion: The Making of a Rounded Individual," 26 and 28.

[51]"Good, Evil, and Beyond," *The Annals of the American Academy of Political and Social Science* 249 (1947), 169-78, here 174.

insight, of sacrifice and prayer, charity and intelligence, there is fully expressed a faith which when reduced to intellectual outlines however correct always seems a little bleak and acrid. And about all this, like the glow which rests upon a perfect landscape, there lies a sacred glory, a loveliness, which transcends every other literary work of man. If those who have been deeply offended by some acrimonious phrase of Catholic apologetic, possibly with a result that they have kept angrily aloof from Catholic things ever since, would only read the texts of the *Missa Solemnis* or the *Missa pro Defunctis* over which Bach and Bruckner pondered!...I have read the Mass for Good Friday many and many a time, but never without being profoundly moved by the vision of an earth there re-created by charity and goodness — an earth upon which Christ's death would have blossomed into that abundant life He so greatly desired. All this, of course, must be *believed*, not toyed with in a mere aesthetic mood. It is only as truth that it is really beautiful, but so it is beautiful beyond comparison.[52]

"Someday we shall restore liturgy to its place as the rhythm and the meaning of Catholic life," he wrote years before the recent liturgical renewal, "and having done that, we shall see rise round the chancel once again the myriad carven forms of man's aspiration, and shall hear the wonderful ecstasy of Heaven even in our profane songs. Liturgy is community religion; art is community intuition."[53]

When presenting Shuster with Fordham University's Insignis Medal in 1959 for distinguished service to God and humanity, University president Father Lawrence McGinley, S.J., remarked that at times there seemed to be two kinds of Catholics in America — George Shuster and

[52] *The Catholic Spirit in America*, 116-17.
[53] *Ibid.*, 117.

all the others.[54] As a citizen of many worlds, Shuster did indeed seem different: he was poet and public official, critic and international educator, college president and Catholic layman. As a man of learning and a man of faith, he saw the need to bridge the apparent dichotomy between American Catholicism and the intellectual life. He respected research and scholarship, found the world of ideas captivating and fulfilling, and was convinced that scholarship and learning could — and should — contribute to one's final perfection as a child of God:

> Scholarly work is viewed as a form of participating in the realization of God's will. . . . It remains as always the quest for truth, to be carried on with sincerity and zeal, but is also a sharing, awesome and sanctifying, with Christ of His world — a world which is coming more and more to seem not a panorama of things fixed in space of [*sic*] time — not for example Mont Blanc or the Justinian Code — but an ever-moving film of the Creator's idea. Reality is for the imaginative scholar a dream, but not one which fades or passes away. It is a phase of the vision which has been held in the Divine mind eternally. Seeing the structure of the molecule we are at His side. And being there must of necessity be good. If this be so, man moving from the shadows of things into their essences at the scholar's behest will gain that awareness of the spirit which no being immured in the illusory material can any longer dispel. At least we may hope that it will be so.[55]

---

[54] *The Ground I Walked on*, 23.
[55] "On Catholic Education," 82-83.

American Catholics and the Intellectual Life: Thirty Years Later

John Whitney Evans

On May 14, 1955, John Tracy Ellis made what many regard to be his most significant contribution to American Catholicism. This was his address before the ninth annual convention of the Catholic Commission on Intellectual and Cultural Affairs, meeting at Maryville College in St. Louis, Missouri. His paper grew out of "observation over a long period of years of the lack of first rate scholarship, serious study habits, casualness of Catholic leaders to the intellectual life, and the failure among Catholics to strive to reach the top in things of the mind."[1] He called his lecture, "American Catholics and the Intellectual Life"; it appeared under that title in *Thought* the following autumn,[2] and as a small book issued by the Heritage Foundation of Chicago the following year.

[1] Ellis (Washington, D.C.) to the writer (Duluth), July 5, 1979; I thank Monsignor Ellis for permission to cite this and other correspondence.

[2] John Tracy Ellis, "American Catholics and the Intellectual Life," *Thought* 30 (Autumn, 1955), 351-88.

This trenchant critique by the then Professor of Church History in the Catholic University of America may well be Ellis' greatest contribution to American Catholic life for two reasons. First, unlike similar criticism that preceded it,[3] his was taken seriously and received favorably. Within eighteen months it had been reprinted or abridged in dozens of learned journals and diocesan papers; circulated in a special edition for Catholic educators; commented upon in college and high school commencement exercises; and discussed in countless classrooms, dormitories, faculty lounges, Newman Centers, convents, and rectories across the country. Of several hundred letters Ellis received during this time, all but four appeared to be in agreement with his analysis, if not with his conclusions.[4] Second, as occasionally happens during the career of an historian, the very act of writing about a subject, e.g., nationalism, moves readers to embrace and promote the ideals advocated by the author. I am not arguing that Ellis' essay on American Catholics and the intellectual life is the lone cause of the positive developments that have subsequently taken place; as he spoke the

[3]See George N. Shuster, "Have We Any Scholars?" *America* 33 (August 15, 1925), 418-19; Francis M. Crowley, "Meeting the Shortage of Graduate Students," *N.C.W.C. Bulletin,* 11 (September, 1929), 29-31; Theodore Maynard, *The Story of American Catholicism* (New York, 1941), 585-86. In 1947, John A. O'Brien, who earlier had edited a book setting forth the opinions of thirteen Catholic intellectuals on the question of developing U.S. Catholic scholars (see *Catholics and Scholarship: A Symposium on the Development of Scholars,* ed. John A. O'Brien [Huntington, Ind., 1938], *passim*), argued that this heretofore neglected volume "should be compulsory reading for every administrator, teacher and researcher in our colleges and universities" — cited in *American Catholicism and the Intellectual Ideal,* ed. Frank Christ and Gerard E. Sherry (New York, 1961), 115-18, 136-37, here 136.

[4]In the fall of 1955 I enrolled in the Theological College at the Catholic University of America. During the next three years I was able to attend symposia there and at Georgetown University on the Ellis lecture, and also to discuss it with the author; anecdotal material used here comes from notes I took between 1955 and 1958.

upgrading had already begun at some places. However, I do think it reasonable to assert that his critique provided a focus and an impetus for dozens of Catholic educators and aspiring intellectuals, who took his analysis as a personal challenge to excellence; as one administrator in a Catholic college said to the professor (and to his great delight) shortly afterwards: "We are refuting you!"[5]

It is now thirty years afterwards — years that have witnessed the widespread movement of Catholics from ethnic ghettoes into mainline suburbs, the election and assassination of the nation's first Catholic president, the convening and closing of an ecumenical council that attempted to open the Church to modernity, the arrival on the campuses of the land of Catholics in numbers exceeding their representation in the general population, and the entrance of their country into what one historian, Henry Steele Commager, has termed "the age of no confidence."[6] It is appropriate to discover some of the things that have happened within the world of American Catholic intellectualism during these tumultuous decades. To do so, I shall simply review the elements of the Ellis critique, and then draw upon subsequent research to find out how these conditions have fared in the interval. This "then-and-now" treatment will generate additional observations reserved for the second section of this essay.

I. 1955 and After

The central thesis that Ellis proposed in 1955 was:

The weakest aspect of the Church in this country lies in its failure to produce national leaders and to exercise com-

---

[5]*Ibid.* The best single source chronicling criticism and response is Christ and Sherry, *American Catholicism.*

[6]Quoted in John Tracy Ellis, "The Catholic Liberal Arts College: Has It a Future?" *Current Issues in Catholic Higher Education* 3 (Winter, 1983), 3-31, here 4.

manding influence in intellectual circles, and this at a time when the number of Catholics in the United States is exceeded only by those of Brazil and Italy, and their material resources are incomparably superior to those of any other branch of the universal Church.[7]

This charge included two points: the presence of Catholics among national leaders and their influence upon other intellectuals. With respect to the issue of leadership, fifteen years later Ellis was able to note that in addition to one president and several presidential and vice-presidential candidates, Catholics had come to constitute the largest religious group in Congress, and appeared to be proportionately represented in cabinet posts, governors' chairs, and state legislatures, "with an impressive proportion of their faith in the highest reaches of the professions and in leadership roles in both management and labor."[8]

More recently, Father Andrew M. Greeley concluded an extensive examination of American Catholics in which he concluded, with respect to their intellectual status:

> Through the decade after graduation. . . a younger generation of Catholics have found no real obstacle between their religion and successful pursuit of academic careers. They have gone to graduate school, obtained their doctorates, have appointments in the elite colleges and universities, are publishing articles, displaying the values and attitudes appropriate to intellectuals, and were, at least before the bottom fell out of Catholic religious practice, not substantially less likely to go to church than any other Catholics of their generation. All of these

[7]Ellis, "American Catholics," 353.

[8]John Tracy Ellis, "The Church in Revolt," *The Critic* 27 (January/February, 1970), 12-21, here 15.

things were more likely to have occurred if the young men and women in question had gone to Catholic colleges; they were still more likely if all their education prior to graduate school was Catholic.[9]

It would seem, then, that the "weakest aspect" that Ellis criticized in 1955, the failure to produce national leaders, has been remedied. And if Catholics do not yet appear to exercise a "commanding influence" among intellectual circles, at least a first generation of them has entered "the mainstream" and constitutes a *presence* there.

But, if the general picture shows improvement, what about the specific points that Ellis raised in support of this central thesis?

In 1955, he offered eleven reasons to explain what he termed the "striking discrepancy" between the material status and civic freedoms enjoyed by United States Catholics on one hand, and their relatively negligible intellectual achievements on the other. In first place stood the persistent anti-Catholic prejudice that rendered "the American intellectual climate. . .aloof and unfriendly to Catholic thought and ideas, when it has not been openly hostile."[10] The "character and background of the major portion of the people who, until a relatively recent date, made up the Church" in the United States constituted a second reason.[11] The well-documented American distrust of academicians was also cited;[12] as was the "absence of an intellectual tradition among American Catholics."[13] As a fifth reason Ellis pointed to one of "the dominant characteristics of our socie-

[9]Andrew M. Greeley, *The American Catholic: A Social Portrait* (New York, 1977), 74, 85.

[10]Ellis, "American Catholics," 353-54.

[11]*Ibid.,* 355.

[12]*Ibid.,* 356.

[13]*Ibid.,* 357.

ty...attachment to material goods and the desire to make a fortune."[14]

Ellis then went on to discuss at some length "the failure of Catholics in posts of leadership, both clerical and lay, to understand fully, or to appreciate in a practical way, the value of the vocation of the intellectual."[15] This led naturally to a seventh explanation for the dearth of scholarly Catholics: the "betrayal" of the Catholic heritage in the humanities and liberal arts, especially "philosophy and theology."[16] Ellis also believed that Catholics had been guilty of a kind of "betrayal of one another" by the multiplication of, and inevitable competiton between, institutions of higher education.[17] As a ninth factor, he listed the "absence of a love of scholarship for its own sake"...and a concomitant "over-emphasis (on) the school as an agency for moral development."[18]

Ellis concluded his buttressing arguments with two final reasons:

> The chief blame, I firmly believe, lies with Catholics themselves. It lies in their frequently self-imposed ghetto mentality which prevents them from mingling as they should with their non-Catholic colleagues, and in their lack of industry and habits of work.[19]

It should be immediately evident that some of these conditions no longer exist. Greeley's research has failed to uncover much evidence to support the popular theory that

[14]*Ibid.,* 362.
[15]*Ibid.,* 365.
[16]*Ibid.,* 374.
[17]*Ibid.,* 375.
[18]*Ibid.,* 376-77.
[19]*Ibid.,* 386.

Catholics lack ambition or industry in economic pursuits. The Irish are "the richest and best educated white Gentile group in America"; second richest are the Italians; and, at least in northern cities, "making more money than British Protestants" are Poles and other Slavs.[20] By the end of the 1970s, Ellis himself thought that "the inhibiting factors" historically preventing Catholic colleges from achieving intellectual excellence, namely poverty, proliferation, their exploitation as "priestly and religious recruitment centers," and employment as "citadels" of apologetics and moralism had all but passed from the scene. He referred to the "openness and maturity of attitude" among these institutions toward accrediting bodies, and the presence among their numbers of eleven chapters of Phi Beta Kappa, an increase of nine since 1955, as other signs of progress.[21]

Other researchers confirm the fact of considerable improvement since 1955 among the faculties and administrative teams, as well as in the financial operations, of many Catholic institutions of higher learning. A Carnegie study released in 1969 found that junior faculty in the colleges tended to be "of superior quality" compared with their seniors, although not yet deserving to be ranked "among the very distinguished younger American academicians." This inquiry also concluded that professors in graduate programs under Catholic auspices compared favorably with those in "third level" institutions, even with some at the "second level"; this was regarded as "notable progress" beyond the situation "even a decade ago." The Carnegie findings also disclosed that changing relationships between college administrators, who belonged to religious orders, and their sponsoring communities, e.g., laicization of

---

[20]Greeley, *The American Catholic,* 57.

[21]John Tracy Ellis, "To Lead, To Follow, or to Drift? American Catholic Higher Education in 1976: A Personal View," *Delta Epsilon Sigma Bulletin* 21 (May, 1976), 40-66, here 43-48.

boards of trustees, appeared to be opening the way for upgrading the "second class" status of lay faculty as well as improving the climate for academic freedom.[22] With approximately 60% of Catholic colleges independent of religious orders in 1982, such faculty trends have continued.[23]

Improved methods of management, financing, and utilization of resources also appeared to be ushering in a "new dawn" for Catholic colleges at the end of the 1970s.[24] Some of these institutions had found no real future for their services, and had "discontinued"; the number of Catholic colleges and universities dropped from a high of 309 in 1965 to 238 in 1983. But others were "radically adapting and redefining their mission" or were abandoning their "expansionist mentality of the past."[25] The Council for Financial Aid to Education provided figures suggesting that, for some major Catholic institutions at least, alumni were giving more generously than ever.[26] At the same time, one observer, familiar with administrators in church-related institutions, described highly successful financial campaigns in the 1970s. In most cases, these efforts garnered the highest totals of income in the history of the schools involved.[27]

While acknowledging in 1979 significant academic progress within what might be termed a "middle group" of

[22]Andrew M. Greeley, *From Backwater to Mainstream: A Profile of Catholic Higher Education* (New York, 1969), 112-14, 121-25.

[23]"Colleges Stress Catholic Identity," *National Catholic Reporter* 18 (March 26, 1982), 14, 16.

[24]Paul C. Reinert, S.J., "A New Dawn for Church Related Higher Education," *The Catholic Mind* 74 (June, 1976), 39-43, here 39.

[25]Reinert (St. Louis) to the writer (Duluth), July 9, 1979. I thank Fr. Reinert for permission to quote from this letter.

[26]See appropriate sections of *Voluntary Support of Education 1971-72* and *1976-77* (New York: Council for Financial Aid to Education).

[27]Reinert to the writer, July 9, 1979.

Catholic colleges, Ellis hesitated to cite any he would rank among the top twenty-five percent, and still believed that "far more than our share" still resided among the lowest quarter.[28] That same year, after reviewing the periodic ratings of American graduate schools, he agreed that the "general state" of Catholic graduate programs had "definitely improved" since 1934, when they first began to appear in such evaluations. But he remained disturbed that "nearly half a century later the rank of 'excellent' still elude[d] Catholic universities of the land."[29]

More objective attempts to evaluate Catholic colleges and universities tend to confirm Ellis' pessimism. For example, one study of "leading" institutions in 1982 listed only nineteen Catholic colleges, although three of these were ranked at the top academically.[30] A 1984 appraisal that included 152 Catholic colleges placed one in the top or "strong" group, five among the "good," and seven at "acceptable plus"; it found eighteen colleges to be "adequate," and 121 were described as "marginal."[31] Catholic graduate programs did not fare much better. A report in 1983 ranked only four "above average" and relegated the rest to somewhere between "adequate" and "marginal."[32]

It seems fair to conclude, then, that over the past thirty years American Catholics have removed or overcome, with varying degrees of success, such familiar obstacles to their advancement in intellectual circles as immigrant status,

[28]Ellis to the writer, July 25, 1979.

[29]John Tracy Ellis, "The Catholic University of America, 1927-76: A Personal Memoir," *Social Thought* 5 (Spring, 1979), 35-61, here 57.

[30]"How the *New York Times* Graded 19 Leading U.S. Catholic Colleges," *National Catholic Reporter* 18 (March 26, 1982), 14-15.

[31]Jack Gourman, *The Gourman [Undergraduate] Report, 1983-84* (Los Angeles, 1984), 7-178, here 158-178, *passim.*

[32]Andrew M. Greeley, "Why Catholic Higher Learning is Lower," *National Catholic Reporter* 19 (September 28, 1983), 1-6, here 1.

poverty, ghettoism, sloth, proliferation, competition, moralism, and clericalism. Yet such achievements appear as yet to have been translated into significant and clearly discernible improvements among only a few Catholic colleges and universities.

What of other impediments that Ellis listed in 1955?

We can begin with his charge that American Catholics had "betrayed" their heritage in the liberal arts and theology. In the mid-1960s, Dr. Manning M. Patillo, Jr., summarized for the College and University Section of the National Catholic Educational Association the findings of a Danforth Study on church-related higher education. He reasserted the need for Catholic colleges to revitalize their traditions of liberal education. Although agreeing that they were hardly alone in neglect of the liberal arts, Patillo insisted that they nonetheless could claim "less excuse than many colleges" for tolerating such neglect.[33] A decade later in the same forum, Ellis said that, in his opinion, Robert M. Hutchins' 1937 "indictment of Catholics for their neglect" of the liberal arts remained valid. Acknowledging that preparation for a career or a profession was "legitimate in itself," Ellis nevertheless regretted that it remained dominant as a "major conditioning factor of Catholic higher education."[34]

Practicalism seems destined to remain a major conditioning factor. High school graduates enter college chiefly to prepare themselves for profitable careers. It would seem that only the wealthiest and oldest Catholic institutions can afford what has almost become a curricular luxury. Hope comes to these schools from reports that liberal arts colleges with "long standing reputations for rigorous standards," now attract more new students and lose fewer upperclass-

---

[33] Manning M. Patillo, Jr., "The Danforth Report and Roman Catholic Higher Education," *The Catholic Mind* 64 (June, 1960), 36-46, here 43.

[34] Ellis, "To Lead, To Follow," 46-47.

men to other schools.[35] But some Catholic schools face an ironic dilemma. They enroll many students who are the academic "pioneers" of their families, i.e., the first to go on for education after high school. Such young men and women tend to seek practical, not liberal, training. As graduates, however, they often choose to send their children to the wealthier Catholic (or private and state) colleges, thus locking their *alma maters* into the role of servicing subsequent waves of "pioneers." Perhaps new attitudes within the business community, which is coming to view the "fruits of a solid liberal arts education [as] remarkably marketable,"[36] will encourage liberal studies in such schools. In 1983, Ellis concluded, "There is no place. . .for pessimism about the future of the Catholic liberal arts college if certain conditions are met;" i.e., the reassertion of the Catholic religious heritage and traditional moral values, and a return to the core curriculum or its equivalent.[37]

What of the outlook for theological studies in the Catholic college? Unlike other liberal arts courses, not until the 1930s and 1940s did majors in theology begin to appear.[38] These courses, however, tended usually to serve an apologetical purpose until the 1950s, when more objective and academically respectable treatments of scripture, liturgy, and doctrine emerged. Efforts were even underway to shape curricula to meet the needs of the laity rather than the priorities of the seminary.[39]

[35]Richard J. Cattani, "Students Pour Onto Campuses," *The Christian Science Monitor* (Midwestern Edition) 74 (September 6, 1978), 1.

[36]Beverly Mindrum, "At Minnesota College, 'Basics' Never Left," *Sunday Pioneer Press* (St. Paul) 129 (October 22, 1978), "City Life," 6.

[37]Ellis, "Catholic Liberal Arts," 9.

[38]Philip Gleason, "In Search of Unity: American Catholic Thought 1920-1960," *The Catholic Historical Review* 65 (April, 1979), 185-206, here 195-96.

[39]John D. Garvey, "Theology in the American Catholic College: An Historical Overview," *Lumen Vitae* 33 (1978), 367-76, *passim*.

However, the development of academic theology did not continue happily throughout the 1960s and 1970s. Efforts to implement the Vatican Council II documents on ecumenism and non-Christian religions expanded the content of offerings, often at the expense of courses exclusively treating Catholic topics. More drastically, the decline in the number, or even the elimination, of courses in religious studies required for graduation left enrollments in them lagging behind overall institutional increases.[40] For example, the College Theology Society, whose membership dropped from 1,236 to 733 between 1967 and 1977, found that teachers had "moved from a solid, integrated body of doctrine which represented Catholic orthodoxy and which was to be taught to Catholic students, most often in the format of a core requirement, to a bewildering variety created by *de facto* theological pluralism, representing such a multitude of possibilities" offered largely on an elective basis, that it was no longer certain that undergraduates could receive a "well rounded introduction to the theological enterprises."[41] The same condition offered little encouragement for a similar treatment of specifically Catholic studies. Some critics believed that over-concentration on biblical research and theological writing since World War II seriously failed "to transmit any lively sense of the Catholic tradition."[42] And even if the archivist of the College Theology Society could note that teachers of religion in Catholic colleges were better prepared than ever for this role,[43] "far more students than

[40]Claude Welch, *Religion in the Undergraduate Curriculum* (Washington, D.C.,), 49-54, 69-72.

[41]Report of a study by Theodore Steeman in *CTS News Letter* [No Vol.] (September, 1979), 1-6, here 4-5.

[42]James Hitchcock, "How is a College or University Catholic in Practice?" *The Catholic Mind* 74 (January, 1976), 7-21, here 9, 13-14.

[43]Dennis Doyle (Washington, D.C.) to the writer (Duluth), August 6, 1979. I thank Mr. Doyle for permission to use information from his letter.

ever before" were approaching their classes "inadequately prepared for college theology courses."[44]

Nevertheless, some findings allowed guarded optimism for religious study in Catholic higher education. By the end of the 1960s, Catholics, at slightly under twenty-seven percent, constituted the highest proportion of doctoral candidates in religious studies responding to a survey. A very tentative evaluation of graduate programs located the S.T.D. at the Catholic University of America among the second rank of "older and established programs," and placed Marquette and Notre Dame among those institutions offering "new and promising programs, some of which are potentially of the first rank."[45] Despite the overall decline in the number of students taking religion courses, observers noted a dramatic increase in the number of students electing their major in theology.[46] Such trends found reinforcement in the fact that about the middle of the 1970s, church-related colleges appeared to be reversing their earlier practice of trying to become academically competitive by de-emphasizing their courses in religion, and were "rediscovering" them.[47]

Moving from the state of the liberal arts and theological study in Catholic academic circles, we can ask again, do "Catholics in posts of leadership... understand... the value of the vocation of the intellectual" any better today than thirty years ago? If we assume that having earned an advanced degree signifies sensitivity to, if not some practical gestures of support for, the intellectual life, then we initially come up with a somewhat negative answer. In 1957, a study

[44]Theodore Hall, "Religious Literacy in the Catholic College," *Homiletic and Pastoral Review* 82 (December, 1981), 57-61, *passim.*

[45]Claude Welch, *Graduate Education in Religion: A Critical Appraisal* (Missoula, 1971), 88-96, 214, 230-35, 240-41.

[46]Welch, *Religion,* 49-54, 69-72.

[47]Reinert, "A New Dawn," pp. 42-43.

of 133 bishops disclosed the following distribution of degrees: forty-one percent had earned either the S.T.D. or J.C.D., thirty-one percent held a "secular" M.A., and nineteen a "secular" Ph.D.; only twenty-three percent had no additional non-honorary degrees.[48] Of 165 bishops responding to a survey in 1971, thirty-four percent held a "theological doctorate," ten percent an M.A., and only eight percent a Ph.D.; slightly over thirty percent had no additional earned degree.[49] More dramatically, one can contrast the situation in West Germany, where, in 1979, eight of twenty-one ordinaries were former university professors,[50] with Greeley's claim that only one of their U.S. counterparts "has scholarly training in a great university."[51] Such reflections underscore Ellis' charge in that same year that "an understanding of what constitutes true university learning...has never been the case" among the American hierarchy.[52] As a leadership corps, prepared in part by some kind of academic training beyond the seminary, Catholic bishops in the United States appear to be moving inversely to the educational advancement of their people in general, as well as to that of the theological educators of these people. This may help to explain why one hears from time to time that clerical leaders of American Catholicism are not only indifferent to scholarship, but fearful of it, especially that of a scriptural or theological nature.

[48]John D. Donovan, "The American Catholic Hierarchy: A Social Profile," in Christ and Sherry, *American Catholicism*, 238-40, here 239. Of course the J.C.D. was often a requirement for appointment in a chancery, and not necessarily an indicator of scholarly orientation.

[49]Andrew M. Greeley, Richard A. Schoenherr, Neal W. McDermott, O.P., and John Mulhearn, *American Priests: A Report of the National Opinion Research Center* (Washington, D.C., 1971), 46.

[50]John Jay Hughes, "The Leadership We Need," *The Commonweal* 106 (June 8, 1979), 331-35, here 334.

[51]Andrew M. Greeley, "U.S. Catholics Grow Up," *The London Tablet* 234 (March 22, 1980), 286-87, here 287.

[52]Ellis, "The Catholic University," 56.

In 1973, Ellis entered the fray that had developed between theologians and bishops following the publication of Pope Paul VI's encyclical, *Humanae Vitae.* Commenting on the "just freedom" that Vatican Council II advocated for scholars, Ellis reasoned:

> Nonetheless, when every allowance has been admitted in the name of freedom, and every distinction made such, for example, as the breadth and depth of freedom proper for a research scientist or a graduate student in contrast to that which is suitable for a freshman, there still remains the area that embraces matters that touch directly on divine revelation, and here freedom of thought and interpretation cannot be absolute, if a university is to be true to the commitment that originally brought it into being as a specifically Catholic institution.[53]

The on-going debate over the appropriate freedom for theologians reached a crucial point with the publication in 1983 of the new Code of Canon Law. Canon 812 required teachers of theology in any institute of higher studies to have a "mandate from the competent ecclesiastical authority."[54] While appearing to appropriate theologians as extensions of the teaching office of the *magisterium,* the new law also seemed to put the bishops into a delicate position. Some canon lawyers speculated that in some states the mere right of a bishop "to remove just one teacher of theology could be enough to bring on a court case or a cessation of state aid."[55]

[53] John Tracy Ellis, "American Catholics in 'An Uncertain, Anxious Time'," *Commonweal* 98 (April 27, 1973), 177-84, here 183.

[54] Canon Law Society of America, *Code of Canon Law: Latin-English Edition* (Washington, D.C., 1983), 305.

[55] Tom Roberts, "Canon Code, Civil Law at 'Troubled' Odds," *National Catholic Reporter* 19 (June 3, 1983), 5. See also Charles E. Curran, "Academic Freedom: The Catholic University and Catholic Theology," *The Furrow* 30 (December, 1979), 739-59, *passim.*

However, other canonists, noting that the final form of the canon had been revised "in order to mitigate the severity of the proposed requirement and to avoid or lessen the appearance of any external intervention in the internal affairs of Catholic post secondary institutions," believed that situations embarrassing to bishops or hurtful to colleges need not arise.[56]

On the more positive side, it is necessary to acknowledge that the three-year process the United States' hierarchy employed in drafting its pastoral letter on war and peace, "The Challenge of Peace," promulgated in 1983, permitted them to utilize the talents and training of the cream of specialists in nuclear technology, strategy, and diplomacy. Their effort stands as a model for bringing the best minds into the service of the Church, as well as for the collegial teaching style of pastorally oriented leaders.[57] A similar process has been followed in preparing pastoral letters on American capitalism, women, and campus ministry. Reforms in the liturgy that the bishops in the United States have promoted have, in the eyes of Catholics in some other countries, placed them in the ranks of the most "progressive" in the universal Church.[58] Furthermore, the American hierarchy has, over the past twenty-five years, taken an increasingly active role in developing the campus ministry in secular institutions, and this has had a positive impact on the professionalization of the chaplaincy in the Catholic college. In this respect, the bishops deserve credit for pro-

[56]See for example Ladislas Örsy, S.J., "The Mandate to Teach Theological Disciplines: Glosses on Canon 812 of the New Code," *Theological Studies* 44 (1983), 476-88, *passim;* and Frederick R. McManus, "The Canons on Catholic Higher Education" (a commentary prepared for, and available through, The Association of Catholic Colleges and Universities, Suite 770, One Dupont Circle, Washington, D.C.) 1-19, here 12.

[57]F. X. Murphy, "U.S. Bishops' New Style," *The Tablet* (London) 237 (December 3, 1983), 1172-74, here 1174.

[58]Margaret Hebblethwaite, "The Crisis in Confession," *The Tablet* (London) 237 (Sept. 24, 1983), 917-19, here 918.

viding means to assist the badly needed integration of faith and learning.[59]

With this brief review of developments among Catholic programs of liberal arts and theology, and of the orientation of the leadership of the United States' Church with respect to the intellectual life, we have touched upon all but one of the obstacles to the life of the mind that Ellis set forth in 1955; we shall examine this last one in the next section.

II. Today and Tomorrow

It is now time to devote our remaining space to an examination of some of the challenges and anomalies attendant upon the developments we have just reviewed. These will include the problems of academic bigotry, the "Catholic synthesis," and activist intellectuals.

Prejudice against "Catholic thought and ideas," as well as a traditional disdain for Catholics as persons, was the first cause inhibiting Catholic scholarship that Ellis cited in 1955. He noted Arthur M. Schlesinger, Sr.'s observation that such a bias was "the most persistent prejudice in the history of the American people."[60] Andrew Greeley senses that it is still operative, and has written a little book on the subject.[61] Support for his thesis comes from a more objective source, E. Digby Baltzell, author of *The Protestant Establishment*. He reflected in 1976 that, when he wrote his book "during the administration of President Kennedy, I still had faith in the ability of the WASP establishment to assimilate talented men and women of other ethnic and

[59]John Whitney Evans, *The Newman Movement: Roman Catholics in American Higher Education, 1883-1971* (Notre Dame, Ind., 1980), 149, 158, 164.

[60]Ellis, "American Catholics," 354.

[61]Andrew M. Greeley, *An Ugly Little Secret* (Kansas City, Kan., 1977).

religious origins into its ranks." He sadly concluded in our bi-centennial year, "I have no such faith today."[62]

Perhaps Catholic intellectuals do not face merely an esoteric form of old-time ethnic prejudice; some years ago Richard Hofstadter described the American intellectual establishment in terms more suitable for a congregation of believers than a community of scholars. He claimed it was generally understood "whether a particular person is inside or outside this establishment." Insiders employed "a double standard for evaluating criticism"; that from within was usually accepted as benign in intent, that from without came from those who might well be "against us," that is, from "marginal intellectuals, would-be intellectuals, unfrocked or embittered intellectuals." As Philip Gleason observed, "We are surely justified in concluding that there is an intellectual orthodoxy involved here." Latitudinarian though it may be, he continued, "one can stray too far from its prescriptions, fall into heresy and be cast, unfrocked, into the outer darkness of anti-intellectualism."[63]

If American Nativism still flourishes in the form of a surrogate religion for intellectuals, this would help to explain why Ellis' suggestive criteria for measuring intellectual excellence — membership in certain elite societies, grants from certain foundations, recognition from faculty in prestigious schools — might amount to little more than invoking a sanctimonious version of "the old boy line." And if anti-Catholic prejudice still operates, in however convoluted a fashion, among foundations and elite graduate faculties, will all the industry and habits of work in the world ever bring highest success? I can think of no other

[62]E. Digby Baltzell, "The Protestant Establishment Revisited," *The American Scholar* 45 (Autumn, 1976), 499-518, here 517.

[63]See Richard Hofstadter, *Anti-intellectualism in American Life* (New York, 1963) quoted in Philip Gleason, "Varieties of Anti-intellectualism," unpublished paper, 1964-65, 12 pp., photocopy. Gleason's words appear on p. 10. I thank Professor Gleason for permission to quote from his paper.

answer for Catholics but that proposed by the closing line in Tennyson's *Ulysses*: "To strive, to seek, to find, and not to yield."[64]

Our second topic, "Catholic synthesis," begins with an anomaly. The past thirty years may have produced Catholics who, by American standards, are intellectuals, but these decades have yet to see the emergence of an embodiment of Catholic intellectualism in America. Is it any longer possible to expect American Catholics to try to carry on "the incomparable tradition of Catholic learning" of which they remain the direct heirs? Is it rational to await a new "Catholic synthesis" of knowledge? As Philip Gleason has noted, American Catholics have committed themselves to a kind of intellectual activity that is not only "unprovided for in their classical pedagogical tradition," but that also "has had the practical effect of destroying the intellectual syntheses" of which that tradition was a part.[65] Karl Rahner, S.J., repeatedly grappled with the contemporary reality that "One has to travel the road [to a world view by] oneself in order to reach the goal in any real sense... and it is precisely this that is impossible today, or at least is possible only to a very small extent."[66]

The emergence of an integral Catholic intellectual tradition during the next two or three generations remains a hope. Nearly half the Catholics in Greeley's studies took up graduate work in arts and sciences.[67] Other research toward the end of the 1960s concluded that, compared with students

[64]Alfred Tennyson, *The Poems and Plays of Alfred Lord Tennyson* (New York, 1938), 168.

[65]Philip Gleason, "American Catholic Higher Education: A Historical Perspective" in Robert Hassenger, ed., *The Shape of Catholic Higher Education* (Chicago, 1967), 15-53, here 48.

[66]Karl Rahner, S.J., "A Small Question Regarding the Contemporary Pluralism in the Intellectual Situation of Catholics and the Church," *Theological Investigations* (Baltimore, 1969), VI, 21-30, here 23.

[67]Greeley, *The American Catholic*, 74.

in engineering, social science, and business departments, those in humanities and physical sciences tended to have the least secularistic, most religious world views.[68] But how is an American Catholic cultural heritage to be developed among these young intellectuals? Greeley would have us refer not "to what must be preserved out of the past, but what contribution, if any, the Catholic religious vision can make in the future of the total American higher educational enterprise."[69]

If by "the past" is meant that effort stemming from Leo XIII's encyclical of 1879, *Aeterni Patris*, to integrate the arts and sciences in the mind of the believing Christian by the inculcation of Thomistic philosophy subalternated to theology in an Aristotelian hierarchy of the sciences, then the advice is quite appropriate. As Father Gerald McCool, S.J., indicated in 1979, in the first place, there never was a common scholastic philosophy in the high Middle Ages, and by the middle of the twentieth century, Neo-Scholasticism had produced "several irreducibly distinct philosophical systems, all of which claimed to be authentically Thomistic." Futhermore, because the natural and social sciences have declared their independence from theology, and also because the philosophical pluralism of contemporary culture cannot be overcome, "it is no longer possible for the theologian to integrate the data of the sciences into his theology on the basis of a pre-given philosophical system."[70] Nor is it possible for the physicist or bio-chemist to integrate a mastered theological or philosophical perspective into his.

[68]Parker J. Palmer, "A Typology of World Views" in Kenneth Underwood, ed., *The Church, the University, and Social Policy* (Middletown, 1969), II, 27-59, here 54-55.

[69]Greeley, *Profile*, 84.

[70]Gerald McCool, S.J., "An Overview of the Scholastic Revival," paper read at the April, 1979, meeting of the American Catholic Historical Association, 16 pages mimeograph, here p. 3. I thank Fr. McCool for permission to quote from this paper.

Thus, rather than speak of an "integral Catholic intellectual tradition," we must use the plural. As historical research over the last century has demonstrated, Catholic intellectualism has been more multi-form than monolithic. Speaking in a broader context, Christopher Dawson has warned "when we talk of Christian culture, we ought not to think of some ideal pattern of social perfection which can be used as a sort of model or blueprint by which existing societies can be judged." Rather, we must look "at the historic reality of Christianity as a living force," which at times "seems to have conquered the world and is able to create a new Christian culture and new forms of life and art and thought."[71] McCool assures the young Catholic scholar that both Thomistic epistemology and the decrees of Vatican II justify, in principle, a plurality of diverse historical and philosophical frameworks. He concludes that a "Patristic or Hegelian theology might be just as true as a theology structured by the Aristotelian metaphysics of act and potency."[72]

If we place Rahner's assertion, that the contemporary world confronts us with questions, objections, methodologies, disciplines, and philosophies percolating in an "unmasterable pluralism," into Dawson's historical context of a plurality of Christian/Catholic cultural expressions down through the centuries, we encounter an exhilarating vision. It is a Catholicism in which intellectuals share in the unity of Catholic faith, while at the same time they work from their own disciplined perspectives at developing one of the several traditions either within the Catholic heritage, or compatible with it.

But it is precisely at this point that the solution encounters new difficulty. Do the new Catholic intellectuals care

[71]Christopher Dawson, *The Historic Reality of Christian Culture* (New York, 1960), 14, 47.

[72]McCool, "Overview," 12-13.

enough about the traditions of their Church to want to see themselves in the role of developing and enriching them? Does the leadership of the American Church care enough about the young intellectuals to want to assist them in this project? Greeley answers the first questions with a "Yes," the second with a "No."[73] McCool observes: the "Church's task of preserving the unity of faith within the diversity of her theologies and cultures will be a difficult one," one for which she is "still inadequately prepared."[74]

Perhaps we must turn to that point in the documents of Vatican II where the Council Fathers, when speaking of all human effort in the world (not specifically that of Catholic scholars, scientists, and technicians), set forth the following guidance: "far from thinking that works produced by man's own talent and energy are in opposition to God's power...Christians are convinced that the triumphs of the human race are a sign of God's greatness and the flowering of His own mysterious design."[75] It would seem necessary for administrators and authorities in the Church constantly to review the Council's lessons on the autonomy of the sciences and to recall Newman's *dictum:* "Great minds need elbowroom, not indeed in the domain of faith, but of thought...so indeed do lesser minds, and all minds."[76]

Complicating this projection of an already complex American Catholic intellectualism of a scholarly or academic sort is a more recent phenomenon, but one that appears to be as permanent as practitioners of Liberation Theology. This is the emergent tradition of the "activist intellectual," the one who is committed to exposing the lies in his society and its institutions as well as seeking truth. Far

[73]Greeley, "U.S. Catholics," 286-87; see also his *The Communal Catholic* (New York, 1976), 180-98 *passim.*.

[74]McCool, "Overview," 4.

[75]Walter M. Abbot, S.J., and Joseph Gallagher, eds., *The Documents of Vatican II* (New York, 1966), 232.

[76]John Henry Newman, *The Idea of a University* (Garden City, 1959), 429.

from placing its adherents "in the mainstream," where Catholics and their institutions now stand, this variant tradition may very well prepare them for a task that is quite alienating and lonely. This was the perspective that David J. O'Brien opened in 1973, when he examined the Ellis 1955 paper.[77] O'Brien cited the American bishops' statement on education that encouraged Christians "to be involved in seeking solutions to a host of complex problems, such as war, poverty, racism and environmental pollution."[78] Catholic intellectuals, claimed O'Brien, "must consider very seriously whether their own efforts might, where appropriate, be directed more specifically to questions of justice and peace."[79]

Involvement with such practical matters might seem opposed to the development of a scholarly tradition; many administrators of Catholic colleges have noted in recent years that members of their religious orders refuse to go on for doctoral studies because they would rather be engaged in a more "relevant" ministry. But O'Brien spoke, not of simple activism, but of "intellectual activists," and cited such examples as Thomas Merton, Paul Hanley Furfey, and Gordon Zahn, who drew upon "the incomparable tradition of Catholic learning" to expose falsehood. The exemplary careers of John A. Ryan and John LaFarge, S.J., represent an older generation whose ideas have had an impact upon the justness of labor-management and race relations in this country. Indeed, the very essay we are here considering might well qualify Monsignor Ellis for the title of "intellectual activist." And one has but to read the scholarly (and merry!)

[77]David J. O'Brien, "American Catholics and the Intellectual Life: Where Do We Go From Here?" paper read at the Spring, 1973, meeting of the American Catholic Historical Association, 18 pages ditto, here 7. I thank Professor O'Brien for permission to quote from this paper.

[78] *To Teach As Jesus Did* (Washington, D.C., 1973), 8.

[79]O'Brien, "Where Do We Go?" 15.

works of Matthew Fox, O.P., to discover how an intellectual, and even a mystical, tradition inspires and nourishes activism.[80]

The case of the intellectual activists is another form of the problem posed by pluralism. If an intellectual may not simply enjoy the play of ideas, but must also sit "in incessant and relentless judgement on his times,"[81] the Catholic intellectual tradition will have to make room for those who seek to "allow the light of the Gospel to be a more effective force in the liberation of men and women from bondage and ignorance, oppression and death."[82] What is more, this is precisely the sort of *institutional* presence called for in the Vatican working paper, "Pastoral Activity in the University Milieu," issued in 1976. The authors of this document suggested that Catholic colleges and universities could perform their function as social critics, in part, "by denouncing — where necessary and opportune — situations prejudicial to truth, to the dignity of the human person and to justice." It is recognized by all that such a proposal enjoys significance in varying ways, according to the nation or region in which Catholic institutions for advanced learning operate. But there is surely a need in our own country for "the disinterested, but committed collaboration of the university in altering public opinion"[83] on a variety of problems peculiarly our own. To the degree that American Catholic intellectuals develop scholarship and traditions acceptable to the mainline of American academicians and foundations, they may very well overcome the kind of scholastic bigotry that

[80]See Matthew Fox, O.P., *A Spirituality Named Compassion* (Minneapolis, 1979).

[81]Robert A. Nisbet, "What Is an Intellectual?" *Commentary* 40 (December, 1965), 93-94, here 93.

[82]O'Brien, "Where Do We Go?" 13.

[83]Joint Committee of Vatican Congregation for Catholic Education and Council for the Laity, "Pastoral Ministry in the University Milieu," *Origins* 6 (September 16, 1976), 197, 199-204, here 201.

Greeley and Baltzell have written about. It is very likely, however, that Catholics who choose to be intellectual activists, as described by O'Brien, may be slower to receive due recognition, at times even within the ranks of their own co-religionists.

Let me now attempt to summarize the central theme of this essay, the status of American Catholic intellectualism thirty years after the criticism that Ellis levelled against it in 1955. Observers leave us with an ambiguous evaluation. According to John T. Noonan, Jr., the 1955 assessment was "far bleaker that what is deserved today."[84] In contrast, Andrew Greeley believes that "[t]he intellectual life, a climate of respect for learning are of less concern" among Catholic bishops and school administrators in the early 1980s than thirty years ago.[85] Ellis himself tends more toward criticism than adulation. Although in 1981 he commented that "considerable improvement" had taken place in "many" Catholic institutions "over those of a quarter century ago,"[86] in 1984, as he prepared his own thirty year retrospective, he commented that the picture was not very encouraging: "We still have a long way to go before we can be said to be really doing our part, given our numbers and resources." Characteristically, he insisted that the "key to our relative failure" remained "our failure to *will to excel.*"[87]

Over my own celebration of the progress of Catholic intellectualism in the United States during the last three decades hovers a Banquo's ghost, or, perhaps, two of them: that these developments have taken place during a time of

[84]John T. Noonan, Jr., "American Catholics and the Intellectual Life," *Cross Currents* 31 (Winter, 1981-82), 433-46, here 442.

[85]Greeley, "Lower," 1.

[86]Eugene C. Bianchi, "A Church Historian's Personal Story: An Interview with Monsignor John Tracy Ellis," *Records of the American Catholic Historical Society of Philadelphia* 92 (March, 1981), 3-42, here 27.

[87]Ellis to the writer, August 9, 1984. Italics in the original.

declining standards, both in academic institutions and in popular taste; and during a time when many Catholic institutions of higher learning may have become less "Catholic." We have yet to actualize our distinctly Catholic intellectual and cultural heritages into a prominent and influential pattern of American traditions, although we may yet do so. And we have yet to develop leadership within the Church for this task, although it may yet emerge. To help us to do both, it will be helpful to keep in mind the Master's warning: "Everyone to whom much is given, of him much will be required."[88]

[88]Luke 12:48.

The History of Spirituality and the Catholic Community in the United States: An Agenda for the Future

Joseph P. Chinnici, O.F.M.

"Why study church history?" With this question John Tracy Ellis has begun his lectures for generations of scholars on "Catholicism since 1800: Some Leading Movements." Invoking the authority of such diverse people as Leopold von Ranke, Thomas Macaulay, Teilhard de Chardin, Lord Acton, and Barbara Ward, Ellis has stressed the close connection between the Catholic Church and the evolution of modern culture. Historical science, in this context, becomes a partial bearer of that culture; a knowledge of history is essential to Western civilization's preservation and growth. Ellis has also quoted Newman on the duty of the historian to provide a coherent structure of knowledge for the human condition's encounter with the divine. Unless this is done, Newman noted,

I shall not be able to trace out, for my own edification, the solemn conflict which is waging in the soul between what is divine and what is human, or the eras of the successive victories won by the powers and principles which are divine. I shall not be able to determine whether there was heroism in the young, whether there was not infirmity and temptation in the old. I shall be wearied and disappointed, and I shall go back with pleasure to the Fathers....[1]

What Newman referred to was the exemplary character of historical truth for action in the present. He called this connection between historical data, the historian's interpretation, and the ecclesial faith life of the contemporary person, when it occurred, "edification." It is a characteristic of history which Ellis himself has labored to reflect. Church history, in addition to being as integral part of our heritage, also teaches by example; it needs to "edify."[2]

In some of his writings and lectures Ellis has elaborated on these connections between culture, history, and "edification" by referring to the Bollandists and Maurists, the founders of modern historical scholarship, and the English Benedictine author, David Knowles. The theme has also appeared in occasional pieces on the sanctity of Mother Seton, the role of the *via crucis* in the life of the priest, and the necessity of truth, honesty, and free inquiry in approaching scholarship, liturgical worship, and religious devotions.[3] History as a discipline, in these more direct ways, has been

[1]John Henry Newman, "The Ancient Saints," *The Rambler* I [New Series] (May 1859), 90-98, here 98.

[2]John Tracy Ellis, "Catholicism Since 1800: Some Leading Movements," opening lecture, manuscript in author's possession.

[3]Confer, for examples, Ellis, *Perspectives in American Catholicism* (Baltimore, Dublin, 1963), *passim*; *A Commitment to Truth* (Latrobe, Pa., 1966); "Whence did they come, these uncertain priests of the 1960's?" *American Ecclesiastical Review* 162 (1970), 145-72, 234-48.

used by Ellis to reveal the spiritual realities with which the Church and believer are concerned. The historical enterprise here becomes a means of discovering and witnessing to truth, which reflects the Master of Truth, Christ himself.

By addressing the question "Why study church history?" and answering it in terms of the interplay between Catholicism and culture, Ellis has reflected within his own discipline the predominant religious problem of the mid-twentieth-century Catholic community in the United States. This problem, as Philip Gleason and William Halsey have shown, revolved around the role of Catholicism in politics, society, and scholarship.[4] In addition, Ellis' emphasis on Newman's understanding of "edification" acknowledged the important impact the historian could make on the creation of that Catholic culture, the building up of both personal faith and the Body of Christ within the context of contemporary society. Scholarship for "edification" was a species of Catholic Action. Lastly, Ellis' insistence on the moral dimension of scholarship as the pursuit of truth certainly rested on an abiding commitment to integrity, the opposite of hypocrisy: "Let us aim at meaning what we say, and saying what we mean."[5]

This essay contends that today the grounds on which we attempt to answer the question "Why study church history?" have shifted from the years preceding and following World War II. The contemporary Catholic historian is still interested in the relationship between the Church and culture, still committed to the pursuit of truth. But since 1961,

[4]Philip Gleason, "Mass and Maypole Revisited: American Catholics and the Middle Ages," *The Catholic Historical Review* 57 (1971), 249-74; Gleason, "In Search of Unity: American Catholic Thought 1920-1960," *ibid.*, 65 (1979), 185-205; William M. Halsey, *The Survival of American Innocence* (Notre Dame, 1980).

[5]John Henry Newman, "Words," preached on June 2, 1839, *Cardinal Newman's Best Plain Sermons*, ed. Vincent Ferrer Blehl, S.J. (New York, 1964), 83, as quoted by Ellis, *A Commitment to Truth*, 78.

our own history has also pressed upon us, with ever increasing urgency and self-consciousness, another issue, that of spiritual experience.[6] As a result, one of the "edifying" functions of history for us has changed. If the historical enterprise is to engage the contemporary believer, as Newman would have it, then historians themselves need to describe, analyze, and provide a coherent structure of interpretation for spiritual experience. In order to answer adequately today the question "Why study church history?", a history of spirituality is needed.

In this essay I would like to trace the shift from history in service to Catholicism and culture to the need for a history of spirituality. I will do this by examining significant works written from World War I to the present on the historical dimensions of the spiritual life in the Catholic community in the United States. In doing so, I hope to take note of the changing definition of "spirituality," present a somewhat comprehensive overview of books and articles in the area, isolate major themes, and provide some directions for future research.

History in Service to Catholicism and Culture, 1921-1961

In 1961 Gustave Weigel wrote a lengthy article surveying the history of American Catholic spirituality.[7] This essay still remains the only comprehensive review of the subject. After noting the almost complete absence of works on the history of the spiritual life in the United States, Weigel described the historical structure or context in which such a

---

[6]For the importance of "experience" as a contemporary category of thought, confer the articles in *Revelation and Experience*, ed. Edward Schillebeeckx and Bas van Iersel, *Concilium* 113 (New York, 1979).

[7]Gustave Weigel, "États-Unis," *Dictionnaire de Spiritualité*, Vol. IV/2 (Paris, 1961), 1428-45.

history could be written. He divided the material into two major periods: I. Before Independence, a section detailing the English, Spanish, and French contributions to colonial America up to 1776; II. From Independence to the 1950s, a slightly longer treatment. In part II Weigel argued that because of the diverse character of immigrant Catholicism and its continual growth, there was a need for organization and the unification of ecclesiastical discipline. This need for order became a dominant characteristic of Catholic spiritual life. Also, one of the most significant traits of the Christian experience during the nineteenth century was the *élan créateur,* which manifested itself in the construction of churches and parochial schools. Weigel concentrated on the contribution of the religious orders, the decrees of the Provincial and Plenary Councils, and the activities of important persons, especially Isaac Hecker and James Gibbons. For him the spiritual life in the United States could best be described as centered on the parish, its cult and numerous activities. The American Jesuit included a short section on the evangelization of the Blacks and Indians. Lastly, after referring to the growth of the retreat, liturgical, and novena movements in the twentieth century, Weigel concluded that the Church in the United States had now entered into its spiritual maturity.

Weigel's article was important not only for its bibliographical references, which were abundant, but also because it exemplified the dominant social and intellectual outlook which shaped people's understanding and practice of spirituality from 1921 to Vatican Council II. The spiritual life rested, above all, on strong institutional and organizational foundations: diocesan synods, ecclesiastical legislation, parishes, religious orders. When these foundations were missing, creating them became a primary indicator of a strong spiritual life. During this time sanctity was defined as a moral virtue combining proper disposition with action. Holiness characterized individuals and those organized into a church who participated in the *élan créateur,* who were apostolically oriented toward good works, and who expressed themselves through liturgy, pious organizations (Marian congregations, third-orders) and devotions (personal mental prayer, parochial missions, novenas, benediction of the Blessed Sacrament). In a telling sentence, Weigel noted that "if there exist spiritual autobiographies, they have not been published."[8]

There was no attempt in Weigel's article to describe the inner life, or what Lucien Febvre calls "religious sensibility," the history of people's emotions or affections, the qualities surrounding the spiritual life.[9] Theodore Maynard summarized the orientation of the American approach when he wrote in *The Story of American Catholicism* (first published 1941; 9th edition, 1954):

> Therefore the most important part of the history of the Catholic Church in America — as in any land — must remain unwritten. External happenings can be recorded, and we may deduce a great deal from them. But the life of the spirit — unique in the case of each individual soul — escapes the historian. Only in one respect are we able to say much about it: it is in the respect under which we have treated it — the communal life of liturgy.[10]

Catholic historians could not model their writing on, for example, Henri Bremond's classic *Histoire littéraire du*

[8]*Ibid.,* 1439.

[9]Confer Lucien Febvre, "Sensibility and history: how to reconstitute the emotional life of the past," *A New Kind of History and other essays, Lucien Febvre,* ed. Peter Burke, trans. K. Folca (New York, 1973), 12-26. For application to the American scene see Joseph P. Chinnici, "Organization of the Spiritual Life: American Catholic Devotional Works, 1791-1866," *Theological Studies* 40 (June 1979), 229-55.

[10]Theodore Maynard, *The Story of American Catholicism* (New York, 1954), 615-16.

sentiment religieux en France. Europeans had the luxury of
analyzing the literary expression of religious experience —
biographies, sermons, devotional works — and to penetrate
into the inner life, the "holy of holies." American Catholics,
on the other hand, as Jordan Aumann noted in 1956, had
been primarily activists.[11] Consequently, their history of
spirituality dealt with institutions, cultic expressions, and
works of charity.

By including such a large section on the colonial period
and stressing the active dimensions of spirituality in the lives
of outstanding Catholics, Weigel capitalized on a current
which had been flowing in the historical reflections on the
spiritual life since the beginning of the century. In 1884 the
Third Plenary Council of Baltimore petitioned the Holy See
to open the cause for canonization of the North American
martyrs, Isaac Jogues and companions. T. J. Campbell,
S.J., elaborated on this theme in his three-volume work
(1908-1911), *Pioneer Priests in North America 1642-1710,*
written to revive "the memory of their heroism and holiness." When the cause for canonization was finally opened
after World War I, the scholarly work began in earnest. F.
G. Holweck, building on earlier compilations in the *American Catholic Historical Researches,* published "An American Martyrology." He listed by calendar dating, January to
December, the martyrs, confessors, and virgins who had
been outstanding signs of sanctity in American history.
People were well aware that the Church in the United States
had as yet no canonized saint. In succeeding years, John
Joseph Wynne (1925), Marion Habig (1939), Amleto Giovanni Cicognani (1939), and Joseph B. Code (1946) wrote
extensively on the holiness characteristic of martyred missionaries, bishops, and members of religious congregations.
Their expositions reflected a hierarchical emphasis on the

---

[11]Jordan Aumann, O.P., "Activism and the Interior Life," *The Catholic Church,
U.S.A.*, ed. Louis J. Putz, C.S.C. (Chicago, 1956), 374-93.

clergy, since, as Cicognani noted, it is "through the administration of the bishops that sanctity is possible."[12]

Perhaps the most significant work of this hagiographical
genre was *The Martyrs of the United States of America,*
edited by James M. Powers in 1957, and containing numerous addresses by John Mark Gannon, Archbishop of Erie.
The book arose out of the hierarchy's commissioning of
Gannon in 1939 to assemble data on the life, labors, and
heroic deaths of the martyrs of the United States. It appears
that when Pius XI had canonized the North American
martyrs in 1930 and beatified Frances Xavier Cabrini in
1938, he galvanized the efforts to uncover the meaning of
holiness in the United States. As Gannon himself noted,
America was a hero-worshipping country; justice required
that Catholic spiritual leaders be finally given their due.[13]

This emphasis on prominent men and women and their
role in Church and society reflected significant values in the
spirituality of the Catholic community in the United States
in the inter-war period. For example, John Wynne, S.J.,
delivered a sermon in 1926 on the beatification of the mar-
tyed priests. He summarized the prevailing attitude:

> These solemnities also will be an occasion for inspiring in
> our Catholic people habits of self-denial, sacrifice, gener-
> osity, attachment to the Church, courage in professing

---

[12]Thomas J. Campbell, *Pioneer Priests of North America, 1642-1710,* Vol. 1
(New York, 1908); Vol. 2 (New York, 1910); Vol. 3 (New York, 1911); F. G.
Holweck, "An American Martyrology," *The Catholic Historical Review* 6 (1921),
495-516; John Joseph Wynne, S.J., *The Jesuit Martyrs of North America* (New
York, 1925); Marion A. Habig, O.F. M., *Heroes of the Cross* (New York, 1930; 3rd
ed., Patterson, N.J., 1947); Amleto Giovanni Cicognani, *Sanctity in America*
(Patterson, N.J. 1939); Joseph B. Code, "The Contribution of Europe to Holiness
in America," *Miscellanea Historica in honorem Alberti de Meyer,* Vol. 2 (Leuven-
Brussel, 1946), 1217-36. Cicognani is quoted in *American Ecclesiastical Review* 102
(March, 1940), 276.

[13]James M. Powers, ed., *The Martyrs of the United States* (Easton, Pa., 1957),
xii.

the Faith. They will help to develop vocations to the priesthood, to the religious life and to the missions, and a greater interest among the laity in all the work of our priests and religious, especially in the missions. They will also be an occasion for making known to the many non-Catholics who revere these men the true character and influence of our religion, and its part in our early history.[14]

For Wynne, holiness meant both the inculcation of virtues (sacrifice, self-denial, generosity) and attachment to the Church (defense of the Faith, promotion of vocations, interest in religious life and the missions). Wynne's sermon underscored a history of sanctity which studied the impact of Catholicism on civilization.

Bishop Gannon constantly reiterated similar values in his addresses. For him the hagiographical work of Catholic historians heralded the role of priests in the foundation of Christian culture; historical work described the antidote to the "hot fever of selfishness," injustice, greed, race prejudice, and class war dominating society in the United States. Now that Catholics had the leisure and ability to do research, Gannon argued, they also could "re-appraise the forces that fused to form the United States of America"; they could rewrite the story of its origin and development.[15] Francis L. Beckman, Archbishop of Dubuque, agreed: holiness was a characteristic of the Church, "a visible society, whose life, marks and works have given evidence of her existence and of her saving and civilizing influence upon humanity and the

[14]Wynne is quoted in "Our American Beatified Martyr-Priests," *American Ecclesiastical Review* 74 (Jan., 1926), 74-75. For the full text of the sermon see John J. Wynne, "Martyrs of North America," *Catholic Mind* 28 (Sept., 1930), 365-76.

[15]Powers, *The Martyrs of the United States*, 36, 192-94; quotation from 194.

institutions of her civilizations."[16] Historians of American Catholic spiritual life saw themselves as describing and furthering the Catholic contribution to culture, the most mature indicator of which was sanctity.

Numerous other historians beyond those working on the hagiographical materials emphasized the relationship between Catholic spiritual life and the spread of civilization. Thomas M. Schwertner, O.P., in his 1926 work on the *Eucharistic Renaissance,* written in anticipation of the gathering in Chicago, traced the history of the eucharistic congresses. He placed the religious revival in catechetics and philosophy in sharp contrast to the self-centered aspirations of the day. In a parallel fashion, the rekindling of interest in the eucharist represented a "scholasticism of the heart" and answered the prevailing hunger for joy. "America," he wrote, "belongs to the eucharist," as it had since the time of Columbus and the first missionaries. In the celebration and festivities of the 28th Congress "we would forget our thirst for gold in the ardors of a holy love; our industrialism for the blessed peace of His presence; our materialism for the spiritual things which will almost become tangible in His nearness."[17] Historians reflecting on the retreat and liturgical movements, two other widespread reforms of the same period, argued in a similar fashion.[18]

---

[16]Cited in M. M. Hoffmann, *Centennial History of the Archdiocese of Dubuque* (Dubuque, Ia., 1938), xix-xx.

[17]Thomas M. Schwertner, *The Eucharistic Renaissance or the International Eucharistic Congresses* (New York, 1926), ix, 362, 365.

[18]For reflections on the retreat movement, confer Gerald C. Treacy, S.J., "The Beginning of the Retreat Movement in America," *Proceedings of the First National Conference of the Layman's Retreat Movement in the United States of America* (Philadelphia, 1928), 13-20; Joseph L. Durkin, "Organization and Progress of the Retreat Movement in America," *ibid.,* 34-47; B. A. Seymour, "The Retreat Movement in the U.S. up to Now," *Proceedings of the Third National Conference of the Layman's Retreat Movement* (Detroit, 1930), 4-7; Joseph R. Stack, "Who was the Father of the Layman Retreats in the United States?" *Records of the American Catholic Historical Society of Philadelphia* 41 (March

The devotional life characteristic of immigrant spirituality also represented for many authors the spread of Catholic culture in an alien world. In 1939 Ralph and Henry Woods compiled *Pilgrim Places in North America;* in 1954 Francis Beauchesne Thornton wrote *Catholic Shrines in the United States and Canada.* The latter work described the Catholic contribution to the architectural and musical heritage of America. It professed to give the "history of noted places of popular pilgrimage: places where the attraction of a saint, an atmosphere, or a devotion has drawn men and women with the compelling magnetism Chartres had for Henry Adams." Thornton hoped that the knowledge of holy places and shrines crisscrossing the country would give a "living message of faith and love" to people of the twentieth century.[19]

The development of Marian devotions came under a similar treatment, the most notable being that of Daniel Sargent in 1940. *Our Lady and Our Land* traced the history of Mary's role in the United States from Spanish times to the present. Sargent believed that "Catholics in the United States need her to establish them in their own American citizenship." Through devotion to Mary, Catholics could perpetuate, as they always had, hopefulness, reliance on God, and a missionary zeal "to add to Christendom." These virtues were consonant with the American soul.[20] Marion Habig, Maurice Grajewski, Margaret Haferd, and Wilfrid Parsons also contributed historical studies on Mary in the

1930), 69-78; Gerald C. Treacy, ed., *Father Sheahy — A Tribute* (New York, 1927). For observations on the liturgical movement see Paul B. Marx, O.S.B., *Virgil Michel and the Liturgical Movement* (Collegeville, Minn., 1957); Robert D. Cross, *The Emergence of Liberal Catholicism in America* (Cambridge, Mass., 1958), 213; Theodore Maynard, "The Spiritual Heritage of America," *Spiritual Life* 2 (Dec. 1956), 235-44, here 243.

[19]Francis Beauchesne Thornton, *Catholic Shrines in the United States and Canada* (New York, 1954), x.

[20]Daniel Sargent, *Our Land and Our Lady* (New York, 1940), 244-45.

United States.[21] The sodality movement, part of Daniel Lord's vision of Catholic Action, attracted others.[22] Sister Mary Anselm Langenderfer, in a departure from the dominant cultural motif, presented "An Annotated Study of Catholic Lives of Christ Published in the United States."[23] Joseph Clifford Fenton, on the other hand, recognized the importance of devotions in the spread of Catholic culture. He wrote a short article detailing the importance of the spread of devotion to the Holy Ghost as it had been advocated by John Keane, Isaac Hecker, and the Paulists.[24] Lastly, *The Catholic Life Annual,* begun in 1958, contained historical studies designed to counteract the trend toward the secularization of holy days. This periodical attempted to interrelate the Christian heritage in the United States with the celebration of Christmas. Most, if not all, of these studies presupposed that if Thomism represented the doctrinal side of the Catholic revival, then devotions too had a place: they represented the emotional side of religion placed at the service of Christendom.

[21]Marion Habig, "The Cult of the Assumption of Our Lady in the United States, 1598-1888," *Studia Mariana* 7 (1952), 83-119; Maurice Grajewski, O.F.M., "The Franciscan Marian Cult in the United States in Our Times," *ibid.*, 120-25; Habig, "The Cult of the Immaculate Conception in the United States Before 1854," *ibid.*, 9 (1954), 11-23; Grajewski, "The Franciscans of the United States and the Cult of the *Immaculate Conception,*" *ibid.*, 133-45; Margaret Haferd, "The Shrine of Our Lady of Consolation, Carey, Ohio," *Records of the American Catholic Historical Society of Philadelphia* 48 (June, 1937), 204-14; Wilfrid Parsons, "Marian Devotion in the Early United States," *Marian Studies* 3 (1952), 236-50.

[22]Roger Baudier, "The First Sodality of the Blessed Virgin, New Orleans, 1730," *Historical Records and Studies* 30 (1939), 47-53; Bernice Wolff [Sister Mary Florence], *The Sodality Movement in the United States, 1926-36* (St. Louis, 1939).

[23]Mary Anselm Langenderfer, "An Annotated Study of Catholic Lives of Christ Published in the United States" (Catholic University of America, M.A. Thesis, 1940).

[24]Joseph C. Fenton, "Devotion to the Holy Ghost and Its American Advocates," *American Ecclesiastical Review* 121 (Dec., 1949), 486-501.

Weigel was not quite accurate when in 1961 he lamented the lack of studies on the history of the spiritual life in the United States. Within the context of the definition of spirituality of the time, there had been substantial biographical studies of holy men and women since the turn of the century. In addition, movements associated with spiritual revival and numerous devotional practices had been investigated. Most of the studies agreed that institutional structures provided the base for a strong Catholic spiritual life. Liturgy, retreats, devotional practices, and the imitation of apostolic bishops, priests, and religious, concretized the Catholic spirit for all to see. Historians defined spirituality in its various personal, ritual, and social expressions as the affective carrier of the structures and message of Christendom. In the process of severely challenging this view, the 1960s would call forth new historical approaches to the spirituality of the Catholic community in the United States.

The Question of Identity and Integration, 1961-1984

Reflection on the spiritual experience of the Catholic community in the United States began to change almost at the same time that Weigel had provided what he thought were the basic structures for such a history. The 1960s witnessed the collapse of the devotional base of immigrant Catholicism, a call for contemplation, and a general critique of a spirituality in service to Christendom. The decline in pious practices — novenas, recitation of the rosary, stations of the cross, mission sermons —had been noted as early as 1959 by Andrew Greeley.[25] By 1965 Dan Herr in the pages of *The Critic* was referring to a "piety void," a fact readily

[25]Andrew Greeley, "Popular Devotions, Friend or Foe," *Worship* 33 (Oct. 1959), 569-73.

acknowledged in the pages of such periodicals as *Spiritual Life, American Ecclesiastical Review,* and *Worship.*[26] Concomitant with the movement away from devotions was an increasing interest in contemplation as a prayer form which had been discouraged by the American bent toward activism. *The Catholic Periodical and Literature Index* noted twenty-two entries for "contemplation" and "mysticism" in 1961-1962; nineteen for 1967-1968; fifty-four for 1971-1972. The same years saw only six, zero, and three entries for "Devotions, popular." Articles by Greeley, Bernard Häring, C.SS.R., Thomas U. Mullaney, O.P., Peter Riga, Benedict M. Ashley, O.P., and others defined prayer not in terms of its cultic or ritual expressions, but as a profoundly personal contact with God and the world.[27] Lastly, in 1969 Greeley wrote a fairly comprehensive article on the "Changing Styles of Catholic Spirituality."[28] The new style emphasized

[26]Cf. Walter Nash, O.C.D., "The Piety Void and Liturgical Renewal," *Spiritual Life* 13 (Fall 1967), 153-59; Daniel L. Lowery, C.SS.R., "A 'Piety Void'?" *American Ecclesiastical Review* 204 (Jan., 1966), 31-8; Carl Dehne, S.J., "Roman Catholic Popular Devotions," *Worship* 49 (Oct., 1975), 446-60. Note also the appeal for popular devotional practices by Richard Portasik, O.F.M., "Popular Devotions," *Homiletic and Pastoral Review* 66 (Sept., 1966), 1017-22.

[27]Andrew Greeley, "Culture, Contemplation and the Religious Revival," *The Critic* 18 (April-May 1960), 17-18, 77; Bernard Häring, C.SS.R., "A Contemplative House," *Review for Religious* 26 (Sept. 1967), 771-78; Thomas U. Mullaney, O.P., "Contemplation: 'In' or 'Out'?" *Review for Religious* 28 (Jan. 1969), 56-71; Peter Riga, "Christian Prayer," *Spiritual Life* 15 (Summer 1969), 105-18; Benedict M. Ashley, O.P., "Toward an American Theology of Contemplation," *Review for Religious* 30 (March 1971), 187-98; George A. Maloney, S.J., "And Now, the Yoga Retreat," *America* 124 (June 5, 1971), 591-93; Sister Marie Agnes Houle, S.S.J., "Toward Tomorrow's Task: Contemplation," *Sisters Today* 42 (Feb. 1971), 300-06; Sister Margaret Rowe, O.C.D., "Current Trends in Prayer," *Spiritual Life* 17 (Fall 1971), 172-85; Walter J. Burghardt, S.J., "Without Contemplation the People Perish," *America* 127 (July 22, 1972), 29-32; Jean Leclercq, O.S.B., "New Forms of Contemplation and of the Contemplative Life," *Theological Studies* 33 (June 1972), 307-19; Herbert F. Smith, S.J., "Contemplation: Option or Human Imperative," *Homiletic and Pastoral Review* 73 (May 1973), 17-24; Thomas Keating, O.C.S.O., "Contemplative Prayer in the Christian Tradition," *America* 138 (April 8, 1978), 278-81.

[28]Andrew Greeley, "Changing Styles of Catholic Spirituality," *Homiletic and Pastoral Review* 67 (April 1967), 557-65.

the practice of social virtue, liturgical celebration, community, the development of personality, and commitment to action within the world. Many articles appeared in succeeding years which reflected the growing awareness among Catholics of an American spirituality.[29] Clearly, the 1960s urgently posed the question: What is American Catholic spirituality?

What all of this meant for the historian of spirituality was summarized in what is perhaps the only comprehensive article on American spirituality to appear since Weigel's. In 1969 Aidan Kavanagh, O.S.B., wrote "Spirituality in the American Church: An Evaluative Essay." The Benedictine's article was significant for four major reasons. First, Kavanagh defined spirituality not with reference to its importance in the spread of Catholic culture, but as the "awareness any religious society has of itself — that is, of its own living relationship with the continuum of faith objects in which it believes." Spirituality consisted of the raw stuff of human experience crystallized into patterns of culto-symbolic forms: worship, devotions, styles of prayer, etc. It was rooted in the subject, based on experience, reflective of and contributor toward the objective social structures of belief: creed, organization, and social position. Kavanagh related spirituality primarily to awareness, the self-consciousness of a community. The crisis of spirituality, he argued, was a crisis of personal and communal identity, continuity, and cohesion.[30]

[29]Cf. Denis Read, O.C.D., "Toward an American Spirituality," *Spiritual Life* 14 (Fall, 1968), 188-92; Andrew Greeley, ed., "Spirituality for the Seventies," *The Critic* 29 (Sept.-Oct., 1970), 19-53; David M. Knight, S.J., "Something is Missing in the Church," *Homiletic and Pastoral Review* 73 (June, 1973), 30-32, 50-56; various articles in two fascicles entitled "The Rebirth of Spirituality," *New Catholic World* 219 (Mar.-April, 1976), *passim*, and "A Spiritual Life Handbook," *Chicago Studies* 15 (Spring, 1976), *passim*; Rawley Myers, "American Spirituality," *Homiletic and Pastoral Review* 78 (Dec. 1977), 59-62.

[30]Aidan Kavanagh, "Spirituality in the American Church: An Evaluative Essay," *Contemporary Catholicism in the United States*, ed. Philip Gleason (Notre Dame, 1969), 197-214; the definition of spirituality is taken from 197.

This conception of spirituality marked an obvious and radical break from the views of historians previous to 1961. Kavanagh used the same materials of religious expression but viewed them anthropologically. What did religious expressions say about the Catholic community's awareness of itself, about its concept of self-identity, its inner spiritual experience? It is clear that within the context of the 1960s and the collapse of the institutional self-understanding which supported the Church of Christendom, "spirituality" had come to signify a community's as well as an individual's own search for their deepest identity in God.

Second, "Spirituality in the American Church" focused on a major problem which Kavanagh believed had characterized the general development of spirituality in Western Christendom. He argued that the rupture between the formal liturgical expression of worship and the more spontaneous, creative outbursts of religiosity in popular devotions symbolized the disintegration between the objective and subjective elements in piety. As a result, "the presbyterate came to assume an almost exclusively cultic character." With the sacralization of ecclesiastical structure, the Benedictine noted, the Church lost contact with the evolution of modern society. In addition, the image of Christ in popular piety became "over-divinized and extra-worldly," thus divorcing Christ from the world, the sacred from the secular, grace from nature. People had access to the divine only through "periodic irruptions of the divinity" in, for example, formal worship.[31] Kavanagh's analysis agreed with that of many of his contemporaries, who complained about the inherited dualism in American Catholic spirituality.[32]

For the purposes of this essay, the significant issue is that the revival in historical reflection on spirituality was engen-

[31] *Ibid.*, 203-06.

[32] Cf. Greeley, "Changing Styles of Catholic Spirituality"; Ashley, "Toward An American Theology of Contemplation."

dered within the context of the contemporary divorce between nature and grace. As a result, the issue of *integration* or the relationship between personal experience, institutional forms, cultic expressions, and the problems of society, now joined *identity* as a major question which historians would pose of their materials.

Thirdly, Kavanagh stressed not only identity and integration, but also the changing nature of Catholic spiritual expression in the United States. He quoted de Tocqueville on the simplicity and lack of "taste for minute individual observances" in pre-immigration (1830) American Catholicism. The Benedictine related the complex of cult, popular devotions, sodalities, attitudes toward the clergy, schools, and national parishes to the necessity of combining faith with ethnic solidarity in a hostile environment. He referred to the differences between medieval and post-Reformation Catholicism and Protestantism and detailed some changes in worship patterns throughout the centuries.[33] In the midst of the crisis of the 1960s, "Spirituality in the American Church" called for both an awareness of change itself and an ability to move beyond the seemingly fixed patterns of previous Catholic spirituality.

Kavanagh's article also pointed to a fourth major element which differentiated recent historical reflection on spirituality from its earlier counterparts. In order better to argue his evaluation of the current scene, the American Benedictine combined the methodological tools of theology, anthropology, sociology, phenomenology of religion, and psychology with those of history. He referred to Michel de Certeau, Marshall McLuhan, and Mircea Eliade.[34] It is not surprising that he wrote from the perspective of liturgical renewal,

[33]Kavanagh, "Spirituality in the American Church," 207-10.

[34]*Ibid.*, 197 n. 1, 198 n. 3. An exceptionally valuable background article on this perspective is Michel de Certeau, "Culture and Spiritual Experience," *Spirituality in the Secular City*, ed. C. Duquoc, *Concilium* 19 (New York, 1966), 3-31.

which, as Mary Collins would later illustrate, provided a unique source for the interaction of various disciplines.[35] Kavanagh went beyond the descriptive narration of the expressions of Catholic spirituality to their meaning as *symbols* in a cultural context. This interdisciplinary method of interpreting historical data would be characteristic of future researches in the field. Influenced largely by European trends, historians in the United States would begin to use the diverse insights of such people as Lucien Febvre, Gabriel Le Bras, Philippe Ariès, Elisabeth Germain, Paul Ricoeur, Mary Douglas, Victor Turner, Carlo Ginzburg, and Jacques Le Goff.[36]

Since 1969, a concern for identity and integration, and an emphasis on development and interdisciplinary studies, have characterized almost all of the scholarship dealing directly or indirectly with the history of spiritual expression in the Catholic community in the United States. The impetus began with the social historians of immigration and ethnicity, who analyzed the spirituality of the community in terms of its function in establishing a cohesive identity and its ability either to hinder or promote acculturation. Martin Marty signaled the new approach in his foreword to Jay Dolan's *The Immigrant Church* in 1975.[37] Since then, ethnic

[35]Mary Collins, O.S.B., "Liturgical Methodology and the Cultural Evolution of Worship in the United States," *Worship* 49 (Feb., 1975), 85-102.

[36]For background on the growth of interdisciplinary method in history, confer: Theodore K. Rabb and Robert I. Rotberg, eds., *The New History, The 1980s and Beyond* (Princeton, 1982), *passim*; Jean Delumeau, *Catholicism between Luther and Voltaire: a new view of the Counter-Reformation*, trans. Jeremy Moiser (London, 1977), 129-53; Raphael Samuel, ed., *People's History and Socialist Theory* (London, 1981), *passim*; Frank E. Manuel, "The Use and Abuse of Psychology in History," *Daedalus* 100 (Winter, 1976), 187-213; Keith Thomas, "History and Anthropology," *Past and Present* 24 (April, 1963), 3-24; E. P. Thompson, "Anthropology and the Discipline of Historical Context," *Midland History* 1 (Spring, 1972), 41-55.

[37]Jay Dolan, *The Immigrant Church, New York's Irish and German Catholics, 1815-1865* (Baltimore, 1975), ix-xii.

historians of the Germans, Irish, Italians, Poles, Czechs, and Hispanics have examined the diverse expressions which concretized the community's spiritual experience: ceremonies surrounding the rites of passage, patronal feast days, processions, superstitious practices, music, Christmas celebrations, attitudes toward the role of the clergy, attendance at the sacraments, popular devotions, lay confraternities, architectural preferences, artistic expressions in paintings, holy cards, and statues.[38] The religious life of the ethnic community was discovered to be multi-dimensional and intricately connected with its experience of society and its understanding of the institutional Church. Sociology, spirituality, and ecclesiolgy were not divorced. Catholicism in the United States, these studies implied, had become a patchwork quilt of spiritualities, a diversity which had previously been acknowledged only in reference to religious orders. Two major themes which the social historians pioneered, popular religion and Americanization, also influenced others studying the problems of spiritual identity and integration.

Scholars have offered various and much-debated definitions of popular religion.[39] For those studying the spiritual experience of the American Catholic community, "popular"

---

[38]For examples, confer the collection of articles in Randall M. Miller and Thomas D. Marzik, ed., *Immigrants and Religion in Urban America* (Philadelphia, 1977). On Hispanic Catholicism, see Frances M. Campbell, "American Regional Catholicism: Dichotomous Developments in 'Anglo' and 'Hispano' Traditions, 1776-1885," unpublished paper delivered at the annual meeting of the American Catholic Historical Association, San Francisco, 1983; Thomas J. Steele, S.J., *Santos and Saints, The Religious Folk Art of Hispanic New Mexico* (Albuquerque, N.M., 1974); Virgilio Elizondo, *Galilean Journey* (New York, 1983).

[39]For the contemporary European debate see Bernard Plongeron, ed., *La reli gion populaire dans l'Occident Chrétien, approches historiques* (Paris, 1976); Carlo Ginzburg, *The Cheese and the Worms*, trans. John and Anne Tedeschi (New York, 1982), xiii-xxvi; Alphonse Dupront, "La religion populaire dans l'histoire de l'Europe Occidentale," *Revue d'Histoire de l'Église de France* 64 (July-Dec. 1978), 185-202.

usually refers to the religious expressions of all the people. The term generally does not carry the dichotomies so frequent in studies of religious expression in Europe: communal/individual; lay/clerical; devotional/cultic; oral/literate. In the United States popular devotions have clearly received the most attention. John Huels has studied the appeal of the Sorrowful Mother Novena from its inception in 1937 to its decline in the 1950s. He found that the novena combined liturgical and Marian themes which responded to the social anxieties of a Catholic body caught in the economic depression and war.[40] Thomas Kselman has related to the war against communism the post-World War II revival in Marian piety expressed in the forms of miraculous medals, the proliferation of Fatima grottoes and popular pilgrimages.[41] The finest general study to date is that by Ann Taves, "Relocating the Sacred: Roman Catholic Devotions in Mid-Nineteenth Century America." Building on, yet critiquing, my own study of 1979,[42] Taves argues that the popularization of devotions in the United States from 1830 to 1880 bridged "the gap between the orally transmitted folk practices of the Irish immigrants and more sophisticated book-based forms of devotion." Indulgences and pious practices also enabled the hierarchy to universalize and standardize local customs. They encouraged Romanization. Thirdly, popular devotions helped define the "Irish Catholic subculture in the United States" by sharply differentiating Catholics from non-Catholics.[43] All four of these studies have clearly attempted to understand the ecclesial

[40] John Huels, "The Popular Appeal of the Sorrowful Mother Novena," *Marianum* 38 (1976), 191-99; and his *The Friday Night Novena* (Berwyn, Ill., 1977).

[41] Thomas Kselman, "Our Lady of Necedah, Marian Piety and the Cold War," *Working Paper Series* 12, 2 (Notre Dame, 1982).

[42] Chinnici, "Organization of the Spiritual Life."

[43] Ann Taves, "Relocating the Sacred: Roman Catholic Devotions in Mid-Nineteenth Century America" (University of Chicago Divinity School, Ph.D. dissertation, 1983), here 3-4.

and social identity of Catholics from the perspective of the concretization of religious experience in symbolic form.

The religious expressions of the people have received further analysis in treatments of education, popular missions, and the liturgical calendar, three key formulators and reflectors of spirituality. In 1976 Christa Ressmeyer Klein wrote a dissertation on "The Jesuits and Catholic Boyhood in Nineteenth-Century New York City," a significant portion of which studied sacramental life and piety. Klein consciously related the annual retreat, stations of the cross, spiritual reading, paraliturgical activities,sermons, novels, and iconography to the educational imperative of self-definition in a hostile society. Noting the shifting images of piety during the period, she described the emergence of "muscular Christianity" in the latter half of the nineteenth century. The literature of the time, she argued, bore witness to "the manly or pious soldier or athlete whose sense of fair play, hard work, self-sacrifice, and obedience to authority would merit success with both God and man."[44] Klein's emphasis on the role of piety in the formation of the Catholic subculture received confirmation in the studies of Jay Dolan on popular missions.[45] Dolan maintained that the "revivals" with their emphasis on sin, death, judgment, hell, and conversion channeled the emotions of Catholics toward the institutional structures of the Church. They strengthened the parish and the authority of the priest, rallied support for the parochial schools, encouraged isolation from the world, and stressed a moralistic approach to the spiritual life. Others argued that mission preachers,

[44]Christa Ressmeyer Klein, "The Jesuits and Catholic Boyhood in Nineteenth-Century New York City: A Study of St. John's College and the College of St. Francis Xavier, 1846-1912" (University of Pennsylvania, Ph.D. dissertation, 1976), here 348, *passim*.

[45]Jay Dolan, *Catholic Revivalism, The American Experience 1830-1900* (Notre Dame, 1978).

using different methods for Catholic and Protestant audiences, helped create the "Church militant," a spirituality which the evangelical Catholic Truth Guild carried into the twentieth century.[46] In addition to schools and missions, John Gurrieri has noted the importance of the liturgical calendar and its evolution for understanding Catholic spirituality.[47] In a scholarly way he traced the movement from a liturgically based spirituality in Anglo-American Catholicism to the formation of an "individualist ghetto-piety" and a Catholic fundamental sabbatarianism.

The ethnic historians' concern with Americanization found another parallel expression in scholars who addressed spirituality from a biographical perspective. Although this trend could be seen to be in continuity with an earlier generation's emphasis on "American martyrs," an important difference divided the two. Cicognani, Weigel, and J. B. Code had emphasized the derivative nature of holiness in the United States, namely, its European origins. In contrast, recent studies concentrate on distinctively American approaches to the spiritual life. John Farina, Martin Kirk, and Mary Lyons have contributed substantial works on Isaac Hecker, the founder of the Paulists.[48] The

[46]For mission preaching, confer: Thomas Joseph Jonas, "The Divided Mind: American Catholic Evangelists in the 1890's" (University of Chicago Divinity School, Ph.D. dissertation, 1980); Mary Lyons, "A Rhetoric for American Catholicism: The Transcendental Voice of Isaac T. Hecker" (University of California, Berkeley, Ph.D. dissertation, 1983); Debra Campbell, "A Catholic Salvation Army: David Goldstein, Pioneer Lay Evangelist," *Church History* 52 (Sept., 1983), 322-32.

[47]John Gurrieri, "Holy Days in America," *Worship* 54 (Sept. 1980), 417-46; and his "Catholic Sunday in America: Its Shape and Early History," *Sunday morning: a time for worship*, ed. Mark Searle (Collegeville, Minn., 1982), 75-95.

[48]John Farina, *An American Experience of God, The Spirituality of Isaac Hecker* (New York, 1981); Martin Kirk, "The Spirituality of Isaac Thomas Hecker: Reconciling the American Character and the Catholic Faith" (St. Louis University, Ph. D. dissertation, 1979); Lyons, "A Rhetoric for American Catholicism."

growing body of literature surrounding the personal histories of Dorothy Day and Thomas Merton symbolizes the
contemporary preoccupation with a Catholic spiritual identity which is peculiarly American.[49] John Courtney Murray,
not usually recognized as a spiritual writer, has also received
treatment from this perspective.[50] Underlying all of these
works is a desire to uncover models of holiness which integrate the Catholic spiritual tradition with American society.

Finally, between 1961 and 1982 historians examined
trends in theology and broader reform movements which
directly related to the spiritual experience of the Catholic
community. Sister Rosemary Rodgers and Gordon Edward
Truitt surveyed the changing patterns of Catholic theology
in studies of the role of Christ in college textbooks and the
approaches to prayer in books and periodical articles.[51] The
Retreat, Liturgical, Sodality, and Pentecostal movements,
were also objects of preliminary investigation.[52]

[49]For Day, see William D. Miller, *Dorothy Day, A Biography* (San Francisco,
1982), *passim*, and Mel Piehl, *Breaking Bread, The Catholic Worker and the
Origin of Catholic Radicalism in America* (Philadelphia, 1982), ch. 7, "Catholic
Spiritual Radicalism in America." For Merton, confer Marquita Breit, *Thomas
Merton: A Bibliography* (Metuchen, N.J. 1974).

[50]John A. Rohr, "John Courtney Murray's Theology of Our Founding Fathers'
'Faith'," *Freedom in Christian Spirituality in the United States: Independence and
Interdependence*, eds. Francis A. Eigo and Silvio E. Fittipaldi (Philadelphia,
1978), 1-30.

[51]Rosemary Rodgers, "The Changing Concept of College Theology: A Case
Study" (Catholic University of America, Ph.D. dissertation, 1973); Gordon E.
Truitt, "A Historical and Theological Analysis of the Main Trends of the Catholic
Theology of Prayer in the United States, 1940-1975" (Catholic University of
America, Ph.D. dissertation, 1981).

[52]Joseph Chinnici, "The Retreat Movement: Changing Structures of a Spiritual
Vision, 1909-1982" (Notre Dame: Retreats International, 1982); Sister Jeremy
Hall, O.S.B. *The Full Stature of Christ, the Ecclesiology of Virgil Michel, O.S.B.*
(Collegeville, Minn., 1976); George E. Ganss, S.J. "The Christian Life Communi-
ties as Sprung from the Sodalities of Our Lady," *Studies in the Spirituality of the
Jesuits* 7 (March, 1975), 45-58; James T. Connelly, C.S.C., "Legitimate Reasons
for Existence: The Beginning of the Charismatic Movement in the American
Catholic Church, 1967-1971," *Working Paper Series* 11, 2 (Notre Dame, 1982).

This brief survey indicates that scholarship has moved a great distance in the last twenty years. Almost all of the works have approached spirituality from within the context of more dominant institutional, social, or intellectual concerns. This approach has necessarily involved subsidiary reflections on Catholic spiritual experience, its development and changing patterns of expression. What emerges is a rich tapestry of approaches, sources, and themes which touch in some way on key elements in the Catholic community's religious self-awareness. There has been a slow but definite shift away from history in service to Catholicism and culture to a history which addresses the issues of identity and integration as these were raised in the mid-1960s.

Spirituality, Dom Jean Leclercq writes in a very recent essay,

> does not identify with the faith and practice implied by Christian life at large, neither with some particular devotions, nor with theology — though it may include all these components. To all of them it adds that element of vital contact with God, of which the first, spontaneous expression is prayer. Thanks to such a personal experience, made available by the Spirit of Christ, the mystery of God and of his work for the world has an immediate impact on everyday life: religious transcendence penetrates into and emerges out of intentions and actions.[53]

The research surveyed here tends to support Leclercq's perspective. Vital contact with God has become the issue of the times. The pursuit of integration and the Catholic community's deepest identity has enabled many people to reflect on the interrelationship between the material, social and

---

[53] Jean Leclercq, "The Distinctive Characteristics of Roman Catholic American Spirituality," *Louvain Studies* 9 (Spring, 1983), 295-306, here 295.

cultural conditions of life, personal experience, and religious expression. Scholars have been preoccupied with both the inner and outer, the subjective and objective, the personal and institutional, the individual and social dimensions of history. The theology of prayer, devotional life, spiritual reform movements, cultic expressions, personal histories, the use of symbols, art forms, and the liturgical calendar have all received attention. Much of this has been made possible by the methodological combination of psychology, sociology, anthropology, and history. The orientation is clear. I believe that it has now become possible to build on the insights of Weigel, Kavanagh, and others, in a more explicit way. What is needed, in both monographs and general surveys, is a history of spirituality itself. Thus, in our own day and for the purpose of Newman's "edification" we can answer the original question: "Why study church history?"

Preserving Manuscripts of Our Religious and Cultural Traditions

Colman J. Barry, O.S.B.

While doing research under the direction of Monsignor John Tracy Ellis for my thesis on nineteenth-century German Catholic immigration to the United States, I was granted a Penfield Fellowship by the Catholic University of America in 1950-51 for study of primary sources in Germany. The rigorous Ellis training in respect for and care of original source materials was an invaluable aid in the elusive tracing of German Catholic emigrants, their ideals and purposes in that movement to the New World.

On my research trip to Rome in 1950 the papers of Abbot Bernard Smith, O.S.B., a Roman agent for English-speaking conservative Catholics, were discovered intact in the Archives of the Abbey of Saint Paul Outside the Walls. This previously unknown deposit of clerical and lay documents opened a balancing dimension for studies of the heated liberal and conservative differences in the American Catholic Church. Similar positions among nineteenth-century German, Irish, English, Canadian, and Australian Catholics were opened and expanded by the discovery of the

Smith Papers which were microfilmed on the spot and are now preserved in the archives of the Catholic University of America and Saint John's University, Collegeville, Minnesota.[1]

During a semi-private audience with Pope Pius XII in Rome on January 4, 1951, that pontiff expressed interest in this author's research studies on German Catholic emigrants and the places where materials are located such as in Rome, Freiburg im Breisgau, Hamburg, Munich, Cologne, etc. He stated: "How many displaced persons the Church must now try to help care for in these years after World War II! It is a major concern of ours. We must assist in caring for their spiritual and material needs, as well as preserving their legitimate and valued traditions. So much of their heritage has already been lost and especially as a result of devastation during the recent war. We must do everything we can to insure that this will not happen again. So much has already been lost...," he sadly repeated.

These two Roman experiences, along with daily searches in West Germany for lost sources and incomplete findings, left an unforgettable impression on this graduate student. Living in a totally defeated Germany with ruins and destruction on every side deepened this awareness. The havoc wrought by conventional weapons was but an all too obvious forerunner to a history student of the destructive potential inherent in possible atomic warfare and a nuclear holocaust.

Wars had devastated countless artistic, cultural, literary, and religious treasures. The fragile and vulnerable state of important manuscripts which had survived the destruction of war, flood, and fire continued as an imminent danger. An opportunity presented itself beginning in the 1960s for a contribution to preserving the manuscript heritage of Western civilization.

[1]Callistus J. Edie, O.S.B., "Letter from Rome," *The Scriptorium* 11 (March, 1951), 21-35.

Saint John's Abbey, Collegeville, Minnesota, had joined in the world-wide effort following World War II to contribute to the assistance, support, and restoration of European Benedictine Abbeys, victims of that devastation. Some of these abbeys were receptive in turn a decade and a half later to a proposal to microfilm their manuscript collections, organize them in one center, and preserve them on film both in America and at the home abbey or deposit of origin. In 1964 Abbot Baldwin Dworschak, O.S.B., sixth abbot of Saint John's Abbey, wrote to European abbots requesting permission to send a monk of Saint John's Abbey to their archives and libraries to organize *in situ* a program for the microfilming of manuscripts which would use local technical workers. Original planning had envisioned initiating the undertaking in either Italy or Switzerland where rich archival deposits were well known, such as the Monte Cassino and St. Gall libraries. However, restrictive state controls over such collections proved to be an insurmountable obstacle especially at the very beginning of such an untraditional and American-sponsored project as microfilming treasured collections or even allowing a copy to be transmitted to a United States center.

The project was conceived as a long-range undertaking to preserve on microfilm the contents of pre-1600 manuscripts still preserved, often precariously, in libraries and archives; and of making these largely inaccessible primary source materials — as, for example, to women students in monastic centers — available to all researchers, scholars, and teachers.

The project was indispensably supported by a pilot grant in 1964 of $40,000 from the Louis W. and Maud Hill Family Foundation of Saint Paul, Minnesota. Established in 1934 by Louis W., son of the Empire Builder, James J. Hill, this foundation's executive director, Mr. A. A. Heckman, had from the very beginning received favorably the proposal of Saint John's Abbey and University to undertake this unique enterprise. He immediately saw the potential for scholars and students everywhere by preserving the manuscript deposits, giving a copy to the donor institution, and establishing a center for research in an American private university center. The members of the Board of the Hill Family Foundation were equally foresighted in their early and on-going enthusiasic support.[2]

Two further supports for the project were on the scene from its inception. One was the enthusiastic encouragement and professional competence of Eugene B. Power, K.B.E., founder of University Microfilms, Inc. of Ann Arbor, Michigan, who continued for a decade personally to supply advice on technical filming procedures, equipment, and storage of the original negative microfilm from each deposit. The second was the choice of the Reverend Oliver Kapsner, O.S.B., of Saint John's Abbey, to be the first field director of what came to be a vast project. Father Oliver, a friend of Monsignor Ellis, had served previously as a catalogue librarian at Saint John's University and then at the Catholic University of America, as well as writer of the theological subject headings for the catalogue cards of the Library of Congress, Washington, D.C.

Father Oliver was further qualified for the pathfinding undertaking by his student experiences at Sant' Anselmo in Rome, knowledge of Latin, Greek, German, and Italian, and his military service in the European theatre during World War II as a field chaplain. He chose to go to Austria after the initial negative responses to the project were received from Italy and Switzerland. He was successful in obtaining entry to the library manuscript book collection of Kremsmuenster Abbey in that nation enjoying a unique

---

[2] Members of the Board of Directors of the Louis W. and Maude Hill Family Foundation who in 1964 established the policy of supporting the program of microfilming pre-1600 manuscript collections included: Louis W. Hill, Jr., Francis D. Butler, Charles J. Curley, Curtis E. Goodson, Philip L. Ray, and A. A. Heckman.

position for its cultural heritage in central Europe, an area preserved from both the Napoleonic and Turkish depravations of the past from the west, east, and south. Here were priceless manuscripts from classical, medieval, and Renaissance periods to be preserved now on microfilm both at home and abroad for future generations.

At Kremsmuenster Abbey, the Austrian microfilm team of Father Oliver and two technicians, Paul Seger and Hans Berger, made the original breakthrough. Positive copies of entire collections, as the project developed, were donated to the donor institutions along with a microfilm reader for the larger collections through the Hill Family Foundation grant. In addition to HMML's security copy (the original negative film), a positive copy for user purposes was mailed to Collegeville where a considerable collection was accumulating in the basement of the new Alcuin Library at Saint John's. A director was needed to organize the collection and prepare a program for its cataloguing, growing availability, and use. This was especially the case since the Hill Family Foundation continued its generous grants for twenty years, from 1964 to 1984, for a total of $1,750,000 in direct support.

Julian G. Plante, doctor of classical and medieval philology from Fordham University, was appointed executive director in 1966. He began the indispensable dimension of the project, namely, organizing a center for the films which were steadily arriving from Austria, and establishing procedures for making the rapidly increasing volume of microfilmed manuscripts available to scholars and research students. The collection was called from 1965 to 1974 the Monastic Manuscript Microfilm Library and later the Hill Monastic Manuscript Library (hereafter HMML), in recognition of the generous support of the project from its inception by the Hill Family Foundation (now entitled the Northwest Area Foundation).

Scholars visiting or investigating the microfilm library at Saint John's in the first years descended to the lower levels of the Alcuin Library to study the documents. In 1974 a grant of $540,000 from the Bush Foundation of Saint Paul enabled HMML to move from its cramped quarters to a new building known as the Bush Center. This two-level facility adjoining the Alcuin Library was designed by Marcel Breuer and Associates and affords 12,500 square feet of space for storage of films, catalog areas, and scholars' carrells, visitors' facilities, as well as administrative offices.[3]

Since spring, 1965, when the initial manuscript was photographed by the team pioneered by Father Oliver Kapsner, at the venerable Benedictine abbey of Kremsmuenster, which celebrated its 1200th year of foundation in 1978, HMML has been engaged in microfilming projects in Austria, Spain, Malta, Ethiopia, Germany, and Portugal. Dur-

[3]Dr. Plante has been assisted in cataloguing, responding to scholarly inquiries, and related services at HMML at different times during the period 1966-1984 by Mrs. Marianne Hansen, Administrative Assistant to the Director and Secretary; Fr. Wilfred Theisen, O.S.B., Assistant Director; Fr. Cloud Meinberg, O.S.B., Research Associate for Art; and Cataloguers Fr. Roland Behrendt, O.S.B., Dr. Getatchew Haile, Dr. William F. Macomber, Dr. Hope Mayo, Dr. Peter Jeffery, Sr. Mary Elizabeth Mason, O.S.B., Dr. Francis Swietek, John Philip Mulvaney, John Germain, Fr. Urban Steiner, O.S.B., Dr. Donald Yates, Fr. Gregory Sebastian, O.S.B., Lynn Bryce, Fr. Knute Anderson, O.S.B., Dr. Richard Gerberding, Dr. Thomas Amos, and Dr. William Ziezulewicz.

Fr. Oliver Kapsner, O.S.B., labored as first Field Director for seven years in Austria (1965-1972). He was succeeded by another monk of Saint John's Abbey, Fr. Urban Steiner, O.S.B., who completed filming operations in Austria (1973) and initiated the project in Spain. Between 1979 and 1983, Rev. William F. Lanahan, priest of the Diocese of Brooklyn, N.Y., served as HMML Field Director in Germany where work was concentrated on collections in Cologne and the Rhineland. In the spring and summer of 1983, Rev. Gunther Rolfson, O.S.B., and Rev. Wilfred Theisen, O.S.B., monks of St. John's Abbey, served for a while as field directors in Muenster during a period of transition. In late summer 1983, another monk of the abbey, Fr. Jonathan Fischer, O.S.B., assumed the mantle of Field Director on a permanent full-time basis, completing work in Muenster and carrying the project forward to Paderborn, Detmold and, now, Trier.

Local workers are always employed in each nation. All films have been processed by Eugene B. Power's University Microfilms, Inc.: the original negatives are deposited in vaults, a positive copy is donated to the host library or archives, and a positive copy is made available to all students in the Bush Center, Saint John's Abbey and University, Collegeville, Minnesota.

ing the years 1965-1973, more than 32,000 manuscripts belonging to seventy-six Austrian libraries were microfilmed.[4] The largest cooperating library in Austria was the Oesterreichische Nationalbibliothek in Vienna, where approximately 14,000 codices and 100,000 papyri fragments were microfilmed. Between 1973 and 1977, with Father Urban Steiner, O.S.B., leading the team, more than 6,000 manuscripts belonging to twenty-nine Spanish libraries and

---

[4]The Austrian collections include Admont, Altenburg, Bregenz (4 libraries: Kapuzinerkloster, Landesarchiv, Landesmuseum, Zisterzienserkloster Mehrerau), Bressanone-Brixen, Fiecht, Geras, Goettweig, Graz (8 libraries: Dioezesanarchiv, Dominikanerkonvent, Minoritenkonvent, Bischoefl. Ordinariat, Stadtpfarre zum Heiligen Blut, Steiermaerkisches Landesarchiv, Universitaetsbibliothek including the Ris Bibliothek Flaurling, Zentralbibliothek der Wiener Franziskanerprovinz), Guessing, Haus im Ennstall, Heiligenkreuz, Herzogenburg, Innsbruck (4 libraries: Servitenkloster, Tiroler Landesarchiv, Tiroler Landesmuseum, Universitaetsbibliothek), Klagenfurt (4 libraries: Bischoefl, Bibliothek, Kapuzinerkloster, Kaerntner Landesarchiv, Studienbibliothek), Klosterneuburg, Kremsmuenster, Burg Kreuzenstein bei Loebendorf, Lambach, Lilienfeld, Linz (5 libraries: Bibliotek der Phil.-Theol. Hochschule der Dioezese Linz, Bundesstaatliche Studienbibliothek, Museum der Stadt Linz, Oberoesterreichisches Landesmuseum, Oberoesterreichisches Landesarchiv), Maria Saal, Melk, Michaelbeuern, Neukloster zu Wiener Neustadt, Novacella (Neustift), Reichersberg, Rein, Salzburg (6 libraries: Erzbischoefl, Konsistorial Archiv, Museum Carolino-Augusteum, Nonnberg Abtei, Sankt Peter Erzabtei, Universitaetsbibliothek), Sankt Florian, Sankt Paul im Lavanttal, Sankt Poelten, Schlaegl, Schlierbach, Schwaz, Seitenstetten, Solbad Hall, Stams, Villach, Vorau, Wien (7 libraries: Dominikanerkloster, Haus-, Hof- und Staatsarchiv, Mechitaristenkongregation, Minoritenkonvent, Oesterreichische Nationalbibliothek, Schottenkloster, Universitaetsbibliothek), Wilhering, Wilten, Zwettl. See *Checklist of Manuscripts Microfilmed for the Monastic Manuscript Library, Saint John's University, Collegeville, Minnesota,* by Julian G. Plante, Vol. 1, 2 parts (Collegeville, 1967-1974). For a prospectus of out-of-print published and unpublished manuscript catalogues currently available in microfilm or Xerography, see *Catalogs of Manuscripts in Austrian Monasteries* (Ann Arbor, Mich.: Xerox University Microfilms, 1972). Catalogues published since manuscripts were microfilmed include: *Catalogue of Manuscripts in the Library of Stift Reichersberg,* by Julian G. Plante; "Institut de Recherche et d'Histoire des Textes. Bibliographies — Colloques — Travaux Préparatoires" (Paris: C.N.R.S., 1973); and Julian G. Plante, "Catalogue of Manuscripts in the Bibliothek der Phil.-Theol. Hochschule der Dioezese Linz" *Traditio* 32 (1976), 427-74. Microfilms of manuscripts from the Kollegialstiftsbibliothek Mattsee and from the Theresianischebibliothek Wien completed the Austrian corpus.

archives were photographed.[5] Also beginning in 1973 and continuing at present is a microfilm project in Malta. To date nearly 6,000 volumes of archival material belonging to the ecclesiastical archives of Malta at the Cathedral Museum in Mdina have been microfilmed.[6] During the

[5]The collections include Barcelona (5 libraries: Archivo Capitular de la Catedral, Archivo Diocesano, Archivo Episcopal, Biblioteca del Seminario Diocesano, Sant Pere de les Puel·les), Gerona (3 libraries: Archivo Capitular, Museo Diocesano, Seminario Diocesano), Huesca, Lérida, Madrid, Academia de la Historia (San Millan de Cogolla and San Pedro de Cárdeña fonds, the Abbeys of Montserrat, Pamplona, Poblet, Seo de Urgel, Silos, Solsona, Tarazona, Tarragona, Tarrasa, Toledo, Tortosa, Vallbona de las Monjas, Vich, Zaragoza (2 libraries: Biblioteca Capitular, Biblioteca del Real Seminario de San Carlos). See *Checklist of Manuscripts Microfilmed for the Hill Monastic Manuscript Library, Saint John's University, Collegeville, Minnesota*, by Julian G. Plante, vol. 2, part 1 (Ann Arbor, 1978), Spanish collections microfilmed.

[6]The three main *fonds* of the Cathedral Museum in Mdina include the Cathedral Archives (*Archivum Cathedrale Melitense*=ACM) containing the official records and administrative registers of the Cathedral Archives; the Inquisition Archives (*Archivum Inquisitionis Melitensis*=AIM) containing the correspondence, legal proceedings, and records of the Inquisitors in Malta both as judges in matters of faith and as diplomatic representatives of the Holy See; the Episcopal and Pro-Vicarial Archives (*Curia Episcopalis Melitensis*=CEM) containing 928 volumes of documents which throw new light on the religious, social, and economic history not only of the Maltese Islands but also on the Mediterranean world in general. They abound with references to Gozo, one of the Maltese islands, which has no records of its own before 1551. The various sections forming this third *fond*, CEM, are *Acta Originalia*, 464 volumes of 21,259 documents; *Conti Originalia*, 213 volumes of detailed accounts of the administration of the various churches and confraternities falling under the Pro-Vicar's jurisdiction. They are the old counterpart of the *Ufficio della Revisione* of the Archiepiscopal Curia and shed important new light on the artistic, religious, economic, and social history of Malta; *Bastardella* or *Protocollo Actorum Originalium* containing first notes jotted down by curia officials and later worked out into the full documents now forming the *Acta Originalia; Mandati*, decrees issued by the bishop and his vicars at the request of the respective procurators authorizing payments; *Citationes*, instructions given to the *alarius* to cite a particular person in the episcopal or pro-vicarial court: *Registers* contain full transcripts, important excerpts or brief summaries of the original documents preserved in the *Acta Originalia*, which break down into *Acta Civilia, Acta Criminalia, Supplicationes, Donationes, Monitorii, Cedulae*, and *Sententiae*. They also throw light on the original structure of the archives and of the curia itself. The CEM also includes 18 volumes entitled *Registrum Ordinandorum Privilegiorum Clericalium* listing ordained candidates with details of date and place of ordination, name of ordaining bishop, etc., documents relative to ordina-

period 1973-1977, a total of 7,573 manuscripts in Ethiopia in cooperation with the Divinity School of Vanderbilt University and the Ethiopian Manuscript Microfilm Library (= EMML) were microfilmed.[7] Microfilms of manuscript collections from Italy and England, acquired through purchase, are also represented at HMML.[8]

tions (*privilegia*), papal dispensations (*breve apostolicum dispensationis*), and permissions to candidates by their bishops to receive orders from another bishop (*litterae dimissoriales*).

Although filming in Malta was concentrated on the ecclesiastical archives of the Cathedral Museum in Mdina, other materials photographed include the musical archives in Mdina, 22 rare Arabic manuscripts in the library of the Franciscan Fathers in Valletta, 46 volumes of materials in the Archives of the parish church in Vittoriosa, 3 volumes from the library of the cloistered convent of Benedictine nuns of St. Peter's Abbey in Mdina, 4 volumes from the Crypta S. Pauli in Rabat. In addition to the manuscripts a certain number of published works by Maltese scholars or writers on Maltese history were filmed so that a coherent collection of materials for the study of Maltese (and Mediterranean) history and culture could be established. These included 152 publications of Dom Mauro Inguanez, O.S.B., 68 publications of Dom Daniel Call, O.P., 14 publications of Fr. Joseph Mizzi. Published guides to the Malta materials filmed include, *Handlist of the Episcopal and Pro-Vicarial Archives (Curia Episcopalis Melitensis or CEM Archives) at the Malta Cathedral Museum*, by Rev. John Azzopardi, "Handlist of the Ecclesiastical Archives at the Malta Cathedral Museum, Mdina," n. 1 (Collegeville, 1975). A register of 13 *codices manuscripti* and liturgical books microfilmed will be found on p. 54. See also *Archives of the Cathedral of Malta Misc. 32A: 1313-1529. The Study and Text of an Eighteenth-Century Index of Transcripts*, edited by Fr. John Azzopardi (with a study by Anthony Luttrell, on the earliest documents transcribed in the Cathedral Archives, Mdina: 1316-1372, and a compilation by Gian Battista Borg, on the text of Misc. 32A: Index Notitiarum: 1313-1529) (Zabbar, Malta, 1977).

[7]See *A Catalogue of Ethiopian Manuscripts Microfilmed for the Ethiopian Manuscript Microfilm Library, Addis Ababa and for the Monastic Manuscript Microfilm Library, Collegeville, Minnesota*, by William F. Macomber, vol. I: Project Nos. 1-300; vol. II: Project Nos. 301-700 (Collegeville, 1975-1976); vol. III: Project Nos. 701-1100 (Ann Arbor: Monograph Publishing on Demand, 1978). On the Ethiopian manuscript microfilm project, see the 20-page brochure *An Ethiopian Manuscript Microfilming Program; a joint venture of Vanderbilt University Divinity School...Hill Monastic Manuscript Library...and the Ethiopian Manuscript Microfilm Library* (Collegeville, 1976), available gratis from HMML.

[8]From Italy, 307 manuscripts from Subiaco, 65 manuscripts from the library of SS. Trinità di Cava de' Tirreni. From England, 226 manuscripts from Hereford Cathedral, 242 manuscripts from Lincoln Cathedral, 399 manuscripts and 30 volumes of the Registers of the Archbishops of Canterbury from the years 615 to

The original scope of HMML's microfilm operations was eventually expanded to include manuscript collections of other libraries and archives, whether of monastic provenance or not, when interest in participation in HMML's program became known. Similarily another of HMML's guiding principles — to include only *codices manuscripti* or the literary and historical type manuscripts in bound form dating before the year 1600 — was altered to permit the inclusion of archival documents and records of the administrative type and of manuscript materials dating after the year 1600 when deemed significant by the librarian or archivist of the collection and/or the HMML project director. The collections of manuscripts from Austria, Spain, and Malta particularly reflect these changes.

With papyri dating from the third century B.C. and the codices back to the fifth century A.D., the manuscript materials photographed to date reflect Western cultural, intellectual, social, political, and religious developments from classical antiquity to the early modern period. While manuscripts of the classical Greek and Latin authors (and subsequent commentaries thereon) are represented in the microfilm collections, the particular strength of HMML collections are manuscripts from the patristic and medieval periods. The literature of the Middle Ages in all its forms, from the earliest period to the Renaissance is the most representative for the Latin tradition. Medieval vernacular literature, though less strong, is an important part of the total collections, especially German and Spanish, and in the Austrian National Library are manuscripts in the other vernacular languages. Important for the social, political, diplomatic, and ecclesiastical history of Europe are the administrative records and documents of the archives in Austria, Spain, and Malta.

1645 from the Lambeth Palace, London, 197 manuscripts from Salisbury Cathedral and some 70 manuscripts from the Warden and Fellows' Library of Winchester College.

While most manuscripts are photographed in black and white, color microfilm is used for manuscripts containing miniatures and illuminations; when possible, two pages are photographed at once. Thus, for Austria the nearly 32,000 codices were microfilmed with 6,331,698 black and white exposures (12,663,396 pages) and 42,155 color exposures; for Spain, 6,206 codies required 1,182,152 black and white exposures (2,364,304 pages) and 8,984 color exposures.

In the years since 1966, which marked the beginning of HMML's cataloguing efforts, the emphasis has been upon cataloguing collections of manuscripts without printed catalogues or for which inadequate guides to the collections have been published. The procedure used at HMML is to analyze, catalogue, and classify each individual work within a manuscript on the basis of the following: author when identifiable, title, *incipit* (the beginning words of both intro- ductory material, e.g., scripture quotations, and the actual beginning words of the writer being copied), subject classifi- cation (usually more than one heading), scribe where known, and provenance where this can be established. Each entry bears the codex name, number, date, and HMML's identifying project number.

For Austria, approximately 21,400 manuscripts or 65.5% of the total filmed for HMML are accessible through good printed catalogues. Another 2,700-plus manuscripts or 8.3% of the total have been catalogued at HMML to date and more than 8,500 manuscripts or 26.2% of the total remain to be catalogued. For Spain, 1,635 manuscripts or 25.8% of the total filmed for HMML are accessible through printed catalogues. About 100 manuscripts or 1.5% of the total have been catalogued by HMML staff and 4,600 manuscripts or 72.7% still await cataloguing. Except for Reichersberg (12 Mss.) and the Bibliothek der Phil.-Theol. Hochschule der Dioezese Linz (11 Mss.) for which cata- logues prepared by HMML have been published, access to the collections is through a card catalogue which contains nearly 19,000 individual entries for the more than 5,000 manuscripts catalogued by the HMML staff.

Under a 1980 three-year grant of $120,000 from the Andrew W. Mellon Foundation, New York, HMML had available to it the services of two additional cataloguers who, in addition to carrying on original cataloguing, edited a vast body of material catalogued to date for publication. HMML began in 1981 to issue printed catalogues of the Latin and vernacular manuscript collections it has on film.

In addition to the three-volume published catalogue of 1,100 manuscripts in Ge'ez and Amharic microfilmed in Ethiopia, a fourth volume, covering another 400 manuscripts, all edited by Dr. Getatchew Haile, was published in 1979. For reasons of time and economy, subsequent volumes of the HMML-produced catalogue of Ethiopian manuscripts, beginning with vol. 5, took the form of an inventory with abbreviated descriptions; approximately 3,500 manuscripts have been inventoried in rough draft in this inventory form to date. A total of 3,500 manuscripts filmed to date remain to be catalogued.

For England, the libraries of Hereford, Lincoln, and Salisbury cathedrals and the Lambeth Palace in London have printed catalogues of their manuscript holdings. Cava and Subiaco, the two collections from Italy on microfilm in HMML, are likewise accessible through printed catalogues.

In addition to the card catalogue, sources of information on the microfilmed manuscripts derive from catalogues, inventories, shelflists, etc., sometimes published, sometimes not, of certain collections. An alphabetical index to these catalogues and inventories does not always exist. However, persons interested in the contents of a given collection will be able to consult these sources which are also present in HMML in reproduction. Inventory cards prepared by the leader of the photographic team and microfilmed at the head of the manuscript also provide some indication as to the contents of a given manuscript. This is particularly valuable for those collections which have neither catalogue nor inventory of their own. These inventory cards are available for consultation by scholars visiting HMML.

To accommodate the scholarly research of art historians and others interested in iconography in medieval manuscripts, a comprehensive analytical index of the miniatures and illuminations photographed in color was undertaken in September, 1968. The cataloguing system adopted is based on that of the Princeton Index of Christian Art. Each manuscript miniature, illumination, or other decorative piece is catalogued according to subject of illustration, author or title with subheadings used for artist, scribe, patron, owner, and century in which the manuscript was produced. These headings are supplemented by a brief description of the manuscript decoration and reference to pertinent bibliographical materials.

At present, some 500 codices containing over 11,000 color frames and representing 24 collections have been catalogued and indexed. During the summer of 1975, HMML's art cataloguer worked at the Index of Christian Art, Princeton University, a microfilm of the 30,000 cards of the Index's authority file and the editor's file was made. In an unprecedented gesture of good will, the Director of the Index, Dr. Rosalie Green, allowed HMML to obtain a copy of these files so as to ensure that HMML's cataloguing of manuscript illuminations would follow the Princeton norms as exactly as possible. Approximately 40,000 color frames of miniatures and illuminations from over 2,000 codices representing the holdings of 42 collections remain to be catalogued and indexed. Since the end of June, 1976, HMML's art cataloguer had to be furloughed for lack of funding.

From the beginning HMML has regarded the cataloguing of uncatalogued or inadequately catalogued manuscript collections as an integral part of making these primary source materials available to scholars. To aid the cataloguers, a collection of reference works and tools has been assembled. The collection of the printed catalogues of manuscripts belonging to the major and lesser known manuscript collections in the world already ranks with similar collections in major university and research libraries. As funds are available and as secondhand copies of catalogues appear in antiquarian and scholarly booksellers' lists, HMML makes a major effort to acquire catalogues which have long been out-of-print. Other strengths of the reference collection in HMML include standard works on paleography, manuscript painting and illumination, manuscript facsimiles, history of libraries, and critical editions of texts.

The creation of HMML's Index of Incipits, which now contains almost 800,000 entries, began as HMML undertook the cataloguing of its microfilmed manuscripts. Approximately 900 printed and handwritten sources are represented and have been systematically garnered; they include indices found in catalogues of manuscript collections, indices found in *opera omnia* and other critical editions in specialized monographs as they are received, articles in journals and *Festschriften*, wherever an *incipit* may be cited. Serial publications such as the *Monumenta Germaniae Historica*, Jaffé's *Regesta Pontificum Romanorum*, and Dreves' *Analecta Hymnica* are examples of types of series whose indices of *initia* have been collected.

No variety of text is excluded from the Index of Incipits, and texts in all western languages are included. The majority of texts are in Latin; however, approximately 100,000 Italian entries (principally extracted from Mazzatinti-Sorbelli) and smaller but valuable collections of *incipits* of texts in Dutch, French, German, Greek, Spanish, and other languages form separate parts of the Index.

Scholars are invited to make full use of HMML's resources by visiting or by corresponding. Questions regarding HMML's holdings or inquires about codicology may be resolved by consulting HMML's Index of Incipits and its codicological files. HMML provides answers to mail inquiries as well as preliminary surveys of the manuscript resources involved in carrying out various research projects.[9]

In November, 1969, Dr. George Fowler, professor emeritus of the University of Pittsburgh's Department of History, spoke for many visiting scholars when he said: "The progress at the HMML is unbelievable. I feel sure that this Institute is already the largest focus for scholarly research in medieval manuscripts in the United States in particular, and among the largest in the world."

Father Oliver Kapsner, O.S.B., stated from the field in 1970 where he was directing filming at the Oesterreichische Nationalbibliothek in Vienna: "My own humble opinion is that after we have finished the Austrian National Bibliothek (two more years) HMML will be second only to the Vatican Library as a focus for scholarly research into medieval manuscripts, having surpassed the British Museum in London, the Bibliothèque Nationale in Paris, and the Staatsbibliothek in Munich."

Visiting scholars, librarians, curators, and classics professors concur that after eighteen years of steady microfilming, cataloguing, endless trans-Atlantic communications, and the continued search for private funding, the St. John's microfilm project has become an international focal point for scholarly research.

Statistics attest to the volume and comprehensiveness of the work. In Austria, in the first seven years of operation more than thirty-two thousand manuscripts, antedating the invention of printing, were photographed at seventy-six

---

[9]Cf. Julian G. Plante, "The Hill Monastic Manuscript Library. Its Origins, Microfilmed Collections, and Activities," *Res Publica Litterarum, Studies in the Classical Tradition,* II (1979), 251-61. This complete account and analysis of HMML is the basic source for full information on the origins, support, resource development, microfilm operation, background, cataloguing activity, and availability of this unique deposit. Dr. Plante's summary of the nature and scope of HMML, along with on-going interviews, has been an invaluable source for this article.

monastic and allied libraries. At the Austrian National Library in Vienna, approximately fifteen thousand manuscripts were photographed. From Hungary, the first shipment of microfilmed manuscripts was sent on exchange to Collegeville in November, 1969, to be catalogued. Those who describe the vast file cabinets of microfilm inevitably ask their audience to visualize a highway. "Since one reel of film is 100 feet long, the photographed manuscripts collected in the HMML at St. John's are over 90 miles long," said a 1969 HMML report. "That means that by the spring of 1970, we had somewhere in the neighborhood of 7.5 million pages microfilmed."

By 1984 HMML has filmed over 62,000 manuscript books. More than 62,000 codices, 100,000 papyri, and countless archival units — totaling in excess of 21 million pages of documentation. Nearly all of it dates from before the invention of printing. In the brief span of eighteen years, HMML has evolved from a concept to a unique, international resource. As a matter of policy, HMML microfilms entire collections of manuscripts whenever possible. Most other similar libraries film selectively, often concentrating on a particular discipline.

Most recently, HMML joined in 1983 with Lutheran Brotherhood, Minneapolis, Minnesota, to cooperate wherever possible and when requested in microfilming documents relating to the Lutheran Reformation, the Catholic Counter-Reformation, and causes leading to the sixteenth-century reform movement in Christendom. The estimated volume of the Lutheran Brotherhood Reformation Research Library project over the next 25 years will be around seventy-five million additional pages of primary source material.

Recognition of its value as a cultural resource and its contribution in the form of services to the community of scholars and educators distinguishes HMML as an international research center. HMML's resources and discoveries have received attention in both print and non-print media, and an increasingly broad-based support from foundations, corporations, and individuals across the U.S. and abroad.

The unsettled conditions of the world today point to the importance and urgency of HMML's work. Political unrest in Ethiopia has forced HMML to curtail its filming operations there, hopefully only temporarily for, according to Fr. Godfrey Diekmann, O.S.B., a Saint John's liturgist and theologian, "the manuscript discoveries yet to be made in Ethiopia may rival, and perhaps even surpass, the importance of the Dead Sea Scrolls for an understanding of the New Testament Scriptures." HMML's record led former-Governor of Minnesota, Elmer L. Andersen, in 1974 to state that HMML is "the most significant historical achievement in this state in the 20th century."

Planning at HMML is conducted by the staff and members of the Board of Overseers in ongoing consultation with a Board of Consultants. Included among the consultants are some of the world's distinguished medievalists and Renaissance scholars.[10] Long-range microfilming plans include continued work in Germany, inauguration of filming in England, and increasing cooperation with Lutheran Brotherhood to film Reformation and Counter-Reformation materials worldwide. In its planning, HMML seeks to assure a degree of flexibility to enable its film teams to respond to unanticipated filming opportunities.

[10]Members of the Board of Overseers are: Fr. Colman Barry, O.S.B., Mr. Ronald Bosrock, Fr. Baldwin Dworschak, O.S.B., Dr. Sheila ffolliott, Fr. Ivan Havener, O.S.B., Dr. A. A. Heckman, Mr. Ronald Hubbs, Mr. Joseph S. Micallef (chairman), Mr. Malcolm MacDonald, Mr. John E. Pellegrene, Ms. Sally Pope, Rabbi Bernard Raskas, Sr. Helen Rolfson, O.S.F., Dr. Alison Stones, Mr. Donald Volkmuth.

Members of the Board of Consultants are: Mr. John S. Borden (Columbia University); Prof. Virginia Brown (Pontifical Institute of Mediaeval Studies, Toronto); Prof. Marvin Colker (University of Virginia); Prof. John J. Contreni (Purdue University); Prof. David C. Lindberg (University of Wisconsin, Madison); Prof. Roger E. Reynolds (Pontifical Institute of Mediaeval Studies, Toronto); Prof. Richard H. Rouse (University of California, Los Angeles); Prof. Robert Somerville (Columbia University).

Cataloguing continues to be an equally important challenge. Uncatalogued microfilm is of limited use to scholars. A continuing high priority will be the seeking of funds to enable the pace of cataloguing not only to continue but to accelerate.

Numerous benefactors in addition to the Northwest Area Foundation made the extensive HMML project a reality: the National Endowment for the Humanities, Bush Foundation, Andrew W. Mellon Foundation, the Minnesota Council of the Knights of Columbus, F. R. Bigelow Foundation, Raskob Foundation for Catholic Activities, the Xerox Corporation Educational Fund, O'Neil Foundation, Alice M. O'Brien Foundation, George A. MacPherson Fund, St. Vincent Archabbey, Tinker Foundation, Grace Foundation, various Weyerhaeuser Family Foundations, Charles Horn, Minneapolis, as well as other individual contributors known as the "Friends of HMML," and anonymous donors. Since the project's beginning in 1964, over $4,500,000 has been donated by some fifty foundations and over five hundred individuals. Support has also been received from foreign foundations including Germany's Fritz Thyssen Stiftung and the Evangelische Kirche in Deutschland Kirchlicher Entwicklungsdienst [KED], Portugal's Calouste Gulbenkian Foundation, and Spain's Comité Conjunto Hispano-Norteamericano para Asuntos Educativos y Culturales.

An annual lecture series featuring prominent scholars began in October, 1968, including Dr. Paul Oskar Kristeller, professor emeritus of philosophy at Columbia University; Dr. Sesto Prete, research scholar at the Vatican Library and professor of classics at the University of Kansas; the late Professor Rudolph Arbesmann, O.S.A., Fordham University; and Professor Giles Constable, Harvard University.

Since HMML was established, there has been a steady increase in the number of scholars using the facilities. Visiting researchers to HMML during the years 1975-78, for example, included 254 individuals. This number is accelerating as HMML becomes better known through the United States, Canada, Australia, and Europe, and as its research holdings expand. The majority of scholars who come to use the facilities of HMML stay more than one day. And increasing numbers are coming back for further research as they recognize its value to their respective projects. There were 1,464 queries from 434 individuals in this three-year period.

Forty-two lectures and presentations were made to visiting classes and tour groups. Most of these groups are classes from colleges and universities in the Midwest and provinces of Canada. Graduate and undergraduate students in such disciplines as theology, art, music, philosophy, history of science, languages, and the humanities in general comprise these groups. A total of 4,342 registered persons (walk-in visitors, group tours, and presentations for individuals) were hosted during the same three years. Over 12,000 persons visited HMML quarters between October, 1966, when the guestbook was first presented, and June 30, 1978; of this number, 9,876 signed the guest register.

Typical of the steadily growing interest in the collection was an article by Kenneth A. Briggs in the New York *Times*, August 12, 1979, on the potential primary sources of the early Church to be found in the Ethiopian collection still in progress:

"The mountainous regions of northern Ethiopia are dotted with hundreds of monasteries, many of them chiseled from solid rock centuries ago. If experts here are right, the monasteries are a storehouse of ancient manuscripts that could greatly alter prevailing views of early Christianity.

"The Coptic church of Ethiopia was founded about A.D. 400 by missionaries from Syria who made their way through Egypt. The Rev. Godfrey Diekmann, a Benedictine monk and a professor of early church history at St. John's University here, believes that invaluable texts of Ethiopian Christianity have been preserved because of several factors.

"These include a penchant of Ethiopian monks for insuring the longevity of texts by using nonperishable materials; the extreme care generally given to sacred documents throughout the Ethiopian church; the dryness of the climate, which would offer another form of protection, and the uninterrupted developments of the country.

"With that belief, Father Diekmann and his colleagues at St. John's are seeking access to the the remote monasteries, as part of the university's long-range goal of microfilming manuscripts tucked away in monastic libraries in Europe and Africa for the last 1,000 years.

"As scholars pore over the writings that have already been microfilmed, which cover subjects including music, astronomy, military tactics and medicine in addition to the tomes of theology, views of the Christian past and of the Middle Ages are being challenged.

"Since 1965, more than 50,000 manuscripts have been microfilmed, catalogued and filed in uniform, numbered rows in a wing of the university library under the guidance of a staff of scholars and librarians.

"While most of the Christian world was disrupted by the Seventh Century Islamic invasions around the rim of the Mediterranean, Ethiopia went unscathed. Therefore, Father Diekmann said, 'the hundreds of manuscripts' kept and revered by the monks are likely to be the 'last untouched reservoir of Christian writing in the world.'

"Many writings of such seminal thinkers as Melito of Sardis, who died about A.D. 160, are referred to by the first major church historian, Eusebius, but have never been found. Ethiopia is considered the last possible repository for copies of these works.

"Six thousand manuscripts from the area around Addis Ababa have been microfilmed, but the northern sources have yet to be examined. So far, the most distinct discovery is a Bible from the 14th or 15th century, the oldest complete set of Scriptures known to exist in Ethiopia. It was found in the pocket of a monk who reportedly knew nothing of its value.

"The purpose of the project, which was begun in 1965, is to insure that the contents of irreplaceable documents do not succumb to the ravages of natural or military disaster and the avarice of unscrupulous scholars.

"Several recent cases have underscored the risks. In 1966, floods in Florence, Italy, destroyed some texts as did the fire that swept the monastery on Mount Athos in Greece in 1968.

"Dr. Julian G. Plante, Director of the project, steers a delicate course in his attempts to convince abbots and others in charge of monastic libraries that the benefits of making copies of the manuscripts far surpass any liabilities. 'Some think it is cultural exploitation,' Dr. Plante said in his library office. 'They're afraid to lose control over their own heritage. My point is that we are helping to preserve their heritage.'

"Through tact and assurance that the documents will be treated with utmost care, the project staff has won permission to photograph materials in 18 nations. In the most extensive project, in Austria, 30,000 manuscripts, the known total, were filmed in seven years under the supervision of the Rev. Oliver Kapsner, a St. John's monk who has been a professional librarian since 1925.

"With heavy support from foundations the project spent $3 million in its first 10 years. The working pace has steadily picked up, and each week 30 new rolls of film arrive to be catalogued.

"Sorting the manuscripts is often a slow, painstaking job. At present, for example, Dr. Hope Mayo, a medieval scholar who catalogues Western manuscripts, is in the final stages of a long effort to classify the contents of the Herzogenburg monastery in lower Austria. The collection, from the 15th century, is fairly typical of those found in the region, and consists mostly of sermons, biblical concordances, limited word dictionaries and treatises on church law.

"As the microfilm collection grows, an increasing number of scholars come to St. John's to conduct research. About

100 researchers are expected to arrive this year to study a wide variety of topics. Among those this week was Merritt Nequette, an instructor at the College of St. Thomas in St. Paul, Minn., whose doctoral thesis on the music manuscripts of Melk monastery in Austria was based on the availability of all the relevant manuscripts at St. John's."

Current 1984 on-going activities by HMML's field microfilming teams, twenty years after the project's inception, are taking place in Germany, Portugal, and Malta. In Germany the documents' exposure rate is on the average 15,000 pages a month. Copying is currently centered in the diocesan libraries and archives of Trier, ancient Roman outpost and first Christian community in Germany which this year is celebrating its 2,000th anniversary of its founding as a city in 16 B.C. In Portugal around 7,500 pages a month are microfilmed and the National Archives have been completed in Lisbon. In the period from January to June 1984 some 1,500 manuscripts have been preserved on film. Two new volumes in the Library's series of *Descriptive Inventories* are in progress; they treat the collections of the Austrian Abbeys of Fiecht and Herzogenburg; the eighth volume of *A Catalogue of Ethiopian Manuscripts* appeared in February, 1985.

Control Data Corporation, Bloomington, Minn., has contributed one of its Cyber 114 Computers to HMML which will expedite cross references and early catalogue identification of the extensive collection. This generous grant of computer hard and software is a major addition to the process of more rapidly serving the requests of scholars and students.

John Tracy Ellis directed and inspired student researchers and teachers both in his classes, addresses, and voluminous writings to hand on carefully and honestly the heritage of our common culture. His example has been a formative and positive source of the intellectual renewal in the contemporary American Catholic Church. One of the derivative and more lasting effects of Ellis' efforts will be the inspiration he gave to the development of this collection by so many dedicated persons. HMML has grown to be the single largest and most comprehensive center of pre-1600 manuscript books and papyri on microfilm in the world. It transcends national and sectarian boundaries. It is a really catholic collection for all students which is still growing and developing. This is what Ellis always taught that the word "catholic" means.

Women in Post-Conciliar Rome: *Evangelica Testificatio* and the International Union of Superiors General

Joan Bland, S.N.D.

The vision of Vatican II inspired, among other things, a desire in many quarters that the universal character of the Church be more visibly and realistically reflected in its government and in the life of its Roman center. Paul VI's determined effort to internationalize was most dramatically reflected in the two conclaves of 1978. It was his appointment of unprecedented numbers of cardinals from the Third World that made these conclaves unique and, probably, made the election of John Paul II possible. In fact, from the outset, Paul had moved to promote international and intercultural communication in the Church's life. A significant but little published example of this policy is the establishment of the International Union of Superiors General of Women's Institutes on December 8, 1965, the day the

Second Vatican Council officially completed its work.[1] Earlier, in 1955, when the Union of Superiors General of masculine religious institutes was formed, the term "international" was not used. It is still the difference which, in common Roman parlance, distinguishes the two groups — the *I*.U.S.G., and the *U*.S.G.[2]

Actually, the women's union is much more international than the men's, partly as a consequence of the tendency of women religious missionaries to initiate local and ultimately independent institutes in the countries where they serve and of the preference in many groups for smaller congregations, so that they divide deliberately as numbers grow. Leadership is often indigenous and most of the women's generalates are not in Rome but spread out over all the continents. These are also among the reasons for the phenomenon of more than 2,000 independent (of each other) institutes of religious women in today's Church.[3]

Ecclesiae Sanctae, issued by the Postconciliar Commission on Religious Life in 1966, presumed associations of the major superiors of religious institutes on both national and international levels.[4] Most of the national conferences, as well as the Union of Superiors General of men (known until 1967 as the "Roman Union of Superiors General") and, for a few months, the International Union of Superiors General of women, were in fact functioning by the time it was published. For the women's union, the Sacred Congregation for Religious had appointed the first president, Mother

[1] Interview with Mother Maria del Rosario Araño, R.J.M., first president of the I.U.S.G., Rome, October 11,1983.

[2] Xeroxed history of the Union of Superiors General, circulated from their headquarters on Via dei Penitenzieri, Rome, March 1, 1979.

[3] Interview with Sister Mary Linscott, S.N.D., Rome, October 13,1983.

[4] *Ecclesiae Sanctae*, in Austin Flannery, O.P., ed., *Vatican Council II, The Conciliar and Post Conciliar Documents* (New York, 1975), 633, paragraph 42.

Maria del Rosario Araño, the Spanish superior general of the Religious of Jesus and Mary, and, as vice-presidents, Mother Felicia Pastoors, of the Ursulines of the Roman Union, and Mother Marie-Paul Bord, of the Soeurs Hospitalières de St. Paul de Chartres.[5] Mother Rosario gave the union what seems to have been generally recognized as excellent leadership[6] until the election of Sister Mary Linscott, the English superior general of the sisters of Notre Dame de Namur, in the fall of 1970. Because the work required a sophisticated understanding of the facts of financial life in Italy, Mother Pasqualina Monti of the Suore di Carità dell'Immacolata Concezione d'Ivrea served as treasurer. From the beginning she and her successors enjoyed the highly competent assistance of Sister Grazia Forleo of the same congregation, who, before embracing religious life, had served as assistant mayor of an Italian town.[7] The secretariat was entrusted to Mère Françoise de Lambilly, who was summoned for the purpose from her post as secretary general of the Society of the Sacred Heart. As assistant (ecclesiastical adviser), the Congregation for Religious chose Father Armand-François Le Bourgeois, Superior general of the Eudist Fathers, who later became Bishop of Autun. He was succeeded by the Reverend Edward Heston, of the Holy Cross Fathers, who was soon to become secretary for the Sacred Congregation for Religious. In 1969 the Reverend Paolo Molinari, postulator general of the Jesuits, succeeded Father Heston.

In the beginning the IUSG rented quarters on Via Pomponio Leto with money provided chiefly by congregations from the more affluent countries.[8] The new officers saw

[5] Interview with Mother Araño.
[6] Interview with Sister Linscott.
[7] *Ibid.*
[8] Interview with Mother Araño.

their responsibility as being especially to the numerous and fast-growing institutes in the developing areas. Many of these had no way of obtaining postconciliar education even for their leaders. Yet they too were obliged to organize renewal chapters and undertake all the complex adaptations inspired or mandated by *Ecclesiae Sanctae* and *Renovationis Causam*.[9]

Soon the IUSG was outgrowing its quarters, as also was Regina Mundi, a theological school in Rome planned especially for Sisters. When a large and excellent facility, adequate for the needs of both projects and ideally located just across the Tiber from the Castel Sant' Angelo, became available, the Mothers General acted promptly. The sale of Regina Mundi's outgrown facilities and a loan on which the IUSG could maintain interest payments sufficed for initial costs. When the building was ready for the Sisters' occupancy, Pope Paul VI came in person to bless it for their use.[10]

According to Mother Rosario, the Union enjoyed complete freedom of operation from the beginning, even though the original initiative came from the Sacred Congregation for Religious. Specifically for communication between that dicastery and the two unions, *Ecclesiae Sanctae* had mandated[11] the Council of Sixteen. Its membership consists of eight superiors general of men and eight of women, who meet with the staff of the Congregation on the last Friday of each month. After a somewhat sporadic beginning, it has functioned effectively since 1972.[12]

The IUSG structure, though twice modified, has always reflected its global constituency. Membership consists of the superiors general of all apostolic institutes of women; its

[9]*Ibid.*

[10]*Ibid.*

[11]*Ecclesiae Sanctae*, 42.

[12]USG brochure, 1979. Verified in interview with Sister Linscott.

general assembly, which includes representatives of every country in which there are members, is designed to "orient" the union; the general council implements the policies made by the assembly. It is composed of the executive committee, resident in Rome, and approximately 30 councillors, chosen for very broad geographical representation. The executive committee consists of the president, vice president, six councillors, the executive secretary, and the treasurer, all of them residing in Rome, but with only the executive secretary serving full time. The executive committee is responsible for carrying out the decisions of the general council and for setting up the commissions necessary for its work. The secretariat has always been staffed by sisters from member institutes, with work divided by language groups. Its quarterly *Bulletin* appears in English, French, Italian, Spanish, German, and Dutch. In the earlier years the sisters serving in the secretariat worked without compensation. Their time was a contribution of their institutes.

The ongoing work of the union involves communication, research, and reflection. It represents religious women not only to the Sacred Congregation for Religious, but also to other pontifical congregations and international bodies. It has cooperated more or less effectively according to their interest level with the national conferences of major superiors of women's institutes.[13]

The first challenge of the new group was simply to find out who and where the institutes of religious women in the world were. Most of this information came from the Sacred Congregation for Religious. From the beginning, possibly the IUSG's most important ongoing service has been to congregations in the Third World. Ways are found to enable

---

[13]*Statutes of the IUSG,* 2nd rev. ed. (Rome, 1977). In the United States of America, the Conference of Major Superiors of Women is known as the Leadership Conference of Women Religious.

their leaders to attend assemblies in Rome, and various projects to counteract their isolation are encouraged.[14]

The USG and the 'Motu Proprio'

As the IUSG was developing its life and structures with enthusiasm and success, clouds were gathering on the horizons of religious life. Perhaps they looked more ominous from Rome's vantage point than from any other. The understaffed offices of the Sacred Congregation for Religious and Secular Institutes (SCR) were deluged with indult applications, as, in the years after the Council, hordes of religious left their institutes. At the same time admission of candidates to religious orders declined drastically. It is not remarkable that a Pope as sensitive and conscientious as Paul VI became more and more concerned. However, it seems to have been on the initiative either of Père René Voillaume, founder and superior general of the Little Brothers of Jesus, or of the Sacred Congregation of Religious itself that a *motu proprio* about religious life was prepared for the Pope's signature.[15] The decision to undertake this work was made sometime prior to May, 1969, when Father Edward Heston, C.S.C., the American procurator general of the Holy Cross Fathers and the ecclesiastical "assistant" for the IUSG, became secretary of the Congregation for Religious.[16] The Cardinal Prefect was still Ildebrando Antoni-

[14]*I.U.S.G. Bulletin,* (Rome 1966), Vol. 1, No. 1.

[15]The minutes of the Presidency Council (Executive Committee) of the I.U.S.G. for November 16, 1970, include a report of the visit of Sister Mary Linscott, S.N.D., President, and Sister Marie-Paule Chauvin, S.F.B., to Cardinal Jean Villot, Papal Secretary of State. He told them that Père Voillaume seemed to have taken the initiative, "perhaps at the request of the Sacred Congregation for Religious."

[16]Germain-Marie Lalande, C.S.C., superior general of Holy Cross, "Memorandum to Father Enrico Systermans, SS.C.C., Secretary of the U.S.G.," dated simply September, 1971, U.S.G. Archives, 9 Progetto *Evangelica Testificatio.*

utti. His old friend, Mother Rosario, had almost finished her term as IUSG president and Sister Mary Linscott would be elected in the fall to replace her.[17]

When, that same autumn, a group of American religious came to Rome to confer with officers of the Congregation for Religious, Father Heston indicated to them that a text was being prepared. The reaction, especially among the women, was very negative; rumors began to fly and anxiety mounted.[18] *Ecclesiae Sanctae* was only three years old and it had provided for a period of experimentation of about twelve years in each religious community.[19] Fears that the impending document would somehow rescind this mandate, or curtail efforts to honor it, were rife. Opinion among many of the leaders of religious orders was strongly negative. In the winter, at a meeting of the Council of Sixteen, Father Heston was asked directly whether such a document was being prepared. Aware by then of the strength of the opposition, he replied evasively,[20] but the rumors continued.

On August 13, 1970, Father Heston called the members of the Council of Sixteen to a meeting. Because notice was short, because many superiors general, especially of women, spend much of their time in travel to areas where their members live, and because, in any case, Rome is left largely to tourists in August, only five men and two women attended. The Secretary gave the members present a text of fifty-seven pages, which they were to return to him after ten days' consideration without keeping a copy.[21] Soon after his

[17]Eligibility for I.U.S.G. office, except for the executive secretary, depends on service as the superior general of an institute. Mother Araño disqualified herself because her term was soon to expire.

[18]Lalande, "Memorandum to Systermans," 1.

[19]*Ecclesiae Sanctae,* 6.

[20]Lalande,"Memorandum to Systermans," 1.

[21]This injunction seems to have been obeyed, since no copy of this version could be located in the U.S.G. archives.

arrival at the Congregation for Religious, he told them, a commission had been established under his presidency to prepare this document. The commission had first met on June 3, 1969, and had held at least thirty meetings since that time. He was now consulting the Council of Sixteen about the "5e" version.

After considerable hesitation, Father Heston read the names of at least some members of the commission to the group. They included a Cistercian, a Benedictine, a Carmelite, two Dominicans, a Redemptorist, a monk of La Grande Chartreuse, an Augustinian, the Jesuit secretary of the Commission for the Reform of Canon Law, and Father Voillaume. But Father Germain Lalande, C.S.C., was convinced that the real leadership of the commission was exercised by Father Dorio Maria Huot, S.M.M., the undersecretary of the Sacred Congregation.[22]

Inevitably the Council of Sixteen, consisting chiefly of the leaders of apostolic religious institutes, objected to the heavily monastic composition of the commission. People who attended USG meetings were conspicuously absent from the list. But Father Heston answered that the text had been reviewed by theologians such as Yves Congar, O.P., Henri de Lubac, S.J., and Karl Rahner, S.J. He said that at the beginning of June the Holy Father had ordered the Sacred Congregation to proceed with consultations. They had sent the draft to some of the Episcopal conferences, with responses due by July 31. Not all had replied and among those who did, some found the document too long and others found it incomplete. In any case, Father Heston said, the text was almost ready for publication. The commission would meet August 25. After the comments of the Council of Sixteen had been considered, in the beginning of September, they would proceed with the translation. Those

22Lalande, "Memorandum to Systermans," 4.

present were to study the text under the greatest secrecy, though experts and councillors serving with the Superiors General in attendance could be consulted as also some Superiors General who were not present.[23]

Father Constantino Koser, O.F.M., Vice-President of the USG, asked if women religious could not be represented on the commission. Father Heston, obviously embarrassed, said they could not be, because the time had not yet come. To a similar question about brothers, the secretary replied that it had not been possible to ask any at the time when the commission was established.[24]

The Council of Sixteeen (or its August remnant) had until the 24th to respond. During those ten difficult August days the USG leaders worked with whoever was in town and could stay there. When Father Lalande heard that Rembert Weakland, abbot primate of the Benedictines and a member of the Council of Sixteen, was back in Rome, he shared the text with him, finding that, monastic as it was, it was not satisfactory to the abbot either.[25]

For the fact that they had a strong and very thorough text ready for the SCR by the 25th, Father Lalande gave special credit to Frère Michel Sauvage, a Christian Brother who represented Brother Charles Henry Buttimer, their superior general and a leader in USG affairs.[26] Because they could not contact the leaders of the IUSG, the Council of Sixteen met without them and sent their critique to the SCR, and also directly to the Pope, in the name of the USG only. Probably most religious would now see this as a providential development, because it led to the separate and ultimately decisive consultation with the IUSG.

[23] *Ibid.*, 2
[24] *Ibid.*
[25] *Ibid.*
[26] *Ibid.*

On August 27, Koser, Lalande, and Buttimer met with Cardinal Jean Villot, the Pope's Secretary of State.[27] They were very eager indeed to prevent the publication of the document they had reviewed.

On September 19, Lalande met with Père Voillaume and learned that he was content with the USG criticism, even though he did not agree with everything in it. He was not satisfied with the text he had worked on, in the version the USG had received on August 13.

In October the SCR called Lecuyer, Koser, and Brother Guzman Basilio Ruedo, superior general of the Marist Brothers, to work with the commission which had prepared a new text since the USG criticism. The meeting went on for a week in early November, 1970, and, during that time, the USG members convened the Council of Sixteen twice, November 3 and November 7. But the meetings of the new commission proved difficult. Minds did not seem to meet. Afterward a new text was prepared, but the three superiors general who had been consulted were not kept informed about it.[28]

The IUSG and 'Sequela Christi'

Brother Charles Henry, meanwhile, had informed Sister Mary Linscott about the document, and she was aware of its contents. In November she and one of the IUSG councillors, Soeur Marie-Paule Chauvin, superior general of the Sisters of the Holy Family of Bordeaux, sought an appointment with Cardinal Villot to request an audience with the Holy Father. They hoped to prevent the publication which seemed imminent. The Secretary of State received them on Sunday, November 15, at 6 p.m. When they expressed their

[27]Lalande, "Memorandum for the U.S.G. Records," August 28, 1970.
[28]Lalande, "Memorandum to Systermans," 4.

concern, the Cardinal told them that many had asked for such a document. He told them something of its history, essentially as it appeared in Lalande's memorandum, adding the information that it was already in print before the Holy Father was told of its existence. He had received his own copy from Père Voillaume. Personally, he was not wholly in agreement with the contents, but neither did he approve of the "too aggressive" criticisms of some of the fathers general. In the end, the Holy Father had not given them an audience. He told the Sisters that the document presented orientations rather than directives, and that the second version was already in print and would soon be published.

The Sisters pointed out that they had not been consulted and that it might not be well received. In any case, at a time when the renewal was in mid-course, a document seemed inopportune. The Cardinal replied that he expected to see the Holy Father the next morning, since he was to accompany him to the Food and Agriculture Organization. The Cardinal thought he would call Father Heston and tell him to give them the text.

On balance, the Sisters reported to the other members of the IUSG Executive that their visit had both positive and negative aspects. On the positive side their conversation had taken place in an atmosphere of confidence and sympathy; they had been assured that they would be consulted; they had been able to discuss frankly the contemporary situation of religious life and the difficulty of communicating with the SCR; they had been informed of the progress of the work on the document; they had learned how they should proceed with the Holy Father. He wanted a written report, and it would be necessary to present a letter about their desiderata, even if an audience were to be granted. They had become aware of the complaints that had reached the Secretariat of State about the need of directives from the Holy See.

On the negative side, they noted a certain hardening of the Cardinal's attitude when the authority of Rome seemed to be touched or when he considered the possibility of a large consultation of Sisters. They realized also that they should not insist on the necessity of an audience with the Holy Father.[29]

A week passed after this interview before word came from the SCR. Meanwhile Sister Mary Linscott had urgent business in the United States of America and she left Rome on November 19. Aware that her business in Rome was still more urgent, and determined that her absence would not deprive the IUSG of the opportunity to be heard, she instructed her generalate to call her immediately if this summons came. It came on Monday, November 23, for a meeting to be held on Tuesday, December 1. When this message was relayed, she asked whether the SCR had called the whole Executive Committee, insisting that she could not come to Rome unless this was done. Investigation revealed that the only other member who had been included was Mother Georgiana Segner, superior general of the School Sisters of Notre Dame. When Father Heston was told that Sister Mary would return only if the whole executive committee was called, he explained that the consultation was personal. In the end, however, since she continued to decline attendance on that basis, the whole executive committee was called to the December 1 meeting. Like the USG they had ten days to respond to the document they were given. They were asked to submit both a group critique and individual ones. Regarding the situation as serious, they decided to call the whole IUSG Council, and, on this incredible notice, 23 superiors general gathered from five continents to work together in Rome.

The whole of the executive committee, based in Rome, participated. Besides Sister Mary Linscott, they included Sisters Marguerite Marie Gonçalves, the Portuguese super-

---

[29]Minutes of the I.U.S.G.Presidency Council, November 16, 1970.

ior general of the Marymont Sisters who was Vice President of the IUSG; Marie-Paule Chauvin, who had been at the audience with Cardinal Villot; Marie Josée Dor, of the White Sisters of Africa; Georgiana Segner, S.S.N.D., who had been called for a personal consultation; Maria Teresa Astray, Mercedarian Missionary of Berriz; Romanus Fitzmaurice, Marist; Pasquela Monti, Immaculate Conception of Ivrea; and Françoise de Lambilly, the able and vigorous executive secretary, who belonged to the Society of the Sacred Heart.

Literally from the ends of the earth came the regional councillors — from Zaire, Kenya, Brazil, Argentina, Chile, Lebanon, Germany, Spain, France, Ireland, Italy. The United States of America was represented by Sisters Margaret Brennan, of the Monroe, Michigan Sisters of the Immaculate Heart; Eucharia Malone of the Sisters of Mercy of Burlingame, California; and Thomas Aquinas Carroll (now known as Elizabeth Carroll) of the Sisters of Mercy of Pittsburgh. From many areas the top leadership seems to have responded. Sister Aida Lopez, for example, was president of the Argentine National Union and vice president of the Conference of Latin American Religious. The Councillors came at short notice, from demanding work, at their own expense. No one could fail to realize how deeply they cared.[30]

What of the document they came to review? Although it bore the same Latin title, *Sequela Christi,* and was written in French, it was clearly not the same document the USG had struggled with in August. It was eighty pages, not counting notes, as compared with the fifty-seven Father Lalande had found long. It must have been somewhat affected by USG criticism, but because the first version could not be found in the USG archives, it is impossible to make a comparison.

---

[30]"Ont eu projet de document pour la S.C.R.: personnes qui sont venues pour contribuer au travail," I.U.S.G.Archives: Presidency Council.

Happily, the version of *Sequela Christi* which the twenty-three women of the IUSG Council assembled to consider is in their archives, both in the original French and in an English translation made hastily, but accurately, at the generalate of the School Sisters of Notre Dame for the benefit of critics who could not easily deal with the French. The corporate response and some of those prepared by individuals are also available. A comparison of the text they received with the apostolic exhortation, *Evangelica Testificatio,* finally released on June 29, 1971, and of the differences between the two texts, with their recommendations should provide some measure of their achievement.

In their report, after three paragraphs of reasons why no text at all should appear, the IUSG councillors state that to this one they have a "unanimous" reaction. Even "the recognition of some 'good' passages did not succeed in dispelling an uneasy feeling 'because' although there are numerous quotations from Council documents, the conciliar atmosphere is missing." Furthermore the text is too long. It is not inspiring. "There is no apparent unity, progression, or harmony of thought. Even where there is a direct reference to concrete situations, there is no vitality in handling them. The style lacks simplicity and warmth; the grave didactic tone seems very unusual today."[31]

The Church in 'Sequela Christi'

The report proceeds to an analysis of the reasons for these immediate reactions. The conciliar atmosphere does not appear, they insist, in the treatment of the Church, even where the term "People of God" is used. For example, in the

---

[31] "Rapport de l'étude du texte 'À la suite du Christ dans état religieux' par les membres du conseil de l'U.I.S.G.," December 9, 1970, I.U.S.G. Archives: Presidency Council.

course of admonishing the episcopate to give religious "pastoral aid," the document refers to the People of God: "More than ever all those who compose the People of God ought to try to understand and to esteem and help one another mutually."[32] Again, in the context of *Lumen Gentium,* the phrase appears: "It is a fact worthy of attention that the council places the question of religious life in the constitution *Lumen Gentium* precisely in the context of the call of all the People of God to holiness."

The IUSG critique acknowledged the effort made in *Sequela Christi* to deal with complementarity of vocations, but found it unsatisfactory. "These states of life [religious and married]," we are told in the SCR document, "while not being on the same plane, are complementary, and equally necessary for the full manifestation of the mystery of the Church. Every baptised person belongs already to a new world built on the glorified Christ." Nevertheless, we are reminded, "He who is engaged in terrestrial tasks cannot identify his life with all the values of the eschatological Christian as profoundly as can he who, by renouncing this world, dedicates his life entirely to the risen Christ so that he may prefigure the Kingdom to come."[33]

The councillors objected to what they considered to be over-emphasis on the hierarchical Church, which teaches and judges, and a relative disregard of the "evolution of charisms."[34] But, *Sequela Christi* insists, "it is the work of the Church to judge charisms and the forms of religious life which they inspire."[35] The IUSG critics considered the treatment of religious consecration one-sided in its emphasis on

---

[32]Sacred Congregation for Religious and Secular Institutes, Schema, *Sequela Christi,* 12, I.U.S.G. Archives.

[33]*Ibid.,* 21

[34]"Rapport," 1.

[35]*Sequela Christi,* 8.

the authority function of the Church. "The Church," according to *Sequela Christi*, receives these vows, "accepting them in virtue of the power which she holds from Christ and in his name, and confirms the special consecration which flows from them."

There is no evidence that the IUSG councillors denied the theological validity of the congregation's draft. Their quarrel was with its emphases and the magisterial character of expressions used.[36]

Relationship between the Church and the World

The Church, according to the Council, as interpreted by the assembled mothers general, "is the Church in the world and for the world; the presence of God in the midst of men."[37] In contrast they found the document they had assembled to review reflected "an attitude which is dualistic, negative, mistrusting, and pessimistic toward the world." They complained that "the text seems to show little understanding of the ambiguity and natural weakness of our human condition and insufficient concern for giving guidance in reading the signs of the times in this ambiguity."

Sequela Christi did, in fact, make what comes through as a rather painstaking effort to deal with the various connotations of the term "world," but it gave more than twice as much space to the negative connotation as to the positive. The IUSG evaluation concludes that "right through these pages, one perceives a dualistic anthropology which does not harmonize much with *Gaudium et Spes,* even though there are references to it." The passage here referred to represents the type of mini-essay, devoted to interesting but not directly relevant subjects, which helped to make the

[36]"Rapport," 3.
[37]*Ibid.,* 1.

document so much longer. It was about socialization and the danger it poses to the individual person and his autonomy.

At the end of the section, the writers point out that the demands of God's love "urge Christians to a more perfect realization of the ecclesial community and of the fraternal human society," and then add, rather apologetically, that "this remark is not without consequences for the religious life."[38]

Religious Life and the Council

The core of the IUSG's objection to the text of *Sequela Christi* was of course its approach to religious life itself. They did not mince words:

> Religious life is seen in the Council documents as being dynamic, the response to a personal call, deeply embodied in the People of God, taking various forms, closely linked to the mystery of life and holiness of the Church. However, the document presents an approach to the theology of religious life which is primarily abstract and which is not relevant to many of the different ways in which this life has evolved.

The criticism conceded some merit in the document, but always with qualifications. The IUSG group was glad to see biblical themes used, which "suggest and give a realistic image of alliance, call and response in faith, of gift and acceptance, of prophecy, of conversion, of openness to the Spirit." But the inevitable negative follows: "They are little or insufficiently inspiring." Again "there are passages which

[38] *Sequela Christi,* 47, 48.

bring out the aspect of encounter with Christ, of the seeking or intimate union with Him," but they "risk being passed over because of the frequent stress on perfection." The superiors general were frankly embarrassed by the document's presentation of religious as analogous to Christ's more intimate followers during his life on earth. They found it elitist.

Ironically, in one sense, the criticism seemed to ask for a more magisterial approach. They "would like to have found some clarification of doctrinal teaching, especially in those areas where the Council texts are rather inexplicit or incomplete." For example, they said, "there are several aspects of consecration which are still vague. The person consecrates himself, God consecrates, the Church consecrates."[39] They objected to the fact that "nowhere can it be found that we live our consecration by means of our vows." In general "the accent," they thought was "too much on the ecclesial aspect of consecration to the detriment of the personal aspect." The treatment of the counsels was generally unsatisfactory to the IUSG. It was regarded as "devoid of inspiration." They were presented as a "protection for the weak" and "treated in a legalistic manner with stress on observance, reduced to a means of avoiding certain imperfections against charity, instead of as an opening to an even greater charity."

"The apostolate," the critics objected, was "reduced to apostolic activities." Participation in the mission of Christ "was a neglected theme," and the "close relationship between the apostolate and prayer" was "not sufficiently developed." Treatment of the whole pastoral dimension was "far from inspiring" and failed to "recognize the actual dynamism of the life of the Church."

---

[39]"Rapport," 2. The Sacred Congregation granted this request definitively in its "Essential Elements in Religious Life," *Origins* 13, nr.8 (July 7, 1983), 134. The answer is, "God consecrates."

The Composition of 'Sequela Christ'

The IUSG councillors had reservations about the content of the document they had been called to consider, but they were even more incisive in their criticism of its style. They began by objecting to the "lack of unity in the text." They felt that the marks of multiple authorship were all too apparent; they objected to the "accumulation of quotations" which "prevent a progression of thought." About the way content was organized also they had reservations, such as these:

> A number of generalized statements fail to convey their message because of the lack of precision. Certain generalizations give an impression of being intended to answer questions applicable to special cases. Platitudes and lengthiness make the text heavy. Frequently, opposing aspects of a truth are considered out of sequence, without any position being taken, and result in a confusion of thought. For all these reasons, the text appears to be very long.

As far as the style was concerned, the council had kind words only for the last few paragraphs. They seem to have satisfied the whole group. One individual evaluation advised that the entire document be rewritten in the same spirit by whoever had composed this material.

> The religious life supposes the folly of the cross. What is necessary for the Church is not so much religious who are reasonable people as men and women capable of being unreasonable for Christ, capable of accepting the insecurity and obscurity of poverty, of being maintained in a very simple style, loving peace, free of compromises, choosing the most complete abnegation, capable of accepting any task, in any place, through a discipline at

the same time free and obedient, spontaneous and stable, — happy and strong in the certitude of faith. This folly, which is that of Jesus Christ, will be given to you in proportion to the totality of the gift which you make of yourselves, without taking it back.[40]

But approval seems to have been pretty well limited to this particular sector, and the stylistic criticisms are the most negative of all, for example:

> The vocabulary is often ambiguous, equivocal and "essentialiste." The tone is negative, moralizing, paternalistic, "triomphaliste," emphatic. This style is not understood today. It would be preferable if such terms as "dear Brothers and Sisters," "venerable," — did not appear in a document of this type.

Conclusion

The evaluation concluded as it had begun with a strong expression of the IUSG's opinion that (1) no document should be published at the time, (2) above all, not this one.

The text, they insisted, was so lacking in unity that people of many points of view would use it to defend their position. The majority of the young, they were very sure, would not feel it concerned them unless to "extinguish all the hope they have."

If, in the future, the SCR decided to publish a text they would prefer one which (1) would allow religious life to develop and which took into consideration the advance in theological teaching since Vatican II, which would help them progress along conciliar lines and would take positive

---

[40] *Sequela Christi,* 40. Personal Evaluation by Sister Margaret Brennan, I.H.M., I.U.S.G. Archives.

attitudes towards change; (2) would not limit religious life by definitions, but would try to present it with a view to the expectations of today's world, taking account especially of its pluralism; would highlight what was good in today's attitude, would grasp the hidden values, the secret desires concealed beneath exaggerations; (3) would explain *Perfectae Caritatis* in a positive way and in two sections: one for contemplatives and one for religious devoted to apostolic works; and (4) would present the words of the Holy Father in a style which would be meaningful to persons accustomed to modern means of communication.

For such a task they recommended that theologians, "both men and women" who were specialists in the study of religious life and who had a living knowledge of contemporary problems, should "begin immediately on the preparation of this text and not only in the role of consultors." Lastly, they insisted on the participation of women religious in this work as "indispensable when one reflects on the importance of religious women and the special way in which women live the present reality."[41]

The Factor of Timing

Any historical analysis of this evaluation must take account of the fact that it was made by people who, like the men religious whose work had been done earlier, were profoundly convinced that no document should appear. At least the more aggressive members of the group certainly came to the work with negative preconceptions. They expressed themselves quite frankly in the introduction to their report:

[41]"Rapport," 3.

Rumors of the coming publication of a document came
as a surprise to a few religious who were not expecting it.
Many who were expecting it were apprehensive, convinced that the time to make definite pronouncements or
to give precise orientations had not come. Others wish to
have this early defined orientation so as to find security,
to put an end to an evolution which is considered dangerous and sometimes destructive, or even to solve specific
problems. All these categories were represented among
the IUSG Councillors.

The councillors insisted, however, that after the study of the
text the reaction was unanimously negative.

As with many other events in the Church of recent years,
the more highly educated, articulate, and aggressive leadership prevailed. The first draft of the report was done by the
American Mother Thomas Aquinas Carroll of the Pittsburgh Sisters of Mercy. It was revised and translated into
French by the progressively oriented leader of the Sisters of
the Holy Family of Bordeaux, Soeur Marie-Paule Chauvin.
The IUSG president, Sister Mary Linscott, English superior
general of the Sisters of Notre Dame of Namur, considered a
splendid chairperson, adept at drawing out and synthesizing
opinions without imposing her own, seems to have coordi-
nated the work, led the discussion, and done some editing of
the final version.[42]

When Father Lalande saw the women's text, as he said,
by a kind of miracle, because it was kept very secret, he
remarked that "the comments of the sisters are perhaps
more radical than ours, even if they are presented with more
delicacy."[43]

The root question is, of course, what the results of this
outpouring of energy and resources on the part of the IUSG

[42]"Note on the Authorship of the 'Rapport,'" I.U.S.G. Archives.
[43]Lalande, "Memorandum to Systermans," 5.

councillors were. The Lalande Memorandum stated that it was very hard to know what happened "after the December text which was criticized so severely by the Sisters."[44] Père Pie-Raymond Régamey, a French Dominican theologian, was called in and worked for weeks on a new text which was quite different from the August or December versions.

When Lalande returned from a long trip to Latin America at the beginning of May the USG officers did not know what had happened, beyond the fact that Père Régamey had prepared a draft. On May 16, the feast of St. Jean Baptiste de la Salle, Lalande went to the generalate of the ever hospitable Christian Brothers and there learned that a text would appear in the near future. Someone was quoting Cardinal Villot as having remarked that no one would be able to say that the Holy Father had not written anything on religious life. Then, a few days before its publication the members of the Council of Sixteen and of the men's and women's councils received advance copies of *Evangelica Testificatio*, which is dated June 29, 1971.[45]

It was called an "apostolic exhortation," an unusual term employed to convey the idea that what the Pope wished to say to religious was not the material for a *motu proprio*, with strict legal prescriptions, but an "exhortation," an encouragement to genuine renewal.

Lalande described its simplicity of style and breadth of view as a great and, obviously, a very pleasant surprise. But he frankly had no idea where it came from. It resembled none of the earlier texts and yet, for reasons he did not mention, Lalande was sure that it was not the Régamey version. He said Régamey's experience had been as disappointing as Voillaume's had been earlier. Father Heston said the Pope himself had worked on it. The original was clearly in French and rumor suggested that Cardinal Villot or

[44] *Ibid.*
[45] *Ibid.*

someone close to him had also been involved. The tone, as Lalande remarked, was infinitely better than earlier drafts. He considered it a good text and told the Holy Father so. Though he found it another "sort of miracle," he did realize that it would not be satisfactory to everyone. He believed, however, that it would be helpful to those who used it without prejudice. At least from those who had seen the earlier versions, criticism was muted.[46]

There is a rather clear relationship between the IUSG criticism of *Sequela Christi* and the character of *Evangelica Testificatio*. They objected to the length of the earlier text. It was about 28,500 words; *Evangelica Testificatio,* about 8,000. The older text devoted about 7,500 words to the vows; the later one, about 3,000. *Evangelica Testificatio* opens with a positive, forthright sentence: "The evangelical witness of the religious life clearly manifests to men the primacy of the love of God." *Sequela Christi* begins with a long and complicated paragraph proving that religious life is important for the whole Church.

Generally, *Evangelica Testificatio* shows a greater tendency to accentuate the positive. For example:

> Certainly many elements, recommended by founders of orders or religious congregations are seen today to be outmoded. Various encumbrances or rigid forms accumulated over the centuries need to be curtailed. Adaptations must be made. New forms can even be sought and instituted with the approval of the Church. For some years now the greater part of religious institutes have been generously dedicating themselves to the attainment of this goal, experimenting — sometimes too hardily — with new types of constitutions and rules. We know well

[46]*Ibid.*

and we are following with attention this effort at renewal which was desired by the Council.[47]

Evangelica Testificatio uses the term "state of life" only once and then not in the context that the IUSG objected to. It does not use the term "perfection" as it appears in *Sequela Christi,* and does speak more of union with the Lord.

The most obvious difference is in style and spirit. *Sequela Christi,* though not prescriptive, was magisterial. The apostolic exhortation is just that, an exhortation, inspirational and encouraging in tone. It is not open to most of the IUSG criticisms of its predecessor.

The evidence we have about the impact of the councillors' work is simply the two texts. Certainly other factors operated in the interval, but no one seems to have found the changes, made before the painstaking and intelligent IUSG council had worked on the version presented to them, at all comparable to the metamorphosis which came afterward. It is also possible that the most effective thing the IUSG did was not the *Rapport* submitted to the SCR and the Holy Father. Shortly after this remarkable group completed its evaluation of *Sequela Christi,* the Executive Committee of IUSG prepared a letter to Paul VI which may have been more effective than its criticism of the ill fated *motu proprio.* It served as cover letter for the *Rapport,* but it was much more than that.

The IUSG Letter to Paul VI

The Councillors were encouraged to take this step by remembering that on October 29 the Pope had received the IUSG Assembly in what they considered a memorable

---

[47]Pope Paul VI, Apostolic Exhortation: *Evangelica Testificatio,* June 29, 1971, in Flannery, *Vatican Council II,* 680-706, here 682, par. 5.

audience. They opened their letter with a reference to this happy experience.[48] They then proceeded to inform the Pope about all the aspects of religious life which they believed the renewal chapters had strengthened, emphasizing seven points. The first, they said, was "a deepening of our consecration to Christ and his mission, understood as a personal relationship, intimate and strong, with the Lord." Since Christ and his salvific mission are inseparable, they saw "the apostolate as integral to this gift." This idea that consecration and mission are inseparable was strong also in their critique of *Sequela Christi*. When *Evangelica Testificatio* defines apostolic life it is in terms which, though more masculine and analytical, seem much closer to this approach than anything in the earlier document. The passage follows one on contemplative life.

> Others are consecrated to the apostolate in its essential mission, which is the proclaiming of the Word of God to those whom He places along their path, so as to lead them towards faith. Such a grace requires a profound union with the Lord, one which will enable you to transmit the message of the Incarnate Word in terms which the world is able to understand. How necessary it is, therefore, that your whole existence should make you share in His passion, death and glory.[49]

Placed second on their list was "an insistence on the primacy of charity, the inspiration for every form of apostolic life." As noted above, *Evangelica Testificatio* begins, "The evangelical witness of the religious life clearly manifests to men the primacy of love of God." The councillors next stressed "a deepening of our life and of the prayer in which we live

[48]I.U.S.G. Presidency Council to Pope Paul VI, December 5, 1970, I.U.S.G. Archives.

[49]*Evangelica Testificatio*, 685, par. 11.

intensely our personal relationship with Christ as a sign to a world which is searching for a path to God." The realization of this thirst prompted them, they said, to try "to find new forms of prayer which correspond to the needs of men today." This is the second time within a few lines that the document refers to personal relationship with Christ. It was seen as the basis of both consecration and mission, and now it is described as a sign to a world searching for God. There is no reference in *Evangelica Testificatio* to new forms of prayer, but it gives much more attention to the idea of relationship with the Lord than *Sequela Christi* did.

As their fourth point the IUSG Councillors turned to "the rebirth of a life of fraternal communion in Christ which speaks strongly to our time." The Christocentric emphasis continued in this passage on community. It was followed by one on the "rediscovery of our place in the Church, and our complementarity with the other people of God." They spoke of "our desire that the Church show itself as truly a sacrament in the world and in our communities." *Evangelica Testificatio's* response to this felt need of religious — to feel their place in the Church and the Church's mission, and to meet the changing needs of a rapidly evolving society — comes through most clearly in its concluding appeal.

> For a living being, adaptation to its surroundings does not consist in abandoning its true identity, but rather in asserting itself in the vitality that is its own. Deep understanding of present tendencies and of the needs of the modern world should cause your own sources of energy to spring up with renewed vigor and freshness. It is a sublime task in the measure that it is a difficult one.[50]

At the same time that religious were exhorted to study the "signs of the times" to comprehend the situation as fully as

---

[50]*Ibid.* 696, par. 33.

possible, they were warned of the recurrent danger of neg-lecting the contemplative dimension of their calling.

> Dear religious, according to the different ways in which the call of God makes demands upon your spiritual fami-lies, you must give your full attention to the needs of men, their problems and their searching; you must give witness in their midst, through prayer and action, to the Good News of love, justice and peace. The aspirations of men to a more fraternal life among individuals and nations require above all a change in ways of living, in mentality and in hearts. Such a mission, which is common to all the People of God, belongs to you in a special way. How can that mission be fulfilled if there is lacking an appreciation of the absolute, which results from a certain experience of God? This does but emphasize the fact that authentic renewal of the religious life is of capital importance for the very renewal of the Church and of the world.[51]

It was to this renewal of the world that the IUSG leaders seemed to feel a special call: "a profound concern about responding to the appeal of the world, in which we perceive the will of God." Yet, as if to reassure the Pope that they did not intend to seek the will of God *only* in the call of the world, they stated very simply as the final positive develop-ment, "a desire to live our apostolic mission in the Church."

They went on to speak of women religious in the "new Churches," reminding the Holy Father that he had himself experienced the "urgency of Kampala," and then remarking on how "the African congregations enter with courage and joy into the living out of the gospel in an African way of life, in spite of the European customs which have often been given to them." In short, the Councillors were convinced

---

[51] *Ibid.*, 34.

that "The Church in Africa awaits this contribution of the religious life for women as an implantation very vital and very close to the people."

They reminded the Holy Father of the special challenges for the Sisters' apostolate in Latin America. "The Sisters in Latin America, faced with a situation of injustice and poverty, search for a form of evangelical life which will respond to it. The newness and the enormity of the problem demands a profound adaptation of life style."

The religious women of Asia "are aware of all the riches of their religious patrimony and wish to share it with the West, and to express it through their presence in the world. In all these differences in culture and in historical background the Councillors saw the need to respond to the Holy Spirit, through a discernment which would allow for extensive possibilities for experimentation. Religious women on each continent, they were sure, were searching in a dynamic way, in a spirit of sincerity and truth. The response to religious life could no longer be made in terms of uniformity. In the October general assembly they had all become vividly aware of the reality of pluralism.

But most of all they were concerned about the young. Inside and outside their communities, the Mothers General saw them as a force for great authenticity and a search for true evangelical life.

> The world of the young overwhelms us with its ardor and magnitude. We learned from an intervention at our assembly that, in certain parts of Latin America, 75% of the population is under 15. The young have little contact with the Church. We have to seek them out: in the universities, in the habitations of the poor, etc. The situation demands that we give very special attention to the formation of the young people who come to us. The Church is already moving in this area because of the instruction *Renovationis Causam,* which has opened up wide possibilities of experimentation and research.

The Councillors stressed also the implications of the new personalism for religious formation and for religious life generally. They pointed out that the world has become intensely conscious of the value and uniqueness of each human person. They expressed concern that this "profoundly Christian idea" was in danger of subversion by "contemporary philosophy" into deformations dangerous for all humanity. "If we are to live fully at the level of our communities," they insisted, "it is necessary to form the conscience of each one." The new direction into which personalism has led us necessitates finding forms of government which, "through sensible cooperation at every level, develops in each one a sense of responsibility as a member of the Church in terms of the apostolate she exercises and in the life of the congregation."

Women, they told the Holy Father, find themselves in a new situation. Everywhere they wish to promote positive values and initiatives in society, not in a controversial or vindictive spirit, but in the desire to serve and cooperate. They were prepared to admit that all these "profound mutations," some aspects of which they had touched on, also involved dangers and risks. Discernment, they knew, was indeed necessary for reading the signs of the times. They were even prepared to concede that some religious had not understood the profound renewal which the Church had asked for and had contented themselves with merely external adaptations and that others actually abused their freedom. These were a minority, but that fact made them all the more conspicuous. They knew these things and suffered also from the attitude of those who risked dying out because they did not see the need of adapting to the needs of the times. They failed to accept the responsibility the Council gave them because they had a static conception of the loyalty they owed their founders. They did respect the anxiety which these sisters felt about change, but they wanted to see them inspired by authentic hope and a greater confidence in the direction of the renewal chapters. They would then avoid anxiety and make the road easier for the sisters who, seriously and with prudence, searched for ways to radiate Christ's love in the world of their time.

This complex and demanding situation had been complicated by rumors that a document on religious life was being prepared. Fifteen days earlier, Father Heston had called them together to review it. They had worked hard, and in loyalty to the Holy Father, they expressed their views about it to him. It seemed to them it would be criticized and become a source of new difficulties, because the theology it presented did not respond to the riches of the Council.

After some rather strong statements about the importance of better communication with the SCR, the IUSG Councillors closed their letter on a note of filial devotion.

> Most Holy Father, we have expressed in all simplicity what is in our hearts and by so doing we have tried to fulfill the mission which was confided to us by the IUSG Assembly. We are sure of your welcome, of your understanding, of your confidence. We regard the future with hope.

The letter, dated December 15, 1970, was signed individually by each member of the IUSG Executive Committee. Their critique of *Sequela Christi* went to the Pope with it. The Holy Father's response took the form both of a private audience for the IUSG Councillors some time later, and, more importantly, of *Evangelica Testificatio*. There is no negative evidence about his reaction. At the Congregation for Religious, at least on the part of Cardinal Antoniutti, it was certainly otherwise.

As was noted earlier, the IUSG had been assigned, from the beginning, a clerical "assistant," the Roman term for something between a theological consultant and a liaison with the Holy See, and, in the fall of 1969 Paolo Molinari,

S.J., had succeeded Theodore Heston, C.S.C., in this capacity. Father Molinari was in Rome when Sister Mary Linscott was called for the consultation, and helped persuade Father Heston to include the whole IUSG executive group. Immediately afterward, however, he had left the city to honor a commitment in England. When, after the IUSG report had been submitted, he returned to Rome, Cardinal Antoniutti sent for him and reproved him strongly for writing such a report for the women religious. Father Molinari replied that he had nothing to do with it, had in fact not even been available for consultation. The irate cardinal then asked who *had* written it for the Sisters. Father Molinari, well aware of the level of their competence, replied, "The Sisters wrote it for themselves." "That is not possible," the cardinal insisted. Father Molinari's response is not recorded. It may well have been a fine Italian shrug, conveying, ever so respectfully, the idea that the cardinal had better adjust.[52]

There is no doubt that the leaders of the group who prepared this effective document were highly articulate, intelligent, sophisticated, self-assured. There is little doubt, either, that the cardinal had no understanding of what this breed of women religious might be or mean or signify. The dreams they articulated so enthusiastically to the Holy Father have hardly had time, in the years since this little drama was played out, to come true. It is obviously a matter of opinion whether they will ultimately prove prophetic. Meanwhile the fundamental question of what forms of religious life are really viable *as* religious life would seem to be determined for some years to come by the new Code of Canon Law. This assumption, however, is more acceptable in some quarters than in others, and the argument threatens to continue.

[52]Interview with Reverend Paolo Molinari, S.J., Rome, October 11, 1983.

The Revised Code of Canon Law in Historical Context

Raymond G. Decker

With the promulgation of the Revised Code of Canon Law on January 25, 1983, and its effective implementation on November 27, 1983, the sage observation of Pierre Teilhard de Chardin seems most appropriate:

> The past has revealed to me how the future is built and preoccupation with the future tends to sweep everything else aside. It is precisely that I may be able to speak with authority about the future that it is essential for me to establish myself more firmly than before as a specialist on the past.[1]

The present operating code is not really "new"; it is, as the very title itself indicated, "revised." Obviously, there has been considerable effort to bring the church's law into con-

---

[1]Pierre Teilhard de Chardin, *Letters from a Traveler,* ed. Bernard Wall (New York, 1956), 207-08 — taken from notes Chardin was jotting down aboard the *Cathay* bound for Bombay under date of September 8, 1935.

formity with the spirit and terminology of the Second Vatican Council, but in much of its content and in most of its form the Revised Code remains faithful to both the structure and legal *Weltansicht* of the Code of 1917. In response to Chardin's observation, therefore, it would be profitable at this time to review the legal attitudes which contributed to the monumental achievement of the Code of 1917 and the suggested directions for its reform, because through this historical exercise we can more readily comprehend the spirit and tone of present church law and its implications for the future.

The very promulgation of the *Codex Juris Canonici* on May 27, 1917, was an historical milestone in the systematization of church law. Since 1317 no official collection of church laws had been promulgated so that by the nineteenth century the legislation of the Church had been exceedingly complicated and disparate. Before the *motu proprio* of Pope Pius X on March 19, 1904, which ordered the codification of church law, the legal system of the Church was a conglomerate of universal papal decrees *(Bullaria)*, decretals, responses from the papal congregations, and diocesan statutes, many of which were countermanding and contradictory.[2] This amalgam of laws making up the *Corpus Juris Canonici* obviously became difficult to administer in a unified and consistent manner. Presented with the task of providing for more uniform administration and adjudication, and motivated by the many examples of codification in the nations of continental Europe,[3] Pope Pius X directed that Canon Law should be codified.

[2] John A. Abbo, "The Revision of the Code," *The Jurist* 20 (1960), 371-97, here 371.

[3] René Metz, *What Is Canon Law?* trans. Michael Durick (New York, 1960), 59.

In keeping with the best of continental civil law traditions, this codification process undertook not simply to resolve existing conflicts and to summarize the laws in the form of a digest or concordance, but much more fundamentally, it undertook deep evaluations of the existing laws in order to provide for an integrated hierarchical structuring. What resulted was precisely that: an integrated and interlocking system providing not only for consistency but for a highly rational and analytic systematization of the whole legal order of the western Church.

This is exemplified by simply glancing in a cursory way at the table of contents of the old Code. The first book, *Normae Generales* (canons 1-86) set forth the general norms and basic juridical principles according to which the entire legal system was to operate. The second book, *De Personis* (canons 87-725) dealt with persons, their obligations and their rights. The third book, *De Rebus* (canons 726-1151) contained everything that did not find a place in the other four books including the sacraments, holy times and places, divine worship, the magisterium of the Church, benefices, and the temporal goods of the Church. The fourth book, *De Processibus* (canons 1152-2194) was concerned with procedure in all its forms: in disputes, criminal processes, marriage processes, ordination processes, causes for beatification, canonization, and administrative procedure. The fifth book, *De Delictis et Poenis* (canons 2195-2414) contained the penal law of the Church, defining the concept of crime, outlining responsibility and ecclesiastical punishments, and enumerating the various breaches of the law for which penalties were provided. The internal portions of these books were, in turn, schematically arranged into logical subdivisions — parts, sections, and chapters. This integrated and interlocking system of laws reflecting a schematic structuring and hierarchical ordering corresponded most accurately to the quality of systematic codification which so clearly characterized the continental civil law of the nintenth century.

Not only did the basic format of the Code reflect the qualities of pandectist systematization, but the preoccupation with order and logical consistency was reinforced after the promulgation of the Code by Pope Benedict XV through his *motu proprio, Cum juris canonici,* in which he gave instructions for making insertions into the Code without even changing the order of the original canons:

> If in the course of time the good of the Church should require that a new general decree be drawn up, the respective Sacred Congregation shall draft it. Should the decree not be in conformity with the prescriptions of the Code, the Sacred Congregation shall inform the Pope of the discrepancy. Once approved by the Pope, the decree is to be presented by the Sacred Congregation to the Commission for the Interpretation of the Code, whose duty it then becomes to draft a canon or canons according to the decree. If the decree is contrary to the Code, the Commission shall indicate to which law of the code the new law is to be added. If the decree deals with a point about which there is no mention in the Code, the Commission shall decide at what place the new canon or the new canons are to be inserted in the Code; in which case, the number of the preceding canon is maintained with the addition of *bis, ter,* etc., so that no canon loses its place and the numbering is not changed in any way.[4]

This spirit of hierarchical structuring and systematization pervaded the legal systems of continental secular society. The Church during the early part of this century was in the throes of a scholastic revival whose spirit was permeated with hierarchical ordering and systematization; and so it was only natural that the spirit which pervaded the theologi-

[4]Pope Benedict XV, *Cum juris canonici* (September 15, 1917), in *Acta Apostolicae Sedis* 9 (1917), 483-84.

cal and philosophical spheres of the Church should likewise permeate its legal system.

Being a "modern legal compendium containing an orderly series of concise and exactly-worded statements of juridical principles and positive enactments covering every aspect of the Church's myriad activities,"[5] the Code of 1917 can be viewed most accurately as an epitomization of continental civil law. This particular spirit was illustrated by some of the accolades given to the Code:

> John Ruskin has remarked that Gothic architecture is frozen poetry. If this be admitted, then it is scarcely intemperate to declare that nearly every canon in the *Codex Juris Canonici* is frozen history. In this monumental work all the ages of ecclesiastical history have given one another rendezvous. Here their various products may be seen altogether; not confused but interfused; not heaped one upon another, as Levy had described Roman Law, but correlated and integrated into a reasonable organic whole for the sole purpose of attaining more effectively the common good of the Church.[6]

From the issuance of the *motu proprio, Arduum sane* of Pope Pius X on March 19, 1904, which initiated the process of codification, until the final promulgation of the Code on May 27, 1917, an intensive period of scholarship was in process, as is generally the case with the issuance of any code in the civil law orbit. Pius X entrusted the responsibility for the codification to a commission of cardinals, and charged them to add a number of consultors chosen from among the most distinguished specialists in canon law and theology.[7]

---

[5]James P. Kelly, "The Law of the Catholic Church," *The Jurist* 3 (1943), 539-44, here 540.

[6]James H. Griffiths, "A Light to the Nations," *The Jurist* 3 (1943), 354-63, here 357.

[7]Metz, *What Is Canon Law?*, 7.

The very important position of secretary to this Commission of Cardinals and president of the Council of Consultors was given to the former professor of Canon Law at the Institut Catholique in Paris, Pietro Gasparri. Gasparri became the central figure around whom the whole process of codification took place. Just as in the histories of codification in most civil law countries one man served to direct and integrate most of the scholarship entailed in the issuance of the new codes, so in the case of the Church's code this function was performed by a man eminently qualified in ecclesiastical legal scholarship and deeply immersed in continental civil law.

Once this administrative structure was established, the body of experts — the Council of Consultors — began the arduous historical and analytic research required for this project. These consultors attained an initial uniformity in their formulations by adherence to a set of rules conceived as expressing desirable characteristics of the Code, and then single items of legislation were assigned to each of two consultors who formulated the appropriate statute without reference to his colleague. The work of these consultors was then submitted for review and amalgamation to each of the two committees into which the Council of Consultors had been divided. The statutes were then passed from these committees to the Commission of Cardinals which had the responsibility of reviewing and amending them at least twice. Through this rather complicated process every statute thus passed through at least four stages of critical and scholarly inspection, and, in fact, some statutes went through ten or more reviews.[8].

The first scholarly task before this Council was historical in nature, in that it had to amalgamate the long canonical heritage of the past before it could begin the process of

[8]The Editors, "The Code of Canon Law: 1918-1943," *The Jurist* 3 (1943), 177-81, here 180.

systematic codification. Starting with the works of Denys the Little (c. 555) through Pope Adrian I (772-795), the Decretum of Gratian (1139-1151), Decretals of Gregory IX (1239), Liber Sextus (1298), the Clementine Decretals (1317), and the Tridentine synthesis, this Council had to amalgamate similar canons and resolve conflicting ones — all of which represented a rather monumental historical survey. However, the creation of a code in the tradition of civil law is not simply the gathering together of existing laws and the resolving of conflicts: it consists, more importantly, of analytical studies which create logical constructs for the orderly systematization of the laws. This aspect of scholarship was accomplished through the creation of the Commission of Cardinals and the Council of Consultors whose function it was through repeated reviews to criticize, catalogue, and organize the statutes into a systematized code. But the scholarship responsible for the *Codex Juris Canonici* was not limited to the thirteen-year period between the creation of the Commission and the promulgation of the Code, for much canonical scholarship had preceded the existence of the Commission and served as the resource materials which made codification possible within such a short period of time.[9]

On September 15, 1917, Pope Benedict XV established a permanent commission to interpret the Code and gave it exclusive competence to declare the authentic meaning and application of canons whose terms might give rise to difficulties. This commission was created to provide ongoing scholarship which would be needed for interpretations and commentaries on the canons. So committed was the Code of 1917 to the continental civil law method of operation that this commission was established to insure its scholarly functioning for the future, and as late as January 25, 1959, with

[9] *Ibid.* 178.

the creation of the commission for the revision of the Code of Canon Law, this concern remained a preoccupation of Church authorities.

Because the Code of 1917 adhered so closely to the civil law characteristics of systematization and scholarship, it almost of necessity had to adhere to the civil law orbit according to its mode of legal reasoning. In the adjudication of cases in this system, attention was not focused upon what new dimension is brought to the law by the contingencies of cases but, rather, how do cases fit into the clear and tightly knit definitions established by the law. The basic process involved in deciding cases is first to ascertain the facts in the case, and then determine what canons apply to the facts at hand. The decision primarily rests upon the application of the canon or canons to the particular facts with little or no reference to decisions made in courts of first, second, or third instance. The legal reasoning process, therefore, does not consist in an analogous application of court decisions in previous cases or with any intention of contributing anything new to the present law, rather, it consists in the maintenance of the existing Code and a deductive application of the Code to the specific case at hand. This process of legal reasoning emanates from the idea that the present law is absolute and all inclusive, and therefore needs only to be imposed.

The occasions for appeal to courts of second or third instance generally involve an appeal to a more general law so that the final arbiter in any case is the general rule as interpreted by *la doctrine* and *jurisprudence permanente* as expressed in the First Book of the *Codex Juris Canonici*. This jurisprudence comes to be recognized as a source of interpretation of the law. Thus Canon 20 of Book One listed as sources from which to fill a legal gap, "The style and practice of the Roman Curia." A single judicial decision therefore had no authoritative binding effect because the permanent practice in a given matter provided for by the

Code should not be disturbed. In a word, the process of legal reasoning in the Code was primarily deductive — the general absolute norms were given and in the process of judicial decision-making they were simply applied without reference to judicial decisions rendered in analogous cases.

In the spirit of the Code of 1917 the law was not discovered, broadened, and expanded by judicial decisions which related to the specificity of concrete cases, but rather by the "scholarly" investigations of the commission established to interpret it; and this commission consistently resorted to the scholastic method of deducing specific principles from more abstract, general, and theoretical principles as enunciated in the Code. In this view, the Code was seen as the only genuine source of law; it was the wellspring from which all future laws were to be deduced. The Pontifical Commission for the Authentic Interpretation of the Code was established primarily to interpret the canons in a manner consistent with the predetermined system, as the name itself implies, and in so doing it protected the future of the Code by deducing those principles which were consistent with the enunciated jurisprudence, as at least expressed in the First Book, and which would not jeopardize the established order of the system.[10] The interpretations of the Commission became the norms for the courts to apply, so that a case was not argued from previous court decisions, but from the scholarly interpretations of the Commission, from the inherent logic of specific canons, or from the basic principles enunciated in the Code. This was a reasoning process which entailed the subsuming of individual cases under the specific categories or general abstractions reestablished by the Code.

This jurisprudential perspective served as the basis for considering the Code as the final expression of church law,

---

[10]Metz, *What Is Canon Law?*, 62.

which needed only to be applied in an ongoing deductive process. Nothing new is brought into the law, it is only deduced from the law, for any developments in the law are somehow already contained in a latent manner in the legal system which is given expression by the Code. This approach to the development of law, which was so typically in accord with the civil law tradition, was also closely aligned with the scholastic concept regarding the development of doctrine. In this view the *depositum fidei* had been entrusted to the Church and contained all that God has revealed to man. However, in the process of history and through certain cultural contingencies, certain truths which lie latent within the *depositum* are unveiled and man's understanding of God's revelation becomes more complete. This same architectonic view is carried over into the legal sphere of the Church in which the legal principle or law has been posited in the Code. The process of legal development, then, does not consist in adding anything new, but in simply drawing out of the existing principles of law what is already latently there. This process of deduction, rather than analogical application of judicial decisions, established the Code as belonging to the civil law orbit.

As early as January 25, 1959, Pope John XXIII expressed the intention of having the *Codex Juris Canonici* updated.[11] Some looked upon this reform as a mere modification in the wording of the canons and an incorporation of the innovations of the Second Vatican Council, leaving the Code essentially as it was. Others moved for more radical change by asking for a re-evaluation of the basic civil law approach of the 1917 Code and requested the adoption of the common law approach, or at least that an eclectic amalgam of both be attempted. This latter movement was particularly prevalent among those within the Church who lived in countries

[11]Abbo, "The Revision of the Code," 371.

belonging to the common law orbit, and most especially those living in the United States. These reformers were pressuring for a deeper evaluation of church law because they found the Code of 1917 totally conditioned by continental legal trends of the nineteenth century, and more personally found themselves functioning schizophrenically in that they were living and reasoning according to the common law in their civil lives and according to civil law in their ecclesiastical lives.

In April of 1970, a report was submitted by the Canon Law Society of America calling for "maximum participation of the universal Church in the present effort to revise the Code of Canon Law," and it regarded this as "an indispensable precondition to its effective acceptance by the community."[12]

The concerns of American canonists were the inflexibility and intransigency of the law as a result of its architectonic ordering.

> ...The legal system of the Church is not open enough, the static and dynamic qualities in it are not rightly balanced. There is an overemphasis on the permanency (not to say perpetuity) of the rules. Stability is favored to such an extent that a wide gap developed between canon law and the active life of the Church. The system does not favor enough the dynamic growth of various Christian communities, nor does it offer an instrument (or instruments) for the speedy creation of new laws for new needs.[13]

[12]Canon Law Society of America in cooperation with Fordham University, "Symposium on Co-Responsibility in the Church," unpublished paper (April, 1970), 4.

[13]James E. Biechler, ed., *Law for Liberty: The Role of Law in the Church Today,* (Baltimore, 1967), 173.

The criticism of the old Code took on the character of the traditional criticisms made against the civil law tradition by those educated or functioning in the tradition of the common law: 1) the bulk of laws was confined to a Code and no rule in the Code could be changed without the initiative being taken by the highest authority, 2) the Code made the conditions for the acceptance of legal customs so stringent that in practice hardly any customs of legal value could develop in the community, and 3) these factors led to the situation in which decision about the need for new legislation was left to the discretionary judgment of the executive organ which as a rule in any governmental form does not have the necessary openness and inspiration for creating new rules and institutions. The critics of the old Code traditionally held that rigidity results from the fact that a Code permeated with civil law jurisprudence attempts through its process of pandectist systematization to be so inclusive of all legal reality that it becomes more concerned with preserving the order of the system than meeting the growing and changing needs of the community it is supposed to serve.

These critics held up the common law as "reluctant to build up a neatly designed legal structure with an air of immobility about it,"[14] and they recommended that instead of revising the *Codex Juris Canonici*, there be established a constitution for the universal Church which would be broad in purpose and scope.[15] As one critic expressed it: "The purpose is not in the first place to compose a well-ordered whole of Canon Law....The first aim is to re-think the whole existing church order in the new spirit that animated

[14]*Ibid.*, 175.

[15]J. Neumann, "Erwägungen zur Revision des Kirchlichen Gesetzbuches," *Tübinger Theologische Quartalschrift* 146 (1966), 301-02; K. Moersdorf, "Streiflichter zur Reform des Kanonischen Rechts," *Archiv für katholisches kirchenrecht* 135 (1966), 38-52, here 46-47.

the Council and was clearly expressed there."[16] They pointed out that a unified code attempting to cover all of the legal needs of the Church would attempt too much and result in a stultified codification lacking sufficient flexibility to meet the ever growing complexity of the modern Christian community. Instead they recommended a general constitution which would allow for the organic development of the law and would not require that every law must fit within the schematic structure created by a code.[17] The constitution was to be so planned as to be valid for all parts of the Church,[18] which meant that it should be general in scope, which in turn would preclude it from being a code in the strict sense of that term.

This debate surfaced a head-on collision between the two orbits of law. On the one hand, there were those who wished simply to revise the present *Codex Juris Canonici* because through its highly systematized form it created a hierarchical and analytical legal structure which provided a sense of stability and permanency. On the other hand, there were those who recommended that only general norms be enunciated in constitutional form, allowing for flexibility and development of the more detailed aspects of the legal system by making possible an easier creation and deletion of laws in order to meet the exigencies of differing cultures and changing times. There was a blatant conflict between the civil law and the common law traditions, with the former insisting upon an integrated and interlocking system of laws and the latter recommending an organic approach to law in a desire for adaptability to contingencies, innovation, and creativity.

---

[16]Neophytos Edelby *et al.*, ed., *Renewal and Reform of Canon Law* (New York, 1967), 28.

[17]Ladislas M. Örsy, "The Problem of Constitutional Law in the Church," *The Jurist* 29 (1969), 29-56, here 50-51.

[18]Edelby, *Reform of Canon Law,* 61.

In a report issued by the Canon Law Society of America, it recommended that "the ongoing work of the Commission for the Revision of the Code of Canon Law be made public and that structures be set up immediately throughout the world for the widest possible consultation and evaluation of its proposals and consideration of other recommendations by the whole ecclesial community."[19] In effect this recommendation called for the involvement of the entire community of the Church in the creation of the new law for the Church, not leaving this task to legal experts and scholars alone. This was a call to all in the Church — laypersons, priests, religious, bishops — to share in the making of the new legal structure. Having experienced a system of laws created by the experts, they criticized it as having created "a gap between the laws and the moving life of the Church"[20] in which "the static and dynamic qualities in it are not rightly balanced."[21] In the estimation of these critics it could be detrimental to a legal system to limit its creation and operation to scholars who at times are out of contact with the genuine needs and problems of the community for which the laws exist.

In keeping with the tradition of the common law orbit these critics would have placed the creation and operation of the legal system more in the hands of the practitioners than in the hands of the scholars, whether they be historians or legal theorists. This was brought out clearly with their insistence upon the importance of collegiality and subsidiarity in the legal system. In calling upon a fuller exercise of collegiality in the creation and operation of church law, these proponents of reform were asking for a greater participation on the part of the nonexpert and nonscholar. They were recommending that all within the Church be given the

---

[19]"Symposium on Co-Responsibility in the Church," 4.

[20]Biechler, *Law for Liberty,* 174.

[21]*Ibid,* 173

opportunity of contributing to the legal structure, and that this not be left to "the legal expert" within the community.

With insistence upon the implementation of collegiality and subsidiarity there was an attempt to decentralize the law-making function in the Church, and consequently there would have been less reason to have a highly systematized and comprehensive code which is dependent upon extensive scholarship. The universal law would have consisted only of general norms governing the functioning of the universal Church, and the more particular laws would have been created on various levels to meet the specificity and contingencies operative on those levels.

One of the structural underpinnings of the common law is its characteristic reasoning process which rests mainly upon the analogous and creative use of judicial judgments. This means that the courts play a most significant part in the creation and operation of the legal system. In accordance with this *Weltanschauung* the American proponents of reform were suggesting that "law can positively facilitate the development of the Church. Ecclesiastical courts should creatively interpret law and, in so doing, contribute to the life and mission of the Church."[22] The old code was criticized in that "the courts are not allowed to make any adaptation of the law to new or unusual circumstances. The result is judicial stability — without creative jurisprudence. Legal history shows that both Roman law and English common law are mainly the creations of the courts."[23] It was the hope of these American reformers that the contemplated revision of Canon Law would envision a broader use of courts for the judicial resolution of conflicts of all kinds and that the value of judicial precedent and the interpretation of

[22]James A. Coriden, ed., *We the People of God: A Study of Constitutional Government for the Church* [Our Sunday Visitor, Inc.], (Huntington, Indiana, 1968), 11.

[23]Biechler, *Law for Liberty,* 174.

law afforded by the adjudication of concrete cases would be adopted.

In essence, what was being called for in these projected reforms was a change from the reasoning process of the civil law tradition in which specific cases are subsumed in an abstractive manner under legal categories established by a code and in which the development of law depends upon the deduction of more specific laws from more general legal norms, to the reasoning process of the common law which tends to focus on the specificity of the immediate case and through a comparative and analogical application of previous court decisions to provide for equity in the specific case at hand and growth in the legal system as a whole. But this call for the adoption of common law reasoning was more than just a recommendation for a change in legal processes; it was an attempt to inculcate into church law the spirit of the common law in which the judge becomes the mediator between the dead letter of the law and the dynamic realities of life, and in which he serves as a vital link between an abstract and universal rule and a particular case.

As the revision of the Code of 1917 took place, it was only natural that those representing different legal traditions would try to inculcate the best of their respective traditions. It is no wonder then that certain groups within the United States, and especially those most concerned with the Church's law — The Canon Law Society of America — pressured for the inculcation of common law approaches into the revision. This society had two major symposia[24] the conclusion of which

> called for many of the values and structures in the future law of the Church which we identify with western constitutionalism. Since it has long been a suspicion (not to say pre-judgment) of many members of the Canon Law

[24]Symposium entitled "The Role of Law in the Church," Pittsburgh, Oct. 8-10, 1966, proceedings edited by James E. Biechler, *Law for Liberty* (Baltimore, 1967). Symposium entitled "A Constitution for the Church," Statler-Hilton Hotel, New York, Oct. 7-9, 1967, proceedings edited by Coriden, *We the People of God.*

Society that the Church could learn from the Anglo-American common law tradition, the proposal for a "constitutional" study was eagerly forwarded....[25]

In order to appreciate the difficulties encountered in revising the old Code, it helps to realize that this involved a long-standing contest between two legal systems: the civil law and the common law. The old Code not only conformed to the characteristics of the civil law orbit, but epitomized them; whereas many of the recommended reforms reflected ideas and concepts specifically associated with the common law tradition.

The revision of Canon Law did not undergo as radical a change as its American critics would have desired because the majority working on the revision were scholars immersed in the civil law tradition. Although Pope Paul VI in an address to the Commission for the Revision of Canon Law on November 20, 1965, intimated the possibility of establishing a general constitution *(constitutio fundamentalis)* for the universal Church, nevertheless the developments of the reform allowed for only a revision of the existing Code. It seems apparent from this historical analysis, however, that tensions even under the revised Code will remain, if for no other reason than those whose legal psyches are conditioned in the common law orbit will be forced to function in a somewhat schizophrenic fashion as long as the civil law tradition dominates the structure and operation of church law. The differences between the two legal systems run quite deep both philosophically and methodologically. As legal structures, they pervade all aspects of life for those living within their respective orbits, and so they serve to structure and condition both collective and individual psyches. Those who are psychically conditioned by the common law tradition will thus continue to find it difficult to function in a system which epitomizes the civil law tradition.

[25]Coriden, *We the People of God,* xiv.

Reflections on the History of the Exposition of Scripture

Roland E. Murphy, O. Carm.

"Church History as the History of the Exposition of Scripture" is the title of a study by Gerhard Ebeling, written in 1946 when he began his illustrious career at the University of Tübingen.[1] The purpose of this essay is not to argue with Ebeling's contention or its presuppositions, but rather to explore some of its implications from the point of view of one who is not a church historian, but a student of the Bible.[2] A brief summary of his perspective is only fair, in view of the apparently radical thesis he proposes.

[1] The English translation (in which "as" [*als*] appears as "is") can be found in *The Word of God and Tradition*, trans. S. H. Hooke (Philadelphia, 1964), 11-31; the original study is *Kirchengeschichte als Geschichte der Auslegung der Heiligen Schrift*, Vol. 189 of *Sammlung gemeinverständlicher Vorträge und Schriften aus dem Gebiet der Theologie und Religionsgeschichte* (Tübingen, 1947); this is reproduced in *Wort Gottes und Tradition*, Vol. 7 of *Kirche und Konfession* (Göttingen, 1964), 9-27. See also G. Ebeling, *Die Geschichtlichkeit der Kirche und ihrer Verkündigung als theologisches Problem*, Vols. 207/208 of *Sammlung gemeinverständlicher Vorträge und Schriften aus dem Gebiet der Theologie und Religionsgeschichte* (Tübingen, 1954), esp. 81-93. The quotations at the beginning of this article are taken from the English translation, with pages indicated in parentheses.

[2] Early on the writer did receive training in European history, and much more, from John Tracy Ellis, to whom he is honored to dedicate this article.

He begins by discussing three problems: the place of church history within the study of theology in general, and within the science of history in general, and finally the relationship between secular and church history. He distinguishes three main forms of church history: the Catholic, the Enthusiastic, and the Reformed, none of them adequate because article VII of the Augsburg Confession was not observed. This article tends to link Church and history, as guided by the interpretation of Holy Scripture.[3] Here an important presupposition appears: the idea of the Church as based on the proclamation of the Word of God; this leads into the concept of church history as the history of interpretation of Scripture. The heart of the definition of church history is expressed in this way:

> But interpretation of Holy Scripture does not find expression only in preaching and doctrine, and certainly not primarily in commentaries; but also in doing and suffering. Interpretation of Holy Scripture finds expression in ritual and prayer, in theological work and in personal decisions, in Church organization and ecclesiastical politics, in the temporal power of the Papacy, and in the ecclesiastical pretensions of rulers, in wars of religion, and in works of compassionate love...(p. 28).

For Ebeling "interpretation" here is both spoken and unspoken, conscious and unconscious, positive and nega-

---

[3]Article VII is translated: "It is also taught among us that one holy Christian church will be and remain forever. This is the assembly of all believers among whom the Gospel is preached in its purity and the holy sacraments are administered according to the Gospel. For it is sufficient for the true unity of the Christian church that the Gospel be preached in conformity with a pure understanding of it and that the sacraments be administered in accordance with the divine Word. It is not necessary for the true unity of the Christian church that ceremonies, instituted by men, should be observed uniformly in all places. It is as Paul says in Eph. 4:4,5 'There is one body and one Spirit, just as you were called to the one hope that belongs to your call, one Lord, one faith, one baptism.'" Cf. *The Book of Concord*, ed. Theodore G. Tappert, *et al.* (Philadelphia, 1959), 32.

tive. The church historian has as his task to uncover the relationship between event and Scripture. Ebeling enunciates certain consequences for the writer of church history:

> The Church historian must pay a greater attention to the history of the interpretation of Holy Scripture in a stricter sense than has hitherto been the case: this may be either a more thoroughgoing use of Church history in the interpretation of individual passages, or by throwing light on the history of the understanding of individual sections or thought-patterns; this may possibly take place, not only in theological literature, but also in its practical interpretation of the event itself (p. 29).

Finally, "[t]he work of the Church historian operates as the radical critical destruction of all that, in the course of Church history, has interposed a barrier between us and Christ, instead of being an interpretation of Holy Scripture pointing to him" (p. 31).

I. Biblical Exegesis

Perhaps the first reaction of a biblical student to Ebeling's lapidary phraseology is the memory of the commentaries of the patristic and medieval periods. It is clear that Ebeling rightly goes beyond this narrow perspective. It is the whole life of the Church, as an explication of Scripture, that is the issue. The old saw about *lex orandi lex credendi* fits in here, at least implicitly. The life style of the Church betrays the way in which she hears, or fails to hear, the Scriptures.

Nonetheless, the history of biblical exegesis in the narrow sense is obviously part of church history, and research in this area deserves greater expansion. Several individual scholarly studies exist, but no critical survey of this history exists — a study that would draw lines of association and dependence among the commentators and also analyze the historical and sociological factors impinging upon the interpreter.[4] One would like to know more about the way in which this exegesis was related to the Church. Ultimately were the commentators writing primarily for themselves? Were their views communicated in preaching to the laity?[5] It is also clear that certain commentators became the giants of the tradition and set an authoritative tone for the interpretation of many biblical books. This was not favorable to originality and variety.

The history of biblical exegesis has come to the fore in recent biblical scholarship. One can point to the noble effort of Brevard Childs to supply this dimension to his commentary on the book of Exodus.[6] This development seems to spring out of the on-going discussion of hermeneutics. The awareness of our own modern presuppositions in interpreting a text has made us more sympathetic to the efforts of the past. Former commentators had their own presuppositions, many of them crippling, but they struggled with the text as much as we do. One cannot deny that the modern situation is a vast improvement over the past. The original texts replaced the Vulgate, and the ensuing discovery of ancient Near Eastern literatures moved biblical scholarship quickly into historical-critical methodology. Despite its limitations, this approach remains fruitful, and has only the more to gain by being integrated into an historical perspective. Some examples from the history of exegesis will illustrate the way in which historical methodology has modified tradi-

[4]General surveys of the history of biblical exegesis are few and superficial. See *The Cambridge History of the Bible*, ed. S. A. Greenslade *et al.* (Cambridge, 1963-70), Vols. I-III. The monumental *Exégèse Médiévale* of Henri de Lubac (Paris, 1959-1964), Vols. 1-2, needs more than an author index to be serviceable. Beryl Smalley's *The Study of the Bible in the Middle Ages* (Notre Dame, 1964) is excellent as far as it goes. Robert M. Grant, *The Bible in the Church* (New York, 1948) is a brief outline. Although brief, the treatment of the history of biblical exegesis of specific books is well done in the *Dictionnaire de Spiritualité*.

[5]This aspect cannot be treated here; see the article on preaching by Hermigild Dressler in *New Catholic Encyclopedia* (New York, 1967), XI, 684-89.

[6]Brevard S. Childs, *The Book of Exodus* (Philadelphia, 1974).

tional exegesis, and hence the way in which the Church continues in its ongoing task of presenting an "exposition of Scripture."

The history of the exegesis of the Song of Songs betrays a remarkable unanimity in interpretation for both Church and synagogue.[7] It was interpreted as describing the love between God and his people: the Lord and Israel, and God (Christ) and the Church. The interpretation was further individualized, and this occurred very early on with Origen, into the mutual love of God and the soul. Further variations, such as the mariological interpretation or recondite medieval philosophical speculation, can also be found, but they are not central to the broad current of interpretation. This traditional understanding has been called "allegorical," since allegory was an entrenched method of explicating the details of the text (Gregory the Great, in commenting on the Song, called allegory a "kind of machine," *quasi quandam machinam*, to elevate the soul to God).[8] It was not until the eighteenth and nineteenth centuries that the spell of traditional interpretation was broken in western exegesis, and the literal historical meaning (the mutual love of man and woman) became firmly established. Indeed, this did not appear as an accepted view among Catholic biblical scholars until the middle of the present century.[9]

This is not the place to argue for one interpretation or the other, or for both.[10] The point is: what does this history tell

---

[7]Friedrich Ohly, *Hohelied-Studien. Grundzüge einer Geschichte der Hohelied-auslegung des Abendlandes bis zum 1200* (Wiesbaden, 1958); George L. Scheper, *The Spiritual Marriage: The Exegetic History and Literary Impact of the Song of Songs in the Middle Ages* (Princeton University dissertation, 1971).

[8]Gregory the Great, *Expositio in Cantica Canticorum*, ed. P. Verbraken, Vol. 144 of *Corpus Christianorum Series Latina* (Turnhout, 1963), 3.

[9]Jean-Paul Audet, "Le sens du cantique des cantiques," *Revue Biblique* 62 (1955), 197-221; André-Marie Dubarle, "L'amour humain dans le cantique des cantiques," *Revue Biblique* 61 (1954), 67-86; Oswald Loretz, "Zum Problem des Eros im Hohelied," *Biblische Zeitschrift* 8 (1964), 191-216.

[10]Roland E. Murphy, "Patristic and Medieval Exegesis — Help or Hindrance?" *The Catholic Biblical Quarterly* 43 (1981), 505-16.

us of the way in which the Church heard this particular book of the Bible? The traditional interpretation is to be viewed against the background of several historical factors: 1) the general tendency of Christian interpreters to allow the New Testament (in this case, Ephesians 5) to determine the direction of exegesis of the Old Testament; 2) the fact that the commentators were largely clerical and celibate, and hence judged divine rather than human love as more congenial; 3) the slowness of the Christian community to come to terms with eroticism on the human level; 4) the popularity of allegory as a method of interpreting Scripture (a literary mistake, if a given work is not written as allegory).

The traditional approach to the Song has a long and glorious history, especially in the Middle Ages. But the "clerical" culture exacted a great price. The Song was not able to be heard in such a way as to contribute to a biblical theology of sex and marriage. Only later, given certain cultural developments as well as historical insight into the ancient world, did another level of meaning become possible. The interaction between the Church and societal culture is an ongoing matrix of interpretation which yields new insights into the meaning of the Bible. To this hermeneutical process the Church must always remain open. Emerging interpretations then react upon the ongoing life of the community.[11]

Another example deserves brief mention here: the way in which the book of Ecclesiastes has been heard in the history of the Church.[12] Because of the strong eschatological trend in church thought and devotion (*conversatio nostra in coelis est,* Phil 3:20), the message of "vanity" (Eccles 1:2 and *passim*) was taken up as a call for asceticism in view of a higher good. One can see this very clearly in the opening

[11]It is interesting to note that a reading from the Song (2:8-10, 14, 16a; 8:6-7a) is now among the selections in the lectionary for the Nuptial Mass.

[12]Roland E. Murphy, "Qohelet Interpreted: The Bearing of the Past on the Present," *Vetus Testamentum* 32 (1982), 331-37.

lines of the *Imitation of Christ*, where we read that all is vanity (and the "preacher" or Ecclesiastes is referred to), except the love of God. This exegetical move fails to do justice to the original message of the book, which is a powerful statement concerning the mystery of God and the inscrutability of his ways. The historical-critical approach prevents the modern reader from yielding to any such domesticated view of the book. Indeed, it opens a much needed option to many moderns who ponder about God.[13]

An extended foray into the history of exegesis would confirm specific interactions of the Church and society. The history of exegesis, however narrowly conceived, reflects the life of the Church, while it also has the potential to improve it, and set it into new pastoral paths.

II. *The Life of the Church*

Before the Reformation and the ensuing Christian debate on Scripture and Tradition it was apparently not possible to describe the history of the Church as the history of the exposition of Scripture. The question would not have been raised in this manner, for it assumes that the Bible plays an *explicitly* normative role, as in Protestant Christianity, whereas it was only implicitly normative in previous centuries. By that I mean the manner in which the Church and her teaching, formed by the Bible in principle, overshadowed whatever private reading of the Bible may have occurred. This is reflected in Augustine's *De utilitate credendi* 14, 31: "From whom did I derive my faith? I see that I owe my faith to opinion and report widely spread and firmly established

---

[13]It is all the more poignant to recall the function of Eccles 1:4 ("the earth remains [stands] forever") in the condemnation of Galileo, as recalled by the famous commentator, Cornelius a Lapide: "Congregatio cardinalium sub Paulo V anno Christi 1616, die quinta Martii, praesente Card. Bellarmino, ex hoc Salomonis loco damnauit Copernici sententiam quae docet terram moueri"— see his *Commentarius in Ecclesiasten* (Antwerp, 1657), 27.

among the peoples and nations of the earth, and that these peoples everywhere observe the mysteries of the Catholic Church."[14] The shift in Roman Catholic emphasis, for which one may be grateful to our separated brothers and sisters, is strikingly evident in the constitution on Revelation in Vatican II. One can now say that for Roman Catholics the Bible is the *norma normans non normata*.[15]

Yet there is a certain paradox in describing the role of the Bible in this way. Such a statement (and that of Ebeling as well) takes for granted that Christianity is a "scriptural religion." The paradox is that biblical faith is not by its nature a scriptural religion; the people of the Bible did not put their faith in a Scripture and give it controlling power for the expression of faith.[16] Scriptural religion emerges only later in the history of Christianity, and in a sharpened form in Protestant Christianity. Although the Bible is a work produced by the community, it became the basic work to guide the community.

This guidance came to play an ever more explicit role in the history of the Church as currents of individualism and nationalism arose. Ebeling's statement is really a very *modern* view in that it seems to be more applicable to a literate society after the invention of printing and the attendant spread of Bible reading in the Christian community. For the preceding ages it applies in a much lower key. In those days Scripture was not a text that the average Christian explicated. Nor was it a text that was thought to be anything other than the source of what one believed, identical with what one believed. Scripture and Tradition were an amal-

[14]Augustine of Hippo, *Augustine: Earlier Writings,* in *The Library of Christian Classics*, trans. J. Burleigh (Philadelphia, 1953) VI, 316.

[15]See Karl Rahner, "What is a Dogmatic Statement? " in *Theological Investigations* (Baltimore, 1966) V, 64, where he describes the Bible as "*norma normans, non normata* of both dogmatic and nondogmatic statements of faith." See also "Scripture and Tradition," in *Sacramentum Mundi*, ed. K. Rahner *et al.* (New York, 1968-1970) VI, 53-57.

[16]James Barr, *Holy Scripture: Canon, Authority, Criticism* (Philadelphia, 1983), 1-32.

gam, and neatly harmonized. The critical edge of Scripture was less obvious in the past than in the present, despite the *Sic et non* and the *quaestio disputata*. The primary means for the exposition of Scripture were the liturgy (both ritual and homily) and various art forms, ranging from church buildings to painting; the *Biblia pauperum* contained vignettes and drawings of New Testament scenes and Old Testament types.

Be that as it may, it is clear today that the biblical dimension of Roman Catholic life has come to the forefront with the Dogmatic Constitution on Divine Revelation of Vatican II. The final chapter presents an ideal description of the function of the Bible in the life of the community:

> Therefore, like the Christian religion itself, all the preaching in the Church must be nourished and ruled by sacred Scripture. For in the sacred books, the Father who is in heaven meets His children with great love and speaks with them; and the force and power in the word of God is so great that it remains the support and energy of the Church, the strength of faith for her sons, the food of the soul, the pure and perennial source of spiritual life.[17]

The statement of Gerhard Ebeling underlines a critical factor that can play a fruitful role in the Church's understanding of herself and her history: how faithfully has the Church heard the Bible? An examination of church history can highlight the failures and the successes in this matter. Would the Church have been as triumphalistic as her history in the nineteenth and twentieth centuries attests, if she had been really listening to the judgments made upon the People of God in the Old Testament? The assurance of Christ's presence (Matt. 28:20) needs to be balanced against the

---

[17]See Chapter VI, #21 in *The Documents of Vatican II*, eds. Walter Abbott and Joseph Gallagher (New York, 1966), 125.

prophetic threats of Amos and other prophets. The emergence of the Church in its jurisdictional and monarchical form needs to be critically examined in terms of biblical data, as well as in terms of political factors. The various episodes in the historical life of the Church need to be analyzed from the point of view of the use of Scripture (one thinks of the Crusades). The Bible can provide a legal bar before which the judgments of church history can be presented.

Considerable courage and wisdom is called for in the implementation of modern biblical insights. These have provided data against which the current practices of the Church can be checked. There is, course, the guidance of the Spirit in the tradition of the Church, but one of the great resources at hand to purify this tradition and to ascertain the presence of the Spirit is precisely a careful attention to the biblical Word. Recently many burning issues in the current life the Church have been addressed by biblical scholars. Exhaustive and pertinent studies of divorce in the New Testament have been made, but these do not seem to have had as yet much effect upon the general theology or practice of the Church.[18] The cutting edge of biblical scholarship does not always sit well with traditional ways. The ever increasing number of difficult issues to which biblical scholarship has spoken makes some kind of action imperative. These issues include Eucharistic ministry, the ordination of women, the nature of priesthood and episcopacy.[19]

[18]An excellent treatment, with complete bibliographical indications, is provided by Bruce Vawter, "Divorce and the New Testament," *The Catholic Biblical Quarterly* 39 (1977), 528-42.

[19]See for example the report of the Task Force of the Catholic Biblical Association on the role of women in early Christianity, published in *The Catholic Biblical Quarterly* 41 (1979), 608-13; note the final sentence, "The conclusion we draw, then, is that the New Testament evidence, while not decisive by itself, points toward the admission of women to priestly ministry." It is an open secret that the report of the members of the Pontifical Biblical Commision likewise found no scriptural warrant for the exclusion of women from priestly ministry. Raymond E. Brown has also addressed this and other critical issues in *Biblical Reflections on Crises Facing the Church* (New York, 1975) and in *The Critical Meaning of the Bible* (New York, 1981).

In these instances the exposition of Scripture can seriously affect the course of church history if the Bible is taken seriously.

This opportunity to consider Ebeling's dictum comes at a propitious time for the present writer. At the annual meeting of the editorial board of *Concilium* at Tübingen in May, 1983, it was decided to combine the issues of Scripture and Church History in a single number of the periodical. Previously Scripture and Church History had separate publications (1965-1972). Then this was felt to be unnecessary since these areas should ideally be reflected in all the other topics (dogma, moral theology, ecumenism, church order, etc.), and separate publication was discontinued (1973-1983). Now the areas are to be joined, almost as if to test or implement the insight of Ebeling.[20]

[20]The collaboration of an international board of editors in the production of a theological periodical is no small accomplishment. The idiosyncracies of an individual can be filtered out in communal discussion and a theological presentation in the spirit of Vatican II can be effected. The tentative topic which the combined boards of Scripture and Church History are developing is the Exodus, and how this biblical theme is reflected (or should have been reflected) in the history of the Church.

New Light on Augustine the Pastor

Robert B. Eno, S.S.

Many of Monsignor Ellis' publications have been concerned with the lives and ministries of bishops. Beyond public statements and pastorals, personal letters often furnish the most striking testimony to their aspirations and intentions. The availability of such evidence cannot always be taken for granted, especially in the case of letters intended for a wider readership. From the ancient period, the letters of Symmachus, the pagan leader, lost much of their interest for the historian when they were rewritten with an eye to publication. One learns more from them about the formalism of late antique prose than about the daily life of the Roman aristocracy. Such details had originally filled the letters but were later excised. In the editor's mind, specific individuals and events paled in significance before the obligation to impress posterity with an alleged purity of style. The letters of bishops like Cyprian and Augustine, on the other hand, reveal the day-to-day lives and pastoral concerns of living human beings.

The recent publication of some hitherto unknown letters of Saint Augustine is a rare and noteworthy event in patristic scholarship.[1] Johannes Divjak of Vienna, while engaged in the project of cataloguing Augustinian manuscripts in France for the Austrian Academy of Sciences, came across a fifteenth century manuscript (A) in the municipal library of Marseille. It had earlier been the property of the Jesuit college of Aix-en-Provence. Divjak later found an older and better manuscript (C, twelfth century) in the Bibliothèque nationale. This manuscript had originally come from the Abbey of St. Cyran.

The new letters are some thirty in number and, for the time being at least, are being designated with an asterisk after the number to distinguish them from the letters of the traditional collection. Of these new discoveries, one is a letter from Jerome to Aurelius of Carthage and two are letters of Consentius to Augustine. The remaining letters were written by Augustine himself. Letter number twenty-seven presumes that letters 23* and 23A* are parts of the same letter. Letter 1* is a complete version of the fragmentary letter known as letter 250A. The letter to Firmus published by Cyrille Lambot in the *Revue bénédictine* in 1939 is also found here as letter 1A*.

These letters were published in 1981 as volume 88 of the *Corpus Scriptorum Ecclesiasticorum Latinorum*. A symposium on this find was held at the Institute for Augustinian Studies in Paris in September 1982. The letters were explored for their relevance to all areas of Augustinian research. In addition, a substantial number of suggestions were made for textual emendations in the Divjak edition. The Institute will publish a revised Latin text with a French translation of the letters.

---

[1] *Corpus Scriptorum Ecclesiasticorum Latinorum*, Vol. 88: *Sancti Aureli Augustini Opera: Epistolae ex duobus codicibus nuper in lucem prolatae* (Vienna, 1981). The year 1982 saw the publication of a second milestone in Latin patristic scholarship: the first volume of the *Prosopographie chrétienne du Bas-Empire. I: l'Afrique* (Paris, 1982) (hereafter cited as PCBE).

Each generation is justifiably impressed when confronted with the volume of the writings and the activities of Augustine the bishop. Hippo regius was not the negligible backwater it is usually presumed to have been. But even if it had been less important than it was, nevertheless, Augustine soon gained fame in North Africa and then in Western circles as a thinker and writer. The volume of requests for letters and treatises on many theological and exegetical questions soon came to assume unmanageable dimensions. He was troubled not only by the ordinary ecclesiastical problems but the need as well to act as mediator in disputes which ordinarily would go to a court of law (the *episcopalis audientia*). His efforts against the Donatist schism required a great deal of conciliar activity. This in turn involved much travel, especially to Carthage. Beyond a major issue like the reunion of the Church, normal duties called him to attend local gatherings of bishops.

In short, Augustine was a man consumed by his calling. He rarely could have had much time to himself, yet his writings are an inexhaustible source of thought, insight, and reflection for others. He exemplified in his life and works the idea that the good shepherd is a man who puts the ideal of *prodesse* (being of service to others) ahead of *praeesse* (being in a position of authority).[2] This essay will look at these newly published letters from the point of view of Augustine the pastor and see how they fit in with our previous knowledge of his episcopal activities.

The new letters make only a modest contribution to the history of the great controversies of the time. While it is impossible to give a precise date to all the letters and difficult to give even an approximate date to some of them , it is

---

[2]See: F. van der Meer, *Augustine the Bishop: The life and work of a Father of the Church*, translated from the Dutch original of 1947 by Brian Battershaw & G.R. Lamb (New York, 1961); Maurice Jourjon, "L'Évêque et le Peuple de Dieu selon St. Augustin," in *Saint Augustin parmi nous* (Le Puy, 1954), 149-97; and Othmar Perler (in collaboration with Jean-Louis Maier), *Les Voyages de Saint Augustin* (Paris, 1969).

clear that the majority of the letters belong to the last ten to twelve years of Augustine's life. Thus it is not surprising that there is little here concerning Donatism. The conference of Carthage of June 411, a meeting which Augustine had done much to bring about, marked the beginning of the end for Donatism. Letters 20* and 28* are concerned with the aftermath of the forced reunion of the Church. In the later letter, Augustine repeats a recommendation he had made on other occasions, viz., that each year during Lent the *acta* of the conference of Carthage be read in the churches so that converted Donatists in the congregation would be enabled to become Catholics interiorly as they had earlier been forced to conform externally. As he put it: "That they may be held in the Catholic peace not only by fear of temporal trials but also by fear of everlasting fire and by love of the truth " (*ep.* 28*.2). These same letters also inform us (*ep.* 28*.7) that some Donatist elements had not changed their earlier, violent ways. A converted Donatist bishop, Rogatus of Assuras, had been attacked and had his tongue cut out and hand cut off. This incident is also noted in letter 185.30 and the *Gesta cum Emerito* 9, thus placing it c.418.

Priscillian[3] had been executed for heresy in 385 but his influence in Spain continued to grow. A lay Christian living in the Balearic islands by the name of Consentius wrote to Augustine seeking counsel.[4] He seems to have been one of those among Augustine's correspondents who might justly be considered nuisances, people who expected long and detailed responses to frivolous questions from a man who had better things to do. It was thought that the Priscillian-ists had a widespread, subversive network of members who appeared outwardly to be faithful Catholics. This network included priests and even bishops. Since they had no scru-ples about lying to protect themselves, some Catholics, including Consentius, claimed the right to lie in order to

---

[3] Henry Chadwick, *Priscillian of Avila: The Occult and the Charismatic in the Early Church* (Oxford, 1976).

[4] The other letters from and to Consentius are : *epp.* 119-20, 205.

infiltrate their ranks. Augustine had been shocked by such a proposition and wrote the treatise *Contra mendacium* as a refutation (420).

The two lengthiest letters of the new collection were written by Consentius (11* and 12*). The first adds little to the serious study of Priscillianism but narrates a long story of an orthodox zealot by the name of Fronto who lied his way into the confidence of some Priscillianists. When he came to expose them, he brought upon himself the wrath of highly placed Priscillianists within the hierarchy. The long letter ends with the remark that some Spanish Catholics perceived Augustine as too moderate in his treatment of the Donatists. Priscillianists and their sympathizers, using the African example as an excuse, complained that they were being treated with unreasonable severity. Would Augustine please write to explain the difference between the two cases, asked Consentius (*ep.* 11*.26). Letter 12* does not have the interest of 11* and is simply annoying. Consentius goes on at great length, repeating in various ways that while he has the greatest difficulty in bringing himself to read anything (including the works of Augustine he had earlier begged for), he seems psychologically incapable of keeping himself from writing unceasingly.

Given the time period of these letters, it was to be expected that the most prominent of the great controversies in these letters would be Pelagianism. In letter 19* to Jerome, Augustine mentions that he has heard of some of Jerome's anti-Pelagian works (*Dialogi contra Pelagianos libri iii*). Of greater interest are letters 4* and 6*, not least because they are written to well-known Eastern bishops, Cyril of Alexandria and Atticus of Constantinople respectively. Such Eastern correspondents are rare, except for letter 179 to John of Jerusalem and, of course, the series of letters to that cantankerous Westerner long resident in Bethlehem, Jerome. In the case of both letters 4* and 6*, there are echoes of the general Eastern lack of comprehension of what Augustine found objectionable in Pelagius. In letter

4*, the messenger who carried to the East a copy of Augustine's *De Gestis Pelagii* (containing his reactions to the exoneration of Pelagius by a Palestinian council) found himself accused of altering the text. The work was sent back to Augustine for verification. He confirmed that the text was authentic and untampered with but once again implied that Pelagian refugees from the West might be sowing the seeds of misunderstanding in the East. He was not able to appreciate that some of his own ideas might be alien to the Eastern outlook.

Letter 6* is especially reminiscent of the bitter battles between Augustine and Julian of Eclanum which saddened the former's last years.[5] Augustine first expressed chagrin at not receiving a letter in return from Atticus, though he also expressed understanding for the reason why no such letter was written, viz., because Atticus had heard rumors of Augustine's death! But Augustine was upset principally because of the "slander" being spread about that he condemned marriage. This was a debate that went on endlessly between Augustine and Julian. In this letter, Augustine's teaching has not changed, but what is unusual is his positive use of the word *concupiscentia*. Carnal concupiscence essentially is the evil of lust, the result of original sin, by which the sexual function is removed from the control of reason. But Augustine adds here, there are also acceptable senses of concupiscence, i.e., the concupiscence of marriage, of conjugal modesty and of the legitimate engendering of children. These are all good senses of concupiscence and may correspond to the three *bona coniugalia* earlier developed by Augustine in his *De bono coniugali*. Unlike many of the Eastern fathers, Augustine had always admitted that even without an original fall, there would have been sexual reproduction in Paradise, but it would have been totally under the control of reason — no lust or passion. It is very

[5]See Marie-Francois Berrouard, "Les lettres 6* et 19* de S. Augustin," *Revue des Etudes Augustiniennes* 27 (1981), 264-77, esp. 269-76.

rare that he applies a positive meaning to the word *concupiscentia* beyond the concupiscence of the spirit fighting back against the flesh.

As we indicated earlier, much of Augustine's valuable time was taken up answering the questions sent to him. Some concerned liturgical or rubrical questions or, more accurately, theological questions posed by liturgical practices (e.g., *epp.* 5*; 28* .3). While some of Augustine's correspondents sought advice on marital problems, there were some married couples who, having taken the vow of continence, now found it difficult to persevere in its observance (cf. letter 127 to Armentarius and Pauline). Augustine was usually very careful to insist that those already married be extremely cautious about embarking on such a course. Above all, they were to do it only with the full and uncoerced agreement of both parties. In letter 3*, the case is different. Here a mother who years before had vowed the continence of her seriously ill infant daughter, if the latter should recover, now when she herself was older and her daughter of marriageable age, wished to transfer the obligation of continence to herself. Augustine condemned such haggling with God, urging that both mother and daughter take the vow. He always was very clear that the younger woman, whatever her mother's wishes, must be allowed to make up her own mind to ratify the vow made in her name or to reject it (*ep.* 3*; cf. also *ep.* 254 and *sermo* 355).

Some people expected Augustine to drop everything and write them a treatise or at least a long letter. There are instances where the same people later admitted that they had not read the work so urgently demanded. It was an honor just to possess a work of Augustine in one's library, and indeed such literary immortality as these people have is due to the fact that they once wrote to Augustine and received a reply. "I craved the treasures of wisdom, but I received less than I wished, although one should not call 'less' a gift bestowed by Augustine, the oracle of the law. . . ." (Audax, *ep.* 260).

Augustine frequently complained of his weariness and overburdened state. After the priest Heraclius had been ratified as his successor by the Christians of Hippo (426), he expressed the hope that he would henceforth be freed from the routine duties he had fulfilled for thirty years, because "both morning and afternoon, I am enmeshed in men's affairs" (*ep.* 213.5). But realistically he concluded, his *otium* (leisure) would always, inevitably, turn into *negotium* (work).

Dealing with the questions and objections of curious pagans was an activity he deemed well worth his best efforts. By the early fifth century, there were few aristocratic families untouched by Christianity. The pattern of conversion frequently brought women into the Church first and left men to be converted much later in their lifetimes, if at all.[6] Augustine, at the urging of Marcellinus, was careful to reply to the queries of the young nobleman, Volusianus (c. 412; cf. *epp.* 132—133, 135,137). Volusianus, however, became a Christian only much later, on his deathbed in Constantinople, attended by his niece Melania (437; cf. *Vita Melaniae* 54—55).

In the new letters, Firmus is the one who best fills the role of the pagan intellectual. He was previously known as the one to whom Augustine had suggested ways in which the *De civitate dei* might be divided — into two or five volumes. That letter caused scholars to envisage Firmus as some sort of literary agent for Augustine. Actually, we find now in letter 2*, Firmus was another of those who professed to be fascinated by philosophical-theological problems. He begged to receive the books of the *De civitate dei* as soon as they appeared. Like many people since, he was more eager to possess such works than to read them. He had read the first ten (especially concerned with anti-pagan apologetic),

---

[6]Peter Brown, "Aspects of the Christianization of the Roman Aristocracy," in *Religion and Society in the Age of St. Augustine* (London, 1972), 161-82.

but apparently not the last twelve (the more positive theological section). Augustine did not object to supplying the books, provided they were read. He hoped that Firmus would be open to the grace of conversion. Firmus had earlier heard an oral presentation of a version of book 18, but no practical result had emerged, complained Augustine.

Firmus put forward three objections to explain why he persisted in his procrastination. His second and third reasons were more intellectual, even philosophical: 2) that it is more reverent to approach the mysteries of religion slowly and hesitantly; 3) we must await God's will in these matters. Augustine deflated these objections by saying that it is clearly God's will that all enter the Church as soon as possible and that much more progress can be made from inside than by waiting outside, skulking about on the margins.

But the real reason, Augustine hinted, was the first excuse, moral weakness, an unwillingness, not unique by any means at that time or since for the male in particular to abandon his privileged position. Augustine fought against the sexual double standard (e.g., *sermo* 392) which allowed men the privilege of philandering while requiring the strictest fidelity of wives. *Virtus* comes from *vir*, does it not? Then why is the "weaker sex" successful in resisting temptation while men who pride themselves on courage and strength plead that the demands of conjugal chastity and fidelity are too much to ask?

> I am not afraid to offend you, when by the example of a woman, I exhort you to enter the City of God; for if this is a difficult thing, the weaker sex is already there; if easy, there is no reason that you may not be stronger there. Therefore, there is nothing to be ashamed of for a man in this matter which demands strength of mind to follow a woman who enters; rather we should be shamed lest while

she enters, you do not at least follow and while she is within, where the virtue of true salvation and piety is attained, you with a greater capacity for virtue, remain outside. (*ep.* 2*.4)

Firmus' wife may not be able to discuss the deep philosophical and theological issues as he can, but, referring to the *disciplina arcani*, Augustine comments: "There are things she knows and you do not yet know that she cannot reveal" (*ibid.*). This letter also contains a version of the proverbial "God writes straight with crooked lines." "[H]e is able to do good things even with evils that are not his" (ep.2*.8).

The reader of these new letters is struck in particular by the magnitude of the social problems of the disintegrating Western empire. The vision of a violent and harsh society intrudes itself relentlessly into our picture of Augustine's social milieu. The shadowy workings of the slave dealers are highlighted in letter 10* to Alypius. The *mangones*, says Augustine, have now become so numerous that they seem to be draining Africa of much of its population, transferring the victims to other provinces across the sea. Sometimes parents sell their own children, not just as servants bound for a set period of time but as true slaves, though this is illegal. Real slave owners, Augustine notes ironically, do not sell their slaves. These unfortunates form a never-ending stream, a great multitude of people going to a form of captivity worse than that experienced under the barbarians. (*ep.* 10*.5)

The slavers are becoming increasingly bold, forcing their way deeper into country areas where they carry off anyone they want. They go into a village, killing the men and taking the women and children. The Church tried to ransom some of these people. Augustine mentioned a little girl so rescued. She told him that slave dealers had broken into her home and taken her away right in front of her parents and brothers. One of her brothers who came to Hippo to get her said they tried to disguise their activities as barbarian incursions.

Augustine points out that such outrages would not happen if: 1) there were not people always ready to do business with such thugs (*praedones*) and worse still, 2) there were not government officials willing to look the other way. An earlier decree of the emperor Honorius decreed that such traffickers be scourged with lead-tipped thongs. Augustine hesitated at such a penalty, noting that it "easily brings about a man's death." (*ep.* 10*.4) Yet in fact the punishment had fallen into abeyance. The law should be used as a deterrent, 1) to stop people from doing such things; 2) to free their victims; and 3) only lastly to punish the guilty. The Roman army in its better days (*cum bene et prospere geritur*) fought to protect Romans from falling into the hands of the barbarians, but who is there to resist these "businessmen" (*talis impietatis negotiatores*)? Who will resist in the name of Roman liberty?

Greed can bring people to do some dreadful things: e.g., the local woman in Hippo who "under the guise of buying wood," beat and sold other women; or one of the Church's *coloni* (tenant farmers), otherwise apparently a good man, who sold his wife. Even a younger member of Augustine's own monastic community was carried off for a short while until he could be ransomed. Once, while Augustine was away, a ship belonging to Galatian slavers docked in Hippo. Christians alerted to this were able to free about 120, almost all of whom, it turned out, had been coerced by violence or deceit. Augustine remarked to Alypius that these 120 represented only a tiny part of the thousands being led into captivity all along the coast. The brigands had friends in high places. They did not give up so easily and sometimes returned with documents to support their claims, even from bishops!

Much of the North African countryside was divided into large estates, some of which were owned by the Church. These estates were worked by tenant farmers whose social and legal status was sinking.[7] In letter 24* Augustine, trying to exercise his episcopal office of mediation among Christians conscientiously, wrote to seek legal advice from one Eustochius. The letter is a witness to the process of the reduction of the *coloni* to the state of serfs, free in theory but in fact tied to the land. Augustine asks, for example, whether free fathers can sell their sons into perpetual servitude or, more precisely, how, he asks, is it possible that a purchaser acquire more authority over the son than the owner of the domain where his father tills the soil? How can the owner make slaves of his tenant farmers or their sons? What exactly is the status of these people? Free-born men are sought for the land and they think they are gaining something by coming to work here. In fact, they find out later that they are letting themselves in for something very serious. They would never have come if they had known the consequences. (Cf. *ep.* 247.) Augustine mentions some laws that have come to his attention and asks Eustochius for explanations. These uncertainties raise questions about the period in which the colonate degenerated into a sort of proto-serfdom. Augustine, to be sure, was not a legal specialist, but he was a well-informed layman in these matters.

A serious source of friction with local government officials was the tradition of the right of sanctuary for the pursued. The issue comes up in the earlier letters of Augustine (cf., e.g., *epp.* 113-115; 268). In the latter case, Augustine expressed the hope that donations from the congregation would help liberate a debtor, Fascius, who had taken refuge in the church. In letter 1*, count Classicianus complained to Augustine that not only he, but his entire family, had been excommunicated by the inexperienced young bishop Auxilius (of Nurco or Murco in Mauretania Caesariensis) for, he claimed, doing his duty (cf. also *ep.*

---

[7]Church-owned estates: e.g., *ep.* 35.4. Is the "Spania" mentioned here to be identified with the "saltus Hispaniensis" of *ep.* 15*.4?

28*.5). Augustine lamented the contempt which officials sometimes showed them because they were clerics and could not enforce their protests against injustice and arbitrary behavior (*ep.* 22*.3). A more serious incident in Carthage is alluded to in several places in the new letters (*epp.* 15*.2; 23A*.1). We do not know the nature of the case, but a number of people had taken refuge in a church in Carthage until pardon arrived from the government in Italy. There is probably a connection to be made between this incident and the reference in letter 203 to Largus, proconsul of Africa, concerning "trials already endured."

The question of the Church and its need for money and the use made by churchmen of the money is as old as the Church itself. The Church, as noted above, owned estates which it probably had inherited. Augustine mentions on several occasions legacies left to the Church and the problems accompanying them. In one case, for example, Augustine refused to accept a legacy from Boniface, a merchant in Hippo, who left the Church his shipping company, because this would involve the Church in conducting a business, a rather high risk one at that (*sermo* 355). In another instance, at about the same time, he was chagrined to find that one of his monks, Januarius, had not divested himself of his property when he became a monk, but when dying made a will with the church of Hippo as his beneficiary. Since Augustine considered it shameful for a monk to keep property in his own name and further, since Januarius had a son and a daughter still living, although they were also in monasteries, Augustine decided that the Church should keep the money only in the capacity of temporary trustee (*ibid.*). Some parishioners thought Augustine's conscience a bit too delicate for the good of the diocesan treasury!

Augustine had become involved in a similar case some years before. A man named Honoratus had been a monk in Alypius' monastery in Thagaste before becoming a priest in the church of Thiave. Here too Augustine was saddened that a monk should have kept his possessions, but he suggested that the money involved should belong to the church where Honoratus served as a priest. The monks at Thagaste claimed at least half the money and suggested that Augustine make up the other half out of his own pocket (c. 405; *ep.* 83). The enthusiasm of the people of Hippo for the proposed ordination of Pinianus was motivated by his fabulous wealth (c.411; *ep.* 126). In the new letter (*ep.* 7*), Augustine handles the delicate question of a bequest from the widow of the tribune Bassus. She may have changed her mind about it but, unfortunately, the Church had already spent some of the money.

Questions of finances are sensitive enough in themselves, but they become much stickier when clerical scandals are involved. For example, the underhanded land dealings of bishop Paul of Cataqua left Boniface, his successor, in a terribly embarrassing position both morally and financially. Augustine in letter 85 (before 408) tried to explain this to Olympius, a government official. In letter 8*, it is not clear whether the addressee, Victor, is a bishop or not. In any event, land swindles are again the subject. Here a Jew named Licinius contacted Augustine to complain that he had been cheated by Victor. The latter bought land from Licinius' mother, but she in fact did not own the land . Upon further inquiry, it emerged that this unpleasant incident was made possible because Licinius and his mother were estranged over a supposed insult from Licinius' wife and her maidservant. Trying to be helpful, Augustine suggested that a reconciliation might be effected if Victor would simply have Licinius flogged in his mother's presence or, have Licinius flog his wife in his mother 's presence. Flogging the servant girl would be the simplest solution of all since she could not protest and all would be satisfied. For all Augustine's unhappy memories of his schooldays, he seemed to suggest flogging rather readily (cf. *ep.* 133. 2 to Marcellinus on how to deal with the Donatists).

Clerical scandals of whatever nature, then as always, seemed to titillate the town gossips. People loved to use the bad conduct of clerics as an excuse for their own indifference or mediocrity (*ep.* 78 .6). Two letters (c. 404; *epp.* 77-78) involved serious recriminations between two monks, Spes and Boniface, including allegations of homosexual solicitation. Augustine packed them both off to Italy to the shrine of the martyr Felix of Nola, presided over by his friend Paulinus. This series of new letters has more than its share of clerical scandals. For example, in letter 9* a man, accused of kidnapping a nun (*sanctimonialis*) for immoral purposes, was then beaten by a group of irate priests; or letter 13*, where a cleric claims that while he was sleeping on the roof on a hot night, a young woman of the house he was visiting (also called a *sanctimonialis*) approached him on the pretext of wanting to talk about her repressive parents, but she actually had something else in mind. He was able to escape only when a downpour ensued; he ran outside, spending the remainder of the night standing under the overhang of the roof. Augustine charitably said he was uncertain whether he should believe the story. It is possible that the cleric involved in letter 13* is the same one spoken of in 18* where Augustine tells the people of Memblibani (?) that the deacon Gitta should be deprived of his office rather than promoted. If Gitta is also the cleric of letter 13*, then the version of the roof incident told there is very much slanted in his favor.

Augustine was a stickler for correctness. He strongly opposed the promotion of bishop Honoratus to the see of Caesarea in Mauretania as successor to Deuterius whom Augustine had recently visited in 418 (see *Gesta cum Emerito* and *Sermo ad Caesarienses*). Honoratus was already a bishop near Cartenna and according to conciliar legislation, such transferrals were not to be permitted. From his tone, however, one might be forgiven for having the impression that canonical objections were not the only ones to Honoratus' promotion (*epp.* 22*.5; 23*; 23A*.5). Augustine told the people of another local church that they might not have a certain cleric as their deacon for similar reasons (*epp.* 21*; 26*).

Augustine knew very well that clerical scandals did a great deal of harm to the Church. He wrote letters to good Christians, trying to help them (and himself?) avoid discouragement on their account. Such, for example, was his letter to Felicia (*ep.* 208). In another place he wrote:

> [S]till, as the Apostle says, the Lord "knows who are his own." He foretold all these scandals to come which sadden us. He warned us not to be discouraged and promised us the reward if we persevere with his help in order that we may live there in eternity with him, where there can be no temptation and scandals but only joy and certainty of eternal joys, blessed immortality and happiness without end. Put your hope in him, my sons and brothers, and may your charity never grow cold so that you may be found tested and proved on the last day. . . . (*ep.* 18*.3)

The longest of Augustine's own letters in this new series concerns a great scandal which was at the same time one of his worst personal trials. This was the case of Antoninus of Fussala about which we already possess his letter 209 to Pope Celestine. Because of the greatly increased numbers of new Catholics brought about by the official suppression of Donatism, Augustine decided that the village of Fussala in the vicinity of Hippo should have its own bishop. He chose a member of his monastic community and asked the primate of Numidia to come to ordain him. In the province of Numidia, there was no permanent primatial see but the honor went to the bishop with the greatest seniority in the episcopate. This almost automatically insured that the position would always be occupied by an elderly and infirm incumbent. The primate at this moment (411/412?) was probably Silvanus of Summa. As he came near Hippo, the monk selected for the new bishopric withdrew and left Augustine with a dilemma. If nothing were done, the elderly primate would have been brought a long distance for nothing. He decided there would be an ordination and

selected a very young lector, Antoninus, a decision he was to
regret for the rest of his years. Antoninus, as letter 209
indicates, was an episcopal disgrace. Letter 20* (422) tells us
more about his background and about his activities as
bishop. This letter is addressed to Fabiola who had charitably taken Antoninus in. She was not Jerome's friend who
had died c.400 (cf. Jerome, *ep.* 77), but is probably the
woman addressed in Augustine's letter 267. She must have
lived near Rome. While Augustine still expressed paternal
feelings for his mean-spirited protégé, he wrote to Fabiola
to tell her his side of the story.

The comings and goings of Numidian bishops in an effort
to do something about Antoninus are recounted. After his
refusal to step down quietly, a council was held at Teglata to
hear his appeal. At one point, the primate of Numidia, now
Aurelius of Macomades, went back to Fussala in the hope
of persuading the people to take him back. They were
outraged at the thought of his return. They refused to speak
out as individuals for fear that their names would be taken
down and Antoninus would avenge himself on them later
(*ep.* 20*.21). He and his principal associates, birds of a
feather, a priest who was also a renegade from Augustine's
monastery and a deacon (*ep.* 20*.6), threatened people,
especially the weak. They extorted "money, furnishings,
clothing, farm animals, produce, wood, and even stone."
Some had their homes taken and demolished to get building
materials. Other things were supposedly "purchased" but
never paid for. Antoninus, the poor boy and erstwhile
monk, did everything he could in a very short time to enrich
himself and above all to build himself a fine house, all at the
expense of the people and the Church.

Upon his initial deposition, bishop Antoninus had
appealed to Rome, to Pope Boniface (418-422), demanding that his case be reviewed so that he might retain his see
and not just the empty title of bishop which the African
council had conceded to him. This was the moment for
appeals to Rome, the time of the controversy concerning the

priest Apiarius who had been disciplined by his bishop, Urbanus of Sicca,[8] the one-time prior of Augustine's monastery in Hippo. The position of the African bishops in relation to the Roman church varied according to the circumstances. In 416, after a Palestinian council, by seeming to give Pelagius a clean bill of health, undermined an earlier African condemnation, the councils of Africa proconsularis and Numidia reiterated their condemnation and appealed to Pope Innocent (401-417) for confirmation.

Later, when Pope Zosimus (417-418), apparently without good reason, accepted the appeal of the priest Apiarius, the Africans conceded the right of appeal from African bishops for the time being (until they verified the "Nicene" canons, alleged as justification by Rome, by comparing the Latin texts with Greek texts newly solicited from the East). Later, when the same priest was caught in the act, he again appealed to Rome, but this time he eventually confessed, and the final result was a forceful and sarcastic letter of protest sent by the African bishops to Pope Celestine (424; *Optaremus*). The debate about appeals to Rome from Africa, even by bishops, is a complex one,[9] but the general picture drawn by scholars is one which minimizes Roman involvement in the affairs of the African church. The African Catholics respected the Roman church as the leader of Western Christians, but wished to run their own affairs without intervention from the great church "across the sea."

The new letters, however, give a somewhat different picture, one of much greater interchange between Rome and North Africa. For example, in letter 1*, when count Classicianus complained that he along with his entire family had been unjustly excommunicated by a young bishop, Augustine noted that the question should be taken up by an

[8]On Urban of Sicca, see PCBE, 1232, "Urbanus 7"; ep 20*.2.

[9]On the issue of appeals to Rome, see W. Marschall, *Karthago und Rom* (Stuttgart, 1971), 161—203.

African council and, if necessary, "questions can be sent to the apostolic see" about the issue. The problem of the episcopal succession at Caesarea in Mauretania was also something that should be considered by Carthage and Rome (*epp.* 22*.6-7 and 23A*.4). Even apparently so trivial an incident as the beating administered to a prominent layman by outraged priests came to the attention of Pope Celestine (*ep.* 9*.1,4).

A few technical questions also have some additional light shed on them in the new letters. Augustine's close friend Alypius, bishop of their native town of Thagaste, made a number of trips to Italy in the last decade of Augustine's life. These missions concerned the Roman government more than the Roman see. From what was previously known, Alypius while in Italy in 419 or 420 received from count Valerius, the recipient of the first book of Augustine's *De nuptiis et concupiscentia*, the four books *Ad Turbantium* of Julian of Eclanum in addition to some of the latter's letters. On his next trip (420 or 421)[10], Alypius brought Valerius the second book of the *De nuptiis* and gave the *Contra duas epistolas Pelagianorum* to Pope Boniface. Julian later called Alypius Augustine's "lackey" (*vernula peccatorum eius*) and claimed that the real reason for the voyage was to bring some eighty African horses to be distributed to government officials as bribes (Julian, in Augustine, *Opus imperfectum contra Julianum* I.7; I.42). Letters 9* and 10* to Alypius in Italy mention that Celestine (422-432) is now pope. Alypius must have made even more frequent trips to Italy in this period than was earlier realized. Finally c. 427 in yet another trip, Alypius received and sent to Augustine the first five books of Julian's *Ad Florum* which Augustine began to answer in his *Opus imperfectum* (429-430).

---

[10]For the dates of Alypius' travels to Italy see Anne-Marie La Bonnardière, *Recherches de Chronologie Augustinienne* (Paris, 1965), 76, n. 2.

We also learn a little more about Augustine's unhappy relations with the general, count Boniface. We know from sermon 114 that Boniface had heard Augustine preach in Carthage. Letter 220.2 mentions a visit by Boniface to Hippo, though Augustine said he (Augustine) was exhausted at the time and did not have much opportunity for a long visit.₁ Letter 17* briefly refers to some people shipwrecked near Hippo. Augustine sent them on to Boniface whom he still regarded favorably as one who sought "eternal peace...even in the midst of the works of war, while you keep faith and love justice in all things" (*ep.* 17*.2).

This brief analysis of these new letters of St. Augustine has pointed out some elements of direct continuity with letters already well known. In addition, I have indicated instances where similar problems and situations are found in Augustine's other works. In his busy life, he accomplished an incredible number of things, being pressed day after day and year after year by problems both theological and pastoral. These new letters add richly to the examples and illustrations found elsewhere in the writings of Augustine to enliven our understanding of late Antiquity as a time when life was often cruel and violent and to appreciate the frustrations of those like Augustine who tried to alleviate the suffering. His ideal of the priest and bishop as servant is clear from his life as well as his teaching. "I live here with you and I live my life for you, and it is my wish and desire that I may live forever with you at the side of Christ" (*sermo* 355.1).

Girolamo Massaino: Another Conciliarist at the Papal Court, Julius II to Adrian VI

Nelson H. Minnich

The triumph of the restored papal monarchy over conciliarism in its various forms was not complete on the eve of the Reformation. The Pisan Council (1511-12), called by emperor Maximilian I and king Louis XII of France and by seven dissident cardinals to censure Julius II (1503-13) for his neglect of church reform and for his military actions in Italy, found support not only north of the Alps, but also in Italy. Defenders of the Pisan Council included not only the eminent Italian canonist Filippo Decio and the learned Benedictine abbot of Subasio, Zaccaria Ferreri, but even a leading curialist at the papal court, Giovanni Gozzadini.[1]

---

[1]For an overview of conciliar thinking at this time, see; Remigius Bäumer, *Nachwirkungen des konziliaren Gedankens in der Theologie und Kanonistik des frühen 16. Jahrhunderts,* Nr. 100 of *Reformationsgeschichtliche Studien und Texte,* ed. August Franzen (Münster/Westfalen, 1971) and Franco Todescan, "Fermenti gallicani e dottrine anti-conciliariste al Lateranense V: un capitolo della teologia politica del secolo XVI," in *Cristianesimo, secolarizzazione e diritto moderno,* eds. Luigi Lombardi Vallauri and Gerhard Dilcher, Nrs. 11/12 of *Per la storia del pensiero giuridico moderno* (Milano, 1981), 567-609, esp. 575-80. For the literary defense of the Pisan Council, see: Josef Hergenroether, *Histoire des conciles d'après les documents originaux,* VIII/1, trans. and rev. Henri Leclercq, (Paris, 1917), 314-23; Pierre Imbart de la Tour, *Les origines de la Réforme,* II:

This former Datarius was not alone in holding such views in Rome.

Girolamo Massaino, a fellow curialist, openly argued that the emperor and kings of Christendom could restrain papal temporal power, while the bishops were a divinely ordained check on the pope's spiritual authority. At the urging of cardinal Niccolò Fieschi, Massaino set down his ideas in a treatise *De conciliis* (1512). So hostile was the cardinal's response to his ecclesiological views that Massaino feared for his life. Far from abandoning his ideas, for the next decade he gathered new arguments to bolster them and incorporated these in a revised treatise, *De conciliis et ecclesiae statu monarchico et aristocratico* (1523) which he submitted to the judgment of the northern reforming pontiff, Adrian VI.[2]

L'Eglise catholique, la crise et la Renaissance, rev. ed. by Yvonne Lanhers (Melun, 1946), 169-72; Francis A. Oakley, "Almain and Major: Conciliar Theory on the Eve of the Reformation," *American Historical Review* 70 (1969), 673-90 and his "Conciliarism in the Sixteenth Century: Jacques Almain Again," *Archiv für Reformationsgeschichte* 68 (1977), 111-32; Myron P. Gilmore, *Humanists and Jurists: Six Studies in the Renaissance* (Cambridge, Ma., 1963), 66-79; Bernardo Morsolin, "L'Abbate di Monte Subasio e il Concilio di Pisa (1511-1512): Episodio di storia ecclesiastica," in *Atti del Reale Istituto Veneto di scienze, lettere, ed arti*, Tomo IV, Serie VII (1892-93), 1689-1735; and Hubert Jedin, "Giovanni Gozzadini, ein Konziliarist am Hofe Julius' II.," *Römische Quartalschrift* 47 (1939), 193-267 and his "Nochmals der Konziliarist Gozzadini," *ibid.* 61 (1966), 88-93.

[2]The treatise *De conciliis*, preserved in the Biblioteca Apostolica Vaticana (hereafter cited as BAV) as Codex Reginensis Latinus 392, fols. 260r-79v, has been described and identified by Andrés Wilmart, O.S.B., as an autograph copy. It is prefaced by a letter to cardinal Niccolò Fieschi dated May 15, 1512, five days after the first formal session of the Fifth Lateran Council. Hereafter this particular manuscript is cited as DC. See Andrés Wilmart, *Codices Reginenses Latini*, Tomus II: *251-500*, in *Bibliothecae Apostolicae Vaticanae codices manu scripti recensiti*, ed. Giovanni Mercati (Vatican City, 1945), 442.

In addition to the autograph at least one other copy of this treatise is extant. This is preserved in BAV, Codex Vaticanus Latinus 3919, fols. 77r-93r. This codex contains a good amount of material relating to the question of whether or not to convoke a council to deal with the Lutheran question and belonged to Girolamo Aleandro. The Massaino fascicle, entitled on fol. 76r *Hiers. Massainus de Conciliis*, consists of 10 sheets folded in half and sewn in the middle at fols. 85v—86r. Each folio measures 21.5 x 29.5 cm. and contains between 22 to 24 lines of text. Folios 76v and 93v-95v are blank. The folios with text have been covered with a

Girolamo's early life was spent in Tuscany. The Massaino family hailed from Poppi in the Casentino, about 25 miles southeast of Florence, near Bibbiena. His father Francesco, the son of *magister* Jacobus de Masseyni was alive in 1480, but had died by 1495. Girolamo was probably born about

browned tissue paper which makes the reading more difficult. The folio paper bears the watermark of a walking duck within an oblongated shield of ten sides which is surmounted by a six-pointed star. This watermark is a variant of Nr. 12,235 in Charles-Moïse Briquet, *Les filigranes: Dictionnaire historique de marques du papier des leur apparition vers 1282 jusqu'en 1600*, 4 vols. (Paris, 1907), IV, among the designs of "oiseau" and II, 613 for the indications that a similar design first appeared in Rome of 1513, with variants in Rome of 1534-46 and Sermoneta of 1536.

Yet other copies of Massaino's treatise are listed in *Concilium Tridentinum: Diariorum, actorum, epistolarum, tractatuum nova collectio*, ed. Görres-Gesellschaft (Freiburg, 1901-), XII (Tractates), ed. V. Schweitzer (Freiburg, 1930), xxi and xxxiv: Bib. Angel. cod. 252 (but no such work exists under that listing at the Biblioteca Angelica of Rome), Archivio Segreto Vaticano (hereafter cited as ASV), Acta Concilii Tridentini 152 (also not under that listing — that codex contains correspondence between Carlo Borromeo and the Council of Trent), and *ibid.* 148, fols. 31r-44v: *J. Massaini, De auctoritate concilii et imperatoris in concilio — 1512* (fols. 31-46 have been extracted from this codex — all that remains is a loose thread).

The revised version of 1523 which has been entitled by a later hand *De conciliis et ecclesiae statu monarchico et aristocratico* (hereafter cited as DCEES) is written in the same hand as DC in Rome and is preserved in the Biblioteca Ambrosiana of Milan with the shelf number P. 238 Parte Superiore, fols. 1r-41v. In addition to the 1512 prefatory letter to Fieschi, DCEES begins with an undated letter to Adrian VI. As indicated by the hand which inscribed the title, this codex is missing its final section (*In fine mutilatus*), yet is still besprinkled throughout with some shrewd, sarcastic, and witty passages (*sed ubique salle respersus*). This manuscript has been foliated in pencil by a later hand in the upper right hand corners. It consists of four quires of five folded sheets each with catchwords on the lower right hand corners of fols. 10v, 21v, 31v, and 41v. Folio 17r, which contains material to be inserted into the text on fol. 18r, is but a half sheet. Each folio is 22.5 x 30 cm. in measurement. The number of lines of text on each side of a folio in the body of the treatise ranges from 31 to 36. Insertions are made in the margins above, below, and on the side of the text. The paper bears the watermark of an anchor inscribed in a circle surmounted by a six-pointed star. The closest approximation to it is figure Nr. 491 in Briquet, *Les Filigranes*; on I, 42 Briquet dates this design to 1519 in Florence and another variant to 1521 also in Florence. The reference in Massaino's dedicatory letter to Adrian to eleven years having passed since he first wrote on this topic places this treatise in 1523, soon after Briquet's earliest dating.

This codex has been mutilated in two ways. The upper right hand corner of fols. 1-4 has been torn off with the loss of portions of from 2 to 4 lines. The text ends abruptly at fol. 41v, the end of the fourth quire, and catchwords indicate that at one

1460, for on June 1, 1482 he was appointed by Sixtus IV rector of the church of Santo Stefano at Calcinaia on the Arno River, some eleven miles east of Pisa, and no mention was made of dispensation for age. Girolamo was an absentee benefice-holder. He appears as a clerical student in the rolls of 1480 and 1493-94 at the University of Pisa, and in the following year is listed as a priest and teacher at the univer-

time the manuscript continued on. Originally there were probably two additional quires. Although the relatively small amount of material in DC which had yet to be incorporated into DCEES (e.g., 269r-v and 273r—78r) would suggest a single quire, reference to a later complete copy of this treatise indicates that almost forty percent of the text is missing from DCEES. Since this missing material is for the most part no more offensive than the rest, it is doubtful that the final quires were deliberately removed. Because the hand which penned DCEES is the same as that which wrote DC and has been identified by Wilmart as that of Massaino himself, a judgment which the numerous revisions made in the text of DCEES seem to confirm, I have cited this manuscript. Where the text was difficult to read or material missing due to mutilations, I have had recourse to the following later complete version.

Under the title *De statu et regimine ecclesiae* (hereafter cited as DSERE), a full version of the DCEES treatise is preserved in the Biblioteca Ambrosiana of Milan with the shelf mark I 228 Inf. (olim F 445 R). This codex, which apparently at one time belonged to Giovanni Vincenzo Pinelli (1535-1601), has been described by Adolfo Rivolta in his *Catalogo dei codici pinelliani dell' Ambrosiana* (Milan, 1933), p. 238, Nr. 266. The paper on which DSERE is written bears the watermark of the stylized outline of a hat with two long string ties — see Briquet, *Les filigranes*, I, 225, Nrs. 3412—18 "chapeau." The earliest place and date he cited for it is Parma 1526. The codex consists of twelve quires, of which the first eleven are of ten sheets folded in half and sewn, while the twelfth is of only eight such sheets. Each folio measures 30 x 21 cm. Folios 125v-28v are blank. The former pagination in ink has been revised in pencil. Because the reviser counted the title page as folio 1, the subsequent numeration had to be raised by one number. I cite the revised penciled numeration of the upper right hand corners. The number of lines of text per folio side varies from as high as 29 in the earlier pages to 20 in the later ones. At least two hands are discernible. The text is in a clear humanist script. This copyist attempted to be precise. Where he could not read a word, he inserted ellipsis periods (e.g., fol. 3r). He proof-read the text and in the margin made corrections of words he would underline or added words, even a whole line (e.g., fol. 115r), he had omitted. Another hand also corrected the text, filling in what the first had missed (e.g., fol. 3r), correcting misreadings (e.g., fols. 73r and 119r), and speculating on what the proper reading should be (e.g., *heus legendum puto* — fol. 106r).

sity of *sacra pagina* and philosophy. He earned the degrees of master of arts and doctor of decrees.[3]

In addition to his university work in theology and canon law, Massaino showed an interest in humanistic studies. He was part of a circle of learned men which included Roberto Pucci, a wealthy lay patron of humanists who had also earned a doctorate in law, and Lucio Bellantio, a noted physician, astrologer, and opponent of Savonarola. Pucci asked Massaino to publish some of Leon Battista Alberti's works lest they fall into oblivion. His ten books on architecture had already been printed. Pucci had to repeat his request, for Massaino was initially intimidated by the difficulty of the task and not sure which of Alberti's works to include in his edition. But once he started to read the materials supplied him by Pucci, Massaino's interest perked. He was amazed at the genius, literary skill, and range of Alberti's expertise. He admired above all his character of temperance and integrity. Because he was not also blessed with physical beauty or financial fortune, Massaino likened Alberti to a new Socrates. He found in him a teacher of the upright life, whose *Momo* ranked with the *Asinus* of Apuleius in that it contained both worldly advice and divine mysteries, and thus merited the Florentine sage a high place among the followers of Plato. Given his enthusiasm for Alberti's works, Massaino took on the difficult task of producing a correct text, overcoming the corruptions, abbreviations, cancellations, and atrocious handwritings of the manuscripts. In the end, he published a collection which included five works: *Opus de commodis litterarum atque incommodis*, an early work of Alberti; his *Libellus de jure* dedicated

[3]Armando F. Verde, *Lo Studio Fiorentino 1473-1503: Ricerche e Documenti*, Vol. III: *Studenti "Fanciulli a Scuola" nel 1480*, Tome I (Pistoia, 1977), 376, nr. 564; Archivio arcivescovile di Firenze, Campagna: Campione Vecchio nr. 1, fol. 222v: Ecclesia S. Stephani de Calcinaria, 1482 "P. Hieronymus Francisci Jacobi de Puppio...," he resigned this church in 1507 to Piero Francesco de Serolis; for his academic degree, see ASV, Register Vaticanus 989, fol. 85r, and 990, fol. 42r.

to Francesco Coppino of Prato; his *Trivia*; the *Canis* or funeral oration for his dog; and his *Centum Apologi* dedicated to Francesco Marescalchio and written in the style of Aesop's fables. Massaino's dedicatory letter to Roberto Pucci, which prefaced this edition, is apparently his only publication.[4]

For about twenty years at least, Massaino then pursued a career at Rome. He won the favor there of the Cypriot cardinal Ludovicus Podocatharus who made him his assistant at the two conclaves in 1503. With the death of Podocatharus on August 25, 1504, Girolamo attached himself to cardinal Galeotto de Franciotti, the favorite nephew of Julius II and the vice-chancellor of the Church, who appointed him his secretary. By 1505 he had been named papal familiar and continuous commensal, titles which gave their holders an advantage in the quest for benefices. On January 28, 1505 Julius II conferred on him the office of apostolic notary. By 1512 he had been promoted to apostolic protonotary.[5]

At the Roman court Massaino accumulated a number of benefices and pensions. As a favor to cardinal Galeotto,

[4]For the dedicatory letter to Roberto Pucci, see *Leonis Baptistae Alberti Opera*, ed. Girolamo Massaino (s.l., s.d.), fol. a1v-a4r. For the place of publication being Florence, the publisher Bartolomeo de Libri, and the date about 1499, see *Gesamtkatalog der Preussische Bibliotheken*, ed. Preussische Staatsbibliothek, II (Berlin, 1932), 722. For Massaino's colleagues, see Luigi Passerini, "Pucci di Firenze," dispensa 158, tavola VI (Milano, 1868), in Pompeo Litta, *Famiglie celebri italiane* (Milano/Torino, 1819-83), and Cesare Vasoli "Bellanti, Lucio," in *Dizionario biografico degli italiani* 7 (Roma, 1965), 597-99.

[5]For his presence at the two conclaves, see *Johannis Burchardi Liber Notarum*, ed. Enrico Celani, 2 vols., XXXII/1 of *Rerum italicarum scriptores*, II (Città di Castello, 1911), 377, and ASV, Reg. Vat. 989, fol. 85r, and 990, fol. 42r which is the papal document appointing him an apostolic notary on January 28, 1505 and describing in passing his presence in the October conclave and his being Galeotto's secretary and a papal familiar and commensal; on DC, fol. 260v he described himself as a protonotary; and for the reference to Galeotto as Julius' favorite nephew, see Loren Partridge and Randolph Starn, *A Renaissance Likeness: Art and Culture in Raphael's 'Julius II'* (Berkeley, 1980), 76-77.

Julius II granted to his secretary free of the provision taxes the parochial church of San Leonardo at Cerreto Guidi, four miles northwest of Empoli in Tuscany, on January 2, 1506. Simone Rucellai contested this provision and not until Feburary 11, 1513 was a settlement finally reached whereby Girolamo resigned the church back into the hands of Julius II who then conferred it on Simone, who in turn agreed to pay Girolamo an annual pension of forty golden ducats from its revenues. This arrangement was confirmed by Leo X on March 19, 1513. On that same date Leo ordered Hugo de Syma, a chaplain and auditor of causes of the apostolic palace, to settle in Massaino's favor the dispute over a vacated canonry and prebend in the church of Mainz which had arisen between the Florentine and Balthasar Grumbach, provided neither one of them nor a third party had a clear right to the benefices. On May 6, 1513, Leo agreed that Girolamo could resign the church of San Giovanni alla Vena in Pisa, which he had received sometime earlier, to Niccolò Gabriele de Vico Pisani in lieu of another annual pension, this time of ten golden ducats. When cardinal Galeotto died in 1507, his brother Sisto not only succeeded to his cardinalitial title, curial office, and benefices, but also took over his staff, employing Massaino too as his secretary. On January 20, 1516 he rewarded him with two churches and a hospital chaplaincy recently vacated in the diocese of Lucca which Sisto administered. Leo X on November 15, 1517 gave him absolution from any ecclesiastical penalties for having held incompatible ecclesiastical benefices involving pastoral care, dispensed him so that he could hold three such benefices, and granted him an expectative on any one of some forty reserved benefices with annual revenues of about one-hundred golden ducats in the dioceses of Salamanca, Palencia, and Bergamo. Whether he actually secured such a benefice is not clear. On December 8, 1520, he was already a canon of the church of Adria in the Veneto and received from Leo X permission to take possession in the diocese of Ferrara of the perpetual chaplaincy in the church at Massa Fiscaglia in the Po River delta. The revenues of these new benefices did not exceed 100 golden ducats. While Massaino was thus able to accumulate handsome incomes from benefices acquired with the support of Julius' two nephews and of his fellow Florentine, Leo X, the official reason often cited for these benefactions was to support him in his studies.[6]

Girolamo seems to have enjoyed a reputation for studiousness. His name appears in the register of those borrowing books from the Vatican Library. Both Julius II and Leo X praised him for his solicitude for study and knowledge of letters. While cardinal Galeotto acknowledged his academic interests, his brother Sisto, whom Paride de Grassi described as someone of very limited intellectual ability, praised him only for his virtues and integrity which he daily observed. Cardinal Fieschi recognized that Massaino held uncommon views and could argue them well. Unlike the popes and fellow cardinals who naively encouraged the Florentine cleric in his studies, Fieschi inquired into his views and was alarmed at their nature.[7]

[6]For the papal documents granting benefices and pensions to Massaino, see ASV, Reg. Vat. 964, fols. 193r-94v (Cerreto Guidi), 1015, fols. 143v-45v (Rucellai settlement), 1039, fols. 135r-37r (Mainz benefices), 1044, fol. 281r (pension from de Vico Pisani), 1116, fols. 10v-12v (absolution, dispensation, and expectative), 1178, fols. 185r-87v (benefices in dioceses of Cervia and Ferrara); for the letter of Sisto de Franciotto granting him benefices in Lucca, see ASV, Reg. Vat. 1209, fol. 27r-v; for examples of support for his studies, see ASV, Vat. 964, fol. 193r, 1044, fol. 281r, and 1116, fol. 10v.

[7]On August 26, 1514 Massaino acted as witness when cardinal Lorenzo Pucci, the half-brother of Roberto, borrowed Roger Bacon's *De naturis metallorum* from the Vatican Library — see Maria Bertòla, *I due primi registri di prestito della Biblioteca Apostolica Vaticana: Codici Vaticani Latini 3964, 3966* (Città del Vaticano, 1942), 99. Sisto de Franciotto was described by Paride de Grassi as: "homo rudis et penitus ignarus litteraturae, et nesciens legere nec minus scribere, sed neque loqui vulgarem sermonem nec intelligere aliquid, sicut unus simplex idiota" — see de Grassi, *Diarium Leonis X,* BAV, Vat. Lat. 12275, fol. 196v. By such a patron Massaino was in little danger of having his writings censored as heretical. For Fieschi's hostility to his ideas, see DCEES, fol. 1v.

Although formally trained in canon law, Massaino rejected its principal sources and current methodology. He questioned the authenticity of collections of ancient papal letters, alleging that they had been deliberately falsified by those who hoped to receive favor from a condoning and conniving papacy for having usurped for it new powers. Massaino claimed this was the case especially for the volume known as the *Decreta patrum* which is taught in the schools and of which all good priests have at home a copy which they read and commit to memory. Its statements are guarded inviolate by canonists, even though they are so full of blatant lies that even children laugh at them. The goal of these modern canonists is to bestow on the pope the fullest power possible. To this end they write tomes whose considerable length is not matched by commensurate wisdom. Although they acknowledge that the pontiff is bound by the four Gospels and other canonical scriptures and by the decrees of the first four ecumenical councils, they get around this limitation by saying that the pope has the power to "interpret" these texts. Massaino doubts that the pope has the ability to make such authoritative interpretations since many popes barely know the first elements of letters, much less grammar, philosophy, and theology. As a result of papal clarifications which are at times contrary to what the universal Church holds, not only has church law from councils and the fathers regarding benefices, tithes, contracts, vows, and marriage been overturned, but so too that law which touches good morals and the Christian faith. Most recently these legal experts have even asserted that the pope can dispose of bishoprics in such a manner that effectively puts the priesthood of Christ up for sale at public auction. To further papal power canonists also favor new laws supporting pomp and wealth. They claim that the pope is above all councils, that apart from him they cannot be assembled, and without his assent their decrees are null. These papal advocates have gone so far as to order us to believe no longer in the Catholic Church but in the Lateran bishop whose words and wishes are said to be the sum of the Christian faith. The pope of the canonists does not speak simple truths, but becomes a larva-like Protean figure who breaks into pieces the law and dogmas of the Church. Their meaning is distorted and disputed by the numerous sophistic arguments and distinctions used by canonists who corrupt everything.[8]

Theologians are also the targets of Massaino's criticisms. Those who teach are accused of having given theology a bad name due to their lack of candor, useless sophistries, and thorny disputations which produce neither flower nor fruit. Massaino seems to have in mind primarily the Nominalists. Theologians spend their energies debating not the substance of an argument but the words used. This they do with great sharpness of mind and tongue. They ask captious questions, extort meanings never intended by the author, and so confuse truth and falsehood as to make the false seem more probable. Their tool in this is dialectics which they waste much time studying. It produces neither truth nor justice and is ultimately opposed to good morals. Instead of listening in silence with a simple heart to the word of God, they doubt everything, calling into question even the immortality of the soul and resurrection of the body — basic truths of the Christian faith. Like Erasmus, Massaino affirmed that true

---

[8]DC, 273v-74v; DCEES, 41v; DSERE, 109r-v. DC, 274r-v: "Condunt nouas de pompis, de diuitiis et luxu inter quas illa quoque extet que iubeat nos non amplius in ecclesiam catholicam credere: sed in episcopum Lateranensem: nec erit quisque qui ultra uerbum addat. Credemus omnem in papam solum cuius uerbis et uoluntate (qualiscumque sit) omnem religionem omnem Christi fidem consistere et contineri dicemus." It is interesting to compare Massaino's concerns with the decree on papal infallibility of Vatican I Council — see *Conciliorum oecumenicorum decreta*, ed. Giuseppe Alberigo *et al.*, 3rd ed. (Bologna, 1973), Vatican I, Session IV (1870), Cap. 4, p. 816: "ideoque eiusmodi Romani pontificis definitiones ex sese, non ex consensu ecclesiae irreformabiles esse" — hereafter this collection of conciliar documents is cited as Alberigo, *Decreta*.

Christian philosophy is marked not by disputation but by
purity of life.[9]

Ancient philosophers are not generally appropriate models for the Christian theologian. The skepticism of the Pyr-
rhonians does not befit a man of faith. The sophistries of the
Pythagoreans were condemned even in antiquity. Socrates
was seen by the Greeks as someone sent by God to purge
false opinions from the souls of men. Plato and the Athe-
nians wanted the sophists excluded from the forum and their
books burnt lest their ideas which appear to be wise contam-
inate all knowledge. Far from heeding these warnings,
Christians today applaud the sophistries of theologians.
Among all pagan philosophers, Aristotle is especially to be
fled, for his teachings are opposed to Christian truths. Tertullian called him the patriarch of all heretics. Nonetheless,
some Christians wish to baptize him and try with all their
might to make him a coreligionist. So greatly do they revere
him that unless they can find in his writings a teaching on the
soul's immortality, they think a Christian should not believe
it. The only Greek philosopher whom Massaino recom-
mends and then with some caution is Plato. Reflecting
perhaps the esteem accorded him by the Florentine followers of Ficino, Massaino calls him the Attic Moses who
taught good and holy morals and with a few modifications
can be considered a Christian. Plato knew the divine mysteries, even those taught by the Egyptians. Nonetheless,
because he inserted many fables into his writings, the first
Christian theologians Justin and Tertullian warn us to be
cautious when reading him.[10]

[9]DC, 274v-75r; DSERE, 70v, 71v-72r, 73r, 74r, 75r. For Erasmus' explanation of
"Christian Philosophy," see his *Paraclesis*, trans. John C. Olin, in his *Christian
Humanism and the Reformation: Selected Writings of Erasmus* (New York, 1965),
92-106, here 100.

[10]DC, 274v; DSERE, 71r, 72r, 73r, 105v-06v. The appeal to Plato to justify the
suppression of dangerous ideas is found also in his earlier prefatory letter — see his
edition of *Alberti Opera*, fol. a3v. For the revival of Greek skepticism in the

The theology which is preached to the people today by the friars is an empty childish discourse. Massaino describes these preachers as philosophasters who blabber about ridiculous things, as noisy dogs who bark in the city squares and taverns their teachings on papal supremacy, as inept orators who violate the rules of Quintilian and yet are considered great. The harsh and bitter way in which the Dominican and Franciscan friars attack each other on minor doctrinal questions, as if they are engaged in some mortal combat, is not worthy of Christian theology. So ludicrous is their message and methods that Massaino is tempted to call them *mareologi*. Such theologians who depart from the teachings of the Bible and of the creeds regarding the nature of authority in the Church are to be considered anathema. They and their memory are to be deleted from the face of the earth.[11]

The type of theology Massaino favors is in the Erasmian mold: based on the Bible, church fathers, and early councils, written in a pure, simple, and clear style employing good

sixteenth century, see Richard H. Popkin, *The History of Scepticism: From Erasmus to Descartes*, rev. ed. (New York, 1964), ix-xii, 17-25. On the role of Aristotle in the debate on the immortality of the soul, see Bruno Nardi, *Saggi sull' aristotelismo padovano dal secolo XIV al XVI* (Firenze, 1958), Etienne Gilson, "Autour de Pomponazzi: Problématique de l' immortalité de l'âme en Italie au début du XVIe siècle," *Archives d'histoire doctrinale et littéraire du Moyen Age* 36 (1961), 163-279, and Giovanni di Napoli, *L'immortalità dell' anima nel Rinascimento* (Torino, 1963). For the influence of Plato and the Florentine Academy of Marsilio Ficino on these debates, see Paul O. Kristeller, *Renaissance Concepts of Man and Other Essays* (New York, 1972), 22-42 and his "Francesco da Diaceto and Florentine Platonism in the Sixteenth Century (1946)," in his *Studies in Renaissance Thought and Letters*, Vol. 54 of *Storia e Letteratura* (Rome, 1956), 287-336.

[11]DC, 267v, 278r; DCEES, 2v, 28v; DSERE, 73v-74r, 75v, and 121v. The only contemporary theologian mentioned by name to ridicule was Cristoforo Marcello, archbishop of Corfù, court theologian at Rome, and a recent literary opponent of Martin Luther — see DCEES, 37r. On teaching authority in the Church, see Remigius Bäumer, "Lehramt und Theologie in der Sicht katholischer Theologen des 16. Jahrhunderts," in his edited work *Lehramt und Theologie im 16. Jahrhundert*, Heft 36 of *Katholisches Leben und Kirchenreform im Zeitalter der Glaubensspaltung* (Münster, 1976), 34-61.

Latin and not that corrupted language used by theologians over the last thousand years. Massaino also refuses to insert into his treatise the typical scholastic divisions of book, chapter, paragraph, and distinctions. He prefers to present his new positive theology in a smooth flowing prose style. When he quotes from or refers to the writings of others, he usually gives only the name of the author and not only fails to provide a precise reference to a passage in the work, but generally does not even cite its title. He apparently does not want to break up his smooth flowing prose style with scholarly citations. He does, however, spice his exposition at times with terms and quotations in the original Greek and from other authoritative sources, with direct address to the reader, interjections of his own views, sarcastic asides, mockery of his opponents, and exclamations of disbelief and indignation. When arguing his own position, Massaino has recourse to the texts and events of Christian antiquity and shuns the speculations of the scholastics and the interpretations of the canonists. His approach is that of a practitioner of positive theology.[12]

A comparison between the treatise dedicated to Fieschi and its revised version submitted to the judgment of Adrian VI eleven years later reveals constancy and change. Almost all of the earlier treatise has been incorporated, often verbatim, into the later version. Changes in the wording were due to correcting facts and dates, providing more precise and explicit information, and adjusting the prose to accommodate new material. In the process of revision, sections were moved about and enlarged with the addition of new arguments and quotations from authoritative sources to bolster old positions. The tone of his attack on canonists and theologians grew more strident and cutting, his criticisms of claims for a papal plenitude of power more radical. He even

[12]DC, 278r; DCEES, 1v, 2v.

ended his treatise with an appeal to secular princes to intervene and reform the Church. The treatise was not thoroughly revised, for the text was not always altered to be in harmony with the insertions and Fieschi (not Adrian VI) is still addressed even in the new sections. While he refused to yield to the criticisms of Fieschi, he explicitly asked the Dutch pope who was both skilled in theology and entrusted with the supreme office of censorship in the Church to judge his treatise, prune away what is useless, evil, or disease-bearing, and if the work is considered by him scandalous and of paltry worth to consign it to the flames.[13]

The list of authors and variety of evidence he drew upon in advancing his arguments are impressive. His favorite books of the Bible were the Acts of the Apostles of Luke and the epistles of Paul where information is provided on how the early Church functioned. He cited the Greek fathers of the Church, notably Ignatius of Antioch, Basil, Gregory of Nyssa, and John Damascene, but more often had reference to the Latin fathers such as Jerome, Augustine, Ambrose, and Hilary, and also popes Leo I and Gregory I. Other early church writers included: Tertullian, whom he considered of all Christian theologians *vetustissimus et quasi primus*; Cyprian, the holiest and most learned bishop of Carthage; Eusebius, bishop of Caesarea; Origen, Lactantius, Cassio-

[13]For examples of: sections dropped — DC, 269r-v and 273r-v; corrections of fact — DC, 275r vs. DCEES, 40v, and DC, 261 vs. DCEES, 3v; of dates — DC, 271 vs. DCEES, 34r; more precise — DC, 263r vs. DCEES, 5r, DC, 266v vs. DCEES, 12v, and DC, 270r vs. DCEES, 36r; Greek words — DCEES, 6v,13r, 40r, and DSERE, 114v; elimination of explanatory phrases — DC, 265r-v, 267r vs. DCEES, 12r-v, 16v; new sections on Donation of Constantine — DCEES, 6v-11r, on two lights and swords — DCEES 17r-28r, on cardinals — DCEES, 30v-32v; sharper attacks on canonist and theologian friars — DCEES, 6r-7v, 11r, DSERE, 70v-75v, 121v; mockery and sarcasm — DCEES, 10r and 37r; fuller criticism of contemporary popes — DC, 265v vs. DCEES, 21r; appeal to secular princes — DSERE, 124r-25r; insertion not harmonized — DCEES, 34v vs. 37v; direct address to Fieschi — DCEES, 30v, 40v; submission to Adrian's judgment — DSERE, 1v.

dorus, Gregory of Tours, and Paul the Deacon. Of the vast number of medieval ecclesiastical writers, Massaino cited only a few: Gratian, Durandus, and Boniface VIII. Of the Renaissance humanists he makes explicit reference to Petrarch, Pius II, and Matteo Palmieri, and shows evidence of Erasmian influences. In keeping with the classical interests of his day, Massaino also had frequent recourse to the writings of Plato, whom he saw as a divinely inspired venerable theologian who was almost Christian, and to Cicero, the *lumen linguae latinae*. Among the others mentioned were Homer, Aristotle, Procopius, Agathius, Virgil, Trajan, Plutarch, Ovid, the ancient Jewish writer Philo, *Judaeorum discertissimus*, and the Byzantine historian Eutropius. His prose was also adorned with allusions to pagan mythology. Ancient inscriptions from around Rome (e.g., on the Tiber bridge, on the Porta Portuense, on the Arch of Constantine, on the Lateran Basilica, and on a tablet in the monastery of Sant' Anastasio), texts taken from the Eucharistic liturgy, divine office, and sacramental rituals, and prescriptions followed in diplomatic protocol and in papal ceremonies were all used to support his arguments. Of particular interest to Massaino were the acts of church councils, especially the general councils of the early Church. But he also made reference to those of the Middle Ages, and the more recent ones of Konstanz, Basel, and Florence. The only references made to the contemporary Fifth Lateran Council (1512-17) are veiled attacks on its avid defenders and opening ceremonies.[14]

---

[14]For some examples of his citations, see: on Luke — DC, 271r, 277r, DCEES, 21v-22r,24r, 36v; on Paul — DCEES, 19v, 24r, 33v, DSERE 72v, 113r-v; on other biblical references — DCEES, 21v, 33v, DSERE, 112v; on Ignatius — DCEES, 19v, 28r, DSERE, 119v; on Basil — DCEES, 20v, 28r, DSERE, 77r-v; on Gregory of Nyssa — DCEES, 35r; on John Damascene — DCEES, 36v; on Jerome — DCEES, 5r, 25r-v, 27r-v, 29v, 36r, 41r, DSERE, 72r, 114r, 117r; on Augustine — DCEES, 6v,9v,19v, 24v, 36r, 37v; on Ambrose — DCEES, 7v, 25v, 26r, DSERE, 121v; on Hilary — DCEES, 19v, 20v, 24r, 25v, 29r, 36v, DSERE, 77r, 120v; on Leo — DCEES, 19v, DSERE, 119r; on Gregory — DC, 273v, DCEES, 29v, 41r; on

The conflicting claims of this council and of its rival, Pisa-Milan, provoked a heated exchange between the theologians of each camp. Massaino participated in the discussions at Rome. Instead of addressing the question of rival claims, he asked more basic questions: to whom pertains the governance of Christ's Church? What are the respective roles of popes, patriarchs, bishops, and emperors in the Church? What are councils and how have they functioned

Tertullian — DCEES, 14v, 18r, 25v-26v, 35r, 38v, 41r, DSERE, 73r, 76v; on Cyprian — DCEES, 20v, 29v, 39v; on Eusebius — DCEES, 6r-v, 36r, 37v; on Origen — DSERE, 78r; on Cassiodorus — DCEES, 4r, 5r, 20r; on Gregory of Tours — DCEES, 6r; on Gratian — DCEES, 31v; on Durandus — DCEES, 32r; on Boniface VIII, DCEES: 23r; on Petrarch — DC, 265r, DCEES, 12r, 31r; on Pius II — DCEES, 8r, 20r; on Matteo Palmieri and Cristoforo Marcello — DC, 265r, DCEES, 37r; for the Erasmian influences — DCEES, 1v (*enchiridion*), 4v and 20v (*Testamentum* as *Instrumentum*), DSERE, 75r (*Christiana philosophia*); on Plato — DC, 272r, 274v, DCEES, 19r, 26v, 27v, 30v, 40r, DSERE, 74r, 78v; on Cicero — DC, 261r, DCEES, 5r, 18v, 26v, 27v, 40r, DSERE, 72r-v, 112r, 113r; on Homer — DC, 268r, DCEES, 24r, 29r, 40r, DSERE, 111v; on Aristotle — DC, 272v, DCEES, 40r, DSERE, 72r-v, 105v; on Plutarch — DCEES, 18v, 21v, 24r, DSERE, 73v; on Quintilian, DSERE, 73v, 75v; on Ovid — DCEES, 24r, 27r, DSERE, 113r; on Philo — DC, 271r, DCEES, 20v, 33v DSERE, 33v, DSERE, 72r, 112r-v; on other ancient writers — DCEES, 6v-7r, 8r, 18v, DSERE, 72v, 112v-113r; for allusions to pagan mythology — DC,274r, DSERE, 70r; for Roman inscriptions — DC,270v, DCEES, 7v, 9v, 20r, 33v, 38v; on liturgical and sacramental texts — DC, 270v, 273r, 277v, DCEES, 10v-11r, 20r, 24r, 31r, 41r; on imperial coronation and diplomats — DCEES, 10v-11r; on earlier church councils — DCEES, 31v, 39v; on later ones — DC, 267r-v, 273r, DCEES, 28r, 41r, DSERE, 108v; and on Lateran V — DC, 267v-68r, 274r.

Whether Massaino read the original works of all these authors and the decrees of the councils he cited or else borrowed his citations from others who had is a question which awaits further research. I suspect a number of his references were culled from the writings and compilations of the very canonists he had so disparaged.

From his Florentine years may have come his esteem for Plato (influence of Marsilio Ficino's circle?) and his tone of moral indignation (Savonarola).

Given his citation of the Venetian prelate and opponent of Luther, Cristoforo Marcello, Massaino was probably aware of the reforming message of Martin Luther. But given the Florentine's acceptance of a divinely instituted hierarchical structure for the Church and of Catholic teachings on the Eucharist, it is doubtful that he derived any of his theological ideas from the German friar. These were well formed before Luther ever burst upon the scene. In his 1523 version, however, he too like Luther looked to the princes to overthrow the whore of Babylon and reform the Church.

over the centuries?[15] While he seems to have backed the legitimacy of the Lateran Council, his ecclesiology was such as to undermine papal supremacy.

Massaino provides the briefest description of the nature of Christ's Church. It is of divine origins. Just as Eve was taken from the side of Adam to be his mate (Gen. 2:21-23), so too the Church came forth from the opened side of Christ on the cross to be His bride (John 19:34). The Church can be considered a most perfect body whose head is Christ (Eph. 1:22-23, 4:15-16). Just as He and the Father are one (John 10:30), so too should the members of His body be mutually joined by the greatest charity (Phil. 2:2). The Church is also the House of the Lord founded by the apostles (Eph. 2:20). It is the congregation of all believers. Its catholicity is affirmed by sponsors at baptism, on all who recite the Apostles', Nicene, or Athanasian creeds, and in the previous century by pope Eugenius IV who instructed the Armenians to believe in the Catholic Church.[16]

The polity given this Church by Christ is that of a monarchy to which has been joined an aristocracy. That the Church is so structured is the teaching of the Old Testament (Moses ruled God's people with the help of seventy elders — Exod. 24:1, 9) and of the New (Christ empowered all the apostles and they ruled together with Peter). To deny this teaching is to reject an article of the faith, to be held in anathema by all good men, and to be deserving of death and the suppression of any personal remembrance.[17]

---

[15]DC, 260v. On the debate between the advocates of the Council of Pisa-Milan and those of the Fifth Lateran Council, see, for example, Olivier de la Brosse, *Le pape et le concile: La comparaison de leur pouvoirs à la veille de la Réforme*, Vol. 58 of *Unam Sanctam* (Paris, 1965), and Remigius Bäumer, *Nachwirkungen des konziliaren Gedankens in der Theologie und Kanonistik des frühen 16. Jahrhunderts*, Nr. 100 of *Reformationsgeschichtliche Studien und Texte* (Münster/Westfalen, 1971).

[16]DC, 273r; DSERE, 2v, 115v, 117r, 119r, 120r. For the relevant passages in Eugenius IV's bull of union with the Armenians (1439), see Alberigo, *Decreta*, 538, 551,553.

[17]DC, 275r; DCEES, 40v; DSERE, 124r.

A monarchical element is needed in the Church. The head as Plato notes is the seat of the ordering principle in man. It is the source of unity. Without it the body cannot be considered perfect, but then it is only part of the whole and needs to collaborate with the others. Its powers are not such that it can dispense with this mutual assistance. Massaino draws his arguments in favor of monarchy more from nature and pagan authors than from Christian writers. Order can be found in all things. In the insect world bees prove the clearest example. The ancients favored the rule by one, claiming as did Homer, that a multitude of rulers is not good. Cicero agreed and noted that kings were rejected in particular cases and then due to personal vices. By His statement on rendering to God and to Caesar what are their due (Matt. 22:21), Christ suggested that the monarchical principle applies also to the spiritual sphere. His Church is thus blessed wisely, prudently, indeed divinely, with a monarch who is the supreme pontiff.[18]

To prevent this monarchy, the best form of government, from slipping into the worst, tyranny, Christ joined to it simultaneously an aristocracy consisting of patriarchs together with their bishops, the successors of His apostles. From secular history Massaino draws many parallels. The ephors of ancient Sparta were instituted as a check on its kings, the tribunes of Rome on the consuls, and the senate on the emperors. Alexander the Great was so impressed by the government of the Indian city of Nysa where the prince ruled together with the optimates that he granted it liberty so that it could continue this form of polity. The most successful modern example of a monarchy joined to an aristocracy is for Massaino Venice. There the doge proposes laws to which others must assent. Should he attempt anything contrary to the good of the republic, the optimates

[18]DC, 260v, 268v-69r; DCEES, 40r-v.

oppose him, pointing out what is not right or just, and forcing him into silence. In the Catholic Church, the patriarchs and bishops should also strive strenuously to prevent any tyranny and see that the pope models himself on Peter or Christ Himself.[19]

An aristocratic constitution was also given by Christ to His Church to assure that difficult decisions were made collegially. He gave equal power to all the apostles who were to collaborate with Peter in its governance. Massaino produces a series of texts from the New Testament and from the church fathers to show that Christ granted not only the power of orders but also that of jurisdiction to all His apostles: He invited all His disciples to follow him, promising that they would sit on twelve thrones judging the tribes of Israel (Matt. 19:21-28), conferring on them all the power of the Holy Spirit to remit sins (John 20:22-23) and of the keys to loosen or bind (Matt. 16:19), calling them all the light and salt of the world (Matt. 5:13-14), the preachers of the Good News with whom He would remain until the end of time (Matt. 28:19-20). Far from showing that Peter exercised a power of universal jurisdiction, the Scriptures never relate that Peter ordered the others to do anything. Instead, he acted always as their equal. When the leaders of the early community in Jerusalem are singled out by name, Peter often appears as one of three, and then not as the most important (Gal. 2:9). Major decisions in the early Church were made collegially by the apostles and elders. In these synods the apostles enjoyed equal authority in speaking and judging, even though James was regarded as the supreme pontiff and leader. Decisions were made under the inspiration of the Holy Spirit and reflected a unity of heart and soul (e.g. Acts 15:6-29). Early church writers and even popes such as Anacletus, Cyprian, Zosimus, Gregory, and Leo IV acknowledged this equality in power among bishops and the

[19]DC, 268v-69r; DCEES, 40v-41r.

obligation on the pope to be subject to the universal Church. The council of Konstanz in 1417 reaffirmed this subordination by requiring Martin V to swear that he firmly held and believed the Catholic faith as taught by the apostles, holy fathers, and church councils. The liturgy of the Church also proclaims in the preface of the Mass for the feast of an apostle that God constituted the blessed apostles as His vicars for guarding His flock on earth. Unfortunately, the Roman pastors forget this truth and imagine what appears as a joke to the learned, namely, that Christ gave immediate power over His Church only to Peter with the other apostles receiving their power from Peter. Such an obviously erroneous teaching appeals only to papal theologians and canonists.[20]

While all bishops have equal power, Massaino assigns special importance to the patriarchs. He refers to the decree of Innocent III in the Fourth Lateran Council (1215) and likens them to the five senses of the body, the patriarch of Rome being sight. Some theologians refer to them as the four living creatures of the Apocalypse or as the evangelists. They were prefigured in the patriarchs of the Old Testament who were pastors of sheep (Gen. 46:32-47:3). If all bishops are successors of the apostles, then patriarchs who are first among bishops and even over archbishops are the heirs of James, Peter, and John, the columns of the early Church (Gal. 2:9). When they reign in the House of the Lord, the Church is indeed catholic or universal; they give it true unity and prevent Christ's tunic from being torn asunder. Given their pre-eminent authority and dignity, even the Roman

---

[20]DC, 275r-76r; DCEES, 40v-41r; DSERE, 108v-09r, 117v-18v, 120r-v, 121v, 123r. Massaino is not always consistent; thus he affirms that the keys were granted both to Peter (DC, 269r) and to all the apostles (DCEES, 38r; DSERE, 120r, 121v), and that Peter was chosen as prince by Christ (DC, 276r) and by the apostles (DSERE, 3r); he invoked the church fathers to justify his interpretation of Matt. 6: 19 as addressed to all the apostles. On the new pope's profession of faith at Konstanz, see Alberigo, *Decreta*, 442, session XXXIX (1417).

pontiffs are forced today to acknowledge that they share
with them the government of the universal Church. Thus
Eugenius IV at the Council of Florence (1439) renewed the
decree of Innocent III recognizing their partnership in providing pastoral care and affirming their rights and privileges. Among their prerogatives are the right to sign
conciliar decrees first, before cardinals and other prelates,
to wear the pallium, to be preceded by a cross anywhere
except in Rome, and to grant absolution in special cases.[21]

Massaino finds perverse the rank assigned to each patriarch by canon law. He notes that the data of the New
Testament were not the deciding factor, but rather political
considerations. Even the order assigned by the Councils of
Constantinople I (381) and Chalcedon (451) reflected non-
scriptural factors, in that the second place was given to the
new city of Constantinople where no apostle had ever
preached but which was destined to be of great importance
due to its geographical location and the seat of the emperor
there. Given this growing prominence and the decline in
Rome's importance, the patriarchs of Constantinople lobbied for first place. They enjoyed a *de facto* primacy in that
they were the presiding prelates at the early general councils
which had set basic Christian dogma. The Roman pontiffs,
when they learned of these conciliar teachings, submitted to
them. The patriarchs also argued that where the head of the
empire resided, there too should be the head of the Church.
Rome responded that the emperor styled himself as the
Roman and not Constantinopolitan emperor and that
Rome was his true base. Emperor Phocas, who was a friend

[21]DC, 271r-72r; DCEES, 33v-35r. The decrees of Innocent III at Lateran IV
(constitutions 5 and 30) make no reference to an analogy based on the five senses —
see Alberigo, *Decreta*, 236, 249. Constitution 5 was incorporated into the decretals
of Gregory IX as Lib. V, Tit. XXXIII, Cap. 23 in *Corpus iuris canonici*, ed. Emile
Ludwig Richter and Emile Friedberg, 2 vols. (Leipzig, 1879), II, 866 — hereafter
this two-volume collection is cited as Friedberg. For the renewal of this order of
precedence at Florence, session VI (1439), see Alberigo, *Decreta*, 528.

of the Roman pope Boniface III, declared in 607 in favor of Rome. His decision was reversed in 630 by emperor Maurice who granted the pallium to the patriarch of Constantinople, called him head of the universal Church, and decreed that he ranked first. In 710 Justinian II went so far as to give precedence to the archbishop of Ravenna over the Roman pontiff, because the exarch who ruled in the West lived in that Adriatic city. Not until the Latins had seized Constantinople and installed the count of Flanders as emperor Baudouin and the Venetian Paulus Maurocraus [Tommaso Morosini, 1204-11] as patriarch did this see submit to Rome and accept the patriarchal pallium from the pope. It soon reverted, however, to its autonomous ways. The position of honor accorded to Rome was also due to considerations apart from the teachings of the New Testament. Rome was blessed with a number of pontiffs who were considered exceptional for their learning and holiness of life. They brought great prestige to the see. As the political titular seat of the empire, Rome also merited special consideration. The backing of emperors such as Phocas also secured the Roman pontiff's position. Although the early popes had protested against the patriarch of Constantinople styling himself as universal patriarch on the grounds that no one should claim such a title, later popes in turn called themselves universal bishop and proclaimed this papal teaching by having inscribed on the Lateran Basilica in letters large the boast of being the mother and head of all churches. The patriarch of Jerusalem who has the strongest scriptural claims to a position of primacy was ironically assigned the last place among the five patriarchs, as if placed in a corner.[22]

[22]DC, 268r-v, 269v-70r, 271r-72r; DCEES, 9r-v, 29r, 33v-35r, 37r-39r. On whether or not the popes protested against the use of the title ecumenical patriarch by Constantinople, see DCEES, 34v (no) vs. DC, 273r-v and DCEES, 37v (yes). For the decrees assigning second place to the patriarch of Constantinople, see canon 3 of Constantinople I (381) and canon 28 of Chalcedon (451) in Alberigo, *Decreta*, 32, 99-100.

By appealing to the data of Scripture and tradition, Massaino proposed the proper ranking of the patriarchs. First place clearly belongs to Jerusalem. Christ so loved that city that He cried over its impending destruction (Luke 19:41). It is the Holy City, the bride of the Apocalypse, a figure of the whole Church (Rev. 21:2). There the Church was born. There its founder, Christ, preached, celebrated the first Mass, died and rose, and sent his Holy Spirit onto His followers gathered in the upper room. His brother James succeeded Him as head of the Church and was appointed bishop of the city by the other apostles. To James as supreme pontiff came Paul (Acts 21:18). Decisions affecting the whole Church were made in councils gathered there under James. His opinions were decisive in formulating doctrine and practice (Acts 15:6-29). This church showed the greatest fortitude in resisting the pressures and persecutions of the Jews. When, after thirty years of rule, James was martyred, the apostles personally chose his successor, something they did for no other church. On the basis of Scripture and tradition it deserves to be considered the true mother and head of all churches.[23] The second position Massaino assigns to Antioch. There Christ's followers were first called Christians (Acts 11:26). There Paul was ordained and preached (Acts 13:1-3). To this city Peter came (Gal. 2:11) and presided as its bishop for seven years. Massaino also reports the claim of Cristoforo Marcello that Peter transferred his seat from Antioch to Rome, but then adds that Marcello did not explain how, by whom, and when Peter was transferred. Massaino doubts whether bishops in the apostolic Church were dispensed to hold two sees. He also wonders whether Peter found merchants and tax collectors who could have paid to the Datary the fees for the bull of

[23]DC , 269v-70r; DCEES, 35v-36v, 38r, 39r.

transfer and for the annates on Rome![24] The see of Alexandria retained its third position in Massaino's listing due to its foundation, according to tradition, by the disciple and evangelist Mark. The clergy of Alexandria faithfully followed the apostolic tradition of Jerusalem by holding their property in common.[25] Because of Paul's teaching there, Rome deserves the fourth place. The Council of Nicaea granted it authority over the neighboring metropolitan churches. The early bishops of Rome were content to be called bishop or metropolitan or patriarch, but never made claims to be universal bishop, such as they do today. The fifth and last place among the patriarchs Massaino reluctantly grants to Constantinople. Its position does not depend on the teachings of Christ or the apostles, but on the wishes of the emperor. More worthy of its place are Ephesus or Caesarea where the teachings of the apostles resounded.[26]

Despite the fourth place Massaino assigns to the patriarch of Rome, he acknowledges that this prelate is head of the Church, that is, first among equal brother bishops. He is successor of Peter with the task of feeding the sheep, a task which is his provided he loves Christ (John 21:15-17). Massaino notes that all good rulers can be considered pastors of the people, a notion found in the writings of the ancients such as Homer. Although head of the Church, the pope is not its lord. His power is within and not over the Church. While first among bishops, he is not the catholic or universal bishop of the whole Church, as if his office included at once

[24]DC , 270r; DCEES, 36v-37r, 38r, 39r, For Marcello's statement on Peter's transfer from Antioch to Rome, see his *De authoritate Summi Pontificis et his quae ad illam pertinent...Adversus impia Martini Lutheri dogmata...*(Firenze, 1521), fol. 27v, Lib. I, Cap. XVIII. In many other ways, too, Massaino's treatise can be seen as a refutation of Marcello's book.

[25]DC, 271r, DCEES, 37r, 38r, 39r.

[26]DCEES, 29r, 33r-v, 38r, 39r. For the decree of Nicaea (canon 6) recognizing Rome's regional jurisdiction, see Alberigo, *Decreta*, 8-9.

the responsibilities and powers of all bishops. Such a title could also imply that he enjoys power apart from the other patriarchs, and would thus detract from the honor owed to his brother patriarchs. For this reason pope Pelagius (556-61) rejected the use of this term. Indeed, there is no justification for a pope to claim this title. He is bishop only of Rome. If he wishes to be called servant of the servants of God, he cannot also be a lord and tyrant. The title of pope has been restricted over the centuries improperly to him alone. It was used by Homer to signify any father and by the ancient theologians and civil officials to indicate a bishop. Once the bishop of Rome became very wealthy, the term was applied ever increasingly only to him. The power of the keys, however, was committed to all the apostles. Their power and that of their successors has remained equal. As the pope's brother bishops, cobishops, and fellow columns of the Church, they enjoy equal authority and power with him. An elder brother does not have rights over his younger siblings. As Aristotle notes, the elder brother manages the household according to the wishes of his brothers. The pope, too, needs the advice and consent of his fellow bishops to govern the Church properly when treating serious matters.[27]

Let the pope follow the example of Peter. This apostle accepted criticism from Paul (Gal. 2:11) and yielded to the more learned and wise. When he strayed from the right path or suggested a course of action that was not correct, he was challenged by the other leaders of the Church and brought around to their opinion. Although entrusted with great power, he did not use it when dealing with insignificant matters. When important decisions were to be taken, Peter never acted by himself, for the government of the Church did not belong to him alone but to the synod of apostles and elders. Although head of the group, he submitted to its

[27]DC, 260v, 268r, 272v-73v; DCEES, 29r-v, 32v; DSERE, 110r-111v.

decisions and was sent by it to preach in Samaria (Acts 8:14). Being the greatest, he sought to be least. A man of God, indeed, seeks correction. He not only bears criticism calmly, but thanks those who offer instruction and admonition. While the pope is not subject to judgment by an individual fellow bishop, he is to obey his brother bishops when they unite in a council. God guides the hearts of the conciliar fathers to establish and govern His Church properly. When a pope obeys a council, he obeys the Holy Spirit.[28]

The pope who merited Massaino's harshest criticisms was the uncle of his two cardinal patrons and employers, Julius II. Whereas in the past popes made trips to compose peace or bring people to the Christian religion, in Massaino's time the pope travels to engage in warfare. He is more like Mohammed than Christ, imitating the Sultan by his use of the sword. Rather than acting as servant of the servants of God, he seeks to be honored by emperors. Rather than turning the other cheek, he lays siege to the Christian town of Mirandola, stomping in the snow among the cannons, and being carried in triumph over the torn-down gates of the conquered town. To open his council in Rome, he marched with infantry, cavalry, and artillery to the Lateran Basilica. The propriety and piety of Julius' actions Massaino seriously questions.[29]

Given Massaino's rejection of the claim of later popes to be the universal bishop and not just head of the particular church of Rome, the prerogatives of the cardinals are also drastically reduced in his ecclesiology. For him cardinals are merely canons of the local church of Rome, and like those of

---

[28]DC, 276r-77r.

[29]DC, 265r, 269v, 274r; DCEES, 21r, 26r; DSERE, 79v; for a first-hand account of Julius' procession to the council, see Marc Dykmans, "Le cinquième Concile du Latran d'après le Diaire de Paride de Grassi," *Annuarium Historiae Conciliorum* 14 (1982), 271-369, here 292, para. 844: 1.

other dioceses such as Trent they elect their bishop. They enjoy this prerogative because Nicholas II took the ancient right away from the clergy and people of Rome and from the Holy Roman Emperor. As bishops, priests, and deacons of the region of Rome, cardinals form when they meet with the pope a provincial synod. Properly speaking the Roman consistory is nothing other than a local assembly and should limit its agenda to local affairs. The concerns of the universal Church are to be treated by the pope and his brother bishops in a general council.[30]

Massaino challenges the position of pre-eminence which cardinals have gained over the centuries in the universal Church. He notes that in the earliest documents of the Christian Church the term "cardinal" does not appear because, he believes, they had not yet been born, conceived, or even imagined. In the patristic Church, the term cardinal was used, but referred to a mere canon of a local church. It is highly doubtful that St. Jerome was in fact a cardinal priest, as canonists like to claim. As reported by Petrarch, cardinals in the Roman Church functioned as ministers to the pope, helping him at funerals and notably at the baptism service at Eastertime when they clothed the newly baptized in white and fed them milk and honey. But instead of remaining humble ministers, cardinals have become proud prelates. Whereas earlier they ranked below an archpriest, they now claim precedence over patriarchs. They are encouraged by ridiculous canonists who call them kings because they are supposedly the hinges or *cardines* of the world and rule over it together with the pope. In keeping with the ridiculous claims of the Donation of Constantine, some cardinals seek to be called "senators" and to have the insignia of S.P.Q.R. placed to their right at ceremonies.

---

[30]DC, 272r; DCEES, 29v-30r, 32v; for the decree of Nicholas II on the election of the pope, see *Decretum*, Prima Pars, Dist. XXIII, Cap. 1, Friedberg, I, 77-79.

When they leave Rome as papal legates, they act as proconsuls going to the provinces. Some are uncomfortable in this role and are embarrassed by such public displays, just as cobblers attired in regal robes feel ashamed to go about the city. Others alternate between displaying and hiding the signs of their new position, as do those who are newly rich at times flash their rings and at others hide their hands. Massaino is of the opinion that cardinals should blush at assuming the name and trappings of the Roman Senate, an institution long ago extinct. Its insignia of S.P.Q.R. has passed to the city of Rome, while the name of senator has been taken over by an official who is really the equivalent of the *praetor* of antiquity.[31]

Massaino traces some of the papal decisions and Roman practices which have advanced the position of cardinals. He attributes major importance to the decree of Nicholas II in 1060 [!] which restricted to them the election of a new pontiff. Innocent IV (1243-54) gave them the external trapping of authority by allowing them to wear the skull cap usually reserved to bishops. To distinguish these Roman clerics from bishops, the cardinal's cap was red with colored tassels. The Third Lateran Council (1179) tried to limit their pretensions by decreeing that a cardinal could have only 25 horses in his suite, while a bishop was to have no more than thirty, and an archbishop fifty. Gregory IX (1227-1241) inserted this decree into his collection of decretals. While exhorting the cardinals to follow with true simplicity and poverty the modesty of Christ and the apostles, Paul II (1464-71) granted cardinals the use of the purple biretta, of the purple *cappa* which had earlier been colored black or sky-blue, of a train to be carried by a servant, and he also

---

[31]DCEES, 10r, 31r-32r.

allowed them to cover their mules with a full cloth of purple.[32]

Cardinals have also successfully laid claim to a title of pre-eminence. At the Lateran Council (1059) under Nicholas II bishops were called "most reverend" and the pope "venerable." The practice today is an unreasonable innovation: cardinals are called "most reverend" and bishops demoted to "reverend." While Massaino does not insist on a return to the former usage, he does urge the pope to call his fellow bishops "venerable brothers" and treat them as companions and friends. He notes that Clement V (1305-14) addressed his cardinals as "beloved sons," a term popes use when speaking to lay persons. Subsequent popes have continued to address their cardinals as sons. From this practice Massaino draws a logical inference and moral. If cardinals are the pope's sons and bishops his brothers, then cardinals are the nephews of bishops. As such they are of inferior status and they violate the moral order when they have bishops as servants. These prelates are expected to stand at attention all day long with head uncovered and bowed, patiently waiting to pick up the towel a cardinal has just soiled when washing his hands — such a menial service even auctioned off slaves are loathe to perform![33]

In attempting to determine the proper place of cardinals in the universal Church, Massaino asks what role they

[32]DC, 272r; DCEES, 29v-31r; for canon 4 of the Third Lateran Council (1179) under Alexander III which limited the number of horses, see Alberigo, *Decreta*, 213. I have been unable to locate where in his decretals Gregory IX inserted this decree.

For a brief over-view with bibliography of the evolution of the office of cardinal, see Karl F. Morrison, "Cardinal, I (History of)," *New Catholic Encyclopedia* (New York, 1967), III, 104-105.

[33]DC, 272v; it is tempting to suggest an influence of Massaino's criticisms on the reform decree of Lateran V, *Supernae dispositionis* (1514), which forbids cardinals to maintain bishops as servants in their households — see *Sacrorum conciliorum nova et amplissima collectio*, ed. Giovanni D. Mansi *et al.*, Vol. 32 (Florence, 1759), col. 878A.

should have in a general council. His answer is simple and clear: none. Just as canons elsewhere who elect the local bishop have no right to participate in a general council, so too neither do the cardinals of Rome. Their responsibilities are restricted to the particular church of Rome, and nothing regarding the universal Church pertains to them. They should not even be considered the least members of a council. Nonetheless, canon law today has assigned to them and the pope the right to convoke a council and preside over it. While Massaino's own line of reasoning demolishes the claims of the Pisan cardinals to have authority to convoke and preside over a council aimed at correcting the scandalous conduct of Julius II, which Massaino himself also condemned, it went too far. If cardinal Fieschi and others at Rome initially praised his treatise, it is no wonder that after a more careful reading of it, which would have revealed that he not only undermined the claims of the Pisan Council but those of the whole college of cardinals, Fieschi's support turned to hostility. What is surprising is the continued patronage and employment offered by the della Rovere cardinal:[34]

The institution which best embodies Massaino's vision of the Church as monarchy to which an aristocracy has been added is a general council which incorporates the pope and his fellow patriarchs with their bishops. When they are gathered in the name of Christ and pray to the Lord for guidance, the Paraclete sent by Christ from the Father breathes in the assembly. He is so present in the council that the Holy Spirit and synod are as one. When the synod is united in unanimous agreement about what is of God and is good to do, then the Church itself can be said to be present. A synod represents that Catholic Church, rules over it, is the Church. It is present and makes decisions in a council.[35]

[34]DC, 272r; DCEES, 30r.
[35]DC, 277r-v; DSERE, 3r.

Councils have functioned as important institutions from the earliest days of the Church. St. Luke reports in the Acts of the Apostles three synods. The first met to choose a replacement for Judas who had betrayed his apostolic office and ministry and selected Matthias in his stead (Acts 1:15-26). The second synod composed of the apostles and a multitude of disciples chose seven deacons to serve the Church (Acts 6:2-6). The apostles and elders in the third synod after prayer and fasting were told by the Holy Spirit to select Paul and Barnabas to preach the Gospel (Acts 13:2-3). These two were ordained, according to St. Jerome, by Peter, James, and John, and sent by the synod to Antioch to do God's work there. Later Paul and Silas were sent to preach elsewhere.[36]

The example set by the apostles of making in a synod major decisions touching the Church was followed by their successors. Beginning with that at Nicaea in 325, the first four general councils were of such importance for the Church that they should be venerated as are the four Gospels. They are also referred to allegorically as the four columns of the Church and the rivers of Paradise. They were the models and source of all other synods. They have enjoyed over the centuries this enormous authority despite the fact that no pope was present at them, nor presided. When the popes sent representatives, as is first mentioned for the sixth council, Constantinople III (680), their delegates did not act as if they had any right to oppose or force the council. When Leo II learned of the decisions of Constantinople III he accepted them and ordered them to be observed, as would have any Christian bishop. The council's

---

[36]DC, 277r-78r. Massaino's description of the third synod is confused and does not agree with Acts 11:22, 12:25 and Gal 2:1-10. On these synods of Jerusalem, see Joseph A. Fischer, "Die ersten Synoden," in *Synodale Strukturen der Kirche: Entwicklung und Probleme*, ed. Walter Brandmüller, Nr. 3 of *Theologie interdisziplinar* (Donauwörth, 1977), 27-60, here 27-33.

authority did not depend on papal confirmation. Canonists today, however, wish in effect to abolish councils, to require papal assent for them to gather, and to insist that conciliar decrees be ratified by the pope or be held null. Thus reduced in power, councils become occasions for papal pomp and triumphal processions, for the pope to force to appear before him and do obeisance prelates adorned not with learning and virtue but with styled hair and silken robes.[37]

But from the history of the early councils, it is clear that councils enjoy much power. They can appoint bishops, as when James was placed over the church of Jerusalem. They can designate dioceses, having sent out the apostles to the different regions of the world. Whatever honor or authority a particular church is endowed with was bestowed on it by councils. The bishop of Rome was called an archbishop and given the jurisdiction of a metropolitan by a council. Given the selection of Matthias by the synod of Jerusalem, it is only fitting that a council which represents the whole body of the Church and contains the successors of the apostles should today select the pope. But instead, cardinals now choose the pope and they together with the pope choose bishops for the whole world. How this group of Roman prelates can properly instruct and set down rules for the whole world is something Massaino finds difficult to understand.[38]

From apostolic times until recently, Peter and his successors have been subject to councils. Peter always acted as an equal with his fellow apostles and never ordered others. Among the apostles it is not clear who held the place of honor. St. Paul lists James, Peter, and John. SS. Augustine and Ambrose call both Peter and Paul princes of the apostles. In the formula of absolution used by a priest in confession, the authority of both Peter and Paul is invoked. That

[37]DC, 261v-62r, 274r; DCEES, 30r; DSERE, 3r.
[38]DCEES. 30r, 41r.

Peter had rights over the other apostles is doubtful: he
always acted either as an equal or as someone of lesser
importance. He never dominated others. His successors in
subsequent centuries have repeatedly subjected themselves
to the authority of councils. Thus the Councils of Konstanz
and Basel did not innovate when they declared that all
Christians are subject to a council. Far from complaining
about this decree, papal canonists should rejoice in it, for it
is a safeguard of Christian liberty and protects the pope
from ever being subject to an emperor. Both the pope and
emperor should wish to be justly and piously under the
authority of a council. As popes have affirmed the decrees of
other councils, so too now should they confirm this one of
Konstanz and Basel.[39] If councils have exercised a major
influence for good in the history of the Church, they have
often done so with the help of the emperors.

Emperors and kings have always exercised the greatest
authority over pontiffs and clerics. The Byzantine emperors'
authority extended beyond Constantinople and the Greeks
to the Latins and was delegated at times to the barbarian
kings in the West. Holy and learned men, even popes, have
acknowledged this.[40]

Emperors, kings, and princes have over the centuries
played a major role in councils. A precedent for this can be
found in the Old Testament where good kings assembled
and gave orders to the priests. The bishops of the patristic
Church greatly desired, consented to, and praised the care

[39]DC, 267v, 277r-v; DCEES, 28r, 41r. For the decrees *Haec Sancta* of Konstanz,
session V (1415) and of Basel, session XVIII (1434), see Alberigo, *Decreta*,
409-410, 477. For three recent studies of this decree, see: Francis A. Oakley,
Council over Pope? Towards a Provisional Ecclesiology (New York, 1969), Walter
Brandmüller, "Besitz das Konstanzer Dekret 'Haec sancta' dogmatische Verbind-
lichkeit?" in *Die Entwicklung des Konziliarismus*, Nr. 279 of *Wege der Forschung*,
ed. Remigius Bäumer (Darmstadt, 1976), 247-71, and Giuseppe Alberigo, *Chiesa
conciliare: Identità e significato del conciliarismo*, Vol. 19 of *Testi e ricerche di
Scienze religiose* (Brescia, 1981), 187-289.

[40]DC, 263v-264r.

which Constantine showed for Christian affairs. They considered his convocation of a council a proper thing and participated in it. Numerous subsequent Byzantine emperors, Frankish kings, and German emperors have also ordered councils to be called. Some have been present at and presided over these assemblies. Even countess Mathilda may have attended the council of Mantua under Nicholas II (1059-61) and the Lateran Council under Gregory VII (1073-85). While Christian rulers attending a council are not to sit in judgment on questions of faith, according to St. Ambrose, they have seen to the enforcement of its decrees. Emperor Valentinian signed the decrees of a council and ordered the bishops to do the same. The decrees of pope Gregory I were later ratified by the signatures of king Theuderich and queen Brunhilda of the Franks (612-13).[41]

Emperors have long had a say in the election of popes. The holiest and most learned pontiffs have acknowledged this authority of the emperors. So that requests regarding the selection of the bishop of Rome would not always have to come to Constantinople, Constantine II (337-40) granted to the Roman clergy, people, and army the right to choose their own pope. Under the Byzantine emperors, however, no pope wanted to enter upon his pontificate unless his election had first been confirmed by the emperor. By the time of Gregory I (590-604) no one was considered pope, even though elected, unless he had secured imperial confirmation. Gregory himself sought ratification of his election from emperor Maurice (582-602). A similar procedure was followed under the Carolingian emperors. Although dutifully elected by the Roman clergy and people, Gregory IV (827-44) did not want to enter his office unless first confirmed in it by Louis the Pious (814-40), son of Charle-

---

[41] DC, 262v-63r; DCEES, 4v-6v. Massaino's source seems to have been in error: Mathilda's mother Beatrice may have attended the Council of Mantua in 1072 which met under Alexander II — see Mansi, *Conciliorum collectio*, XIX, 1033-1036.

magne. Massaino holds that pope Hadrian I (772-95) and the synod at Rome had conferred on Charlemagne the rights of choosing the Roman pontiff and of putting order into the apostolic see. Likewise in the Middle Ages there were bishops who wanted the emperor to have the right not only of confirming papal elections but of selecting the pope, thus transferring to the emperor the right which had belonged to the Roman clergy and people. When papal elections were disputed, the emperors were called upon to resolve the dispute. Even the barbarian king, Theodoric of the Goths (474-526), had settled a disputed election.[42]

Emperors have often intervened to put in order the affairs of the papacy and to castigate erring clerics. When accusations against erring bishops were lodged at Constantinople with the emperor, Constantine set the day for the trial; and when the bishops' teachings were condemned, he ordered their heretical books burnt. Emperors themselves have heard charges against a pope and come to a judgment. Thus Valentinian III (425-54) absolved Sixtus III (432-40) of charges made against him. The German emperor Henry III (1039-56) was not so supportive of the sitting popes. He forced the abdication in 1046 of three rival ones: Benedict IX (1033-44), Gregory VI (1044-46), and Sylvester III (1045). Let the princes of Christendom today, especially the emperor, rise up, cast judgment upon, and throw down the great whore of Babylon, and thus save Christ's spouse.[43]

For their part, the clergy should stay out of secular affairs, not engage in temporal rule or warfare, but confine themselves to the care of souls. The pope's ability to govern should come from the authority he gains from his sound

[42]DC, 263v, 266r-v, 270v; DCEES, 5v, 6r, 9r, 14v, 16r, 17r, 20v. On imperial and royal confirmation of papal elections, see Karl Bihlmeyer and Hermann Tüchle, *Church History*, Vol. 1, trans. Victor E. Mills (Westminster, Md., 1958), 303, Nr. 60: 3.

[43]DC, 263r, 267r; DCEES, 4v, 6v, 16r-v; DSERE, 124r-25r.

doctrine and good morals, and not from force and domination. His superiority is limited to the government of souls and does not extend to temporal affairs.[44]

This is the teaching of scripture and of wise and holy men. In the New Testament Christ set an example. He fled when the crowd tried to make him a king (John 6:15) and taught that his kingdom is not of this world (John 18:36). He warned his disciples not to be like the rulers of the gentiles who lord it over others (Luke 22:25). When asked to settle a disputed inheritance, he refused (Luke 12:14). St. Paul, writing to Titus, affirmed that no one who seeks to serve God becomes involved in secular affairs (Titus 2:12, 3:1). According to what is reported in a papal ritual from the year 1143 by a canon of St. Peter's Basilica, St. Peter also warned his successor Clement not to engage in profane matters. In the patristic period, St. Hilary also admonished Christian priests to avoid the great danger of secular affairs. Pope Leo I (440-61) affirmed that Christ's kingdom is apart from this changing world and is instead eternal. In the Middle Ages, St. Bernard (1090-1153) pointed out to pope Eugenius III (1145-53) that the successors of St. Peter receive the keys to a heavenly and not an earthly kingdom. Even in pagan antiquity such wise men as Homer, Ovid, and Plutarch counseled against the involvement of priests in secular matters.[45]

Over the course of history spiritual persons have acknowledged their dependence on temporal rulers. In pagan times the spiritual office was joined to the temporal. The pagan kings of Rome were considered to be also priests and pontiffs. In the Old Testament the offices were separate: Moses was like an emperor, while Aaron his older brother was high priest; Judah and his descendants ruled, while Levi and his attended to the worship of God; Saul was king, while

---

[44]DCEES, 17r, 24v, 27v.

[45]DCEES, 23v-24r.

Samuel who constituted him such on orders from God was a
prophet. Among the Jewish people, the priests were considered lesser than kings and were subject to them. In the New
Testament Christ taught by word and example that all
should submit to civil authority. He ordered his followers to
render to Caesar what is his, and He Himself obeyed Roman
authority by submitting to the census and tax. In the early
Church the Roman popes were always in fact and also seen
to be and indeed gloried in being subject to emperors both
legitimate and false. From their actions one can discern
both the human and divine laws with which these popes
sought to comply: that man should acknowledge and submit to civil authority, and priests should stay out of secular
affairs. Papal expressions of submission used at times color-
ful words. When the early popes appeared before the
emperor they used to refer to themselves as slaves, dust, and
worms. The early Church paid tribute to the emperor by its
labor and sweat. Pope Gregory I (590-604) warned his
bishops to obey the tribune. Even though the popes
crowned the German emperors, they always submitted to
their authority. In matters of episcopal appointments, too,
popes complied with imperial wishes. Pope Leo IV (847-55)
requested from the German emperor that the church of
Rieti be granted to a certain deacon and that the pope be
allowed to consecrate him. Leo was concerned that priests
who were pleasing to God and to the emperor be appointed
bishop. Some nine hundred years after Constantine, pope
Innocent III (1198-1216) reaffirmed the principle that in
temporal affairs the emperor is supreme. Massaino observes
that popes should not, therefore, be treated as if they themselves were emperors and had their powers. Instead of fighting emperors, they should seek to assist them.[46]

[46]DC, 266r, 267r; DCEES, 13r, 16v-17r, 18r-19v, 25r, on 24v Massaino notes that
pope Gregory IV (827-44), unlike his predecessors, claimed to be greater than
temporal lords.

Roman emperors do not receive their empire from the pope and to claim the opposite is ridiculous. In early Christian times, emperors were not crowned by popes, yet were nonetheless true emperors. Popes have no rights either to confer or to confirm the imperial honor. Both before and after the time of Charlemagne, the popes always called the Byzantine rulers "augustus" and "emperor." This tradition was followed throughout the Middle Ages up to the time of Eugenius IV (1431-47) who at the Council of Florence referred to John VII Paleologus (1425-48) as emperor of the Romans. Some make the silly argument that because Eugenius called him *Imperator Romeorum*, he meant thereby that John was not the true Roman emperor. The empire was translated to Byzantium and with it went the rights and majesty of the emperor, something Eugenius acknowledged by his words at Florence. Those who claim that the papacy transferred the empire to the German rulers are so far from the truth that they contradict each other in proposing at least five different popes who are supposed to have made this transfer. Canonists make the laughable assertion that the German princes merely elect the King of the Romans and that only after he has been confirmed and crowned by the pope is augustus and emperor. But it is obvious that the Germans choose their own emperor and give no king to the Romans who traditionally hate such a ruler. The only "emperor" whom the pope appoints and who really depends on him is that official known as the "captain of the Church" who commands the infantry and siege equipment of the papal army at the pope's good pleasure.[47]

Massaino rejects the "two-swords" theory of the papalists as based on misinterpretations of scriptural texts. Christ's advice to sell one's mantle in order to buy a sword (Luke

[47]DC, 265v-66v; DCEES, 7r, 11r-13v; for Eugenius' use of the word *Romeorum*, see the decrees of sessions IV (1438), V (1439), VII (1439), and IX (1440), in Alberigo, *Decreta*, 521, 523—24, 531, 561.

22:36) was not addressed to Peter alone. Nor was it meant to be taken literally, for otherwise all the apostles and their successors, the bishops, should also have temporal swords and be able to make emperors. Christ's subsequent statement that two swords are enough (Luke 22:38) did not refer to spiritual and temporal arms. Indeed, He expressly warned His apostles against the use of the temporal sword, stating that those who live by it will also perish by it (Matt. 26:52) and counseling them instead to turn the other cheek when attacked (Luke 6:29). Instead of rushing out with the temporal sword to defend the rights of the Church, Massaino urges the pope to follow Christ's counsel. The only sword which is appropriately used by His disciples is the spiritual one of God's word which penetrates a man's breast and divides men. The images of a sword or weapon found in the New Testament have also been interpreted in a spiritual rather than temporal way by such early Christian writers as Tertullian, Hilary of Poitiers, Ambrose, and Jerome.[48]

Massaino also attempts to disprove the "Donation of Constantine." He notes that the defenders of this fabricated document assert that Constantine was so preoccupied with the affairs of the eastern portion of the Roman Empire that he conceded to the Roman pontiffs the city of Rome and Italy. And because Constantine's successors were Greeks living in a colony of the empire they lost any rights they may have had either to approve a papal election or to call a council. Such papalist claims Massaino finds ridiculous and he uses a wide array of counter-arguments to prove it.[49]

The facts of history and the ceremonials of court and Church disprove the Donation. A careful reading of Eusebius' *Ecclesiastical History*, of Augustine's *City of God*, and of Eutropius' *Brevarium ab Urbe Condita* shows that

[48]DCEES, 17r, 25v-26r.
[49]DCEES, 6v, 27r.

the emperors willed the West to their sons. Thus Constantine's son Constantine II succeeded to the empire in the West (337-40). And subsequent emperors continued to rule there until barbarian kings replaced them in Italy, but even these governed with the consent of the emperors in Constantinople. Under emperor Justinian (527-65) the empire in the West was restored temporarily to direct imperial rule. For the three centuries following Constantine's coming to power as emperor, the popes held no dominion over all or even part of Italy, not over Rome or even one of its suburbs, not over a temple or even a chapel. They sought the emperor's permission to convert into Christian churches such pagan temples as the Pantheon and that dedicated to Romulus. It was only due to the humble supplications of pope Vitalian (657-72) that emperor Constans II (641-68) spared certain Christian churches when he came in person to Rome in 660 to plunder its wealth. So lacking in temporal power were the popes that empress Theodora (527-48) ordered the senate and Roman people to send to Constantinople in chains the Roman pontiff. In their correspondence the bishops of Rome openly acknowledged in most humble terms the authority of the emperors. An implicit admission that the emperor rules with power directly from God has even been incorporated into the papal ceremonial. At the coronation ceremonies when handing the emperor his sword, the pope does not refer to him as a papal vicar but as a type of Christ, the Savior of the world. Contemporary court practice also suggests that the pope is not the sovereign ruler of Rome, or else why does the senator of Rome to whom the pope has committed his temporal sceptre yield to the representative of the emperor at diplomatic functions in Rome? Is the pope tacitly admitting that he rules in Rome as vicar of the emperor? Massaino confesses that he often laughs to himself when he sees a senator yield his place to a mere chamberlain of emperor Maximilian (1493-1519).[50]

[50]DC, 270v; DCEES, 6v—10v, 20r; in his survey of those writers who continued to debate the validity of the "Donation of Constantine" even after Lorenzo Valla's

Even if Constantine had conferred on the papacy the western portion of the empire, that donation should not today be considered valid and proper. Did not the victory of the Goths in Italy destroy any imperial or papal temporal authority there and thus nullify the donation, while the later reconquest of Italy by Justinian's forces restore these imperial rights? Should Constantine have made such a gift to the papacy, he would have done so imprudently. The pope should have returned this donation to the emperor because temporal things belong properly to Caesar while the spiritual pertains to priests, as St. Ambrose teaches. The confusion of the two spheres represented by the "Donation of Constantine" is both sacrilegious and pestiferous. But so far has the papacy strayed from the teachings of Christ in this regard that Boniface VIII (1294-1303), in his *Liber Sextus* inserted into the body of canon law, has ruled that anyone who denies in the least way the Donation of Constantine should be held excommunicated and be burnt in the forum![51]

Anyone who has studied history, however, knows that papal power evolved over the centuries and did not come

famous attack on it, Massimo Miglio makes no mention of Massaino — see his "L'umanista Pietro Edo e la polemica sulla Donazione di Costantino," *Bullettino dell'Istituto Storico Italiano per il Medio Evo e Archivio Muratoriano* 79 (1968), 167-232, here 172-74, 189, 223-28, 231; and neither do Domenico Maffei, *La Donazione di Costantino nei giuristi medioevali* (Milan, 1964) or Mario Fois, *Il pensiero cristiano di Lorenzo Valla nel quadro storico-culturale del suo ambiente* (Rome, 1969), 343-45.

For a history of the imperial coronation, see Eduard Eichmann, *Die Kaiserkrönung im Abendland*, 2 vols. (Würzburg, 1942); for the procedure used in the coronation of an emperor, see Agostino Patrizi, *Rituum ecclesiasticarum sive sacrarum cerimoniarum sacrosanctae Romanae Ecclesiae libri tres*, ed. Cristoforo Marcello (Venice, 1516), fol. XXIr — unfortunately Patrizi does not go into the details of the ceremony; for the term "savior of the world" applied to an emperor, see Ernst H. Kantorowicz, *The King's Two Bodies: A Study in Medieval Political Theology* (Princeton, 1957), 87-92.

[51]DCEES, 10r-v, 27r, on the insertion of Boniface VIII, see *Liber Sextus Decretalium*, Lib. I, Tit. VI, Cap. 17, in Friedberg, II, 957-59.

from a single donation of Constantine. Large tracts of land were given to the papacy by such rulers as Liutprand, king of the Lombards (712-44), by Constantine V, the Byzantine emperor (741-75), and by Mathilda countess of Tuscany (1069-1115). The popes themselves also occupied territories and then claimed them as their own, as was done by the ancestral relative of cardinal Niccolò Fieschi, to whom Massaino first dedicated his treatise, pope Innocent IV (1243-54) and as was announced at the Council of Lyon in 1245. The pope's spiritual power in the West also grew over time as evidenced by the acceptance from him of the pallium first by the archbishop of Ravenna and then by the metropolitan of Milan.[52]

To provide revenues commensurate with their claims to worldly power, popes have perverted Christian doctrine and engaged in deception. So adverse is the papacy to Christ's teachings on and example of poverty that John XXII inserted among his *Extravagantes* a laughable but also impudent, presumptuous, and sacrilegious decree anathematizing anyone who claims that Christ and His disciples were poor. Having affirmed a doctrinal basis for clerical wealth, popes have sought ever greater riches, even resorting to nefarious means. Claiming that the taxes they are levying are for a crusade against the Saracens and Turks, they have raised large sums of money which they use instead in military operations against Christian cities, towns, and villages. So limitless is their quest for wealth that everything is for sale in an open and impudent manner: the pope sells to the cardinals, bishops, and protonotaries, they sell to the curates, and these in turn to the chaplains.[53]

---

[52]DCEES, 23r, for three standard treatments of the evolution of papal power, see: Erich Caspar, *Geschichte des Papsttums*, 2 vols. (Tübingen, 1930-33), Walter Ullmann, *The Growth of Papal Government in the Middle Ages*, 3rd ed. (London, 1970) and Peter Partner, *The Lands of St. Peter: The Papal State in the Middle Ages and the Early Renaissance* (Berkeley, 1972), 14-19, 129, 151, 255-58.

[53]DCEES, 27r-28r; for the insertion of John XXII, see *Extravagantes*, Lib. I, Tit. XIV, Cap. 4, in Friedberg, II, 1229-30.

Massaino singles out several symbols of worldly power which he urges the popes to abandon. He finds ridiculous the papal tiara which is so heavy with precious metal and stones that it is said to have caused the death of pope Paul II (1464-71). Is not a single crown enough? Instead of being the servant of the servants of God, popes wish to be mighty lords with the rulers of this world as their servants. Thus they assign to the emperor the function of holding still the palfrey while the pontiff mounts and of leading this horse about for the pope. The French king is to hold the pope's stirrup and spur and to minister to him the water he uses to wash his hands at Mass. The ceremony of kissing the pope's foot is particularly repulsive to Massaino. He notes that Peter protested that he was only a man while making Cornelius rise up when he fell at his feet (Acts 10:25-26). Even the German barbarian ruler Maximus forbade anyone to kiss his foot, saying that the gods themselves had prohibited it. Massaino also opposes the practice of placing before the pope's foot a cross which could be kissed instead. He rejects this as a theatrical subterfuge and pointed out that the cross is an object of cult which the pope himself should be reverencing instead of having it lie at his feet.[54]

In their quest for honors popes have also abused spiritual things. Given that the Eucharist is the true body of Christ and can scarcely be properly honored in a church, it is most impious and impudent to make it part of the papal suite, being carried before the pope as he travels through various towns and over snowy mountains. Titles such as "most holy" and "most blessed" belong properly only to God. Let the popes content themselves with the appellations of "your holiness" or "your beatitude" and have their brother patriarchs and bishops call them such. Given, however, the moral standing of the recent popes, even this modified title would

---

[54]DCEES, 21r-22v; on Maximus, see Frank L. Borchardt, *German Antiquity in Renaissance Myth* (Baltimore, 1971), 142, 190.

be an excessive violation of language and should not be used or heard. Let some emended or changed title for such popes be found.[55].

Massaino's criticisms of the papacy of his day are forceful and at times acerbic. In his dedicatory letter to Adrian VI he suggests that those who cannot stomach his words may be spiritually ill. The food contained in his *enchiridion* is but the teachings of Scripture and of the holy fathers. Should his critics then protest that it is his parenthetical comments that are too sour and pungent, Massaino replies that Christ, Paul, and other good men have been allowed to denounce the evils of their day. May not he, too, point out with accuracy and moral indignation what has gone wrong?[56]

Massaino was reacting to a constitutional imbalance in the Church on the eve of the Reformation. In their efforts to defeat conciliarism and restore the papal monarchy, the Renaissance popes had gone too far. Julius II had tried to create an imperial papacy advancing its claims to temporal power by political alliances, crusade proposals, military might, grandiose building projects, and the resurrected trappings of imperial Rome of antiquity. In the spiritual sphere, the papacy sought even greater control over ecclesiastical appointments and revenues, and increased power, prestige, and wealth for the papal court and Roman curia as reflections of the majesty and authority of the Holy See. Cardinals and curialists profited most from these developments, the losers were the bishops. With few checks on their powers, popes like Alexander VI (1492-1503) and Julius II (1503-13) could pursue policies that harmed the Church universal. Massaino's study of church history, especially of the apostolic and patristic periods, convinced him that the current papacy was an aberration.

[55]DCEES, 22r-v.
[56]DCEES, 1v.

Reform would come with a return to earlier ecclesiological models. He rejected the cardinals as agents of reform, pointing out that their office lacked any scriptural basis. Instead he argued that the bishops under the leadership of their patriarchs or assembled in council could prevent the papacy from becoming a tyranny. Massaino was not alone in calling for a restored episcopacy. At the Lateran Council (1512-17) meeting in Rome while he was revising his treatise, the bishops demanded an end to the pretensions of cardinals, a restitution of their authority in their own dioceses, and a continuing voice in the government of the Church by the establishment in Rome of a permanent, elected college of bishops. Leo X (1513-21) and the college of cardinals skilfully manipulated the conciliar proceedings so that the bishops received very little of what they had wanted.[57] While Massaino makes no mention of this in his revised version, the fact that he ends his treatise with an appeal to the princes of Christendom to overthrow the whore of Rome and thus rescue the Church suggests that he had come to realize that the current episcopacy was too weak to exercise its divine mission of restraining the papacy.

Buried in his books, Massaino had become too enamored with the seeming reasonableness and logic of his own ideas and had not taken into sufficient account contemporary realities. The patriarchs of the East no longer presided over thriving Christian communities, were unable to travel for consultations with the pope, and were alienated from the West by remembered grievances and doctrinal differences. The cardinals were not merely local Roman officials, but often administrators of the Church's central bureaucracy, and bishops or archbishops or even titular patriarchs in their own right. If their role in the government of the Church

[57]On the reforming efforts of the bishops, see my "Episcopal Reform at the Fifth Lateran Council (1512-17)" (Harvard University dissertation, 1976), esp. 370-434, and "Paride de Grassi's Diary of the Fifth Lateran Council," *Annuarium Historiae Conciliorum* 14 (1982), 370-460, here 381-86.

was to be discounted on the grounds that their office and its powers were later developments in the history of the Church, why did Massaino then turn around and claim great authority for Christian emperors and patriarchs who also lacked a scriptural basis? Perhaps most disquieting is his selective reading of the Gospels when treating the Petrine office. Important texts which support papal claims were not even mentioned. Until a critical edition with a complete apparatus of the sources used in his two treatises is published, it will be difficult to determine the accuracy of his arguments based on the Bible and church history.

While we know that cardinal Fieschi was adamantly opposed to the ideas presented in the first treatise which Massaino had dedicated to him, we do not know how the dour Dutchman Adrian VI reacted to the even more biting revision dedicated to him. At least he did not have all copies of it destroyed. His register in the Vatican Secret Archives records no new benefices or pensions for the Florentine whom previous popes had unwittingly praised for his scholarship. Perhaps Adrian read it before his sudden demise. What became of Massaino thereafter is as yet not known. His treatise, however, seems to have had some later influence, for it was included in a collection of materials assembled to help determine the advisability or not of calling a council to deal with the Lutheran question. Given the critical views of even loyal Catholics such as Massaino, it is not surprising that the papacy put off calling a council that might limit its powers and reform its practices.

From *Sermo* to *Anathema*:
A Dispute about the Confession of Mortal Sins

Carl J. Peter

In 1518 Martin Luther published his *Sermo de Poenitentia*, perhaps as an aid in the hearing of Easter confessions that year. His decision to do so was destined to have notable consequences not only for himself but for Western Christendom. This essay aims at presenting the subsequent history of a position which the Reformer espoused in that early work.

The time period covered will be from 1518 to 1551. Lutheran Confessions will figure prominently. The *terminus ad quem* will be the fourteenth session of the Council of Trent. A line of development will be traced in what was at the time a dialectic leading from *sermo* to *anathema*. The precise focus will be on the debate about the obligatory character of the confession of mortal sins committed after baptism.

Sermo de Poenitentia[1]

In that early sermon Luther was at pains to offer advice with regard to the attitudes that Christians should have when confessing sin and seeking absolution. He did not write a detached analysis of what the sacrament of penance involves. Instead he offered reflections and counsel.

After dealing with sorrow for sin, Luther turned his attention to sacramental confession itself. Here he says he wishes to make two points.

The second has to do with the establishment of priorities. It is more important, Luther contends, to determine whether the one who confesses *believes* that his or her sins are actually forgiven by the absolution than whether he or she is truly contrite.[2] There is always room for doubt about the authenticity, certainty, and sufficiency of one's sorrow; this is not the case with regard to faith and Christ's promise of forgiveness through the power of the keys.[3]

It is, however, Luther's first point that is of greater interest in this paper. Again it is the attitude of the one confessing that concerns him:

> First, presume in no way to confess venial and not even all mortal sins. It is impossible for you to know all your mortal sins. And no one is bound to the impossible.[4]

---

[1] *Sermo de poenitentia P. Martini Luther Augustiniani Vuittenbergensis*, Band 1 of *D. Martin Luthers Werke: Kritische Gesamtausgabe* (Weimar,1883), 319-24. Henceforth this edition will be referred to as W.A., followed by citation of the volume, page, and line numbers.

[2] Luther, *De Poenitentia*, W.A. 1, 324,2-3.

[3] *Ibid.*, 4-6: "... contritio numquam est vera satis, quod si esset vera, non est tamen certa, et si esset certa, non tamen esset satis. Fides autem et verbum Christi sunt verissima, certissima, sufficientissima." Luther may well be saying that *objective* grounds for doubt exist with regard to contrition but not with regard to Christ's word of promise and the faith which is its acknowledgement. Cf. as well: *Sermo de Poenitentia*, 323, 34-36.

[4] *Ibid.*, 322, 22-23: "Primum, ut nullo modo praesumas confiteri peccata venialia, sed nec omnia mortalia, quia impossibile est ut omnia mortalia cognoscas."

Luther then looks back and says it was for this reason that in the early Church only some mortal sins were confessed: those that were manifest or of their nature public. With regard to the changed situation of his own day he has a real lament. People confess their sins by relating the latter to the five senses, the seven gifts of the Holy Spirit, the seven sacraments, the eight beatitudes; indeed, they distinguish sins in even more ways than these! It is as if they were concerned that no sin go unconfessed. There are times when no sin at all or scarcely even a venial sin is involved. When they confess in such a fashion, penitents tire the confessor to no good purpose, waste time, and are a hindrance to others.[5]

What alternative did Luther propose in 1518? He would have people confess to a priest all their sins that are clearly mortal and leave all the rest to God.[6] Our good works, he adds, are sins worthy of damnation if God enters into judgment with us. But when we acknowledge this and pray to God for forgiveness, these sinful deeds are forgiven and become meritorious.[7]

In concluding this section on the confession of sins, Luther shows what his real interest and concern are when he offers such admonitions. In fact, he says, one who wishes to confess all his or her sins wishes: a) to leave nothing to divine mercy for forgiveness; b) to trust not in God but in his or her own confession; and c) not to fear God's judgment but to seek security and peace of conscience from the realization that sins have been confessed. God, however, is kindly disposed to those who have fear and yet trust in divine mercy.[8]

Here one finds unmistakable evidence of concern for the tormented conscience of which Reformation historians and theologians have spoken so often and rightly! How is a

[5]*Ibid.*, 28-32.
[6]*Ibid.*, 33-37.
[7]*Ibid.*, 322, 39-40; 323, 1-3.
[8]*Ibid.*, 323, 4-9.

baptized Christian conscious of sin to find peace and consolation through the sacrament of penance in 1518? Luther gives a very clear answer in the form of counsel and advice: "Do not try to confess all your sins; not even all your mortal sins." This stipulation is not his whole answer; it is nevertheless an important part of his answer and had a subsequent history that is worthy of more consideration than it has received.

The Reaction of Cardinal Cajetan

On three successive days Luther met with Cardinal Cajetan during the fall of 1518. In their first encounter, October 12, the papal legate showed he had carefully studied the *Sermo de Poenitentia*.[9] In fact, he had already put down in writing a challenge to what Luther had said in that text about the kind of faith required for a fruitful reception of the sacrament of penance.[10]

There are, wrote the renowned Thomist, two very different kinds of faith: infused and acquired. The first is found in the baptized and is indeed a requirement for the sacrament of penance. By this infused faith, Christians believe that when sacramental absolution is rightly conferred, grace is given to a subject who is properly disposed. There is no way that infused faith can err or be false! The second kind of

---

[9]Cf. Jared Wicks, S.J., *Cajetan Responds: A Reader in Reformation Controversy* (Washington, 1978), 22-23; his "Roman Reactions to Luther: The First Year (1518)," *The Catholic Historical Review* 69 (1983), 521-62, here 544-48; and his "Fides Sacramenti — Fides Specialis: Luther's Development in 1518," *Gregorianum* 65 (1984), 53-86, here 69.

[10]The place was Augsburg. The date given in the Venice edition of 1580 is September 29, 1518. Cf. *Opuscula Omnia Thomae de Vio Cajetani Cardinalis tituli Sancti Sixti in Tres Distincta Tomos Quorum Seriem et Quae in Eis Continentur Sequens Index Indicabit* (Venice, 1580), Tomus 1, Tractatus 18, Q.4, 56v -75 (sic for 57) r; here 57r. September 26, 1518 is the date given in Jared Wicks' translation of the Lyons edition of 1562 emended with the aid of the Venice edition of 1531. Cf. *Cajetan Responds*, 266.

faith (acquired) depends on conditions (e.g., the intention of the confessor) which may or may not be fulfilled in a particular instance. By this acquired faith one believes he or she has actually received grace through a particular confession of sin and conferral of absolution. The contingencies involved in such a situation do not allow for the certainty that characterizes infused faith. But it is precisely that kind of certainty which Luther seems to expect and demand in individual instances of sacramental absolution. For Cajetan this is excessive and unrealistic.[11] Indeed he wrote: "this is to establish a new Church."[12]

More directly to the point of this paper, and again before the meeting of October 12, Cajetan had objected to Luther's denial of the obligatory character of the confession of all mortal sins committed after baptism.[13] He had transposed Luther's counsel or stipulation into the form of a scholastic question by asking whether it is presumptuous to confess venial sins and all mortal sins.[14] Before proceeding to his own carefully nuanced answer, he gives four arguments that aim at making a case for an affirmative reply.[15] They are an almost verbatim reportage of Luther's in the *Sermo de Poenitentia.*

For his part Cajetan contends that it is not presumptuous but virtuous and obligatory to confess all one's mortal

[11]*Opuscula Omnia Thomae de Vio* (Venice, 1580), 56v, col. 1-2.

[12]*Ibid.*, 75 (sic for 57) r, col. 2, A. In their meeting on October 12, Cajetan challenged Luther both about the latter's demand for this kind of faith in the reception of the sacrament of penance and about the effects of indulgences. After their third meeting, the legate no longer insisted that Luther retract what he had written in the *Sermo de Poenitentia* on the first point. Cf. Jared Wicks, "Roman Reactions," 550.

[13]This too he did on September 29, 1518; cf. *Opuscula Omnia Thomae de Vio* (Venice, 1580), Tomus 1, Tractatus 18, Q.2, 55v, col. 2-56r, col. 1, here 56r, col. 1. Wicks gives a synopsis rather than a translation in this case; cf. *Cajetan Responds*, 62-63.

[14]*Opuscula Omnia Thomae de Vio*, 55v, col. 2.

[15]*Ibid.*

sins.[16] The reasons he gives are worthy of note:

a) by the common consent of theologians, integrity is one of the sixteen [!] conditions required for confession;

b) all mortal sins (and not just some) must be confessed because one cannot be forgiven if others are not;

c) as one must be sorry before God for all one's mortal sins, so one must confess them all to the priest;

d) the Fourth Lateran Council in its decree *Omnis Utriusque* specified that all sins must be confessed once a year and the whole Church has understood the *all* to refer not to venial sins but to those that are mortal;

e) it is rash to restrict the object of this obligation to mortal sins that are public or manifest when the Council of Florence restricted it to all those that one remembers.[17]

As for the objection that confession of all one's mortal sins is impossible, such is not the case since in the case of mortal sin one is dealing with voluntary acts rather than spontaneous reactions whose frequency may not be subject to recall. What is more, the texts from *1 Corinthians* 5:11 and *Galatians* 5:19 (which Luther had cited!) do not prove what they were intended to demonstrate: the fact is that neither speaks of confessing sins.[18] Cajetan's reaction would be followed by another that was more corporate in nature.

[16]*Ibid.*
[17]*Ibid.*
[18]*Ibid.*, 56r, col. 1, B.

Censures from Academe

On November 7, 1519, the Dean and Faculty of Sacred Theology at Louvain entered the fray by finding fourteen headings or areas of Luther's theology worthy of censure. The *Sermo de Poenitentia* is listed among the works from which individual assertions are drawn. It is a source for the following position:

> With regard to confession: 'Not all mortal sins must be confessed, because it is impossible for you to know all mortal sins; no one, however, is bound to the impossible.'[19]

The text continues — with Luther's own formulation —by observing that in the early Church only manifest mortal sins were confessed and by giving as evidence the reference to *Galatians* 5:19 ff.[20]

It is impossible to determine from their censure just how negatively the Louvain divines viewed this particular position of the Reformer.[21] Citing it along with others he had taken, they condemned the ensemble globally: "as defamatory with regard to philosophy and the theologians of the previous four centuries" as well as "containing many assertions that are false, scandalous, heretical, and smacking of heresy."[22]

In the *Sermo de Poenitentia*, Luther's counsel or stipulation had been put in the second person, was clearly related to presumption, and included venial as well as mortal sins. To his credit, Cajetan had not missed the second and third of

---

[19] *Facultatis Theologiae Lovaniensis doctrinalis condemnatio doctrinae Martini Lutheri*, W.A. 6, 175-78; here 177.

[20] *Ibid.*

[21] *Ibid.* 176.

[22] *Ibid.*

these facts even though he transposed the language of a *Sermo* into that of a *Quaestio*. Neither is taken into account in the Louvain text. The result is the rejection of a proposition to the effect that not all mortal sins must be confessed because it is impossible for *you* to remember them all. In the retention of the second person there is a trace of Luther's original intention. The fact remains, however, that *you*, in the context of the Louvain censure as in that of Cajetan's *quaestio,* is the equivalent of the indefinite *one.*

A *sermo* intended to give concrete advice with regard to the way in which sacramental confession should take place contains a position that is becoming a thesis calling for judgment and censure. Luther's intent and choice of genre might have been taken more into account than was the case. Language seeking to engage readers and elicit a religious response is being read as if it were a detached, objective analysis of one of the components of the sacrament of penance; namely the confession of mortal sins. Luther's text is faithfully transcribed. But it is acquiring an existence of its own, outside its original literary and pastoral context. What is more, that passage is coming to be taken as a hallmark of the Reformer on the sacrament of penance.[23]

Papal Intervention

On June 15, 1520, Pope Leo X approved the bull *Exsurge Domine*, which threatened Luther with excommunication.[24] Both Cardinal Cajetan and the indefatigable John Eck had

[23]On August 30, 1519 the Theological Faculty of Cologne had condemned certain propositions of Luther. With regard to confession he was described as having given very bad advice (*perversa consilia*) that is contrary to the long-standing (*veterem*) teaching of the universal Church. Cf. W.A. 6, 178-80; here 179.

[24]It was only later that Luther's excommunication took place through the bull *Decet Romanum Pontificem* on January 3, 1521.

been involved in its preparation. The former had argued in favor of producing a document that was theologically precise: to each text taken from the Reformer's writings should be attached the censure or censures it deserved.[25] Such was not to be! The condemnation was global. Six censures were appended to a list of forty-one propositions, which were described as being "heretical or scandalous or false or offensive to pious ears or seductive of simple minds or at odds with catholic truth."[26] The confusion caused by this scatter shot approach was to be lamented later by Eck himself.[27] For all his trouble Cajetan wound up writing to explain, for example, why the bull condemned the following proposition from the *Sermo de Poenitentia*:

> To sin no more and to live a new life are the best kind of repentance; this saying is very true indeed and a better teaching on contrition than any given heretofore.[28]

Of the forty-one propositions that were repudiated in *Exsurge Domine*, no fewer than ten deal with repentance.[29] If one adds to this the fact that yet another eight have to do with indulgences and excommunication, it becomes clear that the Church's penitential system was singled out for

---

[25]Wicks, *Cajetan Responds*, 30.

[26] Henricus Denzinger and Adolfus Schönmetzer, *Enchiridion Symbolorum, Definitionum et Declarationum de Rebus Fidei et Morum* (Freiburg, 1976), 1492 — henceforth cited as D.S.

[27]Erwin Iserloh, Joseph Glazik, and Hubert Jedin, *Reformation and Counter Reformation*, volume 5 of *History of the Church*, trans. A. Biggs and P. W. Becker (New York, 1980), 72. Iserloh notes (*ibid.*) that the opinions given the previous year by the Universities of Cologne and Louvain were used in the preparation of *Exsurge Domine*.

[28]For the text of the proposition in *Exsurge Domine*, cf. D.S. 1457; for Luther's Teutonic and Latin original, cf. W.A. 1, 321, 2-4. The cardinal's defense of the condemnation is given by Jared Wicks; cf. *Cajetan Responds*, 31, 145-46, 280.

[29]*D.S.* 1455-64.

defense against Luther's early criticism.[30] The sacrament of penance was the focal point for a dispute about the nature of justification.

In all, seven propositions cited in *Exsurge Domine* were taken from the *Sermo de Poenitentia* of 1518.[31] This included Luther's counsel about not presuming to confess venial sins and not even all mortal sins since this is impossible and no one is bound to that.[32] The Reformer's words about confession are accurately reported. But outside their original context they fail to convey the pastoral concern that lay behind them in the first place and are easily understood as an attempt to state objectively what God does not expect in the confession of sin. Then the reader or hearer will miss the fact that Luther's words were clearly intended to warn against a kind of presumption; namely, that forgiveness comes because of the completeness of one's confession of sin rather than as a result of God's compassion in Jesus Christ.

To be sure, Luther had written a second sermon on the sacrament of penance — this one in 1519.[33] But with regard to the obligation to confess mortal sins, it was his first endeavor that was decisive for Cajetan, the University of Louvain, and *Exsurge Domine*. As a result, a text that was intended to inculcate a special kind of trust in God came to be taken as Luther's view of what God's saving will does not call for in the confession of sin. Two very different kinds of discourse were at work — without the participants' being fully aware of it. That did not prevent the condemnation of

[30] *D.S.* 1467-74.

[31] *D.S.* 1456-59,1461-62, 1464.

[32] *D.S.* 1458.

[33] *Ein Sermon von dem Sakrament der Busse Doctoris Martini L.A.W.*, W.A. 2, 714-23. In "Roman Reactions," 548, Wicks says this work presents "a more coherently systematic view" than does the *Sermo* of 1518. *Exsurge Domine* drew on the later Sermon when it censured (*D.S.* 1463) the following proposition (W.A. 2, 716, 25-28): "In the sacrament of penance and forgiveness of guilt, a pope or a bishop does no more than the most lowly priest, or where there is no priest, any other Christian, albeit a woman or child."

Luther's view about confession in *Exsurge Domine* from having long-lasting implications. The Lutheran Confessions saw in this bull a negative reply to an attempt to bring about reform with regard to the sacrament of penance. In fact no other authoritative teaching from the Holy See would be available on the matters under dispute (including the confession of mortal sins) until the time of the Council of Trent.

The Diet of 1530

When it comes to the sacrament of penance, the eleventh article of the *Augsburg Confession* stresses that the practice of private absolution is to be retained.[34] Then Melanchthon immediately adds a *caveat*. In confession, the text continues, it is not required that one enumerate all trespasses and sins. Indeed the words of the *Psalm* (19:12) show that this is impossible.[35] There is a family resemblance between this article and the *Sermo de Poenitentia*, though Luther's concern for avoiding presumption in the way one confesses is not reiterated[36]

The final section of the *Augustana* deals with "abuses" about which Christians are not of one mind in 1530. Here too confession is singled out.[37] It is important because of its connection with absolution and because of its potential for consoling terrified consciences.[38] But no one is to be com-

---

[34] *Die Bekenntnisschriften der Evangelisch-Lutherischen Kirche* (Göttingen, 1982), 66 — henceforth cited as BSLK.

[35] BSLK, 66.

[36] One does find something of Luther's concern about presumption in the following article (XII: On Repentance). There the *Confession* rejects the position of those who require us to merit grace through our acts of satisfaction. Cf. BSLK, 67.

[37] *Augsburg Confession*, XXV; BSLK, 97-100.

[38] BSLK, 100.

pelled to enumerate all his or her sins. This is impossible as Scripture attests.[39]

In 1518 Luther spoke of not presuming to confess all sins; he was concerned that for forgiveness one not look to the integrity of his or her confession but to God's mercy. Here the *Confession* speaks of an enumeration of all sins, says this is impossible, and regards any such requirement as an abuse. Luther had distinguished between venial and mortal sins; the *Confession* does not. It has been suggested that the enumeration to which Melanchthon objected was one that encouraged scrupulosity and tormented consciences.[40] If so, then perhaps the two Reformers were rejecting a confession of sin that was made in such a way as to encourage presumption, put conscience to the test, and result in anguish rather than peace. That rejection would not directly contradict a more abstract doctrinal teaching requiring confession of all mortal sins in species and number!

The Response to the Augustana

An answer to the *Augsburg Confession* came from the Catholic party at the Diet of 1530 in the form of the *Confutatio*. Unfortunately the latter is still mistakenly thought by many to have received papal approval. *Confutatio Caesarea* is a far more accurate description.[41] The external authority behind it was that of Charles V.

---

[39]BSLK, 98-99.

[40]Holsten Fagerberg and Hans Jorissen, "Penance and Confession," trans. James L. Schaaf, in *Confessing One Faith: A Joint Commentary on the Augsburg Confession by Lutheran and Catholic Theologians*, ed. by G. W. Forrell and James F. McCue (Augsburg, 1982), 234-61, here 251 — henceforth cited as "Penance and Confession."

[41] Herbert Immenkötter, *Um die Einheit im Glauben: Die Unionsverhandlungen des Augsburger Reichstages im August und September 1530*, 1st ed. (Münster, 1973), 30.

With regard to article XI of the *Confession*, the *Confutatio* notes with approval the former's insistence that private absolution is not to fall into desuetude. Sacramental absolution rests firmly on the Word of Christ as its guarantee; that is the reason for its importance.[42] The agreement between Luther, the *Augsburg Confession*, and the *Confutatio* on this issue is utterly undeniable.

Absolution, however, takes place in the context of confession of sin.[43] At this point the *Confutatio* asks that two things be required by the civil authorities who subscribed to the *Augsburg Confession*.

The first has to to with church law. The constitution *Omnis Utriusque* of the Fourth Lateran Council prescribed annual confession of sin. This practice should be observed.[44]

The second has to do with the proper instruction that preachers should give the Christian people.

> [T]hose who are about to confess may find it impossible to enumerate all their sins individually; still after making a careful examination of conscience they should make an integral confession of all their serious sins (*delictorum*); namely, of all those that they remember after such scrutiny. As for other sins, that are forgotten or escape recall, it is licit to confess them in a general way and to say with the Psalmist: 'From my hidden sins, cleanse me, Lord!'[45]

In article XXV the *Confutatio* returns to the subject of confessing sins.[46] The *Augustana* is said to have erred in

---

[42] *Die Confutatio der Confessio Augustana vom 3 August 1530*, ed. Herbert Immenkötter, Band 33 of *Corpus Catholicorum* (Münster, 1979), 102-05, here 102-03 — henceforth cited as *Die Confutatio*.

[43] *Die Confutatio*, 102-103.

[44] *Ibid.*

[45] *Ibid.*, 102-05.

[46] *Ibid.*, 172-77.

citing John Chrysostom as someone opposed to the requirement of integral confession.[47] Peter Lombard and Gratian
are reported to have replied to that charge over three
hundred years earlier. As to the *Gloss* on the *Decree of
Gratian* (which proposed the enumeration of sins in confession as an obligation arising from ecclesiastical rather than
divine law), it is a clear exception — one challenged and
rejected by specialists in divine law.[48]

The *Confutatio* becomes yet stronger. Integral confession
is necessary for salvation and is the nerve of all Christian
obedience and discipline.[49] The adherents of the *Augsburg
Confession* should be admonished to bring themselves into
conformity with the Church that is correct in its beliefs and
practices (*ecclesiae orthodoxae*). Otherwise they may wind
up with the Montanists, of whom Jerome said twelve
hundred years earlier that they are ashamed to confess their
sins.[50]

The *Confutatio* acknowledges that at times it is impossible to recall all one's mortal sins. On those occasions, it says,
such confession is not required. Presumption and despair
had been the concerns of Luther in the *Sermo de Poenitentia* of 1518 when he dealt with the way in which Christians
ought to confess their sins. The *Confutatio* concerns itself
not with these two undesirable possibilities but with what
the Church has taught about the need to confess one's
mortal sins when this is possible. Promoting the proper kind
of hope is the priority of Luther; believing correctly about
God's saving will is paramount for the *Confutatio*.

It may not exactly have been a dialogue of the deaf. But

[47]*Ibid.*, 172-75.

[48]*Ibid.*, 174-75. Melanchthon had referred to this Gloss in article 25 of the
Augsburg Confession; cf. BSLK, 99.

[49]*Die Confutatio*, 174-77.

[50]*Ibid.*, 176-77.

each side was clearly more intent on pressing its own preoccupation than on listening to why the other side had a different one.

A Lutheran Response

In 1531, Philip Melanchthon replied to the *Confutatio* in his famous *Apology*.[51] He deals with the confession of sin in article XI. There he asserts that Lutheran teaching about absolution (which he calls a sacrament) has brought great peace to troubled consciences.[52] Christians are being encouraged to believe that in absolution God forgives their sins freely for Christ's sake; no longer are they left to think that their works bring this about.[53] Once more faith in the effect of the sacrament has made its appearance!

When it comes to the enumeration of sins in confession, Melanchthon's first stated concern is that consciences not be ensnared. The mention of some sins may be helpful at times in providing the occasion for needed instruction. But the real question at stake is whether an enumeration of sins is called for by divine law.[54]

He asks to be shown where God makes the forgiveness of sins dependent on their enumeration. As to the decree *Omnis Utriusque*, it has in his opinion caused a great deal of anguish by requiring that *all* sins be confessed. In this it commands the impossible. No wonder the devout have been driven to despair: thinking themselves bound by God to confess all their sins and finding this beyond their powers![55]

---

[51]*Apology of the Augsburg Confession*; BSLK, 141-404 — henceforth cited as *Apology*.

[52]*Apology*, XI: 2-3; BSLK, 249-50.

[53]*Ibid.*, XI: 2; BSLK, 249.

[54]*Ibid.*, XI: 6; BSLK, 250-51.

[55]*Ibid.*, XI: 7-10; BSLK 251-52.

In article XII Melanchthon concerns himself with what is involved in repentance. Here again he turns to the subject of the confession of sins. It is false and contrary to Scripture to maintain that the enumeration of sins in confession — as his opponents command it — is necessary by divine right.[56] Confession is to be retained for the sake of absolution. In stressing this he calls attention to the fact that he has already denied that the enumeration of sins in confession is necessary *jure divino*.[57] Those who disagree must not think they have made their point when they object that a judge must hear a case before passing sentence. The reason is clear enough: absolution is a ministry of grace and not of law. Investigating a penitent's hidden sins is not included in Christ's command to forgive.[58] However useful confession and the enumeration of some sins may be, they should not be allowed to ensnare consciences.[59] For its part the *Confutatio* states that complete confession is necessary for salvation; in so doing it teaches something that is totally false and at the same time it commands the impossible.[60]

Luther's concern in the *Sermo* of 1518 is still present. Confession is not to be a work that one trusts as sufficient (*because* and *if* it is complete) to win the forgiveness of sins. At the same time Melanchthon enters into a more traditional type of theological debate. He asks whether an enumeration of sins is necessary in God's saving plan (*jure divino*) for the forgiveness of sins. He is willing to admit that confession of sin was practiced in the early Church; its purpose was to enable priests to impose penalties or works of satisfaction corresponding to offenses. But forgiveness

---

[56] *Apology*, XII: 23; BSLK 256.

[57] *Ibid.*, XII: 99; BSLK 272; and XII: 102-03; BSLK, 272-73. See below n. 80 for my study of the meaning of the term *jus divinum*.

[58] *Ibid.*, XII: 103-05; BSLK, 273.

[59] *Ibid.*, XII: 110-11; BSLK, 274.

[60] *Ibid.*, XII: 111; BSLK, 274.

comes freely as a result of God's mercy in Jesus Christ and not because of the confession or enumeration of one's sins. Two types of theological discourse are at work in this section of the *Apology*. The first looks at the consequences of teaching about the confession of sins. It asks whether such teaching is likely to lead to despair. The other has to do with truth and denies that for the forgiveness of sins God requires their confession and enumeration. Both are evoked by Melanchthon's desire to reply to the *Confutatio*.[61]

Preparation for a Council

When Pope Paul III convoked a Council to meet in Mantua in May of 1537, Luther drew up a position paper in response.[62] History knows this text as the *Smalcald Articles*, which were completed by their author in late December of 1536.[63]

Their *Third Part* is introduced with a preface telling the reader the subjects that follow are not of much interest to

[61] A comparison of the texts leads to the conclusion that the *Confutation* and the *Apology* meant different things by *complete* or *integral confession* when the former described it as necessary for salvation and the latter rejected it as spiritually disastrous. Melanchthon repudiated a tortuous enumeration of *all* sins; the confutators required confession of *all serious* sins that come to mind after a careful examination of conscience. There remain two important questions. In denying that complete confession is necessary (*jure divino*) for salvation, did Melanchthon deny as well that God's law (*jus divinum*) *ever* requires the clear and unambiguous confession of mortal sin for forgiveness? Did he or would he have seen even that confession as a human work or as a condition keeping absolution from bringing divinely intended consolation and peace to the sinner?

Until these questions are answered, one has to remain a bit skeptical about the agreement that Holsten Fagerberg and Hans Jorissen say was possible between the *Confutatio* and the *Apology* on this issue. Cf. "Penance and Confession," 250.

[62] *Smalcald Articles*; BSLK, 405-68.

[63] When he subscribed to these Articles, Philip Melanchthon added a codicil to his signature and thereby indicated the kind of primacy he was willing to accord the pope for the sake of Christian unity. Cf. BSLK, 463-64.

the Pope and his court.[64] After treatments of *Sin* (Article I) and *The Law* (Article II) Luther turns to *Repentance*, which he explains through the themes of *Law* and *Gospel*.[65] By way of contrast he describes "The False Repentance of the Papists."[66] Here he charges his opponents with minimizing the effects of original sin, exaggerating the importance of works, encouraging presumption, and failing to mention Christ or faith. What is more, he says, they demand the confession of *all* sins, thus insisting on the impossible and bringing great torture to penitents.[67] This is, he thinks, a prime instance of promoting works-righteousness. Its fruits are misery, torments, fraud, and idolatry.[68] In Article VII (*The Keys*) he restricts to God alone the power to judge the gravity and number of our sins.[69] Finally he adds in Article VIII (*Confession*) that the individual penitent should be free to decide whether he or she wishes to enumerate sins when seeking absolution.[70] The irenic tone of the *Augsburg Confession* is replaced by a polemic against the Papacy and its works. Luther is concerned with the harmful effects that come from telling penitents they must confess all their sins.

The Council of Trent

Despite the call of Paul III, the Council that was to meet in Mantua never did. Later, in 1541, a serious effort at reunion was made by way of officially sponsored negotia-

---

[64]BSLK,433.

[65]*Smalcald Articles* III, 3; BSLK,436-38.

[66]*Ibid.*, BSLK 438-49.

[67]*Ibid.*, BSLK, 440.

[68]*Ibid.*, BSLK, 441.

[69]*Ibid.*, III, 7: BSLK, 452.

[70]*Ibid.*, III, 8: BSLK, 453.

tions between Lutherans and Catholics. History knows one of these attempts as the Colloquy of Regensburg. After a number of successes (including surprising but short-lived agreements on original sin and justification), the exchanges led to a debacle. The beginning of the end came with the failure of the collocutors to reach a consensus on transubstantiation. To find a way out of the impasse, the subject was shifted to other issues. Among these was the need to confess all mortal sins in confession. Here too the sides wound up at odds.[71]

On October 15, 1551, discussions began that would lead to the Tridentine teaching on the sacrament of penance.[72] Twelve articles had been taken from the writings of the Reformers and were referred to the Council's theologians. The latter were asked to decide whether these articles were heretical and deserving of conciliar condemnation. In the nineteen congregations that followed (the last being held on October 30th), thirty-eight speakers voiced their opinions, including such figures as Laínez, Salmeron, Tapper, Cano, and Gropper.

The fifth article that was proposed for the theologians' judgment was the following:

---

[71] *Corpus Rerformatorum* IV (Hallis Saxonum, 1837) 217-18, 300. See also Peter Matheson, *Cardinal Contarini at Regensburg* (Oxford, 1972), 136-38 and Thomas M. Parker's review in *The Journal of Theological Studies* 24 (1973), 303-07.

[72] There had been earlier discussions of this sacrament when the Council met in Bologna. Although these led to no doctrinal or reform decrees, a point that was explicitly discussed deserves to be mentioned here. Under the heading of provisions that might be made to correct abuses, one finds mention of cautioning confessors not to make unnecessary inquiries into sins confessed (especially concerning chastity). Cf. *Concilium Tridentinum: Diariorum, Actorum, Epistularum, Tractatuum Nova Collectio*, VI/1 (Freiburg, 1950), 404-07 — henceforth cited as C.T. One recalls Melanchthon's insistence that the ministry of absolution does not include a charge to make an investigation into hidden sins. Whatever their differences, this much is clear. Both sides in the dispute recognized that in pastoral practice the actual administration of the sacrament of penance might involve unjustified prying on the part of the confessor.

An enumeration of sins in confession is not necessary for their forgiveness but is free. Rather than being required, it is useful for instructing and consoling the penitent in this day and age. An enumeration was once required for the purpose of imposing canonical penalties. It is not necessary to confess all mortal sins (for example those that are occult and against the last two precepts of the Decalogue) or any circumstances of sins (an obligation thought up by people who had nothing better to do!). To wish to confess all sins is to leave nothing to God's mercy for forgiveness. It is not licit to confess venial sins.[73]

Sources from which the article was derived were cited; the *Sermo de Poenitentia* of 1518 was not among them.[74] But there is good reason to think it figured in the discussions.

On Friday November 6th, the theologians' judgments were presented to the Council in summary fashion. With regard to the fifth article it was reported:

As to that part of the article which says it is not licit to confess venial sins, this should be noted. Some of the theologians warned that Luther does not say this, but rather: 'Do not presume to confess venial sins, etc.'[75]

The words of the *Sermo* are easily recognized here — introduced as a corrective against misunderstanding.

That same day the council Fathers began their own discussion of the articles. On the 16th of November, a small commission was appointed to draft canons and chapters for a decree. After further debate there was a liturgical session

---

[73]C. T., VII/1 (Freiburg, 1961), 235.

[74]The eleventh article began: "Optimam poenitentiam esse novam vitam...." For it the *Sermo de poenitentia* was cited as a source. Cf. *ibid.*, 238.

[75]*Ibid.*, 293.

on November 25th in which solemn approval was given to the Council's teaching on the sacrament of penance.[76]

It will be helpful at this point to recall the content of the fifth article taken from the writings of the Reformers and given to the Council's theologians for their judgment. That article had used the phrase *enumeration of sins* and denied that the latter was necessary for forgiveness. What was the Council's verdict on this?

The matter was dealt with in the seventh canon, which avoided using the term *enumeration*. Instead, it called for a *confession* not of all sins but of each and every *mortal* sin that one remembers after an examination of conscience made with due care. Such confession is said to be required by divine law (*jure divino*) for forgiveness. This obligation includes the confession of occult sins as well as those that are public; it extends to the last two precepts of the Decalogue. Not any and all circumstances, but those that are important enough to distinguish one species of sin from another must be mentioned.[77]

Correspondingly, such confession is more than something that is useful in the instruction and consolation of penitents. It was indeed required in the early Church because of the need to know what penalties should be imposed, but not for that reason only. What is more, those who strive to confess all their sins are not *eo ipso* guilty of wishing to leave nothing to God's mercy for forgiveness. Finally, it is licit to confess venial sins.[78]

Issues had been raised by Luther in his *Sermo* of 1518. He offered advice aimed at helping confessors and penitents. Among other things he was intent on keeping the confession of sins from becoming the occasion of presumption or

---

[76]D.S. 1667-93, 1701-15.

[77]D.S. 1707.

[78]*Ibid.*

despair. It could become either if the penitent thought the completeness (integrity) of his or her confession was the necessary and sufficient condition for divine forgiveness. Thirty-three years later the Council of Trent concerned itself with what God's saving will expects of the baptized in the confession of sin. That saving will (*jus divinum*) was presented as calling for the clear and unambiguous acknowledgement of all mortal sins subject to recall after a careful examination of conscience. Not disinterested with regard to the pastoral effects of such a teaching, the Council expressed a conviction that consolation comes to those who confess in this fashion and receive absolution.[79]

Conclusion

In the Roman Catholic Church at present there is a widespread impression with regard to the position taken by the Council of Trent concerning the oligation to confess mortal sins. Some think the Tridentine teaching so time-conditioned that it may be effectively and safely ignored in the new situations of our day. Others regard that teaching as still binding and as so restrictive as to make general absolution without individual confession of mortal sins something that on dogmatic grounds can be allowed only in the most unusual of circumstances.

This paper has not taken sides in that debate.[80] Its purpose has rather been to trace the history of a cluster of questions that were answered by Luther in 1518 and that led from a *Sermo* of that year to a conciliar *Anathema* in 1551.

[79]D.S. 1682.

[80]The author has done so elsewhere. Cf. his "Auricular Confession and the Council of Trent," *The Jurist* 28 (1968), 280-97; "Integral Confession and the Council of Trent," *Concilium* 61 (1971), 99-109; "Dimensions of *Jus Divinum* in Roman Catholic Theology," *Theological Studies* 34 (1973), 227-50; and "Integrity Today?" *Communio* 1 (1974), 60-82.

The author is of the opinion that the doctrinal teaching of councils is usually in response to some rather precise questions. Perhaps the history recalled here will help to show what the questions were for Trent and what they were not with regard to the obligation to confess mortal sins. Such an historical clarification ought to be of help in the current debate about general absolution.

Duchesne and Loisy
on the Rue de Vaugirard
Marvin R. O'Connell

Twenty-two universities, the glory of the medieval past, had existed in France before 1789. The Revolution had swept them all away, to the regret of only a few vested interests, since they were even more decayed and intellectually moribund, if that were possible, than the Oxford and Cambridge of the same period. Over the next century the very idea of institutions devoted to an inquiry into the whole of human knowledge was abandoned; not until 1896 did France have genuine universities again. Substituted for them during the revolutionary period were the so-called *écoles spéciales*, all of them located in Paris and each of them designed to meet some specialized vocational need. The École Polytechnique, which trained military and civil engineers for the state, was the most highly esteemed among them, but there were many others. The École Normale Supérieure, for instance, provided administrators for the secondary schools, and the École Centrale des Arts et Manufactures technical experts to serve in industry.

To this pragmatic and largely statist system — even the celebrated École des Chartes was chiefly concerned with training the civil servants who would be archivists in the communes and departments — Napoleon I had added the *facultés*, which he set up in Paris and in sixteen provincial towns. The faculties did not belong to a university, since there were no universities to belong to. They had no moral or legal unity with one another. Instead each faculty enjoyed an independent status as an examining board for entry into the various professions. The faculties of law and medicine performed this function adequately enough, but professors of the humanities and the sciences did little more than award degrees to teachers trained elsewhere and deliver popular lectures to local elites. They were miserably paid and often took another job on the staff of a *lycée*, thus blurring whatever distinction there was between higher and secondary education. The most prestigious professors were the likes of François Guizot and Victor Cousin, literary figures and men of the world, but not serious scholars. Research was unknown. Laboratories and libraries went virtually unsupported; in 1869-70 the law faculty at Paris spent less than $200 on its library holdings, and the faculties at Marseille spent nothing at all. The accomplishments of Louis Pasteur and, later, of Jean Martin Charcot were the fruits of individual genius and owed nothing to the educational system of which they were supposed to be a part. Reformers, especially those who admired the booming German universities, deplored this anomalous and inefficient structure, but they could do nothing to change it. They did manage, however, on the eve of the Prussian war, to found another *école spéciale* which was unique in that it neither catered to specific career preparation nor acted merely as a licensing agency. The École Pratique des Hautes Études, small and underfunded as it was, did have nevertheless the distinction of being the first French graduate school and center for advanced and disinterested research.[1]

[1]See Theodore Zeldin, "Higher Education in France," *Journal of Contemporary History* 2 (July, 1967), 53ff.

The shock and humiliation of the defeat of 1870 did not go unfelt within the educational community nor among those politicians for whom education was a constant bone of contention. Positivists like Jules Ferry argued that the bespectacled German soldiers, who could read and calculate, had beaten their French counterparts, because the latter had been either uneducated or else ill-educated in a system disfigured by the influences of clericalism. The Catholics for their part seized the opportunity the debacle had given them to apply the principle of free schools, under the precedent established by the Falloux Law (1850), to higher education. This they did while the Assemby elected in 1871 still had life. By legislation passed on July 12, 1875, private universities received official sanction. Regional groups of bishops scrambled to take advantage of the Act, and Catholic universities were founded within the year at Paris, Angers, Lille, and Lyon, and a little later, at Toulouse. It was a bold venture to move so quickly, without teachers or students or facilities of any kind. But the bishops knew, as everyone knew, that the elections of 1876 would bring a republican majority into the Chamber, and they wanted their new institutions to be in place when that dire day arrived.[2]

Their decisiveness served them only up to a point. Ferry and his colleagues once in power expended most of their energy upon reforming to their taste the primary and secondary levels of education and, above all, upon getting the religious orders out of the schools.[3] They did little in fact to address the problems inherent in the cumbersome apparatus of *écoles spéciales* and *facultés*, aside from adding modest amounts of money to its budget. But they did strike

[2]Édouard Lecanuet, *L'Église de France sous la troisième république. Les dernières années du pontificat de Pie IX, 1870-1878* (Paris, 1931), 251ff.

[3]See Paul A. Gagnon, *France since 1789* (New York, 1964), 198ff. and Denis Brogan, *The Development of Modern France* (London, 1953), 140ff.

down the fledgling Catholic universities which, in 1880, were deprived of the use of that title, deprived also of the right to grant degrees. In a small gesture of vindictiveness, this latter provision was made retroactive to 1875; all degree students had to pass examinations administered exclusively by state-appointed boards.[4] Thus the five *universités catholiques* became the five *instituts catholiques*, and, thanks to sectarian animosities, genuine university education in France was put off for two more decades.

As if official hostility were not trouble enough, the bishops quickly learned that in having founded five universities virtually at once they had seriously overreached their resources. Endowments were non-existent, and fee-paying students were reluctant to attend schools which could not offer recognized degrees. Poverty brooded over the *instituts* as relentlessly as did the enmity of the anticlericals; only the Institut Catholique of Lille gave any evidence of adequate funding.[5]

But as always Paris was the place which mattered, and the *institut* set up there was the most visible and the most important. Under the leadership of the cardinal-archbishop, Jean Hippolyte Guibert, and his coadjutor, François-Marie-Benjamin Richard de la Vergne, twenty-five bishops whose dioceses were relatively close to the capital participated in its founding and sat on its governing board.[6] The real driving force behind the project, however, was Maurice le Sage d'Hauteroche d'Hulst.[7] Born in Paris in 1841, educated at Saint-Sulpice and in Rome, where he

[4]René Aigrain, *Les universités catholiques* (Paris, 1935), 39ff.

[5]See John J. Keane, "The Catholic Universities of France," *Catholic World* 47 (1888), 293, and J. Calvert, "Catholic University Education in France," *Catholic University Bulletin* (Washington) 13 (1907), 191-210.

[6]Alfred Baudrillart, *L'Institut catholique* (Paris, 1930), 16ff.

[7]The standard biography is Alfred Baudrillart, *Vie de Mgr. d'Hulst*, 2 vols. (Paris, 1921).

earned doctorates in theology and in canon law, d'Hulst was ordained in 1865 and served in a working class Parisian parish until the Prussian war, during which he was an army chaplain. Cardinal Guibert made him his secretary in 1872 and a year later a vicar general specially charged with planning for the new university. He became vice-rector in November, 1875, with control of most of the day-to-day operations in his hands; in 1881 he was named rector of the Institut Catholique and a domestic prelate.

Mgr. d'Hulst belonged to the school of Montalembert and Félix Dupanloup, a liberal to be sure but no republican. A lifelong monarchist and an intimate of the Count of Paris, the Orleanist pretender, he comported himself like the aristocrat he was. His long narrow face with its aquiline nose over a severely wide mouth testified to the cultivation and to the self-confidence which only inherited position could give. He sat for a time in the Chamber of Deputies where, amidst the democratic rough and tumble, he was not a notable success. A literary man rather than a scholar, he made his mark in the pulpit of Notre Dame, though some worshippers there claimed he could not be heard, so weak was his voice. His sermons were at any rate published in accord with the convention of the day, and upon them rested much of his reputation. Loisy recalled him mockingly as a great improviser, "who came now to improvise a university."[8] Not so much profoundly reflective or even very well educated, d'Hulst was dedicated and industrious, and he possessed the proper social connections. He gave the best that was in him to the cause of Catholic higher education in France. The times were not propitious for that task, and it may have been just as well that he brought to it something of the spirit of *noblesse oblige*.

The law of 1875 had specified that the private universities it permitted had to be composed of at least three faculties.

[8] Alfred Loisy, *Mémoires*, I (Paris 1930), 73.

At Paris this injunction was duly carried out with the establishment by March, 1876, of the faculties of arts, sciences, and law. Plans were also drawn up for a faculty of medicine, though in the end the obstacles proved too great to achieve that goal. A faculty of theology had not been contemplated at first; the objective of the universities was the advanced education of laymen, not of clerics who alone, it was supposed, had any business studying theology or any interest in doing so. But Rome intervened forcefully, and as a result an École Supérieure de Théologie was attached to the Institut Catholique of Paris in 1878 (and became a full-fledged *faculté* in 1889).

This development caused some awkwardness for Mgr. d'Hulst. Rome's insistence on the point probably derived from a desire to create a counterpoise to the six theology *facultés* which Napoleon I had included among his reforms of higher education. These bodies had in fact never flourished, but Rome continued to regard them with deep suspicion, more perhaps because they remained bastions of old-fashioned Gallicanism than because of their indifferent intellectual quality. The French bishops for their part had sent few students to the Napoleonic faculties and had instead concentrated their resources and energies into building up an imposing system of seminaries, both *petits* and *grands*. The papal initiative therefore tended to bring forward a competition, not so much between the Institut Catholique and the state faculties of theology--which were anyhow suppressed by the Chamber in 1886, their function, such as it was, absorbed into a new *Sciences religieuses* section of the École Pratique des Hautes Études — as between the Institut Catholique and the diocesan seminaries.

So d'Hulst had another problem to wrestle with, along with a chronic shortage of money and a hostile political climate. He pressed on like a good soldier nonetheless, and the theological school was installed within the Institut's compound on the rue de Vaugirard — a hallowed spot for Catholic Frenchmen, because here, in the old Carmelite convent, had died many of the martyrs of the September Massacres of 1792. It was necessary also to incorporate a *séminaire universitaire* to see to the spiritual formation of the talented clerical students who, it was hoped, would come in droves from their dioceses to matriculate in the theological school. D'Hulst entrusted this duty to a staff of three Sulpicians, an obvious choice indeed but a shrewd stroke as well, in that it established a cordial link between the theological school and the Society of Saint-Sulpice which operated the great Parisian seminary. Sulpician patronage proved especially important, because the bishops outside Paris hesitated to send very many of their seminarians to the Institut, and Loisy, who was a member of the first class, did not think they had sent their brightest ones either.[9] The faculty also was small, four professors altogether, including a corpulent Italian Jesuit who taught systematic theology, a Parisian scripturist, and a Dominican who offered a course in scholastic philosophy.

They were eminently forgettable, however much praise d'Hulst lavished upon them at the theological school's inaugural ceremonies in November of 1878. Not so the fourth member of the faculty. Louis Duchesne, the thirty-five-year-old Professor of Ecclesiastical History, had already established a considerable reputation for himself in academic circles. Born at Saint-Servan on the Breton coast, he was a child of six when his father, a commercial fisherman, was lost at sea. Madame Duchesne raised Louis and his five siblings in that stern dedication to religious faith which was a byword in Brittany — so much so that as a grown man her famous son described his holidays as "a two-month retreat under the direction of my mother." At thir-

---

[9] Albert Houtin and Félix Sartiaux, *Alfred Loisy: sa vie, son oeuvre*, ed. Émile Poulat (Paris, 1960), 22

teen he entered the College Saint-Charles, which served as the *petit séminaire* at Saint-Brieuc, where he studied the classics and won all the prizes. The Bishop of Saint-Brieuc was enough impressed by young Duchesne's talents to send him to Rome for his theology and, after ordination in 1867, to assign him to the faculty of Saint-Charles. He taught there for four years, and long afterward, during a sentimental school reunion, he was moved to say, "My roots have always been here."[10]

There was a sense in which this trite remark was profoundly true, if not of the little backwater clerical lycée then at least of Brittany as a whole. Duchesne became the consummate cosmopolitan, at home in salons in Paris and Rome and Alexandria. Life among a provincial intelligentsia could never have satisfied him. Yet part of him remained a Breton peasant — this bald, stocky, thickfingered man, given to hard work, broad humor, and town pump gossip, whose eyes never lost their cast of wariness. The faith he had imbided from his mother perdured too, though many on both sides of later arguments judged him more shrewd and self-serving than sincere in maintaining it.

Duchesne was not at any rate one to keep his opinions to himself, not even at the very beginning of his career. He returned from Rome to Saint-Brieuc a fervent and outspoken ultramontane, much to the annoyance of his bishop who stood with the inopportunist minority at the Vatican Council. The bishop perhaps foresaw that such youthful enthusiasm would pass away, as indeed proved to be the case; in the meanwhile he decided to temper that enthusiasm by dispatching the young priest to the fountainhead of Gallicanism in Paris for higher studies.[11] In 1871 Duchesne

---

[10]Claude d'Habloville, *Grandes figures de l'église contemporaine* (Paris, 1925), 3ff.

[11]Jean-Marie Mayeur, "Mgr. Duchesne et l'université," in *Monseigneur Duchesne et son temps* (Rome, 1975), 318.

duly enrolled in the Sorbonne — now the state theological faculty in Paris which, like all the Napoleonic faculties, was essentially an examining entity — and, at the same time, in the École Pratique des Hautes Études. The latter institution, devoted exclusively to research, offered no degree, but it gave Duchesne his vocation as historian. Under the direction of the finest masters available in France, he plunged into the technical details of philology and paleography and thus began to unravel some of the mysteries of Christian antiquity which had first beguiled him during his student days in Rome. His natural aptitude for this kind of work revealed itself quickly. He determined to do a thesis for the Sorbonne on the *Liber Pontificalis*, a critical edition, in effect, of a sixth-century document indispensable for the history of the early popes as well as for Roman archeology and topography. It was a mammoth task, but Duchesne proved equal to it. Over a two-year period he relentlessly pursued the hundred and fifty extant manuscripts across France, Italy, and the Levant and in the process carved out for himself a permanent place in the scholarly community. His edition, when it appeared, was hailed as a triumph of scientific skill and *critique*.[12]

Here was the important word. Duchesne had shown himself to be a "critical" historian, applying the techniques of modern scholarship to the data of Christian origins. He had moreover shown himself to be a "higher critic," because he was concerned with the authenticity of the document at hand: had it in fact been written by the authors to whom it was attributed, and did it in fact issue from the era claimed for it? The *Liber Pontificalis* had undergone through the Middle Ages constant editorial tampering and additions so that it had become virtually useless as a source for the history of the centuries it purported to treat. Duchesne

---

[12]H. Leclercq, "Monsignor [sic] Duchesne," in *Dictionnaire d'archéologie chrétienne et de liturgie*, 6 (Paris, 1925), 2680 ff.

ruthlessly stripped away the legendary and apocryphal incrustations and let the document, as it were, speak for itself. The performance was impressive and gained favorable notice even from German scholars, which was the ultimate accolade.

Among others impressed were the consultants at the Ministry of Public Instruction. Since 1859 the French government had maintained a research center in Athens which included in its course of study a three-month sojourn in Italy. In 1873 it was proposed to detach this feature from the École française d'Athènes and expand it into a full-fledged program of its own. Thus was born the École française de Rome, and Duchesne was a member of the original staff. He taught Greek paleography and earned thereby a stipend of two thousand francs as well as rich public praise from his superiors for his "lively intelligence, the sureness of his critical science, his paleographical skill, his profound knowledge of the original sources."[13] Nor did the republican victory in the general election of 1876 materially affect his position; Father Duchesne was assured by a succession of governments that his connection with the official *université* might continue as long as he liked, and in the mid-1880s, at the height of the anticlerical crisis over education, he did return to it.[14]

In the meantime, however, he threw in his lot with the new Catholic universities. D'Hulst recruited him for the Paris faculty of arts and — of special note to those attuned to symbolic connections — the aged Dupanloup became his official sponsor with the governing board of bishops, who, in January, 1877, gave unanimous assent to his appointment as professor. The trouble had started, however, even before that. Stories spread out of his home diocese about

[13]A. Geffroy, "La nouvelle École française de Rome," *Revue des deux mondes* 16 (1876), 818ff. Geffroy was the first director of the school.

[14]Mayeur, "Mgr. Duchesne et l'université," 324.

Duchesne's habitual impertinence, his neglect of certain "venerable devotions," his lack of a genuine "ecclesiastical spirit." Had he in fact dismissed the pope's authority and contemptuously referred to the pontiff simply as "Giovanni Mastai?" Had he in fact refused publicly to pray the litany of the Virgin because he could not abide the sentimentality of Marian devotions? Duchesne denied all — his retreat from ultramontanism had left his ideas about the papacy no more radical than those of Dupanloup — and he pointed, with good reason, at the nasty anonymity of his accusers as a *prima facie* reason to disallow their testimony. "I am deeply hurt," he wrote, "that any of my confreres could believe me capable of saying such foolish and irreverent things."[15] Hurt perhaps but hardly surprised that his nameless detractors came from among his "confrères," his fellow priests, schoolmates and Breton *curés* who had nothing to gain from Duchesne's fall save the sweet satisfaction involved in leveling the talented; envy has always been the peculiarly clerical sin.

Not that Duchesne was without defenders. D'Hulst stood by him through thick and thin. The vicar general back in Saint-Brieuc, while admitting that the historian had a weakness for "imprudent language" and for drawing unflattering word portraits of important people — his characterization of the members of the French hierarchy as "mitered sacristans" was widely quoted — nevertheless argued strongly that "these eccentricities" were not the true measure of the man. Similarly the Bishop of Saint-Brieuc intervened in Duchesne's behalf when, during the summer of 1877, his edition of the *Liber Pontificalis* was delated to the Congregation of the Index in Rome. The bishop wrote almost fiercely to Cardinal Jean-Baptiste Pitra, the suave prefect of the congregation, and almost warned him not to meddle in

---

[15]Paul Poupard, "Mgr. Duchesne à l'institut catholique de Paris," in *Monseigneur Duchesne et son temps* (Rome, 1975), 305ff.

what was an issue internal to the French church.[16] It was a bold course for a provincial bishop, who had voted wrong at the Vatican Council, so to confront a powerful curial cardinal, but Pitra responded mildly, once Duchesne announced his willingness to accept a Roman decision; a routine commission was set up, and it recommended merely some minor cosmetic changes should the critical edition of the *Liber Pontificalis* be published.

But Duchesne could not stay out of hot water for long. In 1881, three years after he had begun teaching in the theological school, a disgruntled colleague made public a copy of lecture notes in which Duchesne argued that the traditional doctrine of the Trinity had not been clearly proclaimed in the Church before the definitions of the Council of Nicaea in 325. This argument was savagely attacked in a journal published by the Institut Catholique of Lille, and Duchesne replied in kind, as did d'Hulst.[17] The controversy increased in acrimony until November,1882, when the superior general of the Sulpicians suddenly decreed that from henceforth no Parisian seminarians would be allowed to follow Duchesne's course. Crusty old Henri Picard was not a man to trifle with; the archetype of the austere and unbending Gallican priest, he wielded enormous influence with the French bishops, many of whom, as young men, had been under his charge — he was, for instance, confessor to Archbishop Richard, the coadjutor of Paris. His intervention meant in effect that Duchesne no longer had any students to teach. The theological school arranged for its ecclesiastical historian a hasty leave of absence.[18]

Once again the Vatican was called upon to provide a referee. The celebrated Jesuit theologian, Cardinal

---

[16]D'Habloville, *Grandes figures*, 28 for a partial text.

[17]Leclercq, "Monsignor Duchesne," 2690ff.

[18]Baudrillart, *Vie de Mgr. d'Hulst*, I, 459ff.

Johannes Baptist Franzelin, asked Duchesne, through d'Hulst, to clarify his position. This Duchesne did — his point, he said, had been that the trinitarian doctrine of the ante-Nicene fathers showed development, not from error to truth, but from the less clear and precise to the more — and there, Franzelin apparently satisfied, the matter rested. Yet d'Hulst felt constrained to assure the cardinal, in a letter of February, 1883, that it was not Duchesne "who set the tone" of the instruction in the theological school and that the Institut would soon appoint a second professor of ecclesiastical history whose "inclinations will be different from those of M. Duchesne."[19]

But two years later the rector ran out of room to maneuver. The most venerable legend cherished by the Church in France was that several of its dioceses — Sens, Troyes, Chartres among others — had been founded by one or another of the seventy-two disciples mentioned in the gospel. In an article in the *Bulletin critique* — a journal he had founded in 1880 — Duchesne put this old canard under close historical scrutiny and found it, needless to say, wanting. His tone was tart and scornful. The fury provoked in some circles by this exposé was white hot. The Archbishop of Sens was particularly exercised at the challenge to the apostolic origins of his see; he wrote to d'Hulst complaining bitterly of this assault upon approved tradition and of "the most offensive mockery displayed in various passages of this most regrettable article."

The fuss proved to be the last straw. Duchesne offered to resign and go back to Brittany where his bishop would give him "a little rural parish by the seaside; I shall not be in the least embarrassed, once my scientific career is finished, to become the pastor of fishermen and peasants."[20] It is to be

[19] Poupard, "Mgr. Duqhesne à l'institut catholique de Paris," 309.
[20] *Ibid.*, 310ff.

doubted that Duchesne intended this conventional protestation to be taken seriously. D'Hulst at any rate, with the help of Archbishop Richard, worked out a face-saving device whereby Duchesne went on leave of absence again, this time, it was said, in order to prepare his edition of the *Liber Pontificalis* for the press. He did not in fact ever return to the Institut Catholique, though he remained technically on its books until 1895 when he was appointed by the French government director of the École française de Rome. Before that, however, in 1887, his scholarly productivity, which continued at a remarkable rate, earned him a place on the staff of the École Pratique des Hautes Études, in whose rarefied and anticlerical precincts he wore his soutane as jauntily as ever.[21] But a vein of bitterness ran deep into him. "These absurd attacks," he wrote a friend, "have quite worn me out and left me full of disgust."[22]

Louis Duchesne was not a sparkling lecturer, at least not at the beginning of his ill-starred career at the Institut Catholique. The cutting wit which so enlivened his private conversation did not reveal itself at the podium. His voice was faint and toneless, and some students complained about the tediousness of his presentations.[23] In an era when eloquence and literary flair were so valued that Joseph Ernest Renan was the great academic figure, Duchesne's dry, critical approach to his material was not calculated to win widespread favor. Even so, the quality of his courses was not lost upon a growing circle of young clerics enrolled in the theological school, however difficult they may have found it to listen to him.

[21]P. d'Espezel, "Duchesne," in *Dictionnaire d'histoire et de géographie ecclésiastique*, 14 (Paris, 1960), 966.

[22]Émile Poulat, "Mgr. Duchesne et la crise moderniste," in *Monseigneur Duchesne et son temps* (Rome, 1975), 358.

[23]Poupard, "Mgr. Duchesne à l'institut catholique de Paris," 308. For Duchesne's enormous scholarly productivity, see the final columns of Leclercq, "Monsignor Duchesne," where 429 total published items are listed, 157 of them by the end of 1885.

Alfred Loisy, a member of the first class which began its studies in the fall of 1878, had nothing but contempt for most of the instruction he received. He made a partial exception for Duchesne. "The course in ecclesiastical history," he said, "was very substantial if a little confused." "Father Duchesne," he added, "did not express himself with the clarity and facility one would have liked."[24] Loisy was not, then or ever, a man free with compliments, so that this half-praise of Duchesne might be considered something of a tribute. This first encounter with Duchesne was in any case exceedingly brief, for Loisy stayed only a few months at the Institut. By January, 1879, he was back in the *grand séminaire* of his home diocese of Châlons-sur-Marne, back in his native country, the ancient province of Champagne for which he cultivated so romantic an attachment.

There had been Loisys in the valley of the Marne for hundreds of years. By the late eighteenth century they had grown so numerous that different branches of the family peopled whole villages. It was not an unusual occurrence when, in 1851, Charles-Sébastien Loisy married a distant cousin, Justine Desanlis, with whom he shared a great great Loisy grandfather. They settled on the Loisy family farm on the outskirts of Ambrières, he a quiet, hard-working man who knew how to command and how to make himself obeyed without ever lifting his voice; she a gay and talkative woman, given to kindly sarcasm, much devoted to her housekeeping, her garden, her poultry, her children.[25]

There were three children, of whom Alfred Firmin was the second, born February 28, 1857, and baptized the next day. From the moment of his birth he had to endure the

[24]Houtin, *Loisy*, 22. Houtin quotes from autobiographical notes of 1884 entrusted to him by Loisy in 1907. In much of what follows this account will be used parallel to and sometimes in distinction to Loisy's later published accounts of 1913 and 1930.

[25]Loisy, *Mémoires*, I, 10ff.

cross — the curse, Loisy himself might have said — of a frail constitution. He did not suffer unduly from any particular illness — he lived to a great age — but he lacked the physical size and stamina so important in a culture which necessarily put a premium upon manual labor. While his elder brother ran with the boys of the village, Alfred spent much of his childhood time in the company of his younger sister and her friends. He became adept at sewing dolls' clothes, a skill with which he delighted his nieces many years later. He was not strong enough to perform the heavier tasks on the farm; he could feed the chickens, but work in the fields at sowing or harvest time was quite beyond his capacity. This was a circumstance which greatly depressed him and which eroded his self-esteem. It also led him in later years to romanticize the virtues of rural France in general and of his family in particular.

There was one forum, however, in which Alfred Loisy soon discovered he could compensate, to some degree at least, for his weak body. The schoolroom was a place where he shone as no one else did, where his remarkable intellectual talents could bring a sense of accomplishment denied him in the rough masculine world of physical work and play. As a child and adolescent he won all sorts of local and district prizes for scholastic achievement. When he was an old man he used to look at a primary school report, dated March 7, 1868, which recorded that he had done *très bien* in reading, writing, spelling, history, and geography, and *assez bien* in arithmetic. He did not cease to compete in this arena for the rest of his life.[26]

The religious atmosphere in which Loisy was reared was earnest without being ostentatiously pious. The men in his family regularly went to church, though only the women and children communicated (at Christmas and Easter) and

[26]*Ibid.*, I, 19.

assisted at all the offices of Sundays and feast days. The world of Ambrières, he remembered, "took religion seriously as a wise and austere discipline." It was the old Gallican Catholicism, tinged with Jansenist reserve, in which Loisy pointedly found more enduring good than in "the facile, sentimental, ultramontane religion."[27] The *curé* Loisy recalled best was a big man with a booming voice and a severe air, who had no time for fancy new devotions like that of La Salette; he frightened the people a little, but his catechetical instruction was simple and solid. "He was a priest of the olden time," Loisy said with a nostalgia he reserved for his home country, "a strong man who still belonged to the Gallican church."[28]

In 1869 Alfred matriculated at the secondary school in nearby Vitry-le-François. It was a small, lay establishment attended by farmers' sons who spent a few years there acquiring the rudiments of general education. Loisy had no trouble winning all the prizes in the tiny classics department, but it pained him to be constantly with boys more robust than he, who called him "le petit Loisy." "The hapless 'petit Loisy' did not excel among his schoolmates except on the days of examination." At the end of July, 1870, the pupils were taken to the railroad station to see Napoleon III who was passing through Vitry on his way to the front. As the train slowed down and the emperor stood at the door of his carriage, everybody cheered. "In the simplicity of my ignorance," Loisy remembered, "I cried 'vive l'empereur' like the others. . . . It was, I believe, the only occasion in my life when I raised my voice in a political cause. The thought of it still sticks in my throat."[29]

"Le petit Loisy" came home for the summer holiday in time to witness the remnant of the French army straggling

[27] *Ibid.,* I, 14.
[28] *Ibid.,* I, 20.
[29] *Ibid.,* I, 21.

back toward Paris, German cavalry on its heels. On a hot day in mid-August three troopers rode into the Loisy farmyard and without dismounting, their hands on the butts of their pistols, civilly asked for a drink of water. On August 25 a corps of German infantry invested Ambrières and its environs, and the commanding general, a stiffly courteous old man, settled himself and his staff in the Loisy house. He took pains to reassure Charles-Sébastien that he would allow no looting or disorder: "It is not you who have wanted this war," he said, "it is your emperor." The general was good as his word; the only casualty Alfred Loisy remembered was a cow — "la plus belle vache" — which the soldiers slaughtered and roasted in the middle of the yard.

These troops departed after a few days to be replaced by others similarly well-disciplined. The German occupation lasted into 1871, and all the great events of the intervening months — Napoleon III's surrender at Sedan, the proclamation of the Republic, Gambetta's frenzied efforts to carry on the war, the rising of the Paris Commune — remained merely rumors in Ambrières, because the local newspapers printed only what the Germans let them print. Yet the foreign presence made little real difference in the day-to-day routine of the countryside; the average *paysan champenois* shrugged and observed that surely as the Germans had come, so they would go away again. The unsettled times did affect Alfred Loisy to the extent that his formal schooling was interrupted for two years; he studied instead at home with borrowed books and under the eye of the *curé*. But he still clung to the hope that he might yet take his place shoulder to shoulder with the other men in his family. About this time he composed a little prayer to be said every night that God, through the intercession of our Lady of Lourdes, would grant him enough physical strength to be a good farmer.[30] It was not to be.

[30] *Ibid.*, I, 23.

The *curé* who monitored Alfred's lessons in 1871-72 was new to the village, and his arrival suggested to the fourteen-year-old boy another career option. He had never up till then considered the possibility of becoming a priest. Other people, remarking upon the combination of poor health, precocity, studiousness, and gravity of manner, insisted that he was destined to be a *curé*, but not Loisy himself: "The priests I had known inspired more respect in me than sympathy." But on the Sunday in September, 1871, when the new pastor sang his first high Mass in the parish church, "I felt a singular impression." All of Ambrières was aflutter, for the installation of a *curé* was still a matter of civic importance. The mayor and his council attended wearing their sashes of office. The firemen, in uniform, gave a military salute at the elevation.

> I was in my place in the family pew, to the right of my mother as usual. When the priest at the end of the liturgical procession, led by cross and banners, passed close to us, he appeared very moved, as no doubt he was. An instant later, when he turned to the altar, something said to me that one day I too would turn to that altar and that I too would say Mass in this church.

Loisy afterward considered this experience "a sort of illumination" which, though it was ultimately realized, he never for a moment confused with "a sign from heaven."[31] Indeed, by the time he enrolled in the ecclesiastical secondary school in Saint-Dizier (October, 1872), he had pretty much put the illumination out of his mind.

Yet the idea of the priesthood seemed to possess an ineluctable logic of its own. The school in Saint-Dizier, operated by the secular clergy of the diocese of Langres, was a classics

---

[31]Alfred Loisy, *Choses passées* (Paris, 1913), 10.

collège of the kind authorized by the Falloux Law rather than a *petit séminaire*, but religious and moral training played a large role in its program. Loisy, as usual, stood at the head of his class, and he also displayed a piety beyond the ordinary which his masters took due note of. His school-fellows, at once awestruck at his scholastic performance and contemptuous of him as timid, awkward, shabby, and "no good at games," assumed that he would be a priest, because, as the more malicious among them expressed it, he was clearly fitted for nothing else.[32]

In October, 1873, Loisy decided for himself. During the school's annual retreat he made up his mind that he could best serve God, humanity, and truth — concepts which glitter so brightly for a sixteen-year-old — by heeding an ecclesiastical vocation. Significantly (and, as succeeding years and crises were to demonstrate, typically) Loisy sought no counsel at this moment of profound personal commitment, consulted with no one, neither with the retreat master nor his confessor nor any other officer of the *collège*. His decision once arrived at was a *fait accompli* which needed only the formal endorsement of his parents. They gave their reluctant agreement, after some tears shed by Justine and some sleepless nights endured by Charles-Sébastien, because they also believed that their second son was fitted for little else — at least so their second son chose to think they believed. And now that he had made his choice, he was in a hurry to implement it. He left Saint-Dizier without the baccalaureate and, in October, 1874, entered the *grand séminaire* of the diocese of Châlons-sur-Marne. Charles-Sébastien rode the train with Alfred to Châlons, walked with him from the station to the gloomy old seminary next to the prefecture, and watched

[32]*Ibid.*, 13.

wordlessly as his son donned the soutane for the first time. "I put on the ecclesiastical garb," Loisy recalled, "with less joy than I had anticipated."[33] He wore it for the next thirty-four years.

The bishop of Châlons-sur-Marne, Guillaume Meignan, had once been professor of sacred scripture in the state faculty of theology in the Sorbonne. His mildly liberal publications on various biblical subjects had been numerous. When he came to Châlons in 1864, he removed the Vincentians who had staffed the major seminary there and replaced them with his own diocesan priests in hopes that the institution's intellectual quality might thereby be improved. By the time Loisy arrived ten years later these hopes had gone aglimmering, and Meignan — who was destined for a greater see and a cardinal's hat — contented himself with the cynical observation that his seminary was hardly worse than any other in France.

During the five years he spent there Loisy found a tenuous kind of happiness in the seminary of Châlons. He got along better with his schoolfellows and they with him than had been the case at Saint-Dizier; these older, more mature students — about fifty of them altogether[34] — preparing themselves for a profession placed less value than boys did upon physical strength and proficiency in games. Loisy liked "the regular life, in which the employment of every hour was fixed and in which one had fully half of each day to oneself." The relatively sumptuous celebration of the liturgy and the round of other pious practices gave him much emotional satisfaction.[35]

---

[33] Loisy, *Mémoires*, I, 28ff.
[34] Houtin, *Loisy*, 15.
[35] Loisy, *Choses passées*, 25f.

But what passed for cultivation of the mind in the *grand séminaire* of Châlons was quite another matter. The members of the faculty, with one passing exception, were incapable, in Loisy's harsh judgment, of offering any intellectual training worthy of the name. The vulgar and pretentious professor of moral theology had appointed himself the watchdog of orthodoxy which was defined for him in the strident pages of Louis Veuillot's *Univers*. The professor of dogma and canon law boasted of his two years in Rome during which sojourn he had earned doctorates in both those subjects; "he was a Lorrainer by birth," Loisy observed acidly, "but he might as well have been an Italian, being at once intelligent and lazy." A typical lecture by the professor of scripture and church history — "a holy man as innocent as it was possible to be of the principles of scientific criticism" — explained that St. John in the Apocalypse had prophesied the convening of the Vatican Council. Over this little mélange presided the rector, one abbé Roussel, a veteran parish priest with no scholarly attainments or interests whose sole concern appeared to be the maintenance of firm discipline.[36]

Loisy was put off by Roussel's stern and unbending manner, though in the long run the rector proved to be a good friend. In the meantime Loisy discovered in the young professor of philosophy, abbé Ludot, a helpful mentor. Ludot had no particular philosophical training beyond his own seminary course, but he read widely and had an inquiring mind. He gave Loisy a supplemental reading list which included standard Catholic liberals like Albert de Broglie and Henri-Dominique Lacordaire — not, it should be noted, Immanuel Kant or the German critics or the positivists of whom Loisy remained entirely ignorant. Lacordaire so impressed him that he contemplated for a while becoming a Dominican. He was moved also by Charles Montalembert's

[36]*Ibid.,* 20ff.

Monks of the West. None of these authors was "critical," and so none of them contributed to the development of Loisy's scientific methodology — indeed, as early as 1884 he recorded that "this liberalism was a far cry from my own." Yet, lively and provocative, Montalembert and the others provided him with a taste for history as well as some relief from the humdrum scholasticism which comprised most of his required reading. The higher reaches of philosophical investigation, as the seminary defined them, certainly did not humble him: "I doubted, in spite of myself, the objective reality of metaphysical conclusions."[37]

Ludot, who was known to speak favorably of Félicité de Lamennais and to be less than enthusiastic about the definition of papal infallibility, rapidly became a *persona non grata* to his colleagues. At the end of Loisy's first year at Châlons he was dismissed from the faculty and assigned as *curé* to a large country parish. He went off to his new post cheerfully enough, but his favorite pupil saw the event as an instance of his bishop's "cunning" cynicism. In order to placate a few reactionaries Meignan, himself an anti-infallibilist at the Vatican Council, "had light-heartedly sacrificed a man whom he admired and whose faith, as he knew very well, was sounder than his own."[38] Ludot's departure in any case removed whatever intellectual excitement Loisy had encountered in his seminary curriculum; the new professor of philosophy was a much more conventional type.

As he moved from 1875 onward into the formal study of theology, Loisy, as he remembered it, experienced constant tedium mixed with large doses of inner distress. It was one thing to let the emotions loose in prayerful consideration of the Christian mysteries; it was quite another to subject those same mysteries to rational analysis. He did not yet regard the superstructure of scholastic thought as resting upon the

[37]Houtin, *Loisy*, 16.
[38]Loisy, *Choses passées*, 27.

air; Renan many years before had had this intuition as a seminarian, but Loisy was not so precocious. He suffered rather from doubts about specific doctrines: the Trinity, grace, the divinity of Christ. "Now that I had to think about these things and not just feel them, I was in a state of perpetual agony. My intelligence was unsatisfied, and my timid, child-like consciousness made me tremble before the question which pressed itself upon me, in spite of myself, every moment of the day: is there a reality which corresponds to these theories?" And the moral tracts were equally disturbing. The casuistry he studied was "less the general science of morals, the reasoned conception of duty, than the specific spiritual direction suited to the confessional. That manner of specifying duty confused me as much as the Catholic manner of understanding truth. Could I justify myself in the face of such complicated rules?"[39]

Conscientiously Loisy revealed his problem to his confessor for whom it was no problem at all. Merely excessive scruples, the confessor said, the best cure for which was to think about something else. This simple, well-intended advice did not help much, for though Loisy continued fervent in prayer and felt no desire to return to the secular life, the intellectual misgivings lingered on. At one point he "plunged boldly," on his own and with no direction, into the study of the *Summa Theologiae* of St. Thomas Aquinas. He went through the tract on the Trinity article by article, an exercise he described later with ill-concealed contempt. "The speculations of St. Thomas on the Trinity. . .had upon me the effect of a huge logomachy. . .[and] left, as it were, a void."[40]

Another extracurricular activity brought more solace. Loisy began to study Hebrew under the tutelage of an upper

---

[39] *Ibid.,* 36ff.
[40] *Ibid.,* 42f.

classman who knew a smattering of the sacred language. "Immediately I felt as though I were accomplishing something." Once his tutor's knowledge was exhausted, Loisy continued the work alone. He compared Greek and Latin versions of Genesis to the Hebrew text and reveled in the insights which his extraordinary gift for languages afforded him. "Having no critical commentary to work with, I could make no troubling discoveries."[41]

At the end of June, 1878, his intellect still uneasy but his will firm, Alfred Loisy was ordained a subdeacon and thereby assumed the obligations of celibacy and the daily recitation of the breviary. It was a step he understood to be irrevocable. The following September, at the instance of abbé Roussel, Bishop Meignan sent him for higher study to the new theological school in the Catholic University of Paris. It was Roussel's intention to bring Loisy back to Châlons as professor once he had obtained a degree. But Loisy did not cooperate. He disliked Paris and disliked the theological school even more. He missed the Marne valley and all its associations. The only attractive person he met in Paris was Duchesne[42] — "I succumbed at this first encounter with genuine science" — but even he could not relieve Loisy's homesickness or prop up his always precarious health. At New Year's, his nerves in tatters, Loisy went home to Ambrières where his physician prescribed a month's complete rest and forbade a return to Paris. By the end of January, he had gone back to Châlons.

Bishop Meignan was not amused. The young man had thwarted the episcopal will, and the young man had to pay the price, as Loisy found out upon his ordination as priest, June 29, 1879. Meignan assigned him as *curé* to the worst parish in the diocese, to a village where there survived hardly a glimmer of Christian practice. Loisy stayed there

[41]*Ibid.*, 44.
[42]*Ibid.*, 47.

six months, contemplating his fate in the cold and empty church, until Roussel interceded for him and arranged a transfer to another, rather better pastorate near Ambrières. Altogether Loisy spent about a year and a half as a country priest, and during that time his health improved markedly. He had plenty of leisure to pursue his studies; he even began to plot out in his mind a large book "in which I would prove, from history and philosophy, the truth of Catholicism." But whatever abstract devotion he had for the *champenois* countryside, Loisy did not intend to remain there, banished forever from the academic life. He therefore initiated the "diplomacy" by which he hoped to regain the bishop's favor and to secure for himself, at worst, a professorship at Châllons. Roussel, who died in 1880, could no longer help him but d'Hulst and Duchesne could, by recommending to Meignan that Loisy be allowed to resume his formal studies and earn the appropriate theological degrees. In the spring of 1881 Loisy went to see the bishop and asked permission to return to the Institut Catholique. Meignan received him kindly, called him "mon bon petit Loisy," and, no doubt satisfied that the young man had learned his lesson, acceded to his request. On May 12 Loisy, having shaken the proverbial dust from his feet, arrived in Paris.[43]

Nothing much had changed on the rue de Vaugirard, except of course the name of the institution which by law could no longer call itself a university. There had been since Loisy's brief interlude thirty months before only one notable addition to the faculty; the Italian, Pietro Gasparri, destined for great fame as a Vatican diplomat, now filled the newly created chair of canon law. Duchesne was even more the dominating figure, and it was he who quickly took Loisy in hand. He arranged first that Loisy be awarded the baccalaureate degree within weeks of his arrival. He then persuaded d'Hulst to permit Loisy to count his two months'

[43]Loisy, *Mémoires*, I, 77ff.

residence in 1878 and May and June of 1881 as equivalent to a full academic year, which meant that Loisy could qualify for the licentiate after a single year, instead of the normal two years, of coursework.[44] When the professor of scripture and Hebrew fell ill in the December of 1881, Duchesne saw to it that his protégé was named instructor in Hebrew. All this haste and cutting of corners — which says as much about the parlous state of the infant Institut as it does about Duchesne's influence or Loisy's brilliance — appeared justified when Loisy passed his licentiate's examination *magna cum laude* in June, 1882. D'Hulst at any rate was impressed enough to request the bishop of Châlons to make Loisy's assignment to the Institut a permanent one. Meignan readily agreed and wrote Loisy a cordial letter with a small sting of mockery at the end: "When you visit Châlons do not forget that the bishop's palace will be your hotel. We shall talk about exegesis."[45]

Armed with his license Loisy from 1882 no longer had to attend classes in the theological school of the Institut. D'Hulst suggested that he enroll at the École Pratique des Hautes Études and take courses in Assyriology and Egyptology.[46] This he did, and he also at this time began to follow Renan's lectures at the Collège de France. (Duchesne went with him the first time, lest the formidable reputation of this hammer of orthodoxy overawe le petit Loisy.) He regularly attended these lectures for three years, though he never in all that time attempted to speak to Renan personally. Indeed, as he listened admiringly to this greatest of teachers, Loisy was quietly pondering the elements of a vast intellectual project whereby the rationalism of Renan could be over-

---

[44]For the sake of convenience the terms employed here are the conventional ones. In fact the government forbade their use outside state faculties, so that for bachelor, licentiate, and doctor were substituted, auditor, lector, and master. See Houtin, *Loisy*, 29.

[45]Loisy, *Choses passées*, 383.

[46]Loisy soon gave up the course in Egyptology, because it was of little use for biblical studies. In 1883, however, he began a two-year course in Ethiopian.

turned by the proper application of the very *critique* which Renan championed. The young priest had it for his objective no less than the complete overhaul of Catholic theological teaching. As a first step he determined to write his doctoral dissertation on the thorny issue of biblical inspiration, the basic lines for which "came upon me suddenly in the middle of a night when I could not sleep, early in the year 1883."[47] By May, 1884, he had finished it.

A month later, when he made his annual retreat, he kept a kind of running journal into which, on June 14, he put this entry: "no being comes into existence without a particular purpose determined by God. . . . My vocation seems to be the vocation of a doctor."[48] Alfred Loisy had found his calling within the bare lecture halls on the rue de Vaugirard. The sacred and emotional associations of the place — the memory of heaps of dead priests piled like cordwood on the street outside the Carmelite convent in the early days of September, 1792 — meant little to this small, frail, sharp-featured man with narrow eyes, for whom the scholar's commitment must lead where it would lead, must bring, if need be, not peace but a sword.

[47] Loisy, *Choses passées*, 66ff., 75.
[48] Houtin, *Loisy*, 40.

The Genesis of the German Concordat of 1933

John Zeender

Introduction

For approximately three decades scholars, German and non-German, and more recently the literate lay population of West Germany concerned with the history of the German nation in the Nazi era have shown marked interest in the origins of the Concordat of 1933. Both groups have come to focus their attention pre-eminently, if not solely, on the person of Monsignor Ludwig Kaas, the leader of the German Center party, and on the question of what role he might have played in shaping historic decisions like the Center's approval of Hitler's Enabling Act of March 23,1933, the withdrawal five days later on March 28 of the Catholic bishops' prohibition of Catholic membership in the Nazi party, and, finally, the leaders' dissolution of the Center party on July 5. For a variety of reasons many prominent scholars and many laymen inside or outside institutions of higher learning in West Germany have come to believe that there was a causal relationship between those decisions and the negotiations on a concordat between the Hitler state and the Holy See which appeared to begin in mid-April and which ended in the signing of such a pact on July 20, 1933.[1]

There are several reasons why the above attitudes concerning the probable linkage between the above historic acts and the concordat negotiations are so prevalent. First of all, those acts and the negotiations took place in a restricted time frame, so that one must naturally ask whether they were related. Secondly, the Vatican had sought with firm persistence since 1920 to negotiate a concordat with the German Reich and Ludwig Kaas was its leading adviser on German affairs from that date onwards. Thirdly, Hitler's desire to destroy the two Catholic parties, the Center and the BVP, the Bavarian Peoples party, which had seceded from the Center in 1920, and his belief that it could be done readily by prevailing on the Vatican to ban priests' participation in parliamentary politics are well known. And in fact the German Concordat of 1933 contained such an article (#32).

At this point the reader unfamiliar with the controversy over the origins of the Concordat and its possible connection with German Catholic decision-making in the period March-July 1933 might ask the question, "Why is there any need to write further on the subject if the preponderance of opinion, scholarly or otherwise, is that there was such a linkage?"

Only a few years ago Klaus Scholder, the Tübingen church historian, presented the thesis in the first volume of

---

[1]See the revealing observations of Konrad Repgen regarding his own experiences with both students and older people outside of his university: "Ungedruckte Nachkreigsquellen zum Reichskonkordat: Eine Dokumentation," *Historisches Jahrbuch* 99 (1979), 375-77; also, "Dokumentation. Zur Vatikanischen Strategie beim Reichskonkordat," *Vierteljahrshefte für Zeitgeschichte* 31 (1983), 506-09. The author also provides invaluable bibliographical references for the study of the debates over the major issues in the controversy.

his history of the Christian churches in the Nazi era that Ludwig Kaas had promised Hitler that his Center party would approve the Enabling Act in return for a pledge from the Nazi Chancellor to negotiate a concordat with the Holy See. Scholder's case was based on circumstantial evidence of extensive scope and his findings appeared to fit the logic of the political situation in Germany in the spring of 1933.[2] But two other scholars of considerable reputation, Konrad Repgen of the University of Bonn and Gerhard Scholz, Scholder's colleague at Tübingen, both experts in the field of recent German history, pointed out in review articles that Scholder had not provided verifiable evidence to prove his thesis.[3]

In my own essay, I take a modified Scholder position. Repgen and Scholz are certainly correct that Scholder did not base his conclusions on the hard rock of explicit documentary evidence, but it should be said that one cannot supply what apparently does not exist. Nor can I provide substantial documentation to bear the burden of my own hypothesis which rests essentially on circumstantial proofs, largely borrowed from Scholder, extended knowledge of the personalities involved in the German Catholic decision-making gained from my own earlier research, and the logic of the political situation in which the Catholic Church found itself in the Germany of early 1933. It points to the location of the key to the solution of the problem of whether

[2]Klaus Scholder, *Die Kirchen und das dritte Reich*. Band 1: *Vorgeschichte und Zeit der Illusionen 1918-1934* (Frankfurt/M, 1977), 300-22, 482-524.

[3]In fact, Repgen and Scholder became involved in a prolonged and distinguished debate over the validity of Scholder's thesis. See Repgen's review article: "Über die Entstehung der Reichskonkordats-Offerte im Frühjahr 1933," *Vierteljahrshefte für Zeitgeschichte* 26 (1978), 499-534. Scholder's reply: "Altes und Neues zur Vorgeschichte des Reichskonkordats," *ibid.*, 535-70; and Repgen's "Nachwort zu einer Kontroverse," *ibid.*, 27 (1979), 159-61. And for more of Repgen's articles on the Concordat problem of the spring of 1933, see n. 1 above. Gerhard Scholz, "Neue Kontroversen in der Deutschen Zeitgeschichte: Kirchengeschichte, Parteien und Reichskonkordat," *Der Staat* 22 (1983), 578-603.

an agreement between Hitler and the leader of the Center party existed before the voting on the Enabling Act took place. Scholder sensed that such a key existed, but he passed by the place where it was apparently hidden.

The Vatican's Unsuccessful Pursuit of a German Concordat: 1920-1932

Klaus Scholder associates the driving effort of the Papal Curia to conclude a concordat treaty with Germany after 1919 with its growing emphasis on the centralization of the Catholic Church since the mid-nineteenth century. But he attaches special importance to the completion of the new canon law code in 1917 which put stress on papal authority and uniformity in administrative procedures. Some of the concordats concluded in the 1920s did reflect the prescriptions and spirit of the new code, especially those with Bavaria (1924) and with Italy (1929).[4] And it is not surprising that Cardinal Pietro Gasparri, the Papal Secretary of State from 1914 to 1929 and his successor Eugenio Pacelli were respectively the chairman and secretary of the committee which had drafted the code; each was to be seriously involved in the effort of the Papal Curia to win a concordat with the German Reich.

It may be that Scholder attributes too much importance to the Holy See's desire to shape relations between Church and State in Germany in accordance with the new code of canon law, since the Vatican had certainly tried hard enough through the nineteenth century to use its own diplomatic

---

[4]See Dieter Golombek, *Die politische Vorgeschichte des Preussenkonkordats (1929)* (Mainz, 1970), 58-64. Also Ludwig Kaas, "Der Konkordatstyp des faschistischen Italien," *Zeitgeschichte der ausländisches öffentliches Recht und Völkerrecht,* Bd. III (1933), 488-522.

skills to improve the position of its Church in the various German states. But the German Revolution of 1918 and the Weimar Constitution of the next year, which located ultimate sovereignty in cultural matters in the national government, offered the Papal Curia the attractive possibility of a treaty with the German state which would regulate all relations between the Catholic Church and the state throughout Germany and conceivably in accordance with the terms of the new code of canon law.

There were many German Catholics who believed that the members of their Church lived very well in the new Germany without a concordat. Though not to the same extent as Jews, Catholics had been virtually barred in the old Empire from higher offices in most German states, above all in the giant state of Prussia. Under the new Weimar Republic and at an early date, Catholics frequently held the chancellorship because of the Center's pivotal position in the Reichstag. In Prussia Catholics from the educated middle-classes or the trade unions held a variety of high public offices because the Center was the junior partner of the larger Social Democratic party, a relationship which was distressing to the Catholic episcopate. And in predominantly Catholic Bavaria, the BVP, virtually dominated Bavarian politics from 1920 to 1933. And in that period Catholic associations flowered — when Hitler came to power in 1933 the Catholic Youth Movement had a membership of about 1,500,000.

The Catholic Church itself had benefited from the new conditions. While monarchical controls had not been severe after the late nineteenth century in most parts of Germany, they were in place, and the selection of the bishops, the leaders of the Church, was not a matter in which the cathedral clergy and the Vatican could ignore the individual state governments for either treaty or political reasons. But by 1920 the Catholic Church enjoyed complete freedom throughout Germany. Speaking of the new position of that Church in his country an old Prussian state official complained:

> all that the state had carried through in centuries of concordat negotiations and struggles over education will have been given up for a theory [of freedom] without compensation.[5]

Now the Church elected or appointed its own bishops, priests spoke freely from the pulpit, religious orders had freedom of action, and the Church was able to found new associations at will. Even though there was separation of Church and State, the Center had prevailed on its secular allies in the Weimar Constitutional Assembly to recognize the churches as public institutions and to collect taxes from their members, a task which the states took over for them. The Center was also able to save the denominational schools which remained the dominant form in the larger states like Prussia, Bavaria, Württemberg, and some others.

There is no evidence, however, that any of the twenty to twenty-five bishops of the period 1920-1933 did anything more than recognize the liberal republic as the legal form of governmental authority. The best form of government in their eyes was any authoritarian system based on constitutional principles, preferably one of a monarchical character, which could protect the churches' rights and interests against anticlerical liberals and antireligious Socialists in state legislatures, and maintain certain standards of moral decency through censorship of the stage, cinema, and non-artistic literature. How unready they had been for the separation of Church and State was evident in their anguished cry in February 1919, just weeks after the elections to the

[5]Golombek, *Preussenkonkordat*, 37 n. 49.

Weimar Constitutional Assembly, that if the State and the Church were separated, "the fate of our poor Fatherland would be sealed. Then the peace would be lost as well as the war."[6] In their judgment, what made matters worse was the growth in the influence of Socialism after the lost war and the Revolution, and in their concern they made no distinction in condemning the movement between the Social Democratic party and the more radical variants of Marxist political thought and activity.[7] Since they were regularly engaged in the profession and teaching of religious ideals they tended to overestimate the appeal of the Socialist "free-thinker" and the Communist "Godless" movement to Catholic workers, a fear which sometimes made it difficult for some of the bishops to see what a sham the supposed "positive Christianity" of the Nazi movement really was.[8]

On a day-by-day level, however, the Catholic bishops worried more about two other matters. One was the possibility that the state legislatures would at some future point cut off their approval of their governments' supplementary financial aid to the churches, a worry that was disposed of in any individual state if its government entered into a concordat with the Holy See. But of prime importance was their obsessive fear for the future of the church schools, a concern they had inherited from at least two generations of predecessors. Extensive though those systems were in Germany, they lacked the legal status of the interdenominational form which the constitutional settlement of 1919 had established as the norm.[9]

[6]Günter Plum, *Gesellschaftstruktur und politisches Bewusstsein in einer katholischen Region 1928-1933, Untersuchung am Beispiel des Regierungsbezirks Aachen* (Stuttgart, 1971), 190.

[7]*Ibid*, 155-57.

[8]See my article: "Germany: The Catholic Church and the Nazi Regime 1933-1945," *The Clergy and the State in the Interwar Years,* eds. Richard J. Wolff and Jörg Hoensch (in press).

[9]*Ibid*.

There appears to be no evidence that the German bishops, except possibly for the Bavarians, shared the enthusiasm of the Holy See for concordats, especially one at the national level which would reduce their own freedom of action in church-state affairs. Yet they were seemingly at one with the Vatican that the priority for the Church in its wider German goals had to be a law, either free-standing or embedded in a concordat, that would put a legal flooring under the church schools, providing them with a status equal to that of the interconfessional school system and greater security. Consequently, the leaders of the Catholic Church moved on separate but parallel tracks to achieve that end: Archbishop Eugenio Pacelli, the Papal Nuncio in Germany, sought to negotiate a concordat containing that kind of school article with the national government, and the Center party, acting really on the episcopacy's orders, endeavored to bring a school bill favorable to the church schools through the Reichstag. To put it mildly it was to be an uphill journey for both.

It is evident from Ludwig Volk, S.J.'s magisterial study of the Vatican's efforts to secure a concordat with Germany after 1919 that the prospects seemed most favorable in the early 1920s.[10] Three of the chancellors were Catholic, but more importantly the German state was then headed by a Social Democratic president, Friedrich Ebert, who was acutely conscious that his country was isolated and subject to heavy French pressures over reparations. The Vatican's top diplomat, Eugenio Pacelli, to use a Bismarck expression about one of his own ambassadors, was "the best horse" in the Vatican stable and was to have long service as Papal Nuncio to Bavaria and the Reich (1917-1929). Pacelli was dedicated, brilliant, and gracious though not broad enough

---

[10]Ludwig Volk, *Das Reichskonkordat vom 20. Juli 1933. Von den Ansätzen in der Weimarer Republik bis zur Ratifizierung am 10. September 1933* (Mainz, 1972), 1-31.

in outlook to appreciate all the needs, secular as well as religious, of the German Catholic minority.[11] That he was to have both enthusiastic admirers and critics in that community is understandable.

Despite Germany's own diplomatic needs in the earlier 1920s and Pacelli's impressive gifts, one wonders if there was ever a real prospect for the acceptance of a concordat by a post-1919 Reichstag. There was an old German Protestant fear of the Curial hand in the internal affairs of the German nation and a dislike on the part of German liberals and democrats for the Vatican's efforts to limit the competence of state legislatures to deal with educational questions by concluding pacts with the national or state governments.[12] By 1927 Pacelli had decided for at least the time being to put the whole question of a national concordat on hold and to hope that a national school bill could make its way through the Reichstag, even though its acceptance depended on some liberal backing. The liberals, Social Democrats, and Communists successfully blocked its passage and the measure was finally withdrawn in 1928.[13]

Both the Papal Nuncio and the German bishops were to enter into a new cycle of hope and disappointment in the early 1930s, the years of deep economic depression and political instability in Germany. But before we turn to that period, we need to examine the career of Ludwig Kaas, Pacelli's aide and friend, who had become the national chairman of the Center party in December 1928.

[11]*Ibid.* And see Rudolf Morsey, "Eugenio Pacelli als Nuntius in Deutschland," *Pius XII. Zum Gedächtnis,* ed. Herbert Schambeck (Berlin, 1977). This volume contains numerous other essays on Pacelli which demonstrate his impressive abilities, but it tends on the whole to be reverential in approach.

[12]See Golumbek, *Preussenkonkordat,* 28-45.

[13]For a clear and balanced treatment of this whole question for the early twenties down to 1928, see Ellen L. Evans, *The German Center Party, 1920-1933* (Carbondale, 1981), ch. 16.

That Kaas was a man of many talents cannot be doubted. He had high intelligence, a mastery of the spoken and written word, a warm personality, and marked diplomatic gifts. Whether he was ideally suited for political life, which required more physical and psychological robustness and a wider breadth of outlook than he possessed, may be another matter. In any case the task of trying to walk on a tightrope stretched all the way between Rome and Berlin would probably have been too much for any other Catholic politician as well.[14]

Kaas' membership in the Reichstag, knowledge of German political affairs, training in canon law, and intelligence brought him in 1920 to the staff of Eugenio Pacelli. He and the Nuncio were soon linked in a common diplomatic effort and in close friendship. They successfully negotiated concordats between the Vatican and Bavaria (1924), Prussia (1929), and Baden (1932); but only the pact with the Bavarian state contained school articles, and hence the other treaties made the ideal of a German concordat with the kind of provisions for the church schools that the German Catholic bishops and the Curia desired all the more enticing to Pacelli and Kaas. Both men, but especially Pacelli, who returned to Rome for good in 1929, were frustrated by their failure to get anywhere with their efforts to win a national concordat from the Reich or a school bill of their preference from the Reichstag.[15]

---

[14]See Karl Otmar v. Aretin, "Ludwig Kaas," in *Neue Deutsche Biographie* (Berlin, 1974), X, 713-14. Aretin stresses Kaas's conviction that parliamentary democracy was unsuitable for Germany and the mistake that the Center party made in electing Kaas as its chairman in 1928. See also Volk, *Reichskonkordat,* 37-42 and Heinrich Brüning, *Memoiren 1918-1934* (Stuttgart, 1970), *passim.*

[15]In fact, Pacelli had fought vigorously in a vain effort to persuade the Prussian government to agree to the incorporation of school articles in the concordat between the Vatican and Prussia signed on June 14, 1929 — see Golumbek, *Preussenkonkordat,* 106-07. Pacelli thought it would be easier for him finally to break the resistance of the central German government to a German concordat if the Vatican could point to two state concordats, the Bavarian model and then a Prussian pact, each of which contained the school provisions the Vatican and the Catholic bishops desired. Together they would have embraced eighty percent of the German nation.

In December 1928 Kaas was unexpectedly elected to the national chairmanship of the Center party, the first priest ever to hold that office. The party congress had split over the candidacy of a laborite and Kaas who had a mediating personality had become the compromise choice. Georg Schreiber, who was a priest and who had worked intimately with Kaas on the school bill of 1927-1928, had lobbied energetically for the election of his friend.[16] Ironically enough the election of Kaas to the chairmanship turned out to have more serious consequences than a later series of events in national politics that must have initially impressed and pleased Cardinal Pacelli and the German Catholic clergy a great deal.

In March 1930 the German state machine turned sharply to the right. The Social Democrats and the liberal parties, with the Center serving as a junior partner, had formed a large coalition in 1928, but that alliance had collapsed under the political strains of early depression budget-making. The military and other advisers of President Paul von Hindenburg now saw a chance to get rid of the Social Democrats from government *en permanence* and to put conservatives in their place. For the next two years the chancellor was Heinrich Brüning, a prominent conservative member of the Center, a devout but independent Catholic with close Protestant political associations and a trained economist.[17]

Judging from the height of Eugenio Pacelli's expectations regarding the presence of a conservative Catholic in the chancellorship of the German Reich, his disappointment over Heinrich Brüning's complete lack of interest in concordat negotiations must have been great. Adolf Hitler, concerned about the formal opposition of the German Catholic

[16]On that election, see Evans, *Center Party*, 346-50.

[17]For the Brüning years prior to 1930, see Rudolf Morsey, "Brüning. Ein Staatsmann aus Westfalen," *Zwischen Ruhrkampf und Wiederaufbau*, ed. Walter Forst (Cologne, 1972), 83-94.

628   *The Genesis of the German Concordat of 1933*

episcopacy, had sent Herman Goering on a goodwill mission to the Vatican in April 1931 and had apparently convinced Curial officials that the Nazi leadership wanted to establish good relations with the leadership of the Catholic Church. However, Brüning rejected outright Pacelli's request, made when they met in the Vatican in August 1931, to form a coalition of the right which would include the Nazi party. The Catholic German chancellor had strong views on the subjects of the inclusion of Nazis in his government and a German concordat and was to ignore a second effort made by Pacelli through Kaas on January 1, 1932 to persuade him to work toward an understanding with Adolf Hitler.[18]

It is evident enough why the Chancellor responded negatively to the Cardinal Secretary of State's efforts to influence his own coalition policy. First of all, Pacelli was strikingly insensitive to Brüning's dignity and responsibilities as the leader of a predominantly non-Catholic state. But Brüning probably disliked concordats on principle, having spent most of his career working with Protestants in the interconfessional trade union movement and in politics. More immediately, he was never forgetful of the fact that his government depended on the willingness of the Social Democratic party to tolerate his unpopular economic policies. In all likelihood that dependence on the moderate Marxist party also explains why he did not encourage his own party friends to expect any early action on a new school bill which would put legal flooring under the church schools.[19].

---

[18]Brüning, *Memoiren*, 358-59; Volk, *Reichskonkordat*, 48; and Scholder, "Altes und Neues," 561.

[19]In what was probably a move to loosen the ties between the Center and the Social Democrats in Prussia, the German National Peoples party had introduced a school bill to the Reichstag in October of 1930 which the Center leaders wanted to support, but did not do so — see *Die Protokolle der Reichstag und des Fraktions-vorstands der Deutschen Zentrumspartei 1926-1930*, ed. Rudolf Morsey (Mainz, 1969), 485 and n. 4.

At some point in 1932 a fissure slowly emerged in the relationship between Kaas and Brüning which was fairly wide by the winter of 1932-1933, if concealed from the public. The likelihood is that it originated in Brüning's suspicions that his old friend was no longer loyal to him in the last months of his chancellorship, but that it was expanded by differences over their views on the question of a coalition with the Nazis with Hitler as chancellor. Nevertheless, Kaas was to be severely shaken by Brüning's dismissal in late May 1932 and by his replacement with Franz von Papen who many Centrists thought was a traitor to the Catholic cause in agreeing to succeed the revered Brüning.[20]

Brüning's dependence on the Social Democrats and his failure to break up the Social Democratic-Center alliance in Prussia, if not the immediate cause of his fall, had been deeply frustrating to conservatives inside and outside the presidential circle. But it had also been a matter of some concern to Cardinal Pacelli and Kaas who were also distressed that there could be no hope for a new school law and for a concordat as long as the Chancellor insisted on maintaining good working relations with the moderate Marxist party. We have no reason to doubt Brüning's word that Kaas had held talks with Franz von Papen, one of the closest intimates of President Hindenburg and a reactionary ex-member of the Prussian Center, in January and February 1932 over the legitimacy from a Catholic point of view of a *coup d'état*.[21] It will be remembered from what we have already learned that Pacelli had tried to get Brüning to move politically to the right in that same period.

In view of Kaas' and Cardinal Pacelli's deep desires for a rightwing coalition in Germany, it is difficult to say why

---

[20]Rudolf Morsey, *Der Untergang des politischen Katholizismus. Die Zentrumspartei zwischen christlichem Selbstverständnis und "nationaler Erhebung" 1932-33* (Stuttgart-Zürich, 1977), 46-47.

[21]Brüning, *Memoiren*, 609.

Kaas was undoubtedly shaken by the dismissal of Brüning and his replacement by Franz von Papen. There appear to be two probable explanations. First of all, Brüning had no objections in principle to a school law which would benefit the church schools which had been after all the prime objective of the Vatican's concordat drive.[22] One can probably assume that if he had stayed in office and had strengthened his political position by improving economic conditions and in securing revisions of the unpopular Treaty of Versailles from the Allies he undoubtedly would have tried to improve the legal position of church schools. There would have been concessions of an economic character that he could have made to the Social Democrats to secure their tolerance of such legislation. Secondly, Brüning was enormously popular with the great majority of Catholics who had no reason to think that his position with the Hindenburg circle had undergone serious erosion well before his forced resignation from office. In any case Center support of Papen was not forthcoming, although the new chancellor desperately sought it. Consequently, the number of conservatives who could be considered for the chancellorship was very narrow indeed.

Let us be fair to Ludwig Kaas and define the kind of government that he would have ideally desired. He was a devout churchman, a conservative, an authoritarian, but certainly no fascist. Kaas was also a patriot. His preferred governmental coalition was one of "concentration" (*Sammlung*),[23] a term that had been used in the 1890s to describe

---

[22]This is implicit in his references to the church schools in his memoirs, *ibid.*, 670-71. Conservative politicians, Catholic and Protestant, had to be supportive of them in any event.

[23]He presented his basic views, though without reference to his concordat concerns, in an emotional letter to a Benedictine abbot, dated January 6, 1934 — see "Erste Jahreswende unter Hitler. Ein unbekannter Briefwechsel zwischen Ludwig Kaas und dem Abt von Grüssau. Zum 100. Geburtstag des Zentrumspolitiker am 23. Mai 1981," ed. Ludwig Volk, *Stimmen der Zeit* 199 (1981), 322-23.

the alliance of the conservative and right-liberal parties, in which the Center was a sleeping partner, against the Social Democrats. It was quite clear to Kaas and Cardinal Pacelli that such a coalition had to include the Nazis who were the largest parliamentary group on the right even prior to their great victory of July 1932 which brought them 230 mandates in the Reichstag. But even if he had been tempted by Franz von Papen in February 1932 to agree to a conservative dictatorship, and there is no firm proof that he was, Kaas as the leader of a minority party long devoted to constitutional principles would have had to insist that such a coalition would have to function within the limits of the constitution.

In the later summer, fall, and early winter of 1932 the question of just what role the Nazi party and in particular its leader Adolf Hitler would play in such a coalition became the burning political question in Germany. The Nazi party more than doubled the number of its Reichstag seats (from 107 to 230) and with the Center and the BVP (the Catholic Bavarian Peoples party) constituted a negative parliamentary majority against Papen. If President Hindenburg had consented, which he did not do, Hitler would have become chancellor on or soon after August 10, 1932.

Oddly enough Ludwig Kaas was not a visible figure in German politics in the above period, being absent from Berlin over long periods of time. Rudolf Morsey stresses the apparent breakdown of his health, never strong, after the dismissal of Brüning and his replacement by the unpopular Papen whom the Center party leadership considered to be a traitor.[24] Hence Kaas was to spend most of that time convalescing in northern Italy where he was wont to spend his vacations.

Nevertheless, it seems to me that we should consider another explanation of Kaas' extended absences from his

[24]Morsey, *Untergang*, 48.

leadership post in Berlin. In my judgment he was a hardier human being than he appears to be in the view of Rudolf Morsey and Ludwig Volk; despite his stomach ailments, the strain he was under in the early 1930s, and his great disillusionment with the Nazi regime after 1933, he did live on to just over seventy years of age. It is difficult to avoid the conclusion that during his absences from Berlin he was in communication with his old friend Cardinal Pacelli, discussing the German political situation. He was undoubtedly Pacelli's chief source of information and advice regarding the German political scene, and not Cesare Orsenigo, the Papal Nuncio in Berlin, a competent reporter in more normal times but not in the highly volatile months of 1932.[25]

It is a very important part of Klaus Scholder's argument regarding Ludwig Kaas' unrelenting commitment to the achievement of a German concordat that he looked upon a government led by the National Socialists as the best solution to the German political crisis. Scholder points out that Adolf Hitler himself had made a speech soon after the conclusion of the Lateran concordat between the Fascist government of Italy and the Holy See in 1929 in which the Nazi leader said the treaty proved that Fascism and the Catholic Church had shown that they could make peade with each other. In February 1930 Johannes Stark, a Catholic and Nobel prize winner in physics, had repeated that conclusion but had added that the Lateran pact had provided for the banning of participation by priests in politics. Stark went on to say that it would mean the end of the Center party if a National Socialist state were to enter into a similar treaty with the Vatican.[26]

Scholder had also called attention to the fact that Kaas had practically finished in November 1932, the month in

---

[25]On Orsenigo, see Volk, *Reichskonkordat*, 52-55.
[26]Scholder, "Altes und Neues," 544-45.

which Franz von Papen fell from office, an essay on the Lateran Concordat of 1929. In that essay the author eulogized the two statesmen, Pius XI and Mussolini, who through their diplomacy had restored harmony to the Italian nation and in so doing had benefited it immensely.[27]

In his debate with Scholder, Konrad Repgen has made several objections to the above interpretation of the Kaas article on the Lateran concordat. He claims that there is no sure proof that the article was completed before the negotiations on the German-Vatican treaty of 1933 were virtually over because the issue of the journal containing it was not published before early August of that year. He notes that the author himself had called attention to the fact that some of the provisions of the Italian treaty were not completely compatible with conditions and arrangements in Germany, especially those parts having to do with marriage, education, and especially with the banning of clerical participation in politics. And finally he says that Kaas could not have been thinking of Hitler as a German Mussolini because the Nazi party, having lost five percent of its electorate in the elections of November 6, 1932, was now on a downward slope. Would a man like Kaas, Repgen asks, who had just negotiated with Hitler, "bet on this horse?"[28]

It cannot be proven by verifiable evidence that the Center's leader did want to put his money on just that horse, but there is considerable circumstantial evidence that he believed Hitler to be the best runner in the small group of entries in the chancellor stakes and that the Center, its Church, and the Protestant conservatives of the German National People's party would profit from his victory. Why else would a party leader overburdened with work and responsibility and possibly ill take time to write a scholarly

[27]Kaas, "Konkordatstyp des faschistischen Italien," 491-95.
[28]Repgen, "Reichskonkordats-Offerte," 506-08.

article on a previous Church-State treaty if it were not immediately relevant to German politics in a time of high importance? Center representatives had negotiated on several occasions with Hitler between August and October, when the Nazis and their own party together held a majority of the Reichstag seats, with the purpose of forming a coalition but had apparently been frustrated by Hitler's lack of interest in such a relationship or by his unacceptable terms.[29]

There are reasons to believe that Kaas, despite the failures of the negotiations between his colleagues and the Nazis and despite President Hindenburg's dislike of Hitler, favored a Hitler chancellorship in the winter of 1932-1933. Cardinal Pacelli was still as intent as ever to secure a concordat with the Reich and Nazi support was indispensable to its realization.[30] Franz von Papen, who had started to take up talks with the Vatican on such a pact, fell from office after his government's poor performance in the elections of November 6. His successor, General Kurt von Schleicher, had been peremptory in his handling of another issue which concerned both the Reich and the Vatican and which Pacelli had long hoped to use as a basis for the introduction of talks on a concordat.[31] And only a Nazi-Center-Bavarian Peoples

[29]On those negotiations, see Morsey, *Untergang*, 56-80. Morsey indicates that the Center would even "tolerate" a Hitler chancellorship based on the Nazi and German National Peoples parties if the government functioned on a constitutional basis (p. 80).

[30]Ludwig Volk says of Pacelli in this period, "Decisive for Pacelli's church political assessment of the NS-movement was its stand on concordats." — see his *Reichskonkordat*, 63. And it was probably revealing that Brüning thought it necessary to warn his parliamentary group on January 26, 1933, just two days before Hitler's appointment to the chancellorship, that the Nazis were unreliable with regard to commitments, even when they were recorded on paper — see Morsey, *Protokolle der Deutschen Zentrums*, 608-09.

[31]See Volk, *Reichskonkordat*, 50 n. 27. The Ministry of Defense and the German Catholic hierarchy had long disagreed over the right of the *Reichswehr* to have its own bishop who could make full exemptions from canon law in Catholic-Protestant mixed matters. Unlike the bishops, Pacelli was ready to meet the

party coalition would provide enough votes for the approval of such a treaty in the Reichstag. In fact, it appeared that Hitler, if Hindenburg were ever to appoint him chancellor, would need the Center's support for a constitutional government since the Nazis had lost enough ground in the November elections for the Center to recover its historical pivotal position. However, Papen succeeded in overcoming Hindenburg's aversion to Hitler and his party, with the result that the Nazi leader became chancellor and the leader of a coalition of Nazis and conservative nationalists on January 30, 1933, leaving the Center out in the cold.

The last relatively free Reichstag elections of March 5, 1933, undoubtedly made a significant impact on both the Nazi leader and on Kaas. Hitler's coalition won by only a narrow margin but it secured a majority of the seats. In addition the Chancellor possessed special police powers which Hindenburg had granted him after a young Communist had set fire to the Reichstag on the night of February 27. Still the Center in particular and the Bavarian Peoples party to a somewhat lesser extent had done well in the election.[32] To secure total legislative power Hitler needed to win over those parties or at least the Center, for the approval of the enabling act legislation.

Ministry of Defense's demands on the matter if the German government expressed willingness to enter into concordat negotiations. In October 1932 Schleicher, then the Minister of Defense, attacked the bishops for their opposition to the appointment of a bishop with such powers. Ludwig Volk seems to leave open the question of whether Kaas had acted as a Schleicher adviser on that occasion, but the fact that Georg Schreiber, a priest member of the Center, spoke out strongly in the bishops' defense may indicate that the party itself was cool toward the general. In any event Schleicher, a gifted man, was a general without parliamentary troops of any size and soon fell from office.

[32]The lower Catholic clergy involved itself heavily in the campaign and the priest-leaders of the numerous Catholic associations issued a collective proclamation calling on their members to support the Catholic parties. On that proclamation, see *Atken deutscher Bischöfe über die Lage der Kirche 1933-1945*. I: *1933-1934*, ed. Bernhard Stasiewski (Mainz, 1968), 1-4.

Hitler, Ludwig Kaas, and the Enabling Act

We are now at a point in high-level German politics that is crucial for the introduction and development of this writer's own hypothesis about the origins of the concordat negotiations, the reasons for them, and their effects on Catholic political decision-making and actions in March, 1933.

On March 7, two days after the Reichstag elections, Chancellor Adolf Hitler and his Vice-Chancellor Franz von Papen made remarks in a cabinet session that were about the Catholic parties. Hitler said "that the voters of the Center and the Bavarian People's party will first vote for the national parties after the Curia drops both parties." Konrad Repgen argues that Hitler's words did not necessarily mean that he was envisaging concordat negotiations with the Vatican since he could seek an understanding with the Curia in other ways.[33] It is difficult to accept the plausibility of the Repgen argument for these reasons: 1) the Nazi chancellor's earlier favorable references to the Lateran pact, made either by himself or by others; 2) his need to be *sure* (my italics) that the Center party would not frustrate his desire for an enabling act; and 3) the demonstrated lack of Vatican interest in any kind of an agreement with Germany that was not a concordat containing favorable provisions for the church schools.

The other pregnant remark was the simple statement of the Vice-Chancellor that he had received a visit from Kaas on the previous day, March 6, for the purpose of burying their past disagreements.[34] Those disagreements had undoubtedly been aggravated by Papen's role as the regime's "hatchet man" in the recent election campaign in

---

[33]Repgen, "Reichskonkordats-Offerte," 511-15. His basic argument is, however, that Scholder cannot offer any firm proof that Hitler had a fixed intent to offer Rome a concordat at this time.

[34]Scholder, *Die Kirchen*, 304.

the Catholic districts of northern Germany.[35] The fact that the Vice-Chancellor then remained silent about the meeting led Klaus Scholder to give it no significance in the making of his own thesis that Hitler and the Center leader reached an agreement according to which the Center would vote for the Enabling Act and Hitler would initiate concordat talks with an aim to a final German-Vatican treaty. And while Konrad Repgen believes that Franz von Papen was more interested in early March in a concordat agreement than his Chancellor, Adolf Hitler, he does not attach any importance to the Papen-Kaas session of March 6 either.[36]

There were no records left of that talk and that is probably the explanation of why two such careful scholars as Scholder and Repgen did not bother with it. But that is the very reason why Scholder in particular should have become suspicious about the possible meaningful nature of the meeting instead of interpreting Papen's brief reference to it and his later silence in the cabinet session of March 7 as evidence that his encounter with Ludwig Kaas was relatively inconsequential. After all, Papen, an ex-chancellor himself, was the second man in the realm as Hitler's Vice-Chancellor and Kaas was the leader of the party which could block the passage of the Enabling Act and also the *de facto* Papal Nuncio in Germany. In fact, Kaas appeared to have acted more like a Papal diplomat representing the Holy See than as a party leader because he, as Rudolf Morsey has told us, did not say anything to his party council about his intended session with the Vice-Chancellor and for that matter he was apparently never to let its members in on his secret.[37]

[35]Morsey, *Untergang,* 107.

[36]Repgen, "Altes und Neues," 512-14. However, in a separate place Repgen says that Papen on March 6, the same day on which he met with Ludwig Kaas, paid a visit to the office of Friedrich Trendelenburg, the leader of the division of church affairs in the Prussian Ministry of Cults to ask him about problems connected with negotiations on concordats, *ibid.,* 521 n. 36.

[37]Morsey, *Untergang,* 116.

We know little about that meeting of March 6 beyond Papen's report that the Center's leader wanted to bury the past and offer his party's collaboration to the government, but we are well acquainted with Adolf Hitler, Franz von Papen, Ludwig Kaas, and Eugenio Pacelli. Let us remember that Kaas was a devout Catholic prelate for whom a German concordat had been an ideal objective for over a decade and that Franz von Papen was a pious Catholic who also wanted to demonstrate to Hilter his influence with his Church. There is explicit evidence that Hitler was at this very time wrestling in his mind with the question of how to get rid of the Catholic parties and that he was thinking of approaching the Vatican with that end in view. The future was to show that he would virtually give the Holy See the kind of concordat it wanted if it would ban priests from participating in German party life.[38] There was no reason why Franz von Papen would not have given that message to Ludwig Kaas on March 6, although the Center's leader would have had to depend on Papen's word rather than on a written pledge to that intent. It is certainly unlikely that Kaas would have encouraged Papen to believe at that time that the Holy See would insist on the withdrawal of German priests from political life, but it is equally unlikely that he would have risked ending the prospects of a German concordat then and there by telling the Vice-Chancellor that that subject could not be discussed in the negotiations.[39]

In his own efforts to prove that Kaas and Hitler had met at some date before the Reichstag acted on the Enabling

[38]See below n. 75.

[39]According to his diary notes for April 8, the day he met Papen on the train to Rome, the Vice-Chancellor brought up the question of the depoliticization of the clergy. Kaas said that he did not rebuff Papen on that issue but said that there had to be proof that there would be sufficient political cultural guarantees and that if there were such he would not be "small." Papen even spoke of the giving up of the Center party. See Scholder, *Die Kirchen*, 486-87.

Act, Klaus Scholder has called in Heinrich Brüning as a witness. The chancellor of the years 1930-1932 has said in his memoirs:

> Kaas' resistance became weaker when Hitler spoke of a concordat and Papen asserted that it was as good as assured....Since 1920 Kaas had always hoped to conclude a concordat.... Hitler and Papen will have noticed how Kaas was increasingly attracted by the growing prospect of a concordat.[40]

One has to give respectful attention, however, to the critical reservations Konrad Repgen had expressed about the value of that quotation from Brüning's recollections published after his death in 1970. The ex-Chancellor had once written that Kaas had gone to Rome to put a halt to the concordat negotiations. Repgen also claims that Brüning's later remarks reflected his bitterness against his old friend and colleague. Still other scholars have concluded that Brüning's memoirs have a strong political cast to them so that scholars have to be very careful in their use of them. And if one reads the above quotation critically, it does not seem that Brüning had firsthand knowledge of any meeting. between Hitler and Kaas.[41]

Nevertheless, this writer holds that Brüning's remarks about his former friend and party-leader have some value because of his extensive knowledge of Kaas' political personality. One cannot quarrel with his statement that the

---

[40]Brüning, *Memoiren*, 656.

[41]Repgen, "Ungedruckte Nachkriegsquellen," 393. But it is also remarkable what Ludwig Volk has said about Hitler's lack of confidence in Kaas's pro-concordat convictions. According to Volk, Hitler would not have said anything about his own concordat plans when they met privately on April 7, just hours before Kaas left Berlin for Rome, because he would have feared that the Center leader might work against them at the Vatican! See Volk, *Reichskonkordat*, 97.

One cannot imagine Kaas letting Brüning know under any circumstances about talks with Papen or any other German official about a concordat.

concordat issue was "the question which naturally and understandably interested Kaas most of all."[42] Oddly enough Brüning made no reference in his memoirs to his heated confrontation with Kaas at a friend's home several days before the Reichstag voted on the Enabling Act. Kaas had the reputation among those who knew him well of being both an "indecisive man" and a natural mediator. However, in his quarrel with Brüning he pounded his fist on the table and asked rhetorically, "Am I still the leader of the party or is someone else?"[43] Kaas on that occasion sounded very much like a political leader who had made a commitment and who could not back away from it.

From Rudolf Morsey's account of the debates over the Enabling bill among Center party members in the Reichstag Center on March 23, held before and after Hitler's own speech to the national parliament, it does not appear that Ludwig Kaas had to exert himself to win over a majority of the parliamentary group. Most of the group's members had been in favor of approving the Hitler measure before the debates.[44] They were influenced by a variety of concerns: their personal or political security, the future of their party, and the effect that opposition to the regime could have for the civil servants in its ranks. If they had serious qualms of conscience about voting for the Enabling Act, they undoubtedly felt better when Hitler in his own speech solemnly guaranteed the rights of the major Christian churches in the schools, promised to respect the state concordats, and stressed the regime's high evaluation of Christian values.[45] When Kaas called for a test vote in the parliamentary group after the Hitler speech only twelve to fourteen deputies followed Heinrich Brüning in casting neg-

---

[42]Brüning, *Memoiren*, 636.

[43]Scholder, *Die Kirchen*, 312.

[44]Morsey, *Untergang*, 134.

[45]*Ibid.*, 137.

ative ballots, though it should be added that they included many of the most promising talents in the Center party. Much of Kaas' support, except for a few personalities like Adam Stegerwald, the longtime leader of the interconfessional trade union movement, and the handful of priest deputies, apparently came from the back benches.[46]

Still Ludwig Kaas was undoubtedly a more important figure in the making of the Center's historic decision on the Enabling Act than the Morsey account permits us to conclude. In times of crisis and uncertainty while parliamentarians, especially those from out of the middle and back of the party group, may want to vote the easier way, they will pay heed to their leader. Like any competent party leader Kaas had not intended to let his group's decision depend on the speeches he and his allies would deliver to their colleagues on March 23. As we now know he had lobbied hard to win support from his colleagues for the Enabling Act about the time the Reichstag reconvened on March 20.[47] He had also gotten pledges from Hitler on March 22 to the effect that the government would not introduce a new constitution, that it would respect the tenure of judges, and that cultural matters like the state concordats would not come under the powers of the new Act.[48] From the brief excerpts that Morsey

---

[46]Since Morsey does not list Stegerwald, a longtime conservative laborite, and the other clergymen (besides Kaas) among the members of the Brüning group, whom he names, I have put them among the Chairman's allies. The Brüning followers included several laborites or members of Catholic workers associations and two women. It has been known that Kaas wrote a Prussian official on March 24, 1933, hence the day after passage of the Enabling Act, that he had brought about (*herbeigeführt*) his party's approval of that measure. See Scholder, "Altes und Neues," 553.

[47]Just a few years ago Ludwig Volk uncovered a brief correspondence between Kaas and a Catholic clergyman in which the Center's leader stressed among other things his role in convincing his friends to vote for the Hitler bill. The correspondence brings out Kaas' patriotism, but above all his strong religious feelings. See Volk, "Erste Jahreswende," 322-23.

[48]Morsey, *Untergang*, 131-32.

provides of his speeches to his group on March 23, it is clear that Kaas wanted to impress on his colleagues that the Center's old influence was gone, that the regime would achieve the power it wanted one way or other, and that opposition to it on the Enabling Act could do serious damage to the Center party.[49] On the other hand, if Kaas had chosen to ally himself with Brüning, former Chancellor Joseph Wirth, Eugene Bolz, the Minister-President of Württemberg and their allies, there could be no question but that the majority however much it disliked doing so would have had to follow their lead in opposing Hitler's bill.

An unusual facet of the Center's political activities before and on March 23 was the participation of Albert Hackelsberger in the leadership circle. Hackelsberger, an industrialist from Baden, had apparently elbowed himself onto the Center's electoral list for that state for the Reichstag election of July 1932. Because the Center was a party in which seniority of service and age had always carried considerable weight, it was remarkable that Hackelsberger had early vaulted into the front group of the Reichstag contingent. He was one of the three Centrist dignitaries, of whom Kaas was another, who negotiated with Hitler on March 22. In the debates within the Center's own group on the next day, he emerged as the leader of those Centrists who wanted to vote for the Enabling Act.[50] It is surprising that scholars have not earlier reflected on the importance of the close connection between Ludwig Kaas and Hackelsberger.

[49]*Ibid.*, 139. Morsey notes that a woman colleague observed that Kaas did not appear to be enthusiastic about the Hitler bill on March 23, but then he understood that the Reichstag would be adding to the Chancellor's already considerable power by giving him the ability to legislate at will, something the leader of the Catholic minority could not have contemplated without some inner reservations.

[50]On Hackelsberger, see Heinrich Köhler, *Lebenserinnerungen des Politikers und Staatsmannes 1878-1949,* unter Mitwirkung von F. Zilken, ed.. Josef Becker (Stuttgart, 1964), 40, 126 n. 56, 318, 321, and Morsey, *Untergang,* 131,139.

It is undoubtedly important for an understanding of the Center's decision-making just before and on March 23 to know something about Hackelsberger's connections in the Church itself. He was a close friend of Archbishop Konrad Gröber of Freiburg who owed his high office to the good will of Cardinal Pacelli[51] and perhaps even more to the influence of their mutual friend Kaas. Together Gröber, a churchman of considerable energy, and Pacelli had forced an unwilling Baden Center party to provide the parliamentary backing for the Concordat of 1932 between Baden and the Vatican.[52] After the passage of the Enabling Act and even more after the signing of the Concordat, Kaas, Gröber, and Hackelsberger were to become the frontrunners in the German Catholic effort to build up a long-term relationship between their Church and the Nazi regime patterned on the Italian model. Hackelsberger was apparently their contact person with the Nazi government after the conclusion of the Concordat negotiations.[53] In fact, when some of the bishops were becoming disillusioned with the regime over its party's attacks against the Catholic press and associations and with the government's failure to silence Alfred Rosenberg, the Nazi racist philosopher, Hackelsberger warned his ecclesiastical friends that if "Kerenski" (Hitler) fell he would be followed by someone worse.[54]

One can only speculate as to what would have happened to the Center if Kaas, Hackelsberger, and their allies had joined forces with Brüning and his group on March 23. Brüning appears to have assumed that the regime would

[51]Köhler, *Lebenserinnerungen,* 322 n. 54.

[52]*Ibid.*

[53]Hackelsberger was to be busy negotiating with Nazi governmental officials over the dissolution of the Center and the reception of some Center deputies into the Nazi Reichstag delegation in late June 1933 when Brüning was trying hard to keep his party afloat — see Morsey, *Untergang,* 193.

[54]Stasiewski, *Akten deutscher Bischöfe,* I, 489.

suppress his party if it were to have voted negatively on the Enabling Act.[55] Hitler would certainly have taken his revenge on the Center and its civil servants as Kaas had correctly prophesied, though the future would show that he preferred to put pressure on the non-Marxist parties to dissolve themselves rather than openly to suppress them. In any event we should assume that he would have been careful in his approach to the Catholic Church itself. It will be remembered that Mussolini, even though there was no longer a Catholic party in Italy in 1929, insisted that there be an article in the Lateran Concordat that banned priests from politics. Regardless of what his relations were with the Center, it is likely that Hitler would have at some early point found a road to Rome.

The Episcopal Statement of March 28 on the Nazi Party

On March 28, hence five days after the passage of the Enabling Act, the united Catholic bishops issued a formal statement in which they withdrew their earlier prohibitions of Catholic membership in the Nazi party. They apparently acted without consultation with the executive councils of the Center and the BVP, although both of those parties were inevitably to be damaged by the church hierarchy's change of policy toward the Nazi movement. And by any standard of traditional episcopal conduct the act was hasty.[56]

It is not surprising then that Klaus Scholder, who holds that Franz von Papen, acting for Hitler, and Ludwig Kaas had been moving purposely before the Reichstag voting on

---

[55]Morsey, *Untergang*, 139. He said "it is better to go under gloriously than to experience one by one this fate."

[56]Scholder, *Die Kirchen*, 319-20.

the Enabling Act to smooth the way for a German concordat, insists that either the Vice-Chancellor or the leader of the Center party had turned the leaders of the hierarchy around on the issue of Catholic membership in the Nazi party.[57] On the other hand, Ludwig Volk and Rudolf Morsey assert that there was a direct causal relationship between the extensive guarantees Adolf Hitler had offered to the churches in his Reichstag speech of March 23 and the decision of the bishops to permit Catholics to join the Nazi party.[58] Unlike Scholder, they can point to some explicit documentation to support their views on the issue.

Still the Scholder thesis cannot be dismissed without careful consideration. While the bishops had not spoken out as unitedly and emotionally against the Nazi movement as they had against the Communist and Socialist parties, their language against certain Nazi doctrines and practices, among them racism, state supremacy, and violence had been forceful and sharp enough. In August 1931 Cardinal Adolf Bertram, the Archbishop of Breslau, the Chairman of the Fulda Episcopal Conference, had, on behalf of his colleagues, made up a stiff pastoral letter to pastors which read in part: National Socialism "actually stands in the most pointed contradiction to the fundamental truths of Christianity and with the organization of the Catholic Church created by Christ."[59] How effective the various episcopal prohibitions or warnings against Catholic membership in the Nazi party were was evident from the high degree of loyal support that practicing Catholics gave to the Center party in the last relatively free election of March 1933.

It is especially difficult to understand why Cardinal Bertram, then seventy-four, a churchman of strong mental

[57]*Ibid.*
[58]Volk, *Reichskonkordat,* 73-79; Morsey, *Untergang,* 153-56.
[59]Zeender, "Catholic Church and Nazi Regime."

powers, remarkable work energy, and firm views, but above all marked prudence, would have led his episcopal colleagues in such a hasty change of front toward the Nazi party, though not toward its doctrines. His longtime episcopal colleague and usually loyal supporter Cardinal Josef Schulte, the Archbishop of Cologne, a man of milder temperament but strict on doctrinal matters, had been insistent until March 22 that the hierarchy adhere to its traditional stand toward the Nazi party.[60] And it should be noted, as Scholder has told us, that Franz von Papen visited Cardinal Bertram in Breslau on March 18 in an apparent effort to get him to bring about a change in attitude of the Catholic episcopacy toward the Nazi regime and its party.[61] Even though Papen may have kept Hitler's concordat intentions a secret during that visit we cannot be sure that he did so.

Both Ludwig Volk, who once believed that the hasty action of the bishops bespoke outside intervention in their decision-making, and Rudolf Morsey link up the episcopate's announcement of March 28 on Catholic membership in the Nazi party with Hitler's guarantees to the churches given in his Reichstag speech of March 23. They can point to documentary evidence that Cardinal Bertram moved quickly to try to change the bishops' position directly after the Chancellor had publicly offered his pledges to the Christian churches. And during his visit of March 18 to Bertram, Franz von Papen had undoubtedly reassured the leader of the Fulda bishops' conference concerning the good intentions of the Hitler regime toward the Catholic Church. At that time Cardinal Bertram bluntly told his visitor that he would not change his own policy until the leader of the Nazi movement had changed his.[62] Hitler's speech on March 23

[60]Volk, *Reichskonkordat,* 73.

[61]Scholder, *Die Kirchen,* 309.

[62]*Ibid.*

in its references to matters of concern to the Catholic hierarchy might have seemed to the cardinal to be a direct answer to his own remarks of March 18 to the Vice-Chancellor. That the Chancellor of the German Reich would commit himself in such a manner to respect and uphold the rights and interests of the major Christian churches undoubtedly made a marked impression on the leaders and most of the other members of the German Catholic hierarchy who did not know how readily Hitler could lie. They would learn sooner or later.

Still it is my own conclusion that Cardinal Bertram, as Scholder insists, had gotten wind of the fact that some representative of the Vatican had been or was still talking with government representatives about a concordat. And one cannot leave out the possibility that Papen had told him something to that effect on March 18. But the more impressive claim by Scholder is that Cardinal Bertram, given his exalted position in the German Catholic Church, must have known what the most prominent dignitary in the Protestant Church learned on the morning of March 23, the day of the voting on the Enabling Act. At that time a contact, presumably an official in the German government, called Hermann Kapler, the chairman of the umbrella committee which provided a loose unity among the Protestant state churches, had told him, that in connection with the negotiations over the acceptance of the Enabling Act discussions (*Erörterungen*) were taking place with political or ecclesiastical representatives of the Catholic Church.[63] Ludwig Kaas was most likely at one and the same time a Catholic political leader and also a representative of the Cardinal Secretary of State at the Vatican. And let us remember, as Konrad Repgen has told us, that Franz von Papen had gone to the offices of the Prussian Ministry of Cults on March 6 to inquire about

[63] *Ibid.*, 312-13.

problems connected with negotiations over concordats.[64] It is little wonder that actual reports and not just rumors of concordat talks were circulating in the German and Prussian governments.

The episcopal announcement on the Nazi party of March 28 was the second body blow suffered by the Center party and the BVP within a week's time. The passage of the Enabling Act which transferred all legislative functions to the executive for at least the foreseeable future left the parties without any of their traditional functions and hence without a sense of purpose. The withdrawal by the bishops of their earlier prohibition of Catholic membership in the Nazi party and their silence toward the Catholic parties as they struggled painfully to maintain their existence compounded their difficulties. But what we will want in particular to notice about the episcopal statement is that the leaders of the Catholic hierarchy had not taken into serious consideration what its effects would be on the ability of already weakened parties to survive the loss of their rights to be considered the only legitimate parties for which Catholics could vote. The leader of the Baden Center, Ernst Föhr, a priest, had warned Archbishop Gröber two days before the bishops made their announcement on the Nazi party that such a proclamation could "easily" mean the death of the Center.[65] Since Gröber was a member of the Kaas-Pacelli circle one can wonder just what kind of an impact the Föhr warning had on the Archbishop's thinking about the bishops' plan to rescind the prohibition against Catholic membership in the Nazi party and its various organizations. But the fact that the Church's leaders had unitedly made that decision without any formal discussion about its advis-

---

[64]See n. 36 above.

[65]Morsey, *Untergang*, 156. Morsey is probably correct in his insistence that a much later Föhr charge that the episcopal proclamation was a "deathblow" to the Center is "insupportable."

ability with the leadership groups of the Center and BVP
was revealing regarding the nature of their priorities.

The Concordat Negotiations and the Fate of the Catholic Parties

While the more politically astute bishops undoubtedly
realized that their statement of March 28 had hurt the
Catholic parties, they and their colleagues did hope that
those parties would survive in some form or other. Ludwig
Kaas had indicated in his essay on the Lateran pact of 1929
which banned priests from party politics that the article
which did so was not applicable to conditions in Germany.
With the possible exception of Konrad Gröber, the members of the German Catholic hierarchy were apparently not
confident that they could dispense with their traditional
political shields even after Hitler's reassuring words to the
churches in his Reichstag speech of March 23. Therefore
they looked to Vatican diplomacy to do what it could to save
the Catholic parties.

In recent years Konrad Repgen has striven to rebut the
findings of Klaus Scholder, Karl D. Erdmann, and some
other scholars that the Papal Curia did not really expect to
persuade the Hitler regime to conclude a treaty in which
priests would continue to be members of German Catholic
parties. Of course, Ludwig Volk had shown in his study on
the *Reichskonkordat* that the Vatican's negotiators had
consistently adhered to that position down to July 1/2 when
the negotiations reached their climax. Thus the Holy See
had maintained that principle intact up to that point in time,
even though its representatives in an effort to make it
acceptable to Hitler had agreed after May 14 that bishops
would only grant priests permission to be politically active
in those rare cases where it was necessary in the Church's

interest that they do so.[66] But that meant that the power of decision would still be in the hands of church authorities and that the full-time Center clerics would retain their parliamentary mandates.

Repgen is insistent that the Holy See was committed to the principle of priest participation in parliamentary politics and only yielded its position when the bottom fell out of the political situation in Germany, following the suppression or dissolution of the secular parties between June 22 and 29. He bases his interpretation of Vatican strategy on this issue on a document he found in the Austrian Foreign Office Archives a few years ago which was written by Robert Leiber, S.J., the German secretary of Cardinal Pacelli. Leiber had composed the document, a report, around July 16, hence eight days after the German and Vatican representatives had signed the articles of the concordat. He had also written some days earlier a commentary on those articles, which accompanied this report. Both documents were intended for the eyes of Engelbert Dollfuss, the Catholic Chancellor of Austria, whose government was threatened by its own rebellious Nazis and by the Hitler regime itself. Dollfuss had reason to be unhappy about a concordat that might make Nazism respectable in his own state and which might also through its banning of priests from politics embarrass his own Catholic party which had always depended to some degree on clerical members.

In Repgen's judgment, the report is the key to the Vatican's diplomacy in the concordat negotiations.[67] Leiber, the author, stressed the uniform belief of all officials engaged in Vatican diplomacy that Catholicism and Nazism were incompatible with each other and that those dealing with the Hitler regime were determined to do so in a cautious and

---

[66]Volk, *Reichskonkordat,* 124-34, 171-73.
[67]Repgen, "Zur Vatikans Strategie," 517.

diplomatic manner, taking up each issue in the negotiations in a deliberate way. Repgen is impressed by what he thinks the report reveals about the lack of an appeasement mentality among the Holy See's representatives in the negotiations and the absence of a compulsion to conclude a treaty at any cost. And while the report itself makes no reference to the issue of priests in politics, Repgen thinks it reinforces the thought of a cryptic phrase Rober Leiber had used in a letter to Archbishop Gröber, dated April 20, to the effect that "Lateran Concordat 42.3 does not come into question."[68] In other words the Vatican meant to uphold the right of the German hierarchy to permit priests to hold parliamentary positions.

Aside from the fact that Ludwig Kaas undoubtedly felt a sense of obligation to his old party, Vatican leaders had reason to try to save the Catholic parties because the German bishops wanted them to do so. There was broad satisfaction among the bishops with the report that Konrad Gröber gave of the concordat proceedings to the Fulda Episcopal conference at the end of May, except for the revised version of the article dealing with the clergy in party politics. They insisted that they have wider powers in providing permission to priests to participate in parliamentary bodies, a demand that apparently did not sit well with Archbishop Gröber since he did not mention it in a personal letter to the Cardinal Secretary of State afterwards.[69]

Still there are reasons for doubting that the Vatican really intended from the beginning to pursue a hard line to maintain the right of the Catholic hierarchy in Germany to continue the old tradition of permitting priests to engage in party politics. The Leiber report to Dollfuss was a diplomatic document in which the author had to explain some unpleasant things to the head of a government who

[68]*Ibid.*, 524.
[69]Scholder, *Die Kirchen,* 500-01.

obviously had to believe that a German concordat could worsen his own inability to fend off the Nazi threat. Its basic statements were all of a general nature and did not refer to the specific persons who shaped Vatican tactics in the negotiations. Leiber did not explain why the Holy See abandoned its position on the clergy-in-politics issue, and for that matter he did not even mention it in the report.[70] In reading his brief comment on the article treating their withdrawal from that activity, one has the feeling that he felt some embarrassment that the Vatican had abandoned its fight on that issue. He simply noted that it was not based on the Lateran treaty,[71] a remark that must have puzzled Dollfuss.

Nevertheless, the historian can extricate some material of value from the Leiber report and the commentary on the articles of the Concordat. In the report he stated that "Vatican diplomacy considers the Concordat treaty, *as it is now presented* (my italics), as being favorable overall from the Vatican standpoint...."[72] In fact, Pacelli and Pius XI were highly pleased with their achievement[73] until they learned that Hitler did not share the Vatican's stern views on the commitment of signatories to treaties. One can understand their pleasure when one analyzes the Concordat article by article and in particular when one notes from the Leiber commentary that it not only guaranteed the existence of the Catholic school system where it existed but also permitted the Church to establish it in those parts where it did not

[70]Repgen, "Zur Vatikans Strategie," 530-33.

[71]*Ibid.*, 529.

[72]*Ibid.*, 531.

[73]The Italian ambassador to the Vatican saw Cardinal Pacelli and Pius XI on July 25 and reported to his government, "The Pope and the Cardinal Secretary of State have rejoiced over the Concordat with Germany like children who have been rewarded in school" — see Scholder, "Altes und Neues," 569.

exist.[74] Eugenio Pacelli and Kaas had finally achieved the prize they had sought for thirteen years.

In my judgment, it is difficult to avoid the conclusion that Kaas and the other Vatican negotiators realized from the beginnings of the negotiations that they would have to agree eventually to the Hitler regime's demand that priests be kept out of party politics. Regardless of what Papen said or did not say during their earlier stages for tactical reasons, Adolf Hitler was always insistent that the clergy had to leave political life in Germany. It is necessary to keep in mind that there would have been no concordat negotiations and no Concordat of 1933 if Hitler had not been determined to undermine the Catholic parties by depriving them of their priest members. And when Vatican representatives weighed in their scales a concordat providing for the security and extension of the Catholic school system, the maintenance of state financial aid to the Church, and other benefits against the continued existence of the Catholic parties (something they assuredly did in the early spring of 1933, perhaps earlier), there could hardly have been a doubt in their minds about the decision they would make when Hitler finally presented them with an ultimatum on the issue. It is revealing that even the German bishops at their Fulda meeting of late May, eager to keep the Catholic parties in existence, had not made their eventual approval of a concordat dependent on their right to permit priests to serve in parliamentary bodies, a right the German episcopate had possessed since time immemorial.[75]

Over the course of the past thirty years or so there has been a remarkable increase in the number of important

---

[74]Repgen, "Zur Vatikans Strategie," 529.

[75]And Cardinal Faulhaber was to tell Franz von Papen shortly afterwards that he would not insist on the Church's right to permit priests to be involved in parliamentary politics, and he later made a note to the effect that because of the school question the Concordat could not be allowed to fail. Scholder, *Die Kirchen,* 501.

scholarly publications — editions of sources, monographs, articles, and more general works — which have dealt with different aspects of the German Catholic Church's history from the late Weimar years down to the end of the Second World War and the collapse of the Nazi regime. One thinks of the impressive volumes of primary documents from Church archives published by *Die Kommission für Zeitgeschichte bei der Katholischen Akademie in Bayern* with which Konrad Repgen, Ludwig Volk, and Rudolf Morsey have been prominently associated. One also thinks in this connection of the first volume of Klaus Scholder's history of the Christian churches under the Third Reich which has done so much to revive and advance the old debates over the possible linkage between concordat negotiations and Catholic decision-making on the Enabling Act of March 23, the episcopal statement of March 28, and the dissolution of the Center on July 5, 1933.

Still it is remarkable how little agreement has been reached between scholars on the opposing sides in the debates. Historians like Repgen, Volk, and Morsey are still vigorously upholding their positions, although they have had to permit their opponents to create at least one salient behind their front line. Repgen in his debate with Klaus Scholder in the late 1970s admitted the validity of Scholder's claim that Hermann Kapler, the noted Protestant church dignitary, had received news of discussions (*Erörterungen*) about a Reich's Concordat from an informant on the morning of March 23, the day on which the Reichstag Center had to vote on the Enabling Act. But Repgen insists that Kapler's informant, who had telephoned his information to the Protestant church leader, must have gotten his intelligence only shortly before his call and that he had spoken only of discussions and not of actual negotiation.[76]

[76]Repgen, "Reichskonkordats-Offerte," 516-17.

The Repgen-Volk-Morsey group maintain their positions behind a double line. The inner line is their charge that there is no explicit documentation to support the Scholder thesis that there was a Hitler-Kaas agreement about a concordat before the vote on the Enabling Act and that either Papen or Kaas had informed Cardinal Bertram of such an agreement before the Catholic episcopal leader called on his colleagues to rescind their prohibition of Catholic membership in the Nazi party. It is conceivable that they can hold that line for a long time unless some scholar or scholars turn up sure proof that Hitler and Kaas had reached an agreement for concordat negotiations before March 23.

The outer line of their position is Ludwig Kaas's written statement regarding the time and circumstances when he, as Repgen puts it, first learned of Hitler's intention to conclude a concordat with the Holy See. According to Kaas, he "unexpectedly" met Vice-Chancellor Papen on the express train which ran from Munich to Rome on April 7, 1933, two weeks to ten days respectively after the Center had approved the Enabling Act and the bishops had made their celebrated statement on the Nazi party. The relevant passage below comes from a letter Kaas wrote to Diego von Bergen, the longtime German Ambassador to the Holy See, on November 19, 1935:

> In the course of a conversation initiated by him [Papen] in his compartment [the Munich to Rome express], I determined that the *intention* often discussed even in public of the eventual conclusion of a concordat was *a fact* [Repgen's italics and inserts].[77]

Repgen emphatically stresses certain points about the above Kaas statement. The first is that the Center leader was a person who was most careful and precise about what he

---

[77]*Ibid.*, 517-18.

had to say on anything of importance, an assertion with which we can agree.[78] The second is that Kaas had no knowledge of Hitler's intentions regarding a concordat prior to his "unexpected" meeting with Papen on the train.[79] But from the stress that Repgen also puts on the word *fact* in the Kaas letter to Bergen, it appears that he means that Kaas was sure of the Chancellor's intentions only when he heard from Papen on the train of his commission to initiate conclusive concordat negotiations with the Vatican.[80] Hence there could have been no agreement between the Nazi Chancellor and the leader of the Center party prior to the Enabling Act vote or the bishops' declaration of March 28.

Scholder has taken sharp issue with Repgen's analysis of those important lines in Kaas's letter to Diego von Bergen. He claims that if the public, as Kaas himself said, had had some earlier knowledge of Hitler's intentions regarding a concordat, then Kaas had to have had that knowledge himself.[81] The Scholder argument in this connection is certainly sound enough. Putting aside his and my hypothesis that Hitler and Kaas had reached an agreement about the initiation of negotiations on such a treaty, it is sensible to assume that Kaas would have learned about Hitler's intentions well before the public. Whatever flaws he had as a party leader, no one has ever claimed that Ludwig Kaas, as the head of the Center and as the Vatican's chief adviser on German affairs, did not know the importance of possessing up-to-date information on the government's thinking and planning, especially on matters affecting the Catholic Church.

However, by underlining both "intention" and "fact" in the passage from the Kaas letter to Bergen, Repgen wants us

[78]*Ibid.,* 518.
[79]*Ibid.,* 517.
[80]*Ibid.,* 518.
[81]Scholder, "Altes und Neues," 555-56.

to believe, as I had noted above, that Kaas could not have reached an understanding with Hitler through Papen at any time in March 1933, because Kaas had no guarantee of the Chancellor's honest intention regarding the initiation of conclusive concordat negotiations. In my judgment, Repgen is demanding too high a standard of proof from scholars like Scholder and those who agree with him that Hitler (working through Papen) and Kaas had reached an agreement about the initiation of concordat negotiations at some time before the Center debated what to do about the Enabling Act.

For the purposes of argument let us assume that my hypothesis is correct that Papen, acting for Hitler, assured Kaas before March 23 that the government would initiate negotiations with the Vatican in the near future. What pledge of that intention beyond a firm, gentlemanly handshake and related acts could Papen have provided Kaas to convince him of the integrity of Hitler's intentions? Neither the Chancellor nor Kaas would have been interested at that time in exchanging pieces of paper to commit himself in a formal way to concordat negotiations since both the German government and the Vatican might want to deny rumors that such negotiations were taking place just as the Mussolini regime and the Holy See had insisted that they were not negotiating on a pact prior to the publication of the Lateran Concordat.[82]

Finally we must turn to what Ludwig Kaas had to say about his role in the Center's approval of the Enabling Act. Like Konrad Repgen, we believe that he carefully weighed the words he used when referring in writing to serious political matters. On March 24, 1933, the day after the Center's action on the Enabling Act, Kaas wrote a Hamburg

---

[82]Kaas himself made this statement about the manner in which the Fascist regime and the Holy See carried on their negotiations before the conclusion of the Lateran treaty — see Scholder, "Altes und Neues," 535.

merchant a letter which contained the sentence: "In any case I hope, nevertheless, that the decision of yesterday brought about (*herbeigeführt*) by me finds your approval."[83] In a letter to a clerical acquaintance dated January 6, 1934, he emphasized among other things, how he had remained true in 1933 to his ideal of "concentration," "an inner necessity," and had sought to bring together the politically valuable part of the Catholic population and "the Führer." He then said, "In this sense I had not rested until I became master of the fears around me and brought into being the yes (*das Ja*) of my friends."[84]

In recent years there apparently have been no new developments on the issue of the motivation for the episcopal statement of March 28, 1933. The fronts are apparently still frozen between those scholars who believe like Scholder that at least Cardinal Bertram knew of an agreement between the Hitler regime and a Catholic representative and those who insist that Bertram and his colleagues had simply reacted in the issuing of their announcement to Hitler's formal pledges to the two Christian churches in his own speech of March 23 in the Reichstag.

There has also been no change in the front between those who believe that there was direct linkage between the Vatican's desire to conclude the concordat and the dissolution of the Center on July 5, 1933, and those who vigorously insist that the proceedings between German and Vatican representatives had nothing to do with the Center's end. But it has hardly been a quiet front, as historians like Konrad Repgen, Rudolf Morsey, and Ludwig Volk have not been content to rest on the defensive. As we have already seen, Repgen claimed in an article published in 1983 that a report from Robert Leiber, S.J., Pacelli's secretary, to Chancellor Doll-

---

[83]*Ibid.,* 555.
[84]Volk, "Ein unbekannter Briefwechsel," 317.

fuss of Austria written on July 16, 1933 — eight days after the signing of the articles of the Concordat —demonstrated how determined the Holy See was to uphold the principle that priests, if in very limited numbers, could serve in political parties. The Vatican negotiators only abandoned this position after the bottom fell out of the political situation in Germany as a consequence of the suppression of the Social Democratic party and the dissolution of the secular non-Marxist parties between June 22 and June 29.[85]

The most advanced stand on the controverted issue of whether the Papal Curia's insistence on a concordat was directly connected with the rapid decline of the Center as a viable political organization and with its end on July 5, had been taken earlier by Rudolf Morsey in 1977 in the second version of his earlier book on the collapse of the Center party. In his defense of Ludwig Kaas and the concordat negotiations he makes the categorical and unequivocal assertion that:

> ...Ludwig Kaas had through his collaboration in the coming into being of the Reich Concordat neither caused nor hastened the downfall of political Catholicism.... Kaas had to suffer as a clerical scapegoat and as the embodiment of political Catholicism for that indecision with which he had acted in the field of tension between Church and Politics.[86]

And Morsey, like Ludwig Volk earlier, insists that Joseph Joos, the deputy Chairman of the Center party, misunderstood Kaas's intent when Kaas, in a telephone conversation with Joos on July 2, who was then in nearby Switzerland, asked his former colleague, "Have you dissolved yourselves

---

[85]See above nn. 66-70.
[86]Morsey, *Untergang,* 207.

yet?" Joos interpreted that question to be a masked instruction from the Papal Curia to the Center's leaders that they should terminate the life of their party as quickly as possible. Morsey says, however, in undocumented statements that Kaas was merely seeking information about the Center from his old colleagues and that the ex-leader of the Center really hoped that his party would, for the sake of the concordat negotiations, be able to survive for a few months longer.[87]

Finally, Morsey insists that there was no tie-in between the dissolution of the Center on July 5 and the signing of the paragraphs of the Concordat on July 8, a relationship which Kaas's critics in the Center party believed existed. One of those articles, I might add for clarification at this point, contained the provision that clergymen could not be members of political parties or involve themselves in political agitation.[88] For the most part, however, Morsey refers only rarely to the concordat negotiations in Rome. Indeed, it could be said with only slight exaggeration that he treats them as if they were taking place on the moon.

There is an implicit thesis in Morsey's explanation of the decline and final end of the Catholic parties, in particular the Center itself. He is certainly sound in claiming that the Center's leadership made a disastrous mistake in turning its back on Franz von Papen when he was Chancellor (June 1932 — November 1932) since Papen was the legal head of the government and also the close friend of the President who alone could appoint the Chancellor.[89] Morsey is, of course, on sound ground too in his assertion that Hitler,

[87] *Ibid.,* 195-96.

[88] For the exact text of the final treaty, see *Der Notenwechsel zwischen dem Heiligen Stuhl und der Deutschen Reichsregierung.* I. *Von der Ratifizierung des Reichs-Konkordats bis zur Enzyklika "Mit brennender Sorge,"* ed. Dieter Albrecht (Mainz, 1965), 587.

[89] Morsey, *Untergang,* 219.

when he assumed that office, was ready to take the necessary steps to consign the hated Center to a political cemetery.

By and large Morsey's thesis, although never explicitly stated, is that the Catholic parties were the victims of the unbearable pressures imposed on them by the Hitler regime and its party's organizations.[90] The parties, one and all, had difficulties after the passage of the Enabling Act adjusting to political life without their legislative functions and traditional interaction with each other, a situation I would stress even more than Morsey does. The Center was leaderless until May 6 because of Kaas's absence in Rome and it had lost a sense of purpose until Heinrich Brüning took over its leadership. The Center suffered a continuous loss of members from the civil service who feared for their job security or who wanted to climb onto the Nazi bandwagon. The confidence of other members was also shaken by the terrorist methods of the regime, which included the arrest of some Center personalities on July 1, an experience suffered by over 2,000 members of the BVP (including 200 priests), during a crucial phase in the concordat negotiations (June 29 — July 7). In the parlance of the boxing profession, the Center's leaders were hanging onto the ropes even before that point in time.[91]

One can differ with Morsey over his essentially unilinear explanation of the collapse of the Center party. He recognizes that the bishops' withdrawal of their earlier prohibition of Catholic membership in the Nazi party had to weaken the hold the Catholic parties had had on some of their members, a situation which was aggravated by their later silence toward those parties as they struggled for breath.[92] He even briefly acknowledges that some members felt that the ongoing concordat negotiations in Rome gave

[90] *Ibid.*, 95.

[91] *Ibid.*, Ch. 6, sections 3-5, and Ch. 7.

[92] *Ibid.*, 156-58, 183.

them the right to leave the Center or the BVP.[93] But Morsey does not attribute major importance to those factors as serious causes of the Center's gradual breakdown.

Morsey's heavy concentration on the developments in Germany which were sapping the strength of the Center provides a narrow and, in my judgment, unsatisfactory explanation of the Catholic party's end. It leaves some questions hanging in the air. If the Center was solely a victim of the harsh political conditions in Nazi Germany, why had Heinrich Brüning made the seemingly hopeless effort to keep his party alive after the other parties had disappeared from the scene?[94] And why was Joseph Joos, the Center's deputy Chairman, staying in Switzerland, where telephones were not tapped by the police, while the Reich's and Vatican's negotiators dealt with the question of whether at least some priests could participate in party politics, an issue on which the German representative, Papen, won a victory on July 1.[95] Cardinal Pacelli was to insist to a Catholic correspondent two weeks later that the subject of "the dissolution" of the Center had never been discussed in the concordat negotiations.[96] Actually there had been no need to do so since the withdrawal of Catholic priests from that party would have exactly that effect. Seen against the background of that decision of July 1, it was logical enough that Joseph Joos understood Kaas's question of the next evening, "Have

[93]*Ibid.*, 202.

[94]Brüning was not always consequential in his recollections. In his memoirs he says that the Center might have been saved at the time he became its chairman on May 6 if it had taken the action itself of prohibiting clergymen from accepting parliamentary mandates — see his *Memoiren*, 608. Such an act would have hardly secured the Center's existence for any length of time. It is clear enough from his later remarks that he believed the conclusion of the Concordat would mean the end of the Center's life — *Ibid.*, 671-72; and see Volk, *Reichskonkordat*, 182.

[95]Morsey says that Pius XI approved the text of the Concordat on the next day, August 2 — see his *Untergang*, 196.

[96]*Ibid.*, 196.

you dissolved yourselves yet?" to mean that Vatican officials wanted its leaders to terminate their parties' affairs. Brüning and his colleagues decided soon afterwards to take that step and did so on July 5, a date which the embittered Brüning probably chose to underscore its closeness in time with the crucial decision taken four days earlier in Rome.[97]

In the interest of clarity I will affirm that the Center was primarily the victim of a terminal illness whose prime causes were the products of the difficult political conditions in Germany. However, the immediate cause of its dissolution lay in the turn that the concordat negotiations took on July 1, a development that could have been foreseen at a much earlier date. It must be said that even a healthier Center party working under milder conditions in Germany could not have long survived its loss of priest members. Leaving aside the technical contribution of individual priest members to the effectiveness of the Catholic parties, the clerical members were indispensable as symbols of those parties' close ties to their Church and of the increased reliance of the Center and the BVP on the rank and file of the priesthood throughout Germany.[98]

Like Ludwig Volk at an earlier date, Morsey tells us that Hitler, by approving the Concordat on July 20, paid that price to the Vatican for a prize he had already won: the collapse of the Catholic parties two weeks earlier. The truth

[97]Cardinal Pacelli was annoyed over that act of Brüning and his colleagues since he, according to Ludwig Volk, wanted them to keep their party alive for some weeks more in order to strengthen the Vatican's negotiating position — see Volk, *Reichskonkordat,* 183-84. That seems doubtful to me. The likely explanation is that Pacelli was obviously concerned about the extensive rumors circulating in Germany that the Catholic parties were being sacrificed on the altar of the Concordat. Volk himself observes that the Vatican was slow and not forceful in denying the truth of those rumors — *ibid.,* 182-83. And as we have seen above (n. 96), Cardinal Pacelli's denial of July 16 was beside the mark.

[98]For an informed and penetrating treatment of the Center's heavy dependence on the clergy, see Josef Becker, "Das Ende der Zentrumspartei und die Problematik des politischen Katholizismus in Deutschland (1963)," *Von Weimar zu Hitler 1930-1933,* ed. Gotthard Jasper (Köln, 1968), 344-76, here 357-60.

of the matter is different. In 1929 Mussolini, already governing a one-party Fascist state, had insisted that the Lateran
pact contain an article (42,3) stipulating that priests could
not involve themselves in politics, a provision which guaranteed that there would be no official Catholic effort in the
future to recreate a Catholic party with clerical support. In
the concordat negotiations in Rome four years later, Hitler
made sure that the Vatican gave him the same kind of
pledge. Ludwig Volk has said that the German dictator
wanted to destroy the Center because it was a democratic
party, not because it was a Catholic party.[99] Actually it was
just the other way around. For historical reasons the democratic tradition was weak in Catholic Germany. However,
the tradition of loyalty to the Catholic Church and to the
political parties so closely associated with it was relatively
strong, although not as pronounced as in the nineteenth
century.

In the introductory part of this article I stated that there is
no explicit evidence that there was a causal connection
between the Center's vote in the Reichstag in favor of the
Hitler regime's Enabling Act and the beginnings of negotiations on a concordat between the German government and
the Holy See. But like Klaus Scholder I have been impressed
by the amount of circumstantial evidence that can readily
lead to such a conclusion. Unlike Scholder, however, I have
found it highly meaningful that Ludwig Kaas, the leader of
the Catholic Center party, the chief adviser to the Papal
Curia on German affairs, and the close friend of Cardinal
Pacelli, the Secretary of State of the Vatican, met with
Franz von Papen, the German Vice-Chancellor, on March
6, 1933 — seventeen days before the Reichstag had to vote
on the Enabling Act. While Papen made a terse reference to
that meeting in the cabinet session of the next day, Kaas

[99]Volk, *Reichskonkordat*, 185.

kept permanently silent about it. One would certainly not say that Ludwig Kaas was motivated by ambitious and selfish motives in his political career, but it is also true that few men who played significant roles in the political life of their nations left scantier records of their political activities than he did. Heinrich Brüning did write a substantial memoir, imperfect though it is. Some historians will find meaning in the fact that Ludwig Kaas left only fragments of a diary which began two weeks after the passage of the Enabling Act.[100]

[100]Kaas, "Tagebuch 7-20. April 1933," ed. Rudolf Morsey, *Stimmen der Zeit* 167 (1960-61), 422-30.

The Reverend Monsignor John Tracy Ellis
CURRICULUM VITAE

A. *Life:*

Born:	1905	July 30, Seneca, Illinois
Degrees:	1927	A.B., Saint Viator College, Bourbonnais, Illinois
	1928	A.M., The Catholic University of America
	1930	Ph.D., The Catholic University of America
Theological Studies:	1934-38	Sulpician Seminary, Washington, D.C.
Ordained:	1938	June 5, Chapel of Our Lady of the Angels, College of Saint Teresa, Winona, Minnesota
Domestic Prelate of Pope Pius XII:	1955	December 21

B. *Teaching:* 1930-32 Saint Viator College

1932-34 College of Saint Teresa, Winona

1935-38   The Catholic University of America,
Assistant in History

1938-41   The Catholic University of America,
Instructor in History

1941-43   The Catholic University of America,
Assistant Professor of History

1943-47   The Catholic University of America,
Associate Professor of History

1947-64   The Catholic University of America,
Professor of Church History

1962-63   The Catholic University of America,
Coordinator of the Program of
Ecclesiastical History

1964-76   University of San Francisco, Professor
of Church History

1977-   The Catholic University of America,
Professorial Lecturer in Church
History

C. *Summer*
    Sessions: 1928   College of Saint Teresa, Winona

1930   Saint Benedict's College, Atchison

1933-34   Dominican College of San Rafael,
Pacific Coast Branch, The Catholic
University of America

1935-37   Our Lady of the Lake College, San
Antonio, Director of Southern Branch,
The Catholic University of America

1939-44   The Catholic University of America

1960   Mount Saint Mary's College,
Los Angeles

1962	University of San Francisco
1963	University of San Francisco
1976	Saint Norbert College, DePere, Wisconsin and Saint Charles Borromeo Seminary, Philadelphia
1978	University of San Francisco

D. *Lectureships:*

1955	Walgreen Lectures, University of Chicago, January 24-28.
1965	North American College, Rome, September 15-30
1967	Visiting Professor of Roman Catholic Studies, Brown University, February-June
1967-68	Saint Patrick's Seminary, Menlo Park, California, November-May
1970	Visiting Professor of Church History, University of Notre Dame, February-June
1970-71	Visiting Professor of Church History, Graduate Theological Union, Berkeley, Winter and Spring Quarters
1974-75	Scholar-in-Residence, North American College, Rome, and Visiting Professor of American Catholic History, Gregorian University
1976	Scholar-in-Residence, North American College, Rome, and Visiting Professor of American Catholic History, Angelicum University, February-June

1976	Catholic Daughters of the Americas Professor of American Catholic History, The Catholic University of America, September-December
1977	Visiting Professor of Church History, Mount Saint Mary's Seminary, Emmitsburg, January-May

E. *Other Positions:*

Executive
Secretary   1941-61   American Catholic Historical Association

Managing
Editor   1941-63   *The Catholic Historical Review*

Advisory
Editor   1963-

Offices in
Learned
Societies: 1965-71   Member of the Council of the American Society of Church History

1968   Vice President of the American Catholic Historical Association

Vice President of the American Society of Church History

1969   President of the American Catholic Historical Association and the American Society of Church History

Chairman   1967-71   Sub-Committee on History of the Committee on Priestly Life and

Ministry of the National Conference
of Catholic Bishops

Consultant   1961-71 American Heritage Recordings, Saint
Meinrad Seminary, edited by Adrian
Fuerst, O.S.B.

1965-   Member of the Board of Governors of
the Center for Research and Education
in American Liberties, Columbia
University

1973-76 Member of the Subcommittee on
History of the National Conference of
Catholic Bishops' Committee for the
Observance of the Bicentennial

F. *Awards:*   1956   John Gilmary Shea Prize, American
Catholic Historical Association for
American Catholicism, Saint Louis,
Missouri, December 29

1965   Campion Award of the Catholic Book
Club, New York, New York,
November 26

1969   Research and Scholarship, Alumni
Association, The Catholic University
of America, Washington, D.C.,
November 8

1974   Distinguished Teacher of the Year,
University of San Francisco, San
Francisco, California, June 4

1976   Delta Epsilon Sigma Award, College
and University Department, National
Catholic Educational Association,
Philadelphia, Pennsylvania, February 7

1976   Newman Alumni Association Award,
        City College of the University of New
        York, New York, November 5

1977   Seton Founder's Award, Saint Joseph's
        Provincial House, Emmitsburg,
        Maryland, May 14

1980   Teresa of Avila Award, College of
        Saint Teresa, May 25

1984   Hesburgh Award, Association of
        Catholic Colleges and Universities,
        Washington, D.C.,
        January 24.

        Father Andrew White, S.J., Award
        of the Catholic Historical Society of
        Washington, February 25.

G. *Honorary*
    Degrees: 1954   L.H.D. Mount Mary College,
                          Milwaukee

              1957   LL.D. University of Notre Dame

              1960   LL.D. Belmont Abbey College

                      Litt.D. Loyola College, Baltimore

              1962   L.H.D. Saint Mary's College, Moraga

              1963   Litt. D. Stonehill College

              1969   L.H.D. University of Portland

              1972   LL.D. Fordham University

              1973   Litt. D. University of Florida

              1974   Litt.D. Marquette University

              1977   L.H.D. Loyola University of Chicago

1977	L.H.D. Saint Charles Borromeo Seminary, Philadelphia
1978	Ed.D. The Catholic University of America
1978	Theo.D. Immaculate Conception Seminary, Mahwah, New Jersey
1979	Litt.D. Saint Vincent College, Latrobe
1983	LL.D. University of Southern California
1984	L.H.D. Georgetown University
	L.H.D. University of Santa Clara
1985	LL.D. Saint Anselm College
	LL.D. Saint Bonaventure University

H. *Other Honors:*

Honorary
  Fellowship 1969   American Benedictine Academy, August 1

Honorary
  Membership 1959   Delta Epsilon Sigma, April 2

            1962   Phi Beta Kappa, The Catholic University of America Chapter, May 6

            1972   Phi Alpha Theta, University of San Francisco Chapter, February 26

Medals   1960   Golden Jubilee Medal, Saint Mary's Dominican College, New Orleans, May 30

            1961   Bene Merenti Medal, The Catholic University of America, January 15

	1978	Laetare Medal, University of Notre Dame, May 21
	1981	Cardinal Gibbons Medal, Alumni Association of the Catholic University of America, October 24
	1984	Saint Francis Xavier Medal, Cincinnati, December 2.
Citation	1957	Centennial Citation by Saint John's University, Collegeville, May 17

BIBLIOGRAPHY OF THE WORKS OF JOHN TRACY ELLIS FOR THE YEARS 1923-1985

Mark A. Miller

Abbreviations used in this bibliography:

ABR — American Benedictine Review

ACHS Records — American Catholic Historical Society Records

AER — American Ecclesiastical Review

CHR — Catholic Historical Review

C. Mind — Catholic Mind

CUA Bulletin — Catholic University of America Bulletin

C. World — Catholic World

NCR — National Catholic Reporter

MAJOR PUBLICATIONS

1930

1 *Anti-Papal Legislation in Medieval England (1066-1377)*. Washington, 1930.

1933

2 "Catholic Action for Peace," *The Commonweal* (hereafter cited as *Commonweal*) 17 (1933), 602-04.

3 "Some Catholic Research of 1932," *Catholic World* (hereafter cited as *C. World*) 136 (1933), 426-32.

1934

4 "Another Anniversary; The Golden Anniversary of Pope Leo XIII's *De Studiis Historicis*," *Commonweal* 19 (1934), 378-80.

5 (With William F. Roemer and the History Committee of the Catholic Association for International Peace) *The Catholic Church and Peace Efforts*. Washington, 1934.

1936

6 "Accreditation and the Catholic College," *Catholic Educational Review* 34 (1936), 589-97.

1940

7 "On Whose Side is the Pope?" *The Catholic Life* (Spring 1940), 4-7.

8 (With J. L. McMahon) "Our Envoy to the Vatican," *C. World* 151 (1940), 573-81.

1942

9 *Cardinal Consalvi and Anglo-Papal Relations, 1814-1824.* Washington, 1942.

10 "Washington's St. Sulpice: Twenty-five Years," *The Voice* (St. Mary's Seminary, Baltimore) 20 (November 1942), 17-19, 26. An address delivered at the dedication of Theological College's new statue of Our Lady, October 11, 1942.

1944

11 "A Challenge to the American Church on Its One Hundredth Birthday," *The Catholic Historical Review* (hereafter cited as *CHR*) 30 (1944), 290-98.

12 "Some Student Letters of John Lancaster Spalding," *CHR* 29 (1944), 510-39.

1945

13 "Can We Have a History of the Church in the United States?" *The Catholic University of America Bulletin* (hereafter cited as *CUA Bulletin*) 12 (March 1945), 2-3, 11.

1946

14 *The Formative Years of the Catholic University of America.* Washington, 1946.

15 "A Guide to the Baltimore Cathedral Archives," *CHR* 32 (1946), 341-60.

16 "Some Newman Letters from the Baltimore Cathedral Archives," *CHR* 31 (1946), 438-45.

1947

17 "Cardinal Gibbons and Philadelphia," *American Catholic Historical Society Records* (hereafter cited as *ACHS Records*) 58 (1947), 87-102.

18 "Heirs of an American Catholic Tradition," *Bulletin of the College of St. Catherine* 28 (July 1947), 9-18. Reprinted in 71. Under original title, "The Catholic Tradition in the Northwest," given as the commencement address at the College of St. Catherine, St. Paul, Minnesota, June 2, 1947.

19 "Old Catholic Newspapers in Some Eastern Catholic Libraries," *CHR* 33 (1947), 302-05.

20 "Peter Guilday, March 25, 1884—July 31, 1947," *CHR* 33 (1947), 257-68.

21 *A Select Bibliography of the History of the Catholic Church in the United States.* New York, 1947. For revised editions see 53 and 138.

1948

22 "Armistice Day — Thirty Years Later," *Knight Cap* 9

(November 1948), 3-4. A sermon preached at a Memorial Mass, University of Maryland, November 14, 1948.

23 "Cardinal ,Gibbons' Assistance to Pastor's *History of the Popes:* An Exchange of Letters," *CHR* 34 (1948), 306-18.

24 "A Venerable Church of Maryland," *CUA Bulletin* 16 (November 1948), 8-10. An address delivered at the sesquicentennial of St. Ignatius Church, Bel Alton, Maryland, September 26, 1948.

1949

25 "Sixtieth Birthday of the *American Ecclesiastical Review,*" *American Ecclesiastical Review* (hereafter cited as *AER)* 121 (1949), 261-80.

1950

26 "In Sufferings Linked," *The Voice* 28 (December 1950), 5-6, 31-32. An Alumni Day sermon preached at St. Mary's Seminary, Roland Park, September 23, 1950.

1952

27 "Archbishop Carroll and the Liturgy in the Vernacular," *Worship* 26 (1952), 545-52. Reprinted in 71.

28 "Cardinal Gibbons and New York," *Historical Records and Studies* 39 (1952), 5-32.

29 "The Centennial of the First Plenary Council of Baltimore," *AER* 126 (1952), 321-50. Reprinted in 71.

30 *"Church and State in the United States*: A Critical Appraisal," *CHR* 38 (1952), 285-316. Reprinted in 71. A review article of Anson Phelps Stokes, *Church and State in the United States*. 3 vols. New York, 1950.

31 "The Church in Colombia," *Commonweal* 56 (1952), 625-27.

32 *The Life of James Cardinal Gibbons, Archbishop of Baltimore, 1834-1921*. 2 vols. Milwaukee, 1952. For a condensed edition see 70.

33 "Teaching American Catholic History in Our Schools," *National Catholic Educational Association Bulletin* 48 (May 1952), 7-16.

1953

34 "Church and State: An American Catholic Tradition," *Harper's Magazine* 207 (November 1953), 63-67. Also in *Catholic Mind* (hereafter cited as *C. Mind*) 52 (April 1954), 209-16. Reprinted in 71.

35 "The Church in South America," *The Tablet* 201 (1953), 67-68, 88-89.

36 "A Half Century of Financial Support," *CUA Bulletin* 21 (October 1953), 10-12.

37 *Patriot Churchmen*. A brochure published by the National Council of Catholic Men, 1953. Contents reprinted in 71, under the names of the individual churchmen: John Carroll, John Hughes, John Lancaster Spalding, John Ireland, and James Gibbons. Originally a series of radio addresses delivered on the Catholic Hour, November 2, 9, 16, 23, and 30, 1952.

1954

38 "Young Gibbons of Ballinrobe," *Irish Digest* (January 1954), 20-24.

1955

39 "American Catholics and the Intellectual Life," *Thought* 30 (1955), 351-88. Also published in pamphlet form by the National Catholic Educational Association, and in book form, Chicago, 1956. Under the title "The American Catholic and the Intellectual Life," this essay appears as Chapter 20, pp. 315-57 in *The Catholic Church, U.S.A.*, edited by Louis J. Putz, C.S.C. Chicago, 1956. Excerpts in "Catholic Intellectual Responsibility," *Commonweal* 63 (1955), 143-44. In its original form, the essay was read as a paper at the annual meeting of the Catholic Commission on Intellectual and Cultural Affairs at Maryville College, St. Louis, May 14, 1955. See also 42 and 44.

40 "The Character of St. Patrick," *Washington Post and Times Herald* (March 17, 1955), pp. 1, 15.

1956

41 *American Catholicism.* A volume in *The Chicago History of American Civilization,* edited by Daniel J. Boorstin. Chicago, 1956. For a revised edition see 100. Chapters originated as lectures delivered on January 24, 25, 27, and 28, 1955, at the University of Chicago under the auspices of the Charles R. Walgreen Foundation for the Study of American Institutions.

42 "Catholic Intellectuals: A Spirit of Separatism," *Catholic International Outlook* 17 (October 1956), 13-21. A summary of 39.

43 *Documents of American Catholic History.* 1 vol. Milwaukee, 1956. Revised editions in 66 and 92.

44 "No Complacency," *America* 95 (April 7, 1956), 14-18, 20, 22, 24-25. Reprinted in 71. A report on reactions to 39.

1957

45 "Catholics in Colonial America," *AER* 136 (1957), 11-27, 100-19, 184-96, 265-74, 304-21.

46 "Right Reverend Monsignor John Tracy Ellis," pp. 81-88 in *The Book of Catholic Authors,* vol. V, edited by Walter Romig. Grosse Point, Michigan, [1957?].

1958

47 "Letter from Washington," *Dublin Review* 232 (1958), 363-71.

48 "A Shrine of My Name for All Time," *The Voice* 36 (December 1958), 14-16, 25-26. Under the title, "The Sesquicentennial of an Historic Chapel," preached as the sermon at the sesquicentennial of the dedication of the chapel of St. Mary's Seminary, Baltimore, November 19, 1958.

49 "The Spirit of Achievement," *Marymount College Bulletin* 35 (October 1958), 5-15. Sermon at the diamond jubilee Mass of the Sisters of St. Joseph of Concordia, Marymount College, Salina, Kansas, June 24, 1958.

50 "Three American Letters from the Wiseman Papers,"
CHR 43 (1958), 458-72.

1959

51 "The American Catholic College, 1939-1959: Contrasts
and Prospects," *Delta Epsilon Sigma Bulletin* (June
1959), 3-12. Reprinted in 71. An address delivered at the
annual meeting of Delta Epsilon Sigma, Atlantic City,
New Jersey, April 2, 1959.

52 "Character and the Catholic College Graduate," *Alum-
nae Journal of Trinity College* 33 (1959), 191-96. A
commencement address delivered at Trinity College,
Washington, June 1, 1959.

53 *A Guide to American Catholic History.* Milwaukee,
1959. A revision of 21. Another revision in 138.

54 *Mother Seton in Emmitsburg.* Emmitsburg, Md., 1959.
A sermon preached at a Mass commemorating the
sesquicentennial of the founding of Mother Seton's Sisters of Charity, Emmitsburg, Maryland, July 31, 1959.

55 *The Sanctity of Mother Seton.* Emmitsburg, Md., 1959.
Reprinted in 71. A sermon to a group from the Archdio-
cese of Washington visiting Elizabeth Seton's tomb,
Emmitsburg, Maryland, June 14, 1959.

1960

56 "American Catholicism in 1960: An Historical Perspective," *American Benedictine Review* (hereafter cited as
ABR) 11 (1960), 1-20. Also in *C. Mind* 59 (April 1961),
135-52. Reprinted in 71. A paper read at a symposium
sponsored by the Thomas More Association and the

Library Science Department of Rosary College, at Rosary College, River Forest, Illinois, June 11, 1960.

57 "Honors and Work," *The Evergreen Quarterly* 15 (Autumn 1960), 8-16. An address delivered at the Fall Academic Convocation, Loyola College, Baltimore, Maryland, September 16, 1960.

1961

58 *John Lancaster Spalding, First Bishop of Peoria, American Educator.* Milwaukee, 1961. This small book grew from a sermon preached on October 25, 1960, at a Mass in St. Mary's Cathedral, Peoria, Illinois, during the annual meeting of the School Superintendents' Department of the National Catholic Educational Association. Lengthy excerpts were published in "Crusader for Christian Education in the U.S.," *The Register* (Diocese of Peoria edition), November 6, 1960, pp. B1, 4. Sermon was expanded to become the 1961 Gabriel Richard Lecture.

59 "Saint Patrick in North America," *ABR* 12 (1961), 415-29. Reprinted in 71. A paper read during the Patrician Congress, Dublin, Ireland, June 22, 1961.

60 "Truth and the Responsibilities That Are Owed to It," *Catholic Library World* 33 (September 1961, 11-12, 61. Excerpts from an address delivered at the annual meeting of the Catholic Library Association, St. Louis, April 5, 1961.

1962

61 "The American Catholic Laity — 1962," *The Way* (U.S.) 18 (September, 1962), 13-17. Also in *The Current*

(Harvard), October, 1962, pp. 156-62. Reprinted in 71. A commencement address delivered at St. Mary's College, Moraga, California, June 9, 1962.

62 "The Catholic Layman in America Today," *Commonweal* 76 (1962), 319-22. Under original title, "The Catholic Tradition in the Far West," given as the commencement address at Carroll College, Helena, Montana, May 27, 1962.

63 "The Challenge to Personal Responsibility," *National Council of Catholic Women: Proceedings* 31 (1962), 161-69. An address delivered at the National Convention in Detroit, November 6, 1962.

64 "The Church Faces the Modern World: The Vatican Council, 1869-1870," pp. 113-45 in *The General Council: Special Studies in Doctrinal and Historical Background*, edited by William J. McDonald. Washington, 1962. The chapter cited was reprinted in 71. It was originally a lecture given at the Catholic University of America, March 13, 1961.

65 "Church History and the Seminarian," *St. Meinrad Essays* 13 (May 1962), 1-37. Reprinted in 71. Originally delivered as the Father Cyril Gaul Memorial Lecture, Saint Meinrad Seminary, September 24, 1961.

66 *Documents of American Catholic History*. 1 vol. Milwaukee, 1962. A revised edition of 43. For another revised edition see 92.

1963

67 "The Catholic Press: Reflections on Past and Present," *ABR* 14 (1963), 45-61. Also in *Catholic Journalist* 14 (March 1963), 3-4; (April 1963), 7-8. An address delivered at a meeting of the eastern regional unit of the

Catholic Press Association, Baltimore, November 8, 1962.

68 "The Christian Teacher," *Lasallian Digest* 5 (Summer 1963), 60-65. An oration delivered at the National Shrine of the Immaculate Conception, Washington, on the feast of St. John Baptist de La Salle, May 15, 1963.

69 "The Issue of Religious Freedom," *ABR* 14 (1963), 505-15. Also published under the title, "Conscience and Religious Commitment," *C. Mind* 62 (June 1964), 32-40. Originally delivered as an address to the Medievalists, Cincinnati, Ohio, March 21, 1963. Also a commencement address at Stonehill College, June 2, 1963.

70 *The Life of James Cardinal Gibbons: Popular Edition.* Edited by Francis L. Broderick. Milwaukee, 1963. A condensation of 32.

71 *Perspectives in American Catholicism.* Baltimore, 1963. A collection of topical essays, including reprints of 18, 27, 29, 30, 34, 37, 44, 51, 55, 56, 59, 61, 64, and 65. The following were published here for the first time: "The Cult of Quality," originally a commencement address at the College of Saint Teresa, Winona, Minnesota, June 2, 1958; "Live As Freemen," originally titled "Integrity in the Life of the Catholic Graduate" and preached as the baccalaureate sermon at Belmont Abbey College, Belmont, North Carolina, June 7, 1960; "The Paulist Fathers: A Century in the Apostolate to Americans," originally a sermon preached at St. Mary's Church, Chicago, April 27, 1958; "Saint John's: A Living Tradition," an address at the centennial honors convocation of Saint John's Abbey and University, Collegeville, Minnesota, May 17, 1957 (previously printed in a brochure); and "You Are the Light of the World," originally titled "The Blessing of an Abbot" and preached as the

sermon at the solemn blessing of the Right Reverend Alban Boultwood, O.S.B., as the first Abbot of St. Anselm's Abbey, Washington, in a ceremony at the National Shrine of the Immaculate Conception, Washington, December 30, 1961.

72 "Religious Freedom and American Catholicism," *Cross Currents* 13 (Winter 1963), 3-12. Also in *Wiseman Review* 237 (1963), 128-38. Originally a paper read at a seminar during the First National Institute, Religious Freedom and Public Affairs Project, National Conference of Christians and Jews, Washington, November 18, 1962.

1964

73 "The American Church and Free Experimentation," pp. 57-58, 66 in program booklet published by the National Council of Catholic Women. An address given at the thirty-second National Convention, National Council of Catholic Women, Washington, November 11-14, 1964.

74 "Has History Anything to Say to Social Work?" *Catholic Charities* 48 (1964), 5-12. An address to the Board of Directors, Catholic Social Service of Santa Clara County, San Jose, California, February 6, 1964.

75 "Light and Freedom in the University," *The Way* (U.S.) 20 (July-August 1964), 2-6.

76 "A School for the Lord's Service," *ABR* 15 (1964), 303-15. A sermon preached at the Diamond Jubilee Mass of the Seminary of Mt. Angel Abbey, Saint Benedict, Oregon, May 13, 1964.

1965

77 *Catholics in Colonial America.* Baltimore, 1965.

78 "The Irish in Relation to Religious and Political Freedom," *Wiseman Review* 238 (1965), 328-42.

79 "Jameson and American Religious History," pp. 9-23 in *J. Franklin Jameson: A Tribute*, edited by Ruth Anna Fisher and William Lloyd Fox. Washington, 1965.

80 "Reflections of an Ex-Editor," *CHR* 50 (1965), 459-74.

81 "Religion on the Secular Campus: A Prime Responsibility," *Southern California Quarterly* 47 (1965), 357-77. An address at a dinner hosted by the Newman Center, San Jose State College, California, in honor of its new president, Robert D. Clark, May 10, 1965.

82 "A Seminary Jubilee," *Chicago Studies* 4 (1965), 115-36. Excerpts in *C. Mind* 63 (April 1965), 28-29. An address delivered at the diamond jubilee dinner, St. Paul's College, Washington, January 25, 1965.

83 "A Short History of Seminary Education," pp. 1-81 in *Seminary Education in a Time of Change*, edited by James Michael Lee and Louis J. Putz, C.S.C. Notre Dame, Indiana, 1965.

84 "The Spirit of Cardinal Gibbons," *ACHS Records* 76 (1965), 14-20.

1966

85 "American Catholic Clerical-Lay Relations," *Thought* 41 (1966), 327-48. An address delivered at the annual dinner of the Catholic Press Association, San Francisco, May 12, 1966.

86 "American Jewish-Catholic Relations: Past and Prospect," *C. Mind* 64 (November 1966), 11-24. Also in *ABR* 18 (1967), 44-61. A paper read to the National Community Relations Advisory Council, Washington, June 25, 1966.

87 "Catholicism Midwest Style," *America* 104 (February 12, 1966), 229-30.

88 *A Commitment to Truth.* Latrobe, Pennsylvania, 1966. Originally delivered as the 1965 Wimmer Lecture at St. Vincent College, Latrobe, Pennsylvania, November 23, 1965.

89 "Contemporary American Catholicism in the Light of History," *The Critic* 24 (June-July 1966), 8-19. Originally delivered as the first Thomas J. Walsh Memorial Lecture at Carroll College, Helena, Montana, October 15, 1965.

90 "The Seminary Today," *The Voice* 44 (Winter 1966), 7-11, 89-94. Reappears in 94 as Chapter 5.

1967

91 Article on "United States of America," *The New Catholic Encyclopedia* XIV, 425-48. New York, 1967.

92 *Documents of American Catholic History.* 2 vols. Chicago, 1967. A revised edition of 43 and 66.

93 "An English Visitor's Comments on the American Religious Scene, 1846," *Church History* 36 (1967), 36-44.

94 *Essays in Seminary Education.* Notre Dame, Indiana, 1967. Includes 90.

95 "On Selecting American Bishops," *Commonweal* 85 (1967), 643-49.

96 "The Priest and the Intellectual Life," pp. 186-218 in *Secular Priest in the New Church*, edited by Gerard S. Sloyan. New York, 1967.

1968

97 "Archbishop Hallinan: In Memoriam," *Thought* 43 (1968), 539-72.

98 *The Catholic Church and the Negro*. Huntington, Indiana, 1968. This pamphlet was condensed in an article with the same title in *Our Sunday Visitor*, March 31, 1968, pp. 8-9.

99 "A Commitment Renewed," *ACHS Records* 79 (1968), 131-40. Also published in pamphlet form by *Our Sunday Visitor*. A homily preached at the Mass opening the academic year for the University of San Francisco at St. Ignatius Church, San Francisco, September 17, 1968.

1969

100 *American Catholicism*. Chicago, 1969. A revised edition of 41.

101 "The Ecclesiastical Historian in the Service of Clio," *Church History* 38 (1969), 106-20. A paper read at the annual meeting of the Pacific Coast Branch, American Historical Association, at the University of Santa Clara, August 28, 1968.

102 "On Selecting Catholic Bishops for the United States," *The Critic* 27 (June-July 1969), 42-48, 53-55. A paper read at a study day sponsored by the Senate of Priests, Archdiocese of San Francisco, March 2, 1969.

103 *The Priest in an Age of Revolution.* Detroit, 1969. This pamphlet contains his address at the Silver Jubilee of Sacred Heart Seminary, Detroit, May 28, 1969.

104 "Tradition and Change," *The Priest* 25 (January 1969), 15-20. Also in *ABR* 20 (1969), 65-74. A homily delivered at a Mass for lawyers, St. Ignatius Church, San Francisco, September 5, 1968.

1970

105 "The Aim...Is To Search Out Truth," *Thought* 45 (1970), 5-19. A paper read at the luncheon preceding the installation of Clarence C. Walton as the first lay President of the Catholic University of America, Washington, November 9, 1969.

106 "American Catholics and Peace: An Historical Sketch," pp. 13-39 in *The Family of Nations: An Expanded View of Patriotism,* edited by James S. Rausch. Huntington, Indiana, 1970.

107 "The Church in Revolt: The Tumultuous Sixties," *The Critic* 28 (January-February 1970), 12-21. Given as the 1969 Critic Lecture, sponsored jointly by the Thomas More Association and Rosary College, at Rosary College, River Forest, Illinois, October 12, 1969.

108 "Integrity the Shield of Justice," *The Jurist* 30 (1970), 328-42. A homily preached at a Mass for lawyers, Cathedral of St. Louis, New Orleans, October 6, 1969.

109 "John Henry Newman, A Bridge for Men of Good Will," *CHR* 56 (1970), 1-24. Given as the Presidential address of both the American Catholic Historical Association and the American Society of Church History at a joint luncheon, Washington, December 29, 1969.

110 "A Living Tradition in the Stream of History," *Liturgical Arts* 38 (February 1970), 40-42. A review article of Meriol Trevor, *Prophets and Guardians: Renewal and Tradition in the Church.* Garden City, New York, 1969.

111 "Priorities for the Teacher," *Catholic School Journal* 70 (May-June 1970), 20-21.

112 "A Tradition of Autonomy?" pp. 206-70 in *The Catholic University: A Modern Appraisal,* edited by Neil Gerard McCluskey, S.J. Notre Dame, Indiana, 1970. Originally a paper discussed at a conference of the North American region, International Federation of Catholic Universities, Land O'Lakes, Wisconsin, July 21-23, 1967.

113 "Whence Did They Come, These Uncertain Priests of the 1960's?" *AER* 162 (1970), 145-72, 234-48. Originally the keynote address at a symposium of the Association of Chicago Priests, November 24, 1968. Also given to groups of priests in the Archdiocese of Baltimore and in the Dioceses of Cleveland, Madison, and Manchester.

1971

114 "The Catholic School: Commitment or Compromise?" *Notre Dame Journal of Education* 2 (1971), 13-29. Originally the keynote address at a Teachers' Institute, Diocese of Spokane, November 12, 1970.

115 "The Formation of the American Priest: An Historical Perspective," pp. 3-110 in *The Catholic Priest in the United States: Historical Investigations,* edited by John Tracy Ellis. Collegeville, Minnesota, 1971.

116 "The Future: Does It Need A Prologue?" *C. World* 214 (October 1971), 21-26.

117 "Our Gifts Differ," *Chicago Studies* 10 (1971), 155-69.

1972

118 "Changing Concerns of the American Bishops, 1792-1970," *CHR* 58 (1972), 388-93. A review article of *Pastoral Letters of the American Hierarchy, 1792-1970,* edited by Hugh J. Nolan. Huntington, Indiana, 1971.

119 "The Surges of the Sea That Threaten Us," *Thought* 47 (1972), 507-35. Given as the principal address at the golden jubilee of Weston School of Theology, Cambridge, Massachusetts, February 5, 1972.

120 "Letter to a Bishop," *Origins* 2 (1972), 317-31. Also published under title, "Those Called to Lead — Then and Now," *Canon Law Society of America: Proceedings* 34 (1973), 4-33. Also under latter title in *The Critic* 31 (March-April 1973), 12-29. Originally delivered as an address at the annual meeting of the Canon Law Society of America, Seattle, Washington, October 24, 1972.

1973

121 "American Catholicism in an Uncertain, Anxious Time," *Commonweal* 98 (1973), 177-84.

1974

122 "*Commonweal* at 50: A Golden Jubilee in American Catholic Thought," *Commonweal* 100 (1974), 406-08. A review article of Rodger Van Allen, *The Commonweal and American Catholicism: The Magazine, the Movement, the Meaning.* Philadelphia, 1974.

123 "Fragments from My Autobiography, 1905-1942," *Review of Politics* 36 (1974), 565-91.

1975

124 "Should Cardinal Newman Be Canonized?" *America* 133 (1975), 250-51.

1976

125 "The Role of the Catholic University," *C. Mind* 74 (January 1976), 27-32. A homily preached at the University of San Francisco, September 7, 1975.

1977

126 "Ecclesiastical Archives," *CHR* 63 (1977), 489-90.

127 "The Eucharist in the Life of Cardinal Newman," *Communio* 4 (1977), 321-40. Originally a paper presented at the International Eucharistic Congress, Philadelphia, August 4, 1976.

128 "Lessons of Diversity Within the Church," *Momentum* 8 (February 1977), 6-7.

1978

129 "The Place of History," *Commonweal* 105 (1978), 41-46. Under original title, "Is there a Brighter Hour Dawning for Clio?" given as a dinner address at a regional meeting of the American Catholic Historical Association, College of the Holy Cross, Worcester, Massachusetts, March 18, 1977.

130 "The U.S.A.," pp. 253-317 in *The Christian Centuries*, edited by Roger Aubert and others. Vol. V: *The Church in a Secularized Society.* New York, 1978.

1979

131 "American Catholicism, 1953-1979: A Notable Change," *Thought* 54 (1979), 113-31. A paper read on October 21, 1978, in celebration of the diamond jubilee of the College of New Rochelle.

132 "American Catholics in 1979: Certain 'Signs of the Times,'" *Origins* 9 (1979), 225, 227-34. Also in *C. Mind* 78 (1980), 36-50. An address at the sesquicentennial dinner of *The Pilot,* Boston, September 12, 1979.

133 "The American Priest in 1979: Still an 'Uncertain, Anxious Time,'" *The Priest* 35 (September 1979), 32-33, 37-42. An address at the annual alumni reunion for the North American College, Rome, held in Cleveland, Ohio, June 13, 1979.

134 "Australian Catholicism: An American Perspective," *Journal of Religious History* 10 (1979), 313-21. A review article of Patrick O'Farrell, *The Catholic Church and Community in Australia: A History.* West Melbourne, 1977.

135 "The Catholic University of America, 1927-1979: A Personal Memoir," *Social Thought* 5 (1979), 35-62. A paper delivered March 25, 1979, as the Catholic University of America's second annual Catholic Daughters of the Americas' Lecture.

1980

136 "The Appointment of Bishops and the Selection of Candidates in the United States since Vatican II," pp. 81-84 in *Concilium,* Vol. 137: *Electing Our Own Bishops,* edited by Peter Huizing, S.J., and Knut Walf. New York, 1980.

1982

137 "The Chicago Controversies," *Catholic New York* 1 (February 28, 1982), 24-25. A review article of Charles W. Dahm, *Power and Authority in the Catholic Church: Cardinal Cody in Chicago*. Notre Dame, Indiana, 1981.

138 (With Robert Trisco) *A Guide to American Catholic History*. 2nd ed. Santa Barbara, California, 1982. A revised edition of 53.

139 "In Defense of the Church's Memory," *America* 147 (1982), 185-88.

1983

140 *Catholic Bishops: A Memoir*. Wilmington, Delaware, 1983.

141 "The Catholic Liberal Arts College: Has It A Future?" *Current Issues in Catholic Higher Education* 3 (1983), 3-9. A lecture delivered at St. Ambrose College, October 11, 1982, as part of the diocese of Davenport, Iowa, centenary celebration.

142 "Church, State, and Papal Diplomacy," *America* 149 (1983), 45-47.

143 "From the Enlightenment to the Present: Papal Policy Seen through the Encyclicals," *CHR* 69 (1983), 51-58. A review article of *The Papal Encyclicals, 1740-1981*, edited by Claudia Carlen, I.H.M. Wilmington, North Carolina, 1981.

144 "The Influence of the Catholic University of Louvain on the Church in the U.S.," *Louvain Studies* 9 (1983), 265-83. A lecture given at the Catholic University of

Louvain in celebration of the 125th anniversary of the American College, December 9, 1982.

145 "Recent Developments in American Catholic History," *Louvain Studies* 9 (1983), 251-64. Another lecture delivered on the same date as 144.

146 "Values in a Changing World: Truth's Link to Society's Integrity," *Origins* 13 (1983), 54-59. An address delivered during the baccalaureate service, University of Southern California, Los Angeles, May 12, 1983.

1984

147 "Peter Guilday," *Dictionnaire d'Histoire et de Géographie Ecclésiastiques* (The Catholic University of Louvain). In press.

1985

148 "American Catholic Bishops: Styles of Pastoral Leadership," *Church*, I (January, 1985), 21-30.

149 "Episcopal Vision in 1884 and Thereafter," *U.S. Catholic Historian* (in press). A paper read at the three-day conference entitled "Historians and Bishops in Dialogue," St. Mary's Seminary, Baltimore, Maryland, November 9, 1984.

MINOR PUBLICATIONS

1923

1 "The Elizabethan Age of Literature," *The Viatorian* (St. Viator College, Bourbonnais, Illinois) 40 (April 1923), 14-16.

1924

2 "Our Cardinal," *The Viatorian* 41 (June 1924), 4-9.

1930

3 Review of Leona C. Gabel, *Benefit of Clergy in England in the Later Middle Ages.* Vol. XIV, Nr. 1-4 in *Smith College Studies in History.* Northampton, Massachusetts, 1928, in *CHR* 16 (1930), 229-30.

4 Review of Oscar Albert Marti, *Economic Causes of the Reformation in England.* New York, 1929, in *CHR* 16 (1930), 220-22.

1932

5 Review of Z. N. Brooke, *The English Church and the Papacy.* New York, 1931, in *CHR* 18 (1932), 240-41.

6 Review of C. R. Cheney, *Episcopal Visitation of Monasteries in the Thirteenth Century.* Manchester, 1931, in *CHR* 18 (1932), 106-08.

1933

7 Brief notice of Laurence M. Larson, *A History of England and the British Commonwealth.* New York, 1932, in *CHR* 19 (1933), 379.

8 Brief notice of Dorothy Margaret Stuart, *Men and Women of Plantagenet England.* New York, 1932, in *CHR* 19 (1933), 123.

9 Review of Frederic C. Church, *The Italian Reformers 1534-1564.* New York, 1932, in *CHR* 19 (1933), 210-12.

1934

10 Brief notice of Thomas P. Phelan, *Thomas Dongan, Colonial Governor of New York, 1683-1688.* New York, 1933, in *CHR* 20 (1934), 224-25.

1935

11 Brief notice of George Burton Adams, *Constitutional History of England.* Revised by Robert L. Schuyler. New York, 1934, in *CHR* 21 (1935), 230.

12 Brief notice of C. S. B. Buckland, *Metternich and the British Government from 1809 to 1813.* London, 1932, in *CHR* 20 (1935), 461-62.

13 Brief notice of Arthur H. Noyes, *Europe: Its History and Its World Relationships, 1789-1933.* Boston, 1934, in *CHR* 21 (1935), 118.

1936

14 Brief notice of Arthur Bryant, *The England of Charles II.* New York, 1935, in *CHR* 22 (1936), 350.

15 Brief notice of Andrew C. McLaughlin, *A Constitutional History of the United States.* New York, 1935, in *CHR* 22 (1936), 245-46.

16 Review of Donald Lord Finlayson, *Michelangelo, the Man.* New York, 1935, in *CHR* 22 (1936), 198-99.

17 Review of H. L. Hughes, *The Catholic Revival in Italy, 1815-1915.* London, 1935, in *CHR* 22 (1936), 199-200.

18 Review of Thomas More, *The Last Four Things.* Edited by D. O'Connor. London, 1935, in *CHR* 22 (1936), 69-70.

19 Review of *Saint John Fisher: The Earliest English Life.* Edited with an introduction and notes by Philip Hughes. London, 1935, in *CHR* 22 (1936), 69-70.

20 Review of Eduardo Soderini, *Leo XIII, Italy and France.* Translated by Barbara Barclay Carter. London, 1935, in *CHR* 22 (1936), 84-86.

21 Review of Eduardo Soderini, *The Pontificate of Leo XIII.* Vol. I. Translated by Barbara Barclay Carter. London, 1934, in *CHR* 21 (1936), 461-64.

22 Review of K. L. Wood-Legh, *Studies in Church Life in England under Edward III.* Cambridge, 1934, in *CHR* 21 (1936), 453-54.

1937

23 Brief notice of Sidney R. Welch, *Europe's Discovery of South Africa.* Cape Town, 1935, in *CHR* 23 (1937), 123.

24 [Letter to editor:] "Book Reviews," *Commonweal* 26 (1937), 387.

25 Review of David Mathew, *Catholicism in England, 1535-1935.* New York, 1936, in *CHR* 23 (1937), 209-10.

1938

26 Brief notice of F. Lee Benns, *European History Since 1870*. New York, 1938, in *CHR* 24 (1938), 234.

27 Brief notice of *The Cambridge History of the British Empire*. Vol. VIII: *South Africa, Rhodesia, and the Protectorates*. Edited by A. P. Newton and E. A. Benians. Cambridge, 1936, in *CHR* 23 (1938), 530.

28 Brief notice of F. C. Montague, *The Elements of English Constitutional History*. New York, 1936, in *CHR* 24 (1938), 115-16.

29 Brief notice of *The Writings and Speeches of Oliver Cromwell*. Vol. I: *1599-1649*. Edited by Wilbur Cortez Abbott, with the assistance of Catherine D. Crane. Cambridge, 1937, in *CHR* 24 (1938), 229.

30 Review of Joseph H. Brady, *Rome and the Neapolitan Revolution of 1820-21: A Study in Papal Neutrality*. New York, 1937, in *CHR* 24 (1938), 356-57.

31 Review of Pierre Crabitès, *Victoria's Guardian Angel. A Study of Baron Stockmar*. New York, 1938, in *CHR* 24 (1938), 351-52.

32 Review of Edmund Curtis, *A History of Ireland*. New York, 1937, in *CHR* 24 (1938), 353-54.

33 Review of Carl Conrad Eckhardts, *The Papacy and World-Affairs as Reflected in the Secularization of Politics*. Chicago, 1937, in *CHR* 24 (1938), 190-92.

34 Review of Sidney Bradshaw Fay, *The Rise of Brandenburg-Prussia to 1786*. New York, 1937, in *CHR* 24 (1938), 85-86.

35 Review of Frederick L. Schuman, *Germany Since 1918*. New York, 1937, in *CHR* 24 (1938), 85-86.

1939

36 Brief notice of George Gordon Andrews, *Napoleon in Review.* New York, 1939, in *CHR* 25 (1939), 385.

37 Brief notice of Francis William Coker, *Readings in Political Philosophy.* Revised edition. New York, 1938, in *CHR* 24 (1939), 505.

38 Brief notice of Sister Mary Clare Goodwin, *The Papal Conflict with Josephinism.* New York, 1938, in *CHR* 25 (1939), 231.

39 Brief notice of Ernst Christian Helmreich, *The Diplomacy of the Balkan Wars, 1912-1913.* Cambridge, 1938, in *CHR* 25 (1939), 235-36.

40 Brief notice of E. L. Higgins, *The French Revolution as Told by Contemporaries.* Boston, 1939, in *CHR* 25 (1939), 395-96.

41 Brief notice of Adolf Hitler, *Mein Kampf.* New York, 1939, in *CHR* 25 (1939), 396-98.

42 Brief notice of David Ogg, *Europe in the Seventeenth Century.* Third edition. New York, 1938, in *CHR* 25 (1939), 241-42.

43 Brief notice of Mihailo D. Stojanovič, *The Great Powers and the Balkans, 1875-1878.* Cambridge, 1939, in *CHR* 25 (1939), 410-11.

44 Brief notice of E. L. Woodward, *The Age of Reform, 1815-1870.* Oxford, 1938, in *CHR* 25 (1939), 258.

45 Review of Joseph Bernhart, *The Vatican as a World Power.* Translated by George N. Shuster. New York, 1939, in *CHR* 25 (1939), 187-89.

46 Review of S. William Halperin, *Italy and the Vatican at War. A Study of Their Relations from the Outbreak of*

the Franco-Prussian War to the Death of Pius IX. Chicago, 1939, in *CHR* 25 (1939), 350-52.

47 Review of *The Letters of King George IV, 1812-1830.* 3 vols. Edited by A. Aspinall. Cambridge, 1938, in *CHR* 25 (1939), 206-08.

1940

48 Brief notice of Joan Evans, *Chateaubriand. A Biography.* London, 1939, in *CHR* 25 (1940), 526-27.

49 Brief notice of Theodore Maynard, *Apostle of Charity. The Life of St. Vincent de Paul.* New York, 1939, in *CHR* 26 (1940), 142.

50 Brief notice of Cardinal Merry Del Val, *Memories of Pope Pius X.* London, 1939, in *CHR* 25 (1940), 536-37.

51 Brief notice of Saul K. Padover, *The Life and Death of Louis XVI.* New York, 1939, in *CHR* 25 (1940), 539-41.

52 Brief notice of Luigi Salvatorelli, *A Concise History of Italy.* Translated by Bernard Miall. New York, 1940, in *CHR* 26 (1940), 150-51.

53 Brief notice of Joseph Schmidlin, *Histoire des Papes de l'Epoque contemporaine.* Tome I: *La Papauté et les Papes de la Restauration (1800-1846).* Premiére partie: *Pius VII, le Pape de la Restauration (1800-1823).* Traduction de L. Marchal. Lyon, 1938, in *CHR* (1940), 543-44.

54 Brief notice of Reginald F. Walker, *An Outline History of the Catholic Church.* 2 vols. Dublin, 1938-39, in *CHR* 26 (1940), 412-13.

55 Review of Luigi Sturzo, *Church and State.* Translated by Barbara Barclay Carter. New York, 1939, in *CHR* 26 (1940), 93-95.

1941

56 Brief notice of Catherine E. Boyd, *The French Renaissance*. Illustrative Set Nr. 3 of Museum Extension Publications. Boston, 1940, in *CHR* 26 (1941), 531-32.

57 Brief notice of *The Cambridge History of the British Empire*. Vol. II: *The Growth of the New Empire, 1783-1870*. Edited by J. Holland Rose, A. P. Newton, and E. A. Benians. Cambridge, 1940, in *CHR* 27 (1941), 264-65.

58 Brief notice of Marcus Cheke, *Dictator of Portugal. A Life of the Marquis of Pombal, 1699-1782*. London, 1938, in *CHR* 26 (1941), 533-34.

59 Brief notice of Martin Dempsey, *John Baptist De La Salle. His Life and His Institute*. Milwaukee, 1940, in *CHR* 27 (1941), 127-28.

60 Brief notice of Walter L. Dorn, *Competition for Empire, 1740-1763*. New York, 1940, in *CHR* 26 (1941), 536-37.

61 Brief notice of *An Encyclopedia of World History*. Compiled and edited by William L. Langer. Boston, 1940, in *CHR* 26 (1941), 547-49.

62 Brief notice of Wallace K. Ferguson, *The Renaissance*. New York, 1940, in *CHR* 26 (1941), 537-38.

63 Brief notice of Denis Gwynn, *The Vatican and the War in Europe*. Dublin, 1940, in *CHR* 27 (1941), 258-59.

64 Brief notice of Stuart Ramsey Tompkins, *Russia through the Ages*. New York, 1940, in *CHR* 26 (1941), 561-62.

65 Brief notice of John B. Wolf, *France 1815 to the Present*. New York, 1940, in *CHR* 26 (1941), 564-65.

66 Managing editor of *The Catholic Historical Review* (through December 1962).

67 Review of Carl J. Burckhardt, *Richelieu. His Rise to Power.* Translated and abridged by Edwin and Willa Muir. New York, 1940, in *CHR* 26 (1941), 506-08.

1942

68 Brief notice of Oscar Handlin, *Boston's Immigrants, 1790-1865. A Study in Acculturation.* Vol. L in *Harvard Historical Studies.* Cambridge, 1941, in *CHR* 28 (1942), 521-22.

69 Brief notice of *Inventory of the Church Archives in New York City. The Roman Catholic Church. Archdiocese of New York.* Vol. II. Compiled by Charles C. Fisher, State Supervisor for New York City. New York, 1940, in *CHR* 28 (1942), 142-43.

70 Brief notice of *Inventory of the Church Archives of Michigan. The Roman Catholic Church. Archdiocese of Detroit.* Compiled by Stuart Portner, State Supervisor for Michigan. Detroit, 1941, in *CHR* 28 (1942), 142-43.

71 Brief notice of *Souvenirs de Édouard de Mondésir.* Edited by Gilbert Chinard. Baltimore, 1942, in *CHR* 28 (1942), 419-20.

72 Brief notice of *The Trial of Death. Letters of Benjamin Marie Petit.* Edited by Irving McKee. Indianapolis, 1941, in *CHR* 27 (1942), 526.

73 [Report as Secretary:] "The Twenty-Second Annual Meeting of the American Catholic Historical Association, Chicago, December 29-31, 1941," *CHR* 28 (1942), 71-84.

74 Review of Kenneth Scott Latourette, *A History of the Expansion of Christianity.* Vol. IV: *The Great Century, A. D. 1800-A. D. 1914. Europe and the United States of America.* New York, 1941, in *CHR* 27 (1942), 457-59.

1943

75 Brief notice of *The American Mind. Selections from the Literature of the United States.* Edited by Harry R. Warfel, Ralph H. Gabriel, and Stanley T. Williams. New York, 1937, in *CHR* 29 (1943), 295-96.

76 Brief notice of *Altas of American History.* Edited by James Truslow Adams and R. V. Coleman. New York, 1943, in *CHR* 29 (1943), 288.

77 Brief notice of Henry Putney Beers, *Bibliographies in American History. Guide to Materials for Research.* Second edition, New York, 1942, in *CHR* 28 (1943), 553.

78 Brief notice of William J. Lallou, *The Fifty Years of the Apostolic Delegation, Washington, D.C., 1893-1943.* Paterson, 1943, in *CHR* 29 (1943), 291-92.

79 Brief notice of Jules Lebreton and Jacques Zeiller, *The History of the Primitive Church.* Vol. I: *The Church in the New Testament.* Translated by Ernest C. Messenger. London, 1942, in *CHR* 29 (1943), 292.

80 Brief notice of Albert Post, *Popular Freethought in America, 1825-1850.* New York, 1943, in *CHR* 29 (1943), 418-19.

81 [Report as Secretary:] "The Twenty-Third Annual Meeting of the American Catholic Historical Association, Washington, January 16, 1943," *CHR* 29 (1943), 65-75.

82 Review of Evarts B. Greene, *Religion and the State. The Making and Testing of an American Tradition.* New York, 1941, in *CHR* 29 (1943), 238-40.

83 Review of Theodore Roemer, *Ten Decades of Alms.* St. Louis, 1942, in *CHR* 28 (1943), 526-28.

84 Review of Ellen Hart Smith, *Charles Carroll of Carrollton.* Cambridge, 1942, in *CHR* 29 (1943), 256-58.

85 Review of William Warren Sweet, *Religion in Colonial America.* New York, 1942, in *CHR* 28 (1943), 521-23.

1944

86 [Report as Secretary:] "The Twenty-Fourth Annual Meeting of the American Catholic Historical Association, New York City, December 29-30, 1943," *CHR* 30 (1944), 41-50.

87 Review of Gustavus Myers, *History of Bigotry in the United States.* New York, 1943, in *CHR* 29 (1944), 545-47.

88 "Spare the Humble," *The Sunday Star,* Washington, D.C., August 13, 1944.

1945

89 [Report as Secretary:] "The Silver Jubilee Meeting of the American Catholic Historical Association, Chicago, December 28-29, 1944," *CHR* 31 (1945), 80-90.

1946

90 Brief notice of Covelle Newcomb, *Larger Than the Sky. A Story of James Cardinal Gibbons.* New York, 1945, in *CHR* 32 (1946), 137-38.

91 [Report as Secretary:] "The Twenty-Sixth Annual Meeting of the American Catholic Historical Association, Washington, December 15, 1945," *CHR* 32 (1946), 59-68.

1947

92 Brief notice of James G. Murtagh, *Australia: The Catholic Chapter.* New York, 1946, in *CHR* 33 (1947), 110-11.

93 Preface to Mary David Cameron, S.S.N.D., *The College of Notre Dame of Maryland, 1895-1945.* New York, 1947, pp. vii-x.

94 [Report as Secretary:] "The Twenty-Seventh Annual Meeting of the American Catholic Historical Association, New York City, December 27-29, 1946," *CHR* 33 (1947), 31-42.

95 Review of Philip Hughes, *A History of the Church.* Vol. III: *The Revolt against the Church: Aquinas to Luther.* New York, 1947, in *AER* 117 (1947), 392-95.

1948

96 [Report as Secretary:] "The Twenty-Eighth Annual Meeting of the American Catholic Historical Association, Cleveland, Ohio, December 27-29, 1947," *CHR* 34 (1948), 20-32.

97 Review of Brendan A. Finn, *Twenty-four American Cardinals.* Boston, 1947, in *AER* 119 (1948), 231-37.

98 Review of Dagmar Renshaw Lebreton, *Chahta-Ima. The Life of Adrien-Emmanuel Rouquette.* Baton Rouge, 1947, in *CHR* 33 (1948), 471-73.

1949

99 Brief notice of *Guide to the Records in the National Archives.* Washington, 1948, in *CHR* 35 (1949), 223-24.

100 [Report as Secretary:] "The Twenty-Ninth Annual Meeting of the American Catholic Historical Association, Washington, D.C., December 28-30, 1948," *CHR* 35 (1949), 43-53.

1950

101 Foreword to Maria Kostka Logue, S.S.J., *Sisters of St. Joseph of Philadelphia: A Century of Growth and Development, 1847-1947.* Westminster, Maryland, 1950, pp. vii-x.

102 [Report as Secretary:] "The Thirtieth Annual Meeting of the American Catholic Historical Association, Boston, December 28-30, 1949," *CHR* 36 (1950), 33-42.

103 Review of *Documents on German Foreign Policy, 1918-1945. From the Archives of the German Foreign Ministry.* Washington, 1949, in *CHR* 35 (1950), 449-52.

104 Review of Thomas Merton, *The Waters of Siloe.* New York, 1949. Review was published as a pamphlet by the Critics' Forum, after delivery at the Critics' Forum, Washington, February 1, 1950.

105 Review of M. Raymond, *Burnt Out Incense.* New York, 1949, in *CHR* 35 (1950), 458-60.

1951

106 "Baltimore's Cardinal Gibbons Appealed to Pope Leo XIII for an Encyclical Three Years Before It Was Issued in 1891," The *Catholic Review* (Baltimore), May 18, 1951.

107 Brief notice of *Archivium Hibernicum.* Vol. XV. Edited by Patrick J. Corish. Maynooth, 1950, in *CHR* 37 (1951), 353-54.

108 Brief notice of Denis Gwynn, *The History of the Partition (1912-1925).* Dublin, 1950, in *CHR* 37 (1951), 88-89.

109 [Guest column:] "History," The *Catholic Standard*, December 7, 1951.

110 Letter to Archbishop Karl J. Alter of Cincinnati about building a new altar or making repairs to the cathedral. Extract in *Cincinnati Register-Telegraph*, July 7, 1951.

111 [Report as Secretary:] "The Thirty-First Annual Meeting of the American Catholic Historical Association, Chicago, December 28-30, 1950," *CHR* 37 (1951), 23-35.

112 Review of *The English Catholics, 1850-1950.* Edited by George A. Beck. London, 1950, in *AER* 125 (1951), 231-37.

113 "U.S. Catholics Venerate Archbishop Carroll for Establishing Church in This Country," *Archbishop Carroll High School Dedication News*, September 9, 1951, p. 12.

1952

114 "James Cardinal Gibbons, Churchman and Citizen." Published by the Critics' Forum. Originally delivered as a lecture at the Critics' Forum, Washington, November 13, 1952.

115 "John Tracy Ellis," pp. 156-57, in *Catholic Authors. Contemporary Biographical Sketches.* Edited by Matthew Hoehn, O.S.B. Newark, 1952.

116 [Report as Secretary:] "The Thirty-Second Annual Meeting of the American Catholic Historical Association, New York, December 28-30, 1951," *CHR* 38 (1952), 26-35.

1953

117 "The American Catholic Historical Association." Published in the *Program* of the twenty-fifth biennial convention of the Order of the Alhambra, Washington, August 5-8, 1953. Originally given as an address at the convention.

118 Brief notice of Irving S. and Nell M. Kull, *A Short Chronology of American History, 1492-1950.* New Brunswick, 1952, in *CHR* 38 (1953), 500.

119 [Letter to editor, replying to review:] "Life of Cardinal Gibbons," *The Tablet* 202 (1953), 607.

120 [Report as Secretary:] "The Thirty-Third Annual Meeting of the American Catholic Historical Association, Washington, December 28-30, 1952," *CHR* 39 (1953), 35-47.

1954

121 [Letter to editor:] "Diocesan Archives," *Books on Trial* 12 (1954), 194.

122 [Report as Secretary:] "The Thirty-Fourth Annual Meeting of the American Catholic Historical Association, Chicago, December 28-30, 1953," *CHR* 40 (1954), 46-62.

1955

123 Brief notice of Basil Hemphill, *The Early Vicars Apostolic of England, 1685-1750*. London, 1954, in *CHR* 41 (1955), 107-08.

124 Letter to the editors of *The Voice*, replying to a review. Published in *CHR* 40 (1955), 487-88.

125 [Report as Secretary:] "The Thirty-Fifth Annual Meeting of the American Catholic Historical Association, New York City, December 28-30, 1954," *CHR* 41 (1955), 18-28.

1956

126 [Letter to editor, replying to comments about Major Publication 39:] "Catholic Intellectual Responsibility: Reply," *Commonweal* 63 (1956), 485-86.

127 [Letter to editor:] "Catholic Intellectuals," *America* 95 (1956), 313.

128 [Report as Secretary:] "The Thirty-Sixth Annual Meeting of the American Catholic Historical Association, Washington, December 28-30, 1955," *CHR* 42 (1956), 53-63.

129 Review of Carl Wittke, *The Irish in America*. Baton Rouge, 1956, in *Louisiana Historical Quarterly* 39 (1956), 473-75.

1957

130 [Report as Secretary:] "The Thirty-Seventh Annual Meeting of the American Catholic Historical Association, St. Louis, December 28-30, 1956," *CHR* 43 (1957), 46-56.

131 Review of John M. Daley, S.J., *Georgetown University: Origin and Early Years*. Washington, 1957, in *America* 98 (1957), 377-78.

132 Review of Robert F. McNamara, *The American College in Rome, 1855-1955*. Rochester, New York, 1956, in *America* 96 (1957), 484.

1958

133 [Report as Secretary:] "The Thirty-Eighth Annual Meeting of the American Catholic Historical Association, New York, December 28-30, 1957," *CHR* 44 (1958), 17-27.

134 Review of Robert D. Cross, *The Emergence of Liberal Catholicism in America*. Cambridge, Mass., 1958, in *Theological Studies* 19 (1958), 237-48.

135 Review of Thomas T. McAvoy, C.S.C., *The Great Crisis in American Catholic History, 1895-1900*. Chicago, 1957, in *Theological Studies* 19 (1958), 237-48.

1959

136 "Eulogy of Monsignor Charles A. Hart: Priest, Philosopher, and University Professor." Excerpts in *CUA Bulletin* 26 (April 1959), 8-9. Originally delivered at the funeral in St. Patrick's Church, Ottawa, Illinois, February 2, 1959.

137 [Report as Secretary:] "The Thirty-Ninth Annual Meeting of the American Catholic Historical Association, Washington, December 28-30, 1958," *CHR* 45 (1959), 24-37.

138 Review of *Dictionary of American Biography. Supplement Two.* New York, 1958, in *CHR* 44 (1959), 474-76.

1960

139 Brief notice of R. S. Dell, *An Atlas of Christian History.* London, 1960, in *CHR* 46 (1960), 249.

140 [Letter to editor:] "Religious Tolerance," *America* 102 (1960), 541-42.

141 [Report as Secretary:] "The Fortieth Annual Meeting of the American Catholic Historical Association, Chicago, December 28-30, 1959," *CHR* 46 (1960), 27-42.

142 Review of Arnold Schrier, *Ireland and the American Emigration, 1850-1900.* Minneapolis, 1958, in *Journal of Religion* 40 (1960), 318-19.

143 Review of Gustave Weigel, *Faith and Understanding in America.* New York, 1959, in *CHR* 46 (1960), 205-06.

1961

144 Brief notice of D. W. Brogan, *America in the Modern World.* New Brunswick, 1960, in *CHR* 46 (1961), 509-10.

145 [Report as Secretary:] "The Forty-First Annual Meeting of the American Catholic Historical Association, New York, December 28-30, 1960," *CHR* 47 (1961), 15-28.

1962

146 [Letter to editor, clarifying points in Major Publication 62:] "Letter from Msgr. Ellis," *America* 107 (1962), 451.

1963

147 Brief notice of *Dictionary of American History.* Vol. VI *(Supplement One).* New York, 1961, in *CHR* 49 (1963), 150-51.

148 Letter to members of American Catholic Historical Association, resigning as managing editor of *CHR* in *CHR* 49 (1963), 87.

149 Review of Daniel Callahan, *The Mind of the Catholic Layman.* New York, 1963, in *Commonweal* 79 (1963), 171-72.

1964

150 Brief notice of Martin E. Marty and others, *The Religious Press in America.* New York, 1963, in *CHR* 50 (1964), 119-20.

151 Foreword to Michael V. Gannon, *Rebel Bishop: The Life and Era of Augustin Verot.* Milwaukee, 1964, pp. ix-xvi.

152 "General Introduction," pp. v-xii in *The Christian Centuries.* Vol. I: *The First Six Hundred Years.* Edited by Jean Daniélou and Henri Marrou. New York, 1964.

Introduction by Ellis also appears under title, "A New Church History Series," *AER* 153 (1965), 145-54.

153 Review of Emmanuel Curtis, *Blessed Oliver Plunkett.* Dublin, 1963, in *CHR* 50 (1964), 224-25.

154 Review of Richard Hofstadter, *Anti-Intellectualism in American Life.* New York, 1963, in *CHR* 49 (1964), 580-83.

1965

155 Editor of *Makers of American Catholicism.* Vol. I: *The Life of John Lancaster Spalding, First Bishop of Peoria, 1840-1916,* by David Francis Sweeney, O.F.M. New York, 1965.

156 [Letter to editor:] "American Catholic Scholars," *America* 112 (1965), 301.

157 [Letter to editor:] "The Emerging Nun," *Commonweal* 82 (1965), 202-03.

158 [Letter to editor:] "Responsible Laymen," *Commonweal* 81 (1965), 651, 678-79.

159 [Letter to editor:] "What's Your Last Name, Sister?" *National Catholic Reporter* (hereafter cited as *NCR*), March 10, 1965.

1966

160 Editor of "James Cardinal Gibbons," pp. 477-92 in *An American Primer,* Vol. I. Edited by Daniel J. Boorstin. Chicago, 1966.

161 [Letter to editor, opposing the proliferation of seminaries:] "Free Us from This Madness," *America* 115 (1966), 124.

162 [Letter to editor:] "History and Drama," *The Monitor* (San Francisco), January 20, 1966, p. 18.

163 Review of Maynard Geiger, O.F.M., *Mission Santa Barbara, 1782-1965.* Santa Barbara, 1965, in *Southern California Quarterly* 48 (1966), 212-13.

1967

164 Articles in the *New Catholic Encyclopedia.* New York, 1967. "Catholic University of America, The," III, 332-34; "Gibbons, James," VI, 466-68; "Guilday, Peter," VI, 844-45; "Maguire, John William Rochfort," IX, 75-76; "Washington, D. C., Archdiocese of," XIV, 822-24. See also Major Publication 91.

165 Foreword to James W. Trent, *Catholics in College: Religious Commitment and the Intellectual Life.* Chicago, 1967, pp. v-viii.

166 [Interview by Leonard B. Stevens:] "The Catholic University and Academic Freedom," *The Rhode Islander, Providence Sunday Journal Magazine,* June 11, 1967, pp. 20-21, 23-24, 26.

167 [Interview by James H. Gandrau:] "Church Race Relations Seen in Historical Context," *The Catholic Northwest Progress* (Seattle), July 21, 1967, p. 7.

168 [Letter to editor:] "Honesty in the Church," *America* 116 (1967), 267.

169 [Letter to editor, regarding statement in above letter:] "An Apology," *America* 116 (1967), 612.

170 [Letter to editor:] "The Kingdom of God and the Common School," *Harvard Educational Review* 37 (1967), 270-72.

171 Review of Lawrence H. Fuchs, *John F. Kennedy and American Catholicism.* New York, 1967, in *America* 117 (1967), 507-08.

172 "Zeroing in on Freedom," *Commonweal* 86 (1967), 317.

1968

173 [Letter to editor:] "Catholic U. Only Pontifical University?" *NCR,* December 11, 1968, p. 4.

174 [Letter to editor:] "Liturgy Ruling Sounds Familiar to Tracy Ellis," *NCR,* March 20, 1968, p. 4.

175 [Letter to editor:] "Senates of Priests," *America* 118 (1968), 390.

176 Review of *Academic Freedom and the Catholic University.* Edited by Edward Manier and John W. Houck. Notre Dame, 1967, in *Journal of Higher Education* 39 (1968), 115-17.

177 Review of Claude Leetham, *Luigi Gentili: A Sower for the Second Spring.* London, 1965 in *CHR* 54 (1968), 185-87.

178 Review of E. R. Norman, *The Conscience of the State in North America.* A volume in the *Cambridge Studies in the History and Theory of Politics.* New York, 1968, in *American Historical Review* 74 (1968), 269-70.

179 Review of William A. Osborne, *The Segregated Covenant. Race Relations and American Catholics.* New York, 1967, in *Journal of American History* 55 (1968), 190-91.

180 Review of *The Shape of Catholic Higher Education.* Edited by Robert Hassenger. Chicago, 1967, in *Journal of Higher Education* 39 (1968), 115-17.

1969

181 Review of Charles Stephen Dessain, *John Henry New-man*. London, 1966, in *CHR* 55 (1969), 201-03.

182 Review of Arthur McCormack, M.H.M., *Cardinal Vaughan. The Life of the Third Archbishop of Westminster*. London, 1966 in *CHR* 55 (1969), 206-08.

1970

183 [Interview:] "Does the Church Have a Future? Does Christ?" *NCR*, March 25, 1970, p. 1.

184 Review of *American Participation in the Second Vatican Council*. Edited by Vincent A. Yzermans. New York, 1967, in *CHR* 56 (1970), 204-06.

185 Review of William A. Clebsch, *From Sacred to Profane America: The Role of Religion in American History*. New York, 1968, in *CHR* 56 (1970), 149-51.

186 Review of Andrew M. Greeley, *The Catholic Experience. An Interpretation of the History of American Catholicism*. Garden City, 1967, in *CHR* 56 (1970), 151-57.

1971

187 "Mother Mary Baptist Russell, 1829-1898," pp. 213-14 in *Notable American Women, 1607-1950. A Biographical Dictionary*. Volume III. Edited by Edward T. James. Cambridge, Mass., 1971.

188 Obituary of Sir Shane Leslie, *CHR* 57 (1971), 546-48.

1973

189 [Interview by J. Harrington:] "Is America Falling Apart?" *St. Anthony Messenger* 80 (April 1973), 14-21.

190 [Interview:] "John Tracy Ellis on Faith, Polarization," *NCR,* October 26, 1973, p. 17.

191 Obituary of Joseph S. Brusher, S.J., *CHR* 59 (1973), 161-62.

192 Obituary of Raymond J. Sontag, *CHR* 58 (1973), 654-56.

193 "A Tribute: 'With Prudence, with Courage, with Determination,'" pp. i-xviii in *Days of Hope and Promise. The Writings and Speeches of Paul J. Hallinan, Archbishop of Atlanta.* Edited by Vincent A. Yzermans. Collegeville, 1973.

1974

194 "James Cardinal Gibbons," pp. 418-20 in *Encyclopedia of American Biography.* Edited by John A. Garraty. New York, 1974.

195 "Peter Guilday," pp. 352-54 in *Dictionary of American Biography, Supplement Four (1946-50).* Edited by John A. Garraty and Edward T. James. New York, 1974.

196 "Paul J. Hallinan," p. 202 in *New Catholic Encyclopedia,* Vol. XVI *(Supplement 1967-74).* New York, 1974.

197 Obituary of James Broderick, S.J., *CHR* 59 (1974), 733-34.

1975

198 [Interview by Desmond O'Grady:] "The Church in

America: God Shed His Grace on Thee," *U. S. Catholic* 40 (July 1975), 6-12.

199 Obituary of David Knowles, *CHR* 61 (1975), 331-33.

200 Review of Edward J. Power, *Catholic Higher Education in America; A History.* New York, 1972, in *CHR* 61 (1975), 448-51.

1976

201 Review of John Beevers, *A Man for Now. The Life of Damien de Veuster, Friend of Lepers.* Garden City, 1973, in *CHR* 62 (1976), 502-05.

202 Review of Gavan Daws, *Holy Man: Father Damien of Molokai.* New York, 1973, in *CHR* 62 (1976), 502-05.

203 Review of *On the Side of Truth, George N. Shuster. An Evaluation with Readings.* Edited by Vincent P. Lannie. Notre Dame, 1974, in *CHR* 62 (1976), 679-81.

1977

204 Review of Sister Alice O'Rourke, O. P., *The Good Work Begun. Centennial History of Peoria Diocese.* Peoria, 1977, in *CHR* 63 (1977), 655-56.

205 Review of Frank Sheed, *The Church and I.* Garden City, 1974, in *CHR* 63 (1977), 626-28.

206 Review of John B. Sheerin, C.S.P., *Never Look Back: The Career and Concerns of John J. Burke.* New York, 1975, in *CHR* 63 (1977), 48-50.

1978

207 Foreword to *Italian-Americans and Religion: An*

Annotated Bibliography. Edited by Silvano M. Tomasi and Edward C. Stibili. New York, 1978, pp. v-vi.

208 [Interview:] "The Problems Facing the Church and Society are Unprecedented," *NCR*, May 19, 1978, pp. 7-11.

209 Obituary of Friedrich Engel-Janosi, *CHR* 64 (1978), 544-45.

210 Obituary of John B. Heffernan, *CHR* 64 (1978), 546.

211 Obituary of Douglas Woodruff, *CHR* 64 (1978), 545-46.

212 Review of *The Letters and Diaries of John Henry Newman.* Vol. XXIX: *The Cardinalate, January 1879 to September 1881.* Edited by Charles Stephen Dessain and Thomas Gornall. New York, 1976, in *CHR* 64 (1978), 699-701.

1979

213 "A Notable Birthday," *The Pilot* (Boston), September 1979, sesquicentennial issue.

214 Obituary of Aloysius K. Ziegler, *CHR* 65 (1979), 691-92.

215 Review of *The San Francisco Irish, 1850-1976.* Edited by James P. Walsh. San Francisco, 1978, in *CHR* 65 (1979), 137-38.

1980

216 "Fulton J. Sheen," in *International Biographical Dictionary.* New York, 1980.

217 Obituary of Joseph B. Code, *CHR* 66 (1980), 512.

218 Obituary of Ernst Posner, *CHR* 66 (1980), 510-11.

219 Review of Robert Emmett Curran, *Michael Augustine Corrigan and the Shaping of Conservative Catholicism in America, 1878-1902.* A volume in *The American Catholic Tradition.* New York, 1978, in *CHR* 66 (1980), 258-60.

220 Review of Peter Hebblethwaite, *The Year of Three Popes.* Cleveland, 1979, in *CHR* 66 (1980), 459-60.

1981

221 Brief notice of Edmund Campion, *John Henry Newman. Friends, Allies, Bishops, Catholics.* Melbourne, 1980, in *CHR* 67 (1981), 678-79.

222 Foreword to James Hennesey , S.J., *American Catholics: A History of the Roman Catholic Community in the United States.* New York, 1981, pp. vii-xii.

223 Foreword to J. Derek Holmes, *The Papacy in the Modern World, 1914-1978.* New York, 1981, pp. vii-viii.

224 [Interview by Eugene Carl Bianchi:] "A Church Historian's Personal Story," *ACHS Records* 92 (1981), 3-42.

225 Obituary of Henry J. Browne, *CHR* 67 (1981), 167-68.

226 Obituary of Ernest Edwin Reynolds, *CHR* 67 (1981), 167.

227 Review of Vincent Ferrer Blehl, S. J., *John Henry Newman. A Bibliographical Catalogue of His Writings.* Charlottesville, 1978, in *CHR* 67 (1981), 321-22.

1982

228 Foreword to Gerald P. Fogarty, *The Vatican and the American Hierarchy from 1870 to 1965.* Stuttgart, 1982, pp. xi-xiv.

229 Interview by Louis Jacquet, *The Harmonizer* (Diocese of Fort Wayne-South Bend), March 14, 1982, pp. 10, 13.

230 Obituary of Edward V. Cardinal, C.S.V., *CHR* 68 (1982), 379.

231 Review of Owen Chadwick, *The Popes and European Revolution.* New York, 1981, in *Commonweal* 109 (1982), 56-57.

232 Foreword to Thomas J. Peterman, *The Cutting Edge: The Life of Thomas Andrew Becker, 1831-1899.* Devon, Pa., 1982, pp. iv-v.

1983

233 Brief notice of Paul Milcent, *Jeanne Jugan. Humble, So as to Love More.* Translated by Alan Neame. London, 1980, in *CHR* 69 (1983), 477-78.

234 Foreword to David W. Givey, *The Social Thought of Thomas Merton. The Way of Nonviolence and Peace for the Future.* Chicago, 1983, pp. xiii-xv.

235 Foreword to Sister Evangeline Thomas, *Women Religious History Sources: A Guide to Repositories in the United States.* New York, 1983, pp. ix-xi.

236 Review of Saul E. Bronder, *Social Justice and Church Authority: The Public Life of Archbishop Robert E. Lucey.* Philadelphia, 1982, in *America* 148 (1983), 244-45.

237 Review of Dom Adrian Morey, *David Knowles. A Memoir.* London, 1979, in *CHR* 69 (1983), 87-89.

1984

238 "Church, State and Papal Diplomacy," *America* 149 (1984), 45-47.

239 "The Hesburgh Award: A Response," *Current Issues in Catholic Higher Education* 4 (Winter, 1984), 43-45.

240 Interview with Arthur Jones, *NCR,* February 17, 1984, p. 40.

241 Interview with Gerard E. Sherry, *Our Sunday Visitor,* February 5, 1984, pp. 4-5, 12.

242 "The Selection of Bishops," *ABR,* 35 (1984), 111-27.

243 "It's Not New. 'Religion in Politics' Issue Runs Through U.S. History," *The Catholic Standard* (Washington), October 4, 1984, p. 13.

244 "Catholic Intellectual Life: 1984," *America* 151 (1984), 179-80.

245 "Precedents. Popes Throughout History Were Involved in Politics," *The Catholic Standard* (Washington), October 18, 1984, p. 10.

246 "The Spirit of Maryknoll," *Maryknoll Magazine* 78 (November 1984), 15-19.

UNPUBLISHED WORKS

[This list of unpublished works was compiled from the Ellis Papers in the Archives of the Catholic University of America. The compiler would like to thank Dr. Anthony Zito, Archivist, for his kind assistance. Msgr. Ellis has also delivered addresses other than those listed here.]

1927

1 "George Meredith, the Novelist of Manners," B.A. dissertation, St. Viator College, May 17, 1927.

1928

2 "Anti-Papal Legislation in Medieval England, 1066-1377," The Catholic University of America, June, 1928.

1939

3 "Submission of Anglicans to the Holy See," sermon during Church Unity Octave, National Shrine of the

Immaculate Conception, Washington, D.C., January 20, 1939.

1942

4 "The Catholic Church — The Friend of Freedom Everywhere," commencement address, Mount Saint Scholastica College, Atchison, Kansas, May 27, 1942.

5 Baccalaureate address, Saint Benedict's College, Atchison, Kansas, May 28, 1942.

6 "The Priesthood — The Light of the World," sermon at the first solemn Mass of David J. Murphy and Roland E. Murphy, both O.Carm., St. Cyril Church, Chicago, May 31, 1942.

7 Address to graduates, Mary Manse College, June 2, 1942.

1945

8 "Life's Quest for Beauty," commencement address, Immaculate Conception Academy, Washington, D.C., June 6, 1945.

1946

9 "The American Centennial of the Immaculate Conception," sermon at the National Shrine of the Immaculate Conception, Washington, D.C., May 12, 1946.

1947

10 "The Centennial of St. Thomas Church, Wilmington, North Carolina," sermon given there on May 11, 1947.

11 "Pentecost and Commencement," commencement address, College of Saint Teresa, Winona, Minnesota, June 1, 1947. Also given as commencement address at Marian College, Indianapolis, June 6, 1954.

12 "Saint Matthew, Patron of the Cathedral of the Archdiocese of Washington," sermon at St. Matthew's Cathedral, Washington, September 21, 1947.

13 "The Holy Name Man's Loyalty to Church and to State," address at Holy Name Rally, Archdiocese of Washington, Washington Monument Grounds, October 26, 1947.

1948

14 Address about aspects of relations between Church and State, delivered at a convention of the Holy Name Union of the Archdiocese of Washington, April 25, 1948.

1951

15 "Roots of Anti-Catholic Bigotry in America," lecture sponsored by the Catholic University Conference of Clerics and Religious of the Catholic Students Mission Crusade, Catholic University of America, Washington, D.C., January 12, 1951.

16 "Devotion to the Mother of God," sermon about the history of devotion to Mary, preached on World Sodal-

ity Day, Catholic University of America, Washington, D.C., May 20, 1951.

17 Address at graduation exercises, Towson Catholic High School, June 3, 1951.

18 Address to graduates, Mount Saint Agnes College, Mount Washington, Maryland, June 3, 1951.

19 Commencement address, Marygrove College, Detroit, June 6, 1951.

20 "Saint Francis in the New World," sermon at Mass opening annual meeting of Academy of American Franciscan History, Mount Saint Sepulchre, Washington, D.C., December 9, 1951.

1953

21 "The Mother of God," sermon on CBS radio at the opening of the drive for the National Shrine of the Immaculate Conception, November 29, 1953.

1954

22 "Leo Francis Stock, 1878-1954," eulogy at funeral, St. Anthony's Church, Washington, D.C., March 10, 1954. Mimeographed.

23 Review of John LaFarge, S.J., *The Manner is Ordinary.* New York, 1954.

1956

24 Address to Society of Friendly Sons of St. Patrick, Hotel Mayflower, Washington, D.C., March 17, 1956.

1957

25 Address about Cardinal Gibbons as churchman and statesman, delivered to First Friday Club, Washington, D.C., October 4, 1957.

1958

26 Address about need of American Catholics for a healthy and constructive spirit of self-criticism, delivered at the twenty-second diocesan congress, League of Catholic Women, Boston, May 13, 1958.

27 Baccalaureate address, Mundelein College, Chicago, June 1, 1958.

28 Address about the Catholic Church in the United States having come of age, delivered at a joint communion breakfast, Harvard-Radcliffe Catholic Clubs, Hotel Commander, Cambridge, December 1, 1958.

1959

29 Interview on "The Way to Go," CBS-TV, August 19, 1959.

30 "The Quality of Mercy," sermon at dedication of Generalate of Sisters of Mercy of the Union, Bethesda, Maryland, November 1, 1959.

1960

31 "A Half Century of Dedication," commencement address delivered at golden jubilee of Saint Mary's Dominican College, New Orleans, Louisiana, May 29, 1960.

32 "Church History in the Life of a Religious," address to American Benedictine Academy, Social Service Section, during meeting at Mount Angel Abbey, Saint Benedict, Oregon, August 23, 1960.

1961

33 Address about how laymen can contribute to Christian unity by helping to fashion a correct public image of the Church, delivered at National Council of Catholic Men Study Day, Washington, D.C., February 28, 1961.

34 "Saint Patrick's Fifteenth Centennial," sermon delivered at St. Patrick's Church, Washington, D.C., March 17, 1961.

35 Address about contributions of Cardinal Gibbons to the advancement of individual freedom, delivered at blessing of Gibbons Hall, College of Notre Dame of Maryland, December 10, 1961.

1962

36 "Ecumenical Councils in the Life of the Church," address at clergy conference, Archdiocese of Washington, May 24, 1962.

37 "Americans and Vatican Council I, 1869-1870," speech at fifty-fifth annual meeting, Pacific Coast Branch, American Historical Association, August 29, 1962.

38 "Teaching Church History in Our Schools of Religion," speech to Confraternity of Christian Doctrine Institute, Marin Catholic High School, San Rafael, California, September 8, 1962.

39 "The Apostolate to Truth," lecture at Woodstock College (Maryland), Lecture Forum, October 24, 1962.

1964

40 Keynote address about the problems facing Catholic higher education, delivered at Northwest Regional Meeting, National Catholic Educational Association, Portland, Oregon, January 30, 1964.

41 Lecture in series sponsored by the Paulist Fathers, San Francisco, early February, 1964.

42 Address at annual banquet, United Irish Societies, Sheraton-Palace Hotel, San Francisco, March 17, 1964.

1965

43 Speech at All-Jesuit Alumni Communion and Breakfast, St. Ignatius Church, San Francisco, January 31, 1965.

44 "Three Decades of American Catholicism," interview by John Cogley, "The Catholic Hour," (NBC radio), March 28, 1965.

45 "The Beginnings of Catholic Theological Education in the Middle West," paper read at meeting of the American Society of Church History, Concordia Seminary, Saint Louis, April 24, 1965.

46 "Response to Renewal," keynote address to the thirteenth annual convention, San Francisco Archdiocesan

Council of Catholic Men, Dominican College, San
Rafael, California, May 23, 1965.

47 Commencement address, San Francisco College for
Women, June 5, 1965.

48 Homily about the necessity of maintaining balance in
the use of history for apologetical purposes, delivered at
the forty-sixth annual meeting of the American Catholic Historical Association, Saint Boniface Church, San
Francisco, December 29, 1965.

1966

49 Address to the Philetheia Club, San Francisco, March
3, 1966.

50 "American Catholicism in 1966: An Historical Perspective," lecture at Newman Forum, Newman Center,
Sacramento, March 4, 1966.

1967

51 "A Sense of the Past," lecture in college lecture series,
Seton Hall University, South Orange, New Jersey, February 17, 1967. Also delivered as address at the dedication of the new library, Saint John's Seminary,
Brighton, March 7, 1967.

52 "American Catholicism in the 1960's: An Historical
Evaluation," public lecture, Brown University, April 13,
1967.

1968

53 Letter to editor, *New York Times,* protesting quotation

about Cardinal Cooke attributed to Ellis, March 11, 1968.

54 Prayer at worship service, First Congregational Church, San Francisco, April 3, 1968.

55 Invocation at installation of new student officers, University of San Francisco, May 2, 1968.

56 Interview about Pope Paul VI's encyclical, *Humanae Vitae,* CBS News, July 30, 1968.

1969

57 Letter to editor, *Washington Post*, denying that Ellis was the author of an anonymous article in the London *Tablet* of January 18 about the present state of American Catholicism, February 19, 1969.

58 Sermon at Baccalaureate Mass, University of Portland, May 11, 1969.

59 Letter to editors, San Francisco *Chronicle* and San Francisco *Examiner,* protesting publication of the rumor that the Most Reverend James P. Shannon, Auxiliary Bishop of St. Paul-Minneapolis, had resigned over the issue of birth control, May 30, 1969.

60 Invocation read at memorial exercises, Supreme Court of Louisiana, New Orleans, October 6, 1969.

61 "The National Federation of Priests' Councils: The Problems It Faces," keynote address at conference of bishops and priests, LaFarge Institute, New York, October 6-12, 1969.

1973

62 "Character and Civility Are Their Own Reward," address at retirement dinner for John L. McMahon, President of Our Lady of the Lake College, March 18, 1973.

1974

63 "A Harvard Interval," third annual Thomas T. McAvoy Lecture, about years Ellis spent at Harvard, delivered at the University of Notre Dame, May 2, 1974.

64 Sermon at golden jubilee Mass of Edward V. Cardinal, C.S.V., St. Viator Church, Chicago, June 14, 1974.

65 "The Immigrant Fixes the Pattern, 1790-1866," lecture in American Catholic history, Casa Santa Maria, Rome, October 28, 1974.

66 "The Catholic Church and Industrial Society, 1866-1900," lecture, Casa Santa Maria, November 12, 1974.

67 "The American Catholics of the 1970's: Whence Did They Come?" lecture, North American College, Rome, November 19, 1974.

68 "Groping Toward Maturity, 1908-1960," lecture, Casa Santa Maria, Rome, November 25, 1974.

69 "A Shattered Fixity — An Uncertain Future," lecture, Casa Santa Maria, Rome, December 9, 1974. Also delivered as an address at the Cathedral of Saint Thomas More, Arlington, Virginia, March 25, 1982.

1975

70 "American Catholics and the Intellectual Life," lecture,

North American College, Rome, February 18, 1975. Also delivered at Casa Santa Maria, Rome, March 13, 1975.

71 "Nationalities in Conflict," lecture, Casa Santa Maria, Rome, March 24, 1975.

72 "The Catholic Church and American Politics," lecture, Casa Santa Maria, April 15, 1975. Also delivered at North American College, Rome, May 6, 1975.

73 "'Heresy' in American Catholicism — Americanism and Modernism," lecture, Casa Santa Maria, April 22, 1975. Also delivered at North American College, May 13, 1975.

1976

74 "The Intellectual Formation of the American Priest," lecture, Casa Santa Maria, Rome, March 16, 1976.

75 "American Catholics in 1976: Another Revolution?" lecture, North American College, May 3, 1976.

76 Homily about being open to the modern world but not to the false premises of philosophical liberalism, delivered at farewell Mass for fourth and fifth year students, North American College, May 31, 1976.

77 "Diversity in the Church — A View from History," address to the Department of Chief Administrators, National Catholic Educational Association, Washington, D.C., November 19, 1976. Also delivered at the annual convention, National Catholic Educational Association, April 13, 1977; St. John's Seminary, Brighton, Mass., September 13, 1979; Theological College, Washington, D.C., November 8, 1979.

1977

78 "The Vatican in the World of Politics," address delivered at Mount Saint Mary's College, Emmitsburg, Maryland, April 25, 1977.

79 Address about St. Elizabeth Ann Seton as an example of integrity, delivered at the St. Elizabeth Ann Seton Convocation, Emmitsburg, Maryland, May 14, 1977.

80 Homily at fiftieth anniversary Mass of Antonine Tibesar, O.F.M., Academy of American Franciscan History, Washington, D.C., May 31, 1977.

81 "Responsibility: An Institutional and Personal Response," commencement address, Loyola University of Chicago, June 11, 1977.

82 "A New Chapter Opens in Emmitsburg," address about the role of the Catholic liberal arts college, delivered at inauguration of new administration, Mount Saint Mary's College, September 28, 1977.

1978

83 Address at baccalaureate Mass for the Catholic University of America, National Shrine of the Immaculate Conception, Washington, D.C., May 12, 1978.

84 Commencement address about preparation for the priesthood, St. Charles College, Catonsville, Md., May 13, 1978.

85 "The Spirit and the Intellect: A Union of Enrichment," commencement address, Immaculate Conception Seminary, Mahwah, New Jersey, June 3, 1978.

86 "A High Goal — A Happy Landing," commencement address, Monsignor Farrell High School, Staten Island, New York, June 11, 1978.

87 "A College That 'Brings Out...Things Both New and Old,' The Eve of a Diamond Jubilee," College of New Rochelle, New Rochelle, New York, October 21, 1978.

1979

88 "A Liberal Arts College in the Catholic Tradition," commencement address, Saint Vincent College, Latrobe, Pennsylvania, May 12, 1979.

1981

89 "Communicating the Word of God Today," address at Saint Paul's College, Washington, D.C., January 24, 1981.

90 Homily at funeral of Edward V. Cardinal, C.S.V., December 23, 1981.

1982

91 "Bishops in Politics — A View from History," address, Akron, Diocese of Cleveland, May 10, 1982.

92 "The Importance of Church History for Future Priests," conferences held separately with the Faculty of Theology and with seminarians of the American College of Louvain, December 10, 1982.

1984

93 "1884: The Ark Fortified: 'The Third Plenary Council of Baltimore," Trinity College, Washington, D.C., Febru-

ary 25, 1984. A response to the reception of the Father Andrew White, S.J. Award of the Catholic Historical Society of Washington.

94 "Tradition: A Support for Life," commencement address, Georgetown Preparatory School, Rockville, Maryland, May 26, 1984.

95 "Mary in the Life of the Church," sermon preached at the National Shrine of the Immaculate Conception, Washington, D.C., Sunday, November 18, 1984, commemorating the twenty-fifth anniversary of the dedication of the Shrine's upper church.

96 "Diversity in the Church — A View from History," Xavier University, Cincinnati, Ohio, Sunday, December 2, 1984. A response to the reception of the Saint Francis Xavier Medal.

1985

97 "The Laity: A View from History," Serra International Colloquium, Washington, D.C., January 5, 1985; also, delivered at the golden jubilee meeting of Serra International, New York, July 2, 1985.

98 "The Priesthood: A View from History," Saint John's Seminary, Brighton, Massachusetts, March 11, 1985; also delivered at the Pontifical College Josephinum, Columbus, Ohio, March 22, 1985.

99 "The Parish: A View from History," opening of the diamond jubilee year of Blessed Sacrament Parish, Washington, D.C., April 17, 1985, the Monsignor Corbett Memorial Lecture for 1985.

100 "A Premium for Integrity," homily at the baccalaureate Mass, Saint Bonaventure University, May 19, 1985. ·

CONTRIBUTORS

Aubert, Roger: Canon Aubert, professor emeritus of ecclesiastical history in the Catholic University of Louvain, is internationally recognized as one of the ranking historians of modern Catholicism. For many years he has been editor of the prestigious *Revue d'histoire ecclésiastique*.

Barry, Colman J., O.S.B.: Since the publication in 1953 of *The Catholic Church and German Americans*, the professor of church history in and former president of Saint John's University, Collegeville, has made significant contributions by his books and his editing of source materials in Catholic history.

Bland, Joan, S.N.D.: A sister of Notre Dame de Namur and graduate of the Catholic University of America, she has taught history at Trinity College and has written on the Catholic abstinence movement and on Catholic education and social reform. She is currently director of the Education for Parish Service Program at Trinity College.

Blantz, Thomas E., C.S.C.: Father Blantz has served his *alma mater*, the University of Notre Dame, in a variety of roles, as teacher, archivist, vice-president for student affairs, and chairman of the Department of History. His Columbia University doctoral dissertation added an important chapter to American Catholic social history, and he is now at work on a biography of George N. Shuster, one of the founders of *Commonweal* and a leading Catholic intellectual of his time.

Chinnici, Joseph P., O.F.M.: Following his doctorate from the University of Oxford, the professor of church history in the Franciscan School of Theology and the Graduate Theological Union, Berkeley, has centered his research and writing on a neglected aspect of American Catholic history, namely, spirituality, a field wherein his scholarly efforts offer high promise for the future.

Curran, R. Emmett, S.J.: Chairman of the Department of History in Georgetown University, Father Curran has found time for research and writing on colonial Maryland's Jesuit history and is at present engaged on a history of Georgetown for its approaching bicentennial. His Yale doctoral dissertation, a study of conservative American Catholic thought centered about Archbishop Michael A. Corrigan of New York, was published in 1978.

Decker, Raymond G.: A priest of the archdiocese of San Francisco who took his doctor's degree at the Graduate Theological Union, Berkeley, in 1974. Father Decker's prime scholarly interest has been in the area of morals and the law. He was one of the founders of the National Federation of Priests' Councils, served as assistant dean of the School of Law of Loyola Marymount University, Los Angeles, and at present is on loan to the diocese of Oakland where he serves as Consultant on Public Policy.

Eno, Robert B., S.S.: Chairman of the Department of Church History in the Catholic University of America, Father Eno received his doctorate at the Institut Catholique de Paris. His field of specialization has been the ancient Church, particularly that of North Africa. He served as an editor of the patristic theology section of the *Catholic Theological Encyclopedia* (1966-1970) and is an editor of the *Bulletin de Saint Sulpice*.

Evans, John Whitney: A priest of the diocese of Duluth who holds his Ph.D. degree from the University of Minnesota, Father Evans is associate professor of history and religious studies in the College of Saint Scholastica, diocesan archivist, and author of *The Newman Movement: Roman Catholics in American Higher Education, 1883-1971* (Notre Dame, 1980).

Fogarty, Gerald P., S.J.: Subsequent to receiving his doctorate at Yale University, Father Fogarty has published a widely praised work, *The Vatican and the American Hierarchy from 1870 to 1965*, Band 21 in the series *Päpste und Papsttum* (Stuttgart, 1982). He is associate professor of religious studies in the University of Virginia and is now at work on a history of Catholic biblical scholarship in the United States.

Gleason, Philip: Mr. Gleason, professor of history in the University of Notre Dame, is an authority in the history of American Catholicism whose numerous publications have been centered on the intellectual trends in that religious community.

Handy, Robert T.: The Henry Sloane Coffin professor of church history in Union Theological Seminary, New York, is recognized as one of the outstanding Protestant historians of American Christianity.

Hennesey, James, S.J.: Trained at Loyola University of Chicago, Woodstock College, and the Catholic University of America, Father Hennesey has been one of the most productive among contemporary Catholic historians. His latest book, *American Catholics. A History of the Roman Catholic Community in the United States* (New York, 1981), is recognized as the best survey of that vast subject. He is professor of American Christianity in Boston College.

Lipscomb, Oscar H.: If the Archbishop of Mobile has been so absorbed in administrative duties since he took his doctorate at the Catholic University of America in 1961 that it has prevented him from research and publication, he has lost none of his keen interest in American Catholic history. He is chairman of the Board of Trustees of his *alma mater*, the North American College, Rome, and likewise a trustee of the Catholic University of America.

McNamara, Robert F.: A priest of the diocese of Rochester, Father McNamara is the author of a scholarly history of the North American College, Rome, as well as a history of his native diocese. Educated at Georgetown, Harvard, and the Gregorian University, Rome, he taught church history at Saint Bernard's Seminary, Rochester, from 1938 until the close of the seminary in 1982.

Melville, Annabelle M.: Mrs. Melville long ago established her reputation as the outstanding laywoman in the field of American Catholic history with scholarly biographies of Elizabeth Seton, Archbishop John Carroll, and Jean de Cheverus, first Bishop of Boston. Her last teaching assignment was that of Commonwealth professor at Bridgewater State College, Bridgewater, Massachusetts, and since retirement she has completed a biography of Bishop Louis W. DuBourg.

Miller, Mark A.: A priest of the diocese of Rochester, Father Miller was educated at Saint Bernard's Seminary, Rochester, received a master's degree at the Catholic University of America, and has almost completed the requirements for his Th.D. degree at St Michael's College, the University of Toronto.

Minnich, Nelson H.: Mr. Minnich, associate professor of church history and of history in the Catholic University of America, is a graduate of the Gregorian University, Rome, and earned his Ph.D. degree at Harvard University. He is associate editor of the *Catholic Historical Review* and has published articles on the religious history of the early sixteenth century in Europe.

Murphy, Roland E., O. Carm.: Occupant of the George Washington Ivy Chair of Old Testament Studies in the Divinity School of Duke University, Father Murphy is internationally recognized in biblical circles as one of the editors of the *Jerome Biblical Commentary* and for numerous articles on the Old Testament.

O'Brien, David J.: Mr. O'Brien, graduate of the University of Notre Dame with a doctorate from the University of Rochester, is an authority on social Catholicism in the United States. His most recent project is a biography of Isaac T. Hecker, founder of the Paulist Fathers. He is associate professor of history in the College of the Holy Cross.

O'Connell, Marvin R.: A priest of the archdiocese of Saint Paul-Minneapolis, Father O'Connell is the author of significant volumes on the English Reformation, the Catholic Reformation, and the Oxford Movement. A professor of history in the University of Notre Dame, he is nearing the completion of a biography of John Ireland, Archbishop of Saint Paul.

Peter, Carl J.: The Dean of the School of Religious Studies at the Catholic University of America was trained at the Gregorian University, Rome, and has since distinguished himself for his research and writing in the field of systematic theology as well as for his participation in ecumenical dialogue with non-Catholic Christians. A priest of the archdiocese of Omaha, Father Peter received recognition for his work in being named a member of the Holy See's International Theological Commission.

Trisco, Robert: A priest of the archdiocese of Chicago, Father Trisco studied at Saint Mary of the Lake Seminary, Mundelein, and the Gregorian University, Rome, where he received his doctorate in ecclesiastical history in

1962. In addition to his duties as professor of church history and of history in the Catholic University of America, he is also editor of the *Catholic Historical Review* and Secretary-Treasurer of the American Catholic Historical Association. His achievements have been honored by election to the Bureau of the International Commission for Comparative Church History and more recently by appointment to the Pontifical Committee of Historical Sciences.

Zeender, John K.: Mr. Zeender retired as professor of modern European history in the Catholic University of America in 1984 after a distinguished teaching career there and previously at the University of Massachusetts, Amherst. He completed doctoral studies at Yale University in 1952 and thereafter pursued his specialty in modern German history with emphasis on the Center Party.

INDEX